P9-CSZ-848

COMBAT
WW
II
PACIFIC

Also by DON CONGDON

COMBAT: THE CIVIL WAR

COMBAT: WORLD WAR I

THE THIRTIES: A TIME TO REMEMBER

Also by HERBERT MITGANG

Fiction

KINGS IN THE COUNTING HOUSE

THE MONTAUK FAULT

GET THESE MEN OUT OF THE HOT SUN

THE RETURN

Biography

THE FIERY TRIAL: A Life of Lincoln

THE MAN WHO RODE THE TIGER: The Life and Times of
Judge Samuel Seabury

LINCOLN AS THEY SAW HIM

Criticism

WORKING FOR THE READER: A Chronicle of Culture,
Literature, War and Politics in Books from the 1950s to the Present

Reportage

FREEDOM TO SEE: Television and the First Amendment

Editor

THE LETTERS OF CARL SANDBURG

CIVILIANS UNDER ARMS: Stars and Stripes, Civil War
to Korea

WASHINGTON, D.C., IN LINCOLN'S TIME

SPECTATOR OF AMERICA

AMERICA AT RANDOM: Topics of The Times

Play

MISTER LINCOLN

COMBAT
WW
II
PACIFIC

Unforgettable Eyewitness
Accounts of the Momentous Military
Struggles of World War II

EDITED BY DON CONGDON
FOREWORD BY HERBERT MITGANG

GALAHAD BOOKS

Copyright © 1958, 1963, 1983 by Don Congdon.

Foreword copyright © 1983 by Herbert Mitgang.

All rights reserved. No part of this work may be reproduced or
transmitted in any form or by any means, electronic or mechanical,
including photocopying, recording, or any information storage and retrieval
system without permission in writing from the publisher. All requests for
permission to reproduce material from this work should be directed
to Don Congdon Associates, Inc., 156 Fifth Avenue,
New York, NY 10010-7002.

First Galahad Books edition published in 1996.

Galahad Books
A division of Budget Book Service, Inc.
386 Park Avenue South
New York, NY 10016

Galahad Books is a registered trademark of Budget Book Service, Inc.

This edition published by arrangement with Don Congdon Associates, Inc.

Library of Congress Catalog Card Number: 95-81825

ISBN: 0-88365-944-1

Printed in the United States of America.

Acknowledgments

This page constitutes an extension of the copyright page.

"Pearl Harbor," copyright, 1944, by the Marine Corps Association. Reprinted from the Marine Corps Gazette and *The Marine Corps Reader,* published by G. P. Putnam's Sons, N.Y.C.

"Tragedy in the China Sea," copyright 1942 by Random House, Inc., from *Suez to Singapore.* Reprinted by permission of the publisher.

"The Fall of Singapore," copyright 1959 by Kenneth Attiwill, from *Fortress.* Reprinted by permission of Doubleday & Co., and Frederick Muller, London.

"Bamboo Doctor," copyright 1960 by Stanley S. Pavillard. Reprinted by permission of St. Martin's Press.

"Wake Island Command," copyright 1961 by Lydel Sims and W. Scott Cunningham. Reprinted by permission of Little, Brown & Co. and The Sterling Lord Agency.

"Death March on Bataan," copyright, 1944, by Marajen Stevick Dyess. From *The Dyess Story,* published by G. P. Putnam's Sons, N.Y.C., and reprinted by permission of the publisher.

"Action in the Sunda Strait," copyright, 1953, by Ronald McKie, from *The Survivors,* used by special permission of the publisher, The Bobbs-Merrill Company, Inc., Indianapolis, and the Australian publisher, Angus & Robertson, Ltd., Sydney.

"The Battle of Midway," copyright, 1949, by The Curtis Publishing Company. Reprinted from The Saturday Evening Post where it appeared under the title "Never a Battle Like Midway." Used by permission of the author's agent, Brandt & Brandt.

"Ferdinand on Hollandia," copyright 1946, 1959 by Oxford University Press. Reprinted from *The Coastwatchers* by permission of Ballantine Books and Commander E. A. Feldt.

"Guadalcanal: The Turning Point," copyright, 1947, by Major Frank Hough. From *The Island War,* published by J. B. Lippincott Company, Philadelphia, and used by permission of the publisher.

"Fighting Back in New Guinea," copyright, 1943, by George H. Johnston, from *The Toughest Fighting in the World,* used by permission of the publisher, Duell, Sloan and Pearce, Inc., N.Y.C., and the Australian publisher, Angus & Robertson, Ltd., Sydney.

"Raid on Singapore," copyright 1960 by Brian Connell, from *Return of the Tiger.* Reprinted by permission of Doubleday & Co., and the Author.

"PT Boats in the Slot," copyright, 1944, by John Hersey. Published in *The New Yorker,* and reprinted by permission of the author.

"Tarawa: The Second Day," copyright, 1944, by Robert Sherrod. From *Tarawa,* published by Duell, Sloan and Pearce, Inc., and used by permission of the publisher.

"Suicide Creek at New Britain," copyright, 1947, by William Sloane Associates. Reprinted from *Semper Fidelis,* a Marine Corps Anthology published by William Sloane Associates, Inc. Used by permission of the Leatherneck Association, Inc.

"Action at the Pigpen," copyright 1945 by The Infantry Journal, Inc. Reprinted by permission of the author. From *Island Victory.*

"End on Saipan," copyright, 1947, by Major Frank Hough. From *The Island War,* published by J. B. Lippincott Company, Philadelphia, and used by permission of the publisher.

"Banzai on Guam," copyright, 1946, by Alfred A. Knopf, Inc. From *The Long, the Short, and the Tall.* Reprinted by permission of the publisher, Alfred Knopf, Inc., N.Y.C., and the author, Alvin M. Josephy, Jr.

"The Caves of Biak," copyright 1955 by The George Macy Co., Inc. Reprinted by permission of Dial Press.

"Raid on Balikpapan," copyright 1945 by Captain Donald Hough and Captain Elliott Arnold, from *Big Distance.* Reprinted by permission of Duell, Sloane and Pearce.

"Coral Comes High," copyright 1946 by George P. Hunt. Reprinted by permission of Harper & Brothers, and Harold Ober Associates.

"Submarine vs. Destroyer," copyright, 1951, by W. W. Norton & Company, Inc. From *Battle Submerged,* and reprinted by permission of the publisher.

"The Northern Front in Burma," copyright 1961 by Field Marshal the Viscount William Slim, from *Defeat into Victory.* Reprinted by permission of David McKay Company, Inc., and David Higham Associates Ltd., London.

"Blackpool Block," copyright 1961 by Bengal-Rockland, Inc., from *The Road Past Mandalay.* Reprinted by permission of Harper & Bros., and Laurence Pollinger Ltd., London.

"The Battle for Leyte Gulf," copyright, 1955, by Hanson W. Baldwin. Copyright, 1938, by Hanson W. Baldwin. Reprinted from *Sea Fights and Shipwrecks* by Hanson W. Baldwin, and used by permission of the publishers Doubleday & Company, Inc. (Hanover House) and the London publisher, Museum Press, Ltd.

"Iwo: Jungle of Stone," copyright, 1945, by The Dial Press, Inc., and *The Infantry Journal.* From *U.S. Marines on Iwo Jima,* and reprinted by permission of the publisher.

"Okinawa," copyright 1947 by Frank O. Hough. From *The Island War.* Reprinted by permission of J. B. Lippincott Company.

"The Gallant Fight of the Radar Pickets," copyright 1960 by Samuel Eliot Morison, from *Victory in the Pacific.* Reprinted by permission of Little, Brown & Co.

"Abandon Ship," copyright 1958 by Richard F. Newcomb. Reprinted by permission of Henry Holt & Co.

"The Great White Light," copyright 1961 by Gene Gurney, from *Journey of the Giants.* Reprinted by permission of Coward-McCann Inc.

Contents

Foreword

Let me begin at the end: Hiroshima and Nagasaki. The island and ocean battles across the long Pacific begin to fade in the sunset of memory. But the mushroom clouds from the only two atomic bombs ever dropped in wartime linger as symbols and warnings. It is a terrible thought, but the victims of the plutonium bombs may have made the most important sacrifice for future peace. If so, we are eternally indebted to them. The technology of warfare has moved onward and upward to confrontation in space; defense budgets in the United States, Russia and elsewhere around the world deprive the underprivileged of necessary social needs; and the tensions between the superpowers remain steadfast while cold warriors decline disarmament and still talk theoretically about "limited" nuclear exchange in which merely tens of millions of people would perish. Yet the ugly new "final solution" has not occurred because Hiroshima and Nagasaki have, thus far, served to brake the madness.

World War II in the Pacific was a clear war against military aggression by Japan. The warrior class took over the Japanese government and installed a General, Hideki Tojo, as premier. The Japanese had already conquered parts of the Asian mainland and had occupied island chains in the Pacific ocean when, on that fateful dawn of December 7, 1941, its fleet of carriers and battleships attacked Pearl Harbor. Like the Nazi blitzkrieg that swept across France and occupied western Europe, the Japanese had achieved a brilliant surprise against a sleeping giant.

The United States had already started to inch into the war before Pearl Harbor by helping beleaguered Britain defend itself. More than a year before the Japanese attack, fifty destroyers were given to the British in exchange for naval and air bases in the Caribbean and British Guiana to help defend the Western Hemisphere. The preparation for world war continued with President Roosevelt's "Four Freedoms" speech in January 1941, calling for a world founded on freedom of speech and expression, freedom to worship God in one's own way, freedom from want and freedom from fear. But there was also a military message in that same speech against the isolationists:

"We must always be wary of those who with sounding brass and a tinkling cymbal preach the 'ism' of appeasement. We must especially beware of that small group of selfish men who would clip the wings of the American eagle to feather their own nests. I have recently pointed out how quickly the tempo of modern warfare could bring into our very midst the physical attack which we must expect if the dictator nations win this war. As long as the aggressor nations maintain the offensive, they—not we—will choose the time and the place and the method of their attack."

These prescient remarks before the Japanese attack were not universally admired in the country. Nevertheless, President Roosevelt succeeded a few months later in getting Congress to pass the Lend-Lease Act providing further help to the Allied cause. And, again, the Atlantic Charter formulated by President Roosevelt and Prime Minister Churchill in the summer of 1941, pledged that "after the final destruction of the Nazi tyranny" a peace would be established where people everywhere could live in freedom.

After Pearl Harbor—"December 7, 1941, a date that will live in infamy"—Congress without a dissenting vote declared war against Japan. Germany and Italy, partners with Japan in the Axis, declared war on the United States on December 11, and Congress replied with declarations or war and voted that American forces could be dispatched to any part of the world.

"The true goal we seek is far above and beyond the ugly field of battle," President Roosevelt told the nation. "When we resort to force, as now we must, we are determined that this force shall be directed toward ultimate good as well as against immediate evil. We Americans are not destroyers— we are builders. We are now in the midst of a war, not for conquest, not for vengeance, but for a world in which this nation, and all that this nation represents, will be safe for our children. We are going to win the war and we are going to win the peace that follows."

With these noble words, the American armed forces began the long journey on the watery highway to victory across the Pacific ocean. The names of the battlegrounds on land and sea are here in pain and splendor. Bataan. Sundra Strait. Midway. New Guinea. Guadalcanal. Tarawa. Saipan. Guam. Leyte Gulf. Okinawa. Iwo Jima. And more tales of the South Pacific, and Singapore, Burma and the Asian mainland, alone and with allies, in foxholes and on unmarked seas. In kamikaze assaults from the air and from jungle lairs, the Japanese fought for their Emperor and military ideals to the death.

In his opening paragraph of *Tales of the South Pacific,*
James A. Michener set the strange war scene:

I wish I could tell you about the South Pacific. The
way it actually was. The endless ocean. The infinite
specks of coral we called islands. Coconut palms nod-
ding gracefully toward the ocean. Reefs upon which
waves broke into spray, and lagoons, lovely beyond
description. I wish I could tell you about the sweating
jungle, the full moon behind rising volcanoes, and the
waiting. The waiting. The timeless, repetitive waiting.

And then came the great white light of the atom bombs.
President Roosevelt was dead; the decision belonged to President Truman. In retrospect today, with the knowledge of the
human death and damage caused by radiation and fire, we
wonder if Hiroshima and Nagasaki were necessary. Should
there have been a demonstration of the atom bomb's effects?
Would Japan have surrendered without it? Or would millions
of casualties resulted on both sides in a beachhead invasion
and combat in Japan? We shall never know.

But this is certain: at the time soldiers and scientists, civilians and government officials wanted the war to end sooner
than later and were glad that we, and not Japan or Germany,
possessed the nuclear weapon. In the hands of the dictators,
the atom bomb would have been unthinkable.

From time immemorial, always there have been two wars:
the war, and the war remembered. When Virgil wrote *"Arma
virumque cano"* as the opening line of the epic *Aeneid,* he
began a wondrous tale of warring Greeks and Trojans, full of
glory without purpose and death by primitive sword. And yet
he began his tale with, "I sing of arms and the man." Thus
have come many singers of war afterward, up to our own
time of nuclear overkill and forbearance.

In his Nobel Peace Prize lecture Linus Pauling plucked a
neutron of hope from the core of the dreamkillers: "I believe
that there will never again be a great world war—a war in
which the terrible weapons involving nuclear fission and nuclear fusion would be used. And I believe that it is the dis-
coveries of the scientists upon which the development of
these terrible weapons was based that are now forcing us to
move into a new period in the history of the world, a period of
peace and reason, when world problems are not solved by
war or by force, but are solved in accordance with world law,
in a way that does justice to all nations and that benefits all
people."

The Second World War is now history. Unlike the Viet-
nam war, it was a war of defense. Its battles speak to us
across the divide of nearly half a century. It tells us we must
think the unthinkable—of civilized world law to insure
peace. And we must sing of men without arms.

—Herbert Mitgang

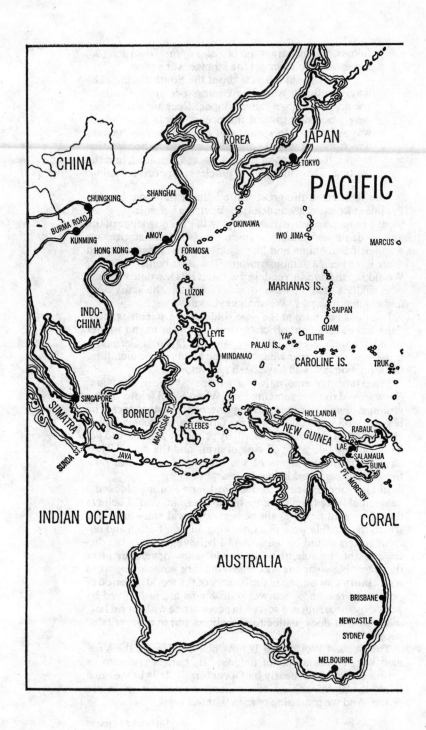

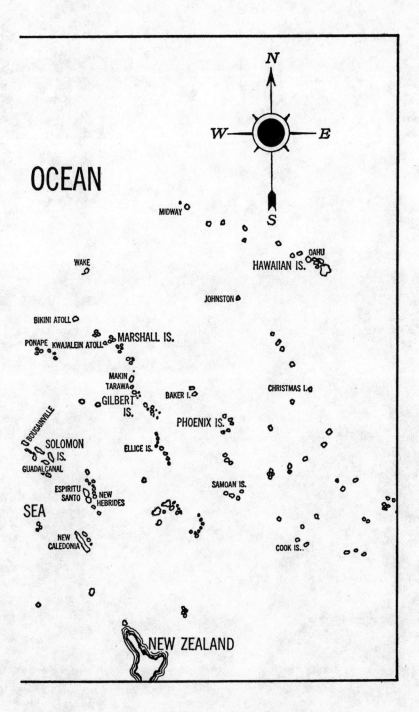

Sunday Morning

Japan attacked Pearl Harbor on December 7, 1941. For the United States it was a catastrophic surprise; for Japan, a logical next step in her drive to rule Asia.

In half a century of aggression, Japan had already won Formosa from China, defeated Russia on land and sea, absorbed Korea and, fighting on the side of the Allies in World War I, had won the Pacific island chains of the Marianas, Carolines and Marshalls from Germany; in 1931 she had occupied Chinese Manchuria, and in 1937 began an invasion of China proper that was to last through 1945.

The United States tried to persuade Japan to drop the war on China; she could pressure the Japanese with economic sanctions (U.S. scrap iron and oil were vital to their war machine) but it was feared that this would only drive Japan to attack the oil-rich Dutch East Indies (Indonesia). She therefore first tried to stop Japanese aggression by diplomacy.

But Japan was dedicated to war. Many Japanese traditionally regarded war as an ultimate good, and their army's past successes helped raise it to an exalted position in the nation's counsels. There were elements in the Japanese government that opposed militarism, but they were clearly in the minority.

And Japan was strong enough to ignore Western protests. In the naval conferences of world powers called in 1921 and 1930 to fix limitations on naval construction, Japan had agreed to a secondary position in a 5-5-3 ratio with Britain and the U.S. But secretly she worked for complete equality with the U.S. and Britain, or better. By Pearl Harbor day Japan's navy was more powerful than the combined British and U.S. fleets in the Pacific area. She had ten aircraft carriers, while the U.S. had only three and the British, one. She had constructed the two largest battleships the world had ever seen, both displacing over 60,000 tons, and armed with 18.1-inch guns. Even more important, Japan was the first nation to fully embrace the strategy of using the aircraft carrier

11

as an offensive weapon (heretofore carriers had been used only to protect big battleships).

Diplomacy didn't succeed in persuading Japan to change her ways. Early in 1938 the U.S. began adopting economic sanctions against her piecemeal, until, in July 1941, trade with Japan was severed and her assets in the U.S. were frozen. A calculated risk had been taken that Japan would not strike at the East Indies before the U.S. was strong enough to deter her. But the American people weren't ready to take the risk of war seriously, and Congress was in no mood to appropriate the sums needed to expand the armed services. With only limited means, Gen. Marshall and Adm. Stark, the heads of the army and navy, now set about relocating their small forces, strengthening wherever possible the commitments the U.S. had assumed in the Pacific. Elements of the 4th Marine Division stationed in Shanghai were to be withdrawn to the Philippines (orders were not delivered in time to prevent their capture by the Japanese in December), an infantry division in training was scheduled to go to the Philippines (war began before they could be sent), and the navy was alerted to the possibilities of imminent war with Japan. In the meantime, the State Department and President Roosevelt were negotiating with the Japanese, for if nothing else could be accomplished time had to be gained for the nation to build up its strength.

But Japan had no time to waste. Suspension of trade with the U.S. caught her with little more than a year's supply of oil on hand. In September 1941, the Japanese military leaders gave their government six weeks to reinstate oil imports from the U.S.; otherwise they would invade the East Indies, accepting the full implications of possible war with the U.S. and European powers, most of whom were too involved in the war with Germany to fight Japan in the Pacific.

By early October the diplomats were still bogged down over the issue of Japan's withdrawal from China. The Japanese army now took over full control of the government, with Gen. Tojo as premier. Early in November Tojo's cabinet, now committed to hostilities, ordered the Japanese fleet to prepare for aggressive operations against the East Indies and the Philippines, and called for a carrier attack on Pearl Harbor. There was to be no declaration of war (as there had been none in Germany's earlier invasions), but a total surprise attack.* The Pearl Harbor

* Official negotiations would continue until the very hour news was flashed to Washington that Pearl Harbor was attacked.

12

striking force would consist of six carriers, two battleships, two cruisers, nine destroyers, and twenty-seven submarines. The fleet left Japan on November 26th, scheduled to strike Hawaii around December 8th, if all went well. To achieve surprise, a course was charted north to the Aleutians, and then south, coming in north of Hawaii. The Japanese naval commander had instructions to abandon his attack if discovered, but because of overcast weather, and because of failures in U.S. reconnaissance at Hawaii on the morning of December 7th, the attack would achieve its purpose—complete and disastrous surprise.

At a point 275 miles north of Pearl Harbor, the Japanese carriers turned into the wind, and launched their planes. But of 423 jammed into the carriers, 353 would see action that day. At 0750 they would find 70 combat ships of the U.S. Pacific Fleet in Pearl Harbor, and only one would be under way when the Japs arrived. Here is an eyewitness report of what happened.

PEARL HARBOR

by 1st Sgt. Roger Emmons

At 7:55 a.m. on 7 December, 1941 (as all the world now knows), the Japanese made a surprise aerial attack on the U.S. Pacific Fleet in Pearl Harbor, Territory of Hawaii. The sole object of the attack was to annihilate the American fleet—battleships in particular.

The *U.S.S. Tennessee*, Captain C. E. Reordan commanding, was one of eight battleships which participated in the battle. On that occasion the *California, Maryland, Tennessee, Arizona,* and *Nevada,* respectively, were moored in single file at Ford Island in the middle of Pearl Harbor. The *Oklahoma* was berthed alongside the *Maryland,* while the *West Virginia* was beside the *Tennessee.* The eighth battleship, *Pennsylvania,* was in drydock at the Navy Yard. Other warships of various types were also present in the harbor.

13

It was a beautiful morning with fleecy clouds in the sky, and the visibility was good. Aboard the *Tennessee* the usual Sunday schedule prevailed. Many of the officers had gone ashore over the week end. The Marine Detachment was drawn up on the fantail for morning Colors, mess tables were being cleared away, some of the men were getting dressed preparatory to going on liberty, while others "batted-the-breeze" over their after-breakfast smoke. In its beginning the day was just another peaceful Sunday at the United States' largest naval base.

A few minutes before 7:55 a.m., several squadrons of mustard-yellow planes flew over the Hawaiian island of Oahu from the southwest, but this caused no alarm as military planes overhead were the usual thing. When those squadrons approached Pearl Harbor, they maneuvered into attack formations at low altitude over Merry's Point. At 7:55 a.m. wave after wave of those warplanes streamed across the harbor and hurled their deadly missiles upon the unsuspecting battle fleet. Every plane seemed to have its objective selected in advance, for they separated into groups and each group concentrated on a specific ship.

When the first wave of attacking planes came over, I was in the Marine Detachment office on the second deck of the *Tennessee*. Pfc George W. Dinning, the clerk, was seated at the desk making out the Morning Report. Suddenly we felt a violent bump which gave us the feeling that the ship had been pushed bodily sideways, and as I did not hear any explosion I remarked that some ship had run into us.

Immediately after that the alarm gongs sounded "General Quarters." I was so surprised that I could hardly believe my ears, but the noise of explosions through the open ports forced it upon me. George never did finish that Morning Report; he jumped seemingly sideways through the door and was gone like the wind. Snatching a detachment roster from the desk, I dashed after him.

My battle station was on the 5-inch broadside guns where I could see what actually was happening around us. I had a hurried look round from the casemates on the starboard side and then went over to the port side. The sky was dotted with black puffs of antiaircraft fire. A plane, trailing a plume of smoke, was plunging earthward over Ford Island. Off in the direction of Schofield Barracks, there was a vast cloud of black smoke. At the same time, two billowing pillars of smoke arose from the Navy Yard and Hickam Field area. The sky was full of planes bearing the Rising Sun emblem of Japan. Overhead droned a flight of horizontal bombers at an altitude of about 10,000 feet. Some sixty enemy planes were diving at our ships.

Then a great many things happened in a very short time. The Japanese planes struck time and time again to get in the killing blows. First came aerial torpedoes, then heavy bombers and dive bombers. Within a few minutes of the commencement of the attack, we were hit direct two times by bombs.

One bomb bursting on the forward turret disabled one gun, and a fragment from it penetrated the shield on the bridge above, killing a sailor and severely wounding Ensign Donald M. Kable. The commander of the *West Virginia,* Captain Mervyn S. Bennion, was mortally wounded by a portion of this bomb when he emerged from the conning tower to the bridge of his ship. The second, a 15- or 16-inch projectile, which the enemy was using as a bomb, hit the aft turret, but fortunately, it did not explode, but pierced the top, killing two men under the point of impact.

At about 8:00 a.m., a terrific explosion in the *Arizona,* astern of us, fairly lifted us in the water. She blew up in an enormous flame and a cloud of black smoke when her forward magazine exploded after a Japanese bomb had literally dropped down her funnel. Her back broken by the explosion, the entire forward portion of the ship canted away from the aft portion as the ship began to settle on the bottom.

It was a scene which cannot easily be forgotten—the *Arizona* was a mass of fire from bow to foremast, on deck and between decks, and the surface of the water for a large distance round was a mass of flaming oil from millions of gallons of fuel oil. Over a thousand dead men lay in her twisted wreck. Among those who perished were Rear Admiral Isaac C. Kidd and Captain Franklin Van Valkenburgh.

A few moments after this disaster, our attention was absorbed in the *Oklahoma*. Stabbed several times in her port side by torpedoes, she heeled very gently over, and capsized within nine minutes. The water was dotted with the heads of men. Some swam ashore, covered from head to foot with thick, oily scum, but hundreds of men trapped in the vessel's hull were drowned.

We had only been in the attack a few minutes when the *West Virginia*, about 20 feet on our port beam, began slowly to settle by the bow, and then took a heavy list to the port. She had been badly hit by several torpedoes in the opening attack. Incendiary bombs started fires which filled her decks and superstructure with flame and smoke.

In the midst of all this turmoil, the *Nevada*, the next ship astern of the blazing *Arizona*, got under way and headed for the channel. As she moved down stream, the vessel was a target of many enemy planes until badly crippled by a torpedo, and after that she ran aground to prevent sinking.

The next picture was a destroyer, name unknown, leaving the harbor under a withering fire from Japanese planes.

But to return to the *Tennessee*. The real story of this ship lies in the splendid manner in which the officers and men on board arose to the emergency. When "General Quarters" was sounded, all hands dashed to their battle stations. There was no panic. The shock found each and every man ready for his job. Antiaircraft and machine guns were quickly manned, the first gun getting into action in less than three minutes after the alarm.

For the next forty minutes, the *Tennessee* was the center of a whirlwind of bombs and bullets. The Japanese planes bombed our ship and then bombed again. They opened up with machine guns in low flying attacks. The ship's gun crews fought with utmost gallantry, and in a most tenacious and determined manner. They had no other thought than to keep the guns going and thereby annihilate those "slant-eyed sons-of-bitches" from the land of the Rising Sun. Hostile planes swooping down on what they thought an easy prey were greeted with volleys from our antiaircraft and machine guns. After such a warm reception, the Japanese airmen gave the *Tennessee* a wide berth.

16

So terrific was the noise of the explosions and our own antiaircraft guns that one could not hear himself speak and had to shout in anybody's ear. The air seemed to be full of fragments and flying pieces. In the general din, there was a *whoosh,* followed by a dull *whoomph* of huge explosives which struck so close to the ship that she shivered from end to end.

The Marines were stationed on the 5-inch broadside guns numbers 6, 7, 8, 9, and 10. They had nothing active to do at the beginning of the action—any firing by the broadside batteries was absolutely out of the question as the port guns trained on the adjacent *West Virginia,* while the starboard guns aimed at Ford Island. They had simply to stand by under a heavy aerial assault unable to reply; or to put it in the vernacular of the Marines in casemate No. 10, "We felt like bastards at a family reunion."

Captain Chevey S. White, in command of the Marines, seeing that it was no use keeping the Marines on the broadside batteries, sent a volunteer crew to man the 3-inch guns on the starboard side of the quarter-deck, and the surplus were given a chance to fight it out with ancient Lewis machine guns placed in advantageous positions about the ship.

There was an interval of comparative calm, which seemed a good opportunity to ascertain the casualties suffered by the Marines and make a report to Captain White. Accordingly, I began a tour of the assumed battle stations, checking the men by that roster which I had brought with me. I counted 76; there had been 81.

My next job then was to take a look round the ship for the men missing. Naturally, my first thought was to see if they were among the wounded. Went below to second deck, where sick bay was located. The passageway outside the ward was covered with men lying on mattresses or on cots. Stepping carefully between the rows of maimed, burned and bleeding, I groped my way to the surgeon's office. A hospital corpsman informed me that no Marines appeared on the casualty list.

Then I crossed over to the Marine office on the port side, and found the lock had been knocked off the door by a working party detailed to secure all battle ports. Thought it

17

would be just as well to gather up our service record books in case it was necessary to quickly abandon ship, so I put the records in my pillowcase and carried them up to casemate No. 10.

Coming on deck again, I met Lieutenant Hugh J. Chapman, who had recently joined the detachment. He was occupied in organizing ammunition supply parties. Throughout the attack, he rendered invaluable service, directing the distribution of ammunition to guns requiring it.

Someone told me there were a few Marines manning the main-top, some 70 or 80 feet above the deck, access to which could be gained by ascending a series of iron ladders running up the interior of the mast. Deciding to have a look there for the missing men, I clambered up the ladders, past the first landing, through a belt of hot, acid, funnel smoke, and was halfway to the top when enemy planes suddenly reappeared and soon we were in the thick of a bombing and strafing attack.

Appreciating that I might momentarily expect to be blown or shot off the mast, I thought for a few seconds, "Should I go up or down," and decided on the former. I didn't waste much time in climbing up the ladder into the top through the "lubber's hole." When I stepped on the platform, my feet slipped out from under me and it was nothing short of a miracle that I didn't fall down the hole and get mashed up. Looked around to see what the trouble was, and discovered the source to be an overturned bucket of aluminum paint. Corporal C. Westover afterwards told me that he was painting there when the blitz started.

It is difficult to write clearly of the details of this attack for the whole thing outdid the most imaginative picture of a battle. The Japs dive-bombed our ships again and again, while low-flying planes, no more than 100 feet above the water, strafed the gun crews. They flew to the end of the bay, made a turn, and came back. For about twenty minutes the strafing attack kept up, the planes going continuously up and down, spraying the low row of battleships with machine gun bullets.

In the general din, I could hear the staccato bark of the pom-poms on the *Maryland* just ahead of us. There was

18

something tremendously heartening about the sound of them, and the very noise was inspiring. After what seemed ages to me, some of the raiders left and the sky was clearer.

On the main-top I found four of the missing Marines, where also were Lieutenant Ernest C. Fusan and Gunnery Sergeant Porter W. Stark. They were craning their necks at the yardarm which had been struck by a bomb.

A terrible scene of destruction was revealed to me as I took a general look round. The *West Virginia* just abeam of us was flaming furiously. Only the bottom of the *Oklahoma* was visible. The *Arizona* was an inferno now, emitting dense volumes of oily smoke which hung over the harbor like a funeral pall. Our next ahead, *Maryland,* was hit by a large bomb on the forecastle which penetrated the deck and made an ugly hole in her port bow. An armor-piercing bomb had exploded in one of the casemates on the *Pennsylvania.* Looking toward the *California,* I noticed that she had a heavy list to the port side, and smoke appeared to be coming from her. The *Nevada* had been run hard ashore, in a sinking condition.

One had a none too cheerful feeling at the thought that five of our eight battleships had been sunk or badly damaged in the attack. In addition to these, three destroyers and a mine layer were sunk. The old target ship, *Utah,* moored at the place usually occupied by the aircraft carrier *Lexington,* had capsized as a result of being torpedoed.

My attention was called by Sergeant Stark to the bridge of the *West Virginia* below us. Her captain was lying there mortally wounded. Rescue parties could not reach him because the bridge was wreathed in fire and smoke. Still capable of movement, he was trying to roll away from the choking fumes and blistering heat.

Sergeant Stark said that during the first attack a low-flying torpedo-carrying plane coming in astern of us was blown into infinitesimal pieces by a direct hit from our antiaircraft batteries. It happened, literally speaking, in a flash; one moment there was an attacking plane; the next moment it was a puff of smoke. When this cleared, there was nothing to be seen save dust settling on the water.

I then got down from the tops and made another tour of

19

the battle stations, and at each found the same picture. The men were cool and in fine spirit. Everyone was doing his utmost, and the things that we had been training for for many months were being achieved. The men had set up machine guns on temporary mounts and were blazing away at the attackers.

Corporal Flood's volunteer crew on the quarter-deck worked the 3-inch gun with the precision and certainty of a well-regulated machine. They might have been at drill for all the excitement they displayed. A Jap plane flew over; the gun flamed, it roared, it leaped to the rear, it slid to the front; the gun was loaded; another target appeared, the gun was fired again, and the projectile screamed skyward. I thought these men performed their duties in a most efficient manner despite the fact that they had no previous experience in the use of that particular type gun. The members of the gun crew were Cpl. Warren K. Flood. Pfc George W. Dinning, Pvts. Robert H. Stinecipher, Jr., George H. Tarver, and Benjamin F. Williams, Jr.

Sergeant Frederick E. Frank (Xenia, Ohio) was in charge of a detail handling the 3-inch ammunition. In constant danger of being blown to bits, the men in this party carried ammunition from aft magazine to the gun with much enthusiasm and energy.

Went up on the bridge and located the last two of the missing Marines. They were manning a .50-caliber machine gun which Field Cook Clay H. Gee had carried to the bridge and set up in the face of severe enemy bombing and strafing. Other Marines on this gun were Pfc Delbert W. Johnson, Pfc Ralph F. Haws, and Pvt. Roy D. Kelly. While there I came upon the body of a sailor who had been killed by bomb fragments which penetrated the bridge shield as if it was tissue paper. He was propped in a sitting position and still wore head phones.

I was astonished to find that the only casualty among the Marines was Sergeant Walter Holland, injured in the right foot by flying debris or bomb fragment while operating with Group I, Machine Guns, but despite his injury, he continued to work at the guns.

Then I went in search of Captain White and found him

20

standing coolly on the quarter-deck, occupied in estimating the situation, giving orders, and receiving reports. I reported to him and then continued touring the battle stations to see how things were faring.

On one of my expeditions I was surprised to find a soldier at a battle station. He had come aboard that morning to visit Pfc Coy R. Tyson, and when "General Quarters" sounded, he was ordered by Sergeant Stark to go along with Tyson to his action station.

Very early in the action an incident occurred which history may record as the first hand-to-hand encounter of the American-Japanese War. A Nipponese plane crashed on Ford Island near us, and the uninjured pilot started running toward a nearby clump of trees when a Marine sentry with a bayoneted rifle intervened. The flier took out his pistol and attempted to shoot the Marine, but the latter plunged his bayonet into the Jap until he was dead. I personally did not see this, but some of the ship's company were witnesses.

Eventually the attackers gradually flew away, and toward 10:15 a.m., I saw one solitary Jap plane disappear beyond the mountain in back of Pearl Harbor. The action for us was ended although we did not think so at the time. The exact number of enemy planes disposed of could not be ascertained with any certainty, but my impression was that it was not very large. We, of course, did not know where the attackers came from, but thought they came from land bases as well as from aircraft carriers.

Most disappointing on this occasion was the total absence of our own aircraft. During the attack on Pearl Harbor itself, there was not one American plane to be seen in the sky. Those who participated in the battle had one thought, one question: "Where in hell is our air force?"

I have said little about the navy personnel in this narrative for I was fully occupied during the action with the Marines and had little time to observe the sailors, except the antiaircraft crews on which the brunt of the fighting fell. They were perfect. Their lot was the hardest, for it takes rugged men to stick to their guns as dive bombers come screaming at them, and low-flying planes spray the decks with machine gun bullets. Ignoring the bombs and strafing, these navy gunners pumped a hail of metal above the harbor just as coolly as if they were at target practice, and accounted for several raiders. No praise can be too high for them.

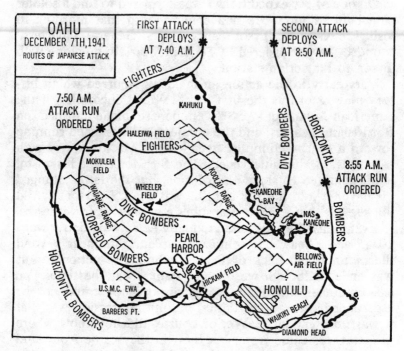

It might be mentioned here that the *Tennessee*'s casualties were only 6 men killed or died of wounds, 1 officer and 36 men wounded, and 1 man missing, which was really an astonishingly light number considering the total casualties in the attack.

The most vivid impression of the battle left to all of us was the suddenness and unexpectedness of the whole incident. Although the powers that be may have known that something more than usual was in the wind, the men were certainly unaware that anything was likely to happen. The first inkling we received that there was something doing was when the Japanese planes streamed across the harbor and hurled their torpedoes into our warships.

It will never cease to be a source of wonder to me that we

did not share the fate of the *Arizona*. One may attribute our comparative immunity to the following:

1. The Grace of God—for an armor-piercing bomb, deflected by the yardarm, struck the roof of the aft turret a glancing blow. Had the yardarm not been in its path, the projectile would have penetrated the turret and detonated in the aft magazine.

2. That the *West Virginia* berthed alongside shielded us from the torpedo planes.

3. The bravery and persistency of our antiaircraft gun crews in fighting to the fullest extent of their ability and equipment. Their fire was so heavy that the Japanese bombers were forced to swerve off course, causing their bombs to fall short of the *Tennessee*.

4. That so few hits were obtained considering the number and proximity of the bombs that fell round us. We compared notes afterwards, and decided that during the battle, about eighteen to twenty bombs fell within 100 yards of the ship.

5. That at times the *Tennessee* was entirely hidden by huge smoke clouds drifting from the *Arizona* and *West Virginia*.

Scenes about the ship, after the battle, beggar description. The water surrounding the *Tennessee* was covered with burning oil, which spread from the *Arizona*, and fire brigades were engaged in a desperate fight for two days to save the ship. During this time, damage control parties fought for many hours to extinguish a large fire that had started aft in the officers' quarters.

In the meanwhile casualties and survivors from other ships began to arrive. That afternoon ten survivors of the *Arizona* Marine Detachment were received on board. Among them was Captain John H. Earle, Jr., who had assumed command on the previous day. Prior to his transfer on the 6th of December, Captain Earle had been detachment officer on the *Tennessee* and we were thankful to see him turn up alive. It was a great shock to us when he informed us that of the eighty-seven Marines who formed the *Arizona* detachment, only thirteen were able to escape.

Most of the survivors had been in the main-top when the

ship blew up and in some miraculous way, in spite of the intense heat and choking smoke, they climbed down the mast, jumped overboard, and swam ashore through patches of oil burning on the water. The only injury received by the swimmers was "sore guts" caused by shock of bombs exploding in the water.

Among those who perished was the First Sergeant of the *Arizona*—Sergeant John Duveene. The survivors told us that after coming up on deck, Sergeant Duveene suddenly went back into the ship with the object of recovering the detachment's vital records. Presently he staggered on deck again, badly burnt all over, his clothing on fire, but carrying the records. He leaped overboard and was never seen again.

During the rest of the night nothing further happened, except that all this time the *Arizona* had been burning fiercely, lighting up the harbor for a great distance, and, much to our discomfort, we were visible for miles round. She burned for two days.

Lightning War in the Far East

The British and Dutch had plenty of warning in Asia and the Southwest Pacific, but were just as vulnerable. The British had been at war with Germany for over two years and Italy for a year and a half and were fully mobilized, but the British commanders grossly underestimated the fighting capabilities of the Japanese. For example, they persuaded themselves in face of evidence to the contrary from the war in China that their outdated planes were a match for the Japanese Zero. Indeed, the Far East commanders paid little attention to the lesson resulting from the Atlantic and Mediterranean naval battles: that battleships and heavy cruisers were easy prey to attacks from the air. The *Prince of Wales* and *Repulse* were permitted to sally out in the China Sea without air cover. Worst of all, the British forces fighting on a world front were spread too thin. They were on the offensive in the African desert, raiding the coast of Europe, defending huge shipping convoys from North America, and picketing the Atlantic Ocean against the threat of German submarines and pocket battleships.

Toward the end of summer, 1941, Prime Minister Churchill was urged to build up British naval strength in the Far East. He dispatched as "the first installment" of the Far Eastern Fleet, the *Prince of Wales*, *Repulse* and four destroyers. The aircraft carrier *Indomitable* was to provide air cover but she had to be left behind for repairs, having run aground. Churchill's "general naval policy was to build up under the remote cover of the main American Fleet in the Pacific a British Eastern Fleet based in Singapore, which by the spring of 1942 would comprise seven capital ships of various quality, one first-class aircraft carrier, ten cruisers and 24 destroyers." *

*Winston Churchill, *The Grand Alliance,* pp. 589-590. Church-

The Japanese were well aware of the weaknesses of the Allies. Furthermore, they were daring and as effective as an aggressor can be who is sure of his objectives. They had waged successful war in China since 1937; now in December 1941 they occupied most of the Chinese coast and the offshore islands. As soon as the Germans occupied France and the Netherlands in Europe, the French Vichy government permitted the Japs to build airfields in Indo-China, while the Dutch East Indies were now sitting ducks. From Indo-China it was easy for the Japs to infiltrate across the border to Siam* and there was only token resistance when they invaded on December 8.

Japan's next move was south along the Malay Peninsula to assault Singapore, the British fortress of the Far East, through the back door.

The British had the 9th and 11th British-Indian divisions for the defense of Malaya which, together with some Malayan and Australian brigades, were expected to stand off the Japanese long enough for reinforcements to arrive from India and the Near East. In addition there was a well-worked-out defense plan to thwart possible invasion. On December 8, the Japanese landed forces at Singora and Patani on the southern coast of Siam, the very area where the British expected them, and on December 10th at Kota Bharu on the coast of northern Malaya. Unfortunately, the British command acted so sluggishly that the defense plan was never initiated.

News of the landings reached Singapore on the 8th, 2:30 a.m. That evening Force Z, made up of the *Prince of Wales, Repulse* and four destroyers set sail from Singapore to attack Jap troopships and supporting naval vessels in the Singora area. Admiral Tom Phillips hoped to surprise the landing forces, shoot them up fast and withdraw quickly before the Japs could launch bombing and torpedo attacks from their airfields in Indo-China. He requested fighter cover for the Singora ac-

---

ill says that he and the British cabinet discussed ordering the *Prince of Wales* and *Repulse* out of Singapore "to take refuge in the islands," and/or to join the already crippled American fleet. Bernard Ash in his recently published *Someone Had Blundered* (Doubleday) labels this wishful thinking on Churchill's part, asking how the ships could possibly be maintained among the islands, and further, how they would get to Pearl Harbor through 6,000 miles of Jap-controlled waters.

*Now Thailand.

tion but was told it might not be forthcoming. Indeed, before he was at sea very long, he was signaled on December 9, that there could be no fighter cover. The Japanese had swept the platter clean in northern Malaya.

"The total number of British aircraft based on airfields in northern Malaya was 110. At the end of the first day only 50 were fit for operations. The Japanese had decided superiority with 530 aircraft. . . . The destruction was so swift that when the Commanders-in-Chief of Far East and Eastern Fleet signaled London on December 9 asking urgently for two squadrons of long range bombers and two squadrons of night fighters to maintain British air superiority, British air superiority had already been lost. Air Command were forced to pull back aircraft from five airfields so that by the evening of the 9th—about 36 hours after fighting began—the combined British bomber and fighter force in northern Malaya contained only ten serviceable aircraft. Within another 24 hours—by December 10—all the remaining fighters and most of the remaining bombers had been withdrawn from Malaya into Singapore island to protect the Naval Base." *

British Force Z was going into battle naked of air cover. And while the *Prince of Wales* had a full complement of anti-aircraft guns, the *Repulse* was undergunned in this respect.

Cecil Brown, CBS war correspondent then stationed in Singapore, was invited to go along on the ill-fated strike and his eyewitness report follows.

TRAGEDY IN THE CHINA SEA
by Cecil Brown

We went aboard the *Repulse* at 5:15 and almost at once we began moving out . . . at half speed. It was a beautiful evening, that twilight of Monday, December 8th. The bright-red sunset silhouetted the palms on the shore.

*Kenneth Attiwell, *Fortress*, p. 35. Doubleday & Co.

Within minutes the *Prince of Wales* drew up alongside and passed us. The crews of each ship stood at attention. Captain William Tennant on our bridge waved his white hat. Two men standing on the bridge of the *Prince of Wales* waved their hats. They were Admiral Tom Phillips and Captain Leach.

Lieutenant Halton of the Royal Marines took us on a tour of all parts of the ship. We went up and down masts, into various control towers, into turrets of the 15-inch guns, down into the engine room, and to the top of the mainmast.

When we finished the tour of the ship we went to the officers' mess and were introduced to Commander Denby, the executive officer, a middle-aged but boyishly husky man who was tough and amiable and who introduced us to each of the officers in the wardroom. At that time there must have been fifteen. It was terrifically hot and we were all soaked in perspiration. By then the *Repulse* and the *Prince of Wales* and four destroyers were out in the South China Sea, moving northeast.

We sat around almost all evening discussing rumors. No one actually knew what was going on. We had dinner and then heard BBC at 8:30. The news wasn't good.

The Japs are in possession of South Thailand. Thai resistance has ceased temporarily. Japanese planes bombed Bangkok.

Tuesday, December 9th:
Gal[1] and I showed up at our action stations on the flag deck at 5:15. We took with us our gas masks, helmets and our anti-flash equipment and lifebelts. The anti-flash equipment is simply a white cloth hood that covers the head and shoulders and leaves exposed only the nose, eyes and mouth. You are supposed to wear it during action to prevent burns from shells bursting on deck. It isn't burns that bother me—it's shrapnel.

Our action station is on the flag deck which is underneath the bridge and is the least protected part of the ship.

[1] O. D. Gallagher, war correspondent.—Ed. note.

28

The flag deck lieutenant is a tough, wiry officer of about twenty-four or twenty-five.

"Is this your action station?" he asked.

"Yes, it is," we said.

"Well, there is one thing about this place. In every action some men on the flag deck get killed."

"That's encouraging," we said.

At about 6:00 a.m. it began to lighten and we found we were about four miles off shore. The *Prince of Wales* was four cable lengths in front. The destroyers flanked us about a mile away. Men all over the ship were sitting and standing by their guns.

At 6:20 an aircraft was reported off the starboard beam, but it kept far away. It might have been a Japanese reconnaissance plane. As dawn came up, lifting the blackness, I felt terribly exposed. One of our catapult aircraft, a Walrus, was put on the track but didn't take off. Gallagher and I were peering into the haze of dawn to see what we could find. He motioned at something.

"You can't tell," he said sardonically, "whether that's an island or five Japanese battleships, ten cruisers, and three aircraft carriers."

"If it's the Japanese fleet," I said, "we won't be interested very long."

The radio is bringing us some news of the attack on Pearl Harbor. It's shocking, but the reaction of the British officers shows how decent these men are. They are amazed by the losses to the American Navy and the heavy attacks on Hawaii, but the general view is:

"Well, the Japanese had the initial advantage of attack. It will take a while to get adjusted."

At 9:45 Lieutenant Halton took us up to the bridge to see Captain Tennant. We hadn't met him before. Halton took me into the captain's sea cabin. This was a room about twelve feet long and five feet wide with glass all across the front. Halton introduced me, and the captain said: "I am very glad to have an American reporter on board."

He gripped my hand hard.

Captain Tennant was dressed in shorts and a shirt with no insignia on the shoulder. His hat was on the shelf. He seemed about fifty years old, with an open, pleasant face, pinkish, smooth skin with wrinkles around the eyes. On the shelf there was a vase of orchids and a picture of his wife.

As he asked me what part of America I came from he paced up and down the cabin, back and forth, peering out of a porthole on each side and the window in front.

"I hope you will excuse me if I move around while I am talking," he said. "The Japs are probably bringing their convoys down over that route. If we are spotted by their aircraft today the Japanese convoy may turn back and they will send two or three battleships and so forth down to meet us."

Captain Tennant was very gay, pleasant, smiling and courteous and seemed confident that we would encounter action.

We told the captain we wondered if the flag deck was the best place to see action.

"Where would you like to be?"

We said we thought we could see more from the after-mast control tower.

"And anyway," I added, "there is a lot of armor protection up there that I would kinda like to have around me."

"Well," the captain said, "I thought the flag deck was better. You can run from one side to the other and watch things from both sides. We'll try that, and if you are not satisfied, perhaps we can put you somewhere else."

"Would you give us an outline of the action after it is over?" Gallagher asked.

"Yes," the captain smiled. "We hope to get some action, and if so I will try to explain it."

It is raining today and it is pretty miserable out. The main 15-inch guns and the secondary armament 4-inch guns are in second degree of readiness. Damage control and supply are at action stations.

At 12:45 a plane was spotted—a tiny dot above the horizon. There was some uncertainty whether it was a Japanese flying boat or a Catalina. Later it was verified as a Catalina and finally it drew closer.

30

While I was up on the flag deck this afternoon the captain came down and said, "We've a couple of knock-kneed destroyers with us. We've got to oil them. We're going to find a few of your destroyers when we get back to Singapore."

This is the first word that American ships are now operating from Singapore Naval Base.

At 1:20 p.m. a message was blinked from the *Wales* to us. It said: "The Japanese have made an air attack on Kota Bharu which was not followed by landings. Major landing ninety miles north of Singapore. Little is known of enemy naval forces in vicinity. It is believed that *Kongo* is only capital ship likely to be met. There are reported three Japanese heavy cruisers and a number of destroyers likely to be met."

I said to the flag deck officer: "A capital ship, three cruisers and some destroyers? That's the fleet we're going to face, eh? Lieutenant, how about calling a taxi to take me back to Singapore?"

He laughed heartily. "Oh, but they are Japanese. There's nothing to worry about."

Another message just came from the *Wales* giving further details: "An *Akaga*-type, *Kako*-type and *Zintu*-type cruiser have been reported."

I checked up on those. One first-class heavy cruiser and two second-class cruisers.

The *Repulse* has never been in action, the men told me. The closest was off Norway when three German planes dropped eighteen bombs, some pretty close, but the *Repulse* didn't fire a shot.

A notice has just been posted: "All officers and ratings from dawn tomorrow are to be at action stations and are to wear clothing to resist burns from flashes of exploding bombs and shells."

Admiral Tom Phillips, as Commander-in-Chief, just sent this message to the *Repulse* and to the four destroyers:

"The enemy has made several landings on the north coast of Malaya and has made local progress. Our Army is not large and it is hard-pressed in places. Our air forces have had to destroy or abandon one or more airfields.

"Meanwhile, fast transports lie off the coast. This is our opportunity before the enemy can establish itself. We have made a wide circuit to avoid air reconnaissance and hope to surprise the enemy shortly after sunrise tomorrow, Wednesday. We may have the luck to try our mettle against some Japanese cruisers or some destroyers in the Gulf of Siam. We are sure to get some useful practice with high-angle armament, but whatever we meet I want to finish quickly and so get well clear to the eastward before the Japanese can mass too formidable a scale of air attack against us. So, shoot to sink."

I was up on the flag deck at 5:20 this afternoon. For the first time there is a break in the thick, black clouds. Far off in the distance—about four or five miles away, just a speck in the sky—an aircraft was sighted. The word came from a spotter in the defense control tower in the aftermast. The word ran through the ship like fire. I watched the aircraft circling, hardly moving.

"It's a Jap, all right," a lieutenant said as he was thumbing through a book of silhouettes of Japanese aircraft. "That means we have been reported to the enemy."

I saw a number of the gunners and other men rubbing their heads and doing dog steps all over the deck. The signal deck yeoman snorted: "Look at them—all this fuss over one aircraft!"

The *Prince of Wales* has just sent us a signal that a formation of aircraft has been reported. All gun crews hop to their stations, eager to get going. Everyone is very brisk and eager-eyed. That reconnaissance aircraft is still four or five miles away and staying well out of range. What a break that is! Just a few minutes ago there was the first gap in the overcast sky in the entire day and as luck would have it we had to be spotted just at that moment.

The lieutenant commander came by on the flag deck and said to me: "I'm afraid he has spotted us and he may go away before we can get a crack at him."

The general opinion of the flag deck is that the reconnaissance aircraft is a Nakajima Naka 93 seaplane.

I have just been told that in addition to the battleship *Kongo* and the three cruisers and a number of destroyers

32

there are many troopships with the warships. Someone said that there are about thirty. Evidently British reconnaissance has spotted them.

Denby said: "The Admiral has delayed up here in order to get at the *Kongo*. There would be a good moral effect to sinking her."

One of our destroyers is going back tonight. It's the *Tenedos,* an antiquated thing, which is running out of oil.

17:58—Captain Tennant piped over the loudspeaker: "We are now being shadowed by enemy aircraft. We are going to revert to third-degree readiness, but we must be prepared to repel aircraft at a moment's notice."

The gun crews are standing down now.

18:30—We are at dinner listening to the BBC. Heavy fighting is going on in Malaya. The fighting is still confused, but BBC says reinforcements should reach there during the day.

BBC says there is no truth in the Japanese reports that an attack was made on Singapore. The Japs have entered Bangkok.

We sat around in the wardroom. There must have been twelve or fifteen officers discussing the news.

"Those Japs are bloody fools," one of them said. "All these pinpricks at widely separated points is stupid strategy. The Japs should have sent over three hundred planes over Singapore, not eleven."

"Bloody fools!" another snorted.

"Those Japs can't fly," one of the officers said. "They can't see at night and they're not well trained."

"They have rather good ships," one of the officers remarked, "but they can't shoot."

I listened to these remarks about the enemy for some time and then remarked to the officers in the wardroom: "You British are extraordinary people. You always underestimate the enemy. You did it time and again, in Norway and France, in Greece, in Crete. I think it's a mistake to underestimate the enemy. It seems to me the best thing is to figure the enemy is twice as good as you are and twice as smart, and then you make preparations in advance."

There was a moment of shocked silence in the ward-

33

room at this criticism and then someone said in a joking manner to cover up the tension: "Oh, but really, the Japanese are not very good."

Another officer remarked: "Yes, I do think it's wrong to underestimate the enemy."

"Well, there is always the danger certainly," I added, "of underestimating the enemy to the point where you are overconfident."

A number of them chimed in, each in his own way. "We are not overconfident; we just don't think the enemy is much good. They could not beat China for five years and now look what they are doing out here, jumping all over the map instead of meeting at one or two places. They cannot be very smart to be doing that."

21:05—We're sitting in the wardroom again and the voice on the loudspeaker has just said: "Stand by for Captain to speak to you."

In an instant Captain Tennant's cool, even voice came through. "A signal has just been received from the Commander-in-Chief who very much regrets to announce having to abandon the operation. We were shadowed by three planes. We were spotted after dodging them all day. Their troop convoy will now have dispersed. It would be very obvious that if we continued, enemy air concentration would be awaiting us and it would be unwise to continue.

"I know that you all share with us the disappointment in not engaging the enemy at this time, but I am sure that you will agree with the C-in-C's judgment. We are, therefore, going back to Singapore."

In the wardroom there were cries and groans of disappointment and even bitterness. I immediately dashed out of the wardroom into the quarters of the ratings to check their reactions. I went into one sailor's mess and the men were sitting around the long tables. Some of the men had tears in their eyes—two a half years in the war and never a chance to engage an enemy.

"How do you fellows feel about that?"

The remarks I got were: "This always happens to the *Repulse*."

"It's a bloody shyme."

34

"We're just an unlucky ship."

Back in the wardroom I stood in the doorway surveying the long faces of the officers sitting in chairs and on divans in front of the fireplace and on the railing around the edge of the fireplace in utter dejection.

Commander Denby and I found a place on a divan and I asked him to explain the type of operation we expected to encounter.

"The essential element of this tip-and-run raid is surprise, and we lost that when that fellow spotted us this afternoon. It amounts to this: we are up against the whole of the Japanese air force with no aircraft protection and no destroyer screen. Well, maybe not the whole Jap force, but at least 50 percent of it."

I slipped up at that moment in not asking what he meant by "no destroyer screen" because we did have four destroyers with us, not much good, but at least destroyers, and one of them was scheduled to be sent back to Singapore that night.

Denby added, "We don't know the extent or nature of the Jap air force or what we would run into. It isn't worth risking two capital ships under the strategic circumstances."

The gunnery officer, a handsome polite Englishman called "Guns" said to me: "How do you feel about turning back?"

"Relieved—and disappointed."

"Well, that's a frank answer," he laughed.

Wednesday, December 10th:

04.00—Awakened after sleeping for about three hours in the steaming cabin. Came up on the flag deck. Pitch dark and I am thirsty as hell. Would like to have tea. No tea on the flag deck, so I went down to the wardroom, but there is no tea there either. It is hellishly hot, so I went back on the flag deck. I see nothing to write in this diary. I can't sleep, I can't rest, and I can't get any tea to drink.

05.05—The call to action stations just sounded. We are still going southward back to Singapore. Instead of hunting

35

the enemy, we are trying to get away from them. Trying to avoid action.

It is a beautiful dawn, the sky is a bright gray, constantly getting lighter. Everyone is on the alert. We expect an attack at any moment.

06.05—The sun is coming up a bright orange.

06.15—"We are changing course," I said to the lieutenant. "Why are we changing course?"

Just as he was about to reply the answer came through the ship's loudspeaker.

"Men, we have just received a message saying the enemy is making a landing at Kuantan. We are going in." That means we intend to shoot up barges and any warships escorting them.

Kuantan is 150 miles north of Singapore on the east coast of Malaya. Gallagher and I remembered it very well as the place where we came down on the water-covered airdrome in our torpedo-carrying bombers. Instead of heading south for Singapore, we are bearing westward for the coast.

06.30—We are putting on cover-alls, anti-flash helmets, and battle helmets. Off to the beam the sky is streaked with gold. All the gun crews are at the action stations. Gallagher and I went down for breakfast of coffee, cold ham, bread and marmalade.

07.20—Back on the flag deck. We are pushing in toward shore very fast. The *Prince of Wales* is ahead; we follow; the destroyers are about a mile or a mile and a half on each side of us. We still have four of them. We can see the shore line and an island far ahead of us.

07.30—The *Wales* just catapulted one of her planes on a reconnaissance. One of the signalers on the flag deck said the reconnaissance pilot had been given instructions not to return to the ship, but to land on the water near the shore after reporting to us on what he found.

07.40—The *Wales* just elevated her 15-inch guns. What a beautiful sight they are! We are speeding in toward shore at about 24 knots. We were watching the Walrus from the *Wales* gain altitude and circle around us once and then disappear out of sight behind two islands shaped like chocolate drops.

"The enemy must be landing behind those mountains," someone on the flag deck said.

But the Walrus reappeared again as a tiny speck in the sky and then flew out of sight once more.

Some of the gunners are putting on asbestos gloves which come up to their elbows and a number of them are wearing goggles. They all look very efficient.

This is a beautiful sight in the brilliant sunlight. I just took a picture of the *Prince of Wales* on the starboard beam. What power there is out here today! The *Wales* is moving with such rhythm, pushing a white wave away from her bow on each side. Every now and then she slaps the water and the spray comes racing over her forward deck.

Our white ensign and hers, too, are rippling out in the breeze.

This is it, I think. This is the way you go in and knock hell out of the enemy.

07.48—We are about eight miles off shore. I can't see anything except green in the foreground, and the mountains rising in the background. I have just taken some more pictures of the gun crews beside their guns.

The communications loudspeaker just announced there is nothing in sight yet; we are going down along the beach.

07.50—The flag officer says, "I think we are too late now. Think they have all gone."

"I wonder," the flag-deck yeoman remarks, "if they have any naval units in there? I don't see a ship anywhere."

One of the youngsters on the flag deck said, "They might be around the bloody corner."

The lieutenant called to the flag-deck yeoman, who was taking signals on the blinker from the *Wales*.

"Is the *Prince of Wales* ready?"

"Yes, they are all ready."

Walrus again came into view.

"That ties it," said the flag-deck lieutenant. "If the Japs were around that Walrus would be down. He can't fight."

08.15—One of the destroyers, I think it was the *Ex-*

press, has just cut across the bow of the *Wales.* The *Express* is going closer into shore.

The land is quite close. I can see many islands.

The destroyer seems very impertinent going in there. I don't understand why we are waiting around here instead of going straight to Singapore as planned.

The reports are that Kuantan Airdrome is being too heavily bombed to get any report from there. I asked an officer what we expected to find in here, but he did not know. It seems quite obvious that the Japs made their landing and then got away.[2]

08.30—We are now going back northward and I understand that we have detached one of the destroyers to go back to Singapore. The one destroyer we sent into shore is going in as close as it can to see what it can find. We are going back northward away from Singapore—the *Prince of Wales,* the *Repulse,* and two destroyers—to see what we can find.

10.10—We steamed northward for about forty-five minutes not far off shore, but we didn't find anything, and we came back and picked up the third destroyer and are moving out to sea.

10.30—I am back on the flag deck again. Fifteen enemy aircraft are reported southeast, but are not in sight. All kinds of signals are being blinked back and forth between the *Wales* and the *Repulse* and between the *Wales* and the three destroyers.

10.40—We are sending off one of our Walrus reconnaissance planes. It goes off the track and just as it does I get a good photograph of it. It dips slightly then climbs up and swings northward. We still have one aircraft left.

10.45—One twin-engined Jap is reported shadowing us. It is the same type that bombed Singapore the first night of the war. It is type 96 Mitsubishi of the Naval Air Service.

The clouds have gone now, and the sky is a robin's-egg blue and the sun is bright yellow. Our ships plow through

---

[2] Actually, the rumor of a Japanese landing was entirely false and cost Force Z precious time.—Ed. Note.

pea-green water, white where the hulls cleave it. Ahead, the *Wales'* 15-inch guns jut, port and starboard, from turrets that bulge like muscles. They seem to quiver, eagerly. The destroyers that flank us are pygmy ships and seem ridiculous and impertinent in such powerful company.

11.04½—The signal yeoman beside me turns away from his spy glass and snaps, "Two masts, one funnel." He jerks it out to one of the signal ratings.

"Report to the bridge. Hop to it." He adds, "We have sighted a ship."

11.06½—The crew of the pom-poms just below us on the starboard is sitting around playing cards, ready for action in an instant. The men on the control towers on the mainmast and after-mast are peering into the sky for enemy aircraft. Men are at the 4-inch high-altitude guns. The men are getting keyed up at the prospect of action. You can almost feel the electricity all over the ship.

Standing on the flag deck, I look down over the decks of the *Repulse*. The guns seem no less eager for combat than the crews themselves.

We're told that Admiral Phillips on the *Wales* has just sent a signal to Singapore asking for aircraft protection.

I haven't had time to shave. I feel bleary and I am terrifically tired. I just took a picture of the gun crew playing cards and another picture of the *Prince of Wales*. Also snapped Gallagher with the flag-deck yeoman.

We are now zigzagging. I only see two destroyers at the moment. The *Prince of Wales* is four cable lengths ahead.

11.07—The communications loudspeaker announces: "Enemy aircraft approaching—action stations!"

I see them: 1-2-3-4-5-6-7-8-9. I would judge them about 12,000 feet, coming straight over the *Repulse*.

11.14—And here they come.

11.15—The guns of the *Prince of Wales* just let go. At the same instant I see the flame belching from the guns of the *Wales*, ours break into a chattering, ear-splitting roar. The nine Japanese aircraft are stretched out across the bright blue, cloudless sky like star sapphires of a necklace.

I've never been so close to so many guns firing at once. The roar of the pom-poms and the hard, sharp crack of the

4-inch high-altitude guns are deafening. The flashes are blinding and suddenly the smell of cordite is strong. I am standing on the port side of the flag deck, in the lee of an air funnel, eight feet from a battery of pom-poms.

I gape open-mouthed at those aircraft coming directly over us, flying so that they will pass from bow to stern over the *Repulse*. The sky is filled with black puffs from our ack-ack. They seem a discordant profanation of that beautiful sky. But the formation of Japanese planes, coming over one behind the other, is undisturbed.

Now they are directly overhead. For the first time I see the bombs coming down, materializing suddenly out of nothingness and streaming toward us like ever-enlarging tear drops. There's a magnetic, hypnotic, limb-freezing fascination in that sight.

It never occurs to me to try to duck or run. Open-mouthed and rooted, I watch the bombs getting larger and larger. Suddenly, ten yards from me, out in the water, a huge geyser springs out of the sea, and over the side, showering water over me and my camera.

I instinctively hunch over, sort of a semi-crouch, and at that same instant there is a dull thud. The whole ship shudders. Pieces of paint fall from the deck over the flag deck.

11.17—"Fire on the boat deck. Fire below!" That just came over the loudspeakers. There are fountains of water all around the ship. Some are near misses. Most of the bombs are hitting the water ten to thirty yards off the port side. Beautiful fountains of thick white at the base and then tapering up into fine spray.

That first bomb was a direct hit. Someone on the flag deck says: "Fire in Marines' mess and hangar."

That bomb struck the catapult deck, penetrated, exploded underneath. The bomb hit twenty yards astern of my position on the flag deck. A number of men (fifty) were killed.

11.21—We got one of the bombers! It is coming down fast, in black smoke. All our guns are still going. I am now near one of the multiple Vickers guns. It is firing 2,000 half-inch shells a minute. God what a racket! That bomber smacked into the water about a half mile away.

11.23—The high-level bombers are gone. We are still zigzagging like mad. The *Prince of Wales* seems to be firing, but I can't tell.

I run back to see the damage, but the bomb penetrated the deck armor and only smoke is coming up. Our aircraft is knocked off its track and a red-bearded New Zealand fleet-air-arm pilot is atop the crane attempting to lift the plane to drop it overside, since its gasoline constitutes a menace.

As I pass the gun crews they seem extraordinarily calm, replenishing ammunition, laughing. I hear someone say: "Let's get them all next time."

A gunner remarks: "Bloody good bombing for those blokes."

When I return to the flag deck I note a three-inch hole in the funnel from a bomb-splinter eighteen inches above the spot where I'd been standing. It's obvious my number isn't up yet.

Smoke is still coming up from the catapult deck and strenuous efforts are under way to control the fire. Four stokers come up to the flag deck to get first aid. They're blackened and scorched and their clothes are water-soaked.

They are very calm but wild-eyed and stunned, and their hands are shaking. The skin is hanging from their hands and faces like tissue paper. Someone says: "Make way for these men."

A stoker croaks tremulously, "Water, I want some water."

A glass is placed to the stoker's lips.

11.26—Just heard a report that there are a number of small fires below, owing to near misses.

The men are giving a big cheer. "They got another one," Gallagher shouts in my ear. I look over in the direction he points. There is a splash two or three miles astern. Some of the gunners are not so certain. A pom-pom gunner says: "Maybe he just jettisoned his bombs."

"Like hell he did," I tell him. "They dropped all the bombs they had on us."

11.40—The *Prince of Wales* seems to be hit. She's reduced her speed and signals, "We've a man overboard." A destroyer pushes up to her side. Standing less than 100 feet away, it's as incongruous as a baby running to protect its mamma. The flag-deck lieutenant says: "Those Japs are good, aren't they?"

I say, "Too good to suit me. How badly is the *Wales* hit?"

The lieutenant says, "I don't know. They haven't told us yet."

We are all lighting cigarettes, sucking deeply, and our exhalations are more like sighs. The pause is too brief.

11.45—Distant specks appear. Now they are identifiable. Nine torpedo-carrying bombers, circling four or five thousand yards away at about a half-mile altitude. Circling in a huge sweep, they are swooping lower. Now they are like moths around our flaming guns.

A bugle blows to stand by. A voice over the ship's communications roars: "Stand by for a barrage!"

Instantly every gun aboard the *Repulse* is stuttering and roaring and the whole ship vibrates and the pom-poms are spitting out empties furiously. But the clatter of empty shell cases on the deck is unheard in the slap-slap of A.A. guns, the crack-crack-crack of 4-inch guns. A voice beside me says, "Look at those yellow bastards come!" The *Repulse* is twisting and snaking violently to avoid torpedoes. My only weapons are a fountain pen, a notebook and a camera, so I sidle beside a multiple Vickers gun spewing 2,000 half-inch bullets every minute.

A few feet to my right an eight-barreled pom-pom is coughing incessantly and a half dozen feet away a 4-inch high altitude ack-ack is crashing, its barrel nearly horizontal instead of skyward, to meet the onrushing torpedo bombers.

A cooling liquid is gushing over the guns and the paint blisters on them are as big as tennis balls. Gunners are moving like a movie running too fast. Some are very young and eager and breathless with excitement, their faces streaked with sweat. The white cloth anti-flash helmets covering their heads, cheeks and shoulders are soaked and discolored. Some are wearing life belts and "Mae Wests."

A whole pom-pom swings this way and that, with its seated trigger man, feet braced, riding with it. That is a dizzy job.

The torpedo-carrying bombers are coming in. We are putting up a beautiful barrage, a wall of fire. But the bombers come on, in a long glide, from all angles, not simultaneously but alternately. Some come head-on, some astern and from all positions on both sides of the ship. They level out.

About 300 yards distant from the ship and 100 yards above the water, they drop their torpedoes.

The torpedoes seem small, dropping flat in the water, sending up splashes, then streaking toward us. Those bombers are so close you can almost see the color of the pilot's eyes. The bombers are machine-gunning our decks as they come in.

I've just seen three more torpedoes drop. Another plane just let go a torpedo. Then it banked sharply. The whole side of the bomber is exposed to us. Shells and tracers are ripping into it. It's fascinating to watch.

Tracer bullets from our guns are cross-stitching the sky, just above eye level, with long, thin white lines, slightly curved. For me this whole picture—orange flame belching from the 4-inchers, white tracers from pom-poms and Vickers guns, and gray airplanes astonishingly close, like butterflies pinned on blue cardboard—is a confusing, macabre game.

But this, I realize, is deadly business, too. Three gunners ten feet from me slump over with Japanese machine-gun bullets in them. It's difficult to comprehend sudden death. But they aren't the only casualties in this terrible moment. A torpedo bomber has just dropped a tin fish and banked without gaining altitude. It glides beautifully, parallel with the *Repulse* at a ten-degree angle, and still tracers are plowing into it. It doesn't seem to me the plane is going to crash, until an instant later I see that it isn't going to pull out and is still gliding toward the sea. It strikes the water and immediately bursts into flame. It burns fiercely, a twenty-foot circle of orange on a blue sea.

I run to the starboard side of the flag deck, where another torpedo bomber is coming in. It is difficult to judge distance, but I guess it's no more than 200 yards away when it swerves. I don't see the torpedo. And with good reason. There's a huge hole in the side of the plane. It's aflame, and instantly it seems to buckle. I got a beautiful picture of this one. As though stricken with a cramp, the bomber dives, shapeless, flaming, seaward. It's just a pillar of fire until it hits the water and spreads out into nothingness.

The men on the catapult deck are still trying to get the damaged aircraft over the side. Its gasoline makes it a fire hazard. That red-bearded New Zealand pilot is working atop the crane trying to heave the Walrus over the side. As the Jap torpedo bombers come in to drop their fish and machine-gun our decks, he is firing at them with his pistol.

There are nine bombers in that attack.

11.51½—Captain Tennant is sending a message to the *Wales:* "Have you sustained any damage?"

The answer comes back: "We are out of control. Steering gear is gone."

The decks of the *Repulse* are littered with empty shell cases. Upon the faces of the sailors there's a mixture of incredulity and a sort of sensuous pleasure, but I don't detect fear. There's an ecstatic happiness, but strangely, I don't see anything approaching hate for the attackers. For the British this is a contest. This facial expression is interpreted by an officer. He turns to me and says: "Plucky blokes, those Japs. That was as beautiful an attack as ever I expect to see."

He'll never see another action. He's at the bottom of the South China Sea.

Our great concern is that the Japs are going to crash-dive the ship. I understand enough about naval warfare to know that the flag deck is a good spot on which to crash-dive. Suddenly it occurs to me how wonderful it would be to be back in Ohio. A voice says: "Here they come again."

12.01—Twelve torpedo bombers launch an attack at all

44

angles. One even launches a torpedo directly astern, which seems silly, since we are twisting rapidly. Planes coming from port and starboard are headed directly at the bow. I see the *Prince of Wales* being subjected to an attack also, and a bomber is coming toward us from a thousand yards, directly ahead.

I think, "Here comes a crash-dive." The smell of cordite is suffocating. My eyes ache with the blows of shell blasts.

Now I am standing in front of the smokestack. The view is good, and I have just taken some more pictures of the bombers coming in. I hear a rat-tat-tat and whine which seems higher and closer than the crash of other guns. I look around to see where it is coming from and then glance overhead. Two feet above my head, drilled in the smokestack, there is a line of bullet holes. I move away from that position. No sense in magnetizing any more Japanese machine-gun bullets.

It's the same as before—amazingly daring torpedo-bombers are targets for mere moments. They rush headlong into our almost solid wall of shells and bullets and are seemingly unaffected. The water is streaked with tracks of torpedoes. A sudden roar goes up on one side of the ship. It's another bomber down, but I didn't see it.

If it wasn't so awe-inspiring it would be routine: the way planes rush in, drop a tin fish, machine-gun the decks of the *Repulse* and roar away.

During this attack, as during the first wave of bombers, Captain Tennant on the bridge of the Repulse *directly above the flag deck is saying in the coolest, calmest possible voice: "Thirty degrees port. Thirty degrees starboard. Thirty degrees port . . ." zigzagging this 32,000-ton battle cruiser out of the path of those torpedoes.*[3]

12.14—Now all the bombers are gone. Captain Tennant has just ordered this message flashed to Admiral Tom Phillips on the *Wales* up ahead: "We have dodged nineteen torpedoes thus far, thanks to Providence."

[3] Italics denote scenes and remarks which I did not actually witness or hear.

Those who are able light cigarettes. The decks are littered with the debris of battle. There are a number of dead men around the guns, and wounded too. More ammunition is being passed up. Everyone around the guns is soaked in sweat, with blackened faces.

I glance at the notes in this diary. Hastily written. And I've twisted the point of my fountain pen, a green Parker, Martha's pen. I check the pack film in the Plaubel Makina suspended by a strap around my neck. There are four pictures left in the pack, enough, I think. No use taking time to change the pack. I rip open another packet and peel off the tape around the metal container, to be ready for a quick change. My ears ache atrociously and my mouth is cottony. The whole place stinks with cordite. I take off my tin hat. This anti-flash hood is like putting your head in an oven.

A young sailor, about eighteen, is standing there wide-eyed. I grin at him.

"They're sure giving us hell, aren't they?" I ask him.

He grins back. I'm as scared as he is.

A few of the sailors are blowing up their lifebelts, I note. I wonder why but only for an instant and forget about it. My lifebelt is stuck up in a small shelf in the roof of the flag deck, too awkward to wear. I feel bulky enough with the cover-alls over the bush-jacket, the camera around my neck, notebook in my left hand and fountain pen in the right hand.

12.19—I see ten bombers approaching. It's impossible to tell whether this will be a high-level or a torpedo attack. They come closer, lower. It's definitely a torpedo attack.

12.20—The communication pipes again, "Stand by for barrage!" and hell breaks loose. A plane is diving straight for the middle of the ship off the port side, 500 yards away, and tracers are rushing to meet it, but it comes on. Now it seems suspended in the air 100 yards above the water, and the torpedo drops.

It is streaking for us. There is a deadly fascination in watching it. The watcher shouts, "Stand by for torpedo." The torpedo strikes the ship about twenty yards astern of my position. It feels as though the ship has crashed into dock. I am thrown four feet across the deck but I keep my feet. Almost immediately, it seems, the ship lists.

The command roars out of the loudspeaker: "Blow up your lifebelts!"

I take down mine from the shelf. It is a blue-serge affair with a rubber bladder inside. I tie one of the cords around my waist and start to bring another cord up around the neck. Just as I start to tie it the command comes: "All possible men to starboard."

But a Japanese plane invalidates that command. Instantly there's another crash to starboard. Incredibly quickly, the *Repulse* is listing to port, and I haven't started to blow up my lifebelt.

I finish tying the cord around my neck. My camera I hang outside the airless lifebelt. Gallagher already has his belt on and is puffing into the rubber tube to inflate it. The effort makes his strong, fair face redder than usual.

The ship is heeled over at a nasty angle. Gallagher says: "You all right, Cec?"

"Yeh, I guess so. No air in my belt though. The hell with it."

"Better blow it. This is it, Cec."

"Yes, Gal. I guess it is. Good going, Kid."

"We'll stick together."

We grin at each other, a weak grin.

Captain Tennant's voice is coming over the ship's loudspeaker, a cool voice: "All hands on deck. Prepare to abandon ship." There is a pause for just an instant, then: "God be with you."

There is no alarm, no confusion, no panic: We on the flag deck move toward a companionway leading to the quarter deck. Abrahams, the Admiralty photographer, Gallagher and I are together. The coolness of everyone is incredible. There is no pushing, but no pausing either. One youngster seems in a great hurry. He tries to edge his way into the line at the top of the companionway to get down faster to the quarter deck.

A young sub-lieutenant taps him on the shoulder and

says quietly: "Now, now, we are all going the same way, too."

The youngster immediately gets hold of himself.

We move swiftly down the fifteen-foot companionway to the quarter deck. Abrahams is carrying his expensive camera like a baby, cradled in his arms. He goes over to a wooden lifebelt locker, about three feet long, carefully opens the lid, gently places his camera inside, and carefully closes the lid.

Beside a pom-pom two men are dead, stretched in grotesque positions of violently won peace. There is blood all around this gun, hot and silent, its base littered with used and never-fired ammunition, too.

I see four sailors carrying Lieutenant Page up the slanting deck of the ship toward the edge. He had been brought up on the deck when the action with the Japanese was joined. He still couldn't walk. Two lifebelts were wrapped around him "in case anything happened." Now he is being lifted to the edge of the ship. The four men heaved, and Page went sailing overboard, so he would have a chance for rescue. Gallagher and Abrahams seem to have disappeared.

I see a lifeboat jammed with seamen and a half dozen officers, still on its davits, still not swung out.

The only way to reach the boat is by a cable. I jump for it and go hand over hand about ten feet, dangling like a monkey by its tail.

I swing myself into a tiny, precarious corner of the lifeboat, first my feet then using my arms as levers on the cable to get all of me inside. I just settle there when someone shouts: "This boat will never get off!"

We all pile out, streaming over the side of the lifeboat, back onto the deck of the *Repulse*. I drop ten feet, hit the slanting, slippery deck, slide about eight feet and crash into a bulkhead. I am dizzy when I pick myself up. Then I fall back on my hands and knees and scramble up the side of the deck, grabbing cables and deck protuberances to reach the edge of the ship.

The *Repulse* is going down.

The torpedo-smashed *Prince of Wales*, still a half to

three-quarters of a mile ahead, is low in the water, half shrouded in smoke, a destroyer by her side.

Japanese bombers are still winging around like vultures, still attacking the *Wales*. A few of those shot down are bright splotches of burning orange on the blue South China Sea.

Men are tossing overboard rafts, lifebelts, benches, pieces of wood, anything that will float. Standing at the edge of the ship, I see one man (Midshipman Peter Gillis, an eighteen-year-old Australian from Sydney) dive from the Air Defense control tower at the top of the main mast. He dives 170 feet and starts to swim away.

Men are jumping into the sea from the four or five defense control towers that segment the main mast like a series of ledges. One man misses his distance, dives, hits the side of the *Repulse,* breaks every bone in his body and crumples into the sea like a sack of wet cement. Another misses his direction and dives from one of the towers straight down the smokestack.

Men are running all along the deck of the ship to get further astern. The ship is lower in the water at the stern and their jump therefore will be shorter. Twelve Royal Marines run back too far, jump into the water and are sucked into the propeller.

The screws of the *Repulse* are still turning. There are five or six hundred heads bobbing in the water. The men are being swept astern because the *Repulse* is still making way and there's a strong tide here, too.

On all sides of me men are flinging themselves over the side. I sit down on the edge of the *Repulse* and take off my shoes. I am very fond of those shoes. A Chinese made them for me just a few days ago in Singapore. They are soft, with a buckle, and they fit well. I carefully place them together and put them down as you do at the foot of your bed before going to sleep.

I have no vision of what is ahead, no concrete thoughts of how to save myself. It is necessarily every man for himself. As I sit there, it suddenly comes to me, the overwhelming, dogmatic conviction. I actually speak the words: "Cecil you are never going to get out of this."

I see one man jump and land directly on another man. I say to myself: "When I jump I don't want to hurt anyone."

Down below is a mess of oil and debris, and I don't want to jump into that either. I feel my mind getting numb. I look across to the *Wales*. Its guns are flashing and the flames are belching through the grayish-black smoke.

My mind cannot absorb what my eyes see. It is impossible to believe that these two beautiful, powerful, invulnerable ships are going down. But they are. There's no doubt of that.

Men are sliding down the hull of the *Repulse*. Extending around the edge of the ship is a three-inch bulge of steel. The men hit that bulge, shoot off into space and into the water. I say to myself: "I don't want to go down that way. That must hurt their backsides something terrible."

About eight feet to my left there is a gaping hole in the side of the *Repulse*. It is about thirty feet across, with the plates twisted and torn. The hull of the *Repulse* has been ripped open as though a giant had torn apart a tin can. I see an officer dive over the side, dive into the hole underneath the line, dive back inside the ship.

I half turn to look back on the crazy-angled deck of the ship. The padre is beside one of the pom-poms, administering the final rites to a gunner dying beside his gun. The padre seems totally unconcerned by the fact that the *Repulse* is going down at any moment.

About forty-two men have made their way through the tangled, destroyed, burning interior of the ship, crept, stumbled and scrambled and have clambered through the inside of the dummy smokestack to the top. They find the wire screen across the top of the stack is fastened on the outside. Someone hears their cries but by then it is too late. The men are trapped.

Midshipman Christopher Bros, from St. Andrews, is in the fifteen-inch transmitting station, at the very bottom of the ship. There are twenty-five men with him in the small room, and the sharp list of the ship is making it difficult to get out. The water is pouring in.

"Fall in, everyone! March. Up you go," Bros orders.
The men start streaming out, starting a climb up six
decks. One by one they pass out of the room. The water
is coming higher. The water comes in faster than twenty-
six men can get out. The twenty-sixth man is trapped.
Midshipman Kit Bros, tall, slim, Rugby graduate from
Scotland gets all his men out. He is the twenty-sixth man.

I slide down the hull of the *Repulse* about five feet.
There I brace myself in a porthole, take off my tin hat and
white cloth anti-flash hood and place them at my feet in the
porthole. I lie on the side of the *Repulse*, watching this incredible scene—men bobbing in the water, black oil spreading over the debris-filled, blue sea, the *Wales* obviously
sinking, the sky still filled with aircraft and black puffs of
anti-aircraft fire.

I don't want to jump, to leave the relative security of
this steel for that mess down below. I have no panic in
me, no particular fear, just this numbness. I know I'll have
to jump sooner or later. I know I cannot lie here and let
the water come over me without fighting back somehow.
There's no hurry. To jump into the water will hasten the
inevitable.

Captain Tennant on the bridge turns to the navigating
officer: "It looks a bit different from this angle, doesn't
it, pilot?"
The navigating officer nods, but says nothing. The
group of officers on the bridge look at each other, and at
the skipper.
"Well, gentlemen," Captain Tennant says quietly, "you
had better get out of it now."
"Aren't you coming with us, sir?" two or three eagerly
demand simultaneously.
The captain smiles, shakes his head negatively, then
says impatiently: "Off you go now. There's not much
time." They are all hanging on to something, one leg
braced to keep an even keel as the ship heels over more
and more.
"But, Captain," the lieutenant commander says, "you

must come with us. You've done all you could for this ship. More than most men could."

Captain Tennant does not budge. The men are getting restive. Almost by prearrangement they all move toward their skipper. They push him forcibly through the narrow doorway and onto the deck. The Repulse *is almost on her beam ends. Captain Tennant will go no farther. The officers and men of the bridge seize Captain Tennant and push him over the side. Then they jump into the sea.*

I seem to be glued to the hull of the *Repulse*. Just my head is loose. I turn it from side to side, watching the last-minute evacuation of the ship. Someone slides down the hull, pauses for a moment at the bulge, stands up and makes a beautiful swan dive. That galvanizes me, and I stand up in the porthole and jump, the camera wildly swinging from its strap around my neck.

The jump is about twenty feet. The water is warm; it is not water, but thick oil. My first action is to look at my stop watch. It is smashed at 12.35, one hour and twenty minutes after the first Japanese bomb crashed into the catapult deck of the *Repulse*.

It doesn't occur to me to swim away from the ship until I see others striking out. Then I realize how difficult it is. The oil soaks into my clothes, weighting them, and I think underwater demons are tugging at me, trying to drag me down. The airless lifebelt, absorbing oil too, tightens and tautens the preserver cords around my neck. I say to myself: "I'm going to choke to death, I'm going to choke to death."

I have a ring on my left hand which Martha bought for me on the Ponte Vecchio in Florence when we were on our honeymoon. It is rather loose on my finger. With oil on my hands, I'm afraid I will lose it. I clench my fist so that it won't slip off.

I start swimming away with the left hand clenched. With my right hand I make one stroke, tug at the cord around my neck in a futile effort to loosen it, then make another stroke to get away from the ship.

That ring helps save my life. Something like it must have

helped save the lives of hundreds of men. Your mind fastens itself on silly, unimportant matters, absorbing your thoughts and stifling the natural instinct of man to panic in the face of death.

I see a life preserver eighteen inches long and four inches thick. It is like a long sausage and I tuck it to me. A small piece of wood appears inviting and I take that too. A barrel comes near, but I reject that because the oil prevents my getting a grip on it. All around me men are swimming, men with blood streaking their oil-covered faces.

The oil burns in my eyes as though someone is jabbing hot pokers into the eyes. That oil in the eyes is the worst thing. I've swallowed a bit of oil already, and it's beginning to sicken me.

Fifty feet from the ship, hardly swimming at all now, I see the bow of the *Repulse* swing straight into the air like a church steeple. Its red under plates stand out as stark and as gruesome as the blood on the faces of the men around me. Then the tug and draw of the suction of 32,000 tons of steel sliding to the bottom hits me. Something powerful, almost irresistible, snaps at my feet. It feels as though someone were trying to pull my legs out by the hip sockets. But I am more fortunate than some others. They are closer to the ship. They are sucked back.

When the *Repulse* goes down it sends over a huge wave, a wave of oil. I happen to have my mouth open and I take aboard considerable oil. That makes me terribly sick at the stomach.

As I swim in the water, other men are hanging on to pieces of wood, floating lifebelts and debris. Four or five times I see blood- and oil-covered hands loosen their grip and slide beneath the water.

I do not see Gallagher anywhere. It is difficult to recognize anyone through the oil on his face. About fifteen yards away I see someone struggling and fighting in the water. I finally recognize Sub-Lieutenant Page. There are two men near by. The injured Page is struggling to get out of the two lifebelts wrapped around him, the belts he had on when he was tossed overboard.

"I'm hurt," Page is crying. "I'm hurt. I'm no good any more. You take the belts."

The men can't swim, but Page is insisting and sobbing, peeling out of the belts. "Take them; I'm no good any more."

Page prevails on the two men to accept the belts. They are saved, and Sub-Lieutenant Page slips underneath the water.

Someone calls to me, "Are you all right, War Correspondent?"

"Yes," I say, opening my mouth to say it, and I take aboard more oil. I decide if anyone asks me any more questions I will wave my hand, if I have the strength. I am terribly tired.

A small table, about three feet square, floats by. I grab hold of one leg, but it is too slippery and I know I will lose it. I scramble up on top and lie there for a moment. And then I watch the *Prince of Wales* go down, a big, dark thing sliding into nothingness.

Now the sea seems really deserted, with just men and mess floating on the surface.

As I swim I hear one man yell, "An electric eel just shocked me!"

There are no sharks that I can see, although this area of the South China Sea is usually filled with sharks.

There is a Carley float about three-quarters of a mile away, and a destroyer about two miles distant. I have no intention of trying to reach them. I only want to rest on top of the small table. The conviction that this is my finish is still strong within me. Besides, I want to conserve my strength, want jealously to guard it during the hours before death comes.

I say to myself, "I've gotta remember all this; I gotta remember all this." And the next minute, "What the hell's the use? I will never be able to report this story."

It's so easy to close your eyes, shut out this sight, and fiercely forget what the eyes already have seen.

Strangely enough, I don't think of my wife, my family, or my childhood. I constantly glance around to see if I recognize any of the men, and I am especially watching for Gallagher. I don't see him but I do recognize two or three officers and we smile wanly at each other.

As I lie on the table I pull off my heavy cotton khaki socks. They are soaked and weighted by oil, as heavy as iron. I let the soaked socks slip into the water and feel five pounds lighter. As the warmth of the South China Sea slushes between my toes I think, "That feels wonderful on my feet."

The effort, little as it is, exhausts me. The drag of the camera around my neck and the choking by the life-preserver cord convince me I ought to do something about them. But the water-and-oil-soaked cord of the preserver is knotted and I can't unfasten it. As for the camera, I feel I'd rather drown than throw it away.

I know that I should somehow try to get rid of some of my clothes. The oil makes their weight feel like tons. Tears are pouring out of my eyes from the oil, and I sense tiny salty rivulets running down my oil-covered face.

That oil! It coagulates around each body, around the debris, around the men. One officer in the water shouts, "Spread out a bit, men, and let's get out of this oil." Some of the men do it; others are reluctant to get away from pieces of wood. Others depend on absorbing some strength from men around them. Not only miserable but drowning men love company.

One officer swims by me and says, "Let's make for the raft." I shake my head no, and he swims on.

About ten yards from me I see two youngsters—they must be about eighteen—laughing and joking, and I hear one say, "I'll race you to Singapore." We are fifty miles from shore and one hundred and fifty miles north of the city those youngsters are talking about.

It's the tide, not my efforts, that bring me near the Carley float. The Carley contraptions are rafts, fifteen feet long, ten feet wide, and bounded on all sides by a foot-high bulge. Extending around the bulge is a rope on which men can grab hold.

The raft toward which the tide carries me is jammed. There are men inside, men sitting solid on the bulge at the edge, and every handhold on the rope is occupied. Obviously there is no room for me, so I make no effort whatsoever, letting the tide carry me where it wants. It carries me to that raft.

A Royal Marine sitting on the edge calls to me when I am ten feet away, "Just a bit more, just a bit more." I don't answer, just look at him across that ten-foot chasm.

Gradually I draw nearer. He extends his hand as far as he can and I stretch out my hand. For five minutes our hands are three inches apart, but I don't have the energy to bridge that tiny gap. Once again the tide does it for me. Our hands meet, clasp and I'm yanked toward the raft, leaving the small table which thus far has saved my life.

The twenty-year-old marine, Morris Graney, pushes one of the men sitting on the bulge back inside the raft, on top of another man, to make way for me. Then he pulls me onto the bulge and holds me there.

His first remark is: "My Lord, do you still have your camera?"

"Yes."

"Are you all right?"

I nod.

"Can you sit here?"

I say, "Yes, I am all right."

Actually I'm not, and almost fall face forward into the water. Graney grabs me, takes one of my hands—my right hand, since my left is still clenched to prevent my ring from falling off—and forces it to grasp the lifebelt of a man inside the raft.

"Hang onto him," Graney says.

I hang on.

The raft tosses and heaves with the swell of the sea. Men are bobbing and swimming on all sides near the raft, some trying to reach it, some hoping eventually to get a hand hold on it. We want to reach a destroyer which is stationary about a mile or a mile and a half away. There is one paddle on board, and someone inside, using the paddle, is calling, "Heave ho, heave ho!"

Graney says, "Let's all sing." Not many voices join in his choice, "When Irish Eyes Are Smiling," but the voices that do are cheerful.

56

Graney wears only shorts and his thick chest is covered with oil. His brown hair hangs over his forehead and into his eyes. I think just the sight of Graney helps many a man. He is almost six feet tall, husky, almost barrel-chested. Above a square jaw he has a slim, delicate mustache and blue, kind, shy eyes. All the time the only one definable emotion expressed in those eyes is amusement. Graney's amusement is enough, though, as the raft tosses. I am deathly sick at the stomach, and dizzy, too, and again almost fall forward, Graney grabs me.

"You stay right here," he says, slapping me on the shoulder.

"I am very tired," I say, "and I want to rest down there."

Graney slaps me across the face, saying, "Now, none of that. You stay right here with me."

"No. Those other men aren't on the raft," I say. "I am tired, and I can rest better in the water."

Graney's hand is digging into my arm and shoulder. It hurts, but somehow I don't protest. I just know it hurts.

"We're watching those other men," Graney says sharply. "They're all right. You stay right here with us."

I'm not convinced, and twist my head around to look inside the raft. It's the wrong time to do that. Men inside are vomiting and glassy-eyed, all of them black with oil. Two men have just died and their bodies are being gently hustled over the side to make room for more men. I feel a twinge of pity at the sight of it, but it seems an eminently practical thing to do.

Six or seven Jap bombers are roaring over again at about 5,000 feet.

"They're coming over to machine-gun us!" someone says.

"Shut up that guff!" Graney growls, because we all feel bad enough as it is.

"If they come over to machine-gun us," a voice suggests, "dive under the water."

I think to myself: "If I have to dive under the water, I'm never coming up again."

They don't swoop down on us and they don't drop bombs. They just go on. It isn't Japanese chivalry or

57

Bushido. They're just out of bombs and ammunition. With the planes gone and heads turned from the sky to the horizon, we get the impression that the destroyer is getting farther and farther away. In fact, we see one of our destroyers steam away. Someone calls in panic, "They're all going." A reply comes from somewhere inside the raft: "They'll wait for us, don't worry."

As the minutes go on and we seem to be getting no nearer to the destroyer, the morale on the raft begins to slip lower and lower. Graney is one of the first to recognize this. "Keep kicking, keep paddling!" he shouts. "We will soon be there!"

As we drew near the destroyer he said, "All right, now, it's 'Anchors Aweigh'!" And again he starts singing. Almost everyone joins in then, because for the first time we seem to have a chance of rescue.

Rafts and men are converging on the destroyer from all directions. We can already see dripping figures being hauled onto the deck of the ship. Through a megaphone an officer on the bridge is shouting something at us, but we can't make it out.

The oil around the destroyer seems about two feet thick, solid oil. To me it looks like dirty black castor oil. And it tastes the same.

A rope with a loop at the end is tossed thirty feet from the destroyer to us. We miss it. The rope is hauled back and again is hurled. Someone grabs it, but Graney tears it out of his hands and roughly passes the loop over me. "We have an American war correspondent here," he shouts at the destroyer. Then he waves and shouts, "Heave up, heave up!"

He asks solicitously, "Can you hold onto the rope?"

"Of course. Don't worry about me."

And the men on the destroyer pull me off the edge of the Carley float. I sink underneath the oil, and for ten feet while I'm dragged underneath the surface I feel I'm plowing my way through some kind of a solid wall. The pressure pounds at my head like a great rubber hammer.

Then I'm beside the destroyer. A wooden ladder hangs over the side.

58

A frenzied voice calls, "Hang on, hang on! But hurry!"

I get up the ladder and four men drag me over the taffrail. The deck is burning hot on my bare feet. They strip off my clothes and someone hands me a heavy woolen parka. I put it on, and one of the officers says, "Are you all right?"

"I'm fine," I say. "Who has a camera on board this ship?"

The officer doesn't know, but he calls over another man, saying, "Find this man a camera. There must be one on board."

The rating scoots off, and I stand there while Graney, who has just been brought on board, keeps urging me to sit down and rest.

"There's plenty of time for that," I insist. "I've got to get a camera."

Graney empties the pockets of my cover-alls, bush jacket and shorts, and hands over the precious notebook in which I kept this account of the battle. I open the notebook, and see every page is water-and-oil-soaked but still legible.

About a half dozen men are dead on the deck of the destroyer. Others are being sick from the oil. Some men are laughing and joking.

The hospital of the sick bay is jammed, and some of the dead are being carried out and laid on the deck. Men with blood on their faces are being carried back to the sick bay for attention. Still more survivors are being brought on board, and I snap pictures. I use up all the film. They find me another camera and I use all that film.

The destroyer is the *Electra,* which took 1,100 men out of the hell of Dunkirk to England.

There is no bitterness among these men this afternoon about the absence of aircraft protection, just regret that they've lost their ship. One man is wailing that he'd lost the pictures of his girl friend, his mother, his dad.

After about an hour, three Brewster Buffaloes come roaring over, sweeping ten feet from the ship. The Japs are long gone by now.

In the steaming hot wardroom of the *Electra* forty or fifty officers are drinking tea, most all naked to the waist. The heat is stifling, and as we sit there—I taking notes—

the sweat pours out of us as though we are under a shower.

As the sweat drips from me, I remember how exactly twenty-four hours before I sat in the comfortable wardroom of the *Repulse,* talking with the officers of the battle cruiser, and thinking of the British tendency to underestimate the enemy, to look at them solely through British eyes. "It's better," I said, "to consider your enemy twice as good as you are and twice as smart. Then you won't be surprised."

The British officers, twenty-four hours before had been amiable, cheerful and skeptical. Now in that smelling, sweltering wardroom of the *Electra,* one of the officers of the *Repulse* comes up with a rueful smile on his face and says: "You told us not to underestimate the enemy."

"Yes, I know," I say, "but I take no satisfaction in that now—not even grim satisfaction."

I want to know about Captain Tennant. One man speaks up: "I saw him floating face down in the water."

Down there in the wardroom I am told the sequence of attacks on the *Prince of Wales.*

The attack was similar to our own. High-level bombers and torpedo-carrying bombers. With four torpedoes in the *Wales,* Admiral Phillips said: "Tell the *Express* (which was then alongside the *Wales)* to signal to Singapore for tugs to tow us home."

It was obvious the Admiral hadn't yet made up his mind that the ship was going to sink.

I ask a lieutenant commander from the *Wales* about Admiral Phillips and Captain Leach.

They were last seen standing on the bridge of the *Prince of Wales.*

"The admiral and the captain stood there together," the officer says. "They would not go. As we started away, Captain Leach waved, and called out: 'Good-by. Thank you. Good luck. God bless you.'"

Then the water rose up to meet them, meeting and then covering them.

Disaster in Malaya

As December 1941 wore on, the British-Indian 11th and 9th Divisions fell back before the Japanese thrusts down both west and east coasts of Malaya. The invaders maintained pressure on the front, and at the same time made amphibious landings on the coastal flanks; then their troops sliced inland to harass and roll up the supply lines. The Japanese troops were trained jungle fighters and their tactics were so effective that soon the morale of the Allied troops disintegrated. As in Bataan, the certain knowledge that they were fighting only a delaying action did not enable the Allied troops to put up an effective defense. Unlike Bataan, where the native Filipino troops were invaluable, the Malayans had little stomach for this battle.

As Kenneth Attiwill says: "the jungles, mangrove swamps and thickly treed areas of cultivation present a peculiar and difficult problem. Visibility is limited, the opportunity for ambush lies almost everywhere. There are no fields of fire, tactical features tend to lose significance and roads and tracks become important. All-around protection is essential. Movement, though possible, is severely restricted—yet static defense spells defeat. Movement is easier in rubber plantations, but the interminable lines of evenly spaced trees and the limited view make it difficult for troops to keep direction. Control is difficult, emergencies crop up unexpectedly, and junior commanders' actions assume greater influence. Their errors of tactics, judgment and decision may easily decide an action.

"Brooding above all, adding weakness to morale as well as to military efficiency, lies the jungle itself—a terrifying morass of tangled vegetation, steamy heat, nerve-racking noises and the discomfort of insects; mosquitoes by the myriad, moths, beetles, insects of all kinds, biting, buzzing, irritating and debilitating. Rubber, too, with its gloom, dampness and sound-deadening effect breeds a feeling of isolation. The enemy may be anywhere—everywhere—in front or behind—to left or to right. Noise is difficult to pinpoint; men appear and disappear like wraiths. Rumor begins to spread. In the monsoonal season there is the added handicap of torrential rain, hissing down incessantly upon the greenery, dripping dankly on heads and bodies, humid, sweaty, destructive. . . .

"Within a little more than a month the Japanese had advanced from Siam all the way down the peninsula into northern Johore—and the British were back to their last line of defense outside Singapore Island.

"If there were reasons why the speed tactics and fire power of the enemy should have bewildered and surprised the British commanders, their tactics should now have been plain. Time and again the enemy had surprised the defenders by his ability to move more rapidly over all types of terrain; time and again he had used enveloping tactics rather than the direct onslaught. Yet in Johore the defending commanders chose to try to defend one strongpoint, only to be destroyed piecemeal. Elsewhere, a weak brigade was asked to hold the most likely road for the Japanese advance, while three brigades were allocated to the area they did not assault directly. The result was defeat again and again in Johore, until it became apparent by the last week of January 1942, that a withdrawal into Singapore Island was inevitable.

"That was the pattern—errors by commanders; insufficient or inadequately trained troops; continuous under-estimation of a savage, speedy, highly skilled and highly mobile enemy; spreading confusion and panic. As the 'Great Run' lengthened eyes grew red with sleeplessness, limbs became weary with incessant effort, minds sluggish with exhaustion, nerves frayed, morale and discipline and efficiency constantly diminishing.

"To the troops who did not know the truth about Singapore, the island loomed in their minds like an oasis. In Singapore there would be proper accommodations, proper food; above all, a place to lie down in peace for the one night's sleep they all craved." *

But was Singapore the fortress the troops and, for that matter, the rest of the world had been led to believe? Prime Minister Churchill in a letter to General Ismay on January 16, 1942, more than a month after the invasion of Malaya, was shocked to hear of the island's vulnerability. "I must confess to being staggered by Wavell's telegram of the 16th. . . . It never occurred to me for a moment . . . that the gorge of the

Fortress, pp. 44-51. Doubleday & Co.

fortress of Singapore, with its splendid moat half a mile to a mile wide, was not entirely fortified against an attack from the northward. What is the use of having an island for a fortress if it is not to be made into a citadel?" *

A few days later in a telegram to General Wavell, Churchill said, in part, "I want to make it absolutely clear that I expect every inch of ground to be defended . . . and no question of surrender to be entertained until after protracted fighting among the ruins of Singapore City." **

But this telegram had little effect upon the authorities in Singapore. Four days later, a Lieutenant-Colonel of the 11th Indian Division who had led a group of sappers from the action on the Siam borders in the retreat to Singapore, reported:

"I was dumbfounded when I sent to the Chief Engineer's office and learned that there was not a trench and not a bit of barbed wire on the whole of the north-east and north-west side of the island. We thought that during our time up-country all these defences would have been installed." ***

When he went to the Ordnance Depot to get barbed wire, he was told, "Half holiday!" The staff had taken the afternoon off to go to the "pictures."

Little was accomplished to strengthen the defenses between the 25th and the night of February 8 when the first Jap landing barges were observed making their way across the Straits of Johore.

"The approach of the enemy should have been the signal for a blaze of searchlights to light them up for the defenders and a savage counter-barrage to blow the enemy out of the water. The searchlights stayed dark and the guns remained silent. Strict instructions had been given to the searchlight crews that they were not to expose beach lights except on the specific instructions of the unit commanders—it was thought that, once exposed, they would inevitably be destroyed—but by the time the assault was launched all the communications had been cut and those lights which had survived the barrage were never exposed. Because calls for the planned defensive artillery fire never reached the batteries the guns did not open up and it was not until

*Winston Churchill, *The Hinge of Fate,* p. 50. Houghton Mifflin Co.

**The Hinge of Fate,* p. 53.

***Fortress,* p. 77. This quote is from a British book.

the S.O.S. light signals sent up by the infantry were seen that any of the guns went into action. In any event, there wasn't enough artillery to cover the whole brigade front; and in some areas—particularly on the front of the 2/18th and 2/19th A.I.F. Battalions—the infantry was left without artillery support. Some gun positions did not see the warning Very light and stayed silent.

"The Australians fought in darkness broken only by gun flashes and the blaze from burning barges, and without the comfort of a counter-barrage from their own artillery. Too widely spaced, and with untrained reinforcements in their ranks, it is not surprising that the Australians could not keep the Japanese off the Island. The enemy was soon ashore—though in places only at the second or third attempt—and they quickly infiltrated the gaps between the Australian positions.

"By one o'clock on the morning of the 9th—only three and a half hours after the invasion had been first sighted—the Australians in the forward areas were withdrawing, under orders, to their battalion perimeters. Groups of men became separated from their comrades in the bewildering darkness. Others lost their way. Many died. The effect of the withdrawals was to dislocate the whole Brigade area, and by ten o'clock on the morning of the 9th—less than twelve hours after the assault had been sighted—the 22nd Australian Brigade, on whose fighting power had rested the defence of the north-western area of the Island, was no longer a cohesive fighting force." *

THE FALL OF SINGAPORE**

by Kenneth Attiwill

From the events of the desperate days of Monday the 9th, Tuesday the 10th, Wednesday the 11th, and Thursday the 12th, there emerges a painful catalogue of error, folly, indecision and indescribable confusion. When the

*Fortress, pp. 172-173.
**Condensed from Fortress, Chapters 11, 12 and 13.

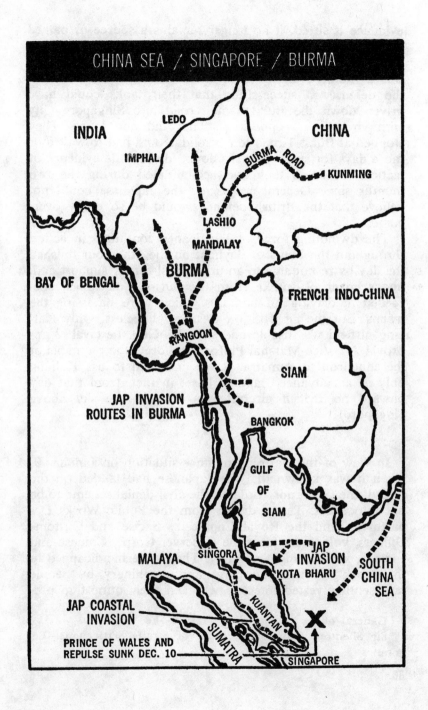

CHINA SEA / SINGAPORE / BURMA

INDIA

LEDO

IMPHAL

CHINA

BURMA ROAD

KUNMING

LASHIO

MANDALAY

BURMA

BAY OF BENGAL

FRENCH INDO-CHINA

RANGOON

SIAM

JAP INVASION
ROUTES IN BURMA

BANGKOK

GULF
OF
SIAM

SOUTH
CHINA
SEA

MALAYA

SINGORA

JAP
INVASION

KOTA BHARU

JAP COASTAL
INVASION

KUANTAN

X

PRINCE OF WALES AND
REPULSE SUNK DEC. 10

SUMATRA

SINGAPORE

evidence is sifted, it no longer remains a source of pained astonishment that Singapore held out for only seven days. The miracle is that it held out for so long. Indeed, there was a moment on the 11th when the Japanese had split the defense so successfully that their tanks could have driven down the Bukit Timah road into Singapore City with virtually no opposition. They did not do so. They stopped at Bukit Timah to consolidate and had to wait four more days for surrender. No doubt, despite the evidence of tactical weakness they had accumulated during the two months since December 8, even the Japanese could not believe that the British defence would be so easily overcome.

The dwindling force of Hurricanes continued in action throughout the hours of daylight on the 9th. Four finished the day by responding to an urgent call for air support and, under cover of smoke from the burning oil tanks, succeeded in driving off bombers which were harassing the troops. But the air position was now hopeless. Only Kallang airfield was usable and with Lt.-Gen. Percival's [1] approval Air Vice-Marshal Pulford withdrew the remnants of the squadron to Sumatra. It was intended to use Kallang only as an advanced landing base; in fact, from that day onward no British aircraft was seen in the sky above Singapore.

In view of the alarming military situation on January 9, when it was known that the Japanese had landed on the Island, the Governor [2] ordered the civil denial scheme to be put into effect. Teams drawn from the Public Works Department, and the Royal Engineers, Excise and Customs Officers, volunteers from the Observer Corps, Chinese and Indians, worked night and day. They were handicapped in their task of smashing plant and machinery by people representing vested interests who did their utmost to pre-

[1] General officer commanding Malaya.—Ed. note.
[2] Sir Shenton Thomas, Governor of Straits Settlements.—Ed. note.

vent the destruction of private property. They lodged appeals with the local authorities. Some companies with head offices in Britain, Australia or India petitioned their home Governments. A few actively intervened to prevent the denial teams getting to work. It was more important to these people—unnamed—that their property should be available for them at some future time, if and when the invader was defeated, than that war potential should be denied to the enemy.

Denial was further hampered by the Governor's orders on the 10th to withdraw all the European Supervisory Staff from the Singapore Harbour Board installations; and again by the unauthorized departure of some officials and key civilians who ran away from Singapore on February 9, 10 and 13. "Nevertheless," says *The War Against Japan*,[8] "with certain exceptions the work was completed by the day of surrender. The exceptions were the installations captured by the enemy before they could be destroyed and those exempted by the Government on the plea of the effect of the denial operations on morale." They were still worrying about morale! The result was that the installations of about forty Chinese firms and the workshops and vehicles of two large motor dealers and their subsidiaries remained intact, and the Japanese received "a welcome present of new vehicles and well-equipped workshops."

Two of the tasks which were accomplished successfully were the destruction of the State money and private stocks of liquor. Mr. Eric Pretty, acting Federal Secretary, burned 5,000,000 Straits dollars in the Treasury—the equivalent of about £600,000. "I never imagined I'd have so much money to burn," he said. Memories of Japanese atrocities in Hong Kong, when their troops got drunk on looted liquor and ran amok, prompted Sir Shenton Thomas's ban on liquor. It came into force at noon on Friday the 13th, but long before then work had begun on the colossal task of destroying every drop of strong drink on the Island.

Gradually the life of Singapore was slowing but still

[8] From *The Loss of Singapore*, Vol. 1. Her Brittanic Majesty's Stationery Office.

Reller's Band played selections at the Adelphi Hotel and people queued for the cinemas. Apologists said it was good for morale, as when the people danced in Brussels on the eve of Waterloo. Raffles Hotel and the clubs and canteens were packed with staff officers who did not know what to do except sit and hope for the best. "All the red-tape from all over Malaya was packed into this little Island," said Capt. Charles Corry, Malayan Civil Service Volunteer with 3rd Corps.

Of Singapore in general, Maj. G. Wort, Wiltshire Regiment, wrote: "It seemed that the spirit of holding on and, if necessary, dying at your post had gone out of the make-up of things altogether. Perhaps in some cases it was because no definite orders were issued by the local Government as to policy. In many cases, one got the feeling that the one idea was to get to hell out of it, and the country too, if you could." The streets were daily becoming more dangerous. Fifth Columnists were liable to be anywhere in Singapore now. It was pitch dark by seven o'clock in the evening, and a long night lay ahead with plenty of opportunities for disguised Japanese and pro-Jap quislings to sneak into the city and occupy good sniping positions in the many flats and offices that were now empty. Sniping was a constant danger along the main streets. Ted Fozard and Eric Pretty said that they dodged bullets near the Supreme Court building. There were plenty of windows in multi-storied business houses, tall blocks of flats, hotels and Chinese lodging-houses—though heaven help the pro-Jap if the loyal Chinese got hold of him.

By the morning of Black Friday the Thirteenth, British withdrawal to the perimeter positions was completed; and except in the south-west and north, where the Japanese continued to make gains, the line was more or less stable. It was a false picture, for Singapore's situation was irretrievable. You would not have guessed it, however, from the second issue of the one-page *Straits Times* which appeared that morning. The title had been garnished with the Governor's famous slogan, printed in heavy type:

"Singapore Must Stand; It SHALL Stand." The three columns carried nine news items from which the beleaguered defenders and civilians of Singapore could read that Chiang Kai-shek had seen Mr. Nehru of India, that the United States was planning to raise its Air Force to an ultimate total of two million men, and that Chinese forces had been successful in a small engagement against the Siamese on the Indo-China frontier. It also announced in a half-column story that an air battle had been fought between Japanese and Dutch East Indies forces over the Java Sea. Closer at home, the inhabitants of rural areas were warned that it was an offence to refuse to accept Malayan currency notes; families of Volunteers were told where to find temporary accommodation, potential readers of the sheet were told how to obtain their copies, free; and it was formally announced that from noon it would be an offence to possess intoxicating liquor. The "lead" story, which was headed "Japanese Suffer Huge Casualties in Singapore—R.A. Gunners Stick to Their Posts," contained only five paragraphs—all quotations from British and Australian newspapers. You could not guess that in the streets of Singapore City, black under the pall of oil smoke, the dead lay uncollected and unburied. Administration had broken down. The Army was hard pressed and running short of everything it needed—food, water, petrol, ammunition. Anti-aircraft guns—especially the Bofors on top of buildings—still blazed away at the non-stop procession of enemy planes which dropped their bombs and then returned to Johore to re-load, but they made little impact. Fighters machine-gunned the arterial roads with impunity. Shelling was incessant and no area was spared. Now that the defence line was drawn tight round the City, the whole of Singapore was a legitimate military target.

The City was crowded with armed deserters. An officer patrol rounded up 1,100 of them in the last few days, but there were still too many to be controlled by the Military Police. They skulked through the town, or hid in the basements of concrete buildings, or looted Chinese shops. Col. Chamier saw them going about with their rifles on their

69

shoulders and their shirts stuffed with cigarettes and tinned food. Mr. Dick Mullaly described the municipal building and all the big buildings of Singapore on the seafront as "solid blocks of Australians sitting on the stairs." Some tried to get aboard the boats that were still leaving the stricken Island. There were instances of deserters threatening and even firing their rifles to try to force their way on board. It is impossible to say how many got away. Lionel Wigmore, in *The Japanese Thrust,* a volume of the Australian official war history, reports that Mr. Bowden cabled the Australian Government on February 12 that "a group of Australians and others had boarded a vessel without authority and in it had sailed to the Netherlands East Indies." He also records that on February 14 groups of soldiers, including Australians, were at large in Singapore seeking to escape and that a few, armed with tommyguns and hand grenades, threatened to open fire on the launch *Osprey* unless they themselves were taken on board. "When the *Osprey* moved out at 11.30 p.m. with thirty-eight on board, rifle shots were fired at it but no one was hit." On Friday the 13th Australian 1st Corps headquarters in Java learned that "a party of 100 reported to be deserters" had arrived from Singapore. On the 14th, one officer and 165 other ranks "presumed to be deserters" were placed under guard in a Dutch prison in Batavia. When questioned, the men said: "Singapore was in a state of confusion, men were unable to contact their units and were ordered by officers whom they did contact to make their way to port and evacuate." In the absence of an official charge or evidence from the master of the vessel that had carried them, or O.C. troops, it was decided that their retention in prison was illegal. They were set free, and fought with Blackforce during the operations in Java.

The War Against Japan describes those troops who left the Island, or tried to, as "most . . . were deserters from administrative units, and men who had recently arrived in Malaya as reinforcements, inadequately trained and disciplined."

By this time, more and more exhausted troops were losing confidence in their leaders and morale was begin-

70

ning to crack. But the well-trained units still fought stubbornly.

At two o'clock in the afternoon Lt.-Gen. Percival held a conference at Fort Canning. Others present were Lt.-Gen. Heath, Maj.-Gens. Gordon Bennett, Keith Simmons, Beckwith-Smith, and Key, and senior staff officers. They took stock of the situation.

Food was down to seven days' supply of military stocks, though there were still ample civilian supplies. There was sufficient ammunition for the 25-pounders, the Bofors A.A., and the mortars. Petrol was down to one small dump plus the amount still in vehicle tanks, plus the Asiatic Petroleum reserve tanks on Palau Bukum Island. Water was running to waste because breaks in the mains were gaining on repairs. Only low pressure was available at street level, and hospitals were running short. At the docks all civil labour had disappeared, in the town area debris from bombing and shelling remained untouched and the dead lay unburied.

Percival gave orders for the fuel reserve at Palau Bukum to be destroyed—a task which was only partially successful—and discussed the question of a counter-attack. His generals were unanimous that no counter-attack could be launched because the men had been fighting day and night and were approaching complete exhaustion. Gordon Bennett recorded:

"It was unanimously considered that new enemy attacks would succeed and that sooner or later the enemy would reach the streets of the City, which were crowded with battle stragglers. . . . It was decided to send a message to General Wavell urging him to agree to immediate capitulation."

When Wavell's reply arrived shortly afterwards it said uncompromisingly: ". . . Fully appreciate your situation but continued action essential."

The conference also discussed the evacuation of selected personnel from the Island in the final withdrawal of boats. Gordon Bennett said: "Owing to the limitation of shipping, accommodation for only 1,800 from the Army could be arranged. The A.I.F. allotment was 100. It was decided that

71

only those whose capabilities would help our ultimate war effort should be evacuated and also that the proportion of officers to other ranks should be as one is to fifteen."

All that day and throughout the night the chosen few—and some who had not been chosen—made their final preparations. When the men who could not be evacuated heard of it, their morale was not improved.

Altogether about 3,000 people were sent away officially that night—Army nurses, Service officers and technicians, and civilian specialists. Others—the runaways—went furtively. Women and children were pushed on board wherever room could be found. They sailed from Singapore in a miscellaneous fleet of small boats—the last of the gunboats and patrol motor-launches, coastal steamers, tugs, harbour launches, outboard motor-boats, yachts, dinghies, tongkans and sampans. Some were seaworthy and some were not.

Tokyo Radio said that night: "There will be no Dunkirk at Singapore. The British are not going to be allowed to get away with it this time. All ships leaving will be destroyed."

Many were destroyed. Some never got past the minefields and harbour wreckage. Most were attacked by Japanese light naval craft and aircraft in the Banka Strait. None knew when they sailed that the Japanese Fleet now stood between Singapore Island and the haven of the Dutch East Indies. Singapore could not tell them because signals from Sumatra were in code—and the man with the code-book had taken it away with him to Java. Singapore received the messages but could not read them. . . .

Lt. H. Gordon Riches, R.N.V.R. (Malaya) took his 75-foot motor-launch out from Singapore as one of six vessels in tow by a tug. All were sunk at the breakwater except the tug, which took survivors on board and reached Palembang. On the way up the Moesi River they picked up two R.A.F. pilots who were sitting out in trees overhanging the river. They had been shot down.

A group of Army nurses and soldiers from one of the wrecked ships reached Muntock Beach on Banka Island, and surrendered to the Japanese. A party of Jap soldiers marched the men along the beach out of sight; and presently returned, wiping their bayonets. The nurses, who wore the Red Cross emblem, were then ordered to walk into the sea. When they were waist deep in the water, still facing out to sea, the Japanese machine-gunned them. Only one soldier and one nurse survived that outrage.

The *Li Wo*, a former Upper Yangtse river steamer of 707 tons, requisitioned by the Royal Navy for Malayan patrol duty in 1940 and commanded by Lt. T. S. Wilkinson, R.N.R., sailed from Singapore with many passengers in addition to her eight officers and 68 crew. She was attacked repeatedly by aircraft but managed to evade the bombs. On the morning of the 14th she encountered part of the Japanese invasion convoy bound for Sumatra. Although armed with only one old 4-inch gun—for which she had just thirteen shells left—and two machine-guns, Lt. Wilkinson turned the *Li Wo* to attack the Japanese transports and hit one and set it on fire. For an hour and a half she fought against hopeless odds, taking heavy punishment from the escorting Japanese cruiser. When all thirteen shells had been fired, Lt. Wilkinson turned his crippled vessel full steam ahead—and rammed the burning Japanese transport. The cruiser then blew the *Li Wo* out of the water. There were only ten survivors, and the gallant Lt. Wilkinson was not one of them. Years later, when the story at last reached London, Wilkinson was posthumously awarded the Victoria Cross.

Most of the people who left Singapore in the last few days failed to reach freedom. The majority were cast far and wide among the myriad islands south of Singapore and suffered tormenting privations. Some were rescued by fishermen and taken step by step along an escape route which remained open for several weeks. Some were picked up by the enemy and taken back to Singapore, Sumatra or Java. Some were never picked up. Many were never heard of again after they left Singapore.

On Singapore Island the noose tightened remorselessly round the tortured body of the City. In the north and in the south-west the Japanese advanced steadily against a desperate defence. That night—the night of the 13th/14th —the Japanese ran amok in Alexandra British military hospital. The story of that black episode has been preserved in a typescript of unknown authorship which has found its way to the British Imperial War Museum. It states:

"During the morning the water supply was cut off. Shelling and air activity was intense. Bursting shells, mortar bombs, with an occasional shot from our own artillery.

"The enemy were approaching the rear of the hospital from the Ayer Rajah Road. The number of incoming patients had lessened considerably and there was little or no traffic in the wards. During the morning, routine work continued. Japanese troops were seen for the first time at about 13.40 hours, attacking towards the Sisters' quarters.

"Japanese fighting troops were about to enter the Hospital from the rear. Lt. Weston went from the reception room to the rear entrance with a white flag to signify the surrender of the Hospital. The Japanese took no notice of the flag and Lt. Weston was bayoneted to death by the first Japanese to enter the Hospital. The troops now entered the Hospital and ran amok. They were excitable and jumpy, and neither the Red Cross brassards nor the shouting of the word 'hospital' had any effect.

"The following events started at about the same time.

"(a) One party entered the theatre block. At this time operations were being prepared in the corridors between the Sisters' bunks and the main theatre, this area being the best lighted and the most sheltered part of the block. The Japs climbed in through the corridors and at the same time a shot from the window was fired, wounding Pte. Lewis in the arm. About ten Japs came into the corridor and all the R.A.M.C. personnel put up their hands. Capt. Smiley pointed to the Red Cross brassards but the enemy appeared very excited and took no notice. The Japs then motioned them to move along the corridor, which they did, and then for no apparent reason, set upon them with bayonets. Lt. Rogers was bayoneted through the throat

74

twice and died at once. Capt. Parkinson was bayoneted to death as also was Cpl. McHewan and Pte. Lewis. A patient on the operating table was bayoneted to death. He was later identified as Cpl. Holden of the 2nd Loyals. Capt. Smiley was bayoneted but he struck the blade away and it hit his cigarette case which was in his left breast-pocket. He was again lunged at and was wounded in the left groin, the previous thrust having wounded his left forearm. He then pretended to be killed, and pushed Pte. Sutton to the floor calling to the others to be quiet. The Japanese then left the corridor.

"(b) Another party of Japs went into the wards and ordered the Medical Officer and those patients who could walk outside the Hospital. In one ward two patients were bayoneted. The Japs then went upstairs and gave similar instructions. These Japs appeared to be more human and motioned the patients on stretchers to stay behind. Patients and personnel numbering about two hundred were taken outside, their hands tied behind them with a slip knot, one length of cord being used for about 4 or 5 persons. Some of the patients could only hobble, others had only one arm, while some were still in plaster and others were obviously very ill.

"Many of the seriously ill showed signs of great distress, one or two collapsed and had to be revived. The party was marched by a circular route to the old quarters, where they were herded into rooms, 50 to 70 persons per room, the sizes of which varied from 9 by 9 to 10 by 12 feet, where they literally jammed in and it took minutes to raise their hands above their heads. Sitting down was out of the question and they were forced to urinate against each other. During the night many died, and all suffered severely from thirst and the suffocating atmosphere. Water was promised but none came. When dawn arrived Japs could be seen with cases of tinned fruit which they kept for themselves. By the evening the shelling was at its maximum and shells were bursting all round. One struck the roof, blowing off doors and windows and injuring some of the prisoners. When this happened, 8 men tried to escape, some were successful but others were hit by machine-gun bullets. Previous to this Japs were leading small parties out of sight where afterwards we heard yells and screams, then a Jap soldier returning and wiping blood from his bayonet which left little doubt as to their fate.

"Except for a few that escaped none of these parties was ever seen again.

"(c) A party of Japs came into the reception room shouting and threatening the staff and patients who had congregated there. Sgt. Sheriff was killed. It was difficult to understand the reason for this barbaric attack on the Hospital. Investigations were carried out to find a possible explanation—rumours had it that a party of Sappers and Miners were digging a trench at the rear of the Hospital and on the approach of the Japs made a run for it. When the Japs passed through the Hospital there were about 40 or 50 herded into the corridor and a guard placed on them. Later the guard went away, and Capt. Barlett went out but could find no trace of the Japs."

Early on the 14th, General Percival was told that a complete failure of the water supply was imminent. Breaks in the water mains caused by bombing and shelling meant that more than half the supply from the reservoirs was being lost. The supply might last forty-eight hours, perhaps for only twenty-four hours. Sir Shenton Thomas warned the G.O.C. of the danger of an epidemic if a large proportion of the population was suddenly deprived of water; but Percival replied that though the shortage was serious it did not make the defence of the city impossible. He intended to go on fighting. Sir Shenton signalled the Colonial Office in London, pointing out that one million people were concentrated within a radius of three miles, with water for only twenty-four hours longer. Percival signalled Wavell in Java, asking, "Would you consider giving me wider discretionary powers?" Wavell replied, "In all places where sufficiency of water exists for troops they must go on fighting. Your gallant stand is serving purpose and must be continued to limit of endurance."

South-west of the city there was further heavy fighting,

but the enemy attacks were beaten off by the 1st Malaya Brigade after bitter hand-to-hand fighting. The Australians were subjected to heavy shelling; and were mortified to observe the Japanese moving west, without being able to shell them. Ammunition was being rationed.

Singapore City was again heavily bombed and shelled. Streets were blocked by the wreckage of smashed buildings, broken telegraph poles and tangled wires. The civil hospitals were crowded with wounded, and the ground floors of many large hotels and buildings were being used to house casualties. The grounds of the Singapore General Hospital were a shambles. Its once smooth, bright green lawns and rich flower-beds were gashed with huge pits dug for the burial of the dead. Bodies were carted out of the hospital and added to the stench, and lime was thrown on top. It was a gruesome business. Inside it was even worse. There were blood and guts and death everywhere. The stench was foul despite the disinfectant. Yet the Matron, Miss Kathleen Stewart, the Sisters and nurses worked on amid the human butchery. Patients, some alive, some dead, were in thousands. They were on the beds, under the beds, between the beds, overflowing out of the wards and filling the corridors. They were even lying on the stairs. Doctors, helped by nurses and orderlies, moved about finding the dead and hauling them out for burial in the loathsome pits outside. Army and civilian doctors had joined forces and worked as a team. The operating theatres were like butchers' yards. Surgeons amputated shattered limbs as fast as they could operate. There was no time for the delicate treatment which might have saved many limbs. The nursing girls stood by and helped. "Those girls were bathed in blood the last few days," said Sqdn. Ldr. Pat Atkins. "Sister Mollie Hill was a very brave girl. She was the head nursing Sister and she worked the clock round. A pretty woman in her late thirties. South African. They were all brave girls. They had no thought for themselves. Completely selfless." Water was short and instruments were sterilized in water that had been used again and again. Towards the end nurses were washing their hands in bottled mineral water.

During the night of the 14th/15th there was little enemy

activity and the general line still held at daybreak on the 15th, despite some gains by the enemy in the west. This was the only crumb of comfort for the defenders as the sun rose on the burning city. Even the ocean seemed to be on fire. The blazing soap factory on Singapore River threw grotesque patterns on the nearby buildings. Out west at Normanton more oil tanks were burning. Alexandra was ablaze. Timber sheds at Kallang shot up huge tongues of flame—one observer said they reached a height of 600 feet. Godowns and warehouses along the waterfront were afire. Paint and oil from anchored lighters spilled and spread on the water, still blazing. Stocks of rubber smouldered and stank.

The Governor watched it from the windows of the Singapore Club. Beside him stood Mr. Pretty. "My chief thought was tremendous relief that my wife and children had gone early on and were safe," said Mr. Pretty. "From where we stood, overlooking the Inner Basin, the whole place seemed to be a blazing inferno. The Governor was very upset. He kept saying 'Isn't this terrible?' or words to that effect."

General Gordon Bennett wrote of Black Sunday the 15th: "Today opened with a hopeless dawn of despair. There is no hope or help on the horizon. The tropical sun is sending its steamy heat on to the dying city which is writhing in its agony.

"The flanks of the Army continue to fall back. The enemy has advanced past Pasir Panjang towards the City. Enemy troop movement along Bukit Timah Road has been shelled by our artillery, as also have enemy troops opposite our own A.I.F. front, but the momentum of the enemy advance goes unchecked."

Early that morning Wavell signalled Percival:

"So long as you are in a position to inflict losses and damage to enemy and your troops are physically capable of doing so, you must fight on. Time gained and damage to enemy are of vital importance at this juncture. When you are fully satisfied that this is no longer possible I give you discretion to cease resistance. Inform me of intentions.

Whatever happens I thank you and all your troops for gallant efforts of last few days."

It was the wider discretion which Percival had requested two days earlier. The decision was now in his hands.

On that same day Wavell sent a long telegram to the Prime Minister in London. Its terms were very different. According to one staff officer, "It was mainly about personalities and it did not pull any punches."

In England, Percival's daughter Margery was celebrating her twelfth birthday.

Lt.-Gen. Percival went to early morning church service at Fort Canning and then called a conference of all senior commanders and key civic officials. The Governor was not present. The G.O.C. told them that the Supreme Commander had granted him the power to capitulate and then they discussed the situation. In Percival's opinion there were two alternatives: to counter-attack in an effort to regain the reservoirs and military food depots captured by the enemy at Bukit Timah, or to surrender. His generals were convinced that a counter-attack was out of the question. The troops were too exhausted and dispirited and had insufficient ammunition and supplies.

Gordon Bennett's diary records: "Silently and sadly we decided to surrender."

At that conference on Black Sunday the 15th, General Percival produced a letter, addressed to him from the Japanese commander, Yamashita. The Japanese had littered Singapore with leaflets; and on February 10 several small wooden boxes had hit the ground. They contained copies of the following:

Lieut. Gen. Tomoyuki Yamashita
High Com. Nippon Army
Feb. 10th 1942

To:—The High Com. of the British Army in Malaya.

Your Excellency,
I, the High Com. of the Nippon Army based on the

spirit of the Japanese chivalry have the honour of presenting the note to your Excellency advising you to surrender the whole force in Malaya.

Many sincere respects are due to your army which, true to the traditional spirit of Great Britain is bravely defending Singapore, which now stands isolated and unaided.

Many fierce and gallant fights have been fought by your gallant men and Officers, to the honour of British warriorship.

But the developments of the general war situation has already sealed the fate of Singapore and continuation of futile resistance would not only serve to inflict direct harm and injuries to thousands of non-combatants in the City, throwing them into further miseries and horrors of war, but also would not certainly add anything to the honour of your Army.

I expect that your Excellency, accepting my advice, will give up this meaningless and desperate resistance and promptly order the entire front to cease hostilities, and will dispatch at the same time your parliamentaire according to the procedure shown at the end of this advice. If, on the contrary, your Excellency should reject my advice and the present resistance continue, I shall be obliged, though reluctantly, from humanitarian considerations, to order my army to make an annihilating attack on Singapore.

In closing this note of advice I pay again my sincere respects to your Excellency.

Tomoyuki Yamashita.

1. The Parliamentaire should proceed to Bukit Timah Road.
2. The Parliamentaire should bear a white flag and the Union Jack.

On Friday the 13th some more Japanese boxes were airdropped. They contained the following:

ADMONITION

I have the honour of presenting to you this Admonition of Peace from the standpoint of the Nippon Samurai Spirit. Nippon Navy, Army and Air Force have conquered the Philippine Islands and Hong Kong and annihilated the British Extreme Oriental Fleet in the Southern Seas. The command of the Pacific Ocean and the Indian Ocean as well as the Aviation power in the Southern and Western Asian Continents is now under the control of the Nippon Forces. India has risen in rebellion. Thai and Malaya have been subjected to Nippon without any remarkable resistance. The war has almost been settled already and Malay is under Nippon Power. Since the 18th Century Singapore has been the starting point of the development of your country and the important juncture of the civilisation of the West and East. Our Army cannot suffer as well as you to see this district burn to ashes by the war. Traditionally when Nippon is at war, when she takes her arms, she is always based upon the loyalty and breaking wrong and helping right and she does not and never aims at the conquest of other nations nor the expansion of her territories.

The War cause, at this time, as you are well aware, originated from this loyalty. We want to establish new order and some of the mutual prosperity in the Eastern Orient. You cannot deny at the bottom of your impartial hearts that this is divine will and humanity to give happiness to millions of East Orientals mourning under the exploitation and persecution. Consequently the Nippon Army, based upon this great loyalty, attacks without reserve those who resist them, but not only the innocent people but also the surrendered to them will be treated kindly according to their Samuraism. When I imagined the state of mind of you who have so well done your duty, isolated and without rescuer, and now surrounded by our Armies, how much more could I not sincerely sympathise with you.

This is why I do advise you to make peace and give you a friendly hand to co-operate for the settlement of the Oriental Peace. Many thousands of wives and children of your Officers and Soldiers are heartily waiting in their Native Land to the coming home of their husbands and fathers and many hundreds of thousands of innocent people are also passionately wishing to avoid the calamities of War.

I expect you to consider upon the eternal honour of British Tradition, and you, be persuaded by this Admonition. Upon my word, we won't kill you, but treat you as Officers and Soldiers if you come to us. But if you resist us we will gibe swords.

Singapore   Nippon Army.
13 Feb. 42

The "parliamentaire" set off from Fort Canning. Lt.-Col. Chamier, Commandant, Intelligence Corps, Malaya, saw them go. "I was coming up to Fort Canning and a car came out and passed me at the gates. It was an open car with the hood down. Brig. Newbiggin (Administrative Branch, Malaya Command) was in the car, with Hugh Fraser, the Colonial Secretary, Capt. Wild, the Japanese-speaking interpreter, and another chap.

"Sticking out of the back of the car were two flagpoles. One was a furled Union Jack. The other was a furled white flag."

This first party was sent off to discuss truce terms. Yamashita would not even see them. "Send Percival," he said, and the party returned for the General Officer Commanding.

The British drove to a point near Bukit Timah and there the G.O.C. and his party alighted from their car and marched under Japanese escort to the enemy Headquarters, set up in the Ford Motor Factory. Percival had to carry the white flag in person to Yamashita.

Their conference lasted fifty minutes and the G.O.C. has not revealed—either in his book or his dispatch to Parliament—what took place there. The Japanese were

82

less reticent—it was not painful and humiliating for them. They published the following account of the final conversation:

> *Yamashita.* We have just received your reply. The Japanese Army will consider nothing but unconditional surrender.
>
> *Percival.* It is 9.15 p.m. Japanese Time, I fear we shall not be able to submit our final reply before midnight.
>
> *Y.* (loudly) Reply to us only whether our terms are acceptable to you or not. Things have to be done swiftly as we are ready to resume firing in the evening.
>
> *P.* Won't you please wait until you formally file into Singapore?
>
> *Y.* It is impossible. In the first place, why not disarm all the British troops here, leaving only about 1,000 armed gendarmes for maintaining peace? In the second place, under no circumstances can we tolerate further British resistance.
>
> *P.* One of your terms handed to us demanded that we turn over certain representatives of the Chungking régime to you. Their names are not clear to us.
>
> *Y.* By that we mean that you arrest and turn over to us Ching Kam Ming, one of the Chinese liaison men.
>
> *P.* I ask that the Nippon Army reciprocate with us in discontinuing attack.
>
> *Y.* Agreed. What has become of the Nippon citizens in Singapore?
>
> *P.* They have all been transferred to India. We do not know exactly where. The British troops would like to cease fire at 11.30 p.m.
>
> *Y.* That is too late. By 11.00 p.m. we shall place part of our Army in Singapore proper.
>
> *P.* Unless you allow us to 11.30 p.m. I fear that I shall not be able to transmit the order to all my troops.
>
> *Y.* Then 11.30 will do.
>
> *P.* Please do not allow the Nippon Army to enter Singapore until tomorrow.

Y. Why not assemble all your arms immediately in the heart of Singapore so that our Army can check them?

P. Why not let us arrange that tomorrow morning?

Y. It is a matter we can arrange as a side issue.

P. Even 11.00 p.m. is a little late for all troops to cease fire. Why not let them cease hostilities in their present positions?

Y. In that case we shall continue firing until 11.30 p.m. I would advise you to order cessation of hostilities immediately.

P. I shall see that they cease firing immediately I return to my H.Q., and that the firing ceases by 11.30 p.m. In the City area the firing will cease immediately and in the distant areas not later than 11.30 p.m.

Y. As proof of your good faith we shall hold the Highest British Commanders and the Governor of the Straits Settlements in custody at our headquarters. (A look of amazement was noticed on General Percival's face.)

P. Cannot the Nippon Army remain in its present position so that we may resume notifications again tomorrow at 7.00 a.m.?

Y. What! I want the hostilities to cease tonight and I want to remind you that the question is strictly a matter of this. If you can discontinue resistance by 11.30 p.m. we shall hold the Highest Commander and the Governor of the Straits Settlements in our custody. If you cannot do this, the Highest Commander and the Governor must come to our H.Q. by 10.00 p.m.

P. We shall discontinue firing by 10.00 p.m. Nippon Time. Had we better remain in our present positions tonight?

Y. Speaking on the whole, see that your troops remain in their positions and assemble tonight, disarmed, at the prescribed places. I approve of the cessation of hostilities at 10.00 p.m. After we have finished firing, all the British troops should disarm themselves save 1,000 men whom we shall permit to carry arms to maintain order. You have agreed to the terms, but you have not yet made yourself clear as to whether you have agreed to unconditional surrender or not.

(General Percival, with bowed head and in a faint voice, gave his consent. It was 7.30 p.m.)

Y. If you have accepted our terms I would like to hear them from your own lips once more.

P. The British troops will cease hostilities not later than 10.00 p.m. Nippon Time.

Y. The British troops shall disarm themselves completely, except 1,000 men whom the Imperial Army will allow to carry arms in order to obtain peace and order. If your troops infringe upon these terms, the Imperial Japanese Army will resume hostilities immediately

P. I agree. I have a request to make. Will the Imperial Army protect the women and children and the British civilians, men, women and children?

Y. We shall see to it. Please sign this truce agreement.

The Commander of the surrendered British Garrison affixed his signature at 7.50 p.m. on the 15th February 1942.

Survival Under the Jap

In victory, the Japanese proved to be arrogant, cruel and merciless to prisoners. At Singapore some were massacred and tortured in the first few hours after the surrender. In the days, weeks and months that followed a more subtle form of killing was practiced. Rations were at a starvation level and very few medical supplies were granted. In consequence, disease caused most of the deaths. Those who lived survived at levels hitherto unimagined by them.

A sense of humor and an ironic appreciation of the vagaries of life helped. One man who had both, as well as the will to survive, was Stanley Pavillard, a young doctor from the Canary Islands, only recently come to Malaya, and a P.O.W. in the Singapore capitulation. He was taken into Siam to help build a railroad from Bangkok to Rangoon for the Japanese. Work parties were sent to jungle camps where they first cut down the jungle growth, then built embankments over which the track would be laid. Dr. Pavillard was Medical Officer for one of three battalions of workers at Camp Wampo.*

On the long marches through the jungles, many prisoners came down with malaria and those who hadn't already contracted dysentery did so now. Dr. Pavillard managed to scrounge medical supplies from the most unlikely places, including the Japs themselves. But the morale of the men was the most serious problem. He says:

"Once a man lost the will to live drugs and treatment were useless. We used every possible subterfuge to keep the men cheerful, even sometimes inventing false news of the progress of the war, and sometimes we succeeded. If a man was past caring about such things it was now and again possible to make successful use of the deeply ingrained habit of military discipline: one could order a man to recover, and even threaten him with court martial if he died. This may seem a little far-fetched, but I have known it to work. I followed the principles of occupational therapy whenever possible, improving men's morale by

*About 1,500 P.O.W.'s.

86

giving them something to do. We devoted much time and effort to the pursuit and capture of bugs and lice, which we then slipped in vast quantities into the Japanese soldiers' huts. Techniques of the chase varied. One man was an expert on louse catching, having been a P.O.W. in the First World War, and he told me that the thing to do was to place a small piece of cottonwool on my navel when retiring for the night. I thought he was pulling my leg, but I tried it, and sure enough, next morning I found in the cottonwool at least two dozen fat juicy parasites. We gave weekly lectures to the men on hygiene, for the individual's own sake and for the common good: negligence gave dysentery even wider scope. In particular we told men always to dig a hole and fill it up afterwards when they obeyed the call of nature in the jungle. I made use of this form of sanitation myself, since I had caught dysentery and was anxious to scrutinize the signs of its progress day by day more precisely than would have been possible in the confusion of the communal deep latrine. Walking off on one occasion into the jungle for this purpose, I suddenly heard a hissing sound, and saw almost at my feet a large black cobra, already in the striking position: hood fully opened, head swaying from side to side, beady black eyes watching me, forked tongue flickering. I stood there like stone for an instant, and then ran so fast that I forgot my original purpose for two whole days afterwards.

"Daddy Richardson and I built two bamboo platforms in the M.I. room; at night we slept there, in the day we used them as examination couches. The M.I. room had a little door leading into the main hospital ward, behind which we had built a small bamboo hut to serve as a mortuary. We very seldom had any occasion to carry out a post mortem, since when the men died it was usually for very obvious reasons; the mortuary was only made necessary by the fact that the Japs did not always give permission for burial immediately.

"It always surprised me that so many men recovered after operations performed in such primitive conditions on patients in such very poor health. We only operated as a last resort, which meant that those who came under the knife—under the cut-throat razor, rather—were already suffering from malaria, gross malnutrition, and varying degrees of avitaminosis, particularly beri-beri and pellagra. Many of them had acute or chronic bacillary and amoebic dysentery as well, not to mention big tropical ulcers.

"Since we never had enough drugs to treat everybody properly, we were constantly being faced with the most appalling decisions. Drugs were withheld as a matter of course until life depended upon their use, but then we had to decide who was to have them. On these occasions I gave preference to married men, especially those with many children, though I often knew that some personal friend of mine would have to die in consequence of this decision. I think I did right: God alone knows how hard it was to decide such a matter. Over and above this, we had to carry the burden and responsibility of easing, so far as we could, the misery and terror of those who were not going to recover. Sometimes we gave them an injection of plain water, making believe it was emetine, or whatever else was needed but not available. In the last stages one had a task like that of comforting a frightened child. I had one man, a sergeant-major in the S.S.V.F., a big burly fellow of tremendous personality and a tower of strength in the Battalion; now he went down with diphtheria, which caused paralysis in his throat, so that whenever he tried to swallow fluid it regurgitated up his nose. Then the nerve type of beri-beri attacked his left foot; I have never seen a man so full of the desire to live, and all I could do was to sit beside him and hold his hand until he calmed down and in the end died quite quietly." *

BAMBOO DOCTOR

by Dr. Stanley Pavillard

As work on the railway progressed, the Japs found it necessary to break us up into three detachments. This meant that I was parted from "D" Battalion: they were sent down to Wampo South, while I and the other doctors had to stay behind in the old camp, travelling backwards and forwards every day to visit our patients.

A new camp had to be built at Wampo South, and then our men got to work on an exceptionally strenuous and even dangerous part of the job. The camp was built on a piece of flat ground quite near the river, on the other side

Bamboo Doctor, pp. 100, 101, 105, 106. St. Martin's Press.

88

of which was a high cliff of solid rock. A ledge a quarter of a mile long had to be carved out of this, to carry the railway; working up there, sixty feet above the river, completely exposed to the blazing sun, our men suffered terribly, and many of them collapsed from heat exhaustion. This was the result, not only of the heat, but also of the glare of sunlight reflected from the bare rocks all round; those men who managed to improvise sun glasses out of odd bits of coloured glass managed much better. In the same way, it was possible to make shoes of a sort out of jungle leaves and tree bark, so as to reduce the pain of walking on scorching rock. Even with the aid of such devices, only the strong ones could carry on, working blindly, in a jerky mechanical fashion as if hypnotized or dazed, aware only of the harsh sunlight boring mercilessly through their eyeballs. The body has a natural and automatic heat-regulating mechanism, but this can only be over-taxed so far: for many of the men there came a time when the brain lost control of the situation. Then they would lie there, chest heaving, heart throbbing, face grey and streaming with perspiration. I got these cases into hospital as quickly as I could, but they were suffering very severely from shock and often died quite soon afterwards.

The actual burden of the work was made easier than it might have been, however, by the fact that the Japs provided material and equipment for blasting. The vast explosions which took place could be heard at enormous distances. I remember the first: I was doing my ward rounds at the time, and I had not known that there was going to be any blasting. So when I heard this terrific bang I flung myself flat on the ground at once; everyone else did the same, our reflexes having been thoroughly conditioned during the battle of Singapore. We got up sheepishly, feeling rather fools.

The Japs had a peculiar sense of humour, and very often they used to fire the dynamite charges embedded in the rock without first sounding the warning signal: they did this for the fun of seeing the P.O.W.s run madly for shelter. This amusing game led to many accidents. The first victim was a cook, who was working at the time in the camp, across the river from where the blasting was taking place. A small piece of rock hit him on the forehead between the eyes: Pinky Riley 'phoned for me at once, and when I came I found the man suffering badly from shock. I examined him and I could actually see his brain tissue with small splinters of bone adhering to it. I cleaned the wound very carefully with boiled water and removed the bone fragments, then filled the cavity with three M. and B. 693 tablets crushed to powder, and applied a dressing. Fortunately the brain tissue itself did not appear to be damaged, and after four weeks in hospital the patient had fully recovered and never developed any after-effects.

The next victim was not so lucky: a large piece of rock hit him on the face, damaging the tear duct and leaving a nasty lacerated wound which extended from the inner angle of his left eye to the outer margin of the left lip. I put in eighteen stitches and he recovered all right, but with a mild degree of facial paralysis: careful plastic surgery after the war improved matters somewhat, but he was disfigured for life. We made repeated representations to the Japs about this aspect of their behaviour: they explained to us that it was our men's own fault and that they should get out of the way quicker.

Once a week we had a half-holiday, and the Japs would often enlist our help in large-scale fishing. The river was teeming with fish; a party of P.O.W.s who were able to swim waited by the riverside, and a Jap threw several hand-grenades into the river some two hundred yards up-stream, so as to explode under water. Enormous quantities of stunned fish floated down stream, to be landed by the waiting swimmers, and the Japs always posted several lookouts to make sure that all the fish was brought ashore so that they could pick the best.

Here again one could diddle them: it was just a question of thinking up the right trick. The way to embezzle fish under these circumstances is as follows: you tie a stout wire round your leg, which is of course out of sight while you are wading or swimming, and when a suitable fish comes along you push the loose end of this wire through its gills and allow it to hang there, out of sight and troubling nobody. Then at some convenient moment you can unhook the wire, with several fish on it, from your leg, and fasten it unobtrusively to the underwater roots of a tree by the edge. When the party is over, you can come back and claim your prize.

But the fish in this river were not all beer and skittles: some of them bit. There was one particularly vicious variety, only about two or three inches long but fond of hunting in enormous shoals, and their idea of a joke was to attack us while we were bathing and bite off small bits of our private parts. The scars which resulted were capable of subsequent misinterpretation by insurance doctors or by ever-loving wives, so I gave certificates to the victims making it quite clear that V.D. was not responsible. These certificates were written on any old dirty scrap of paper and read as follows:

To Whom It May Concern
This is to certify that........................
whilst a P.O.W. in Siam lost a portion of his
Foreskin
————— as a result of a fish bite whilst swimming,
Scrotum
naked, in the river.
Sgd.
Captain: M.O., 1st S.S.V.F.

On 10th April, 1943, I was walking up towards the officers' hut to see Bob Lucas, the Adjutant of "D" Battalion, who was down with malaria, when glancing down a jungle path I was surprised to see a strange party approaching. They were British P.O.W.s escorted by Jap guards and they were carrying heavy packages slung on long bamboo poles. There were eighteen of these packages and I saw with great surprise that they were field medical panniers of the standard army type. It seemed almost unbelievable that the Japs should be sending medical supplies up to Wampo; I watched carefully, wondering what to make of it, while the party reported to the Jap guard room and then unloaded their cargo at the camp rice store, not far from the hospital, placing it carefully under lock and key.

Full of curiosity, I got talking to a member of the party; I gathered that these panniers contained British drugs captured at the fall of Singapore and that they were only going to be left at Wampo for one night. Early next morning the party was to continue its journey, carrying these medical supplies another stage towards their ultimate destination, which was on the frontier between Burma and Siam: they were to be used for the benefit of Jap soldiers fighting the British.

I thought hard. The panniers were not padlocked, but only tied with bits of wire and string. We were running short of medicines, and a move up country was rumoured. The rice store where the panniers had been locked up was only the usual kind of bamboo-and-palm-leaf hut: it had an entrance quite near the hospital, known as the smithy, since a certain amount of ironwork in connection with the railway was done there. Separating the rice store from the smithy was an inner wall or partition, about ten feet high, not reaching to the roof of the hut.

Without telling Daddy Richardson what I was up to I got hold of Pinky Riley and made him keep a sharp lookout near the smithy and let me know if any Japs turned up. Then I scrambled up quite easily over the bamboo partition and into the rice store: the first pannier I opened was full of tins, each tin containing one thousand M. and B. 693 tablets. This was wonderful, as this particular drug was very effective with many tropical diseases. I placed a tin inside my tattered old shorts and tied the pannier up again, and then departed very quickly, with a bulge in front of me that must have made me look at least six months pregnant.

I went back to the hospital and told Daddy Richardson what I had done, and then buried the tin.

This was excellent, but something more substantial was obviously called for, and there was very little time. I went to the officers' hut and explained the situation to Lt.-Col. Lilly, the British Camp Commandant; I pointed out that if we moved up country soon, which seemed very likely as the Wampo stretch of line was nearly completed, our medical situation would be very acute. So I wanted to plan a raid.

Lilly called together the commanding officers of "D" and "F" Battalions, and they weighed the matter up very seriously. Soon they came to the conclusion that my scheme was quite impractical: the Jap Commandant lived practically on top of the rice store, and it was more than likely that extra guards would be laid on to look after these precious supplies. Anyone caught taking part in such a raid would be decapitated at once. The camp administration did not approve and would have nothing to do with the plan.

I went away, feeling well and truly put in my place. But I could not accept this situation for long: and I knew much better than those officers did exactly what a move up country was likely to mean, in medical terms.

So I went to the men's lines and called out four individuals: I explained what I was going to do, and described the dangers and the consequences of being caught. They responded absolutely, without any hesitation at all.

I swore them to secrecy and we worked out every detail of my plan, going over and over again until we had it all by heart. Nobody else was to be told; a few trustworthy men were to be brought along to act as sentries and give a pre-arranged whistle if any Japs appeared, but they were not to be told what was going on.

We planned to start at 9 p.m. sharp. It was obvious that the panniers could not be properly examined in the rice store; each one would have to be lifted over the ten-foot bamboo partition and carried smartly along to the hospital M.I. room twenty-five yards away. There Richardson, Pinky and I would examine the contents of each pannier with a light and take out a suitable quantity of what we needed, but so as to avoid making it obvious that the panniers had been interfered with.

I arranged to go in with the raiding party on their first entry and show them where the panniers were, and then to stay in the M.I. room. I had enlisted four men: two to lift the panniers over the partition, and two to carry them through the smithy and along to the hospital. Pinky was to take the stolen drugs and bury them as we went along.

Eventually the time for action came: we made sure that the coast was clear and that our sentries were alert, and

93

then we went into the smithy and started to climb the bamboo partition, very carefully, very quietly. But just then we distinctly heard the pre-arranged danger signal. We dropped off the partition and crouched in the darkest corners we could find, our hearts pounding: slowly a Jap guard's footsteps marched towards us. Time stopped, agonizingly, and the universe was full of nothing but those footsteps. Furiously, we turned not only our eyes but even our thoughts away from the guard: I had often thought that thought-waves or something similar can betray a man who is trying to hide, and now I made myself imagine that I was falling out of an aeroplane, tumbling and somersaulting, until in my mind's eye I could see only a whirl of earth and sky. This ugly thought was powerful enough to distract my mind and to prevent it from wandering off and attracting the attention of that man just outside.

After what seemed an infinite time of suspense we heard the guard's footsteps receding into the darkness. The all-clear signal was given and soon we were over the partition and at work. I helped the men get the first pannier over and along to the hospital, and soon we had it opened.

And so the work went on, easily and rhythmically: as soon as we had finished extracting a few items from one pannier, another would arrive. It was wonderful and sad to see such a stock of life-saving drugs: sad because of the men now dead for lack of them. We worked with fierce accuracy and speed.

Only one episode, but that an alarming one, interrupted the smooth progress of our work. I put my hand into the last pannier but one to take out a small bottle, and felt a searing pain, as if a red hot poker was being driven into the middle finger of my right hand. I let out a scream of agony, thinking that a snake had bitten me. The pain was unbearable, and within a few seconds I was bathed in a cold perspiration and felt like fainting. I told Richardson and Pinky to look for the snake, since it was important to know what kind it was: I held the hurt finger tight with my left hand, ready to have it slashed open with a razor and dipped in a strong solution of permanganate. But to my relief we found not a snake but a big armour-plated scorpion. My

94

finger throbbed all night and was quite numb for a week afterwards.

Eventually we were told that it was all over: the last of the panniers had been put back exactly as before. I looked at my watch: it was 2 a.m. I thanked the men and commented on the speed with which they had manhandled those heavy panniers over the ten-foot partition. They said, apologetically, that they had opened the door of the rice store from the inside and had brought the panniers out that way, instead of over the partition as they had been told. I nearly had a fit: the front door of the rice store was right opposite the hut of the Jap Commandant in charge of railway construction.

Next morning, with a sigh of relief, I watched the Jap guards and the prisoners carrying the panniers move together out of our camp. Obviously they suspected nothing; I have seldom been so glad to see anybody off the premises. When they had gone I told Lt.-Col. Lilly what I had done, and explained that we now had a year's supply of medicines. The old man replied, "I had a notion you would do it, Pav; as a matter of fact I haven't slept a bloody wink all night."

I arranged that the loot should be left buried for several days in case of unexpected and delayed repercussions, and that it should be shared out equally between "D," "B" and "F" Battalions if all went well.

When I got back to England in October 1945 I submitted a report to the War Office, describing this episode and suggesting that the bravery and devotion of the men concerned should receive official recognition. None was given, and for the record their names are as follows:

No. 5707 C.Q.M.S. Metcalfe, J.M., F.M.S.V.F.
No. 7830 Private Wadsworth, K.T., F.M.S.V.F.
No. 7396 Sergeant Cassidy, T.P., F.M.S.V.F.
No. 13610 Lance-Corporal Miles, E.T., F.M.S.V.F.

I have no doubt that the knowledge that they had put a fast one across the Japanese and had saved the lives of any number of their comrades was then, and still remains, worth more to them than any medal.

Our Wampo stretch of line was almost finished: only part of the work on the cliff face remained to be done. To speed things up the Japs brought in two thousand more P.O.W.s and started what we called the "Speedo Period." Everything had to be done literally at the double. The weekly half-holiday was abolished. The men set off to work before dawn and returned late at night; they had no chance to wash themselves or air their bedding and the number of bugs and lice in action against us increased rapidly. Skin diseases, especially scabies and ringworm, attacked everyone, while malaria, dysentery, and deficiency diseases took full advantage of our exhaustion. Imperial Japanese Army Headquarters had given orders that guards were to bash hell out of the P.O.W.s if they did not work harder.

The worst of the acute and dangerous diseases which we were faced with, apart from cholera, was malignant tertian malaria with its cerebral complications. From this time on we were faced with cases of this sort almost every day. Patients were being brought in with temperatures of 105° to 107°, and unless the proper diagnosis was made and the proper treatment given at once, the patient would sink into delirium and then into a coma, and his temperature would rise to 110°: after this there was no hope of recovery as his brain was literally cooked. The important thing therefore was to keep the temperature down. We took it rectally as soon as the patient arrived in hospital, and if it was 105° or more he would be put on the ground naked, fanned, and soused continually in cold water. Meanwhile, quinine well diluted in saline was slowly injected intravenously. This procedure was not devoid of danger, as it could lead to sudden heart failure, but it was the only life-saving technique we had.

Patients who recovered from severe cerebral malaria had, in general, no recollection of what had happened; but this loss of memory was only temporary, and as a rule recovery was complete.

It was impossible to cope with malaria and its complications properly. At first we never had sufficient quinine; later on, and until our rice-store raid, atebrin had to be kept only for emergencies. Many men refused to take quinine either for prevention or cure: we often found the pills they were supposed to have taken hidden under their rice-sack pillows after they had died. We were always on the move and always at work, and never got a chance to oil the breeding grounds of mosquitoes: the men had no clothing to speak of and certainly no mosquito nets.

Eventually the railway line reached Wampo North. We had been working against our will and in the interests of the Japanese, our enemies; but it was impossible not to feel a certain pride and excitement at the completion of our work. So there we stood one morning, very early, straining our eyes and peering down the line, waiting until eventually the first train to pass over our own railway emerged from the mist and rattled by in a cloud of steam.

Our work at Wampo was done, and the Japs told us that at the end of April 1943 all the men there were to be moved up country. "D" Battalion was the last to leave: our destination was Tonchan South, ten miles to the north of Tarsau. This meant another forced march of about twenty-five miles; as before we had to carry all our kit and cooking utensils. We arrived dead beat after twenty hours.

At first this march followed the railway tracks, and then we left them behind and marched over ground which had been levelled and prepared for them. Further north there were wooden bridges to be crossed: these had been built out of tree trunks, across a number of deep ravines, and it felt very unsafe and alarming to walk across them. They had been built in a crude and clumsy fashion from jungle trees, and the men who built them had taken every opportunity for sabotage: spikes and bolts were put in in the wrong places or left loose, so that when in due course the Japs started to send heavy goods trains over these bridges, many of them collapsed, sometimes causing the locomotive to explode at the bottom of a deep ravine.

When we arrived at Tonchan South we found that the camp already held three thousand P.O.W.s. Another camp had been built to house the labour force which the Japanese had impressed from among the Asian population: there were three thousand of these unfortunate people also, and both the two camps, theirs and ours, occupied less than half a square mile between them. These Chinese, Malays, Indians and Eurasians were in a far worse situation than ours: they had no doctors or medicines and no leaders of any sort, no record was kept of their names and whereabouts, they were fed occasionally when the Japs felt like it, and they were totally ignorant of sanitation. The whole situation was ripe for an epidemic.

I felt very disturbed, but as far as "D" Battalion was concerned, things could have been worse. Before we left Wampo I had lectured the men on cholera precautions, and they had a natural advantage in that their average age was thirty-seven, with eleven years' residence in the Far East. This meant that they were completely acclimatized to a tropical environment, they had a certain sense of responsibility and could be relied on to carry out medical instructions given for their own good, and in most cases they were married and had something to live for. Many other units in Siam were made up chiefly of young men without these advantages, and their survival rate was much lower: a fact which came home to one poignantly when one inspected the rough inscriptions in the various jungle cemeteries.

The Japanese Camp Commandant at Tonchan South was Staff-Sergeant Hiramatsu, a man of few words, tough, rough and brutal: they called him Tiger. But he did have a sense of justice, and the ruthless discipline which he imposed was as bad for the Jap guards as it was for us. We were all afraid of him.

The day after we arrived at Tonchan South he sent for me and for the P.O.W. camp interpreter, who warned me that the Tiger knew English and that I should be careful what I said. Apparently it was beneath the great man's dignity to speak the captives' language or admit that he understood it.

I came into the Tiger's hut and he barked out at me through the interpreter, "You are the new doctor!" I felt like a new boy at school and I nearly answered, "Yes sir"; but I remembered that I was dealing with a bully and I looked him straight in the face and said, "That is so." He looked me up and down and paused and thought a little, and then asked me in a slightly different tone why there was so much sickness amongst us prisoners.

There was plenty to say in reply to that one: I gave him the obvious elementary answers, and pointed out that the conditions we had been living under made sickness inevitable. Men fed on such a poor and defective diet, overworked to the point of collapse, and compelled to do without proper sanitation were not likely to be pictures of health. I ended up by saying, "I am proud of "D" Battalion: they want to work, and I will keep them fit, but you must help me."

Tiger glared at me for a long time: I could see that he was angry and I wondered if I had gone too far. But eventually he smiled in a cunning way and explained to me that the sickness was caused by our men being lazy, sleeping on the wet ground and without shirts to protect them from mosquito bites. Controlling my temper as well as I could I pointed out the various fallacies in this statement of the situation, and I explained that malaria was a menace even in the best conditions: I had always taken proper precautions in the tropics, but I had still caught malaria.

This made Tiger laugh immoderately, and he advanced what seemed to him a tremendously witty suggestion that if I, a doctor, had caught malaria, it must have been in consequence of taking girls into the jungle at night. I pretended to share his amusement at this brilliant joke and laughed loudly, and the interpreter did so too: the atmosphere relaxed and I realized that Tiger and I understood each other. When he stopped laughing he asked me in a business-like way what I needed to ensure my men's health and ability to work. At once, before he had time to change his mind, I made my terms: 26 ounces of uncooked rice per man every day, one cow or buffalo and six large baskets of mixed vegetables every other day, adequate amounts of tea and sugar, and a half a day's rest every week. This half-holiday was needed very urgently: the men were still sleeping on the ground and had no time to wash what few garments they had. The Tiger thought this over and then agreed, but in a quiet, threatening way: he expected results. I felt very pleased at this diplomatic success, although I had some difficulty at first in making our people believe what I said had happened: it sounded too good to be true. But Staff-Sergeant Hiramatsu was a man of his word.

Three days later he sent for me again: I arrived with the interpreter, very puzzled, and found Tiger lying on the floor under a blanket, obviously in the throes of a malarial attack. He produced an ampoule of quinine, pointed to a saucepan in which a hypodermic needle had been boiled, and told me to give him an intravenous injection.

The situation had its humorous side, and I could not resist turning to the interpreter and saying, "Ask him if he has been taking a girl into the jungle." The interpreter did not have time to translate a word: Tiger roared "Kurrah!" at the top of his voice and grabbed furiously at a sword by his bedside. But he controlled himself and smiled through his shivers and asked me to be less comic and to get on with the injection. I did so, and he was up next day.

We now heard that cholera had broken out at a place called Takanun, which was less than one hundred miles from us up the river. This was very serious news; "D" Battalion had all been inoculated against cholera and I had lectured on the subject, but there were now so many men crowded together in such a small area that an outbreak of cholera could wipe us all out in a matter of days.

Cholera is usually endemic in parts of Siam during the dry season; you catch it by drinking contaminated water from a river or shallow well, or by eating food which has been handled by someone suffering from cholera or carrying it. There have been vast epidemics at various periods of history: Thucydides refers to it in the fifth century B.C., while in modern India there were eight million cholera deaths between 1904 and 1924. I had never seen a case, but I was almost obsessed by the fear of it: the section of my textbook on tropical diseases which dealt with cholera was the only part of that book which escaped being used as cigarette paper.

Now this terrifying thing was at work and near us; I

gave further and more urgent lectures, and insisted that full precautions were to be rigorously observed. Only boiled water was to be used for drinking or for cleaning the teeth, bathing in the river was to stop absolutely, eating utensils were to be dipped in boiling water before use, any food touched by flies or ants was to be thrown away, and each man had to take great care to keep his hands away from his mouth. One additional warning I gave, which was that paper used for making cigarettes should not be licked: the men used any old scrap of dirty paper for this purpose.

In practice these rules could not be enforced as strictly as one would wish, and of course they were wholly ignored in the Asian camp next door.

On the morning of 8th June, 1943, Vincent Bennett, the M.O. of "F" Battalion, sent a message to my tent asking if I could come over at once to see one of his men who was very ill. At the time it was raining heavily, and as I left the partial shelter of my leaky tent the cold rain sloshed over my body and soaked my loin cloth, so that by the time I reached the hospital I felt as if I had a wet nappy on.

The man was lying on bamboo slats looking extremely ill, very pale and with a drawn anxious expression on his waxen face. His nose had a pinched appearance and his eyes were sunken; his finger tips were crinkled like a washerwoman's, his skin was cold and clammy, and his temperature below normal.

I asked him several questions. In a barely audible whisper, he told me that he had been vomiting and passing large quantities of stools like barley water, and that he was now getting excruciating pains in his calf muscles. I told him not to worry, and made various vague and sadly dishonest promises of healing medicines.

Vincent and I walked away and as soon as we were out of ear shot I turned to him and said, "Christ, it's caught up with us, Vincent! There is no doubt, that's cholera!"

"I know, Pav, it's a textbook case." It was a great shock and we felt very bitter: one would think we had suffered enough.

We returned to the hospital and gave the man a shot of morphia, since by this time the cramps in his legs were making him scream out in agony. The cholera poisons make the muscles contract suddenly and so violently that individual muscle fibres actually snap: the pain of it is almost unendurable.

Then Vincent and I went to tell Tiger what had happened. It took him a moment or two to realize the full implications of what we had said: then he started to shout and rave like a lunatic, as if it had been our fault. Eventually he calmed down, and we told him that we must at once clear a small area in the jungle, not far from the camp, to serve as a cholera compound for this case and the others which were bound to occur. This sent Tiger raving again and he screamed that the man had to be sent at once to the Base Hospital at Tarsau. We replied that under no circumstances was the man to leave Tonchan South, as to move him would only spread the disease. Finding his will opposed, Tiger went very red in the face, pulled his sword out and brandished it in front of us screaming, "It is an order of the Imperial Japanese Army that the man be moved to Tarsau!"

I thought that a more conciliatory tone might help, so I said. "It shall be done as you say; since there is a Japanese doctor at Tarsau, why not 'phone him first? If this man goes to Tarsau and spreads the disease there, your doctor will make trouble for all of us." Tiger picked up the telephone with a grunt and started jabbering in Japanese, and after a while he turned to us and said, "Japanese doctor now come—you take man to jungle."

So off we went and arranged for a working party to go and make a clearing in the jungle, a quarter of a mile from the camp. Here we rigged up a tent provided by the Japs; it was full of holes where the canvas had rotted. We put the patient inside, but we could do nothing for him except for an injection of morphia to ease the pain and a drink of water which he immediately vomited.

Before the afternoon was over, we had packed ten more cases inside that small tent; and our first patient had died.

We felt uneasy about burying him, since the ground sloped slightly and rain water might soak through the earth and contaminate the river. So we made an attempt to

102

burn the body, using jungle vegetation to build a funeral pyre: after several attempts we managed to get the green wood alight, but the cremation was not a success, and eventually we had to bury the body in a deep grave only partially charred.

The epidemic which now started did not take me wholly by surprise: I had given the men of "D" Battalion a shot of cholera vaccine before we left Wampo, and I had also worked out plans for making a water distillation plant.

The distilled water was required to form the basis of a saline solution to be administered intravenously. The treatment of cholera is aimed in general at the immediate replacement of body fluids lost by vomiting and diarrhoea, so that the body never becomes dehydrated but remains able to function. I managed to save many lives in this way, pouring anything up to eight or ten pints of my saline solution into the patients' veins every twenty-four hours. But there were various dangerous complications: muscular cramps and, more seriously, complete kidney failure or beri-beri. Both of these very often proved fatal. One curious feature of the epidemic which I noticed was that a man liable to attacks of malaria would find them cured on his recovery from cholera: as if the cholera germs had destroyed their malarial colleagues.

As well as salines, we used M. and B. 693 tablets. If given early enough, before the pernicious vomiting started, this made the disease much milder or enabled the patient to by-pass it altogether.

Even so, we had two hundred cases within two days from our diagnosis of the first. The Japanese flatly refused to give us extra tents, and matters were made worse by the fact that many of the Asians in the camp next door panicked and fled into the jungle. Their only possible route was by the river and its tributaries, and so in a very short time these men contrived to contaminate every available source of water supply. Later on, our working parties found their bodies in the jungle.

The men were now dying at such a rate that I persuaded Tiger to let me have a working party to dig a communal grave. This was granted and we dug a pit, 20 feet long,

10 feet wide, and 20 feet deep; we used jungle vines as ropes, to hoist the earth and the workers out of the pit.

The men were thrown into the pit as soon as they died; and every evening, before leaving the compound, the doctors and orderlies together used to shovel a thin layer of earth over the swollen and distorted bodies.

When a new patient was admitted we placed him on the ground and started to administer intravenous salines at once. This was often difficult, since his veins had usually collapsed as a result of dehydration caused by copious vomiting and diarrhoea. We could not locate a vein with our finger tips: we had to cut the skin in an approximate fashion where we knew there ought to be a vein, and then patiently to dissect the tissues around the vein until it was exposed. The best vein for this purpose was the one on the inner aspect of the foot, just above the ankle bone. Once the vein was located a linen thread was passed under it and it was eased clear of the wound; a hollow bamboo needle was pushed into the vein and tied with the thread, and then connected by means of a rubber tube to the saline bottle. We had two dozen such bottles, glass jam-jars or Japanese beer bottles, and they were all in constant use. The operation was carried out without any local anaesthetic, since none was available; but fortunately the shocked and collapsed condition of the patients was as good as an anaesthetic. The thickened blood inside their veins looked like black treacle and flowed slowly.

One of the worst things about cholera was the painfulness of the muscle cramps; we gave morphia when we could, but there was not nearly enough to go round, and from the compound there arose continually, therefore, a faint desperate moaning which was terrible to hear, punctuated at intervals by appalling shrieks as some unfortunate's muscles snapped.

The compound was hellish in every way. The stench from the burial pit was everywhere. When one approached the pit to use it one saw bubbling millions of maggots. The cholera victims from the Asian camp had no doctors or orderlies to look after them, and the Japanese made no provision at all for them to have food or water. They were just dumped in our camp to lie on the ground in the open until they died or were taken by us into a tent. We did what we could to alleviate their sufferings; when some of our own cholera cases recovered, they volunteered to stay in the compound and help.

We could not keep the bodies too long before burial because of the ants; I usually tried to wait a few hours before burial, just to make sure, and in doubtful cases I cut the man's wrist with a razor blade. Flowing blood would show that he was alive, and could then be stopped by artery forceps.

In describing these days, I may have given an impression of callousness, as though I and the other doctors were past feeling and suffering the situation. In a sense our emotions were anaesthetized: we could not have remained sane otherwise. But then and for a long time afterwards we were liable to find memory reasserting itself at night-time, and to wake up screaming from the black depths of nightmare: this still happens to me from time to time, and once again I see the jungle, the rain, and my friends turning liquid in a pit of flies and maggots.

When I left the compound in the evening, I used to go back to a little tent in the main camp, which I shared with five other officers. On one side of me Bob Lucas slept, and on the other was Captain T. E. Abrams, R.A., known to us all as A.B. He and I were good friends and I shared his blanket.

I remember how he came with me one day to Tonchan main camp; I wanted to get some more rubber and glass tubing for our distillation plant, and he came too, walking the weary twelve miles there and back simply so that I could have someone to talk to. We came to a place where the ground was covered with small brown pebbles such as are used for drives and garden paths in England, and A.B. said to me, "Look, Pav: these pebbles remind me of the path leading to my house. Let's rest here for a bit." We sat down and chatted about our homes, idly picking up these pebbles and flinging them in the jungle, listening to the rustling of the leaves as various birds and reptiles moved away from this bombardment. This episode and these thoughts of home came back to me a few days later, when A.B. woke me up in the middle of the night with agitated whispers. I groped for his hand instinctively: it was cold and clammy, and I could feel the ridges on his finger tips. Very sadly, because I knew what had happened, I said to him, "Tell me, A.B., where have you been shitting?" He answered in a whisper, "Just by the tree outside the tent." I lit a candle: it was four in the morning. By the flickering candle light I could see that his eyes had sunk into their orbits and his skin had become pale and waxy. "Listen, A.B., you are not to worry," I said. "It is a good job we have caught it early—here, take these tablets." But only with great difficulty could he swallow the four M. and B. 693 tablets which I gave him. I woke up the other people in the tent and at frequent intervals we carried poor A.B. outside by the tree where he vomited and passed large watery stools. There was not much more we could do till daybreak. After a while, he started complaining of pain in his calf muscles: I boiled a morphia tablet in a spoon with a little water over a candle flame, sucked the liquid into a syringe, and injected it. This relieved the pain, just for a while.

Dawn came at last. I examined his stools: they had a typical cholera appearance. I organized a carrying party and we took A.B. along to the cholera compound on a stretcher made from two sacks and a couple of bamboo poles. Then before following on, I gave instructions that the tent was to be moved and a fire built where it had stood, and also by the tree, in order to disinfect the ground; already the ants were everywhere, and I strongly suspected them of helping to spread the cholera germ, although I have never seen this in a textbook.

Luckily, several bottles of saline were already sterilized and ready: I warmed them to body temperature and dissected my way down to a vein in A.B.'s right foot. I got several pints of saline into him at once, and more later in the day: his cramps were severe and he had to be given morphia. Sometimes he was delirious; but once he took my hands in a tight grip and said in a barely audible whisper,

106

"Pav, write to my wife, tell her I love her." Soon afterwards, he sank into a coma and died; it was 5 p.m.

I had not the heart to throw his body into the common pit, since we had lived as brothers, sharing what little we had. So I took a shovel and dug a deep grave by a jungle tree, and his men in the lines afterwards erected a rough wooden cross there with his name inscribed with a red-hot iron.

On 26th June, 1943, Tiger gave me permission to visit Tarsau ten miles away, to see whether I could get some more rubber and glass tubing for our distillation plant. This apparatus worked day and night now, which enabled us to find plenty of saline sterilized and ready for use when we came to the compound in the morning. But the rubber tubing was starting to perish because of the heat.

I went by myself, taking with me a pass in Japanese characters which Tiger had provided in case I should be stopped. He told me to be back by nightfall. I set off in the early morning along a narrow track, carrying a bamboo cane and making a loud noise so as to frighten away snakes and wild animals. Wild life was very plentiful in the Siamese jungle: at night we could hear elephants fooling around quite near the camp, which made the Japanese get nervous and start banging away with their rifles; tigers had been reported and sometimes we smelt them. Large committees of baboons used to hang around our camp quite often, eyeing us in a disapproving way. The last time I had been out on this errand, A.B. had been with me, and now he was dead: it was hard to believe, and very sad.

After walking several hours, I saw a column of men marching towards me. As they approached I began to feel that there was something familiar about the man who was leading the column. "Dr. Livingstone, I presume?"—it was Lt.-Col. Newey, the C.O. of my wartime Battalion, the 1st S.S.V.F. We had parted a year previously at Changi, and here we were meeting by chance in the middle of a Siamese jungle.

The Jap guard in charge of this party allowed me to talk to them for a while. They were mostly Malayan Volunteers, part of an outfit which the Japanese had designated as

"H" Force. They had just come from Singapore; the Japs had told our administration at Changi that they were forming two units, "F" Force and "H" Force, and that all sick men in Changi who were able to walk should be included in these parties, since they were to be sent to a hill station where it was very healthy, with excellent food and first-class hospitals. The camp authorities had no alternative to accepting this lie; in fact, no arrangements had been made to feed these men at all. During the subsequent few weeks we quite often saw parties of these men from "F" Force and "H" Force on their way through Tonchan South: they appeared to be very near starvation, and we gave them what food we could. Now when I told them that they were walking straight into a cholera area, they were completely shattered by the news; they were quite plainly in no state to cope with any epidemic. In fact, the mortality among the men of these two units was extraordinarily high; they had suffered much more than we had.

I left them, and continued my march to Tarsau. The Jap medical officer there gave me the glass and rubber tubing I had come for, and after talking to various friends I set out on my weary and lonely walk home, moving fast, since starvation had made me night-blind and I was afraid of getting lost. The Japs had given me written permission to carry a walking stick at night, and I was to produce this if a Jap guard questioned my being in possession of what they classed as a dangerous weapon. Usually the guards clouted first, before I could produce the document out of my G-string. Even with the stick I was very liable to fall into holes and bump into trees.

This time I was lucky and got back to camp well before sunset. My friends of "H" Force were there trying to find shelter and scrounging around for food, which we provided as well as we could.

That evening when I held my usual sick parade, many of the Malayan Volunteers of "H" Force came along so that I could do something about their blisters and especially their tropical ulcers. These tended to start in consequence of a bamboo scratch or a blistered foot; at the best they were slow to heal, and unless they were treated at once

108

they increased rapidly in size, spreading and eating up the tissues very deeply until even the bone was affected and started to disintegrate. Then secondary infection set in, accompanied by a sickening smell. The doctors of "H" Force had practically no medicines with them; they tried various ways of treating these tropical ulcers such as scraping them clean without any anaesthetic, the patient being held down meanwhile, or the deliberate placing of live maggots in the ulcer so that they would eat it clean. This form of treatment originated during the First World War; severely wounded men who had to lie out on the battle field for several days before they could be rescued often had wounds which were seething with maggots, but incredibly clean and free from any tendency to go gangrenous.

Following this theory, some of the P.O.W. doctors started putting live maggots into ulcers. This form of treatment would probably have been excellent for fit and well-fed men, but I did not approve of it for anyone in our physical and psychological condition: the sight of a bubbling mass of big fat maggots crawling in and out of even the strongest-minded P.O.W.'s ulcer would be enough to send him round the bend.

Instead, I used the "permanent ulcer dressing," as developed during the Spanish Civil War for the treatment of compound fractures. The Spanish doctors used to encase the shattered limb in plaster of paris and leave it to stew for several weeks in its own pus; when the plaster was removed the fracture was seen to be joined and the wound healed. So now with these ulcers: I cleaned them as well as I could and applied a little iodoform or M. and B. 693, and then slapped on elastoplast, covering this with bandages made from old sheets or banana tree bark.

After three weeks the ulcers had vanished completely unless they had been very big, and even then we saw healthy granulation tissue and the process of healing completed itself soon afterwards.

I treated a great many tropical ulcers in this way and no amputations resulted, except in the case of one man who insisted on being evacuated down-river against my advice. If he had done as he was told, he would have kept his leg.

109

The Heroic Island

One of the most heralded last-stands in modern American military history occurred at Wake Island in December 1941. On this atoll, with its shore line of twenty-one miles, a handful of Marines and construction workers fought off heavy bombing raids and one full-fledged invasion attempt before the Japs managed to get ashore.

Wake was 2,000 miles closer than Pearl Harbor to Japan and considered a part of the U.S. Pacific defense line, a kind of stationary "carrier" from which strikes could be made at the Jap-held Marshall Islands. At the time of the invasion, the island was under the command of W. Scott Cunningham, Commander, U.S.N. He had visited the island twice before. "Aside from the tiny Pan American Airways installations on Peale [island] the atoll in 1940 was virtually the same desolate spot it had been when Mendana de Neyra looked it over, snorted, and departed in the sixteenth century. From time to time there had been talk in Washington about developing Wake's possibilities . . . but its strategic importance had generally been lost on a nation intent on peace. . . . Officially it bore the designation of a bird sanctuary." *

But when Cunningham arrived in November 1941, there were 1,100 civilians hard at work building roads, air strips, and other installations intended primarily for a base to be utilized by amphibious patrol planes; a Marine defense battalion, not up to full strength, was under command of Major James Devereux, and was charged with building the defense installations. Major Devereux had arrived in October bringing three batteries of coastal defense guns, gleaned from retired battleships, and three batteries of anti-aircraft guns. The firepower of the island consisted of the six batteries, plus eighteen machine-gun emplacements of fifty-caliber, and thirty machine guns of

*W. Scott Cunningham, *Wake Island Command*, p. 26. Little Brown & Co.

thirty-caliber. There was no radar, and it was hard to hear warnings from sirens or whistles because of the unusually loud, booming surf.

Radio broadcasts of the Pearl Harbor attack reached Wake on December 7th; on the 8th, Wake received its first visit from Jap bombers based in the Marshalls. Though the Wake defenders were expecting raids, this first one of thirty-six enemy bombers managed complete surprise; considerable damage was caused.

Commander Cunningham had stationed four planes patrolling over the atoll at 12,000 feet, but the Japs flew in at 2,000 feet out of low cloud formations. Even the roar of the approaching planes was smothered by the noise of the surf.

After the first raid, the defending personnel numbered 379 Marines, seven officers and eighteen enlisted men in the Marine air force to man the planes still in working condition. Out of the approximately 1,100 civilian construction workers, only a few were ready and willing to volunteer for combat duty.

Bombing raids occurred at noon the next two days in succession, but these were met with all the firepower the Wake defenders could muster. Some damage was done, but Cunningham says:

"As the news [two Jap bombers had been downed and perhaps a third was damaged] went round the atoll, morale shot up. We had taken three massive raids in as many days, and we were shaken and hungry and so tired we could fall asleep on our feet, but the situation was looking up. . . . We were learning about war and how to take care of ourselves. . . . We had four planes of our own and a fifth almost ready for action again. . . . We turned to repairs and preparations for the fourth day." *

On December 11th, although no Jap had yet set foot on the island, they announced to the world that their flag flew over Wake. On that day they confidently expected to land their troops; but a surprise awaited them.

*Wake Island Command, p. 82.

WAKE ISLAND COMMAND

by Commander W. Scott Cunningham

The telephone roused me about three o'clock on the morning of the eleventh. I stumbled out into the hallway of the cottage, trying to fight off the stupor of sleep into which I had fallen, and reached for the receiver.

"Cunningham."

"Captain, this is Gunner Hamas at the battalion command post."

I came awake fast. Elmer Greey's head appeared in his doorway and he watched me inquiringly.

"Major Devereux reports ships sighted on the horizon." For all his formality, John Hamas's voice was crackling with excitement. "He requests permission to illuminate with searchlights."

Ships on the horizon! The softening-up process was over, then, and they were moving in for the kill. And what could six old five-inch guns do against the batteries of longer-range weapons they were sure to have?

Our only hope was to ambush them. We must lie silent and dark until they steamed in so close our guns would be effective, and then we must hit them with everything we had.

"No," I said flatly. "Don't use the searchlights. And don't commence firing until further orders."

I slammed down the phone and began dressing. Greey and Keene came into my room to learn the news, and I told them to notify Putnam's command post and any other points they could raise. Then I set off at a run for my truck outside.

It was a perfect tropical night. A half moon was coming up over the ocean and the air was cool and soft. The

112

former bird sanctuary lay peaceful and serene before me as I turned on my blued-out lights and began the ride down the pockmarked coral road to the communications center. Inside, the dimly lighted room hummed with activity. Radio men hung over their equipment; the talker exchanged words in low tones with someone on the telephone; a decoding officer stood by to translate messages arriving or going out.

It had been Wesley Platt, the strong-point commander on Wilkes, who had first got word of the ships from one of his lookouts. And now, as we waited, the alert and the warning to keep the lights dark and the guns silent had gone the rounds. At Peacock Point, at Kuku and Toki, men waited in the dim moonlight for the order to open fire, or dug their foxholes deeper against the shelling that might begin at any moment. At the airstrip, the planes were ready but silent.

So Wake lay, inactive but alert, as the tiny specks on the horizon grew larger.

Three-thirty . . . four o'clock . . .

I was scared, plenty scared, though I tried not to show it. My muscles ached from tension.

Four-thirty . . .

"They're getting closer. An awful lot of 'em."

Five o'clock.

The advance ships in the task force were only about four miles off Peacock Point now.

BOOM!

We could hear it above the surf. The invaders had opened fire.

Still our guns remained silent, our searchlights dark.

A column of Japanese ships moved parallel to Wake's southern shore, advancing from Peacock Point toward Wilkes. Then it turned toward the atoll, moved in closer, turned again, and began steaming back toward Peacock. Other ships advanced toward Wilkes. The guns continued to sound, with increasing frequency.

The telephone talker motioned to me. I grabbed the phone.

"Captain?" It was Hamas again. "Lieutenant McAlister

113

reports a destroyer, range four-six-hundred, off Kuku Point. Lieutenant Barninger has ships in his sights off Peacock. Major Devereux ordered me to notify you."

I took a deep breath and looked at my watch. It was 6:15. The long silence was over.

"What are we waiting for, John?" I yelled. "Cut loose at them!"

And as Gunner Hamas relayed the order to the batteries around the atoll, I could hear the five-inchers open up.

It was a sweet, wonderful, glorious shoot-up.

Barninger's guns opened up on Peacock and hit a light cruiser on the second salvo. She turned and began to run; the guns scored twice more before she got out of range.

McAlister opened on Wilkes. He had a problem—his fire control equipment was virtually worthless after the bombing of the day before—but that didn't interfere with the work of Battery L. Nothing could bother Battery L this moonlit morning. Battery L was red hot. Three ships were in sight; the guns chose one and let fire. Dead on target! As the crews cheered, it blew up before their eyes and sank.

Another ship; another hit.

Another, perhaps a transport, and another hit.

And yet another, this one a light cruiser from its silhouette, and, by God, another hit!

And now the guns on Peale had their chance to get into the fight. They had been waiting for something to come within range, and the Japs obliged. Three ships slipped on past Wilkes and turned north toward Toki Point, and Kessler's men at Battery B opened up.

They hit the leading ship. The enemy let loose a hail of fire in answer, and the communications lines between the fire control equipment and the guns were shattered. Battery B kept on firing anyhow.

And then, only forty-five minutes after our first gun had sounded, it was all over—at least, so far as the shore batteries were concerned. The task force sent out to take possession of Wake had had enough, and was running for cover.

But it was not all over for the Japs. As the invader retreated out of range behind a heavy smoke screen, Paul Putnam's impatient flyers moved in for their share of the banquet.

They had gone aloft when we opened fire. After discovering, with some amazement, that no planes accompanied the invaders, they had circled beyond range of our own guns and bided their time. Now they struck.

Putnam was up there himself, with Elrod, Freuler and Tharin, and thanks to Freuler's hard work in the brief days of peace, the little Wildcats carried their lethal cargo of bombs that didn't properly fit the bomb racks. It was the first chance they had had to use them, and they made them good.

The Japs threw up all the antiaircraft fire they could, but the Wildcats kept attacking. They bombed and strafed two light cruisers, knocking out the torpedo battery of one and the radio shack of the other. Freuler set a fierce gasoline fire raging on a transport.

As they expended their bombs and machine gun belts, they came roaring back to the airstrip for more, time after time. Two other pilots, Kinney and Hamilton, got their turns. The fleet continued to race for home, and the four little fighters continued to harass them. And it was Hank Elrod, apparently, who scored the greatest victory from the air. He dropped a bomb on a destroyer; minutes later Kinney sent his plane screaming down toward the same ship just in time to see it blow up in his face.

And that was that. The Japs limped away over the horizon and were gone. We had sunk at least two ships and scored hits on maybe half a dozen others. And we had suffered no casualties.

Not until after the war would we know exactly what we had accomplished, or the size of the fleet Japan had sent out to scoop up the remains of Wake's defenders. Rear Admiral Sadamichi Kajioka, commander of the enemy's 6th Destroyer Squadron, had been on that light cruiser Barninger's men hit when the firing opened at Peacock Point; it was the *Yubari*, flagship of a force numbering two other light cruisers, six destroyers, two patrol boats and

115

two medium transports, with a pair of submarines out ahead to run interference.

Rear Admiral Kuninori Marumo had commanded the other two light cruisers, *Tenryu* and *Tatsuta*. There were 450 landing troops in the patrol boats—two old converted destroyers—and a force of garrison troops in the transports.

Despite a heavy sea, they were already beginning to put their troops into small boats when our fire opened. As Admiral Kajioka pulled his battered flagship out of range, the destroyer *Hayate* was sunk by Battery L on Wilkes, which then scored hits on the destroyer *Oite*, one of the transports, and one of Admiral Marumo's light cruisers. It was the destroyer *Yayoi* that had been hit by Kessler's men on Peale, and the destroyer *Kisaragi* that Elrod had sunk from the air.

Having lost two destroyers and at least five hundred men, and with five or six of his remaining ships damaged, Admiral Kajioka withdrew to Kwajalein in the Marshalls. It was, as a Japanese authority would write after the war, "one of the most humiliating defeats our Navy had ever suffered."

And it was more. It was the first authentic victory of the war for our forces. The *Hayate* and *Kisaragi* were the first enemy ships to be sunk by U.S. naval forces since the fighting had begun. The fact that little Wake Island had turned back an invasion fleet would be an incalculable boost to the morale of a nation dazed by the destruction at Pearl Harbor.

We did not know all this on the morning of December 11, but we knew enough to celebrate. And in less than two weeks we would see further proof of the shocking surprise we had given the Japanese. They had been so confident of taking the atoll that they had laid out all their plans for its administration; the copies of an Imperial Rescript issued to us after our capture were dated December 11.

If we had been confident on Wednesday, we were delirious now. At the airstrip, where I went after the shore guns ceased firing, sweating members of the ground crews shouted and pounded one another on the back. Even the loss of two planes—Elrod's fuel line had been cut, and he had to crash-land on the beach, and Freuler nursed his plane back with an engine hopelessly wrecked by enemy flak—could not dampen our spirits. We would wish desperately for those planes in the remaining days of the defense, but now we couldn't be bothered. We had turned back the enemy in force. We had beaten off an invasion. And we had suffered no casualties!

I went down to the defense battalion command post on the southern shore to congratulate Devereux on his men's performance, and then a group of us headed happily for the nearby Marine Officers' Club. There was a little beer left, though the refrigerator was not working, and we felt entitled to a celebration.

It was like a fraternity picnic. War whoops of joy split the air; warm beer was sprayed on late arrivals without regard to rank; already the memories that would last a lifetime—a tragically short lifetime for some—were being recalled, relived, and even embroidered.

Big John Hamas pushed his way through the crowd to the corner where I sat on an empty ammo box, drinking my beer in sleepy, relaxed, triumphant peace.

"Captain," he gloated, "you told us to cut loose at them, and boy, did we cut loose at the sons of bitches!"

I grinned at him happily. He stood there a moment, towering over me, and then he set down his beer can with an air of finality. "Well," he said, "the celebration's over for me . . . sir. Got to round up my civilians and get some more ammunition over to Wilkes." Gunner Hamas was not one to rest too long on his laurels.

I had work of my own to do, the proudest task of my Navy career: report the good news to Pearl Harbor. At that point we were not sure just how many ships, or what kind, we had actually sunk. But we knew beyond doubt that two had gone down—we thought they were a destroyer and a cruiser—and I decided to stick to the positive facts rather than make any claims we couldn't support. I drove back to my command post, dashed off the message, handed it to one of the decoding officers, and looked at my watch.

Only 8:45. I would have sworn the day was half gone already.

Word of our victory brought a response that was all we could have desired, aside from a promise of reinforcements. Back came a commendation from Pearl saying we had performed our duties "in accordance with the highest traditions of the Naval Service."

I read it to Putnam, Devereux and the others as soon as I had a chance, but there was some unavoidable delay. At nine o'clock the Japanese bombers arrived for a fourth raid. And now we had only two planes left to fight them off.

This time there were seventeen of them, coming in from the northeast, and for the first time in four raids I found myself protected by concrete and steel. The unfinished magazine that formed my communications center and command post had its disadvantages—there was no door, for example—but after the plywood at Camp Two, the brush near Camp One, and the foxhole at the airstrip it was a comforting sensation to look up and find a solid roof over my head.

The magazine brought us through the raid without a scratch, though I promised myself we would lay in a supply of sandbags to protect the entrance hereafter, and when I went on my routine post-raid inspection I found the same was true of the entire atoll. No one had been hurt, and on top of that, Lieutenant Davidson in one of the two Wildcats had shot down two more bombers. On this day of victory nothing could stop us.

Gunner Hamas had come as close as anybody to getting killed this time. With a crew of six civilian volunteers he had loaded a truck with shells, powder, detonators and hand grenades for John McAlister's battery on Kuku Point, and they had driven down to the boat landing only minutes before the bombers were sighted. There Kirby Ludwick, the sailor in charge of the boat crews, took the truck aboard one of the launches and set out across the channel.

They had just cleared the landing when the bombers swept in. Hamas and Ludwick looked at each other and agreed without saying a word that they had a job to do. The battery needed the supplies more now than ever. So on across the channel Ludwick guided the boat with its load of explosives, and all hands crossed their fingers and waited for a bomb.

They made it all right—we all led charmed lives that day—and Hamas's crew of civilians abandoned him, with his blessing, to stay on Wilkes and help out wherever McAlister needed them.

Bryghte Godbold's three-inch battery at Toki Point on Peale had attracted a large part of the enemy's fire. Again, no damage had been done, but it was clear Battery D might be wise to take a leaf from Battery E's book and move while there was time. So, late in the afternoon, the job was begun. Two hundred and fifty civilians pitched in to help move the battery almost the entire length of Peale, from Toki Point to a spot near the bridge.

Meanwhile, Pearl Harbor had given me a small assignment for the day: locate a confidential publication relating to direction finders, which had been in the possession of Pan American, and report its destruction. It was easy enough to report *that*. Not only that publication but all others at Pan American's headquarters, and the headquarters itself for that matter, had been destroyed. The Japs had saved me the trouble.

But we had another job to do, along with the usual repairs, and it was one that could wait no longer. Our dead must be cared for.

They had remained in the big refrigerator until now, those who had not been buried where they fell, and I did not dare wait any longer to pay final honor to them and give them as decent a burial as possible.

We did the best we could. A civilian dragline operator scooped out a long trench, and a handful of us stood in reverent silence while the bodies of the dead were laid into it. A firing squad gave a last salute and a bulldozer covered the grave. There was no chaplain on Wake, but one of the contractor's employees, a lay preacher named John O'Neal from Worland, Wyoming, said a short prayer.

I gave orders that in the future our dead would be

buried where they fell or in the closest practical space. There would be no more mass burials—and, I confidently hoped, there would be no need for them.

We had lost twenty-six officers and men of the fighter squadron, two sailors, and three enlisted men of the defense battalion. And how many civilians were dead? Thirty-five, perhaps, or forty or even more, counting those whose bodies had not been found.

It was a sad note on which to end the day. I tried to shake off my feeling of depression, to regain the spirit of victorious confidence we had all shared earlier, to remember the battered task force and the two bombers shot down by Lieutenant Davidson.

And then somebody was running toward me through the dusk, shouting something I could not hear above the surf, and I stopped stiffly and strained my ears to hear.

It was something about Lieutenant Kliewer, and now as the man came closer I could hear.

Kliewer had sunk a Jap sub.

He had found it basking on the surface as he flew the dusk patrol, and he had torn into it with bombs and machine guns. He had gone so low that fragments from the explosions hit his plane, and he had stayed to see the sub disappear below the surface and an oil slick appear where it had been.

Pearl wanted us to conduct unrestricted warfare, did they? Well, we had done it today. Surface ships, bombers, and now a submarine. If they'd just give us enough time we'd lick the whole Japanese Navy by ourselves.

I went back to my cottage thinking the hell with the dangers of a night raid, threw open the window to the soft breezes and the soothing sound of the surf, and slept like a baby.

Nine times during the next eight days the Japs hit us, and not at regular intervals as they had done at first, but spasmodically, at noon or by moonlight, singly or in masses of as many as forty-one bombers in a single raid.

Despite the variations in time and number, despite the

occasional loss of life, despite everything, it grew increasingly monotonous. Nerves remained tense for so long that they grew listless and flabby; the time came when we had to remind ourselves that our lives were the stakes in the tiresome game we were playing. I actually found myself nursing a small-boy resentment against the enemy one day because there was no raid to report to Pearl Harbor.

At the airstrip, work continued daily on the jigsaw task of arranging battered parts into planes that would fly. Two Wildcats were in working order on Friday; on Saturday Lieutenant Kinney's crew was able to get a third into the air, but on that same day a crash-landing brought the score back down to two. Sunday a bomb hit left only one effective; Tuesday we had two again; later in the week, briefly, three planes were flying. By Friday the nineteenth, the count was back down to one.

But aside from skilled work like this, most of the man-hours on the atoll during those eight days were spent in uneasy idleness. There was simply nothing to do the majority of the time but wait. The foxholes were all dug, the shelters covered and reinforced; the time that might have been spent in repairing damaged guns was cut to almost nothing because we had no parts for repairs.

Paul Putnam could not shake off the terrible memory of the destruction that had visited his squadron on that first day. He continued to push himself relentlessly at the airstrip, trying to improve and extend the ground works, and increasingly he grew impatient with Wake's civilians. One day he came to me in an angry frame of mind.

"Captain," he asked, "will you give me authority to use some armed Marines to round up these civilians and make them work? Dammit, they've got to hold up their end."

I turned him down. It was true that many of the civilians had taken to the bush and could not be found except when food was being distributed. And others, after being detailed to working parties, would fade away like old soldiers. There was even a report that one group of civilians had headed for the beach with their suitcases when the Japanese ships approached on the eleventh, determined to be the first to board what they thought were evacuation ships.

But the situation was not as simple as it appeared to Putnam.

For one thing, these men—or the great majority of them —had had no previous military training of any kind. They had not been drilled in that automatic response to discipline which is the first necessity of any fighting force. And they had no government insurance, no hope of veterans' benefits, no prospect of pensions in case of injury. Furthermore, they had been given to understand they would be evacuated, by some means that was never quite spelled out, before Wake was hit by the enemy. Many of them felt cheated and abandoned as the days rolled by and nothing was done about this pledge.

But when all this was considered, the fact remained that a surprisingly high number of them did pitch in and help, faithfully and at personal hazard—far more than Putnam could see from his limited vantage point at the airfield. Already they were stationed all over the atoll in support of the defense battalion's gun crews; they worked at filling sandbags, moving guns, delivering food and ammunition, operating heavy equipment to scoop out personnel shelters. At the airstrip itself they had accomplished much since the war began, bulldozing the surrounding area, making bunkers for the airplanes, helping to mine the landing strip, putting the radio station underground, assisting with personnel dugouts. And their group had suffered the highest number of casualties on the atoll.

Meanwhile, we had begun to get messages from Pearl that indicated thought was being given to the problem of reinforcements. On the twelfth the office of the Pacific Commander in Chief, Admiral Kimmel, asked for a confidential report on the status of aviation matériel for maintaining planes. I replied that, while we could operate two squadrons under the physical setup, maintenance work was limited to the salvaging of spare parts from the wrecked planes. The same day we were asked for, and gave, a report on the ammunition situation, which was still reasonably good.

A silence followed these reports, and on Sunday the fourteenth I made a few requests of my own, listing some of the many supplies we so urgently needed. At the end of the list I added the one thing that, at the outset, we had needed most of all:

"One radar."

On Monday I gave a general report on the effects of the raids to date, and added a request for 300,000 sandbags. We had plenty of coral sand, but by now the crews of civilians and Marines were having to put it in empty ammunition boxes for want of bags.

Still no word came from Pearl on what we could expect. We waited hopefully, and then on Wednesday we received a message whose unconscious irony was overwhelming:

> HIGHLY DESIRABLE CONTINUE CHANNEL DREDGING. ADVISE FEASIBILITY UNDER PRESENT CONDITIONS WITH EXISTING EQUIPMENT. GIVE ESTIMATED DATE COMPLETION. . . .

I suppose I must have blown my top. I did not answer for almost twenty-four hours, except for a message reporting yet another raid—the twelfth since the war had begun—and when I did, it was with some heat. Friday morning, we enjoyed nearly forty-eight hours of peace, the longest stretch of relief during Wake's defense.

It was about midway in this week that we first heard a strange and, in some ways, exasperating story from the home front. There were a number of short-wave radios on the atoll, private property of civilians and servicemen alike, and occasionally one of them brought us a creditably clear portion of a broadcast from America.

We had heard with pride that President Roosevelt himself had hailed Wake's resistance effort, and we had tried to discount as propaganda for enemy consumption the gloomy reports that relief for Wake could not be expected. But now we heard something that set our teeth on edge.

When Pearl Harbor asked the defenders of Wake if there was anything that could be done for them, the story went, an answer came back:

"Yes. Send us more Japs."

If there was anything we didn't need at Wake it was more Japs. I had sent no such message, and since the release of dispatches was at all times under my direct control, I dismissed the story as a reporter's dream, as did most of the others on the atoll who heard it.

Not until years later, in fact, did I learn through Bucky Henshaw, one of the decoding officers, how the story began. Bucky got it from his fellow-decoder, Bernard Lauff, when they met in Honolulu after the war, and so far as I know this is the first time the details have ever been published.

Part of the decoders' job was to "pad" messages with nonsense at the beginning and end as a device to throw off enemy code-breakers. Such padding was either entirely meaningless or, on occasion, something involving a private joke between Henshaw and Lauff on the one hand and their opposite numbers at Pearl Harbor on the other; it was not expected that the padding would be filed with the text of the message.

On the morning we turned back the invasion fleet, Lauff said, he had done the padding on my message. He had begun it:

> SEND US STOP NOW IS THE TIME FOR ALL GOOD MEN TO COME TO THE AID OF THEIR PARTY STOP CUNNINGHAM MORE JAPS. . . .

So what the world took as a gesture of defiant heroism from Wake Island was actually nothing of the kind and was never intended to be.

The battle continued, and each day we grew weaker. We had been returning shot for shot, and by now an impressive number of enemy planes lay under the waters off Wake along with the two ships we had sunk, but still they came back with more. Twenty-seven bombers were in the Friday raid.

The list of parts and supplies I had requested from Pearl was an indication of the gravity of our matériel needs. We were short on everything, from recoil fluid to range finders, from firing pins to height finders, in addition to the tremen-

124

dous shortages with which we had begun—and by now I could have sent another list just as long as the first. Our personnel losses had been cut to almost nothing, but it was the machines of war rather than the men who served them that would finally settle the issue of Wake.

We went into our second Saturday of the war sleepy, lean, weary, confident of our ability to hold out unless the Japs threw still bigger blows at us, but wondering more and more whether Pearl had in truth written us off as beyond reach of relief.

And then, at 7:10 on that rainy Saturday morning, an electrifying message arrived from Midway:

DEPARTED MIDWAY FOR WAKE ONE PREP SAIL PREP.

A Navy patrol bomber was headed our way. At last we could hope to learn when, or whether, relief might arrive.

The PBY arrived about 3:30. I went down to the remains of the Pan American installation to meet it and took the pilots, Ensigns Murphy and Ady, to my command post. As we bounced along in my pickup truck past bomb craters and the wreckage of Camp Two, their eyes opened wide in surprise. Like some of the dispatch-writers back at Pearl, it appeared, they had not realized the extent of the damage the Japanese had done us.

The orders they brought—and about which they of course knew nothing—contained good news. We were to prepare to receive another fighter plane squadron. Ground troop reinforcements and needed matériel were on the way. All but about 350 civilians were to be evacuated; the remainder, selected by specified trades, would remain to work on construction projects. Pearl Harbor had still not abandoned its conviction that the ship channel across Wilkes must be completed.

Many questions were left unanswered; even the estimated date of arrival of the promised help was not indicated. But it was enough to send our spirits soaring. With reinforcements, with supplies to repair our guns, with more planes

125

to take the air over Wake, we would be strong again. And there should be plenty of time; after the ignominious retreat of the Japanese invasion fleet less than ten days before, I felt it would be many days or even weeks before another landing attempt was made.

I passed the news on to Keene, Devereux, Putnam, Greey and Teters, and as it filtered down through the ranks the atmosphere of Wake took another turn for the better. Teters got busy drawing up rosters of men who would remain; talk of what we would do to the enemy when our reinforcements arrived was indulged in freely by all hands; letters and reports were hastily written to send back to Pearl on the PBY when it left the next morning.

In the report I wrote for Admiral Bloch, I tried again to make the picture of destruction clear, and praised the work of the fighter squadron and the defense battalion.

"Our escape from more serious damage," I wrote, "may be attributed to the effectiveness of AA fire and the heroic actions of the fighter pilots, who have never failed to push home attacks against heavy fire. The performance of these pilots is deserving of all praise. They have attacked air and surface targets alike with equal abandon. That none has been shot down is a miracle. Their planes (two now remain) are full of bullet holes. Two forced landings, fortunately without injury to pilots, have occurred with loss of planes."

As a matter of fact, relief was miles closer than I dreamed as I wrote my letter, though I was not to learn just how close it was until after the war was over.

As early as the second day of the war, Admiral Kimmel, the Pacific Commander in Chief at Pearl, had begun planning our relief. And he had planned on a grand scale, hoping not only to succor Wake but to score a major naval victory that would punish the enemy for the destruction at Pearl.

It was to involve three Pacific Fleet carrier forces. Admiral Bull Halsey, with a group built around the *Enterprise,* would move out beyond Johnston Island, covering Pearl and standing by to support the main action if neces-

126

sary. Admiral Wilson Brown and a task force built around the *Lexington* would head for the Marshalls for a raid to keep the enemy busy to the south of us. And Admiral Frank Jack Fletcher, with a force built around the *Saratoga*, would dash to Wake with a new fighter squadron, ground reinforcements, ammunition and equipment. With three task forces on the prowl, the chance to engage and defeat an enemy naval force would be bright.

There had been the inevitable delays. The *Saratoga*, bearing the fighter planes, had been off San Diego when the war began. With an escort of three destroyers she began racing for Pearl, but it was the morning of December 15 before she arrived. Meanwhile, the other units of Admiral Fletcher's force had been made ready. The *Tangier*, with ground reinforcements, and the oiler *Neches*, escorted by a division of destroyers, left by order of Admiral Kimmel on the same day the *Saratoga* arrived for refueling. By the next day, the big carrier had set out to catch up with them, accompanied by three cruisers and a destroyer squadron. On the seventeenth, they overhauled *Tangier* and *Neches*, released their destroyer escort, and continued toward Wake.

Meanwhile, Admiral Brown's task force had left Pearl on the fourteenth on its bombing mission to the Marshalls, and Admiral Halsey's group sailed shortly after the *Saratoga* had departed.

It had been a slow start, but there was still time. My messages from Wake, which Admiral Fletcher was reading, indicated the need for urgency. Throughout his task force, men worked in a fever of activity to get ready for what they knew might be an opposed landing at Wake. Planes and guns were checked; the radar that was headed for us at last was explained by experts to the men who would use it; plans for lightering men and equipment ashore off Wake's south shore were studied and re-studied.

But now a complication arose. The oiler *Neches* could travel at a top speed of less than 13 knots, as opposed to the 34 knots which the *Saratoga*, as well as the cruisers and destroyers, could make. Admiral Fletcher set the pace of his task force to match that of the *Neches*.

Even at this speed, they made progress. The seas were

127

calm and there was no sight of the enemy. When the PBY arrived on Wake, relief was already well on the way. By Sunday, when the PBY departed, the task force was less than 700 miles away.

Ensigns Murphy and Ady and their crew took off at seven Sunday morning for their return trip, sped on their way by the optimistic thanks of all of us. Besides the letters and reports we had written, they took with them Major Bayler, the Marine specialist who had been waiting for transportation off the atoll since before the war began. But the unfortunate Mr. Hevenor of the Budget Bureau, who had missed the last Clipper, was left again. This time a routine regulation stood in his way: there was no parachute available for him.

We waved good-by to the big plane and went back to our posts with high spirits. And then, less than two hours afterward, a new move by the Japs staggered us.

Twenty-nine dive bombers accompanied by eighteen fighters—obviously from aircraft carriers—roared down on Wake.

If enemy carriers were within striking distance, our plight was far more critical than we had dreamed. Nothing but the greatest speed could bring us relief now. I reported this new development in a dispatch to Pearl marked *Urgent*.

It was during this first carrier-plane raid that Major Putnam added further luster to the brilliant reputation he had acquired during the defense of Wake. At the time the planes came over, he was in a dugout a few hundred yards from my command post, conferring with Commander Keene and Dan Teters. It was immediately apparent that the planes were from a carrier, and Paul Putnam wasted no time. He grabbed a phone, called me, and asked permission to drive to the airstrip, take off in one of our two surviving planes, and go out to look for the carriers themselves.

An attempt to reach the airstrip while the raid was in progress would be hazardous in the extreme, but Putnam was eager to try it and I knew that if he could locate the

128

enemy ships the information could be of incalculable value to Pearl Harbor. I told him to go ahead and to be careful.

He got into a truck and began the ride of perhaps a mile to the airstrip while the planes roared overhead. Twice along the way he was strafed by enemy fighters and had to leave his truck and take cover. But neither he nor the truck was hit, and he did get to the field, where he took off and made a long search for the carriers. That he was unable to locate them in no way dimmed the heroism of his exploit.

At noon we were hit again, this time by land-based bombers, and destruction to the remnants of our fighting equipment was considerable. The obliteration of Camp Two was completed, Peale took another shellacking, and Battery D on the islet was badly hit. One bomb here took the life of Sergeant John Wright, who thus became the fourth casualty of the defense battalion. Four others were wounded.

And now our defensive position was critical indeed. Battery D's director was a complete loss; Battery F had never had one. The only director on the atoll now was at Battery E inside the head of the wishbone on Wake Island. And Battery E had no height finder.

Assisted by a work crew of 125 civilians, Captain Godbold accordingly sent a portion of his battery down to Battery E so we could have one antiaircraft unit at full strength. One gun, the height finder, and a power plant made the move; Godbold's three remaining guns were moved once more, northward from their second position, to be used on the beach against surface targets.

I went to sleep on my sandbag pillow that night hoping the promised relief would arrive in time. Enemy carriers were in the area and we had only one effective antiaircraft battery now to use against the swift fighter planes we had seen that day for the first time.

Monday began on a hopeful note with a message from CINCPAC asking the condition of our runways. But that was the only bright spot in the day. Shortly after noon we had our second attack by a combination of land and car-

129

rier-based planes. They came in greater force than ever and they looked even newer and more deadly than the day before.

Against their overwhelming numbers, Captain Freuler and Lieutenant Davidson tore in to do what they could with our two tattered Wildcats. Freuler shot down two or perhaps three of the fighters, but his plane was damaged by the explosion of one of his victims and he was barely able to nurse it back to a crash-landing that destroyed it. Freuler himself, hit twice by machine gun bullets, went to the hospital.

Lieutenant Davidson did not return.

So ended the glorious record of the Marine flyers, at least so far as flying operations were concerned. Paul Putnam and I went to the hospital later to see Freuler and tell him the sad news about Carl Davidson. Putnam, who was filled with a grim pride in the record his men had made, pretended to be angry with Freuler.

"What do you mean," he demanded, "mixing with those Jap fighters when we told you to stick to the bombers?"

Freuler grinned wearily. We left him then, and Putnam walked back to the airstrip, collected his few remaining able-bodied men and the dozen or so faithful civilians who had refused his orders to take cover in the bush. Together they all went to Devereux's command post and reported for duty as infantry.

I would have been even more uneasy than I was as I settled down to rest that night if I had known what was going on in the waters northeast of Wake occupied by the task force sent for our relief.

Grimly determined to keep the oiler *Neches* with him—though his ships had adequate fuel and he could have doubled his speed if he had chosen—Admiral Fletcher had actually lost ground during the day.

By noon of Sunday the twenty-first he had known we were under attack by carrier planes and therefore in serious trouble, but he neither increased his speed nor refueled. The earlier he accomplished the refueling, the earlier he could get rid of the *Neches,* but still he waited.

130

He waited until the morning of the twenty-second—and then, as if to emphasize his poor judgment, the weather changed from favorable for refueling to unfavorable. Heavy seas hampered the operation, and the wind direction forced the ships to steam in a direction that actually increased their distance from Wake. During the entire day only four destroyers were fueled, leaving four more for the next day.

By eight o'clock on the night of the twenty-first, postwar studies were to show, the *Saratoga* was only 600 miles from Wake. At a speed of 25 knots, she could have been close enough by noon of the twenty-second to launch planes. But by eight the next morning, the carrier was still 515 miles from us. And twelve hours later she was no closer.

Meanwhile, Admiral Kimmel had been succeeded at Pearl on December 17 by Admiral W. S. Pye, serving in a caretaker capacity until the arrival of Admiral Chester Nimitz. On the twentieth Admiral Brown's task force, whose mission was to make a diversionary attack in the Marshalls, was directed to turn northward to support the relief expedition. When Admiral Pye reported this to Washington he was told in reply that Wake was considered a liability, and he was authorized to evacuate it rather than reinforce it if he thought best.

The situation was confusing, but there is no indication that Admiral Pye made it less so. On December 22, Wake time, he first ordered Fletcher to send the *Saratoga* ahead to launch her planes; then he countermanded the order and directed that the *Tangier* go ahead to evacuate the garrison. As I went to sleep that night, neither plan had been put into action.[1]

Shortly after midnight on the twenty-second I received a call reporting flashes of light to the north. I climbed onto

[1] I am indebted to Samuel Eliot Morison's *The Rising Sun in the Pacific* (Little, Brown and Company, 1950) for information on which this brief look at the relief expedition's unhappy record is based. Neither I nor the American public back home knew the details until long after the war was over.—W. S. C.

131

the top of my concrete igloo and studied the display, which was evidently at a considerable distance from the atoll. The lights would blaze up, then sink slowly like parachute flares from star shells. With several others I watched this display for some time, wondering what it meant. We had seen other unexplained displays of lights and rockets off-shore at night from time to time. No definite conclusion as to their meaning was ever reached. In the light of later information it has been theorized that enemy ships who had got off course were firing somewhere at what they thought was Wake Island, but the mystery has never been completely cleared up.

I went back inside my command post and was about to try for a little more sleep when the first blow fell.

Watchers reported barges and landing boats had been sighted near the beach on the south shore of Wake and Wilkes.

This night we had no moon to help us see the enemy, as we had had on the morning of the eleventh. The night was intensely dark; visibility was limited to only a few yards at best. And this time the enemy had profited from its earlier mistake of firing as it approached. The ships had crept in, silent and unseen, until they were ready for the invasion.

At first, conflicting reports pouring into my CP indicated there might be some possibility of error. There were no landings, only the mysterious lights; there were landings; ships were approaching but no boats had attempted to come ashore.

But gradually the truth began to emerge. A Japanese fleet was in the immediate vicinity. Two old destroyer-transports had run in so close in the dark that the five-inch guns on Peacock and Kuku points could not fire on them. Landing craft had definitely been sighted.

At 1:45, after the report of the lights, I had messaged to Pearl Harbor: GUNFIRE BETWEEN SHIPS TO NORTHEAST ISLAND. The message was directed to Admiral Bloch's headquarters. Now, at 2:50, I could no longer hope we were experiencing another false alarm. Guns had begun to flash in the darkness offshore. I sent a second message, this one directed to the Pacific Commander in Chief:

ISLAND UNDER GUNFIRE. APPARENTLY LANDING.

The enemy had arrived, and this time surely they would be coming in greater force and with greater determination than before. Fighter planes could be expected at any moment. Casting about for some hope of help, I remembered Pilly Lent and the *Triton*.

I yelled to the radio operator to send a message in plain English—it was no time now to concern ourselves with codes—directing the *Triton,* if it received us, to attack enemy ships to the south.

At 3:19 a chilling reply came. It was not from the *Triton,* but from Admiral Pye's headquarters.

NO FRIENDLY VESSELS SHOULD BE IN YOUR IMMEDIATE VICINITY TODAY, it said. KEEP ME INFORMED.

Reading it, I did not know how bitter the whole truth was—that the *Triton* had been recalled earlier to keep it out of the way of the relief expedition, which had now been called off—but I knew enough.

We were on our own.

The mishandling and final recall of a relief expedition that almost without doubt could have saved Wake from the enemy, and scored a great naval victory in the process, was one of the darkest marks on the Navy's entire war record.

If Admiral Fletcher had been endowed with some of the energy exhibited by the Japanese invaders in the closing days of December, 1941, he could have arrived ahead of them and forestalled their landing. And he could have delivered a smashing blow to the Japanese Navy—for, if after contacting the enemy he had decided they were too much for his task force to handle alone, there was another

133

task force under Admiral Brown, built around the *Lexington,* within supporting distance. And still a third, Admiral Halsey's, was close enough to join the action if a real battle developed.

It is true our battleships in Pearl Harbor had been hard hit on December 7. Otherwise, though, we had escaped with remarkably little damage. Our carriers were untouched, our cruiser, destroyer and submarine strength was very little reduced, our fuel supplies and workshops at Pearl were intact. We even had some of our shore-based airplanes left.

But there is no question that the attack had also hit us hard in another area—our morale. The pendulum had swung from contempt of the Nipponese to an exaggerated fear of their capabilities. It seems fair to say that neither Admiral Pye nor Admiral Fletcher really wanted a battle, unless they could be certain of superiority of forces. And while the odds were all in favor of this superiority, the desire for certainty held them back.

An American victory would have been a glorious Christmas present for the American people. And here was the opportunity. The Japanese were within reach, and our officers and men should have been smarting with rage over Pearl Harbor and anxious for revenge. And they were; in the *Saratoga* and elsewhere in the task force, it developed when the facts were finally revealed, there was general dismay and even mutinous feeling when Fletcher received and carried out his order to retire while we on Wake were actively engaged with the enemy.

Both in the progress of Admiral Fletcher's task force and in the orders from Pearl that culminated in the withdrawal, our Navy failed, in short, to make the most of a great opportunity to fight back.

All I knew of this in the stormy pre-dawn darkness of December 23, as the Japanese began to swarm ashore on Wake, was that help was not coming—and that even such help as we might otherwise have counted on from the *Triton* had been withdrawn. We were alone against the enemy.

134

So the battle began, in an atmosphere of desperate confusion from which only one clear factor emerged—the overwhelming numerical superiority of the invaders.

This time, the postwar records would show, the Japanese were taking no chance on another humiliating defeat. Rear Admiral Kajioka, who had been given a chance to redeem himself, had a vastly stronger force for his second try. The two destroyers we had sunk had been replaced. A third had been added. Three other ships, a minelayer, a seaplane tender and a transport, beefed up the original force. More landing troops were aboard, some two thousand according to best estimates. And in addition to all this, two other impressive forces had been assigned as support—four heavy cruisers with accompanying destroyers from Truk under command of Rear Admiral A. Goto, and two aircraft carriers, two cruisers, and still more destroyers under Rear Admiral Hiroaki Abe, detached from the fleet that had struck Pearl Harbor. This latter force had more than 100 planes, the first of which had struck us on Sunday.

Wake's geography, and the multiple landings of the invaders, made it inevitable that almost from the first we would be cut up into relatively ineffective pockets of defense. And the early breakdown of communications completed the isolation of our various fighting units.

The telephone system was so laid out that all defense positions fed into Devereux's command post. Peale Island, Keene and Teters's dugout, and perhaps one or two other positions on the north portion of Wake were on a common line with me to the battalion switchboard, and I could talk directly with them. But I was not in direct touch with any of the stations on the south part of Wake, or with Wilkes Island, and had to depend on Devereux for information regarding all the positions that actually were engaged with the enemy. The telephone wires were all above ground. As the Japanese landed and crossed them, they cut them. Soon after the first enemy troops got ashore all communications with Wilkes were severed, and the various strong points along Wake's south shore were isolated shortly thereafter. Only the northern portion of the network remained effective. I was able to direct portions of the defenders on Peale to reinforce the troops on Wake, but from the opening phase of the battle most of the other units were forced to act on their own.

It is worth noting that communications almost never turn out to be fully effective under the stress of battle. Conditions change with lightning speed, mistaken observation results in faulty information, orders become inapplicable to the situation before there is time to carry them out. Accounts of battles frequently suggest that the commander has moved each of his formations around like men on a chess board, but this is seldom the way it happens. After the fighting begins, most decisions are made by subordinate commanders on the spot.

For battles don't go according to plan. There is always confusion, whatever the advance preparation may have been. And there was confusion in plenty on Wake. Little groups of defenders came under enemy attack and fought back without a chance of co-ordinating their actions with any over-all plan. Both our own troops and the Japanese were at times firing toward friends as well as foes. From my command post, trying vainly to establish what was going on over the entire atoll, I could see tracer bullets flying in all directions, and there is no doubt some of the reports I had to assess were based on mistaken assumptions as to who was firing the bullets. Further, the cut-off groups naturally tended to believe they were about the only ones left, and what few reports we did get from them reflected such views.

So it was that the picture which eventually emerged of the last defense of Wake could only be pieced together after it was all over and the various unit commanders told their stories. At the time neither Devereux nor I had, or could have had, more than a dim and often totally false idea of what was happening.

The invaders grounded two destroyer transports off the south shore of Wake and sent troops ashore from both. Two barges unloaded onto the beach at Wilkes. Two other landing craft put men ashore on Wake just east of the channel entrance. Other troops, as best can be determined,

136

landed on Wake's inner shore from rubber boats that entered the shallow lagoon from the northwest.

As these landings began, the bulk of the active defense on Wake fell to mobile forces comprised of Marines, sailors and civilians, for a major portion of the defense battalion's strength was immobilized at the three-inch and five-inch guns. The area from Camp One eastward toward the airstrip was defended by Lieutenant Poindexter and the defense battalion's mobile reserve, augmented by Boatswain's Mate Barnes and fifteen sailors, and a considerable number of civilians. Each end of the airstrip was guarded by machine-gun crews. Near the airstrip's western end, Lieutenant Kliewer of the fighter squadron took a stand with three others at the generator which was wired to set off the mines along the strip. The three-inch gun on the beach south of the airstrip was manned by Lieutenant Hanna and another Marine and three civilians. A defensive line was formed around the gun by Major Putnam, other surviving members of the fighter squadron, and a dozen civilians.

These were the hot spots on Wake as the fighting began.

Hanna and his crew at the three-inch gun poured fifteen rounds into one of the destroyer transports within minutes after it was grounded, and then began firing at the other, but the invasion troops were already swarming ashore. As they advanced on the gun position, Putnam's little defense line fought back, giving ground stubbornly until at last it formed virtually a circle around the gun. Some Japanese remained to contest the position while others proceeded past the pocket and into the brush.

At Camp One, landing craft approaching the channel were fired on by machine guns. When they grounded on the reef offshore, Poindexter, Barnes and others began throwing hand grenades. Barnes scored one direct hit just as the troops began to disembark, but it was not enough to stop them. They began to pour ashore as the Camp One defenders grouped and fought back.

Devereux had done his best to maintain contact with his units, but it was fast becoming impossible. Within half an hour after the first landing, telephone communication had been lost with Camp One, Lieutenant Hanna and the defensive line under Major Putnam, and Battery A on Peacock Point. And reports from Wilkes were becoming more and more fragmentary. We knew only that a considerable force had landed there and was being resisted. Later, contact was lost altogether.

From Peale, the only area where no landings had been made, Lieutenant Kessler reported by telephone that he could use one of his five-inch guns on a destroyer off Wake. I told him to go ahead. I also authorized Captain Godbold to send some of his men down to join the fighting. It could have been a mistake if troops were about to land there too, but we had a real crisis on Wake that took precedence over a possible one on Peale. Accordingly, a truckload of men under Corporal Leon Graves came roaring down the north-south road and were directed to go in support of Major Putnam's group. But in the confusion they never made it; eventually they wound up in a defensive line set up at Major Devereux's command post.

In the midst of everything else, a ludicrous problem arose for me to deal with. A civilian cook came boiling into my command post, drunk as a lord from that evil concoction known as "swipes" about which I had been warned before the war began. He wanted to go out and tackle the Japs single-handed. It was quite a while before we could get him quietly disposed of.

Meanwhile the enemy was moving deeper into the island from its beachheads, and beginning to spread out through the brush. Lewis's Battery E, inside the head of the wishbone, had been firing in answer to the steady shelling we were receiving from the cruisers offshore; now his position came under fire from invasion troops. And down at the point of the wishbone, mortar fire began to fall on the five-inch gun positions of Lieutenant Barninger's Battery A.

At the machine-gun setup on the eastern end of the airstrip, Corporal Winford J. McAnally was in command of a force of six Marines and three civilians. An hour before dawn he reported the enemy was beginning to attack strongly up the north-south road—evidence either that the

138

invasion of our south shore had been successful or that the Japs were landing at yet another spot.

By now I knew beyond doubt that the enemy had landed at three places and perhaps more. As yet no planes had arrived, but we could expect them by dawn. The off-shore shelling continued without letup.

Admiral Pye had asked me to keep him informed. I decided it was time to do so. At five o'clock I messaged:

ENEMY ON ISLAND. ISSUE IN DOUBT.

This message, interpreted as a final gesture of defiance, was to provoke great comment back in America when it appeared in the accounts of Wake's defense, but as a matter of fact no bravado was intended. At the moment I began to write the dispatch, a phrase I had read sixteen years before came into my mind. It was from Anatole France's *Revolt of the Angels*. He was describing the assault made upon the heavenly ramparts by the legions of Satan. "For three days," he wrote, "the issue was in doubt."

Why I should have recalled those words at such a time I do not know, but they seemed appropriate and even hopeful. In France's story, the victory had gone to the side of the angels. And while I knew we were outnumbered and outgunned, I was still unable even to consider the prospect of defeat. It would be more than an hour before the notion actually sank into my mind that we might not, somehow, make out.

In one sector our forces were indeed making out, and would shortly do far better than that. That was on Wilkes.

A force of one hundred Japanese had landed there to wipe out the defenders—Captain Platt, with seventy Marines and a number of sailors and civilians. The enemy had captured Gunner McKinstry's three-inch gun emplacements but had been blocked from expanding their beachhead. Even as I sent my dispatch, Captain Platt was reorganizing his forces for a counterattack that, before seven o'clock, would virtually wipe out the invaders, killing at least 94 and ending all immediate threat to Wilkes.

It was a substantial setback to the enemy, but I did not

139

know of it until after the surrender. Among the various reports I received was one at dawn that Wilkes had fallen.

This word came from observers on Peale, who were about a mile away from Wilkes across the lagoon. When daylight came they could see Japanese flags displayed at many places on Wilkes, and concluded that the islet had capitulated. As I had no reason to question the report, the assumed loss of Wilkes was one of the considerations I had to take into account in sizing up the situation.

But brilliantly as Wesley Platt had conducted his operation, still Wilkes was only a small fraction of the total defense, and even the truth about conditions there could not have altered the final outcome. On the big islet, Wake, were concentrated most of the defenses and the defenders, and on Wake the situation was steadily deteriorating. Each group of defenders was pinned down while the enemy enjoyed wide freedom of movement.

As the build-up of enemy strength increased the pressure northward, chiefly against the machine-gun position held by Corporal McAnally, Devereux ordered Major Potter to set up a final defensive line south of his command post. But the unrelenting pressure continued. And as dawn came, the carrier-based planes swarmed over us like angry hornets.

Devereux and I had been in regular contact throughout the battle, and each time he reported to me he described the situation in darker terms. My own word to him that no relief could be expected made the picture even worse. At 6:30, when it appeared that his was the only position not yet overwhelmed, he reported enemy pressure there was getting heavy and gave the opinion that he would not be able to hold out much longer.

I knew the time had come to consider the question that only a few hours ago had been unthinkable. Accordingly, I asked for his opinion. Would I be justified in surrendering, in order to prevent further and useless loss of life?

Devereux evaded a direct answer. He said he felt the decision was solely up to the commanding officer. I was well aware of that, of course, but I was not willing to act without reviewing the situation as fully as possible.

We talked a while longer. He asked if I knew that Wilkes had fallen. I said that I did. At last I took a deep breath and told him if he felt he could hold out no longer, I authorized him to surrender.

I hung up the phone and sent a final dispatch to the Commander in Chief, reporting two destroyers grounded on the beach and the enemy fleet moving in. Then I had all codes, ciphers and secret orders destroyed, and ordered the communicators to haul down our transmitter antenna. It would be too easy for the Japanese dive bombers to spot. Besides, I had no more messages to send.

Devereux called me again about 7:30 and asked whether I had reached the Japanese commander by radio. I told him I had not. He repeated his statement that he could not hold out much longer, and I repeated mine that he was authorized to surrender. He said he was not sure of his ability to contact the enemy, and asked me to try. I promised to see what I could do.

But before I could do anything, it was all over. Devereux rigged a white flag, left his command post, and moved south down the road toward the enemy, giving our troops the cease-fire order as he reached them. I became aware that the surrender had begun when someone reported that bed sheets could be seen flying above the civilian hospital near Devereux's command post.

I looked around me at the men in my command post and could think of nothing to say. In a sort of a daze I walked out of the unfinished magazine, tossed my .45 pistol into a nearby latrine, got into my truck, and drove away.

I went, not south to the enemy, but north to the cottage I had occupied in the early days of the defense. It was battered and badly damaged but, moving mechanically through the debris, I took off the dirty old khakis I had been living in night and day, shaved and washed my face, and put on a clean blue uniform. Then I got back into the truck, drove down the road, and surrendered.

Philippine Defeat

The Japanese had won a stunning victory at Pearl Harbor—and we had helped them. The state of mind of the naval commanders in Hawaii explains much. They underestimated Japan's offensive power; they couldn't imagine the possibility of an attack at such long range, and a few hints from the U.S. command weren't enough to convince them. (After all, it took the Pearl Harbor trauma to shock a whole nation into action.) President Roosevelt and Secretary of State Hull had warned the military leaders of possible attack from Japan, but they had the advantage of the latest developments on diplomatic and economic fronts, as well as military; without this background, the local commanders in Hawaii couldn't appreciate the seriousness of the warnings they received.

And at Pearl Harbor (as in the Philippines), there was tactical failure in reconnaissance; when signs of unknown ships and planes were picked up, observers on the spot failed to appreciate their significance. When, for instance, planes were noted on a radar screen, still 125 miles away to the north, and duly reported to an officer, nothing was done about it because a flight of U.S. planes was expected from approximately the same direction. (For similar reasons, surprise through air attack was accomplished many times later in the war; in Doolittle's B-25 raid on Tokyo, the Japanese received prior warnings of enemy ships approaching offshore, but paid no attention.)

Japan gained enormously by crippling the American Pacific Fleet, but she was very much mistaken in thinking she had thereby crippled the United States. The surprise attack was "a low blow" that would arouse the American nation, as surely as smoke from a fire arouses a hornets' nest. The people of the United States were suddenly knit together in common purpose. But this in itself did not produce weapons for defense, let alone counterattack. There would be more defeats, tragic for those called to sacrifice themselves so the country could gain the time necessary to gird for battle.

The Philippines were next on the Jap schedule. The islands did not offer many economic advantages to Japan, but to secure their lines of communication for the attack on the East Indies, the Philippines had to be neutralized. Again the initiative was entirely Japan's; the U.S. had waited too long to reinforce the islands.

News of the Pearl Harbor attack had been flashed to the American commanders in the Philippines several hours before Clark and Nichols airfields were attacked on Luzon. The Japs intended to reduce the airfields quickly so that their invasion landings would have unopposed fighter support. The first raid alert in the Manila area found American planes in the air ready to do battle, but no Jap planes appeared; later in the day a real bombing strike, for which no warning had been issued, caught many planes on the ground, destroying a third of the fighters and half of the bombers.

After that the Japs bombed and strafed army and navy installations almost at will. Small invasion forces were put ashore on Luzon almost daily until December 22nd, when the main amphibious operation hit the beaches of Lingayen Gulf. All forces were consolidated for the drive south to Manila, forcing the U.S. 11th and 21st Infantry Divisions under Gen. Wainwright to retreat before them; on December 27th, Gen. MacArthur, over-all commander of the Philippines, decided Manila could not be properly defended, and withdrew his troops into the Bataan Peninsula. Supplies and reinforcements could not be got through the Jap naval and air blockade, and, with rations growing scarce, defeat for the defenders of Bataan was inevitable. During February and March, 1942, Gen. MacArthur and other top personnel were taken off the peninsula. On April 8th, Gen. Wainwright, now in command, transferred naval personnel and the Filipino scouts to Corregidor, and on April 9th, surrendered the troops left in the southern extremity of Bataan. Prisoners were herded together for the infamous Death March back up the peninsula. A moving account of this ordeal is found in the next selection.

DEATH MARCH ON BATAAN

by Lt. Col. William Dyess

North of our narrow flying field stood Mount Bataan, its jagged crater rising 4,600 feet above us into the clear, cool sky. From these upper reaches came the drone of Jap dive bombers, circling endlessly. To the south, smoke still was rising from the rubble which a few days before had been Mariveles.

Three miles away, across the harbor's blue-green waters, the rocky eminence of Corregidor stood unconquered, still guarding the sea approaches to a Manila that had fallen. Grayish smoke puffs blossomed along the sides and pinnacles of the Rock as high-flying Jap bombers dropped their loads.

The dust that enveloped Mariveles field was being stirred up by the wheels of trucks and gun carriages. Jap artillery was preparing to open fire on Corregidor from the sunken rice paddies and near-by ridges. From the pall of smoke and dust new prisoners—American and Filipino soldiers— emerged in lines and groups to join those of us already there, awaiting the pleasure of the Imperial Japanese army.

The first thing I heard after our arrival was an urgent whispering which came to us from all sides. "Get rid of your Jap stuff, quick!"

"What Jap stuff?" we whispered back.

"Everything; money, souvenirs. Get rid of it!" We did so without delay—and just in time. Jap noncommissioned officers and three-star privates were moving among us ordering that packs be opened and spread out. They searched our persons, then went through the other stuff, confiscating personal articles now and then.

I noticed that the Japs, who up to now had treated us

144

with an air of cool suspicion, were beginning to get rough. I saw men shoved, cuffed, and boxed. This angered and mystified us. It was uncalled for. We were not resisting. A few ranks away a Jap jumped up from a pack he had been inspecting. In his hand was a small shaving mirror.

"Nippon?" he asked the owner. The glass was stamped: "Made in Japan." The soldier nodded. The Jap stepped back, then lunged, driving his rifle butt into the American's face. "Yaah!" he yelled, and lunged again. The Yank went down. The raging Jap stood over him, driving crushing blows to the face until the prisoner lay insensible.

A little way off a Jap was smashing his fists into the face of another American soldier who went to his knees and received a thudding kick in the groin. He, too, it seemed, had been caught with some Japanese trifle.

We were shocked. This treatment of war prisoners was beyond our understanding. I still didn't get it, even after someone explained to me that the Japs assumed the contraband articles had been taken from the bodies of their dead. I was totally unprepared for the appalling deed that came next.

I was too far off to witness it personally, but I saw the victim afterward. We had known him. A comrade who had stood close by told me later in shocking detail what had taken place.

The victim, an air force captain, was being searched by a three-star private. Standing by was a Jap commissioned officer, hand on sword hilt. These men were nothing like the toothy, bespectacled runts whose photographs are familiar to most newspaper readers. They were cruel of face, stalwart, and tall.

"This officer looked like a giant beside the Jap private," said my informant, who must be nameless because he still is a prisoner of war. "The big man's face was as black as mahogany. He didn't seem to be paying much attention. There was no expression in his eyes, only a sort of unseeing glare.

"The private, a little squirt, was going through the captain's pockets. All at once he stopped and sucked in his breath with a hissing sound. He had found some Jap yen.

145

"He held these out, ducking his head and sucking in his breath to attract notice. The big Jap looked at the money. Without a word he grabbed the captain by the shoulder and shoved him down to his knees. He pulled the sword out of the scabbard and raised it high over his head, holding it with both hands. The private skipped to one side.

"Before we could grasp what was happening, the black-faced giant had swung his sword. I remember how the sun flashed on it. There was a swish and a kind of chopping thud, like a cleaver going through beef.

"The captain's head seemed to jump off his shoulders. It hit the ground in front of him and went rolling crazily from side to side between the lines of prisoners.

"The body fell forward. I have seen wounds, but never such a gush of blood as this. The heart continued to pump for a few seconds and at each beat there was another great spurt of blood. The white dust around our feet was turned into crimson mud. I saw that the hands were opening and closing spasmodically. Then I looked away.

"When I looked again the big Jap had put up his sword and was strolling off. The runt who had found the yen was putting them into his pocket. He helped himself to the captain's possessions."

This was the first murder. In the year to come there would be enough killing of American and Filipino soldier prisoners to rear a mountain of dead.

Our Jap guards now threw off all restraint. They beat and slugged prisoners, robbing them of watches, fountain pens, money, and toilet articles. Now, as never before, I wanted to kill Japs for the pleasure of it.

The thing that almost drove me crazy was the certainty that the officer who had just been murdered couldn't have taken those yen from a dead Jap. He had been in charge of an observation post far behind the lines. I doubt that he ever had seen a dead Jap.

Gradually I got control of myself. By going berserk now I would only lose my own life without hope of ever helping to even the score.

The score just now was far from being in our favor. The 160 officers and men who remained of the 21st Pursuit

146

Squadron were assembled with about 500 other American and Filipino soldiers of all grades and ranks. They were dirty, ragged, unshaven, and exhausted. Many were half starved.

Swirling chalky dust had whitened sweat-soaked beards, adding grotesquerie to the scene. It would not have been hard to believe these were tottering veterans of 1898, returned to the battlegrounds of their youth.

We stood for more than an hour in the scalding heat while the search, with its beating and sluggings, was completed. Then the Jap guards began pulling some of the huskiest of our number out of line. These were assembled into labor gangs, to remain in the area.

I doubt that many of them survived the hail of steel Corregidor's guns later laid down on the beaches and foothills of Bataan. These were men who for months had faced American iron, thrown at them by Jap guns.

Now, it appeared, they were to die under American iron thrown into their midst by American guns. As the remainder of us were marched off the field our places were taken by other hundreds of prisoners who were to follow us on the Death March from Bataan.

We turned eastward on the national highway, which crosses the southern tip of Bataan to Cabcaben and Bataan airfield, then veers northward through Lamao, Balanga, and Orani. From there it runs northeastward to San Fernando, the rail junction and banking town in Pampanga province.

Ordinarily, the trip from Mariveles to Cabcaben field is a beautiful one with the grandeur of high greenclad mountains on the north and a view of the sea on the right. The white of the road contrasts pleasantly with the deep green of the tropical growth on either side.

But on this day there was no beauty. Coming toward us were seemingly interminable columns of Jap infantry, truck trains, and horse-drawn artillery, all moving into Bataan for a concentrated assault on Corregidor. They stirred up clouds of blinding dust in which all shape and form were lost.

Every few yards Jap noncoms materialized like gargoyles from the grayish white pall and snatched Americans out of

147

line to be searched and beaten. Before we had gone two miles we had been stripped of practically all our personal possessions.

The Japs made no move to feed us. Few of us had had anything to eat since the morning of April 9. Many had tasted no food in four days. We had a little tepid water in our canteens, but nothing else.

The ditches on either side of the road were filled with overturned and wrecked American army trucks, fire-gutted tanks, and artillery our forces had rendered unusable. At intervals we saw mounds of captured food, bearing familiar trademarks. These had fallen almost undamaged into Jap hands.

As we marched along I rounded up the 110 officers and men of the 21st Pursuit. I didn't know yet what the score was, but I felt we would be in a better position to help one another and keep up morale if we were together.

We hadn't walked far when the rumor factory opened up. In a few minutes it was in mass production. There were all kinds of reports: We were going to Manila and Old Bilibid prison. We were going to San Fernando and entrain for a distant concentration camp. Trucks were waiting just ahead to pick us up. We doubted the last rumor, but hoped it was true.

The sun was nearing the zenith now. The penetrating heat seemed to search out and dissipate the small stores of strength remaining within us. The road, which until this moment had been fairly level, rose sharply in a zigzag grade. We were nearing Little Baguio.

I was marching with head down and eyes squinted for the dual purpose of protecting myself as much as possible from the dust and glare and keeping watch on the Jap guards who walked beside and among us. Halfway up the hill we reached a level stretch where a Japanese senior officer and his staff were seated at a camp table upon which were spread maps and dispatches.

As I came abreast he saw me and shouted something that sounded like, "Yoy!" He extended his hand, palm downward, and opened and closed the fingers rapidly. This

148

meant I was to approach him. I pretended I didn't see him. He shouted again as I kept on walking. His third "Yoy!" vibrated with anger. The next I knew a soldier snatched me out of line and shoved me toward the table.

"Name!" shouted the officer. He was staring at the wings and my uniform. "You fly?"

I told him my name without mentioning my rank and said I had been a pilot.

"Where you planes?"

"All shot down." I made a downward, spinning motion with my hand.

"No at Cebu? No at Mindanao?"

"No Cebu. No Mindanao."

"Yaah. Lie! We know you got planes. We see. Sometimes one . . . two . . . sometimes three, four, five. Where you airfields?"

I shook my head again and made the spinning motion with my hand. But I located the airfields for him on his map. I pointed to Cabcaben, Bataan, and Mariveles. He knew about these, of course. He made an impatient gesture.

"One more. Secret field!"

"Nope. No secret field."

"True?"

"Yes. True."

"Where are tunnel? Where are underwater tunnel from Mariveles to Corregidor? Where are tunnels on Corregidor Rock?" He held the map toward me.

"I don't know of any tunnels. No tunnels; no place. I never was on Corregidor. I was only at Nichols field and Bataan."

"You flying officer and you never at Corregidor Rock!" His eyes were slits. His staff officers were angry, too. "LIE!" he shrieked and jumped up.

He was powerfully built, as are most Jap officers. He seized my shoulder and whirled me around with a quick twist that almost dislocated my arm. Then came a violent shove that sent me staggering toward the line. I expected a bullet to follow the push, but I didn't dare look back. This would have been inviting them to shoot. As I reached the

149

marching line, the officer shouted something else. The guards shoved me and motioned that I should catch up with my group.

I wanted to be with them, but the double quick up the hill in the scalding heat and dust almost finished me. I had the thought, too, that the guards I passed might get the idea I was trying to escape. My bullet expectancy was so high it made my backside tingle from scalp to heels. I caught up as we were passing through Little Baguio. In a short time we were abreast the blackened ruins of Hospital No. 1, which had been bombed heavily a couple of days before.

Among the charred debris, sick and wounded American soldiers were walking dazedly about. There was no place for them to go.

Their only clothes were hospital pajama suits and kimonos. Here and there a man was stumping about on one leg and a crutch. Some had lost one or both arms. All were in need of fresh dressings. And all obviously were suffering from the shock of the bombing.

They looked wonderingly at the column of prisoners. When the Jap officers saw them, these shattered Americans were rounded up and shoved into the marching line. All of them tried to walk, but only a few were able to keep it up. Those who fell were kicked aside by the Japs.

The Japs forbade us to help these men. Those who tried it were kicked, slugged, or jabbed with bayonet points by the guards who stalked with us in twos and threes.

For more than a mile these bomb-shocked cripples stumbled along with us. Their shoulders were bent and the sweat streamed from their faces. I can never forget the hopelessness in their eyes.

Eventually their strength ebbed and they began falling back through the marching ranks. I don't know what became of them.

About a mile east of the hospital we encountered a major traffic jam. On either side of the congested road hundreds of Jap soldiers were unloading ammunition and equipment.

Our contingent of more than 600 American and Fili-

150

pino prisoners filtered through, giving the Japs as wide a berth as the limited space permitted. This was to avoid being searched, slugged, or pressed into duty as cargadores [burden carriers].

Through the swirling dust we could see a long line of trucks, standing bumper to bumper. There were hundreds of them. And every last one was an American make. I saw Fords—which predominated—Chevrolets, GMCs, and others.

These were not captured trucks. They bore Jap army insignia and had been landed from the ships of the invasion fleet. It is hard to describe what we felt at seeing these familiar American machines, filled with jeering, snarling Japs. It was a sort of super-sinking feeling. We had become accustomed to having American iron thrown at us by the Japs, but this was a little too much.

Eventually the road became so crowded we were marched into a clearing. Here, for two hours, we had our first taste of the oriental sun treatment, which drains the stamina and weakens the spirit.

The Japs seated us on the scorching ground, exposed to the full glare of the sun. Many of the Americans and Filipinos had no covering to protect their heads. I was beside a small bush, but it cast no shade because the sun was almost directly above us. Many of the men around me were ill.

When I thought I could stand the penetrating heat no longer, I was determined to have a sip of the tepid water in my canteen. I had no more than unscrewed the top when the aluminum flask was snatched from my hands. The Jap who had crept up behind me poured the water into a horse's nosebag, then threw down the canteen. He walked on among the prisoners, taking away their water and pouring it into the bag. When he had enough he gave it to his horse.

Whether by accident or design we had been put just across the road from a pile of canned and boxed food. We were famished, but it seemed worse than useless to ask the Japs for anything. An elderly American colonel did, however. He crossed the road and after pointing to the food and to the drooping prisoners, he went through the motions of eating.

A squat Jap officer grinned at him and picked up a can of salmon. Then he smashed it against the colonel's head, opening the American's cheek from eye to jawbone. The officer staggered and turned back toward us, wiping the blood off.

It seemed as though the Japs had been waiting for just such a brutal display to end the scene. They ordered us to our feet and herded us back into the road.

We knew now the Japs would respect neither age nor rank. Their ferocity grew as we marched on into the afternoon. They no longer were content with mauling stragglers or pricking them with bayonet points. The thrusts were intended to kill.

We had marched about a mile after the sun treatment when I stumbled over a man writhing in the hot dust of the road. He was a Filipino soldier who had been bayoneted through the stomach. Within a quarter of a mile I walked past another. This soldier prisoner had been rolled into the path of the trucks and crushed beneath the heavy wheels.

The huddled and smashed figures beside the road eventually became commonplace to us. The human mind has an amazing faculty of adjusting itself to shock. In this case it may have been that heat and misery had numbed our senses. We remained keenly aware, however, that these murders might well be precursors of our own, if we should falter or lag.

As we straggled past Hospital No. 2 the Japs were setting up artillery and training it on Corregidor. The thick jungle hid the hospital itself, but we could see that guns were all around it. The Japs regarded this as master strategy; the Rock would not dare return their fire. I wondered what the concussion of the heavy guns would do to the stricken men in the hospital wards. The cannonade began after we had passed by.

A few minutes later a violent blow on the head almost sent me to my knees. I thought one of the Jap guns had made a direct hit on me. My steel helmet jammed down

152

over my eyes with a clang that made my ears ring. I pulled it clear and staggered around to see a non-commissioned Jap brandishing a club the size of a child's baseball bat. He was squealing and pointing to the dented helmet. He lifted the club again. I threw the helmet into the ditch and he motioned me to march on. Like many of my comrades, I now was without protection against the merciless sun.

Jap artillery was opening up all along the southern tip of Bataan. The area behind us re-echoed to the thud and crash of heavy gunfire. Grayish smoke puffs speckled Corregidor's sides. The Rock was blasting back at the Japs, but most of its shells were falling in the Mariveles region whence we had come.

At sundown we crossed Cabcaben airfield, from which our planes had taken off not thirty-nine hours before. Here again Jap artillery was going into action. We were marched across the field and halted inside a rice paddy beyond. We had had no food or water, and none was offered, but we were grateful of the opportunity to lie down on the earth and rest. The guards kept to the edges of the paddy, leaving us plenty of room.

I was just dropping off when there came an outburst of yelling and screeching. The Japs had charged in among us and were kicking us to our feet. They herded us back to the road and started marching us eastward again. During the brief respite leg muscles had stiffened. Walking was torture.

It was dark when we marched across Bataan field, which with Cabcaben field I had commanded two days before. It was difficult walking in the darkness. Now and again we passed the huddled forms of men who had collapsed from fatigue or had been bayoneted. I didn't kid myself that I was safe simply because I was keeping up the pace. I would not have been surprised at any time to feel a Jap blade slide between my ribs. The bloodthirsty devils now were killing us for diversion.

The march continued until about 10 p.m. When we were halted some naïve individual started a rumor that we were to be given water. Instead we were about-faced and marched back to the westward. For two more hours we stumbled over the ground we had just covered.

It was midnight when we recrossed Bataan field and kept going. We were within a short distance of Cabcaben field when the Japs diverted the line into a tiny rice paddy. There was no room to lie down. Some of us tried to rest in a half squat. Others drew up their knees and laid their heads on the legs of the men next to them. Jap guards stood around the edges of the little field, their feet almost touching the outer fringe of men.

I heard a cry, followed by thudding blows at one side of the paddy. An American soldier so tortured by the thirst that he could not sleep had asked a Jap guard for water. The Jap fell on him with his fists, then slugged him into insensibility with a rifle butt.

The thirst of all had become almost unbearable, but remembering what had happened to the colonel earlier in the day we asked for nothing. A Jap officer walked along just after the thirsty soldier had been beaten. He appeared surprised that we wanted water. However, he permitted several Americans to collect canteens from their comrades and fill them at a stagnant carabao wallow which had been additionally befouled by seeping sea water. We held our noses to shut out the nauseating reek, but we drank all the water we could get.

At dawn of the second day the impatient Japs stepped among and upon us, kicking us into wakefulness. We were hollow-eyed and as exhausted as we had been when we went to sleep. As we stumbled into the road we passed a Jap non-commissioned officer who was eating meat and rice.

"Pretty soon you eat," he told us.

The rising sun cast its blinding light into our eyes as we marched. The temperature rose by the minute. Noon came and went. The midday heat was searing. At 1 p.m. the column was halted and Jap noncoms told American and Filipino soldiers they might fill their canteens from a dirty puddle beside the road. There was no food.

During the afternoon traffic picked up again. Troop-laden trucks sped past us. A grimacing Jap leaned far

154

out, holding his rifle by the barrel. As the truck roared by he knocked an American soldier senseless with the gun's stock. Other Japs saw this and yelled. From now on we kept out of reach if we could. Several more American and Filipino prisoners were struck down.

At 2 p.m. we were told it would be necessary to segregate the prisoners as to rank; colonels together, majors together, and so on. This separated all units from their officers and afforded opportunity for another hour of sun treatment. There was no mention of food.

The line of march was almost due north now. We reached Balanga, about twenty miles from Cabcaben field, at sundown. We were marched into the courtyard of a large prison-like structure, dating to the Spanish days, and told we would eat, then spend the night there.

At one side of the yard food was bubbling in great caldrons. Rice and soy sauce were boiling together. Jap kitchen corpsmen were opening dozens of cans and dumping vienna sausage into the savory mess. The aromatic steam that drifted over from those pots had us almost crazy. While we waited we were given a little water.

We imagined the rice and sausages were for us, though we saw hundreds of ragged and sick Filipinos behind a barbed wire barricade near-by who had only filthy, fly-covered rice to eat. After drinking we were ordered into the line for what appeared to be a routine search. When it was finished an officer shouted something and the attitude of our guards swiftly changed.

They ordered us out of the patio and lined us up in a field across the road. As we left, grinning Japs held up steaming ladles of sausage and rice. The officer followed us to the field, then began stamping up and down, spouting denunciations and abuse. When he calmed enough to be understood, we heard this:

"When you came here you were told you would eat and be let to sleep. Now that is changed. We have found pistols concealed among three American officers. In punishment for these offenses you will not be given food. You will march to Orani (five miles to the north) before you sleep."

The accusation was a lie. If a pistol had been found, the

155

owner would have been shot, beaten to death, or beheaded on the spot. Besides, we knew that the searchers hadn't overlooked even a toothbrush, to say nothing of a pistol. The Japs simply were adding mental torture to the physical. The Jap officer saw he wasn't believed. He did just what a Jap might be expected to do. Shortly after we resumed the march a staff car pulled up beside us.

Three American officers were dragged out of line and thrown into it. This in the words of Gilbert and Sullivan's Pooh Bah was "corroborative detail, intended to lend artistic verisimilitude to an otherwise bald and unconvincing narrative." We never saw the three officers again, though it is not hard to guess their fate. Men who had stood near two of them during the search said no guns had been found.

Our guards had been increased for the night march, and rigid discipline was imposed. We were formed into columns of fours. A new set of guards came up on bicycles and we were forced to walk practically at double quick to keep up. After two hours these guards were replaced by a group on foot who walked slowly with short mincing steps. The change of gait so cramped our leg muscles that walking was agony.

We had learned by rough experience that efforts to assist our failing comrades served usually to hasten their deaths and add to our own misery and peril. So we tried the next best thing—encouraging them with words. Talking had not been forbidden.

It was during a period of slow marching that an old friend, a captain in the medical corps, began dropping back through the ranks. Presently he was beside me. It was plain he was just about done in. I said:

"Hello, Doc. Taking a walk?"

"Ed," he said slowly, "I can't go another kilometer. A little farther and I'm finished."

"Well, Doc, I'm about in the same fix," I told him. Nothing more was said until we had covered two or three kilometers. Every now and then Doc would begin to lag a little. When this happened, the fellow on the other side of Doc would join me in slipping back some and giving him

156

a little shove with our shoulders. He always took the hint and stepped up. At length he spoke again.

"I'm done, Ed. You fellows forget me and go on. I can't make another kilometer."

"I don't think I can either, Doc. I feel just about as you do."

That was the way we passed the night. Kilometer after kilometer crawled by, but Doc didn't fall out. If he had, his bones would be bleaching now somewhere along that road of death that led out of Bataan.

The hours dragged by and, as we knew they must, the drop-outs began. It seemed that a great many of the prisoners reached the end of their endurance at about the same time. They went down by twos and threes. Usually, they made an effort to rise. I never can forget their groans and strangled breathing as they tried to get up. Some succeeded. Others lay lifelessly where they had fallen.

I observed that the Jap guards paid no attention to these. I wondered why. The explanation wasn't long in coming. There was a sharp crackle of pistol and rifle fire behind us.

Skulking along, a hundred yards behind our contingent, came a "clean-up squad" of murdering Jap buzzards. Their helpless victims, sprawled darkly against the white of the road, were easy targets.

As members of the murder squad stooped over each huddled form, there would be an orange flash in the darkness and a sharp report. The bodies were left where they lay, that other prisoners coming behind us might see them.

Our Japanese guards enjoyed the spectacle in silence for a time. Eventually, one of them who spoke English felt he should add a little spice to the entertainment.

"Sleepee?" he asked. "You want sleep? Just lie down on road. You get good, long sleep!"

On through the night we were followed by orange flashes and thudding shots.

At 3 a.m. of April 12, 1942—the second day after our surrender—we arrived half dead at Orani, in northeastern

157

Bataan, after a twenty-one-hour march from Cabcaben near the peninsula's southern tip. That thirty-mile hike over rough and congested roads had lasted almost from dawn to dawn.

Near the center of the town the Japs ordered us off the road to a barbed wire compound a block away. It had been intended for five hundred men. Our party numbered more than six hundred. Already in it, however, were more than 1,500 Americans and Filipinos.

The stench of the place reached us long before we entered it. Hundreds of the prisoners were suffering from dysentery. Human waste covered the ground. The shanty that had served as a latrine no longer was usable as such.

Maggots were in sight everywhere. There was no room to lie down. We tried to sleep sitting up, but the aches of exhaustion seemed to have penetrated even into our bones.

Jap soldiers told us there would be rice during the morning. We paid no attention. We not only didn't believe them, we were too miserable to care. The sun came up like a blazing ball in a copper sky. With the first shafts of yellow light the temperature started up and, it seemed to me, the vile stench of the compound grew in intensity. Breathing the heavy heated air was physically painful.

As the sun climbed higher, Americans and Filipinos alike grew delirious. Their wild shouts and thrashings about dissipated their ebbing energy. They began lapsing into coma. For some it was the end. Starvation, exhaustion, and abuse had been too much for their weakened bodies. Brief coma was followed by merciful death. I had a blinding headache from the heat, glare, and stench. Several times I thought my senses were slipping.

When it was observed that men were dying, Japanese noncommissioned officers entered the compound and ordered the Americans to drag out the bodies and bury them. We were told to put the delirious ones into a thatched shed a few hundred feet away. When this had been done the grave digging began.

We thought we had seen every atrocity the Japs could offer, but we were wrong. The shallow trenches had been completed. The dead were being rolled into them. Just

158

then an American soldier and two Filipinos were carried out of the compound. They had been delirious. Now they were in a coma. A Jap noncom stopped the bearers and tipped the unconscious men into the trench.

The Japs then ordered the burial detail to fill it up. The Filipinos lay lifelessly in the hole. As the earth began falling about the American, he revived and tried to climb out. His fingers gripped the edge of the grave. He hoisted himself to a standing position.

Two Jap guards placed bayonets at the throat of a Filipino on the burial detail. They gave him an order. When he hesitated they pressed the bayonet points hard against his neck. The Filipino raised a stricken face to the sky. Then he brought his shovel down upon the head of his American comrade, who fell backward to the bottom of the grave. The burial detail filled it up.

For many of those who had been taken into the shade of the thatched shed the respite came too late. One by one their babblings ceased and their bodies twisted into the grotesque postures that mark a corpse as far as it can be seen.

During the long afternoon, stupor served as an anesthetic for most of the prisoners in the compound. There was no food. Toward evening the Japs allowed Americans to gather canteens and fill them at an artesian well. It was the first good water we'd had. Night brought relief from the heat, though there still was no room to lie down, despite the number of dead and delirious removed from the compound.

Dawn of April 13—our fourth day since leaving Mariveles—seemed to come in the middle of the night. Its magnificent colors and flaming splendor meant to us only the beginning of new sufferings. We averted our heads as the coppery light flooded our filthy prison. The temperature seemed to rise a degree a minute.

At 10 a.m., just as I was wondering how I could get through another day, there was a stir at the gates. Guards filed in and began lining us up in rows. Out of one of the dirty buildings came kitchen corpsmen, dragging cans of

159

sticky gray rice which they ladled out—one ladleful to each man. Those of us who had mess kits loaned the lids to men who had none. There were not enough kits and lids to go around, so some of the prisoners had to receive their dole in cupped hands. The portion given each man was equivalent to a saucer or small plate of rice.

The food was unappetizing and was eaten in the worst possible surroundings, but it was eaten. Make no mistake about that. It was our first in many a day. I began feeling stronger immediately, despite the growing heat. There was not enough of the rice, however, to stay delirium and coma for the weaker prisoners. There were those for whom it came too late. Scenes of the previous afternoon were repeated. There were babblings and crazy shouts. There were additional burials in shallow graves.

The rest of us passed the afternoon in stupor. We continued to sit while the sun dropped behind the western mountains. In the twilight we were ordered to our feet. It still was light as we were marched out of the compound, toward the road. We looked at the artesian well, but the Japs warned us not to try to fill our canteens.

During the next four hours of marching we were tortured by the sound of bubbling water. Artesian wells lined the road. It seemed to me I could smell water. But we knew a bullet or a bayonet awaited the man who might try to reach the wells.

About midnight rain started falling. It was chilling, but it cleansed the filth from our stinging bodies and relieved the agony of parched dryness. Those with mess kits or canteen cups held them up toward the rain as they walked. The rain lasted about fifteen minutes and we shared the water with those who had no receptacles.

We were refreshed for a time, but as the grinding march continued men began falling down. The energy derived from the morning rice and the few swallows of rain water had been depleted. When I saw the first man go down I began counting the seconds. I wondered whether the Jap buzzard squad was following us as it had two nights before—the night of April 11.

A flash and the crack of a shot answered my question.

160

The executioners were on the job to kill or wound mortally every prisoner who fell out of the marching line. All through the night there were occasional shots. I didn't count them. I couldn't.

Just before daybreak the guards halted the column and ordered us to sit down. I felt like a fighter who has been saved by the bell. The ground was damp and cool. I slept. Two hours later we were prodded into wakefulness and ordered to get up. The sun had risen.

Our course was northeasterly now and we were leaving the mountains and Bataan behind. The country in which we found ourselves was flat and marshy. There were small rivers and creeks and many rice paddies. This was Pampanga province.

I was somewhat refreshed by the rest, though walking now was much more difficult. Our stay on the damp ground had caused leg muscles to set like concrete. Even my bones seemed to ache. This was the cool of the morning, yet my throat still was afire with thirst.

And just across the road bubbled an artesian well. Its splashing was plainly audible and the clear water, glistening in the morning sun, was almost too much for my self-control. I thought once if I could reach that well and gulp all the water I wanted the Japs could shoot me and welcome. The next minute I told myself I was balmy even to entertain such a thought.

The Japs were aware of the well and they must have known what was passing through our minds. I have no doubt that they were expecting the thing that happened now. A Filipino soldier darted from the ranks and ran toward the well. Two others followed him. Two more followed these, then a sixth broke from the ranks.

Jap guards all along the line raised their rifles and waited for the six to scramble into the grassy ditch and go up on the opposite side, a few feet from the well. Most of the Filipinos fell at the first volley. Two of them, desperately wounded, kept inching toward the water, their hands outstretched. The Japs fired again and again, until all six lay dead. Thus did our fifth day of the death march start with a blood bath. I needed all the control I could muster.

161

Men had been murdered behind me all night, but the deeds had been veiled by darkness. There had been nothing to veil the pitilessness and wantonness of the murders I had just seen. I walked a long time with my head down and my fists clenched in my pockets, fighting to think of nothing at all.

I was partly successful, enough so that from then on I practiced detaching myself from the scenes about me. I have no doubt my cultivated ability to do this saved my sanity on more than one occasion in the days to come. I remember little of the two miles we walked after the six murders at the well. We were at the outskirts of Lubao, a sprawling city of 30,000, before mutterings about me brought me back to earth to look upon a new horror.

I saw that all eyes were directed toward an object hanging on a barbed wire fence that paralleled the road. It had been a Filipino soldier. The victim had been bayoneted. His abdomen was open. The bowels had been wrenched loose and were hanging like great grayish purple ropes along the strands of wire that supported the mutilated body.

This was a Japanese object lesson, of course. But it carried terrible implications. The Japs apparently had wearied of mere shootings and simple bayonetings. These had served only to whet the barbaric appetite. What might lie ahead for all of us we could only guess.

These thoughts still were in mind as our scarecrow procession began passing through the rough streets of Lubao. We were in a residential section. Windows of homes were filled with faces turned to us that bore compassionate expressions. News of our arrival raced down the street ahead of us.

Presently from the upper windows of a large house a shower of food fell among us. It was followed quickly by other gifts, tossed surreptitiously by sympathetic Filipinos who stood on the sidewalks. There were bits of bread, rice cookies, lumps of sugar and pieces of chocolate. There were cigarettes.

The Jap guards went into a frenzy. They struck out right and left at the Good Samaritans, slugging, beating, and jabbing bayonets indiscriminately. Japs tried to stamp

162

on all the food that hadn't been picked up. They turned their rage upon us. When the townsfolk saw their gifts were only adding to our misery they stopped throwing them.

Some Filipinos asked the Jap officers if they might not help us. The petitioners were warned to stay away. I recall a merchant who wanted to open his store to us. We could have anything we wanted free, he said. A Jap officer denounced him, warned him to keep his distance. This was at San Tomas or Santa Monica, the two small settlements between Lubao and Guagua, about three miles to the northeast.

In Guagua the Filipino civilians also tried to slip food to us. For that they were beaten and clubbed—as we were. We passed through the hot streets without a halt.

Our next stop, just outside the city of Guagua, came near being a permanent one for me. At a long, muddy ditch we were allowed to dip up drinking water. After canteens had been filled I determined to soak my aching feet in the ooze at the ditch's edge. I was doing so when the order to resume the march was sounded unexpectedly. Putting on my shoes delayed me a few seconds.

I heard a guard shout in my direction, but I continued to struggle with the footgear. When I looked up the guard was raising his rifle. I snatched my shoes and plunged through the ditch toward the column of prisoners. I dodged from side to side with a prickling feeling all over my back. But the bullet didn't come. The guard probably would have missed—the Japs are bum shots—but I didn't think so then.

As I fell in step beside Doc, he pointed toward an officer just ahead of us. This was Captain Burt, who had given the alarm on our last night at Bataan field. He was eating a long sugar lump he had managed to secrete.

"I'm glad somebody got something," Doc said.

But in a minute or two Burt had dropped back beside us and was holding out the sugar. We each took a bite and tried to give it back. Burt shook his head.

"Split it, fellows," he said. "I've already had more than that."

163

I've never had such a quick reaction from anything. Strength flowed into me. I told Doc I felt as if I'd had a turkey dinner. This was an exaggeration, of course, but it illustrates what just a little food would have done for all of us. The Japs were starving us deliberately.

We neared San Fernando, Pampanga province, during the afternoon of our fifth day's march. It was at San Fernando, according to rumor, that we were to be put aboard a train and carried to a concentration camp.

From among the six hundred and more American and Filipino military prisoners who had started with me from Mariveles, many familiar faces were missing. We had come almost eighty-five miles with nothing to eat except the one ladle of rice given to us more than twenty-four hours before.

We had struck the railroad at Guagua and now could see the tracks which ran alongside the highway, amid the lush vegetation of the flat, marshy countryside. We could have entrained an hour before. I doubted, therefore, that the railroad figured in the Japs' plans for us. I was becoming certain that this was to be a march to the death for all of us. And the events of the next quarter hour did nothing to banish this belief.

Just ahead of me, in the afternoon heat, were two American enlisted men, stumbling along near the point of collapse. I wasn't in much better shape. At this moment we came abreast of a calasa [covered cart] which had stopped beside the road.

An American colonel who also had been watching the two enlisted men, observed that no Jap guard was near us. He drew the two soldiers out of line and helped them into the cart, then got in also. The Filipino driver tapped his pony. The cart had moved only a few feet when the trick was discovered.

Yammering Jap guards pulled the three Americans from the cart and dragged the Filipino from the driver's seat. A stocky Jap noncommissioned officer seized the heavy horsewhip. The enlisted men were flogged first. The crackling lash slashed their faces and tore their clothing. The searing pain revived them for a moment. Then they fell to the ground. The blows thudded upon their bodies. They lost consciousness.

The colonel was next. He stood his punishment a long time. His fortitude enraged the Jap, who put all his strength behind the lash. When the American officer finally dropped to his knees his face was so crisscrossed with bloody welts it was unrecognizable.

The trembling Filipino driver fell at the first cut of the whip. He writhed on the ground. The lash tore his shirt and the flesh beneath it. His face was lacerated and one eye swollen shut. When the whipper grew weary, he ordered the driver on his way. The colonel, bleeding and staggering, was kicked back into the line of American prisoners.

I don't know what became of the enlisted men. I never saw them again. During the remaining two miles we marched to San Fernando I listened for shots, but heard none. The soldiers probably were bayoneted.

The sun still was high in the sky when we straggled into San Fernando, a city of 36,000 population, and were put in a barbed wire compound similar to the one at Orani. We were seated in rows for a continuation of the sun treatment. Conditions here were the worst yet.

The prison pen was jammed with sick, dying, and dead American and Filipino soldiers. They were sprawled amid the filth and maggots that covered the ground. Practically all had dysentery. Malaria and dengue fever appeared to be running unchecked. There were symptoms of other tropical diseases I didn't even recognize.

Jap guards had shoved the worst cases beneath the rotted flooring of some dilapidated building. Many of these prisoners already had died. The others looked as though they couldn't survive until morning.

There obviously had been no burials for many hours.

After sunset Jap soldiers entered and inspected our rows. Then the gate was opened again and kitchen corpsmen entered with cans of rice. We held our mess kits and again passed lids to those who had none. Our spirits rose. We watched as the Japs ladled out generous helpings to the men nearest the gate.

165

Then, without explanation, the cans were dragged away and the gate was closed. It was a repetition of the ghastly farce at Balanga. The fraud was much more cruel this time because our need was vastly greater. In our bewildered state it took some time for the truth to sink in. When it did we were too discouraged even to swear.

We put our mess kits away and tried to get some sleep. But the Japs had something more in store for us. There was an outburst of shrill whooping and yelling, then the guards poured into the compound with fixed bayonets. They feinted at the nearest prisoners with the sharp points.

Those of us who were able rose to our feet in alarm. Evidently we did not appear sufficiently frightened. The Japs outside the compound jeered the jokesters within. One Jap then made a running lunge and drove his bayonet through an American soldier's thigh.

This stampeded several other prisoners who trampled the sick and dying men on the ground. Some prisoners tripped and fell and were trampled by their comrades. The Japs left, laughing. There was little sleep that night. The stench was almost unbearable. Hundreds of prisoners were kept awake by sheer weariness. There were shouts of delirium. There was moaning. There were the sounds of men gasping their last.

At dawn of April 15, 1942, the sixth day of our ordeal, we were kicked to our feet by Jap guards and ordered to get out of the compound. The Japs did not even make a pretense of giving us food or water. Our canteens had been empty for hours. Only muddy scum inside them reminded us that we had filled them at the ditch outside Guagua the afternoon before.

Enough prisoners had been brought out of the compound to form five companies of 115 men each. In this formation we were marched to a railroad siding several blocks away where stood five ancient, ramshackle boxcars. None of these could have held more than fifty men in comfort. Now 115 men were packed into each car and the doors were pulled shut and locked from the outside.

There was no room to move. We stood jammed together because there wasn't sufficient floor space to permit sitting.

166

As the day wore on and the sun climbed higher the heat inside the boxcars grew to oven-like intensity. It was so hot that the air we breathed seemed to scorch our throats.

There was little ventilation, only narrow, screened slits at the ends of the cars. A large per cent of the prisoners was suffering from dysentery. The atmosphere was foul beyond description. Men began to faint. Some went down from weakness. They lay at our feet, face down in the filth that covered the floor boards.

After a seemingly interminable wait the train started with a jerk. A jolting, rocking ride began. Many of the prisoners in the boxcar in which I stood were seized by nausea, adding to the vile state of our rolling cell. The ride lasted more than three hours. Later I heard that a number of men had died in each of the five cars. I don't know. I was too far gone to notice much at the journey's end.

When the doors were opened, someone, I can't remember who, said we had reached Capas, a town in Tarlac province, and that we were headed for O'Donnell prison camp —named for the town of O'Donnell.

When the prisoners tumbled out into the glaring sunlight the wretchedness of their condition brought cries of compassion from Filipino civilians who lined the tracks. The surly Jap guards silenced these sympathetic voices with stern warnings.

We were marched several hundred yards down the tracks to a plot of bare scorching ground amid the tropical undergrowth. It was another sun treatment. There was no breeze. The ground was almost too hot to touch. The heat dried the filth into our pores.

The Jap guards formed a picket wall around us to forestall the friendly Filipinos who had come to give us food and water. Some of these, however, hurled their offerings over the heads of the Japs, hoping they would fall into our midst. Then they took to the bush, outrunning the guards who pursued them.

We sat for two hours in the little clearing before the Japs ordered us to our feet. A seven-mile hike to O'Donnell prison was ahead of us. As we filed into the narrow dirt road that wound through the green walls of the jungle,

167

it became obvious that more than a fourth of our number never would be able to make it.

We expected mass murder of those too weak to walk. Instead, the Jap officers indicated the stronger ones might assist the weaker ones. This was something new. There were precious few stronger ones, however.

As we straggled on we had ample reason to bless the kindly Filipinos of Capas. Having seen other prisoners pass that way, they had set out cans of water among the bushes and in high grass along the road.

The Japs found many of these and kicked them over before our eyes. But some were overlooked and a few of us were able to take the edge off our thirst. One gaunt American officer said he believed he owed his life to the good and thoughtful townfolk of Capas.

My first good look at O'Donnell prison was from atop a rise about a mile off. I saw a forbidding maze of tumble-down buildings, barbed wire entanglements, and high guard towers, from which flew the Jap flag.

I had flown over this dismal spot several times, but never had given it more than passing appraisal. I wondered as I looked at it now how long I would be there; how long I could last.

As we stood, staring dazedly, there came to me a premonition that hundreds about to enter O'Donnell prison this April day never would leave it alive. If I could have known what lay in store for us all, I think I would have given up the ghost then and there.

Sharp commands by the Jap guards aroused me. We started moving.

Java Sea

On May 6, 1942, Wainwright surrendered Corregidor and the Philippines were firmly in the Japs' grasp. Guerrilla activity would increase throughout the rest of the war, with the aid of the U.S., but until the American landings in Leyte Gulf in 1944, there was no more organized fighting.

In the meantime, the Japs had attacked and overrun the islands of Wake and Guam, and had swept down the Malayan Peninsula, capturing Singapore and the thousands of British troops stationed there. And the first big naval action had been fought in the Java Sea.

In the last days of February, Japan had sent a powerful three-pronged striking force, totaling four carriers, four battleships, heavy and light cruisers, and many destroyers, to protect the troop transports for the impending invasion of Java.

Java's sea defense was in the hands of an Allied Naval Group, under the command of Dutch Adm. Doorman, and consisting of two heavy cruisers (the *U.S.S. Houston* and the British *H.M.S. Exeter*), three light cruisers (two Dutch, the *Java* and the *De Ruyter*, and the Australian *H.M.A.S. Perth)*, and eleven destroyers. On February 27th, Doorman struck at the Japanese force attacking from the northeast (a group consisting of cruisers and destroyers only). In an engagement of more than seven hours, the Allies lost half their ships including Doorman's flagship, the *Java.* The Japanese had one destroyer damaged; all their troop transports came through unscathed.

The two opposing forces were not unevenly matched, numerically speaking. The Allies took their licking because they lacked air reconnaissance, because of an astonishingly cumbersome system of communications,* and "the enemy's vast superiority in torpedo materiel and tactics." **

* S. E. Morison, in *The Rising Sun in the Pacific* (p. 342), says the Allied command under Dutch Adm. Doorman had never worked out a set of signals that were common to all; his signals

The two cruisers, *Perth* and *Houston*, escaped to fight another day, and, indeed, before the next day was over, they would be fighting for their very lives. Next morning, February 28th, they put into a Javanese port for badly needed repairs. However, orders were issued to all ships in the Java area to leave the Jap-infested waters at once. Both ships put to sea, heading for the Sunda Strait through which they hoped to escape into the Indian Ocean. They came upon Jap transports landing troops on the beaches of Banten Bay and, on the run—for their orders were to avoid action and escape—they shelled and sank four transports.

Later that night they ran head-on into a Jap force consisting of light and heavy cruisers and destroyers, which barred their entrance to the strait. The *Perth* and *Houston* fought back with everything they had, but the salvos of shells and torpedoes flung at them were simply too much to withstand.

The following selection is a description of the action from on board the *Perth*.

ACTION IN THE SUNDA STRAIT

by Ronald McKie

Saturday: 11:06 P. M.

At 10:45 p.m. Babi Island light was three miles to starboard, and a few minutes later *Perth* and *Houston* were opposite Banten Bay, near the northwest end of Java, and five miles off shore.

They were nearing Sunda Strait at last through waters where much history had been made—where Chinese battle junks had sailed, where men had fought for pepper and

---

had to be translated by a U.S. liaison officer who sent them on to other English-speaking ships; there was no recourse when the orders were conflicting, as often happens in quick actions.

** S. E. Morison, *The Rising Sun in the Pacific*, p. 358.

nutmegs and bases and personal power, where the tide of religion had ebbed and flowed. . . .

With Sunda Strait almost in sight, *Perth* increased her speed and *Houston* followed. They were steaming at 28 knots now, shuddering, straining, creaking under the vibrations of their mighty engines and thrusting screws.

In another hour, perhaps, they would be almost through Sunda Strait. In two hours or less they would be in the Indian Ocean—and out of the trap.

Then, at 11:06 p.m., when five miles from St. Nicolas Point, the extreme northwest tip of Java, with the Java Sea on its right and Sunda Strait on its left, Captain Waller sighted a ship close in to the headland.

"Challenge," he ordered. "It's probably one of our corvettes patrolling the strait."

The chief yeoman, Bert Hatwell, grabbed his Aldis lamp and winked the code letters.

The other ship replied. Her lamp was a strange pale green. Her reply was strange.

"U.B., U.B.," Waller said. "Repeat the challenge."

But as *Perth*'s Aldis winked again the other ship began to turn and make smoke, and as she showed her full silhouette Waller said: "Jap destroyer . . . sound the rattles . . . forward turrets open fire."

Then he called: "One unknown."

Perth's bow swung to bring the broadside to bear on the enemy. Then at point-blank range, her 6-inch guns spewed shells and orange flame.

In the plot below the bridge, Supply Assistant Ronald Clohesy kicked Tiger Lyons on the shin.

"It's on," he said. He might have been announcing lunch.

Lyons jerked upright and was just in time to hear the captain's order to the guns, and his words, "One unknown." That was Lyons' cue to break radio silence and report action to all shore stations. He scribbled the code signal and handed it to Clohesy who ran to the radio room behind the plot as the guns opened up.

And only Darwin, away to the southeast, ever acknowledged that signal that the Battle of Sunda Strait had begun.

Fear now was in Lyons' guts, fear cold and hard like a chunk of ice lodged between his solar plexus and his navel. Fear stayed with him for minutes, urgent and degrading, and in those minutes he felt physically dirty and hated himself. Then his panic ebbed as a shell hissed under the ship —hissed deep under the racing keel with the sound a soda siphon makes when it spits into a glass of whisky.

Now *Perth*'s guns were crashing like houses falling down, and through the speaking tube he heard someone on the bridge above say, "There are four to starboard," and another voice, "There are five on our portside"; and then a surprised "By God, they're all around us," he recognized as from Allan McDonough, the Royal Australian Air Force flying officer with the ship.

Lyons heard the captain order divided control to the guns, and soon after independent control so that each gun could pick its own target. There were plenty, too. His plot of the action already showed thirteen Japanese destroyers and two cruisers attacking them—and that was only part of the enemy force. He knew then he and his shipmates were in for a dirty night, but his early panic never returned. His plot showed that the farthest Jap was only three miles away, the closest less than a mile. The Japanese cruisers were firing over and through their own destroyers, and he thought, I hope the bastards sink one another. The Japanese and Australian and American gunners were almost looking down one another's guns.

As he plotted *Perth*'s zigzag course, Lyons, who in his steel room never saw one gun flash of that action, knew through his instruments that she was turning in a big circle with a diameter of about five miles. Waller's object, he could tell, was to circle and protect *Houston*'s blind stern and to maneuver against torpedo fire. The course changes were so frequent and violent as Waller swung his racing cruiser that Lyons jerked from one side of the plot to the other. It was like being in a car skidding badly on a slippery road. Mechanically, he recorded these course changes, watched his dials, jotted down times, speed, engine revolutions, enemy positions. He was not afraid—not even worried now. Instead, he felt a strange detachment—like being an onlooker watching the action from some independent vantage point. But his shirt stuck to him like wallpaper, and sweat dripped down his fingers and down his pencil onto his pad.

At 11:26 p.m. he noted down that *Perth* collected her first shell—in the forward funnel—with a burst of steam like a locomotive blowing off, and then another somewhere near the flag deck at 11:32. And at 11:50 she got another, near the waterline, which burst in the ordinary seamen's mess. But she was still unharmed, although the Japanese had flung thousands of shells at her. Forty-four minutes after action started she was still fighting with every gun she had, except her useless machine guns, and so was *Houston.*

Then, at 12:05 a.m., a torpedo went into the forward engine room on the starboard side, and Lyons felt *Perth* lift and hang as though she were actually floating in the air. He thought, When will she come down? Then hundreds of ship identification photographs poured on top of him from pigeonholes in a cabinet on the bulkhead above. They frightened him more than the torpedo. He cursed.

"Wouldn't it!" an assistant said. "Now it's a bloody snowstorm."

This was Fred Lasslett, one of his electrical mechanics who was waiting in the plot for damage reports. Lasslett began to pick up the photographs, and David Griffiths, the other mechanic, helped him. They gathered them in bundles, sorted them into rough order, and stuffed them back into the pigeonholes.

Then a second torpedo hit—and all the photographs poured out again. Lasslett shrugged and left them there. He took a slab of chocolate from his pocket and began to eat, gazing at the dials with their flickering needles. Shells howled over, but he didn't even look up.

"Do you reckon we'll make it?" Clohesy asked casually.

Lyons shook his head. "Doesn't look like it."

Clohesy opened a tin of biscuits scrounged from Tanjong and started munching. Lyons noticed with admiration how calm this thin-faced slender kid was. He showed no fear, no emotion except a sort of amused nonchalant de-

173

tachment as though what was happening outside the plot were little concern of his. Lyons remembered then lying flat on the deck beside this youngster when the Jap bombers dropped a stick across them at Tanjong before the Java Sea fight, and watching him, amazed, as he played tittat-toe with a pencil stub on the deck as the bombs burst.

And watching him, eating biscuits now as though he were in his father's shop somewhere in Victoria, Lyons suddenly felt proud to be in action with a boy like this—and humble before such bravery.

John Woods had just reached No. 2 Lookout on the lower bridge when *Perth* opened fire. As the first gun flashes died he looked aft and saw *Houston* switch on a searchlight, and at the end of the cold blue shaft were the silhouettes of Japanese merchant ships packed close together against the Java shore like cattle sheltering against a windbreak. Then all *Perth*'s guns were firing, and the crashing against his ears from then on was continuous. It was like holding his head against a thin wall someone was trying to batter down from the other side.

All round him now the yellow lights that winked were Japanese guns, but he had no sense of fear. This surprised him. He had often wondered what point-blank action would be like, and, now he knew, he decided it was not half so exciting as a good football match.

He had nothing to do except watch. He tried to estimate the position of enemy guns by the shell splashes in the water round the ship, but soon abandoned that. There were too many guns and too many splashes. Yet in all that battle he heard only one shell—one that came in very low and skimmed the bridge like a train a few feet above his head.

When the first torpedo hit he wondered what had happened. He thought it was a shell. When the second torpedo hit, he knew, for he felt *Perth* jump out of the sea, jump ahead and fall back again. Then, quite calmly, he thought of his mother and prayed.

"Look after the family at home, God," he said, "and try to look after me if you can."

But in all that hell let loose and guns winking and metal flying, he was still not afraid.

The general alarm bells woke Len Smith. He knew what to do. He ran to his starboard torpedo tubes and took the pins off the warheads while his No. 2 and No. 3 opened the breeches and put the charges in, and his No. 4 and No. 5 swung the tubes out and trained them. Ten seconds after the alarm he reported to the bridge by phone, "All ready."

He still did not think *Perth* had run into serious trouble, but three minutes later he knew he was wrong. From the torpedo officer on the bridge came the order, "Bearing red 20. Enemy ships. All tubes ready." He waited. The next order, "Changing target," countermanded the first. The third order was, "Bearing three cruisers." Then, ten minutes after action started, came the order to fire, and the four fish leaped outward with that metallic rattling they make—like an old car jerking along a road full of potholes.

"Torpedoes running," Smith reported.

He ran to the portside and got off four more fish. As he watched them run he counted twelve Japanese destroyers under the light of star shells. Then he saw two big explosions and yelled, "You beaut!"

He grabbed the phone. "We got a couple of hits."

"We did better than that," the torpedo officer yelled back. "We killed with the first batch of fish, too."

With all his torpedoes gone, Len Smith detailed some of his crews to damage control on deck. They ran out fire hoses, while others joined the men carrying ammunition to the 4-inch guns.

But Smith still wasn't overworried. He still felt that Hec Waller would get them through, even when, just before the first torpedo hit, he counted eighteen Japanese destroyers attacking in packs of six—like gray beetles with red eyes rushing toward them. Then the second torpedo came in with a roar that even smothered the gunfire and left men dazed. Then water poured down on Smith and his men as if someone had cut the bottom out of a tank.

The water fell and slid away. Slowly he wiped his face

with his sleeve and felt the sting of salt, and thought, Now we're a goner.

Bill Davis was dreaming that a telephone was ringing beside his bed. He tried to reach for it but could not move his arm. Then he was awake and the action buzzer was going above him. He had only one feeling—surprise that of all people Bill Davis should be in two major actions within twenty-four hours.

He was supposed to get to his Red Cross action station, but, without knowing why, he joined the line of men carrying shells from the magazine to the 4-inch, and from that moment time ceased for him and noise replaced it. At first he noticed how the men about him worked as though they were at a practice, but soon they were running with the shells, talking, shouting, pushing one another out of the way, cursing. They cursed the Japs, they cursed one another, they cursed the gun crews. And the gun crews, serving the guns like maniacs, cursed everyone as they operated their mechanism.

One of the ammunition party sang in a shrill tenor that the gunfire cut to pieces, so that Davis heard only stray notes divorced from one another and high like the crying of a sick child. Another man kept yelling, "Flog the Japs, flog the Japs," in an endless chant. Another shouted, "You beaut!" as he ran cradling a shell.

Davis never doubted they would get through. He kept thinking, I wonder what time we'll get to Tjilatjap. He knew Waller would save them, even after the first torpedo hit, even after the direct hit on one of the 4-inch guns. He never forgot that. One moment he saw a gunner sliding a shell into the breech. Then a flash like a scarlet cloth seemed to wipe the man, the crew, and the gun itself into the sea. One moment there was a gun in action and men were yelling and cursing as they served it. The next moment there was only an empty space on the deck where the gun had been, and the sour stink of an exploded shell.

The guns woke Gavin Campbell, and the first thing he thought about was his tin hat. Wearily he picked it up and

176

put it on, but forgot about his antiflash hood and gloves. He growled to Douglas Findlay, the A.B. with him on the multiple gun, "The bastards never let you sleep."

Then he heard the gong in "Y" turret just below him, and the sound reminded him of a Sydney tram bell—brassy and urgent. It told him "Y" turret was about to fire. His body tightened as he waited for the shock. Then it came and the blast, as it poured over him, was like the heat wave from a bush fire. The flash momentarily blinded him, and his sight was just back to normal when the guns fired again, and again and again. Soon, every time the 6-inch fired he pleaded with them to stop. Soon, the tension was almost pain itself, and he felt his inside would burst if the guns fired any more. But they did fire—crash, crash, crash. And then he was angry, angry because of his own helplessness above the big guns, because of the futility of standing beside his useless gun like a shag on a rock, angry because he had always wanted to fire the four black barrels and exult in their metallic argument and couldn't now because there was no time between the blinding flashes of the 6-inch for him to focus on a target. He cursed and Findlay cursed, and their faces were like quick close-ups on a screen as the guns flashed.

Once, during a sudden pause in the firing, he saw enlarging spots of light on two Japanese destroyers and knew they were opening the shutters of their searchlights. Then the 4-inch cracked and put the lights out. And as the lights went out something crashed against the gun shield close to his head and spun into the deck at his feet. A star shell flowered, high and brilliantly soft, and he looked down and saw a chunk of jagged metal, about six inches long, impaled in the deck. The jagged piece of shell looked exactly like a map of New Guinea.

He was facing astern as the first torpedo hit. He felt *Perth* rise and drop, and then everything was, for a long moment, as hushed as the bush at noon, before a great pillar of water and oil collapsed on him. When he wiped his eyes he was still facing astern and saw the dim shape of *Houston*, and from the shape was pouring stream after

177

stream of red and blue and amber tracer as though madmen were throwing electric light bulbs across the sky.

Down in "Y" turret lobby Keith Gosden jumped up as
he heard a clatter in the turret above. He knew what that
meant and thought, as he always did at these moments, Is
this it? Then the automatic hoist squealed and began to
move, and he started feeding shells into her. And, above,
the guns went off.

For an hour he worked like a machine to keep the shells
up to the guns. Only twice, before he fed into the hoist a
dozen practice shells, and realized, with a shock, with sudden dismay, that the magazine below was empty, did he
have time to think or notice what was going on around
him. Once, he shouted, "What are you doing up there?"
and the turret captain, Alfie Coyne, yelled back, "You can
pick your own target—there are hundreds of the bastards."
Once, Jesse Garrett, one of his helpers, collapsed with the
heat and lack of air, and he propped him against the bulkhead and went on feeding shells into the hungry hoist.

Then the first torpedo hit, and lifted Gosden off his feet
and dropped him on his face. And as he scrambled up he
saw that the lobby was leaking through the rivets. His
youngest assistant, a brave boy of eighteen, saw the water,
too, and began to yell. He grabbed the boy's shoulders
and shook him back to control. When the second torpedo
came the water poured into the lobby. At the third torpedo
the three men were up to their knees in water.

They watched it rising, climbing up the sides, up the
shell hoist. Then the others looked at Gosden and he
thought, God, we must be sinking! We'll drown if we don't
get out of this.

And then he wanted to scream.

Polo Owen woke to see two rockets falling. They were
chartreuse and scarlet and soft against the night sky. They
dropped lazily and he thought of Guy Fawkes Night when
he was a child in Western Australia, and of how his brother
once set off a Chinese basket bomb under his bottom. Then

the guns opened and he jumped to his feet, but could see nothing, as he pulled on his antiflash gear, except *Perth*'s superstructure dim and high ahead and the shadowy faces of his companions.

"What the hell are we firing at?" one of the gun crew asked.

Then the cruiser suddenly increased speed, and seemed to run away from under them. The stern where they were stationed seemed to Owen to dip almost under the sea as the ship jumped forward and began to fling about like a destroyer as guns on every side flashed and went out, flashed and went out.

He noticed "Y" turret swinging on an aft bearing, and he and the others flattened behind the Carley float, which was lashed down near their gun position, as the 6-inch fired. The flash poured over them like dragon's breath and singed the hair on their arms above their antiflash gloves. The anchored Carley jumped six inches and fell back. The guns swung away, searching for the next target, and a searchlight reached out and grabbed *Perth*'s stern.

In that blinding blue glare Owen felt twenty feet high, naked and more helpless than he had ever felt in his life. It was like looking down the barrel of a gun and knowing that the gun was about to fire. The faces of his companions looked pale green and distorted—faces from another planet. In the paralytic tension of the searchlight's beam an inner voice told him that *Perth* was doomed. He heard the 4-inch snap, as though from a great distance, and the searchlight went out. Then, as "Y" turret swept round and roared again directly aft, he dived for the deck behind the Carley float.

Lying there, angrily conscious now of the futile part they were playing, he said to Ralph Lowe, "This is bloody stupid. We can't do a thing. Let's get to hell out of here."

Lowe nodded. "We'll get blown overboard if we don't."

And the others agreed.

They all ran along the quarter-deck to the torpedo space under the 4-inch-gun deck. Owen, on the starboard side, was just in time to see four torpedoes like gray cigars leap

179

into the sea, and as he watched them he thought, Where can I go where I won't get hurt? and knew there was nowhere to go.

All along the horizon now the Japanese gun flashes were like electric lights switching on and off, and he saw the shell splashes, in the light of *Perth*'s and the Jap guns, were pale blue topped with soft white plumes which waved gently as they fell back into the sea.

Then he heard a splintering crash forward, followed by a silence, which rushed in and replaced all sound, more terrifying than the din of battle. He ran to the port torpedo space, but it was empty of men. He felt powerless, useless. He thought, This is bloody awful. If I only had something to do—something to occupy my hand or my brain. He turned to the gun at the stern, but it was now twisted metal and parts of the Carley float, draped round the barrel stumps, made the remains of the gun look like a scarecrow in a paddock. He was thinking, I missed by seconds being like that, when the second torpedo hit, and the whole ship seemed to crumple and splinter. He felt he was standing on a matchbox and it was collapsing beneath him. Three sailors ran aft bawling "Abandon ship," and with them he tried to unlash the stacked pilgrim rafts. He tore his fingernails, but the knots would not move. The blast of the 6-inch guns had made them as rigid as metal.

"Anyone got a knife?" he asked, thinking, The Carley was my abandon-ship station. Now it's the rafts or nothing.

The men shook their heads, and ran back along the quarter-deck.

Perth was already listing to port, but still moving. He went to the starboard side and looked over. The screws were slow-thumping and one was almost out of the water. It seemed so close he felt he could touch it. He went forward along the portside. The deck was deserted now, and somewhere forward steam was escaping with a thin high wail. He looked over the side and the sea seemed very near. He thought, There's nothing I can do now, as he climbed the rail.

180

Sam Stening swung off his bunk as the guns opened. As he pulled on his boiler suit and slid his feet into his sandals he thought, The guns shouldn't have gone off. We're done for this time. He ran across the flat to the wardroom. His men there were white-faced and silent. None of them had been in action before, except in the Java Sea.

"This is it, boys," he said, hoping desperately that the cold tightness he felt did not show in his face or voice.

"What do I do?" asked Mathieson, the chaplain.

"Just sit down," Stening said. "There's nothing to do. We just wait."

He could think of no other reply, but for some reason of association he suddenly remembered the time the chaplain, a teetotaler, had drunk cider and thought it was soft drink. Stening smiled secretly at such a stray and meaningless thought at a time like this. But he felt better, steadier. The tightness like a belt round his chest had loosened a hole or two. He said to himself, Don't panic, you bloody ape. Do your job.

But he and his men had only one job—to wait for casualties. And waiting in a closed steel room was infinitely worse than being on deck, watching, doing. Waiting was enough to break the bravest of men. He sat on a chair beside the operating table, but the ship heeled and tipped him out. He tried again, and the same thing happened. He noticed some of the men grinning and thought, They're better now—they're all better.

Perth was flying about like a crazy thing, 7,000 tons of metal changing course every few seconds it seemed. He studied his men as the racket above got worse. They were trying not to show what they felt. One man sat with his eyes closed, but could not keep his fingers still; another licked his lips with a furry tongue, like a lizard; a third . . . He thought, Thank God, they're solid.

And then, as they waited while all hell was loose above, hatred of war welled in him like sudden anger, hatred of its futility, its endless destruction of life and material, its failure to solve any of the basic problems of overcrowded, ignorant, hungry mankind.

Stening had lost all consciousness of time now, and when a man in a repair party yelled from the wardroom flat, "Casualty on the 4-inch gun deck," he did not know whether the action had lasted minutes or hours and didn't care. He detailed four of his men, and they left with a stretcher. He waited perhaps ten minutes, but they didn't return. They never returned. He noticed that boiling water was slopping from the sterilizer, and sizzling down its polished sides, and that one of the men aimlessly combed his fingers through his hair. He had another party ready to go when he heard a shout, "We've been hit forward."

"That doesn't concern us," Stening told his men.

But he thought, What a silly statement! Of course it concerns us—it concerns all of us. This is life or death for these men, for myself.

Then the first torpedo hit and *Perth* seemed to jump.

Hell, he thought, that was something pretty big!

It reminded him of the time in the Mediterranean when a bomb nearly lifted his destroyer out of the water. He had been sunk that time, by dive-bombing Stukas, in the Australian destroyer *Waterhen* along the "Spud Run" to Tobruk. He had no wish to be sunk again.

As *Perth* seemed to flop back into the sea and steady, an order came over the loud-speaker. Mixed with the crash of gunfire it sounded like "Prepare to ram," and he shouted, "Everybody lie down." The men dropped and lay there, but nothing happened, and slowly they got up and watched him—sheeplike, patient, but tense. He looked at their eyes. He could tell now they knew they would soon all have to swim. Calmly he thought, Soon I'll be in the sea.

Less than a minute after action stations, Frank Gillan had climbed into his overalls, put his torch in his pocket, and pulled on his Mae West and only partly inflated it. He was not to know until later that this last decision probably saved his life.

He left his cabin and ran forward along the alleyway, and as he ran sailors slammed the watertight doors behind him and locked the dogs. He reached the airlock above "B" boiler room, closed the steel door, and then went

182

through and down the feet-polished ladders into the stoke-hold, twenty feet below the waterline. Here he was in a familiar world—so familiar that when Gillan dreams he always dreams of engine rooms—of boiler fires and steam and pumping pistons and the whine of turbines. The air stank of hot steel and oil and cordite sucked in by the turbo fans which thundered above like aero engines. The glare from the fires was terra cotta on naked chests of men in front of oil burners, and red on their cheeks as, with heads swung sideways, they watched the hand signals of Chief Stoker Reece. Above, among the tubes and ladders and wire and gauges, the white insulated steam pipes, as thick as a man's body, were like enormous copulating grubs.

"Pretty sudden, wasn't it?" Gillan yelled at Tuersley as he reached the bottom of the ladders. The warrant officer grinned.

Gillan went to the stocky chief stoker and stood beside him. Reece, his backside propped against the electric oil fuel pump, was watching the pressure gauges, and close to him were the discharge valves like rows of organ stops.

The racket now made even bellowed speech almost inaudible. The fans were pumping in the crash of gunfire, and the noise seemed to come in solid and fall on top of them. The ship was twitching like a man in an epileptic fit. The water in the long gauges above the boilers was bouncing and the water levels in the gauges reflected the light of naked bulbs like diamond facets. Every time the 6-inch fired the huge boilers, generating 20,000 horsepower, jumped up and back as though a giant fist had slugged them. They jumped, Gillan noticed, when the guns actually recoiled, not when they fired, and he could tell which way the guns were firing by the way the boilers shifted. Steam pipes, too, were vibrating and jumping as though they were alive, and from them little pieces of asbestos packing were floating down like gentle snow.

"How on earth did I get myself here?" he asked. "God knows what's going to happen."

And instantly he realized he was talking to himself—aloud.

He yelled in the chief stoker's ear, "I say, chief, it's time we had a cup of khai."

Reece just heard him because he yelled back, "I had mine before I came down, but I'll get some organized."

He signaled to a big redheaded stoker and pointed to his mouth. The stoker grinned, made the cocoa and brought Gillan a cup.

The heat, despite the gale from the fans, was getting worse. It seemed to press inward on Gillan's eyes and ears, and to press down on his cap. He was used to it—heat was part of his life—but he saw one of the stokers, a first-trip man, stagger and recover and reach for the salt tray and drop a pinch into his mouth.

Now Gillan lost all sense of time. His only concern was steam and more steam for the engines. Time became oil and burners and the thundering pulse of steam. Then the fans sucked in a terrific explosion he knew wasn't a gun or a shell. He and Tuersley and the others jerked into the air like puppets, and as they landed the plates slammed against their heels and jarred their spines and teeth. To Gillan it felt like driving a draft horse in a springless cart over a 12-inch log at a hand gallop. He knew a torpedo had got them, knew, but only later, it had hit between the forward boiler room and engine room, and in that engine room the officers he had dined with only a few hours before and all the others with them had died instantly. Three men, too, he also learned later, had been standing on a grating above the engine room when the Jap fish hit. Instantaneously the grating went red under their feet, melted in seconds, and they fell in and died in seconds. The sea followed the torpedo and boiled and thrashed among the red-hot ruin. The men there died without knowing what had hit them.

But the only damage in Gillan's boiler room was a broken water gauge. As water sprayed and sizzled down the boiler, he jumped to the turning handles and shut off the cocks sending water into the gauge. Tuersley signaled to one of the artificers, who shinned up the ladders and started fitting a new glass to the gauge.

But Gillan noticed now that the ship had lost life. One

184

moment she was almost human—swinging, bounding, swaying. The next she was sluggish and listing slightly to starboard. Then she straightened, but slowly, almost reluctantly. She seemed tired, listless. He looked at the sides of the boiler room and said, "If a fish comes in there it's finish." And once again he realized he was talking aloud.

Then one of the turbo fans cut out; but Tuersley, who had all the answers, knew what to do. He had been in the Mediterranean, and was no stranger to breakdowns of this kind. He climbed, hand over hand, without once using his feet, grabbing pipes and handrails until he reached the top of the boiler room where he fiddled with the fan until it came in again with a pulsating whine. Then he slid down and glanced at Gillan as much as to say, "Easy, wasn't it?"

After another big explosion, the ship listed and seemed to go down a little by the head. Then she leveled out, lost way, and rolled to port. She was still steaming, but Gillan felt the plates under him moving like a ship in a rough sea. Then came another explosion, and the boilers began to scream and blow off at their safety valves.

Gillan grabbed the phone to the engine room. It was dead. He tried to call damage control. Dead. He called the bridge. Dead. He tried to ring the telegraph to the engine room. The telegraph was jammed. As the ship listed again, Tuersley said calmly, "We'd better shut the boilers down," and Gillan nodded, and Tuersley shut off the oil supply to the burners.

Then Gillan saw that everyone, every man in that stokehold, was looking at him. The ship had a 45-degree list, he noticed, and then he thought, God, she's going! *Perth* was dead now except for the fans which were still whining and the lights which were still on, so that he knew the boiler room diesel generator was still working. The ship rolled again and seemed to slide away from him. He looked round at the men standing there, near naked, waiting, calm, and their quiet courage gave him courage. He signaled upward with both arms. But there was no rush, and he thought, What men to serve with! As they moved up the ladders, he said to Tuersley, "We ought to shut the oil fuel off completely. If we don't she'll catch fire while we're escaping." As they shut everything they could, Gillan saw that the bottom of the stokehold was now empty of stokers. Then he waved Reece and Tuersley on up the ladder.

Please God, not again! Lloyd Burgess thought as the action started. In the dark he fumbled for his shoes, found his tin hat, and stumbled on to the bridge. He was still half asleep and testy as an overtired child, and didn't care if five hundred ships were attacking them. All he wanted was sleep, but every time the guns went off he jumped and his tin hat fell down over his eyes and that woke him up and made him mad.

He could see the dim shapes of the captain standing forward on the bridge, John Harper the navigator, near the binnacle, Peter Hancox the gunnery officer, Johnson the first lieutenant, Willy Gay the officer of the watch, Guy Clarke the torpedo officer, Bert Hatwell the chief yeoman, Allen McDonough the R.A.A.F. flying officer, Frank Tranby-White the paymaster middy. And every time the guns flashed the men on the bridge were deep-etched against the violent light as though in a brilliantly clear photograph.

Between the gun bursts he heard Waller's voice, "Starboard twenty," the ship swung; "Midships," the ship steadied; "Port fifteen," the ship swung; "Midships," the ship steadied. On and on it went like a monotonous chant in a jungle of light and dark. He heard Waller call, "What about those targets on the port bow?" and the navigator's quick reply, "They're islands, sir."

The only light on the bridge was the almost hidden glow under the hooded chart table. Burgess tried to take notes of the action, writing in the dark by feel, forming his words as a child forms them, large and crude. Then the gunfire rattled the chart table to pieces. He propped the pieces up, fixed the hood, and carefully edged his head and shoulders under to check his notes. Then the table collapsed again and he backed out from under the ruin and left it there.

A searchlight got them and Waller called, "For God's sake shoot that bloody light out!"

186

Behind and below Burgess heard the 4-inch barking. The light blacked out.

In a silence that lasted only seconds, Burgess felt his heart hammering and all sound was within himself, so that he could almost hear the blood pumping through his body. Then the deck heaved as the first torpedo got them.

"Forward engine room out . . . speed reduced," came the report.

"Very good," Waller said.

Aft, a shell wrecked the plane and catapult with a crash like two trains meeting head on.

Then "B," "X" and "Y" turrets reported to the gunnery officer that they were out of shells and were firing practice bricks with extra cordite.

Then "A" turret reported five shells left.

Then the 4-inch reported they were firing star shells— and the last of those.

Hancox told the captain.

"Very good," he said.

The second torpedo seemed to hit right under the bridge —and among other things it jammed the hatch in "B" turret magazine, and the men there went down alive. The ship seemed to leap from the sea, straight up, and drop back. Those on the bridge went up with her and came down on their knees. When Burgess fell, he was facing aft, looking up at the director tower, and he wondered if it would fall on him. Then with a noise like escaping steam, water and oil fell on the bridge and knocked some of the men over.

"Hell," Waller said, "that's torn it! . . . Abandon ship."

"Prepare to abandon ship, sir?" Hancox queried.

"No—abandon ship."

The fateful signal went over the intercom—for those who could hear it.

"A" turret fired again—her defiant last—and Burgess' tin hat again fell over his eyes. When he pushed it back the bridge was empty, except for Waller, Gay and himself. The captain was standing far forward blowing into his Mae West.

187

As Burgess went down the ladder he heard Waller say, "Get off the bridge, Gay," and as Gay left Waller was standing with his arms on the front of the bridge looking down at the silent turrets.

Sunday: 12:07 A.M.

As Burgess went down the bridge ladder shells were fluff-fluffing over and Japanese searchlights were opening up like a summer carnival. He had one objective now, and only one: escape.

He yelled, "Abandon ship!" as he went across the flag deck. There were bodies among the shadows, and the darker shadows were shell gashes and blood. He crawled under the wreckage of the catapult and reached his abandon-ship station, a Carley float on the portside, and as he got there a shell hit an ammunition locker and hot metal whined and cried above him like kittens in a basket, and he dragged his tin hat down over his ears.

Three men were already at the Carley. One of them, John Harriss, an A.B., was grinning.

"Did you hear of Chips King?" he said. "He was lugging a four-inch star shell when we got abandon ship. He jumped overboard with the shell in his arms."

Burgess wasn't amused—not then. He wanted to get off, and as soon as possible. They tried to move the float, but it was too heavy. Then, as *Perth* listed, they were able to slide it down the deck and into the sea and jump after it and pull themselves aboard.

The first thing Burgess did when he was free of the ship was to go through his pockets. He threw away a sodden packet of cigarettes, tore up his notebook with the notes of the action in it, and took off his shoes and tossed them into the sea. Then he looked up, as the dying cruiser moved past them and away, and thought, Thank God, I'm clear of that!

"No—abandon ship."

The captain's voice, clear and hard, came down the

speaking tube to the plot. The men there looked at the deck-head, and then at Lyons.

"Shoot through," he said to Clohesy, who was still eating biscuits.

He shook hands with him, and with Lasslett and Griffiths, and with Tony Spriggins, the P.O. telegrapher, who was standing in the door of the plot. He followed them out, but remembered his code books and went back and heard voices on the bridge, including the captain's, but couldn't hear what was being said. He had just grabbed the code book when a shell hit the bridge, ripped the side off the plot with the clatter of a foundry at full blast as it burst upward, and flung him against his table. Then the lights went out and he thought, This is a bloody silly place for a schoolmaster to be in.

For a moment he panicked and rushed for where he knew the door must be. Then he recovered, groped back to the speaking tube and yelled, "Plot stopped." There was no answer—no voices now. He called again, "Bridge, this is the plot." Then as the ship sagged to port, he felt his way out to the flag deck where he slipped and fell to his hands and knees. He fumbled for his torch and turned it on. There were broken bodies all round him, and blood under him, and sticky on his hands, and one of the dead smiled, and another had no face. There was a pile of bodies, stacked up by blast, in an alleyway. He swung the torch. There was a body beside him, without head, legs or arms. He looked at it and wanted to be sick. He got to his feet, jumped to the ship's side, grabbed a paravane rope, swung out and dropped, and as he came to the surface through thick oil someone was calling plaintively for help and purple tracers were going over low—*zip, zip, zip*— and a sailor swam up to him and said, "Did you get any souvenirs, mate?" and before Lyons could answer lifted from the water a heavy pair of binoculars slung round his neck and added, "These bastards'll make a good hock when I get back to Sydney." Lyons was so amazed he opened his mouth and took in fuel oil, and the oil made him vomit. After that he kept his mouth shut.

He swam slowly toward voices on the water and reached *Perth*'s cutter and crawled with other men over the side. But she was jagged with shell holes and filled and sank, and a sailor panicked. He kept going up and down, up and down, screaming and gurgling until he drowned. Then a packet of Jap shells landed perhaps one hundred yards away. The concussion slammed against Lyons, and a spurt of water, as though from a pressure pump, rushed into his bowels and out again. He was sick, and someone called, "It smashed my guts," and Lyons thought, This is bloody awful. It's Saturday night—our only night free from the kids. I should be dancing with my wife.

He was on his own now, but he knew he would not die. Then he saw two men clinging to a 44-gallon drum, and as he swam up to them one said, "I'm leaving," and the other groaned, "Oh, God," and disappeared. Hanging to the drum, slippery with oil, Lyons looked about him and saw the last of *Perth*. She was over on her portside sliding down by the bows. Her screws were high in the air, naked and almost indecent above the sea, and one was still turning as though it was tired. Then she disappeared. He didn't know then, but Burgess on his float also saw the ship go and looked at his watch—the watch he had paid £5 15s. for. It was still going, and the time in the glare of searchlights was 12:25 a.m.

Lyons heard a man call, so he swam away from the drum toward him and met Yeoman of Signals Percy Stokan, who asked cheerfully, "Having any trouble?"

"Plenty," Lyons said. "The ship's sunk, I've lost thirty thousand cigarettes, my neck's stiff, and this bloody Mae is worrying me."

"Okay, okay, I'll hang onto you while you get your clothes off."

As Lyons pulled off his uniform and his shoes a sailor swam up and said, "You blokes got a knife?"

"Hell—what for?" Lyons asked.

"What for?" the sailor said. "There's a team of floggin' Japs in the water over there and I've got a few floggin' bills to pay with the floggin' little Shinto bastards."

190

Woods climbed down from the lower bridge and helped cut a Carley float adrift and get it into the sea on the portside. But an inner voice warned him, Don't get into it—keep away from it. He noticed that the others too seemed reluctant to leave the ship. Not a man moved, and as the float drifted away one said, "What if the old girl is afloat in the morning?" and another snapped, "Don't be a bloody fool—she's almost under now." But, still, not one of the eight men there could leave the ship, and they watched the float drift astern and disappear.

This momentary mood of indecision died as a shell hit the 4-inch-gun deck and showered sparks like an oxy-welding torch and crying lumps of metal. Woods saw a raft in the water and dived over the side, and the others followed. This was one of the pilgrim rafts—copper tanks encased in timber with trailing life lines. Soon many men were on or around it. Mechanically, Woods counted twenty-eight heads.

"Me mate here's hurt," someone called.

Those on board lifted the man from the sea and laid him across the raft. In star-shell light Woods saw that his face was green-tinged and twisted and that his eyes were closed, and he thought, What will we do? And then he got his first sickening, frightening taste of fuel oil—something every survivor will remember for the rest of his life—and for the first time he was afraid, afraid of fear, afraid of the water, afraid of dying, afraid.

Another star shell burst, and as he watched its slow sinking, brilliant yet soft way above, he remembered a book he had read before the war which described how oil fuel on the water caught fire, and how the fire swept through the lifeboats and how . . .

His guts heaved and he vomited over the man beside him in the sea.

Even when Smith knew *Perth* was sinking he was still a product of his long naval training. The average man thought instinctively of himself. But Smith thought, What needs doing before I go over the side? He went aft to the

191

depth charges, pulled the primers out, put the keys in and made them safe. He felt glad now because he knew that if he had not done this the charges, which were set for different depths, could have exploded as *Perth* was going to the bottom and killed every man in the water. Generally, depth charges are not at the ready at night, but Captain Waller had ordered them to be kept ready. Smith had wondered why at the time.

Then he remembered the radio direction finder, near the torpedo space, which he had orders to destroy in an emergency. He found a hammer among the torpedo tools and beat the R.D.F. apparatus into scrap.

Then, for the first time, he thought of Len Smith. *Perth* was well down by the bows as he walked to the stern and sat on the rail. Will I keep my boots on? he asked himself as he listened to the propellers still churning, and the answer was, Keep them on. There's coral along this coast and you'll need them, and your knife. He never had a doubt that he would live to remember Sunda.

As *Perth*'s stern lifted higher; he said aloud, "You'd better go now, Lennie boy." He saw a Carley float and dropped almost onto it and climbed aboard where John Deegan, an A.B., and Davis, his torpedo gunner's mate, welcomed him.

They picked up twenty others as they drifted closer to the Java coast—so close that when they saw Japanese landing craft, in the light of a searchlight, going in to invade, Smith warned, "We'd better get out of this, boys, or we'll be in trouble."

They started to paddle away from the land, but the float kept turning—turning in crazy circles—like a dodgem car at a fun fair.

Davis was terrified only once during the action—right at the end when he saw his shipmates going over the side and remembered he could not swim. He was wearing his Mae West, but was afraid it would not hold him up. Frantically, he searched for a lifebuoy, but could not find one, and then, with surprised discovery, he said to himself, Don't be a fool. You can't swim more than a few yards,

192

but you can float longer than the best swimmer can swim. You've often done it in the baths at home. He remembered the test at Garden Island, Sydney, years before when he had to swim fifty yards fully dressed, but without his boots, then float for three minutes. He had only just been able to dog-paddle the distance and then, exhausted, had turned on his back, put his arms at his sides, and floated—and gone to sleep. He had still been floating, still asleep, when the instructor discovered him a long time later and yelled, "Get to hell out of that water, you flaming seal." Remembering this he climbed the rail near the quarter-deck on the portside and tensed himself to jump.

His next memory was of lying two feet from the opposite rail on the high starboard side covered in belts of pom-pom ammunition and strips of twisted metal.

Good God, he thought, another torpedo must have got me!

In those moments he knew exactly what to do, but they were his only lucid moments for days. He pushed the belts and wreckage aside and tried to rise, but his right leg was useless. Cautiously, he felt the leg from the thigh down, and his fingers and a stab of pain told him it was smashed below the knee. The ship lurched then and he said aloud, "You'll have to leave in a hurry." He dragged himself to the side, dragged himself through the rail and fell into the sea, and saw a paddle waving above him and grabbed it and felt arms grip him.

All that night and part of the next day, as the cloud drifts in his mind lifted and closed in, he remembered pain and thought someone was twisting his leg. He didn't know that the sea was slopping against his fracture as he slumped on the side of the raft with his legs in the water.

Campbell's earphones to gunnery control clicked and went dead. He took them off and heard men on the deck below bawling, "Abandon ship!"

"Hell," Findlay said, "I've left my Mae West in my locker!"

"Then you'd better go after it," Campbell advised.

As he climbed down from his gun position he blew

into his own Mae and then, very carefully, and almost reverently, placed his beloved tin hat on the quarter-deck. He didn't drop it or throw it down. He placed it gently on the deck, and then didn't want to leave it. He had worn it in *H.M.A.S. Hobart* during a bombardment of Italian Somaliland, and again in *H.M.A.S. Canberra* off East Africa when they found the two supply ships of the Nazi pocket battleship *Admiral von Scheer*. This hat was the one thing he had always promised himself he would bring home from the war, and now he had to leave it, and he felt like saying good-by to an old friend.

From below came the grinding, tearing sounds of things shifting, sliding as the ship heeled. He went to the stern and looked over and heard the screws and said aloud, "Not for you, old son," and walked back to near "Y" turret where he straddled the rail and peered down. The swim ahead didn't worry him; he had covered two miles in the sea when at school in Melbourne and was confident he could double that distance if he had to. But he had never been able to dive or even jump from a high tower, yet now, as the same horror of height came to him, he thought, It's now or never.

Then he was falling, falling through endless space, and when he was conscious again he was floating and noticed *Houston* way ahead of him still firing, and heard shouts and saw a raft. He started to swim, but felt like a fish with a damaged fin, and knew two things had happened to him. His shoes and socks had been blown off by the torpedo blast that had knocked him overboard. And his leg was broken.

"No, no—please not that," he pleaded.

He reached under water. His left foot flopped in his hand. His throat tightened and he thought he would choke.

"I haven't a chance now," he whispered. "I'll die in the water."

Then he saw Frank Watson, a petty officer, floating near him, and called, "My leg's broken," and Watson called back. "Don't be bloody silly." But when Watson felt the break just above the ankle he said, "Sorry, but hang on. I'll blow more air into your blimp—and then we'll get you onto that raft."

But they were both only just on the raft when a Japanese destroyer passed at speed. Her bow waves were like slices of spongecake. Her wash tipped them off. In the water again, Campbell thought, calmly now, I'll be a handicap to the others. I might as well drown. And then a small voice argued, You've been unlucky so far. Hang on a bit and your luck will change. He swam, trailing his smashed leg, to another raft where Bob Collins, an A.B., asked, "What's wrong?" and Campbell told him. "Okay," Collins said, "let's see if I can help it."

He dived in, collected driftwood, split it with his knife, cut off one leg of Campbell's overalls, tore the material in strips, and splinted the broken leg. When this was done, Campbell looked at his leg and then at Collins and felt like crying. He held out his hand. The A.B. gripped it and said, "We'll get you through."

For the first time Campbell felt that luck was turning his way. But then he saw something which made him chill and weak. Two big shark fins were circling a box not ten yards away. He shivered, groping for memory of words he had once read about the sharks of Sunda Strait, and finding the words and hearing a man on a raft call, "What's that there?"

"Porpoises," Campbell said.

"They look funny to me."

"Sharks," Campbell whispered to Collins who nodded.

"We'd better tell 'em."

"Pull your legs in," Campbell said to the others, "they're sharks."

The men jerked up their legs and nearly upset the raft. Everyone watched, still suspended above a new kind of death in a sort of hideous anesthesia of frozen bodies and terrified eyes. The sharks circled—once, twice. One of the fins disappeared, there was a thrashing swirl, and the box disappeared. Then the pieces came to the surface and floated away—and slowly the other fin sank and was seen no more.

And a voice in the dark said, "If any of youse blokes see me in the Bondi surf after the war youse can kick my arse."

"Outside," Stening ordered his men, and waved his arms upward.

"Where do we go?" a youngster said.

Stening pointed. "There's a hatch right outside, and the quarter-deck hatch is on the next flat."

They ran from the wardroom and climbed the nearest ladder. As they climbed, Stening hurried to his cabin to get a block of chocolate he kept there for an emergency like this, but his cabin was a ruin of crumpled steel and splintered wood. Back in the quarter-deck lobby he saw the dogs of a hatch being turned from below. He jumped to the hatch, loosened the dogs and let three men out and followed them up the ladder, but just before he reached the deck he remembered the torch he was carrying and threw it away as now useless. On deck at last he saw men milling in the moonlight like cattle about to stampede. He climbed the ladder to the 4-inch-gun deck and tried to reach his abandon-ship station forward, but when heaps of wreckage blocked him he returned to the quarter-deck. It was now bare as a washed plate, though he had left it only a minute or two before, and all around him the silence was like sound. Then something inside the ship rolled and crashed. He ran to the stern, blew into his Mae, and was about to vault over when another torpedo struck. The rail reared and smashed his nose. He jerked into the air and fell on his back. Then water poured down and across the deck and washed him overboard. As he broke surface he saw the ship, gigantic it seemed, above him, and thought it was rolling over on him. He yelled and yelled and tried to paddle away. Chief Petty Officer Kiesey heard him, saw a blond head in the water, grabbed the hair and pulled him aboard the copper painter's punt he was on.

Stening, with a fractured skull, a broken nose, and an injured eye and knee, was shocked and silly. He stared wildly at Kiesey and yelled again because he thought the sinking ship was going to crush him. Then he jumped off the punt. Three times he jumped and three times the C.P.O. grabbed him and pulled him from the water. The third time Kiesey pulled him in he had to quieten him with a punch on the chin.

Later, Stening held out a paddle to Bill Davis in the water, and helped pull him onto the punt—but he doesn't remember that. Nor did he know at that time that the three other men on the punt with him were all badly injured. Kiesey's back had been burned by flash. Davis had a broken leg. And Leading Seaman Ben Talbot had a smashed collar-bone, cracked ribs, and other injuries.

In "Y" turret a gunner bellowed, "Abandon ship," and below in the lobby Gosden forgot about the rising water and remembered the five men in the shell room underneath him. He grabbed the phone to the shell room. It was dead. He rang the bell signals to the shell room. He got no reply. He yelled down the hoist to the shell room. There was no answer.

I must let them know, he thought, I must, I must. I can't let them die there like rats.

He waded across the flooding lobby and tried to open the door which led to a passage and the shell-room hatch. The door was jammed. There was nothing more he could do—except look at the water and want to be sick.

His two assistants had already gone up the ladder through the motor room and up again into the turret itself and out to the deck. Now he followed them.

On deck at last a searchlight blinded him. Then it swung away and he remembered his watch and £100 in notes in his locker, but decided they could stay there. He saw Alfie Coyne and with him tossed pilgrim rafts overboard, as though they were empty fruit cases, and recalled that at Tanjong four men had been needed to carry each of these heavy rafts aboard.

And then a torpedo hit. He went up, up, up—so high that he was above the top of "Y" turret. He felt extraordinarily light, and almost gay, in that mad moment. He wanted to sing and dance on the air. Then, as he fell, the torpedo wave swept across the deck and tumbled him over and over into the sea.

He went down, down. He opened his eyes against pressing blackness, like a hood over his head, but through the blackness he could see his mother crying as she opened a

197

telegram reporting his death in action. He could see the typed words on the telegram. He felt he could touch his mother's face. Then he shot to the surface and shook the water from his eyes and saw *Perth*'s stern, clear and high, against the moon.

Near him a man called, "Help, I can't swim," but Gosden lay back in the water and laughed as the sailor swam toward him and passed him doing the finest crawl stroke he had ever seen.

If he can't swim, Gosden thought, then I'm done for.

He felt carefree now. He began to swim, but he was heavy and sluggish and realized he still had his boots on. He trod water and argued with himself. Would he get rid of them? Then he thought of the walking he would have to do when he got ashore, and decided to keep them. He began swimming again and found a Carley and got on board with Lieutenant-Commander Clarke and the R.A.A.F. corporal, Bradshaw. Later they picked up a man whose right leg was gone at the thigh. He was unconscious as they laid him across the float, and he died in twenty minutes. Then, as the float became more and more crowded, and as space was needed for the living, they slipped the body back into the warm sea.

In perhaps an hour a Japanese destroyer came alongside and tossed them ropes.

"Come aboard," a Jap shouted in English.

But Gosden and the others pushed the float away from the destroyer, and one of the boys yelled, "You know where to stick it, mug—we'd rather drown."

"So," the Jap yelled back. "You say Nippon no bloody good. You wait till tomorrow."

The destroyer went away. Later Gosden felt someone grabbing at his legs and trying to get onto the float. He looked down and saw a Japanese soldier. He was so surprised he nearly fell off the float. The soldier, as far as he could see, was wearing full equipment. He even had his rifle slung around him. Then Gosden saw other Jap soldiers in the water, their rifle barrels like periscopes. Some of the soldiers were swimming, some were floating, already drowned.

The Jap beside the float looked up and spoke. Gosden

didn't understand—and didn't care. Japs and pity did not go together. He put his boots on the flat face and pushed. The Jap clutched his boots, but Gosden jerked free and kicked at the face again and again. Around him now others on the float kicked out and splashed every time a Jap soldier tried to approach. At every kick a soldier snarled, "You killed my mate, you bastards, you killed my mate." Soon the Japs kept away or the current took them away. Soon the sea around the drifting float was empty except for the untidy bundles that were the drowned.

As Owen dived overboard he realized he had forgotten to inflate his Mae. He trod water and bent his head and tried to blow into the valve, but every time he tried he went under. In disgust, he pulled off his blimp, and then his shirt and shorts, and let them float away. Then he emptied his bowels—an act which pleased him—and for the first time was conscious of the water, warm and silky and soothing against his body, and black as the inside of a cupboard.

He began to move away from the slow-moving *Perth*, and ahead could see a long low line of fire that he knew was *Houston* burning, and from the fire leaped sparks that were guns still in action. He wanted to call for help, but could not make a sound. The small inner voice of pride prevented him. It said, Stand on your own feet, and then he smiled and thought, What a ridiculous idea with fifty fathoms of water under me! But later—much later—he heard movement near him and asked, almost apologetically, "Is anyone there?" and someone called, "Swim over here, mate." He joined three men holding to small pieces of driftwood, and hung on with them while he got his wind. Then a wavelet slapped against his face and he took in a mouthful. It was hot and salty and thick and he knew immediately it was blood. He spat. "Who's wounded?"

The man beside him spoke slowly and thickly. "Is that you, Polo?"

He knew it was Lieutenant McWilliam, and said, "Are you hurt, David?"

McWilliam didn't speak for some minutes. Then he said, "I don't think I'll live much longer, Polo."

"You'll be all right, David," Owen said, but he knew the words were meaningless. "Hang on, old boy."

Later, as they drifted among some Carleys, Owen got a mouthful of oil and began to vomit, and when the sickness eased he called to one of the floats and asked if they would take McWilliam aboard.

"Go to hell," a sailor said. "We're full."

But someone on another float called, "Sure, bring him over here. We'll make room for him."

They lifted McWilliam aboard, and Owen, before he pushed off, called, "Cheerio, David, you'll be all right now."

Soon he and Tyrell, a P.O., found a wood and metal recreation seat, which had been on *Perth*'s deck, and they hung to it. It floated with the metal back down, but held them up.

"What do you reckon our chances are?" Tyrell asked.

"We'll be all right—once we hit the beach."

Men on a raft were singing now, and farther off one man was singing "Matilda," and Owen could see the profile of Java against the sky. He felt happy—strangely happy and confident. He locked his arms across the recreation seat and felt the warm sea caressing his naked body, and a gentle peace, as soft as a woman's body, enfolding him.

He slept.

"God, you know what's going to happen, I don't." Gillan prayed as he followed Reece and Tuersley up the stokehold ladders. The ladders were almost horizontal now, and he realized, with surprise mixed with a still sort of horror, that the ship was nearly on her side.

A stoker lost his grip and fell past Reece and Tuersley, but Gillan managed to grab the man's overalls and steady him till he could start climbing again. Then the fans stopped and the only sound Gillan heard was a silent singing sound deep in his ears, and the only thing he felt was the ship sliding away beneath his feet.

When the four men reached the air lock at the entrance to the stokehold, Gillan saw that they were standing on one wall of this pressure room, and that the steel door had now become the roof. The stoker was trying to open it.

200

"It won't move," he yelled.

"Let's all push," Gillan said.

They heaved at the thick steel door and it began to move —up, up, until it fell aside with a crash and they pulled themselves up and through into the alleyway. Gillan now saw that the true floor of the alley had become a wall, and that they were standing on the opposite wall which had become the floor, so that the overhead lights were now burning beside them instead of above them. They all knew there was a manhole farther aft, which led into the enclosed torpedo space below the 4-inch-gun deck. They hurried along the alley, and ahead saw the other stokers climbing through. And then they stopped and looked blankly at one another.

"Hell!" Reece said in alarm.

With the ship on her side, an across-ship alleyway had now become a deep well five feet wide between them and the escape manhole.

"We'll have to jump across," Gillan said.

The lights flickered, but stayed on.

The stoker he had saved in the stokehold was first. The man jumped, but his boots slipped as he was taking off and he fell screaming into the well. The other three looked down into the awful blackness and yelled. There was no answer.

"Oh, God," Reece said.

Reece and Tuersley jumped and ran forward. As Gillan followed he saw water start coming through the manhole, and saw Reece and Tuersley get through, and then water came through the manhole in a spout like a thick green tube.

The lights went out.

For a split second Gillan could not move. Terror anchored him. Then, with the picture of the spouting manhole still before his eyes in a blackness, he dashed those last few yards, took a deep breath, and forced himself against the water and through the manhole.

Most other men would have panicked and drowned inside that ship which was at that moment nearly under water. But Gillan kept his head. In those few seconds after he had pushed through the manhole he reasoned this way: He knew that *Perth* had now turned almost turtle, and that he was not only inside her and under water, but virtually underneath her; he knew also that she must have been badly battered, that there would be wreckage about everywhere, and that if he struggled or tried to force himself anywhere he would get caught in ropes and twisted steel and drown; he knew the ship was sliding to the bottom bow first, that this forward movement would be displacing water, and that the displaced water would be flowing backward. He decided in those seconds, or split seconds, of trapped under-water reasoning, that he had one chance, and only one, of living—to float free and unresisting and to let the water itself wash him out of the ship.

He tucked himself into a ball, his knees and chin almost meeting, and let the backward-moving water roll him over and over inside that sinking ship; and as he rolled he thought, Thank God my Mae isn't fully inflated! I'd be up against the roof if it was and would never get out. He brushed against ropes, bumped into wreckage, but rolled on.

At last he hit the ship's rail and knew he was out of the enclosed torpedo space and on the submerged deck. And then he nearly drowned. The cord of the miner's lamp he was wearing on his cap became tangled in the rail wires and floating ropes. But instead of panicking, he pulled off his cap, which the water had not dislodged, broke the cord which led to a battery in his hip pocket, pulled out the battery and dropped it, and wriggled through the rails.

There the current grabbed him, as though it had hands, turned him over and over, pushed him upward, and then pushed him downward. As he went down he thought, This is like being on the big dipper at Luna Park. Then he was in a whirlpool, because he spun like a propeller, sometimes head down, sometimes feet down, and his heart was hammering and his ears were hammering and he saw scarlet, green and purple lights flicking on and off.

Suddenly the hammering ceased and everything was still. He was still within himself, and around him was stillness, and everything was stillness, and he felt peaceful and happy and never wanted to move again. And yet at that moment he thought, If I don't struggle now I'll drown.

He began to fight his way upward, to claw his way upward, like trying to climb a ladder made of treacle. He dog-

202

paddled upward, clutching and snatching and pulling down at the water, fighting to get away from this under-water world of incredible peace and quiet he had got into where the stillness was like a charm, soft, beautiful and insidious, and where he wanted to lie back and rest and rest and rest forever.

And then, with a rush like falling upward, he catapulted up and broke surface through two inches of oil and saw a biscuit tin and grabbed it with both arms And as he hung there on the surface of the water, gulping air, he saw, thirty yards away, the tip of one of *Perth*'s propeller blades sinking into the sea.

A long 18-inch plank bumped into him, and he crawled onto it and sat on it, and past him floated a white solar topee, bobbing up and down, up and down, as though someone was walking jauntily underneath it. He thought, The sun's going to be hot tomorrow—I'll need you. So he grabbed the topee and put it on his oil-covered head, and it fitted.

Then he looked up at the stars, the brilliant clusters of stars, and spoke to them aloud.

"I'm the last man out of that ship alive," he said. "God, I thank you."

Shangri-La and Coral Sea

The *Perth* was sunk just after midnight. The heavy cruiser *Houston* continued to fight, but there was too much fire power concentrated on her. She went down, less than an hour after the *Perth*, carrying almost 700 Americans with her; 368 survivors were destined to spend the rest of the war in Jap prison camps.

The Japs struck next at Ceylon via a carrier raid, sinking two British heavy cruisers, the aircraft carrier *Hermes*, and a number of merchant ships.

On January 23, 1942, the Japanese had occupied Rabaul on New Britain, using its fine harbor as a jumping-off point for the invasion of New Guinea; on March 8th, they occupied the strategic villages of Lae and Salamaua, on New Guinea's northern coast. They were getting uncomfortably close to Australia.

So far, their conquests had been gained at a remarkably cheap price. From December 7th to May 1st, the main Jap carrier force alone, ranging from Pearl Harbor to Ceylon, had sunk five battleships, one aircraft carrier, two cruisers, and seven destroyers, damaging many other ships; the Japanese themselves lost no ship larger than a destroyer.*

The Japanese took no time out to consolidate their gains. Their strategy now called for an invasion force to sail around the eastern end of New Guinea, and take Port Moresby on the southern coast. If they succeeded, the western approach to the Coral Sea would be secured. Simultaneously, Tulagi Island in the Solomons was to be occupied, protecting the flank of the Port Moresby invasion. The ultimate aim of Japanese strategy was to bring the U.S. Pacific Fleet to decisive battle and annihilate it.

Before the Coral Sea action could take place, however, Doolittle's sixteen B-25 bombers struck Tokyo and three other cities on the Japanese mainland. The plan for the raid, conceived in January 1942 by Adm. King's staff as a much-needed shot in the arm for American mor-

* S. E. Morison, *The Rising Sun in the Pacific,* pp. 385, 386.

204

ale, was completely daring; close calculations were needed for the launching of the army's land-based B-25's from carriers (planes of this size had never taken off from a carrier); there was need for secrecy, too. The two carriers, *Enterprise* and *Hornet,* and their escort were to penetrate Japanese-controlled waters to within 500 miles of Tokyo, where they would be extremely vulnerable to bombers. On April 18th, the raiding force was spotted by Jap patrol boats while still more than 600 miles from Tokyo; their discovery meant the carriers must turn and run. The B-25's were launched; from this distance there was great risk they wouldn't make the China coast, their destination after dropping their bombs.

Ironically, Tokyo had just completed a trial air raid at noon on April 18th, when the first B-25's arrived overhead. While little important damage was done, the raid revived the spirit of the Allied peoples. Not a plane was lost over Japan; one landed at Vladivostok, U.S.S.R., and the rest made it to China; four crash-landed there, eleven had to be abandoned by crews forced to bail out.

This raid was the first offensive punch thrown by the U.S. The first defensive success was to come in the Battle of the Coral Sea, which was the first naval action in history fought almost entirely between aircraft carriers.

The Allied Command had prior notice from intelligence sources of the Coral Sea invasion, and guessed correctly that the main strike would be aimed at Port Moresby. On May 3rd the Japanese staged successful landings on Tulagi, but were bombed and strafed the next day by planes from the carrier *U.S.S. Yorktown.* The *Yorktown* then rendezvoused with the carrier *Lexington,* and a course was fixed for a surprise attack on the Jap invasion forces now rounding the end of New Guinea. On May 7th, a destroyer and an oiler, separated from the main U.S. forces, were destroyed by Jap carrier planes; the same day planes from the *Lexington* and *Yorktown* caught the Jap light carrier *Shoho,* and sank her.

The next day, May 8th, planes from the two big Jap carriers, *Shokaku* and *Zuikaku,* traded air attacks with the two U.S. carriers. *Shokaku* was severely damaged and *Zuikaku* lost a number of first-line fighting planes and pilots.

The *Lexington* sustained several bomb and torpedo hits. Damage seemed to have been brought under control, and it was not until some time later that fires and explosions broke out; a motor generator had been left running, igniting gasoline vapors released by an earlier torpedo hit. The condition of the ship worsened until, in the evening, the *Lexington* had to be abandoned; she was then torpedoed by one of her own escorting destroyers.

No clear-cut victory could be claimed by either side. But the U.S. had forced the Japanese to turn back their invasion forces from Port Moresby; and two of the big Jap carriers were damaged so badly they wouldn't be on hand for the battle of Midway—where they just might have turned the tide. Morison, the naval historian, says: "The Coral Sea battle was an indispensable preliminary to the great victory of Midway."

The enemy's naval commanders stuck to their grand strategy—to occupy Midway and build up an outer perimeter for the new Japanese Empire, stretching from the Aleutians to the Solomons. They intended to land on the Aleutians just before their attack on Midway to draw part of the U.S. Navy north. If they could then take Midway itself, they would hold in their hands the jumping-off point for an attack on Hawaii.

THE BATTLE OF MIDWAY

by J. Bryan, III

The Battle of Midway was one of the most furious in all history. Even before the last salute to its dead was fired, we and our Allies hailed it as a great American victory. So it was—but how great is only now becoming plain. Documents recently made available show that it was the turning point of the war in the Pacific. They also show how narrowly it missed being a defeat. If a certain Japanese scout had taken a longer look; if a young American cryptanalyst had been less acute; if a dive-bomber pilot from the *Enterprise* had guessed wrong; if the signal for an emergency turn had reached Captain Soji promptly—if any one of such seemingly trivial components had been different, years later the United States might have been struggling to dislodge the Japanese from Hawaii.

Beyond that, Midway is unique. It is the only battle in

which nine tenths of the men engaged never saw the prize for which they fought; the only battle ever waged across the one meridian where a warrior could rest tonight from tomorrow's strife.

These facts are clearly recorded, but others, far more important, are already becoming lost. Confusion is the first weed to grow on a field of combat. Historians have never ceased sifting Agincourt and Malplaquet, Brandywine and Jena, for moldy "whens" and "wheres" and "whys." Hundreds of years from now they will be sifting Midway. Today, most of Midway's veterans are vigorously alive, with memories not yet misty and papers not yet tattered. Many of these men have told me their stories. What I have learned from them I am setting down here, in the hope that it will leave fewer gaps in the chronicle of this prodigious battle, and that it will help preserve some precious fragments of American heroism that otherwise might have slipped into irretrievable oblivion.

Although Midway was fought on June 3-6, 1942, it had been precipitated six weeks before, on April eighteenth. At eight o'clock that morning, Vice Adm. William F. Halsey blinked a signal from his flagship, the carrier *Enterprise,* then 650 miles off Tokyo, to Capt. Marc A. Mitscher, of the carrier *Hornet,* near by. The signal read: LAUNCH PLANES X TO COL DOOLITTLE AND HIS GALLANT COMMAND GOOD LUCK AND GOD BLESS YOU.

As Doolittle had hoped, his raid deceived the Japanese into assuming that he had jumped off from a land base—"Shangri-La," President Roosevelt announced jocosely. Officers of the Imperial General Staff measured their charts. Excepting the sterile and unlikely Aleutians, the American outpost nearest Tokyo was Midway Island, 2,250 miles eastward. Not only must this be Shangri-La, the Japanese concluded, but it was additionally dangerous as "a sentry for Hawaii," 1,140 miles farther. They had long contemplated seizure of "AF," their code name for Midway. The commander in chief of their navy, Adm. Isoruku Yamamoto—a stocky, black-browed man with two fingers missing from his right hand—had only to designate the forces and set the date. This he now did. By the end of April the ships chosen for Plan MI—Midway Island—were being mustered from the fringes of the empire.

Right then, a full month before the first gun was fired, Yamamoto lost the battle—for the same reason that, precisely a year after the Doolittle raid, he would lose his life. Certain ingenious men in the United States Navy had broken Japan's most secret codes, and when Yamamoto flashed Plan MI to his subordinate commanders, these phantoms were eavesdropping at his shoulder.

Their hearing was not quite 20/20. They weren't entirely sure whether D Day would be at the end of May or early in June—nor whether AF was Midway or Oahu. COMINCH, Adm. Ernest J. King, thought Oahu at first, but CINCPAC, Adm. Chester W. Nimitz, thought Midway. He flew out there from Pearl on May second, along the curve of those small, sparse wave breaks with the oddly polyglot names: Nihoa, French Frigate Shoal, Gardner Pinnacles, Lisianski Island, Hermes Reef, and finally Midway.

The lagoon is about six miles across, and the islets, Sand and Eastern, lie just inside the southern reef. Sand Island is about 850 acres; its highest point is thirty-nine feet. Eastern, less than half the size, also has less freeboard. Both are arid, featureless and uninhabited, yet they are far more important than many larger, lusher islands. The name of the atoll tells why—midway across the Pacific, it is strategically invaluable.

Accompanied by Lt. Col. Harold D. Shannon, commanding the 6th Marine Defense Battalion, and Comdr. Cyril T. Simard, commanding the naval air station, Adm. Nimitz inspected both islands. Each had its own galleys, mess hall, laundry, post exchange, power house and dispensary. The chief difference was that all the aviation facilities, except the seaplane hangars, were on Eastern. For a whole hot day Nimitz strode and climbed and crawled through the establishment, peering at firing lanes, kettles, ammunition dumps, repair shops, barbed wire, underground command posts. He said nothing about his secret information, but he asked Shannon what additional equipment was needed to withstand "a large-scale attack." When Shannon told him, Nimitz emphasized the point again: "If I get you all these

208

things you say you need, then can you hold Midway against a major amphibious assault?"

"Yes, sir."

Soon after Nimitz returned to Pearl, he wrote Simard and Shannon a personal letter, addressed to them jointly. He was so pleased with what they had accomplished that he was recommending them for promotion. The Japanese, he continued, were mounting a full-scale offensive against Midway, scheduled for May twenty-eighth. Their forces would be divided thus, and their strategy would be so. He was rushing out every man, gun and plane he could spare. He hoped it would be enough.

By now Nimitz knew for certain that Midway was the objective. A smart young officer, Comdr. Joseph J. Rochefort, in Combat Intelligence's ultrasecret Black Chamber at Pearl, had suggested instructing Midway to send a radio message, uncoded, announcing the breakdown of its distillation plant. Midway complied, and two days later Pearl's cryptanalysts intercepted a Japanese dispatch informing certain high commands that AF was short of fresh water.

Nimitz's letter had a violent impact, but Midway was not dislocated. Although its war had been "cold" so far—begging those few dozen shells—the garrison had stayed taut. Every dawn, patrol planes fanned out westward over a million and a half square miles of ocean. The galleys served only two meals a day. The Marines carried their rifles and helmets everywhere, even to the swimming beaches. At night, everyone went underground, except lookouts. So Simard and Shannon had to make no radical adjustments; they had only to assign priorities to their final efforts, and to absorb their reinforcements as smoothly as possible.

On May twenty-fifth Nimitz wrote them again: D Day had been postponed until June third. The reprieve let them put the last touches on their defenses. Shannon's garrison now numbered, 2,138 Marines. Simard's fliers and service troops numbered 1,494, of whom 1,000 were Navy personnel, 374 were Marines and 120 Army. Midway was a thicket of guns and a brier patch of barbed wire. Surf and shore were sown with mines—antiboat, antitank, antipersonnel. Every position was armed with even Molotov cocktails.

Eleven torpedo boats would circle the reefs and patrol the lagoon, to add their AA to that of the ground forces and to pick up ditched fliers.

A yacht and four converted tuna boats were assigned to the sandspit islands near by, also for rescues. Nineteen submarines guarded the approaches from southwest to north, some at 100 miles, some at 150, the rest at 200.

Defensively, Midway was as tough as a hickory nut. Before a landing force could pick its meat, a bombardment would have to crack it open. That is what worried Simard and Shannon. If enough Japanese ships stood offshore, under a fighter umbrella and out of range of Midway's coast defenses, and began throwing in a mixture of fragmentation and semi-armor-piercing shells, it would take a lot of planes to beat them off. On June third, the first day of enemy contact, Midway had 121—thirty of them patrol planes, slow and vulnerable, almost useless in combat; and thirty-seven others, fighters and dive bombers, dangerously obsolete. Worse, some of their crews were Army, some were Navy and some Marine, and interservice liaison was little more than a wishful phrase.

Midway's fliers would write one of the most heroic chapters in the history of forlorn hopes. Their glory is the glory of the Light Brigade and of Pickett's charge. But if Midway's security had depended on its air arm alone, its ground arm might have had to throw the Molotovs. Nimitz, however, in addition to fortifying the shores of his orphan island, also fortified its seas. Only a few ships were available, but he sent them all—the aircraft carriers *Enterprise* and *Hornet,* with six cruisers and nine destroyers, comprising Task Force 16; and the carrier *Yorktown,* with two cruisers and five destroyers, comprising Task Force 17. Rear Adm. Raymond A. Spruance, commanding TF 16, flew his flag on the *Enterprise.* Rear Adm. Frank Jack Fletcher, the over-all commander, flew his on the *Yorktown.*

The two task forces sortied from Pearl Harbor and rendezvoused on June second at "Point Luck," 350 miles northeast of Midway. A signal searchlight on the *Yorktown* began to blink, and Spruance's flag secretary made an entry in the war diary: "Task Force SIXTEEN [is] directed to

maintain an approximate position ten miles to the southward of Task Force SEVENTEEN . . . within visual signaling distance" [so as not to break radio silence]. Next day he
added, "Plan is for forces to move northward from Midway during darkness, to avoid probable enemy attack
course." Then, "Received report that Dutch Harbor was
attacked this morning."

Yamamoto had chosen Dutch Harbor for the opening
scene of his Plan AL—Aleutians—which was parallel to
Plan MI and had the dual purpose of seizing Aleutian territory and weakening Nimitz's strength by luring part of it
north. Word of the attack was still flashing from command
to command when another flash outshone it. Spruance's flag
secretary logged it thus: "Midway search reports sighting
two cargo vessels bearing 247 [degrees from Midway], distance 470 miles. Fired upon by antiaircraft."

The report was made by Ens. Jewell Reid, who had lifted
his Catalina from the Midway lagoon at 4:15, forty minutes
before sunrise. Chance did not lead him to the enemy in
that waste of water. Nimitz had written Simard, "Balsa's
air force [Balsa was the Navy's code name for Midway]
must be employed to inflict prompt and early damage to
Jap carrier flight decks." Rear Adm. Patrick N. L. Bellinger put it otherwise: "The problem is one of hitting before
we are hit." As Commander Patrol Wings Hawaiian Area,
Bellinger's job was not merely to state the problem but to
find the solution. This is it:

"To deny the enemy surprise, our search must insure discovery of his carriers before they launch their first attack.
Assuming that he will not use more than 27 knots for his
run-in [to the launching point], nor launch from farther out
than 200 miles, Catalinas taking off at dawn and flying 700
miles at 100 knots will guarantee effective coverage. With
normal visibility of twenty-five miles, each Catalina can
scan an eight-degree sector. It is desirable to scan 180 degrees [the western semicircle], so twenty-three planes will
be needed."

Nimitz gave them to him. Not all twenty-three were Catalinas. To share the patrol, the Army sent some Flying Fortresses, Lt. Col. Walter C. Sweeney, Jr., commanding, from

the 431st Bombardment Squadron; eight arrived on May thirtieth and more later. Simard assigned them to the southwest sector—the least likely source of attack—because their crews were comparatively unskilled in recognition of ships, and much depended on clear, accurate reports of the enemy's power. Besides, the heavily armed and armored Fortresses had little to fear from a brush with an overlapping Japanese patrol from Wake.

Meanwhile, one Catalina had met a direr threat than any enemy plane—a weather front, deep and wide, which developed 300 miles to the northwest and hung there, mocking Bellinger's calculations. Such a front would let the enemy creep up to its edge unseen and launch a night attack impossible to intercept. Midway's only comfort was the probability that the weather screening the enemy from observation would also screen the skies from the enemy, preventing accurate navigation and forcing postponement of his attack until dawn allowed him a position-fix.

But even though—if this guess was good—bombs would not fall until 6:00 a.m. or perhaps 6:30, Simard could not risk an earlier attack's catching him with sitting ducks. Accordingly, as soon as the search planes were air-borne, the remaining Catalinas and Fortresses also took off, to cruise at economical speed until the search had vouchsafed the first 400 miles, by which time these heavy planes—including such of the Catalinas as were amphibious—would have consumed enough gas to permit their landing on the cramped, 5,000-foot strip without jettisoning their bombs or burning out their brakes. The smaller planes—fighters, dive bombers and torpedo planes—did not take off, but they were manned and warmed up, ready to go.

The patrol crews' schedule was brutal. Midway had enough food, water and sleeping space for essential personnel only. Since maintenance crews were luxuries, the patrol crews were topping their fifteen-hour searches with hours more of repairing and refueling. Worse, a few days before, a blundering sailor had tripped the demolition charges under the aviation fuel tanks—"They were foolproof," a Marine officer said, "but not sailorproof"—and from then on, all planes had to be refueled by hand from unwieldy fifty-five-gallon drums.

The hard grind was forgotten, however, when Ensign Reid reported, "Two cargo vessels—" and twenty-one minutes later, "Main body bearing 261, distance 700 miles. Six large ships in column." Reid was wrong. This was not Yamamoto's main body; it was only a small part of one task group in his occupation force. His main body had not been sighted yet, nor had his striking force.

The occupation force, approaching from the southwest, consisted of two battleships, one seaplane carrier, six heavy cruisers, two light cruisers, twenty-nine destroyers and four assorted ships, escorting sixteen transports. The invasion troops aboard them were 1,500 marines for Sand Island; 1,000 soldiers for Eastern; fifty marines for little Kure, sixty miles west of Midway; two construction battalions and various small special units. Vice Adm. Nobutake Kondo commanded, from the battleship *Kongo.*

The striking force, hidden by the weather front in the northwest, consisted of two battleships, four carriers, two heavy cruisers, one light cruiser, sixteen destroyers and eight supply ships. Vice Adm. Chuichi Nagumo, who had commanded the striking force at Pearl, commanded again, from the same flagship, the carrier *Akagi.*

The main body, far to the west, consisted of seven battleships, one light carrier, three light cruisers, thirteen destroyers and four supply ships. Yamamoto commanded from the new battleship *Yamato.* She and her sister ship, the *Musashi,* were the most formidable in the world—63,700 tons (our *Iowa*-class battleships are 45,000) and mounting nine 18.11-inch rifles (the *Iowas* mount nine 16-inchers).

Plan MI was an exact plagiarism of Simard's and Shannon's fears. It called for the striking force to crush Midway's defenses with a three-day air attack, the main body to follow up with a big-gun bombardment, and the occupation force to put its troops ashore on beaches where only maggots moved. The Japanese unanimously admit this much, but they disagree on the plan's next provision. Some say there was none, beyond holding on. Others say that Midway

213

and Kure were to have been steppingstones to Pearl Harbor.

All morning, radio reports crackled through Midway's earphones, as search pilots spotted the converging elements of the occupation force. Simard wanted to hit them with the Fortresses, but Nimitz had ordered "early damage to Jap carrier flight decks," and no carriers had been sighted. Then, at eleven o'clock, Ensign Reid sent a correction: there were eleven ships, not six. By now the Fortresses were back and refueled. Simard decided to attack.

Nine Fortresses, Sweeney leading, took off at 12:30, and four hours later sighted a force of "five battleships or heavy cruisers and about forty others." Sweeney broke his flight into three V's and stepped them down at 12,000, 10,000 and 8,000 feet. Extra fuel tanks in their bomb-bays left room for only half a bomb load, four 600-pounders apiece, but the bombardiers thought they hit a heavy cruiser and a transport. The Fortresses had not yet landed when four Catalinas with volunteer crews took off to make—it is still almost inconceivable—a night torpedo attack. Catalinas are not built to lug torpedoes, and their crews are not trained to drop them. Still, three pilots managed to find the enemy force—the one the Fortresses had annoyed that afternoon. They approached from down-moon, to silhouette the ships, and Lt. William L. Richards' torpedo blew a hole in the tanker *Akebono Maru*. The attack would have been no more bizarre if the tanker had torpedoed the Catalina.

The weary crews turned their planes back toward the dawn. They were almost home when Midway radioed them that it was under air attack. . . .

Reveille had sounded at three o'clock as usual, and at 4:15 as usual the dawn search took off—eleven Catalinas, scouting for Nagumo's carriers. As soon as they were clear, the Fortresses—there were now fifteen—flew out to reestablish contact with the occupation force. The planes left behind were motley. Four were Army—Marauders, normally a medium bomber, but here jury-rigged to carry torpedoes. Six more were Navy—Avengers, torpedo planes of a brand-new type. The rest were Marine, belonging to the two squadrons of Marine Air Group 22, Lt. Col. Ira L. Kimes commanding. The fighter squadron, VMF 221, had some stubby little Buffaloes, so slow and vulnerable that they were known as "Flying Coffins," and a few Wildcats, new and tough and fairly fast. The scout bombing squadron, VMSB 241, also was mongrel, with new Dauntlesses and old Vindicators—so old that the Marines called them "Vibrators" and "Wind Indicators."

All had been manned since 3:15. Their crews watched the sun rise, grumbling that battle would be better than this everlasting waiting around. Even then battle was approaching, at 200 miles an hour. For more than half the men it would be the last battle they would ever see.

The Japanese striking force had run from under its sheltering weather front shortly after midnight. Dawn gave Nagumo his position, 200 miles northwest of his target and just astride the International Date Line. At 4:30 he turned his four carriers into the southeasterly breeze and began to launch "Organization No. 5"—thirty-six fighters, Zeros, and seventy-two bombers, Vals.

Midway received its first warning at 5:25, when a Catalina reported "in clear," uncoded, "Unidentified planes sighted on bearing 320, distance 100 miles." The same Catalina reported again at 5:34: "Enemy aircraft carriers sighted 150 miles, 330 degrees." At 5:52, another Catalina corrected and elaborated this sighting: "Two carriers and battleships bearing 320, distance 180, course 135 [toward Midway], speed 25." The fourth report was from the radar station on Sand: "Many planes, 89 miles, 320 degrees."

Midway sounded the alarm, and even as its planes were taking the air, Simard radioed his flight leaders: "Fighters to intercept, dive bombers and torpedo planes to hit the carriers, Fortresses to forget the occupation force and head north—"your primary target is the carriers!" By a few minutes past six every plane was air-borne that could leave the ground, except one noncombat utility plane. Visibility was excellent, the sea calm.

Fighting 221's twenty-five operational planes were organized into five irregular divisions. The squadron's skipper, Maj. Floyd B. Parks, led a group of three divisions, consisting of eight Buffaloes and four Wildcats. The executive officer, Capt. Kirk Armistead, led the other two, of twelve

Buffaloes and one Wildcat. Parks' group made the first contact. They had climbed to 14,000 feet and had left Midway thirty miles astern when one of his pilots called, "Tallyho! Hawks at angels 12 [bombers at 12,000 feet], supported by fighters!" Parks pushed over. The time was 6:16.

The Vals were flying in two V's of V's, one far behind the other with the Zeros below both. Parks' group, then Armistead's, fell on the Vals like sheep-killing dogs, but the Zeros fell on the Marines like wolves, slashing and springing back for another slash. Outnumbered as the Marines were and—they immediately realized—hopelessly outclassed, their only chance of escape was to dive at full throttle for the cover of ground fire. Few reached it. Zeros set ablaze one plane after another, then whirled and machine-gunned two of the pilots in their chutes.

The Vals closed their ragged ranks and pressed on. Midway was waiting. All guns were manned, and radar had tracked the flight steadily since 5:55, when it had been picked up. At 6:22, D Battery reported, "On target, 50,000 yards, 320." And at 6:30, Colonel Shannon ordered, "Open fire when targets are within range." One minute later, every AA battery was firing. The first wave had arrived exactly on the schedule that Shannon and Simard had hypothesized.

These were horizontal bombers, at 10,000 feet. Of the original thirty-six, ground observers now counted only twenty-two. The opening bursts of AA were short, but the next scored direct hits on the leading plane and one other. The rest dropped their 533-pound bombs on Eastern and the northeast shore of Sand and were gone before the two broken planes had crashed to earth. Simard and his operations officer, Comdr. Logan C. Ramsey, were watching the plunge, from the entrance to their underground command post on Sand. When the Vals struck near by, Simard shouted to the gunners, "Damn good shooting, boys!"

A Negro steward's mate ran to the wreck of the leader's plane and heaved his body from the cockpit. Ramsey was searching the pockets when the guns opened up again. He and Simard ducked below.

The second wave was dive bombers, the eighteen—half of them—that Fighting 221 had left. The flight leader

216

dropped his huge 1,770-pounder, followed it down, rolled onto his back, and flew across Eastern at fifty feet, thumbing his nose. The AA crews were too astonished to draw beads, until a storm of bombs woke them to his purpose— to distract their attention. Even so, they shot him down almost regretfully. The other Vals pulled out over the lagoon, into the torpedo boats' fire. When they crashed, they threw up white plumes instead of black. Zeros circled and strafed both islands, then followed the bombers home. Midway's only air attack of the war had lasted seventeen minutes.

The AA gunners had shot down ten Japanese planes and they swore that if their visibility hadn't been cut by smoke from a burning oil tank, they'd have shot down ten more. The Japanese admit only three losses to ground fire, but Admiral Nagumo's report mentions the "vicious" AA.

Lieutenant Tomonaga, commanding the strike, radioed Nagumo at 7:00: "There is need for a second attack," but at 7:07 another report assured him, "Sand Island bombed and great results obtained."

Simard and Shannon had assayed them by then. Casualties were few—ten dead, eighteen wounded; and ground-defense equipment had suffered only slightly—one height finder had been damaged; but many of the less important installations were either flat or sieved or in flames. On Sand, in addition to the oil tank, which burned for two days, the seaplane hangars were afire. The dispensary was a shambles —a section of its roof had been hurled high into the air, and the sight of its red cross spinning would not be forgotten.

The laundry was also gone. When Commander Ramsey reported back to Pearl on June twelfth, still in his uniform of that morning, Nimitz told him, "I understand you're crawling with—er—'eagles,' so maybe you'd like these silver ones," and showed him a dispatch recommending his promotion to captain.

Eastern lost its powerhouse, mess hall, galley and post exchange, but the airstrips, a dump of gasoline drums and all radio and radar facilities were untouched—the Japs presumably intended using them. One freakish bomb had opened the door of the brig. Another—a direct hit on the post exchange—had scattered cigarettes and beer cans like shrapnel. One can plugged a machine gunner in the solar plexus. When his wind came back, he gasped, "I never could take beer on an empty stomach!"

As soon as "all clear" sounded, Colonel Kimes broadcast the order: "Fighters land, refuel by divisions, fifth division first." No one landed. He broadcast again. Still no one landed. He changed the order to "All fighters land and re-service." Ten of the original twenty-five touched down, several blowing their tires on the jagged bomb fragments that littered the runway. Of the pilots, six were wounded. Of the planes, only two were fit for further combat.

Fighting 221 had taken fearful punishment, but how much it had inflicted was uncertain. Since there was no way to reckon the missing pilots' scores, Intelligence accepted only the claims of the ten survivors, as verified by ground observers: forty-three enemy "sures," for thirteen Buffaloes and two Wildcats. The enemy's own preposterous figures are forty-one Marine sures for four Vals and two Zeros.

Even if the Marines had known of this disparity at the time, it is doubtful if they would have roused themselves to argue it. They were too dumfounded by the performance of the Zero. Its speed, climb and maneuverability surpassed anything they had ever seen. One pilot said bitterly, "I saw two Buffaloes trying to fight the Zeros. They looked like they were tied to a string while the Zeros made passes at them."

Fighting 221 would not fight the Zeros again for nine months—its ordeal was suspended until Guadalcanal; but the other squadrons' ordeals were just beginning—the ordeals by fire that too often ended in ordeals by water.

When Simard radioed his flight leaders the bearing and distance of the enemy fleet, his intention was a simultaneous strike by all squadrons—by such a swarm of planes attacking from so many directions and elevations that, although they would neither be co-ordinated nor have fighter cover, the enemy could not protect all his carriers against them. The plan was excellent in theory, disastrous in practice.

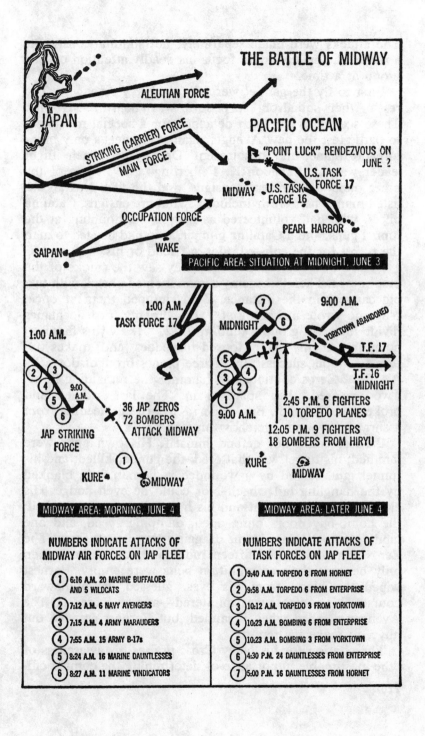

THE BATTLE OF MIDWAY

PACIFIC OCEAN

ALEUTIAN FORCE

JAPAN

STRIKING (CARRIER) FORCE

MAIN FORCE

OCCUPATION FORCE

SAIPAN

WAKE

"POINT LUCK" RENDEZVOUS ON JUNE 2

U.S. TASK FORCE 17

MIDWAY

U.S. TASK FORCE 16

PEARL HARBOR

PACIFIC AREA: SITUATION AT MIDNIGHT, JUNE 3

1:00 A.M.
TASK FORCE 17

1:00 A.M.

9:00 A.M.

JAP STRIKING FORCE

36 JAP ZEROS
72 BOMBERS
ATTACK MIDWAY

KURE

MIDWAY

MIDWAY AREA: MORNING, JUNE 4

NUMBERS INDICATE ATTACKS OF MIDWAY AIR FORCES ON JAP FLEET

1. 6:16 A.M. 20 MARINE BUFFALOES AND 5 WILDCATS
2. 7:12 A.M. 6 NAVY AVENGERS
3. 7:15 A.M. 4 ARMY MARAUDERS
4. 7:55 A.M. 15 ARMY B-17s
5. 8:24 A.M. 16 MARINE DAUNTLESSES
6. 8:27 A.M. 11 MARINE VINDICATORS

9:00 A.M.

MIDNIGHT

YORKTOWN ABANDONED

T.F. 17

T.F. 16
MIDNIGHT

9:00 A.M.

2:45 P.M. 6 FIGHTERS
10 TORPEDO PLANES

12:05 P.M. 9 FIGHTERS
18 BOMBERS FROM HIRYU

KURE

MIDWAY

MIDWAY AREA: LATER JUNE 4

NUMBERS INDICATE ATTACKS OF TASK FORCES ON JAP FLEET

1. 9:40 A.M. TORPEDO 8 FROM HORNET
2. 9:58 A.M. TORPEDO 6 FROM ENTERPRISE
3. 10:12 A.M. TORPEDO 3 FROM YORKTOWN
4. 10:23 A.M. BOMBING 6 FROM ENTERPRISE
5. 10:23 A.M. BOMBING 3 FROM YORKTOWN
6. 4:30 P.M. 24 DAUNTLESSES FROM ENTERPRISE
7. 5:00 P.M. 16 DAUNTLESSES FROM HORNET

The attacks were made separately, not simultaneously. As a result, the enemy could focus his deadly attention on one group at a time.

First to fly the gantlet were the six Navy Avengers. The rest of their squadron, Torpedo 8, was aboard the *Hornet*. These six crews had been detached for a special mission— to battle-test the new Avenger against the fleet's only other torpedo plane, the obsolescent Devastator. Their flight leader was Lt. Langdon K. Feiberling, USN. Four of the other pilots were reserve ensigns, and the fifth was an enlisted man. Their crews included two more ensigns, Catalina pilots, who had volunteered as navigators, doubling at the tunnel guns, and a Catalina gunner, who had begged to man the turret for the enlisted pilot, a friend of his.

Before Midway faded astern, they saw the smoke of the first bombs. Then the enemy screen loomed ahead, with two big carriers in the distance. Zeros jumped them at once. Nagumo wrote in his log at 7:10, "Enemy torpedo planes divide into two groups," and at 7:12, "*Akagi* [his flagship] notes that enemy planes loosed torpedoes [and] makes full turn to evade, successfully. Three planes brought down by AA fire." Zeros continued to hammer the remaining three. Two wavered, then splashed in. The last, riddled and broken, and its pilot, Ens. Albert K. Earnest, bleeding from a shrapnel wound, somehow lurched on.

Earnest could not defend himself. His own guns were jammed; his turret was shattered, the gunner killed; and his tunnel gun, served by a wounded radioman, was blanked by the dangling tail wheel. Nor could he even dodge. His elevator control was cut and his hydraulic system smashed; the bomb-bay doors hung open, damping speed, and one landing wheel hung down, dragging the plane askew. The Zeros chased him for fifteen miles and turned back then only because their ammunition belts were empty. Earnest wiped the blood from his eyes, guessed his homeward course—his compass was splintered—and staggered in. The Avenger crashed when it landed, but Earnest crawled out alive, to make his report.

The citation for his Navy Cross praises his awareness of "the inestimable importance of determining the combat efficiency of a heretofore unproven plane." Admiral Spruance distilled the triumph—and sixteen men's epitaphs—into one crisp statement to Admiral Nimitz: "The new Avenger should be substituted for the Devastator as soon as possible."

Nagumo's respite was brief. He had hardly shaken off the Avengers when he was under torpedo attack again, by the four Marauders of the Army's 69th Medium Bombardment Squadron, Capt. James F. Collins, Jr., commanding. They had been the last to leave Midway, beating the bombs by mere minutes, but their speed had overtaken the Dauntlesses and Vindicators, now trudging astern. Even as Collins sighted the enemy force, a line of Zeros swung toward him. He led his flight straight at them, then ducked toward the water. One pilot yelled, "Boy, if mother could see me now!" A black wall of AA solidified ahead. Two Marauders crashed into it and fell, but Collins and Lt. James P. Muri broke through. Again the *Akagi* was the target. Collins dropped his torpedo at 800 yards; Muri closed to 450 and barely cleared her flight deck on his pull-up. Each thought he had scored, but Nagumo recorded at 7:15, "No hit sustained."

Zeros chased them out to the screen, wrecking Muri's turret and killing his tail gunner. Collins' turret could fire only in jerks, and his tail gun was jammed. Yet their two crews shot down three Zeros, maybe four, and the crippled Marauders—one's landing gear had been shot away, and the other, burning, had more than 500 holes—held together just long enough. When they touched down at Eastern, they were junk.

Meanwhile, Sweeney's fifteen Fortresses, heading westward since before dawn in search of the occupation force, had turned north as soon as they picked up Simard's six-o'clock relay of the position report on the striking force. They sighted it at 7:32, but Sweeney held his bombs. His primary target was the two carriers, and both were hidden by clouds. He began to orbit at 20,000 feet, hoping that they would venture out.

Actually, four of them were down there, all veterans of the attack on Pearl: the *Kaga* ("Increased Joy") and *Akagi*

("Red Castle"), slightly smaller than our big Essexes; and the sisters *Soryu* ("Blue Dragon") and *Hiryu* ("Flying Dragon"), slightly smaller than our light *Independence* class. The *Akagi* and *Hiryu* were unique among the type; their superstructures—"islands"—rose from their port sides.

In twenty minutes Sweeney had his hope. The *Soryu* reported, "Fourteen [sic] enemy twin-engine [sic] planes over us at 30,000 meters [sic]."

Nagumo logged at 7:55: "Enemy bombs *Soryu* (nine or ten bombs). No hits." And a minute later: "Noted that the *Akagi* and *Hiryu* were being subjected to bombings."

The carriers fired a few bursts of AA, then ran back under the clouds, leaving further defense to their CAP— combat air patrol. The Zeros had no stomach for the stalwart Fortresses; their passes were cautiously wide.

Sweeney was surprised: "Hell, I thought this was their varsity!"

As he resumed his watchful orbit, the Marines poured in —Scout Bombing 241's first attack group, sixteen Dauntlesses, Maj. Lofton R. Henderson commanding. Ten of the pilots had not joined the squadron until the week before, and thirteen were totally inexperienced in Dauntlesses, so Henderson decided not to dive-bomb, but to glide-bomb, a shallower, easier maneuver. He was spiraling down from 9,000 feet to his attack point at 4,000 when the Jap fighters caught them. The Marines rearseatmen splashed four, but the Jap pilots and their ships' AA splashed six Dauntlesses, two in flames. One was Henderson's. Seeing him burn, Capt. Elmer C. Glidden, Jr., second in command, moved into the lead. Below him was a cloud bank. He dived for it to lose his pursuit and broke through dead above the *Akagi*. Three fighters had just left her deck. She had gone to battle speed when she first spotted the Dauntlesses, and now she was writhing in her course.

Glidden pushed over and dropped his bomb from 500 feet, with the nine other pilots strung out astern. All managed to get clear of the Japanese force, but on their way home, damage dragged two more planes into the sea, and of those that landed, another two would never fly again. The pilot of one, 1st Lt. Daniel Iverson, Jr., mentioned that his throat microphone had been shot away, and added that his plane had been hit "several times." His rearseatman later counted 259 holes.

Henderson's group reported that their 500-pounders scored two hits and a near miss, and Captain Aoki of the *Akagi* has testified that this is the exact tally of her injuries, which proved fatal. However, there is also evidence that she suffered them in a subsequent attack. The *Akagi* would be a proud memorial, but the men of Scout Bombing 241 do not need her. They have another in the name of Henderson Field on Guadalcanal.

Parks, Feiberling, Henderson: three flight leaders had been killed, and the battle was not yet two hours old.

Meanwhile, the carriers' evasive tactics were intermittently taking them under open sky, so the Fortresses, still at 20,000 feet, began to potshoot. They reported three hits on two carriers, then turned homeward, their bombs exhausted.

That was at 8:24. Three minutes later, Nagumo wrote: "Enemy planes dive on the [battleship] *Haruna*." The Marines were striking again. These were VMSB 241's second attack group, eleven lumbering Vindicators, led by Maj. Benjamin W. Norris. The pilots were as green as Henderson's—nine of them had never flown a "Vibrator" before May twenty-eighth. They approached the enemy force at 13,000 feet and had just sighted it, twenty miles off, when three Zeros, doing graceful vertical rolls, ripped through their formation. One amazed Marine said, "Those Japs put on a good show—very good for us, since more attention to business might easily have wiped out eleven of the slowest and most obsolete planes ever to be used in the war."

The concentrated .30-caliber fire of four rearseatmen knocked one Zero down. More Zeros joined in, and another went down. Norris headed for the clouds at top speed. When he burst out, at 2,000 feet, he expected to find the carriers below. Instead, he was short, and directly above the *Haruna*, zigzagging in the van of the formation near her sister, the *Kirishima*.

Norris now faced a split-second decision. The carriers were his target, but his low altitude would make it suicidal to attempt taking these vulnerable planes—their skin was partly fabric—through the intense AA of the whole force. On the other hand, the *Haruna* not only was close below but might not be alert against attack, as the carriers certainly were. He chose the *Haruna.* The air was so rough with shell blasts that the Marines could hardly hold their planes in a true dive. Geysers rose near the *Haruna,* and one splashed on the *Kirishima*'s fantail, but Nagumo wrote: "No hits."

The Zeros were waiting at the screen. They shot down two Vindicators and shot away another's instruments and elevator control; the pilot limped as far as possible, then ditched in the sea near Kure. The scattered rest made it back as best they could. Even in his harried dive, Norris had radioed them: "Your course is one-four-zero," but there were only four plotting boards among the group, and most of the pilots navigated by thumb until they could home on the black pillar from the burning oil. The last of them touched down at ten o'clock.

They had left Midway neat and taut. Now it was debris. The spring morning stank of ruin. Buildings were a jackstraw pile of charred timbers. The upheaved sand, littered with thousands of dead birds, was still cold under foot. Silence lay on the once-buzzing airstrips. Two thirds of the combat planes were smashed or lost; half the aircrewmen were killed or missing. And the enemy's four deadly carriers were still intact.

Ashore, the situation seemed grave. But afloat, our own carriers had joined the battle.

Dawn on June fourth found the American forces about 220 miles northeast of Midway. A four-knot breeze blew from the southeast. Clouds were low and broken, with visibility twelve miles. Admiral Fletcher's Task Force 17, built around the [carrier] *Yorktown,* was steaming ten miles to the north of Admiral Spruance's Task Force 16, built around the [carriers] *Hornet* and *Enterprise.* Fletcher, the Senior Officer Present Afloat and Officer in Tactical Command, knew that the enemy's occupation force had been sighted west of Midway, but he did not close its position. His target was the striking force, which was expected to approach from the northwest. The *Yorktown*'s scouts had searched that sector on the third; half an hour before sunrise next morning, Fletcher sent them out again. An hour later, at 5:34, he intercepted the first of the reports that the Catalinas were flashing back to Midway, but not until 6:03 did they give him what he wanted: "Two carriers and battleships," with their bearing, distance, course and speed.

His staff laid out the data on a plotting board. The carriers were too far to be reached with an immediate strike. However, if the Japanese commander held his course—and likely he would, to take advantage of the head wind in landing his first attack wave and launching a second—an intercepting course would soon bring him within range. At 6:07 Fletcher ordered Spruance: "Proceed southwesterly and attack enemy carriers when definitely located. I will follow as soon as my planes are recovered."

Spruance headed out at twenty-five knots. The range had closed sufficiently by seven o'clock. His task force swung into the wind, and the first plane roared down the *Enterprise*'s deck. Her Air Group 6 launched fifty-seven in all: ten fighters (Wildcats), thirty-three dive bombers (Dauntlesses), and fourteen torpedo planes (Devastators). Near by the *Hornet*'s AG 8 was launching almost identically: ten Wildcats, thirty-five Dauntlesses and fifteen Devastators. Each group was ordered to attack one of the carriers, now an estimated 155 miles southwest. The launch was completed by 8:06. The task force swung out of the wind and the six squadrons sped away.

But if Fletcher blessed the scout who found Nagumo, Nagumo had one of his own to bless. At 7:28, halfway through Spruance's launch, Nagumo's scout sent back this message: "Sight what appears to be 10 enemy surface ships in position bearing 10 degrees, 240 miles from Midway. Course 150, speed over 20 knots."

Nagumo at once ordered his force, "Prepare to carry out attacks on enemy fleet units!"; then told the scout, "Ascertain ship types and maintain contact."

"Enemy is composed of 5 cruisers and 5 destroyers," the scout replied. Presently he added, "Enemy is accompanied by what appears to be a carrier."

225

By now the *Enterprise* had picked him up on her radar and had sent her combat air patrol to make the kill. He was still there, still transmitting—"Sight two additional enemy cruisers in position bearing 8 degrees, distance 250 miles from Midway. Course 150 degrees, speed 20 knots"—but the CAP pilots could not find him. It made little difference; the damage was already done. A few minutes later he signed off: "I am now homeward bound." The time was 8:34, he had been in the air since five o'clock, and the needles of his fuel gauges were drifting toward "empty."

Major Norris' old Vindicators were swarming over the *Haruna* and *Kirishima* just then, and Nagumo had no leisure until 8:55, when he curtly ordered the scout: "Postpone your homing. Maintain contact with the enemy until arrival of four relief planes. Go on the air with your long-wave transmitter" [to give them a radio bearing].

Nagumo then told his captains, "After completing homing operations [recovering the planes that had struck Midway], proceed northward. We plan to contact and destroy the enemy task force." They had built up speed to thirty knots when, at 9:18, a lookout sighted fifteen American planes, close to the water. They were the *Hornet*'s Torpedo 8, Lt. Comdr. John C. Waldron commanding—the rest of the squadron whose six Avengers had already flown from Midway to enduring glory.

It will never be known how, of the six squadrons launched, Waldron's plodding, 120-knot Devastators were the first by half an hour to find the enemy. It is known only that they did not rendezvous with the rest of the *Hornet*'s strike, as they should have; said a fighter pilot who saw them, "They just lit a shuck for the horizon, all alone."

Although the Japanese carrier force was now far from its predicted position—it had maneuvered radically to dodge Midway's planes, then had turned northeast to attack Spruance—Waldron flew a confident course, straight into its guns. He had lost his own fighters, and Zeros were ahead, astern and around him. The AA was almost thick enough to screen the twisting ships; it gored huge holes in wings and fuselages, cut cable, smashed instruments, killed pilots and gunners. Plane after torn plane—fourteen of them—

226

plunged into the sea, burned briefly and sank. A rearseat-man in another squadron, miles away, overheard Waldron's last words: "Watch those fighters! . . . How'm I doing? . . . Splash! . . . I'd give a million to know who did that! . . . My two wingmen are going in the water. . . ."

The rest of Torpedo 8 is silence, except for the voice of its sole survivor, Ens. George H. Gay. He heard Waldron and he heard his own gunner cry, "They got me!" Then he was hit himself, twice, in the left hand and arm. He squeezed the bullet from his arm and popped it into his mouth. His target was the *Kaga*. He dropped his torpedo and flew down her flank, close to the bridge—"I could see the little Jap captain jumping up and down and raising hell."

A 20-mm. shell exploded on his left rudder pedal, ripping his foot and cutting his controls, and his plane crashed between the *Kaga* and the *Akagi*. He swam back to get his gunner, but strafing Zeros made him dive and dive again; the gunner sank with the plane. A black cushion and a rubber raft floated to the surface. Gay was afraid to inflate the raft; it might draw the Zeros. He put the cushion over his head and hid under it until twilight, peeking out to watch the battle. Tossed by the wash of Japanese warships, wounded, alone, the only man alive of thirty who had been vigorous a few moments before, Gay remembered their training at Norfolk, and how a farmer had complained that their practice runs were souring his cows' milk.

When Winston Churchill was told about Torpedo 8, he wept.

Gay was shot down at about 9:40. At 9:58, Nagumo wrote: "Fourteen enemy planes are heading for us." They were the *Enterprise*'s Torpedo 6, Lt. Comdr. Eugene E. Lindsey commanding. Not only had they, too, lost their fighter cover, but they were attacking an enemy alerted by the previous attack. Before a torpedo pilot can drop with any hope of a hit, he must maintain a steady course and altitude for at least two minutes. A full squadron of Zeros pounced on Torpedo 6 at this vulnerable time. Ten of the Devastators, including Lindsey's, were shot down at once, most with their torpedoes still in the slings. The other four escaped only because the Zeros were called away to meet a new threat, the *Yorktown*'s Torpedo 3.

The principal contact report had mentioned only two enemy carriers, but Intelligence had warned Fletcher that two more would be present. Rather than risk their planes' catching the *Yorktown* with hers on deck, he decided to send about half of them to reinforce the *Hornet*'s and *Enterprises*'s and to hold the rest until the two missing carriers were reported.

The *Yorktown* group—twelve Devastators, seventeen Dauntlesses and six Wildcats—was in the air by 9:30. This once the torpedo planes had the cover they needed so desperately; their fighters clung to them the whole way. Better yet, the *Enterprise*'s fighters, which had become separated from their own torpedo squadron, joined up in support. They sighted the enemy at ten o'clock, but they still had fourteen miles to go when Zeros caught them. The sixteen Wildcats were outnumbered two to one. The fast Zeros splashed three, then sped after the Devastators. By now their commander, Lt. Comdr. Lance E. Massey, had worked his way within a mile of the *Akagi*. As he turned to make his run, a Zero shot him down in flames. Six more of his squadron fell. The remaining five made their drops, then the Zeros shot down another three. The last two escaped.

Of the forty-one torpedo planes which the American carriers had sent into battle, thirty-five had now been lost. Of the eighty-two men who flew them, sixty-nine had been killed, including the three squadron commanders. And of the torpedoes they dropped, not one had scored a hit. Yet these men did not die in vain. The valor that drew the world's admiration also drew the enemy's attention. His dodging carriers could not launch a new strike. And while every gun in his force trained on the torpedo planes, and every Zero in the sky fell on them, our dive bombers— unopposed, almost unnoticed—struck the *Kaga*, the *Akagi* and the *Soryu* their death blows.

The thirty-three Dauntlesses of Scout Bombing 6, led by Lt. Comdr. Clarence Wade McClusky, Jr., commanding the *Enterprise*'s air group, had climbed up the estimated bearing of the enemy force until they should have been on top of it. McClusky cocked his wing and looked down. Visibility was perfect, except for a few small clouds. From his altitude of 20,000 feet, he could see more than 95,000 square miles of ocean. A hundred miles southeast of him was a tiny blur—Midway. But Midway was all he saw; the rest of the ocean was empty. He held on for another seventy-five miles. Still nothing, and time was running out. Merely finding the enemy carriers would not be enough. McClusky had to find them before they could launch a strike against our own carriers. Where were they? He had to guess fast and guess right.

When the *Hornet's* group reached the estimated position and faced the same guess, their leader sent twenty-two of his bombers home and pressed forward with the rest—thirteen Dauntlesses and ten Wildcats. Like McClusky, he held southwest for half an hour, but then—with emptiness still ahead—he turned southeast, toward Midway, and then northeast. His determination to attack ignored the insistencies of his fuel tanks, and when he finally abandoned the search, it was too late for most of his planes to make even Midway. The Wildcats gasped and ditched, one after another, all out of fuel; only eight of the pilots were rescued. Two of the Dauntlesses died over the Midway lagoon; their crews waded mere yards to the beach. The other eleven landed with their last pints, at 11:20. Their welcome was something less than effusive. Not expecting the Dauntlesses, and seeing them jettison their bombs offshore, the Marine lookouts mistook them for enemy planes, blew the air-raid siren and even scrambled one of Fighting 221's riddled fighters to intercept them.

But McClusky decided that the enemy had reversed his southeast course—Capt. George D. Murray, of the *Enterprise,* called it "the most important decision of the entire action"—so he headed his bombers northwest. They had already burned up nearly half their fuel; if he didn't find his target soon, our task forces would lose his planes as well as their ships. Fifteen minutes passed, twenty, twenty-five, before his eye caught a faint white streak below—the wake of a lone Japanese destroyer; and presently, far to the north, three carriers, veering and twisting among their escorts, slid out from the broken overcast—the *Soryu* in the lead, with the *Kaga* to the west and the *Akagi* to the east. The *Hiryu,* bringing up the rear, stayed under the clouds and was never seen.

McClusky split his attack: half for the *Kaga,* half for the *Soryu.* He took a last look around—still no Zeros—and pushed over. The enormous red "meat balls" on the yellow flight decks became as sharply defined as bull's-eyes. . . .

Nagumo's strike against the American carriers was just about to take off. The *Kaga* had thirty planes on her flight deck and thirty more on her hangar deck, all armed and fueled. They were awaiting the signal when four bombs struck her, shattering her bridge and killing every man on it, including Captain Okada. Explosions leaped from plane to plane, from deck to deck. A solid pillar of fire shot 1,600 feet into the air. Smoke shrouded her, a black pall slashed with scarlet, and the blinded helmsman let her run wild.

The *Soryu* also had sixty planes aboard. Three bombs spattered blazing gasoline fore and aft on her hangar deck. A magazine exploded; both engines stopped; she lost steerageway. Captain Yanagimoto shouted from the bridge, "Abandon ship! Every man to safety! Let no man approach me! *Banzai! Banzai!*" He was still shouting *banzais* when flames rose around him. Most of the company struggled to the forward end of the flight deck, out of the fire and smoke, and huddled there until a violent explosion blew them into the sea.

The *Enterprise*'s Bombing 6 struck the *Kaga* and the *Soryu* at 10:23. At the same minute, unknown to them, the *Yorktown*'s Bombing 3 was plunging on the *Akagi,* Nagumo's flagship. Some of her Midway group had not yet returned, so she had only forty planes aboard. Her fighters tried to get clear. As the first of them gathered speed, the first bomb smashed among them, near the midships elevator, and another hit the portside aft. Damage did not seem severe, but when Captain Aoki ordered the magazines flooded, the after pumps would not function. The bridge took fire from a burning fighter below and the fire spread. Nagumo summoned a destroyer to transfer himself and his staff to the light cruiser *Nagara.* Within an hour, the *Akagi*'s flight

230

deck flamed from end to end. When her engines stopped, an officer investigated. Her whole engine-room staff was dead.

The torpedo attacks had drawn the Zeros to water level, so they needed only a short sprint to catch Bombing 6 after the pull-out. Eighteen of McClusky's thirty-three Dauntlesses splashed in—he himself was wounded in the shoulder —but fuel exhaustion was to blame for some of them. Bombing 3 returned intact to the *Yorktown*'s landing circle, only to have her warn them away. Before the *Enterprise* could take them aboard, two of the seventeen ran dry and ditched. Worse, a *Yorktown* fighter pilot, shot in the foot, crash-landed on the *Hornet* without cutting his gun switches. His six .50's jarred off, and the burst killed five men and wounded twenty.

The *Yorktown* warned away her planes because her radar had picked up an incoming strike. Two hours before, at ten o'clock, Nagumo had reported Task Force 17's position to Yamamoto: "After destroying this, we plan to resume our AF attack." At 10:50 he admitted, "Fires are raging aboard the *Kaga, Soryu* and *Akagi*," but added firmly, "We plan to have the *Hiryu* engage the enemy carriers." And at 10:54 the *Hiryu*'s blinker boasted: "All my planes are taking off now for the purpose of destroying the enemy carriers."

"All" was an exaggeration; the strike consisted of only nine fighters and eighteen bombers. As soon as they appeared on the *Yorktown*'s radar screen, at 11:50, her combat air patrol dashed to intercept them. Ten bombers went down at once and AA knocked down five more, but three bombs struck the ship, and one of them hurt her. It tore through to her third deck and exploded in the uptakes, blasting out the fires in two boilers and flooding the boiler rooms with fumes. It also set the paint on her stack ablaze and ruptured the main radio and radar cables. Steam pressure fell; she lost way and went dead in the water.

Fletcher took a quick turn around the flight and hangar decks. When he climbed back to the flag bridge, he found it wreathed in smoke so dense that his blinkers and flag hoists were blanketed. With all communications gone, he and the key men of his staff slid down a line and transferred to the heavy cruiser *Astoria*. Meanwhile, the *Yorktown*'s repair

231

gangs patched her decks, and the engineering force coaxed her up to twenty knots. By two o'clock she was shipshape again—she even hoisted a bright new ensign to replace one stained by battle smoke. It had scarcely shaken out its folds when another ship's radar picked up a second attack group, thirty miles to the west—six fighters and ten torpedo planes, from the *Hiryu* as before. Fletcher's task force was now alone. Spruance was thirty miles eastward, farther from the enemy, since launching and landing had kept the *Hornet* and *Enterprise* on an easterly course. However, Spruance had sent Fletcher two heavy cruisers, and two destroyers as AA reinforcements. The *Yorktown*'s CAP and the combined AA splashed six of the torpedo planes, but four broke through and made their drops at her. The heavy cruiser *Portland* tried in vain to interpose herself. Two torpedoes struck the *Yorktown*'s port flank, almost in the same midships spot. A witness said, "She seemed to leap out of the water, then sank back, all life gone." The time was 2:45.

Dead, dark, gushing steam, she drifted in a slowing circle to port. Her list increased to twenty-six degrees; her port scuppers were awash, and she seemed about to capsize. Stretcher bearers threaded her steep passageways, collecting the wounded. At 2:55, Capt. Elliott Buckmaster ordered, "Abandon ship!" Destroyers stood in. Swimmers climbed aboard and clotted their decks in a whispering death-watch, but the *Yorktown* floated on. The late afternoon was beautiful, with a calm sea and a flamboyant sunset. A CAP pilot above Spruance's force, still steaming eastward, looked back at the stricken ship, deserted except by a destroyer. He thought of her as a dying queen, and his eyes were hot with sudden tears.

So far, no American had seen more than three Japanese carriers at one time, and three were known to have been crippled at 10:23. However, this torpedo-plane attack, nearly four and a half hours later, strongly supported the prediction of a fourth carrier. Fletcher had not long to wait for positive corroboration. Even as the *Yorktown* still reeled, one of her scouts reported, "1 CV [carrier], 2BB [battleships], 3 CA [heavy cruisers], 4 DD [destroyers], lat

232

31-15 N, long 179-05 W [about 160 miles west of Spruance's task force], course 000 [due north], speed 15."

Fletcher ordered the *Enterprise* and *Hornet* to strike immediately. The *Enterprise* completed her launch first. By 3:41, she had twenty-four Dauntlesses in the air, including fourteen refugees from the *Yorktown*. They had flown about an hour when they saw three large columns of smoke from the burning *Kaga, Akagi* and *Soryu*. A few destroyers were standing by them; the rest of the force was some miles to the north, fleeing with the surviving carrier, the *Hiryu*. The bombers swung westward in order to dive out of the blinding afternoon sun, and pushed over from 19,000 feet. They lost three planes to Zeros, but they laid four heavy bombs on the *Hiryu*'s deck and three more just astern, starting such enormous fires that the last pilots in line saw that she was already doomed and kicked over to bomb a battleship near by. When the second half of the strike— sixteen more Dauntlesses, from the *Hornet*—arrived a half hour later, they ignored the *Hiryu* completely and dropped on a battleship and cruiser. All the *Hornet*'s planes returned.

The *Hiryu*'s forward elevator was blasted out of its well and hurled against the bridge, screening it and preventing navigation. She had only twenty planes aboard, but they were enough to feed the fires, which quickly spread to the engine room. Her list reached fifteen degrees. She began to ship water.

Of the four carriers, the *Soryu* was the first to sink. A picket submarine, the *U.S.S. Nautilus,* spied her smoke, crept within range, and shot three torpedoes into her at 1:59. Her fires blazed up, but died by twilight, and boarding parties were attempting to salvage her when she plunged, at 7:13. Fifty miles away, Ensign Gay, under his black cushion, had been watching the burning *Kaga*. Several hundred of her crew were still huddled on her flight deck when a heavy cruiser—Japanese—began firing pointblank into her water line. Two explosions tore her apart. She sank twelve minutes after the *Soryu*.

The *Akagi* and the *Hiryu* also sank within minutes of each other, but not until next morning, June fifth. The

Akagi was stout. Her dead engines, staffed by dead men, suddenly came to life and turned her in a circle for nearly two hours, until they stopped forever. Still she would not sink. One of her destroyers torpedoed her at dawn.

The *Hiryu* was the flagship of Commander Carrier Division 2, Rear Adm. Tamon Yamaguchi, an officer so brilliant that he was expected to succeed Yamamoto as commander in chief. Burly, with a face like a copper disk, he was an alumnus of the Princeton Graduate College and had been the chief of Japanese Naval Intelligence in the United States. When he and Captain Kaki, of the *Hiryu,* saw that she could not be saved, they delivered a farewell address to the crew, which was followed "by expressions of reverence and respect to the Emperor, the shouting of *banzais,* the lowering of the battle flag and command flag. At 0315 [3:15 a.m.], all hands were ordered to abandon ship, His Imperial Highness' portrait removed, and the transfer of personnel to destroyers put underway. . . . The Division Commander and Captain remained aboard. They waved their caps to their men and with complete composure joined their fate with that of their ship." The destroyer *Makigumo* scuttled her with a torpedo at 5:10.

All four carriers were gone. With them went more than 2,000 men. Spruance reported that we now had "incontestable mastery of the air."

To the top commanders at Midway, meanwhile, June fourth had been a day of deep anxiety. The meager reports that reached them during the morning—only one enemy carrier damaged—made the ruins around them prophetic of worse. Incredibly—but for the confusion of battle—Lieutenant Colonel Sweeney, commanding the Fortresses, had not yet been told of the two United States Navy task forces offshore. Believing that Midway was fighting alone and hopelessly, he sent seven of his planes—all that were ready for instant flight—back to Oahu, both to save them from destruction and to help defend the Hawaiian Islands against the invasion which he assumed would follow Midway's imminent fall. Although Commander Ramsey, the Air Operations Officer, was better informed, even he thought it "quite

234

possible that we would be under heavy bombardment from surface vessels before sunset."

Midway's air strength was now reduced to two fighters, eleven dive bombers, eighteen patrol planes and four Fortresses, plus aircraft under repair. Sweeney led the four Fortresses in the first strike of the afternoon, against the scattered carrier force. Two more, patched up, took off an hour later for the same target. At 6:30, as the pilots made their bombing runs, they sighted another six Fortresses a mile below—a squadron which had flown from Molokai, southeast of Oahu, straight into the battle. All three formations reported bomb hits, but Nagumo's log acknowledges none.

The Marines tried next. Their eleven dive bombers, Major Norris commanding, went out at dusk, but squalls thickened the moonless sky, and they had to abandon their search. Only the blue glare from their exhausts kept them together until Midway's oil fires guided them home. Ten returned safely; Major Norris did not return. Midway mounted one more strike that evening. Eleven torpedo boats dashed out at 7:30, hoping to cut down a straggling ship, but they, too, found nothing.

As the torpedo boats left, the Molokai Fortresses landed, with alarming news: Zeros had jumped them during their attack. Midway had learned by now that the enemy's fourth —and presumably last—carrier had been crippled at 4:30, so Zeros aloft two hours later implied that a fifth carrier was present. Actually the Zeros were orphans from the burning *Hiryu*, but Midway could not know this. Nor did it know that a patrol craft's report, at nine o'clock, of a landing on Kure, sixty miles west, derived from simple hysteria. On the contrary, each report strengthened the other. The possibility of invasion became a probability.

Midway radioed its picket submarines to tighten the line against the approaching enemy, and launched two Catalinas with torpedoes to support the interception. The Catalinas took off at midnight. At 1:20, an enemy submarine suddenly fired eight rounds into the lagoon, then submerged. Midway's belief that this was a diversion to cover a landing party seemed confirmed within an hour, when one of its own submarines, the *U.S.S. Tambor,* reported "many unidentified ships" only ninety miles westward.

The garrison already had done its utmost. There was nothing left now but the ceaseless service of the planes—eighty-five 500-pound bombs to be hung by hand, 45,000 gallons of fuel to be pumped by hand—and waiting out the direly pregnant night.

Far northeast of Midway, the American warships were also waiting. Fletcher's task force, maimed by the loss of the *Yorktown,* now merely sheltered battleships behind Spruance's. The *Hornet* and *Enterprise* were unimpaired, but Spruance was wary of the fast Japanese battleships and "did not feel justified in risking a night encounter. . . . On the other hand, I did not wish to be too far from Midway next morning. I wished to have a position from which either to follow up retreating enemy forces or to break up a landing attack on Midway. At this time the possibility of the enemy having a fifth CV [carrier] somewhere in the area . . . still existed."

Spruance had cruised slowly east, then a few miles north, east again and a few miles south, when the *Tambor's* sighting ended his aimlessness. He headed toward Midway at twenty-five knots.

There, as the morning of the fifth dawned, the Catalinas were off at 4:15, followed by the Fortresses, and at 6:30 the first report came in: "Two battleships streaming oil," with the bearing, distance, course and speed. They were not battleships but heavy cruisers, the *Mogami* and *Mikuma.* The Catalina pilot's mistake in identification was excusable. These sister ships and their other two, the *Kumano* and *Suzuya,* were Japan's notorious "gyp cruisers"—professedly built to the conditions of the London Naval Conference, but really far larger and more powerful. They were longer, indeed, than any battleship at Pearl Harbor.

The four, a vanguard for the occupation force, had been given a screen of destroyers and sent ahead to bombard Midway in preparation for the landing. They were steaming at full speed when a lookout spotted the *Tambor* even as she spotted them. An emergency turn was ordered, but the *Mogami* missed the signal. She knifed into the *Mikuma's*

236

port quarter, ripping it open and wrenching her own bow askew, so that neither ship could make more than fifteen knots. The collision occurred soon after 2:00 a.m. At 2:55, Yamamoto's subordinate commanders received an astonishing dispatch: "Occupation of AF is canceled. . . . Retire. . . ."

Thus far, the enemy's motives and maneuvers at Midway have been reconstructed from official documents; but on this critical point—why Yamamoto decided to break off the battle—the files are silent. He himself is dead, so only conjectures are left. The most obvious, suggested by chronology, is that he was influenced by the collision of the cruisers, but this was, after all, only a minor mishap to his powerful fleet. Likelier, the true factors were older than the collision, but new to Yamamoto, owing to faulty fleet communications. At 6:30 the evening before, a scout pilot from one of Nagumo's ships had reported sighting "4 enemy carriers, 6 cruisers and 15 destroyers . . . 30 miles east of the burning and listing carrier. . . . This enemy force was westward bound." The pilot was myopic. The American force had only two operational carriers by then, and was bound eastward. Still, Nagumo had no reason to doubt the sighting, and although his log does not say so, presumably he informed Yamamoto at once. Yamamoto seems not to have received the message, for at 7:15 he was broadcasting:

> *1. The enemy task force has retired to the east. Its carrier strength has practically been destroyed.*
> *2. The Combined Fleet units in that area plan to overtake and destroy this enemy, and, at the same time, occupy AF. . . .*
> *4. The Mobile Force [Nagumo], Occupation Force . . . and Advance Force [submarines] will contact and destroy the enemy as soon as possible.*

Nagumo has written: "It was evident that the above message was sent as a result of an erroneous estimate of the enemy, for he still had 4 carriers in operational condition and his shore-based air on Midway was active." Accordingly, at 9:30 p.m. he repeated the pilot's sighting, and again at 10:50. One of these messages must have reached Yamamoto. When it did, the shock of learning that the

American force, which he believed crippled and quailing, was both on the offensive—which it wasn't—and stronger by two unsuspected carriers—which it wasn't—may have jolted him into ordering the retirement.

All this, it should be emphasized, is conjecture. But it is a fact that the Battle of Midway was over, except for skirmishes.

The first of them was touched off by the Catalina's 6:30 report of "two streaming oil." The Marine dive bombers jumped to the attack. Two Vindicators had been repaired overnight, so there were six now, led by Captain Richard E. Fleming, and six Dauntlesses, led by Capt. Marshall A. Tyler. As the *Mogami* and *Mikuma,* accompanied by two destroyers and trailing the *Kumano* and *Suzuya,* limped westward, their torn tanks left an unmistakable spoor, and the Marines followed it to their quarry. Through a storm of AA, the Dauntlesses dived on the *Mogami* at 8:05 and bracketed her with near misses that riddled her topsides. Then the Vindicators glided down at the *Mikuma.* Smoke gushed from a hit on Fleming's engine, but he held his course. The men behind him saw his bomb drop, saw his whole plane burst into flames, and saw him crash it into the *Mikuma*'s after turret. Captain Akira Soji, of the *Mogami,* said, "He was very brave." The Marine Corps agreed; Fleming was the first Marine aviator of the war to receive the Medal of Honor.

This was Midway's last successful action. The Fortresses made three more strikes that day, against the two cruisers and other units, but none was effective and one was tragic. Two planes, out of fuel, had to ditch, with the loss of ten men—the Fortresses' only casualties in the air battle.

The 6:30 report of "two battleships" reached Spruance too, but the weather was foul in his area, so he kept his planes on deck, hoping for better flying and a fatter target. Presently he had both. At eight o'clock, with the skies clearing, another Catalina reported: "2 battleships, 1 carrier afire [imaginary: the last enemy carrier had sunk three hours before] and 3 heavy cruisers, speed 12." Their position, far to the northwest, was beyond Spruance's range, but he headed out and waited for his superior speed to narrow the gap. No further reports came in, however, and as the day wore on, Spruance felt that the morning position was growing "rather cold." It was the best target offered, though; and at 3:00 p.m., when he had closed to an estimated 230 miles, he began to launch.

A group of *Enterprise* dive bombers searched for 265 miles while a *Hornet* group searched 315 miles on a slightly different bearing. By now the weather had worsened. Each group found one small ship—the same one, a straggling destroyer; each attacked it unsuccessfully; and each lost a plane—the *Enterprise* to AA, the *Hornet* to fuel exhaustion. The weary rest landed in darkness. Disheartened, Spruance set a westward course, although the empty ocean ahead promised little for next day, especially since he had to slack off his full-speed pursuit—his destroyers were low on fuel—and there was always the possibility of a night ambush by fast battleships. Still, luck might bring him across those two lame cruisers. . . . He ordered the *Enterprise* to send a dawn search over the whole western semicircle.

The *Kumano* and *Suzuya* had taken no part in defending their sister against the Marines; they merely stood by a few miles away, and when Fleming's crash further reduced the *Mikuma*'s speed, they increased their own and fled. Through the fifth and the early hours of the sixth, the cripples limped on with their two loyal destroyers. Their plight was desperate; they knew it, and Spruance soon learned it. The *Enterprise*'s scouts spotted them at 7:30 and shouted their position. The *Hornet* began to launch her dive bombers and fighters at 7:57. They struck at 9:50, and as they returned, the *Enterprise* launched. They, too, struck and returned, and the *Hornet* launched again.

In all, the Dauntlesses dropped eighty-one bombs. Five hit the *Mogami*, killing more than 100 men. Ten gutted the *Mikuma*. Her survivors climbed aboard the destroyer *Arashio*, where a direct hit killed nearly all of them. Another bomb burst open the second destroyer's stern. Between bombings, the Wildcats spattered the burning hulks with .50-caliber bullets. The last planes, racks empty,

239

headed home at 3 p.m. The *Mikuma* sank about two hours later. The *Mogami* and the two destroyers, all afire, their broken decks littered with dead men, made their painful way back to Japan.

Spruance's fuel was almost gone; enemy submarines were prowling the area, and further pursuit would take him within range of Wake, which was packed with Japanese planes once expected to base at Midway. He reversed course and withdrew toward his tankers. As his pilots stripped off their flight gear and relaxed, the Fortresses made their final attack—and Midway's. Flying at 10,000 feet, they dropped their bombs on a vessel which they reported as "a cruiser that sank in fifteen seconds." The "cruiser" proved to be the *U.S.S. Grayling,* a submarine. Happily, her sinking was only a crash dive.

Midway's fighting was done, but its work was not—the work that had begun early on June fourth, when the first American pilot parachuted from his flaming plane. All that day, the next, and for weeks afterward, Catalinas searched the ocean for rafts and life jackets. They found Ensign Gay on the afternoon of the fifth. A medical officer asked what treatment he had given his wounds.

Gay said, "Soaked 'em in salt water for ten hours."

On the sixth, they picked up another pilot, a lieutenant (j.g.) who had been clutching the bullet holes in his belly for two days. The Japanese had strafed him in his raft—to prove it, he brought in his splintered paddle. The Catalinas rescued more than fifty men. Thirty-five were Japanese, from the *Hiryu's* engine room. They had drifted thirteen days and some 110 miles.

The biggest aftermath job was salvaging the *Yorktown.* It started auspiciously. The destroyer *Hughes,* standing by her on the night of the fourth, rescued two wounded men, who had been overlooked when she was abandoned, and one of her fighter pilots, who paddled up in his raft. Early next morning, Captain Buckmaster and a working party of 180 returned with three other destroyers, and that afternoon a mine sweeper took her in tow for Pearl Harbor. Repairs crept as slowly as the *Yorktown* herself, but by noon of the sixth, jettisoning and counterflooding had begun to reduce her list, and with the help of the destroyer *Hammann*, lashed to her starboard side and supplying power and water, her fires were being brought under control. Then, at 1:35, a lookout sighted four torpedo wakes to starboard. The *Hammann*'s gunners opened fire, hoping to detonate the warheads, and her captain tried to jerk her clear with his engines, but nothing availed. One torpedo passed astern. One hit the *Hammann*. The other two hit the *Yorktown*. They were death blows for both ships.

Geysers of oil, water and debris spouted high and crashed down. The convulsive heave of the decks snapped ankles and legs. Stunned men were hurled overboard, then sucked into flooding compartments. The *Hammann*'s back was broken; she settled fast and sank by the head. Almost at once, her grave exploded. The concussion killed some of the swimmers outright; others slowly bled to death from the eyes and mouth and nostrils.

The *Yorktown*'s huge bulk absorbed part of the two shocks, but her tall tripod foremast whipped like a sapling, and sheared rivets sang through the air. The rush of water into her starboard firerooms helped counter her port list at first, but Buckmaster knew that she was doomed. Too many safety doors had been sprung, too many bulkheads weakened. He mustered the working party to abandon ship. A few did not appear—the torpedoes had imprisoned them in compartments now inaccessibly submerged. An officer phoned one compartment after another. When a voice answered from the inaccessible fourth deck he asked, "Do you know what kind of a fix you're in?"

"Sure," said the voice, "but we've got a hell of a good acey-deucey game down here. One thing, though—"

"Yes?"

"When you scuttle her, aim the torpedoes right where we are. We want it to be quick."

They did not need to scuttle her. Early the next morning, "she turned over on her port side"—in Buckmaster's words—"and sank in three thousand fathoms of water, with all her battle flags flying." As her bow slid under, men on the destroyers saluted.

So ended the Battle of Midway. The United States had lost a carrier, a destroyer, 150 planes and 307 men. Japan had lost four carriers, a heavy cruiser, 253 planes and 3,500 men. It was a decisive American victory. Exactly six months after Pearl Harbor, naval balance in the Pacific was restored. It was also Japan's only naval defeat since 1592, when the Koreans under Yi Sunsin, in history's first ironclad ships, drove Hideyoshi's fleet from Chinhai Bay.

Tactically, Japan's sunken carriers and dead combat pilots—some 100 of her finest, plus another 120 wounded—caused drastic changes in her whole naval establishment. To replace the carriers, she had not only to convert seaplane tenders, thereby curtailing long-range reconnaissance, but to rig flight decks on two battleships. The pilots could never be replaced. Said Capt. Hiroaki Tsuda, "The loss affected us throughout the war."

Strategically, Midway canceled Japan's threat to Hawaii and the West Coast, arrested her eastward advance and forced her to confine her major efforts to New Guinea and the Solomons. Moreover, her efforts were no longer directed toward expansion, but toward mere holding.

The initiative that Japan dropped, the United States picked up. We moved forward from the "defensive-offensive," in Adm. Ernest J. King's phrases, "to the offensive-defensive," and thence to Tokyo Bay. What ended there had begun at Midway. Said Rear Adm. Toshitane Takata, "Failure of the Midway campaign was the beginning of total failure."

Our commanders may have recognized it at the time, but they restrained their optimism. Immediately after the battle, Admiral Nimitz announced only that "Pearl Harbor has now been partially avenged. Vengeance will not be complete until Japanese sea power is reduced to impotence. We have made substantial progress in that direction." Then his jubilation broke out in a pun: "Perhaps we will be forgiven if we claim that we are about midway to that objective."

The Coastwatchers

Ferdinand was the code name of a highly effective intelligence group of several hundred men (planters, missionaries, government officials and the like) working under the supervision of the Australian Navy who reported Jap movements' in the tropical islands in the Southwest Pacific. Its network kept under surveillance an area of more than half a million square miles. Their story, as E. A. Feldt, their Commander, describes it is one of "damp, dimly lighted jungle camps, of hidden treetop lookouts; of silent submarines landing a few intrepid men on hostile beaches in the dead of night; of American airmen mysteriously rescued from enemy-held islands surrounded by enemy-dominated seas; and how Allied coastwatchers managed, in strange and devious ways, not only to exist under the noses of the Japanese, but also to radio vital military information.

"The story of its origin goes back to 1919 and to the problem of protecting Australia's long, undefended coast line. The island continent, its population of seven million largely concentrated in its southeast corner, presents large areas where, in wartime, an enemy might operate without hindrance and, in fact, without anyone's being aware of it. Pondering this problem after the last war, the Navy hit on a scheme of appointing selected civilians in the coastal areas as coastwatchers. Frugality was the governing factor in the design of the system, for the Navy had little money in peacetime. The coastwatchers were unpaid, and it was not possible for the Navy to supply them with radio equipment." *

Eventually administrative personnel in Papua, New Guinea, and the Solomon Islands, along with planters, were added to the organization. In September 1939, Commander Feldt was sent out to visit those members living in the islands who had teleradios. He visited men in New Guinea, New Britain, the Solomons, and elsewhere, enrolling more tele-

---

*E. A. Feldt, *The Coastwatchers*, p. 7. Oxford University Press.

radio operators, teaching them code, what to report, etc. Back in Australia, he persuaded the government to increase the number of coast-watchers operating teleradios, and by August 1940 the additional sets had been placed. As Commander Feldt says, "the instrument had one serious disadvantage, it was difficult to carry—requiring 12 to 16 porters" to move it any distance.

"When, a month after Pearl Harbor, the hurricane of war struck at the Northeast Area, it worked havoc with our island intelligence chain. Here and there, parts of the chain were left freakishly intact; in other places it was destroyed or its links dislocated.

"There was, for instance, C. C. Jervis, planter and retired Navy telegraphist on Nissan Island, who watched an enemy ship move toward the lagoon entrance of his low, undefended atoll; he calmly coded and sent a report of its presence, and was never heard of again.

"There was J. Daymond, assistant district officer at Gasmata, a noisome, marshy native prison island off the south coast of New Britain, who warned Port Moresby of its first air raid, giving the town ample time to prepare, and then was betrayed, unwittingly, by his countrymen: the news was broadcast in Australia that enemy aircraft had been sighted over Gasmata, direct information to the Japanese that we had a reporting station at that point. Promptly the enemy bombed and gunned Gasmata station. For the nonce, Daymond and his staff were saved, having wisely moved with their teleradio across to the mainland. Unsatisfied, the Japanese landed a force at Gasmata two weeks after the fall of Rabaul. According to the story that percolated through, they asked the first native they saw where the kiap was, and were led, in innocent simplicity, to Daymond and his assistant, who had returned to the island. A third member of the staff radioed the bare facts of their capture, and that was the last heard from him, too. We did not even receive an acknowledgment of our reply to his desperate message.

"There was, on the other hand, L. G. Vial, a young assistant district officer evacuated by the Air Force from Rabaul, who was swiftly commissioned an Air Force Pilot Officer, supplied within a week with teleradio, codes, food, and instruction, and flown to Salamaua on the New Guinea coast a few days before the Japanese moved in. Hidden in the hills above Salamaua airfield, for six months, in his quiet unhurried voice, he reported aircraft on the way, their types, numbers, course, and height. His was the voice most listened for at Port Moresby, and at last a correspondent dubbed him 'the Golden Voice,' a title

244

which embarrassed him considerably. At the end of his watch, he was awarded the American Distinguished Service Cross.

"There was D. G. N. Chambers on Emirau Island, north of Kavieng, who made a remarkable escape by launch, passing enemy-held Rabaul at night. Next morning, driven ashore by an enemy destroyer, his launch wrecked, he managed to find a party of other refugees and to make his escape with them. His experience was typical of a number of the watchers who were forced to flee their posts but who survived to serve *Ferdinand* another day.

"There were W. L. Tupling on Ningo and J. H. McColl on Wuvulu, small coral islands in the Admiralty Group, 250 miles northwest of Rabaul. When the radio station at Rabaul was silenced, they tried desperately to raise Port Moresby on their teleradios, but distance and the intervening mountain ranges were too much. So, uninstructed, they remained at their lonely posts to warn a small detachment of Commandos in the islands of approaching ships, to help in destroying everything of use to the Japanese, and finally to aid in evacuating the soldiers. At last one of their signals was picked up, they were instructed to evacuate, and in a plantation launch they made their way, like Chambers, to safety and to future service." *

By 1944, as the war moved closer to Japan, the coastwatchers were no longer needed for intelligence information. It is the belief of Commander Feldt that "Had *Ferdinand* not existed, Japan would still have been defeated but victory would have come later and at a higher cost of life. . . . Without the coastwatchers, the U.S. Navy would surely have faced still stronger enemy forces when it advanced through the Central Pacific." **

The selection that follows tells the story of one of the coastwatchers in the last days of their epic fight.

*The Coastwatchers, pp. 20, 21.
**The Coastwatchers, p. 236.

245

FERDINAND ON HOLLANDIA

by Commander E. A. Feldt

The Allied forces, after taking the Admiralty Islands, decided to land at Aitape far to the west on the New Guinea border and at Hollandia in Dutch New Guinea, thereby neutralizing the Japanese at Madang, Hansa Bay, and Wewak. Headquarters wanted on-the-spot information of Japanese strength and positions in this area.

Under the Allied Intelligence Bureau system, the Dutch should have been delegated to provide information from Hollandia. But the Dutch had so few people that they could not provide a party. Stavermann and his group, who had attempted to reach Hollandia in the first part of 1943, had been killed before they even crossed the border. In fact, the Dutch had no one in their scant forces who had ever even been to Hollandia.

So it was decided that *Ferdinand* should provide a party, to which the Dutch would add an Indonesian sergeant as interpreter. And at *Ferdinand* headquarters, it was decided that here was a job for "Blue" Harris.

Harris had been pestering *Ferdinand* for a real job. He had assisted in the New Britain evacuation, then had sat on the Rai Coast for about eight months, bickering with the other idling watchers there while he waited for the war to come his way. At Talasea and Witu he had escaped the enemy in the nick of time. He had landed for two nights and two days at Finschafen and had stared into the eyes of a Japanese there, but nothing more had come of it. He had been scheduled to land in the Admiralty Islands, but the attack had taken place without any preliminary reconnaissance, and his job had been cancelled. To "Blue," this just didn't add up to enough.

246

The Hollandia job was just what he wanted. It meant a landing on an enemy-held coast, among natives who were an unknown quantity and whose reactions and thoughts would be difficult to judge.

With the meager information already at our disposal, he prepared as carefully for the job as he could. He painstakingly studied every chart and air photograph available. His team was already made up—the one he had prepared for the Admiralty Islands work. It consisted of Lieutenant R. B. Webber, Sergeant R. J. Cream, and Privates J. I. Bunning, G. Shortis, and P. C. Jeune, all of the Australian Army; Julius McNicol, able seaman in the Australian Navy; and Sergeants Yali, Mas, and Buka and Private Mariba of the New Guinea native police. Webber had been a soldier in the Admiralty Islands when the Japanese had occupied them, and McNicol, Yali, and Mas had all been with Harris on the Rai Coast and at Talasea. To this party, Sergeant Launcelot, the Indonesian interpreter, was added.

The party planned to land from a submarine thirty miles west of Hollandia, then push inland to the mountains, without any contact with local natives if possible. To ensure communication, a party under Captain C. J. Millar, who had been with Bridge in New Guinea, was landed by plane in the Idenburg River, a hundred miles south of Hollandia, where the enemy had not penetrated. If base stations could not receive Harris' signals, owing to the distance, Millar was to relay them on. Harris was to remain ashore for fourteen days and to be picked up at the end of that period by submarine.

The party embarked in the U.S. Submarine *Dace* on 18 March 1944. Four days later the submarine was off Cape Tanamerah, the landing point selected. A day was spent examining the shore through the periscope, and a site chosen, but as the submarine surfaced after dark and approached the shore, a powerful light was sighted just where the party was to have landed. So the submarine held off, and next day, after further examination, a small beach on the open coast was decided upon, even though there were several native huts near by.

With true *Ferdinand* caution, Harris decided to land with

247

a reconnaisance party before committing the entire coast-watcher group. With him he took Webber, Shortis, Mas, and Launcelot, arms, a walkie-talkie and a flashlight. Code signals were arranged—"Groggo" to indicate that all was well and the remainder of the party was to be sent ashore; "Washout" to indicate that the remainder should stay aboard the sub, which was anchored more than a mile offshore.

The reconnaissance party set off in the rubber boat on the dark, calm sea. Suddenly, before it knew what had happened, it was in trouble. The low ground swell, innocuous in deep water, bunched itself into heavy breakers at the edge of the reef. The reef had not been observed through the periscope, and the rubber boat was against it and tossed by the breakers before the men realized it was there. They tried to shoot across, but the boat struck on the reef and Harris and Shortis, with some of the equipment, were washed overboard. They and the other three struggled to shore, about a hundred yards away, dragging the swamped boat with them. As they reached the sand, tense and shaken, a fire flared up in a near-by hut.

Any attempt at concealment was useless, and a bold front seemed the best move. Harris, Launcelot, and Mas walked to the hut, while Webber and Shortis unpacked the soaked and battered walkie-talkie, to find it completely ruined.

The natives in the hut, questioned by Harris through Launcelot, said that the nearest Japanese were two and a half miles away to the westward. They appeared friendly; on the surface there was no reason for Harris to be suspicious of them, but he was not satisfied. Years of dealing with New Guinea natives had given him an instinct more to be relied on than reason.

On the strength of his hunch, he ordered the signal "Washout" to be given. Webber flashed the signal with a light, and then sent a further signal asking that the submarine return the following night. No acknowledgment was received from the submarine, so Webber climbed to higher ground to repeat.

From the slight eminence, he was startled to see the other two boats with the remainder of the party just outside the breakers. He watched them repeat the process of overturning and of wading ashore, dragging what equipment they could. On board the submarine, it seemed, some flashes of light not sent by Harris' group had been seen. Imagination had filled in the gaps to make "Groggo," the signal that all was well. Only Sergeant Cream, who had had an attack of malaria, had remained aboard.

A worried and sleepless coastwatcher party awaited the dawn. Harris reflected that if the natives were unfriendly they would report the party in any case. If they were friendly, or in doubt, a show of trust might hold them to him. To his own party he put on a show of confidence. With the morning, he said, they could strike inland and try to reach the Idenburg River.

Dawn showed that the eleven in the party had twelve firearms among them, of which four were submachine guns, two carbines, and the rest pistols and revolvers. A box of hand grenades, some medical kits, the codes and maps, and about one week's rations had been saved.

There had been four natives in the hut. In the morning they were joined by another, who appeared to have some authority over the others, and who agreed that one of the youths in the hut should guide the party clear of the occupied area.

Hiding their rubber boats as best they could, the party packed up and moved off. They crossed the jungle that fringed the beach, continued inland, and finally made camp in a creek bed. At this point their guide left them, explaining that he would seek a better camp site. When he did not return, the coastwatchers feared he had gone to betray them.

Actually, their landing had been reported to the Japanese as soon as they left the beach. The natives in the hut had waited only until they were out of reach of reprisals from the party. Harris had been right when he signaled "Washout."

Next morning, with still no sign of the guide, the party left its camp in the creek bed and followed a path leading through the jungle. It led them up a spur to an open patch of kunai, and they halted at its edge before going into the open. Harris had given his carbine to Yali—perhaps to raise confidence, perhaps because he felt there was trouble ahead and he would give Yali the best chance while he, the leader, took the worst.

As they paused, voices were heard behind them and Webber, dropping his pack, started back to investigate. Dimly he saw a line of Japanese moving forward in the jungle, and he ran to warn Harris, who, meantime, was hurrying the party across the open patch to the shelter of the jungle on the other side. Yali, Mas, Buka, and Mariba were leading, and they had just reached the far jungle when firing broke out. At the same moment, Webber ran into the open and dropped to earth. McNicol bore to the left and reached the jungle. Harris, Bunning, Shortis, and Launcelot struck to the right under heavy fire, while Jeune, who was last in line, lay still near Webber.

Machine guns and mortars joined in the firing. The position was surrounded and the Japanese were moving in on the open patch. Mariba, wounded, fell after the first burst of fire. Harris, Bunning, and Shortis, still in the open, kept up an accurate fire, drawing the enemy on themselves. McNicol crawled to the edge of the jungle, at a place where there was no firing, and beckoned Harris to come to him. Harris, wounded in the left shoulder and with his pistol in his right hand, waved McNicol away toward the south.

Sadly, McNicol moved off, seeing that he could do no more for his leader. His movement was seen by the enemy soldiers, two of whom turned to fire at him. Firing in return, he escaped. Then, coming upon two dead Japanese, killed by their own mortar fire, he took the rifle of one. While searching the bodies for cartridges, he heard more Japanese approaching and had to retreat.

Yali and Buka remained hidden on the edge of the jungle, not knowing in which direction to move, while Mas slipped off toward McNicol. Launcelot, uninjured, reached the edge of the jungle, a few yards from Harris, who was still in the open. Jeune crept over to join Webber and the two remained concealed.

The Japanese attack converged on Harris, Bunning, and Shortis. The final phases can only be reconstructed from captured Japanese reports, but these are clear enough. The three men kept up the action for four hours, until at last Bunning and Shortis lay dead and Harris, wounded in three places, faced the enemy alone with an empty pistol. Then they rushed him.

"Blue" Harris faced his captors unflinchingly. The Japanese dragged him to a tree in the open and propped him against it. They questioned him about the party, about the ship that had landed it, about future attacks and movements. But Harris faced them with dumb contempt. He knew his wounds were mortal and that he need fear nothing from their threats or even worry that any weakness of the flesh might betray him. His lips remained closed and his eyes defied them until, exasperated, they bayoneted him and, all of their questions unanswered, gave him the release of death that he desired.

Launcelot lay hidden for four days in the one spot, hardly moving, while the Japanese searched within a few yards of him. He had two tins of emergency rations of which he ate a small portion, and licked the rain drops from leaves. When at last the enemy seemed to have left, he set off for the beach, keeping to the jungle. A few days later he met a friendly native who fed him and hid him until our forces landed a month later. When he saw the convoy, he paddled out in a canoe and was taken to General Eichelberger, to whom he told his story. Launcelot, at this time, believed himself to be the only survivor.

But five others, also, had managed somehow to live through the massacre.

Webber and Jeune had crawled into the jungle, where they remained until dusk the next day. Then, taking stock, they found they had an Owen gun, a pistol, two knives, one tin of emergency rations, five bouillon cubes, some medicines, and a compass. They set out through the jungle, heading first east, then south.

After five days they realized they had no hope of reaching the Idenburg and that their only chance lay in keeping to deep gullies and trying to survive until our forces landed. Seven foodless days later they found two small caves where they hid for another fourteen days, with only the raw hearts of palm tops as food.

By this time very weak, they heard the air raids and, on 21 April the bombardment that heralded the attack. Next morning they set out for the beach, and late that afternoon found natives who gave them a hot meal of taro and sweet potatoes, the first real food they had had for four weeks, and sheltered them for the night. Next morning they again set off, guided by two natives. But Jeune was so weak that he could hardly walk, so the natives, by signs, suggested that he be left in a hut while Webber searched for an American patrol. Webber gave his Owen gun to a native to carry, while he supported Jeune, but kept his revolver. Webber tells in his own words what happened next.

When we reached within ten or fifteen feet of the hut, a Jap rushed out and charged us, armed with a sword. I called a warning to Jeune of the presence of the Japanese, released him, and turned to take my gun from the native. I was sure there would be more Japs in the area. The natives were already running.

Jeune, somehow, while my back was turned, was closest to the Jap, therefore was attacked first. He fended off a sabre blow and hung on to the blade.

Overestimating my strength, I tried to knock the Jap out with punches to the face and throat rather than use my pistol for fear of bringing more on to the scene. After a struggle, during which the Jap nearly got possession of my pistol, I shot him by forcing the barrel into his stomach, thereby hoping to deaden the sound. This struggle required the combined strength of both Jeune and myself. Jeune told me later he forced his two fingers into the Jap's nostrils and the remaining fingers and hand into his mouth. This caused partial suffocation, thus enabling me to use my pistol effectively. Then, to prevent any outcry he might make, Jeune stabbed him through the heart with his sabre.

As it turned out, he was alone and I could have used my pistol earlier than I did without jeopardizing our safety.

252

Jeune had suffered cuts on the ear, neck, forearm, and hand, and was still further weakened by the struggle. The two remained hidden awhile, then continued for the beach, Webber scouting ahead and supporting himself on the sabre, while Jeune staggered along, using a long stick for the same purpose. Frequent halts were necessary, but late in the afternoon they met up with American soldiers and were taken to a battalion hospital. Both were evacuated and both recovered, although Jeune's health was permanently affected.

McNicol, who had met up with Mas briefly during the heat of the attack, had lost track of all the members of the party. Late in the afternoon of the day of the ambush, he heard firing near the beach and made his way toward it. He saw about fifteen Japanese, but could not make out at what they were firing, so he hid and worked his way back toward the scene of the ambush. Next day he searched for survivors and, finding none, set out for the mountains, following Harris' last orders to him.

Next day he met Mas again, and for thirty-two days the two men lived in the jungle with hardly any food. When they heard the bombardment and reasoned that it must be the landing, Mas was so weak and ill that McNicol set off alone for the beach. He reached an American medical unit and was promptly put in a hospital. All the while, his voice a whisper from a skull, his large eyes pleading, he begged that they go after Mas.

A patrol was sent out almost immediately, but failed to find him. Later another search was made, but with no success.

Yali and Buka had fallen to the ground during the ambush, when Mariba was shot beside them. Buka was unarmed, but Yali fired in the direction of a machine gun that was spitting bullets at Harris. Several of the Japanese wheeled and advanced on them. Yali fired, then he and Buka escaped into the jungle.

The two searched for two days, but could not find any other members of the party, so they struck out for Mandated New Guinea. So far as they knew, the nearest friendly forces were at Saidor, more than 400 miles away, but they faced the journey fearlessly. This is Yali's story:

> We had many narrow escapes while walking to Vanimo. As we had no food or matches and could not cook any of the food we stole from native gardens, we grew weaker.
>
> When near Vanimo, Buka became ill and weak. One day we were walking near the beach and heard a launch engine near by. I decided to investigate as I thought it might be American soldiers.
>
> I left Buka in the bush as he was too weak to come down with me, and then walked down to the beach. Upon arrival at the beach, I ran into some Japanese soldiers who saw me and shouted out to me, asking if I were an Australian policeboy. I then ran into the bush and kept away from the area where Buka was, as I did not want the Japs to follow me back to him.
>
> Later, I returned to the spot where I had left Buka but could find no sign of him. I searched the vicinity for two days and then decided that he had been captured by the Japs.
>
> I then decided to push on to Aitape, and after arriving at Vanimo, I received help from the natives and here learned of the American landing at Aitape. I arrived at Aitape where I contacted the Angau officer in charge.

So reported Yali to Lieutenant Ben Hall, planter and labor-recruiter, a man not likely to be sentimental about a native. Hall added to the report that Yali's story "does not relate fully the courage and determination displayed by this man in his return to the Allied lines, a journey of a hundred and twenty miles."

Mariba, he who had been the first wounded by the ambushing Japanese, turned up, incredibly, eight months later. He had been captured and held prisoner, but had escaped and made his way back to our lines. His return gave us some faint hope for Mas and Buka.

254

Throughout the world there have been foolish arguments on racial virtues. There are those who contend that mixed races inherit the worst traits of both parents, and there are others who hold that complete mixture of races, once stabilized, is best. Others say that all men are creatures of their environment and training. Coastwatchers wouldn't know the erudite points of such matters. They only know that the half-caste Julius McNicol and the full-bred native Yali can have a place in any party where courage and resource are the qualifications.

Among the coastwatchers, the disaster to the Hollandia party spread a gloom which no other casualties had caused. "Blue" Harris was the most striking personality among a bunch of notable individualists, a man whose vitality was such that his death was, at first, unbelievable. Harris, Shortis, Bunning, Mas, Buka—all had been lost; hearing it, men muttered the meaningless blasphemies and obscenities which had replaced prayer in their vocabularies.

The Solomons

While the Australians and the Americans were fighting in New
Guinea, American Marines had invaded Guadalcanal in the Solomon
Islands. Once Tulagi was occupied (the only successful part of the en-
emy's original Coral Sea scheme), the Japanese had begun work on

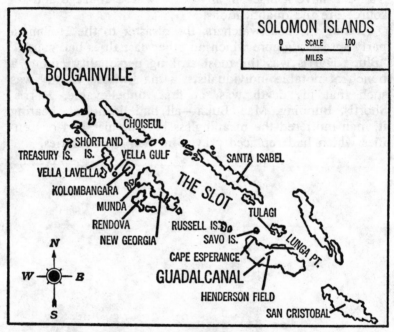

SOLOMON ISLANDS

0 SCALE 100

MILES

BOUGAINVILLE

CHOISEUL

SHORTLAND
IS.

TREASURY IS.   VELLA GULF

VELLA LAVELLA

SANTA ISABEL

KOLOMBANGARA

THE SLOT

MUNDA

TULAGI

RENDOVA   RUSSELL IS.

NEW GEORGIA   SAVO IS.

LUNGA PT.

CAPE ESPERANCE

N

GUADALCANAL

W   E

HENDERSON FIELD

S

SAN CRISTOBAL

an airfield on nearby Guadalcanal. When the American naval commanders heard this news, they rushed the 1st Marine Division, then
in New Zealand, to attack Guadalcanal. Japanese air forces, once
firmly established on Guadalcanal, could raise havoc with the supply
lines stretching from New Zealand and Australia back across the
Pacific to Hawaii and the U.S.

The account which follows is a chapter from Maj. Frank Hough's
remarkably fine book* about the Marines in action in the Pacific.

*The Island War.

GUADALCANAL: THE TURNING POINT

by Maj. Frank Hough

"Now hear this! *Now hear this!* All hands man your battle stations. . . . *Darken Ship! Darken Ship!* Secure all ports and bulkhead doors. The smoking lamp is out on all weather decks. . . . *Now hear this! . . .*"

Moving through empty, placid seas, some thousands of Marines were learning to obey the omnipotent voice of the "bull horn," or PA (public address system); were learning a hundred dull details of life aboard a transport. Many of them, landbound until now, had found a certain thrilling novelty in all this during the first few days, but that had quickly worn off. Others had been denied even this transient pleasure: old-timers, who had traveled a dozen seas aboard the plodding Navy transport *U.S.S. Henderson*, which had been hauling Marines around for thirty years; organized reservists, who had spent months on extended amphibious maneuvers in the Caribbean and off the Atlantic coast.

For the First Marine Division was going to war, though the truth was that none of them, from the Commanding General down, expected that they would actually meet war in the very near future. Although much of the personnel had been in training for more than a year, the units had been brought up to war strength only recently by incorporation of many men fresh from boot camp, and the full combat teams had had comparatively little opportunity to work together as units. The plan was to set up training bases in New Zealand where this deficiency could be remedied. The word was that they would not be called upon for combat action until January, 1943. And this was only late spring of 1942. . . .

Condensed from the author's *The Island War.*

So they settled down resignedly to the dullest life the mind of modern man has been able to devise: to a routine of boat drills, calisthenics, mess formations; to monotony-whiling poker and blackjack (craps showed a notable decline in popularity), cribbage, checkers and a surprising amount of chess. At night they sweltered four and six deep in fetid holds served by overworked blower systems which too often broke down, or groped about the darkened decks, watching the bright tropic stars close above the gently swaying mastheads, speculating vaguely on the strange land toward which they were headed.

The forward echelon, including Division Headquarters, had left Norfolk, Virginia, on 20 May aboard the *U.S.S. Wakefield* (former *S.S. Manhattan*) and two smaller ships, and had reached Wellington, via the Panama Canal, on 14 June. The men liked the people and the country. For two weeks they worked hard and cheerfully at establishing their training base, anticipating a long period of abundant liberty among a hospitable, congenial populace.

But that dream was to be short lived. On 25 June the High Command arrived at a momentous decision, and the Division was ordered to prepare to move into combat at the earliest possible moment. The second echelon, which had traveled by train from New River to San Francisco, reached Wellington on 11 July, only to be put immediately at unloading their ships and reloading, combat style.

Combat-loading, at this stage of the war, was mainly a theory, and not a fully developed theory, at that. Its object was to stow the gear aboard in such fashion that those items most urgently needed on a beachhead could be got at easily and unloaded quickly, the less urgently needed items to follow according to a complicated system of priorities. Space economy was no object; at least, not the primary object. Thus, trucks, jeeps and other rolling stock which had been disassembled on the trip out to conserve space, now had to be reassembled for immediate use and loaded with ammunition, food, etc. This was highly wasteful according to commercial standards, and much valuable cargo was necessarily crowded out.

Furthermore, there was considerable lack of unanimity

of opinion regarding priorities, which led to what turned out to be some regrettable errors. From the outset it had been the fate of the First Division to do things the hard way. As the pioneer unit in the field, it had served as the proving ground in which trial and error developed the methods and techniques of the entire Marine Corps. And it was destined to continue so until, as some cynics put it later, the Division kept on doing things the hard way throughout its career from sheer force of habit.

Other things went wrong, too, unavoidably. The Quartermaster Department, not having expected to go into combat for some months, was lacking in certain essentials which were all but impossible to obtain on short notice. New Zealand labor unions placed some difficulties in the way of loading at first, and with the exception of a few civilian crane operators the Marines handled all the cargo themselves, working continuously in shifts. Then the rains came: torrential downpours which ruined supplies, equipment and dispositions. It was a disgruntled and exhausted Division which shoved off from Wellington on 22 July for a destination still unknown to most.

It was not unknown, of course, to the Division command. Our smashing naval victory at the Battle of Midway had set the stage for a quick followup offensive on our part, and the activities of the Japanese themselves provided the cue to where it could be launched with the best prospects of decisive success.

The archipelago known as the Solomon Islands runs from a point about five degrees below the Equator, adjacent to New Britain, for several hundred miles in a southeasterly direction. The several large islands and innumerable smaller ones lie in two parallel chains, separated by a wide channel which came to be known as the "Slot." Geologically they were described as old coral deposits on an underwater mountain range which had been thrust above the surface by volcanic action at some time in the remote past. This made for rugged, mountainous country, slashed by precipitous ravines and gullies, abounding in natural caves. Centuries of tropical climate had blanketed this with lush jungle.

259

All through the spring, Coastwatchers lurking in the hills had reported steady Japanese penetration southeastward along both of the twin chains. By mid-May, the Japanese had seized the provincial capital of Tulagi, located on a small island in a splendid harbor formed by the larger adjacent island of Florida. Captain W. F. M. Clemens, a British officer who had been a member of the civil Government, had escaped across the channel to Guadalcanal where he had taken up the duties of Coastwatcher, together with two Australians and supported by a small group of loyal natives. From this point of vantage, he was able to verify, early in July, what up until then had been mere rumors: that the Japanese had sent troops and laborers into Guadalcanal where they were building a sizable airfield near the mouth of the Lunga River with such despatch that it might be expected to be operational by mid-August.

Guadalcanal was the next to the last island in the southern end of the two chains which bounded the Slot. It was about ninety miles long, with width up to twenty-five miles over much of its length, its longitudinal axis roughly paralleling that of the chain itself. In common with the other larger Solomons, it possessed a backbone of high, rugged mountains—but with a notable difference. Whereas on the southern shore the mountains dropped sharply to the sea, to the north, save for the northwestern area, they gave way to foothills which in turn flattened out to a comparatively level coastal plain which reached a depth of eight miles in some places.

This was practical terrain for the construction of airfields. Furthermore, it was more open than is usually the case with tropic islands. The jungle was dominant, being thickest and most continuous along the courses of the numerous rivers which drained the region. Elsewhere it was frequently broken by glades and prairies. Much of the shore line was taken up with the evenly spaced palms of extensive coconut plantations. Inland, the plain was checkered with open patches grown to coarse kunai grass, often six to seven feet tall.

These general features were known, but that was about

260

all. No reliable maps could be located. Aerial surveys showed the outline of the coast and location of possible landing beaches, but little else in the inland tangle of jungle and kunai grass. And time was desperately short, because it was imperative that we strike before the enemy aircraft could begin using the new field.

A few New Zealanders were found who had visited one part or another of the Solomons, or had worked in the coconut plantations or missions there. Colonel Goettge, Division Intelligence Officer (D-2), flew to Australia to solicit the services of others with similar knowledge. Little information of value was obtained, but several men with some firsthand knowledge of the area volunteered to accompany the expedition. This would be all we would have to go on until contact could be made ashore with Captain Clemens and his friendly natives.[1]

The Division was far from complete as a unit. Earlier in the year one of the infantry regiments, the 7th Marines,[2]

---

[1] Captain Clemens entered the Marine lines a week after the landing, as soon as convinced that this was not a hit-and-run raid. Like the proverbial Englishman-in-the-tropics, he emerged from the jungle immaculately clad and accompanied by his retinue. Among his followers was a remarkable native, Sergeant Major Vouza, recently retired from the local constabulary, whose subsequent yeoman service was to win him high decorations from both Britain and the United States.

[2] In the Marine Corps, regiments are designated by the term "Marines" following the regimental number, as above. Infantry regiments are numbered 1 through 9 and 21 through 29; artillery regiments 10 through 15; engineer regiments 16 through 20. Army regiments are numbered and designated by branch of service, i.e., 9th Infantry, 25th Field Artillery, 5th Engineers, etc. A common mistake even among well-informed newspapermen was to refer to the Fifth Marine Division, for example, as the 5th Marines. This led to some unfortunate misunderstandings, as at Iwo Jima where a dispatch about the heavy casualties being suffered by the "Fifth Marines" scared the daylights out of relatives of men in the 5th Marines (regiment) which happened to be some two thousand miles from Iwo at the time.

with reinforcing elements, had been detached to strengthen the defense of Samoa, where they were still in garrison. To make up the deficiency, the 2nd Marines, of the Second Division, were temporarily attached, together with the 1st Raider Battalion, 1st Parachute Battalion (minus parachutes), and 3rd Defense Battalion, the composite being designated First Marine Division, Reinforced.

The two convoys carrying the several elements rendezvoused near the Fijis. Off the island of Koro it was planned to hold a dummy run (rehearsal for the coming operation). Again the business was fouled up. The new elements had not been fully integrated into the Division as a whole. Control facilities proved inadequate for an operation of such magnitude. Landing boats milled around aimlessly trying to find the line of departure or figure out what they were supposed to do. When the first wave was finally formed and rushed shoreward, many landing boats piled up on the fringing reef hundreds of yards from dry land, while others barely managed to swerve away. None of them ever did get to shore.

Again, the First Division had done things the hard way. And, again, events were to prove that their efforts had not been wasted.

From there on in, the Division's luck seemed to change. The sea was calm, the weather hazy for the most part. The last two days were overcast, with a low ceiling which hid the convoy from aerial observation. Unmolested, apparently unobserved, the transports and their naval covering force rounded the northwestern end of Guadalcanal during the night of 6/7 August at 0310. Here the convoy separated into two parts for the two primary missions of the operation. The northern force passed to the north of Savo Island and headed for Tulagi Harbor. The main force slipped silently, darkly, between Savo and Guadalcanal, moving to the southeast. Not a sound broke the night stillness, and dawn commenced breaking with tropical placidity.

Then, at 0614, there came a thundering unfamiliar to these parts, and great tongues of crimson and orange flame lit the graying sea. . . .

The beaches selected for the Guadalcanal landing were situated about three miles east of the nearly completed airfield, primary objective of the operation. They were fine wide beaches, backed by the evenly spaced trees of a big coconut plantation. The day was clear and calm, the surf running low. Not a shot sounded from the island as the assault waves swept shoreward. Here began the legend of "First Division landing-luck," which was to endure to a bloody termination on the beaches of Peleliu, more than two years later.

The naval covering force and carrier-based aircraft had given the beaches a quick going over and had thoroughly plastered the airfield area, where aerial reconnaissance and such meager intelligence as had been obtained indicated the Japanese were concentrated. In contrast to the fiasco off the Fijis—and mainly because of it—the assault waves formed with quiet efficiency, crossed the line of departure on schedule and moved in to hit the beach at 0910. While units assembled and moved inland to predetermined phase lines, the Higgins boats returned to the transport area for more troops and for supplies which had been so painfully combat-loaded for the occasion. All was quiet, and it was a fine war, that clear morning of 7 August. Later waves, rushing ashore with high consciousness of history in the making, found members of the waves which had preceded them eagerly trying to hack open coconuts with machetes and bayonets.

The initial assault troops consisted of two battalions of the 5th Marines which landed abreast, the 1st Battalion (1/5) [3] on the right, the 3rd Battalion (3/5) on the left. Their mission was to set up a perimeter defense some distance inland which would secure the beach against counterattack, thus covering further troop landings and obtain-

---

[3] This form of designating battalions of regiments is standard in reports from the field and is used here for economy and convenience. Thus, 1/5 without further designation was 1st Battalion, 5th Marines. There were three battalions to a regiment, each consisting of four companies, lettered "A" through "M." This number was later reduced to three.

ing dispersal areas for the supplies to be brought ashore. The 1st Marines began landing in column of battalions at 1100 and advanced immediately inland through the perimeter in a generally westerly direction. 1/5 thereupon moved up on their right, following the shore in the direction of Lunga Point, leaving beachhead security to 3/5.

Once through the coconut grove, they met the jungle. The time would come when these Marines would be as much at home in the jungle as any fighters in the world; when, upon rare occasions, they would find it a friend. But that time was in the future. On this, their first meeting, it was an enemy, enigmatic and implacable, which impeded their progress, caused units to lose contact and direction, and filled them with a hundred unnamed fears as night closed in.

The jungle of the Solomons is the type known as "rain forest," indigenous to the larger islands of that general area of the Pacific, notably New Guinea and the Bismarck Archipelago. It is characterized by giant hardwoods, which tower well over a hundred feet into the sky, with boles six and eight feet in diameter, flared out at the base by great buttress roots. Among and beneath the trees thrives a fantastic tangle of vines, creepers, ferns and brush, impenetrable even to the eye for more than a few feet. Exotic birds inhabit its upper regions; the insect world permeates the whole in extraordinary sizes and varieties: ants whose bite feels like a live cigarette against the flesh, improbable spiders, wasps three inches long, scorpions and centipedes. The animal kingdom is less numerous, represented by species of rats, some distant relatives of the possum, lizards ranging in length from three inches to three feet, a few snakes mostly of the constrictor type, and some voracious leeches peculiar in that they live in trees and drop upon the unwary passer-by from above.

No air stirs here, and the hot humidity is beyond the imagining of anyone who has not lived in it. Rot lies everywhere just under the exotic lushness. The ground is porous with decaying vegetation, emitting a sour, unpleasant odor. Substantial-looking trees, rotten to the core, are likely to topple over when leaned against, and great forest giants

264

crash down unpredictably in every windstorm. Freshly killed flesh begins to decompose in a matter of a few hours. Dampness, thick and heavy, is everywhere, result of the rains which give the forest its name; unbelievably torrential in season, never ceasing altogether for more than a few days at a time. Mosquitoes, bearers of malaria, dengue and a dozen lesser-known fevers, inhabit the broad, deep swamps which are drained inadequately by sluggish rivers where dwell giant crocodiles, the most deadly creature of this particular region.

Through this steaming wonderland, Marines of the First Division moved toward the airfield, hacking their way through the undergrowth, bogging down in swamps, fording sluggish streams, struggling through occasional "open" patches of tough kunai grass higher than a man's head. Units lost contact and alignment, wandered about aimlessly, wondering where they were. Men shouted and cursed and fired at shadows and generally created sufficient din to reveal their positions to anyone within hundreds of yards. Later, jungle-hardened officers and men alike looked back with horror at this amateurish advance. A wily and determined enemy, familiar with the ground, might have wiped out great segments of the force in detail.

But there was no determined opposition; only a few scattered snipers. Progress was euphemistically described as "satisfactory," and advanced units set up perimeter defenses for the night.

The 1st Marines reached the airfield late on the second day (D+1), the 5th continuing along the shore to Kukum, a native village beyond the mouth of the Lunga. The Japanese bivouac areas showed every sign of having been precipitately abandoned. Many of the enemy had been cooking their breakfasts when the bombardment had struck, and their pots still hung over dead fires. Damage was surprisingly light. Later intelligence disclosed that the defenders had orders to take to the hills in case of attack, but this would not account for their failure to destroy the large stocks of food and building materials which were shortly to prove a boon to the captors, or the fine refrigerating and generating plants which were captured intact. All in all, the Guadalcanal attack can be rated as one of the greatest strategic and tactical surprises achieved in this or any other war.

Meanwhile, matters on the beach were anything but "satisfactory." The dummy run off Koro which had ironed out the worst difficulties in landing procedure had never reached the beach; hence, there had been no rehearsal for the shore party. Both planning and personnel proved wholly inadequate to cope with the flood of supplies which poured ashore in the wake of the troops. As big tank lighters and ramp boats brought in the artillery, rolling stock and other heavy equipment, the scene on the beach passed through confusion to chaos.

As anticipated, the enemy's reaction was prompt and violent. The first air alert sounded about 1300 on D-Day, practically par for the Japanese getting a flight down from Rabaul after receipt of the alarm. Fighter-escorted bombers swept in fearlessly through a sky blossoming with flak air bursts—and proceeded to ignore their main chance with a shortsightedness which seemed incredible at the time, and still does. Perhaps they were acting under orders; perhaps the temptation was simply too great to resist. Whichever the case, this flight and those that followed concentrated entirely on the convoy, ignoring the supplies piled all over the beach in plain sight. Had those supplies been destroyed or even seriously damaged, the expedition would have been doomed at a single stroke, as events were to prove. As it was, all the Japanese accomplished was to inflict minor damage on the shipping, including one destroyer. A heavier raid [4] the following day caused a few casualties and set fire to the transport *George F. Elliott* which burned brightly all night before sinking with a large quantity of much needed supplies.

But that we could still outblunder the Japanese at this stage of the war was soon to be demonstrated. Early the following morning (0200, 9 August) disaster struck.

[4] Coastwatchers on Bougainville radioed the word as soon as this flight passed over, thus furnishing the first concrete example U.S. troops were to have of the value of these gentry.

266

Throughout the day air reconnaissance had reported enemy naval units lurking to the west and northwest within striking distance of Guadalcanal. About dusk a delayed report came from a Coastwatcher of a heavy cruiser task force on the move. In order to screen the vulnerable transports, two cruiser-destroyer groups, including both Australian and U. S. ships, were posted on either side of small Savo Island, in the channel between the northwestern tip of Guadalcanal and Florida, to intercept any Japanese coming down the Slot from the direction of their bases.

How the enemy were able to elude the alertness of a force posted specially in expectation of their arrival has never been entirely explained. But approach they did, undetected. The first intimation of their presence to the men aboard the loafing ships came when they were suddenly blasted at point-blank range by the big guns of what were apparently a number of heavy cruisers. Wholly unprepared, silhouetted by flares and the light from the burning transport *Elliott*, our ships were so many sitting ducks. In approximately thirteen minutes from the opening salvo, the heavy cruisers *U.S.S. Astoria, Quincy* and *Vincennes* and *H.M.A.S. Canberra* were either sunk or sinking, and *U.S.S. Chicago* severely damaged.

Whereupon the Japanese, with that curious knack for losing opportunities which they were to display so often, hurried back the way they had come without entering the transport area where their attentions might well have been catastrophic.[5]

As events proved, this would be the most brilliant and effective naval victory the enemy would achieve in the whole course of the war. But there was no way of knowing that at the time. The Savo Island action had to be taken as a routine demonstration of the efficiency of Japanese

---

[5] Long after the event, it was learned that a lucky shell from one of our dying cruisers struck the Japanese admiral's control room, destroying his charts and evidently giving him the jitters. This, together with fear of being caught in daylight by our aircraft, caused him to turn back without attacking the transports, as he had orders to do.

sea power, and viewed in that light the U.S. Navy faced a grim prospect indeed.

When dawn came the transports began weighing anchor. With what remained of their convoying warships in attendance, they silently stole away to the south, and by evening the Marines were on their way. Very, very much on their own.

The reasons behind this unexpected move were not clear at the time. It was only natural to associate it with the Savo debacle and conclude that the Navy had simply taken to its heels in panic, an impression which caused much bitter criticism and hard feeling. Actually, Admiral Turner had notified General Vandegrift of the proposed move more than three hours before anyone had any inkling that the Japanese were going to strike. The more rational explanation is that the planes of the carrier task force had suffered considerable casualties and were running out of fuel, and it was deemed inadvisable to leave the helpless transports in so dangerous a region without air cover.

Anyway, go they did, taking with them more than half of the cargoes—inadequate to begin with—which they had not had time to unload. All that the Marines ashore had to sustain them during the month to elapse before another convoy arrived was that piled-up litter on the beach which the enemy aviators had not bothered to destroy: that and the supply of rice and fish heads which the hurriedly departing Japanese had considerately left in their bivouac area.

The Marines, of course, could not foresee all this at the time. Most of them did not even know what had happened off Savo Island; they had heard the guns and some had seen the flashes, but so sanguine had their own experience made them it never occurred to most of them that we could have suffered a serious setback. Nor did they realize the full significance of the convoy's departure.

With the men and supplies available, it was obviously impossible to attempt any extensive mopping up of enemy remnants in this unfamiliar territory and still insure the safety of the important ground already taken. Indeed, there were not enough men to form a continuous perimeter cordon at a safe distance around Henderson Field, as the Marines had named the captured airdrome.[6] A defense system was set up with flanks resting on the sluggish Tenaru River to the east and a grassy ridge two miles short of the Matanikau to the west.

Patrols exploring the near-by territory encountered enough opposition to show definitely that there were Japanese fighting men on the island and that they were organizing, mainly to the northwest, farther along the coast. But the men in the ranks were not greatly concerned. Even as the rate of enemy air attack stepped up and increasing patrol activity was encountered along the perimeter, they were more uncomfortable than worried.

Hadn't they accomplished their primary mission as Marines? They had seized and secured an excellent beachhead and a strategic airfield; from here on, the job was the Army's. It was just a case of holding until the Army relieved them, then all hands would go back to New Zealand, about which fabulous stories had already grown up. How long would that be? Scuttlebutt said three weeks, maybe four. . . .

Actually there were no really heavy air attacks during the first two weeks on Guadalcanal; not heavy, that is, judged by the standard of what was to come. But there were repeated small raids: six or seven bombers cruising the field at leisure and unloading just about as they pleased. That was the aggravating part of it: the lack of opposition. The air strip had been completed within the first few days, and a PBY had landed as early as 12 August; yet no fighter protection arrived during those two weeks. AA guns of the 3rd Defense Battalion brought down an occasional raider,

---

[6] Named after Major Loften R. Henderson, Marine flier killed at Battle of Midway. As planned by the Japanese, the original landing strip was 3,778 feet long by 160 feet wide. At the time of its capture, it had been completely graded and all but 197 feet surfaced with coral, clay, gravel and dry cement.

but were inadequate for complete protection and altogether lacking in camouflage netting, one of the many items which turned out not to have been unloaded from the hurriedly departing transports.

And there were various minor nuisances. A carrier-based Japanese fighter plane known as "Louie the Louse" came by occasionally to drop light bombs or flares over the airfield. The latter usually signaled naval action coming up, whereupon Louie would hang around and call the shots for his friends. More persistent was "Washing Machine Charlie," a big twin-engine flying boat, so nicknamed because of the irregular sound of its unsynchronized motors. Charlie had great staying power and would cruise up and down over the Marine positions most of the night, dropping bombs at intervals just to make sleep difficult and wear down the nerves. A submarine (or submarines) called "Oscar" loafed around offshore, surfacing now and again to observe the situation and throw a few rounds into the area or at the slow Higgins boats which were all the water transportation our people had at this stage. Japanese destroyers moved about as they pleased, shelling our installations when the spirit moved them and, it was rumored, landing troops beyond our perimeter. So long as they stayed out of range of our half-track 75's, they were as safe as though in their home waters; coast defense guns were another of the many items which had failed to come ashore. The implications of this complete air and sea superiority did nothing to raise the Marines' morale.

The enemy on shore also proved more of a nuisance than a menace during this period. After the first few days, increasing numbers of sad-looking characters began slinking out of the bush and giving themselves up in hopes of getting something to eat for a change. But as we soon found out, these were not soldiers, but laborers; most of them not even Japanese, but Koreans. The men christened them "termites." They showed no compunctions against telling all they knew of the enemy's strength and dispositions; but they didn't know much, having been kept in a condition of virtual slavery by the military, who had abandoned

270

them to their own devices once the shooting had started.

From what our Intelligence could piece together, there had been about two thousand of these people on the island when we had landed, guarded and supervised by some six hundred troops: naval personnel and members of the Special Landing Forces, the Japanese equivalent of our own Marines. This force had evidently regained some semblance of cohesion following their inglorious flight on D-Day, and indications were that their point of assembly was Matanikau village, just beyond the mouth of the river of that name, some three miles west of our perimeter.

One of this group was finally wounded and captured. From him it was learned that his companions were running short of supplies and that some of them might be inclined to surrender. At least, this was what some of his interrogators believed they learned. On the whole, the prisoner was sullen and unco-operative, not one to inspire any great degree of confidence. At this time there was much we did not know about Japanese psychology, and our technique of prisoner interrogation was still rudimentary.

On the basis of this dubious information, Colonel Frank B. Goettge, Division Intelligence Officer (D-2), determined to lead a patrol into the Matanikau region. The project did not arouse much enthusiasm in other quarters, but Colonel Goettge was insistent. "The way to get intelligence about the enemy is to go where the enemy is," he declared.

And go he did, taking a patrol of twenty-one enlisted men and four officers, including a surgeon and an interpreter. The now terrified prisoner was also brought along.

The party set out in a Higgins boat late on the evening of 12 August and proceeded down the coast beyond Point Cruz. Some time was wasted as they cruised about offshore while the prisoner tried to pick a likely spot to land. Whether he deliberately led them into ambush is problematical; the din of the boat's motor was quite sufficient to alert all the Japanese in the neighborhood. In any event, they had scarcely moved inland from the beach when they were greeted by a withering fire. Colonel Goettge and the prisoner, in the lead, were killed, apparently instantly, and the rest of the patrol pinned down on the beach.

A desperate fire fight lasted through the rest of the night. The Marines, fighting in strange territory in total darkness, did not have a chance. The captain who succeeded to the command dispatched a sergeant in an effort to get through to the perimeter and bring help. The sergeant drew fire some distance down the beach, and, fearing he had been killed, the captain sent a corporal on a similar mission. Actually both men got through safely but not in time to save the doomed patrol. Only one other survived: just before dawn a sergeant, the only one remaining who was not too badly wounded to swim, plunged into the sea, by-passed the Jap-held territory and finally reached the small naval operating base at Kukum. With the coming of daylight, the Japanese closed on the helpless survivors on the beach and massacred them all.

The fate of the Goettge patrol resulted in the first really earnest efforts to wipe out the troublesome pocket of the enemy. Three company-strength patrols of the 5th Marines moved into the region immediately west of the Matanikau. Two native villages were cleared out and a number of Japanese killed in a series of skirmishes, but final results were inconclusive. Veteran jungle fighters, with the great advantage of knowing the terrain intimately, the enemy's major parties were able to slip away from any enveloping movement we tried to throw about them.

Our greatest difficulty was the lack of men to do the job as it needed doing. The object of the campaign had been to seize and hold the airfield. The area included was sufficiently large to stretch the perimeter defense dangerously thin. To draw men in any number from this line might well be fatal to the safety of the field, and the mobile reserve was absurdly small for a mission of these proportions.

The entire Marine force on the island at this time included only two infantry regiments with their reinforcing elements. The Raider Battalion, Parachute Battalion and most of the 2nd Marines were still in the Tulagi area. The 7th Marines, one of the Division's original components, was still on garrison duty in Samoa. General Vandegrift had requested urgently that it be brought to the scene as soon as possible. Until it arrived, however, his scope of offensive action was strictly limited. He and his staff had to strike a delicate balance of safety factors against the urgency of the situation practically every time a combat patrol was organized.

With these inadequate means, he was still trying to eliminate the enemy to the west, when, to the east, the enemy struck what was to prove his first major blow.

This fell on the night of 20/21 August. Only the previous afternoon, the first squadron of Marine fighter planes had, at long last, established themselves on Henderson Field. They were to prove their usefulness sooner, perhaps, than even the most optimistic had expected.

There were many features connected with the so-called Battle of the Tenaru[7] which were puzzling to people as slightly acquainted with Japanese military psychology as were our officers at that early stage. They learned much during that night and the day that followed, but much that they learned remains inexplicable to the American mind to this day.

What, for instance, could the enemy reasonably hope to accomplish by attacking two reinforced regiments with a mere twelve hundred men? True, they could throw an overwhelming weight of numbers against any point of the thinly held perimeter line they might select; yet that force amounted to a small fraction of the strength we could muster against them once the breakthrough was made (if it were made) and we were able to concentrate. They could hardly have expected to drive us into the sea, or even to hold the airfield permanently—provided they ever got to the field. They could not have been planning destruction of our planes because, when their plans were made, we had no planes on the island; the first ones arrived by pure chance only after the Japanese were moving into position for the attack.

[7] Really the Ilu. A former resident, accompanying our troops, mistakenly transposed the names of these two rivers, and they were carried thus on our makeshift maps for some months. They are used here as they were during the campaign.

Perhaps they grossly underestimated our numbers; there were plenty of instances later to demonstrate the faulty functioning of enemy combat intelligence. Perhaps they took their own propaganda too literally and honestly believed themselves supermen, each worth easily ten of us decadent democrats. Whatever went on in their oriental minds, the net result was that twelve hundred first-class Japanese fighting men became unavailable for more important operations to come where their strength might conceivably have proved an important factor.

They not only failed to get to the airfield; they failed even to break through the thin perimeter. In fact, they didn't even come close.

This force had been landed within the past few days, apparently from destroyers, some distance to the east of our positions. We had had some intimations of such an event, but the lack of air observation had prevented us from verifying it or estimating the numbers involved. The enemy was commanded by one Colonel Ichiki.

On the nineteenth a Marine patrol in the Koli Point region had surprised and annihilated an enemy patrol which was obviously the advance party of a much larger force. The dead were found to be clean, well dressed and splendidly equipped, obviously new to the island.[8] Very evidently, something was cooking. A few strands of barbed wire were strung in front of our most exposed positions; wire salvaged from an old plantation fence, since our own wire was another of the necessities which had failed to come ashore in sufficient quantity before the flight of the transports. All hands were exhorted to remain especially alert.

These precautions paid off richly. The Japanese did not bother to bring up artillery. They did not call for a preliminary fire mission from their ships, which had been able to shell us with complete impunity for the past two weeks.

[8] Later one of the few prisoners taken declared, perhaps with tongue in cheek, that not only had he never heard of Guadalcanal but thought they were attacking Catalina Island off the California coast.

Relying entirely on surprise, they moved as silently as possible from their assembly area to the east bank of the Tenaru, then suddenly hurled an overwhelming force of infantry across the sand spit that completely blocks the mouth of that sluggish river at this season.

The alert Marines opened up with everything they had. The carnage on that narrow spit was ghastly. But the impetus of their rush carried the Japanese forward over their own dead and dying. Until they hit the newly installed wire. This seemed to take them completely by surprise, though a few actually got into Marine foxholes; the rest milled around in bewilderment. High-pitched screams of pain, fury, frustration rose above the raving of the automatic weapons which were piling up their dead.

It was hot work for many minutes for the handful of Marines at the point of contact. Japanese grenades reached the nearer foxholes, and men were killed and wounded there. Then the crazy tide receded, leaving its broken debris strewn across the sand spit.

The enemy attacked again and again, both across the spit and at other points just inland from the river's mouth. A hardy handful succeeded in reaching the western bank a couple of hundred yards farther inland, only to be pinned down there and eliminated at leisure when daylight came. A few managed to get around the wire and, creeping along the reverse slope of the beach, attempted unsuccessfully to infiltrate our shore positions. That was all.

The sector where the assault struck was manned by elements of the 2nd Battalion, 1st Marines, plus two platoons of the Special Weapons Battalion, operationally attached to that regiment. It was commanded by Lieutenant Colonel E. A. Pollock, battalion CO. He proceeded as quickly as possible to where things were hottest and took the situation in hand personally. By skillful employment of his few reserves, he had the position greatly strengthened by the time dawn came.

With the new day, Colonel Ichiki contributed another Japanese tactical gem to the general confusion. Instead of drawing off his battered force while he still had time, he chose to dig in among the widely spaced trees of the coconut plantation on a narrow point at the mouth of the river, and opened a fire fight with the Marines on the opposite bank. The Japanese used mortar and small-arms fire; the Marines replied in kind, with the addition of artillery and strafing attacks by the newly arrived planes. It was an absurdly unequal contest from the outset.

Having failed to break through a thinly held line in the darkness, did Ichiki really believe he had a chance of doing so in broad daylight, with the entire Division alerted? It was all quite incomprehensible to the occidental mind. Some officers clung to the belief that he was acting as spearhead for a more powerful force, or at least staging a feint to cover a major attack on some other sector. But when scouting planes failed to detect troop movements elsewhere, all hands decided that theirs was not to reason why. If this strange character wanted to encompass his own destruction, far be it from us to disoblige him.

The 1st Battalion, 1st Marines, currently in Division reserve, was brought up from its bivouac in the Lunga area. The men forded the Tenaru more than a mile above its mouth, deployed to cut off retreat inland or toward the east, and moved slowly through the jungle toward the coconut grove on the point. Downriver the unequal fire fight continued. Some Japanese, frantic with shell shock or terror, plunged into the ocean and tried to swim away. Marine veterans of a dozen rifle ranges happily lined the sights of their 03's upon the futilely bobbing heads.

On the east bank an increasing volume of small-arms fire could be heard as 1/1 closed in inexorably. About three o'clock five light tanks ambled across the corpse-strewn sand spit and into the grove, maneuvering easily among the well-spaced trees. Then 1/1 debouched from the jungle, and the final trap was sprung. Colonel Ichiki wrote "finis" to his peculiar campaign by burning the regimental colors and shooting himself through the head.

Nothing remained now but to bury the dead. With rare consideration, many of the Japanese supplied their own shovels, another of the many implements of which the Marines stood in sore need.

276

The first flight of Marine planes which moved in to base on Henderson Field on 20 August consisted of one fighter squadron and one dive bomber squadron: Captain John L. Smith's VMF-223 (19 Gruman Wildcats) and Major Richard C. Mangrum's VMSB-232 (12 Douglas Dauntlesses). None of the personnel had ever been in combat, but this was a deficiency which was remedied in short order. It so happened that their very timely arrival coincided with a marked stepping-up of Japanese activity in all departments. From the outset, the air force—these units and others which were to reinforce and relieve them from time to time—was employed as a tactical arm of the utmost importance. Never have two arms of any service worked in closer co-ordination than did the Marine Air and Ground Arms at Guadalcanal, and seldom have such efforts been so successful.

The Japanese had begun landing troops on the island in comparatively small contingents within the first few days of our occupation. Aside from the Ichiki detachment, their first—or first-known—attempt to bring in reinforcements on a large scale precipitated the Battle of the Eastern Solomons, 23-25 August. This occurred when a U.S. carrier task force intercepted an enemy convoy some distance short of Guadalcanal. The surface forces did not make contact; it was a case of planes vs. ships on both sides, with the dive bombers from Henderson Field flying missions in support of the Navy carrier-borne planes.

The result was not especially conclusive, and the enemy losses were never fully verified. They are believed to have been considerable. At any rate, for some time after this flight the Japanese showed a marked disinclination to risk their vulnerable heavy transports within range of our land-based bombers and resorted to other methods of piecemeal reinforcement of their garrison: bringing the troops down in smaller craft, traveling only by night along a chain of staging points on other islands; and carrying them as deck loads on destroyers and fast cruisers which could slip in under cover of darkness, unload, and be well out of the area before our planes could spot them in the morning.

Perhaps this was not the fastest way to build up a formidable attacking force, but obviously it was working after a fashion. There were increasing indications that another major assault to recapture the field was impending. If the Japanese had learned anything at all from the fate of the unlamented Colonel Ichiki, this one might really be serious. Marine combat patrols resumed their activities in the Matanikau-Kokumbona region in an effort to nip the threat in the bud, but with the resources at hand they were still unable to bring the enemy to decisive action.

The Japanese could land to the east of us or to the west, and all that made it impractical for them to land directly behind us, to the south, was the width of the island and the height and ruggedness of the mountains which formed its backbone. The same factors—jungle and lack of roads —which deterred the enemy from moving about freely, operated against us whenever we tried to get at them.

The air force was very useful in detecting these landings and helping to frustrate them, but the planes were helpless to a great extent in coping with the night sneaks. To handicap them still further, the Japanese began staging more frequent and heavier air attacks on Henderson Field. Life on Guadalcanal was becoming distinctly unpleasant.

Except for Colonel Ichiki's detachment the persistent landings of the Japanese had been concentrated to the northwest, where a force of formidable dimensions was being built up in the Tassafaronga-Kokumbona region. At 0200 on 2 September, however, a convoy was spotted unloading troops near Taivu Point, some miles to the east. When such activities were observed on several nights following, and ground patrols had verified them, it was decided to strike there by land.

This assignment was given to the Raider Battalion, newly arrived from Tulagi, with the Parachute Battalion in reserve. They embarked at Kukum on APD's[9] and landed under covering fire of the ships' guns early on the morning of 8 September. From here they moved against the rear of the main Japanese position, which had been located at Tasimboko village, not far to the west.

[9] Old destroyers converted into light transports.

278

There had been reports, subsequently verified, that the enemy force numbered up to five thousand. Yet all that the Raiders encountered was disorganized and unusually ineffectual resistance from what turned out to be a small rear echelon. In what had been the enemy bivouac area, supplies and equipment in considerable quantities were captured, together with six field guns. The main enemy forces had moved inland a day or two earlier, cutting a trail as they went, in a generally southwesterly direction.

The Raiders were to meet them a few nights later, however, when the whole howling mob boiled bloodily up out of the jungle to hurl themselves against the south-central sector of the airfield perimeter.

The enemy attack was planned with all the elaborate detail of which Japanese staffs are occasionally capable. It called for a co-ordinated three-pronged drive against the east, center and west sectors of the inland perimeter, supported by heavy air bombing by day and naval gunfire by night. In fact, it took practically everything into consideration—except the terrain in which it would have to be executed.

As a result of this omission, plus some hard fighting by us, the effort ended in as complete frustration as Colonel Ichiki's, and on a considerably larger scale. So difficult were communications in that country that the three assaults were poorly co-ordinated. The eastern force, after days of cutting trail and lugging gear through the dense jungle, arrived in position late and too exhausted to attack with determination. The western force did not attack at all until the main effort, in the center, had been completely defeated, and they were beaten off with comparative ease.

There was nothing easy about the fight in the center, however. This action, known as the Battle of the Ridge—sometimes called Bloody Ridge, Raiders' Ridge or Edson's Ridge—turned out to be one of the hottest things of its kind the campaign was to produce. It began in the evening of 12 September, accompanied by heavy naval shelling, and lasted with varying intensity all that night and the following day, not to be definitely decided until shortly

279

before dawn on the morning of the fourteenth. The defense line was breached at several points, some units were temporarily cut off, and there was wholesale infiltration, one small group of Japanese even penetrating to the Division command post which had been placed dangerously far forward. At one stage, Colonel Edson found himself holding a particularly vital position with some three hundred men against an attacking force estimated at two battalions.

The Ridge extended about a thousand yards due south from a point about a mile beyond the airstrip, which it commanded. Its crest and upper slopes were open and grassy, but the lower slopes and the valleys which flanked them were densely jungled. The defense line ran across the ridge itself and down into the jungle on either side. The left was held by two attenuated companies of the Parachute Battalion, the right by "C" Company of the Raiders whose flank lay near the Lunga River.

The right bore the brunt of the first night's fighting and was forced back, necessitating a withdrawal all along the line in order to maintain contact. When daylight efforts on the thirteenth failed to drive the enemy from their newly won positions, Colonel Edson decided on a further strategic withdrawal. This shortened his lines to about 1,800 yards, but they were still dangerously thin and not so well integrated as would have been desirable, owing to the rugged terrain.

The second night's attack was concentrated mainly on the Ridge itself, where the Paramarines and Company "B" of the Raiders were now in position. The Japanese reached deeply into the bag of tricks with which we were to become increasingly familiar as the war progressed. They talked in loud voices when approaching in order to draw fire that would reveal our position prematurely. They spread a smoke screen and shouted, "Gas attack!" They shouted other things in English of varying quality: insults, threats, faked commands. They cut in on the wave length of the portable radios to issue confusing reports. They charged down the length of the Ridge and swarmed up out of the jungles that flanked it. They obliged Colonel Edson to rec-

280

tify his lines again. At one crucial point he had only sixty men holding the Ridge proper. But they held it.

Action was intense from six in the evening until past midnight, with enemy cruisers and destroyers firing occasional missions on our positions as they had done the previous night. Our own artillery was in action on a large scale all night, firing with amazing speed and accuracy. Often the infantry of both sides were too intermingled in the viciousness of close combat for the fire of the 75's and 105's to be effective, but its end result was devastating. A lull in the fighting occurred during the early hours of the morning, broken by a large infiltration to the left rear. This, too, failed of accomplishment, and by 0500 there were unmistakable signs that the pressure was relaxing.

The reinforced defenders, attacking in their turn, succeeded in pushing the enemy back along the Ridge. Our planes, coming over to strafe at dawn, found a general retreat in progress toward the south and west. More than six hundred Japanese dead [10] were counted on the field of battle; how many were killed elsewhere or died during the retreat is problematical, though the number is known to be considerable.

The Japanese secondary attack to the east was delivered against elements of 3/1 holding a sector southeast of the airfield and a short distance west of the bank of the Tenaru. It began shortly after nine on the evening of the thirteenth with a fire fight, developed several assaults in considerable strength, and flickered intermittently all night. Our troops here were well dug in, behind wire, and the enemy was unable to penetrate anywhere. Throughout this engagement, their troops displayed a lack of spirit and determination remarkable for the Japanese at that time and place. It was not until later that we discovered that they were close to exhaustion before the assault even started. This futile gesture cost them about two hundred dead. Our losses were four dead, three wounded.

[10] Freshly killed Japanese turn a curious shade of lemon-yellow, the characteristic death pallor of their race. This does not last long, however; in the tropics decay sets in in a few hours.

The attack to the west did not even commence until late afternoon on the fourteenth, by which time the main enemy force was in full retreat. It struck a sector about midway between Kukum and the Matanikau, held by the 3rd Battalion of the 5th Marines. The Japanese charged in with the bayonet in broad daylight, one of the very few instances of daylight attacks in the entire campaign, and they were beaten back easily. Other sporadic attacks occurred during the day, uniformly futile.

What made the Guadalcanal campaign such a terrible experience for the personnel participating was the unending pressure to which all hands were subjected. There were no rest areas on the island, no recreation facilities; nowhere a man could go and nothing he could do to recuperate nerves rubbed raw by the strain of what amounted to perpetual combat. There was scarcely a day or night during the four months the First Marine Division was on Guadalcanal when they were not attacking or being attacked, by land, sea or air, and in many instances all three. Few troops in all the world's history have been subjected without relief to a pounding so intense and so sustained.

They had to do everything the hard way. Guadalcanal was a laboratory in which the techniques of future victories were developed by painful experimentation. We knew nothing of the Japanese except that up until now they had swept everything before them in this war. They were an oriental people; their tactics, psychology and battle ethics were utterly foreign to us. Our knowledge of the jungle and jungle fighting proved to be rudimentary. We lacked much in knowledge and in the means to cope with tropical diseases: malaria, dengue, scrub typhus, dysentery, the ever-present fungus infection familiarly known as "the crud."

Furthermore, the Marines who landed on Guadalcanal were essentially assault troops; their mission was to seize and secure a limited objective, then turn it over to troops better prepared to hold and exploit it. They were neither trained nor equipped for a protracted defensive action, and much of the equipment they had intended to bring

282

ashore had been hauled away upon the premature departure of the first transport convoy. But the first Army troops did not arrive until mid-October: one regiment, that came as reinforcements, not relief.

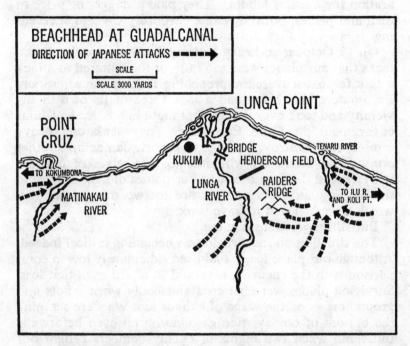

BEACHHEAD AT GUADALCANAL
DIRECTION OF JAPANESE ATTACKS ━━━▶
SCALE
SCALE 3000 YARDS

LUNGA POINT
POINT CRUZ
TENARU RIVER
BRIDGE
KUKUM
HENDERSON FIELD
TO KOKUMBONA
RAIDERS RIDGE
LUNGA RIVER
TO ILU R. AND KOLI PT.
MATINAKAU RIVER

The complete domination of air and sea which the Japanese had enjoyed at the outset had been considerably diminished by the arrival of our planes at Henderson Field. The enemy could harass and retard, but not seriously check, the arrival of our supplies and reinforcements, and we could do just about the same to him. During the two weeks' lull that followed the Battle of the Ridge, nightly parades of warships and landing craft poured Japanese into the Tassafaronga area, to the northwest, while we in turn received an important reinforcement by the arrival, on 18 September, of the last remaining regular element of the First Division: the 7th Marines.

Inside the Marine perimeter tension was mounting, and no clairvoyant was needed to figure out the shape of things to come. The Japanese had begun stepping up the intensity of their air attack late in September, and the tempo continued to mount as October progressed. They were obviously trying to knock out Henderson Field and its planes in preparation for a major landing. They paid a staggering price in men and planes, but they came perilously close to succeeding. In a sense, they did succeed.

On 11 October so heavy and continuous were the air attacks that our planes were too busy or too battered to attack a task force discovered approaching early in the afternoon. Fortunately, our Navy had a task force of its own in the vicinity and took over the job that night in a fierce half-hour engagement off Cape Esperance. They sank one heavy cruiser, four destroyers and a transport, damaging another cruiser and destroyer, with loss to themselves of one destroyer. And the next morning our planes did get up, found the limping survivors and set fire to two more destroyers which were believed to have sunk.

But still more were coming.

The situation on the airfield was becoming critical indeed. Although our plane losses had been ridiculously low in comparison with the enemy's, we could ill afford even that loss. Surviving planes were battered and badly worn, pilots and ground crews on the verge of exhaustion. We were scraping the bottom of our aviation-gasoline barrel even before the thirteenth when two flights of enemy bombers caught our planes on the ground, set fire to one of our few remaining fuel dumps and made a shambles of the landing strip. Clearly a crisis was near. It came that night.

The Japanese heavy artillery had opened on the field early in the evening, and there had been repeated air alerts. Beyond the Matanikau, enemy ground troops were throwing up signal rockets. All hands were expecting a land attack. This never materialized, but it was about the only thing that didn't.

Later in the evening Condition Red sounded again. This time it was Louie the Louse. He dropped a flare over the airfield, and all hands dove for their dugouts. They knew the invariable signal for a naval bombardment. They had lived through many. But they had never lived through anything like that night and, praise God, would never have to again.

This time the Japanese had battleships. For an hour and twenty minutes they lay off Savo Island, pouring in a steady stream of twelve- and fourteen-inch shells. Cruisers added their sixes and eights. Destroyers swung in close with their fives, while bombing planes came over in relays and the heavy artillery ashore contributed its bit to the general chaos.

Of thirty-nine Marine dive bombers which had been operational the day before, only four were in condition to leave the ground in the morning—after the strip had been repaired sufficiently for them to take off.

Late that afternoon one of these hardy survivors, scouting between more air raids, discovered the enemy's main troop convoy coming down the Slot: seven large transports, escorted by destroyers. Meanwhile, ground crews had repaired nine more of the Dauntless dive bombers. These attacked as evening was drawing on, sinking one transport and damaging another. The five survivors plodded on and were soon lost in the closing night. Another naval shelling, lasting from 0105 to 0220, provided them further cover, and at dawn we needed no scouting planes to locate them: they were calmly discharging troops and cargo about fifteen miles up the coast to the west.

The night's bombing and shelling had left us only three bombers in operating condition, and so badly pitted was the runway that two of these were wrecked attempting to take off. The Wildcat fighters, which had been less hard hit, went at the transports with machine guns. More dive bombers were hurriedly put in shape. The Japanese responded with flights of Zeros, float planes, and a storm of AA from the screening warships. Before the day was over, we had thrown in everything we could glue together, including General Geiger's PBY (big, clumsy Catalina flying boat), which attacked successfully in the guise of a torpedo bomber. The Army sent over a flight of B-17 Flying Fortresses from their base at Espiritu Santo in the New Hebrides. 1100 that morning found one of the transports sunk, two beached and burning, the other two damaged and in flight.

But no doubt the Japanese considered them expendable. A large part, at least, of their mission had been accomplished.

It was during this hectic period that the first U.S. Army troops reached the island. If ever soldiers were pitchforked abruptly into battle, it was the men of the 164th Infantry. They landed under air attack on the thirteenth and reached their bivouac area just in time for the naval shelling that the Japanese dished out that night. They were to prove themselves one of the finest fighting units it has ever been the privilege of Marines to serve with. This was fortunate, for their mettle was to be tested in short order.

The Japanese attack which was now in the making was under the direction of Lieutenant General Hyakutake, Commanding General of the XVII Army, recently arrived from Rabaul to take personal charge. Essentially the attack was similar to the one which had failed at Bloody Ridge more than a month before. Hyakutake had fresher men and more of them, that was the main difference: a full division, heavily reinforced. It never seemed to occur to him that the basic tactics might be faulty. Or were these the only offensive tactics the Japanese knew? As the war progressed, we were to see them repeat previous mistakes time and time again.

Once more they moved deep into the jungle to the south, cutting trail and lugging gear. This time, at the cost of prodigious labor, they achieved a degree of tactical surprise: the trail went through so far below the perimeter that our patrols failed to discover it. We were expecting an attack from somewhere in the general direction of the Matanikau for obvious reasons, and we got it, though it proved only a single phase of the whole complicated operation. What prevented the troops to the south from effecting serious surprise was that all hands in our perimeter had been alerted for so long that they were prepared for practically anything, anywhere. That—plus the steadiness and determination of the Marines and soldiers who bore the brunt of the assault; plus, again, the same lack of co-ordination which had doomed the enemy's previous all-out effort.

Japanese patrol activity increased along the lower Matanikau on 20 October. During the following night, tanks could

286

be heard moving up toward the west bank. Artillery chased them back, how far we did not know, and we took the hint to bring half-tracks and 37's into the area. To make their intentions even more evident, enemy planes came over at dusk and strafed our forward positions along the river. But nothing further developed that night or the next. The lone battalion which constituted our sole mobile reserve was not lured into that sector.

The Matanikau attack finally developed shortly after dark on the night of the twenty-third, with Hyakutake trying to throw two full infantry regiments against the narrow front held by 3/1. It was preceded by the closest equivalent of a barrage that the Japanese, with their odd ideas of using artillery, had yet put on. Then their tanks, which we had been hearing for some time, dashed out of the jungle and started for our positions. There were ten of them, in two waves: little 18-tonners, exceedingly vulnerable. The only practicable crossing was the sand spit at the river's mouth, narrow and without cover. Only one made it, overrunning a machine gun emplacement and several foxholes. A Marine, crouching in one of the latter, calmly slipped a hand grenade under one tread, crippling its steering mechanism. It reeled around into the surf where a half-track 75 destroyed it.

Meanwhile, the 11th Marines had opened up with the heaviest massed fire the campaign had produced to date, saturating the area. They had been registered on this particular target for weeks. The carnage was terrible. The Japanese infantry, which had been grouped to follow the tanks, never left the cover of the jungle, where they could be heard yelling and screaming. One column did attempt to force a crossing farther up but was easily repulsed. When our patrols explored the region a few days later, they counted some six hundred dead. Japanese reports captured subsequently indicated that two battalions of the 4th Imperial Infantry had been annihilated.

This abortive attack failed entirely of effect. Again that lack of co-ordination: the troops who were to stage the enemy drive from the south, which presumably was to be simultaneous, did not get into position until the following

287

night, while a secondary blow evidently designed to distract us still further did not come off until the night following that.

The main attack from the south developed about midnight of 24/25 October, hitting a sector below and to the east of Bloody Ridge where the previous drive had been turned back. This was held by the 3rd Battalion, 164th Infantry, with the 1st Battalion, 7th Marines, tying in with their right. After ten days of being bombed, shelled and strafed, the soldiers were spoiling for a chance to fight back. They got it that night and handled it like veterans.

The Japanese attack followed the familiar pattern: a power thrust against a narrow front. Our artillery quickly zeroed-in on the ground it would have to cross, and pounded the enemy assembly area in depth. A torrential downfall of rain hampered both attackers and defenders. Men of the 2nd Battalion, 164th, posted in reserve, groped forward through the pitch darkness to reinforce their comrades. The position, well wired-in, stood firm as a rock. With the approach of dawn, the surviving Japanese fell back sullenly to regroup.

That day (25 October) became known to the battered defenders of Guadalcanal as "Dugout Sunday." Intense enemy air activity gave ample evidence that they considered the battle far from over despite the two bloody repulses they had already suffered. This air activity was unopposed at first, the rains of the night before having reduced the airfield to such a state that it was impossible for our fighters to take off. Japanese warships moved in with impunity to sink or chase away the few auxiliary vessels we had available, before turning their guns on the shore positions, the first occasion when they had approached so close during the daytime since arrival of our planes.

Prodigious work by Engineers and Seabees, however, finally got the field operational again despite hell and high water, bombs, shells and mud. And once our planes did get aloft, the toll was enormous. Fighters went after the enemy's Zeros and bombers, and presently the sky was full of falling aircraft—not ours. Dive bombers chased off the surface ships, sinking a cruiser and seriously damaging at least one other craft.

All these signs and portents were not lost on the men at the front, who spent the day repairing wire and generally improving their positions. Sure enough, with darkness the enemy to the south began to move again. This time their immediate objective was a little to the west of the previous night's attack: the sector held by 1/7, under Lieutenant Colonel Lewis B. Puller.[11]

The first assault hit the defenders' wire about 2200, and from then until after dawn the firing was almost incessant. It would rise to a furious crescendo as each successive onslaught reached its full height, then gradually taper off as the Japanese fell back to reorganize and work themselves up to the proper pitch for another try. The battle developed a rhythm of its own as the same thing happened time after time; a tempo you could almost set your watch by.

And the full force of the attack always struck in the same place, which made it very convenient for the strung-out defenders. Later Colonel Puller asked a captured Japanese sergeant why, after repeated repulses, they had not probed other parts of the line for weak spots, something they had proved quite adept at doing in some other instances. The Japanese shrugged. This particular attack, he explained, had been very thoroughly planned, and no unit would think of deviating from the letter of its orders. Here was another instance of that curious inflexibility of the Japanese military mind which we were to encounter so often.

By 0530 the following morning, Colonel Puller's command had withstood six separate assaults of undiminishing fury. Now a seventh, launched with final desperation,

[11] Much-decorated "Chesty" Puller has never been noted as one of the Marine Corps' least colorful characters. With seven assorted shell fragments in his anatomy, he submitted reluctantly to medical attention. The corpsman on the scene took one look and began writing out an evacuation tag. "Take that damned label and paste it on a bottle!" yelled the colonel furiously. "I remain in command here!"

achieved a small breakthrough; but even this was to be short lived. Before they could exploit their gain or even dig in to hold it, daylight came. Caught in a savage cross fire, the pocket became a deathtrap. Few, if any, of the enemy got back through that gap in our wire.

Once more the Japanese wave subsided into the jungle, beyond artillery and mortar range. After the toll exacted by these two nights of savage fighting, they were through as a major offensive force. And they had not come within a mile of the airfield they had set out to capture.

While the fighting just described had been in progress, during the early morning hours of 26 October, another enemy force launched a furious assault against the inland flank of the Matanikau sector, about four miles to the west. As a diversion, this came at least two days too late to have any effect. It was not organized in sufficient strength to constitute a major threat in itself, but it did provide plenty of trouble during the time it lasted.

Dawn showed 227 Japanese dead in, and immediately in front of, the position, with many more in the ravine below. By conservative estimate, the enemy had lost 3,400 killed during the entire three-way, three-day action.

The Matanikau ridge sector was not attacked again, but the next two days saw some further fighting south of the airfield. It was directed mainly against Colonel Puller's sector and the point where his flank joined that of the 164th. It never achieved the proportions of the first two nights and gradually diminished until it petered out into random sniping.

It was the Japanese who chose to make Guadalcanal a major issue. This was all to the good, as things turned out, but at the time we would have preferred to pay a minimum purchase price, had the choice been ours.

Perhaps they were motivated by that strange oriental fear of losing face. Perhaps, clinging to their singular conceptions of decadent democracies, they fully believed that a serious setback at this remote spot would convince our nation once and for all of the futility of attempting to com-pete with supermen. Whatever the reason, they threw at us everything that they had within reach, and that was a good deal. As someone expressed it, Guadalcanal became a sinkhole: a bottomless pit into which they poured ships and planes and men: ships and planes and men which would never be used against us elsewhere. Nowhere in the Pacific did they pay so high a price to lose a piece of real estate of comparable size and strategic importance.

Before the end of the campaign fifty thousand Japanese, by conservative estimate, had died either on Guadalcanal or on ships attempting to reach it. Dark rumors of the "Island of Death" seeped back to more remote posts of the Imperial Army, and more than a year later Radio Tokyo was still referring to the First Marine Division as "the Guadalcanal butchers."

The part played by the Navy air and surface forces in the campaign cannot be minimized. Without their daring and skillful efforts not even survival would have been possible, let alone victory. Already we have seen how, after the initial setback off Savo Island, they had turned the enemy back in the Battle of the Eastern Solomons on 23-25 August and off Cape Esperance 11 October. On 26 October, while the Marines ashore were still beating back the major Japanese threat, opposing carrier task forces were fighting the plane vs. ship Battle of Santa Cruz, seven hundred miles to the northeast, again inflicting losses that hurt. And our greatest and most decisive victory was yet to come.

But the troops ashore could not know this as that bloody October drew to a close. All they knew was they had smashed the enemy, that they were deathly tired from heavy fighting and months of bombing and shelling—and that, instead of getting the rest they had so well earned, they were moving out to attack once more.

The Japanese were coming again; coming in the greatest strength they had yet displayed. Several separate naval task forces were on the prowl. A transport convoy of twelve large ships lurked somewhere to the northwest, prepared to make the final dash. If their previous defeats had taught them anything, it was that they needed more of everything: more ships, more planes, more troops. This time they planned to land two reinforced divisions to join the battered, scattered survivors of earlier catastrophes.

But we had received some additional troops ourselves. The 8th Marines, Reinforced, a Second Division unit, had landed on 4 November, and much needed replacements arrived on the eleventh. By the twelfth, with the landing of two battalions of the 182nd Infantry, together with reinforcing elements, a large part of the Army's American Division was ashore. These included more artillery: 105's and big 155's. Air reinforcements had brought our strength on Henderson Field to five Marine squadrons, four Navy squadrons and one Army squadron. The ground forces shortened and strengthened their lines and waited confidently.

The Japanese employed the same tactics which had so nearly succeeded in mid-October: to neutralize Henderson Field by intensive air and naval attack in order to permit the vulnerable transports to come in unmolested by our air force. The intensity of their bombing attacks was stepped up sharply on 11 November and during the succeeding day. But now we had much greater strength with which to oppose them. Few of their bombers were able to get through to the field; those which were not shot down in the attempt wasted their ammunition in ineffectual attacks on the shipping which had brought in the reinforcements, still unloading offshore.

During the night of 12/13, a powerful Japanese task force closed in for the kill. About 0100 Louie the Louse flew over the field and dropped flares, the conventional signal that the shelling was about to begin. But at this juncture something occurred which seems to have been quite outside the enemy's expectations.

The transports which had brought in our reinforcements had been escorted by a small task force of cruisers and destroyers in two groups, under command of Rear Admiral Daniel J. Callaghan and Rear Admiral Norman Scott, respectively. As night drew on, Admiral Turner, in over-all command, had herded his transports out to sea and dispersed them in order to avoid the enemy force which was bearing down, turning his combat vessels over to Admiral

Callaghan. About the time Louie's flares were lighting up Henderson Field, this able officer hurled his force with stunning suddenness squarely into the enemy fleet northwest of Savo Island.

He was ridiculously outnumbered and outweighed. The enemy were moving in three parallel columns, and Callaghan led the American force straight down between them, blazing away to port and starboard with fine impartiality. Within fifteen minutes practically every U.S. ship had been damaged. In approximately half an hour the survivors had passed through the entire enemy fleet, whereupon they broke off the action and slipped away into the darkness, leaving the enemy milling about in too great confusion to shell anybody ashore, what remained of the several columns firing into each other long after their attackers had disappeared.

This was an exploit of which any Navy could be proud. But it was not achieved without cost. A shell struck the bridge of the flagship, *U.S.S. San Francisco,* instantly killing Admiral Callaghan and the ship's commander, Captain Cassin Young. Admiral Scott went down with his flagship, the light cruiser, *U.S.S. Atlanta,* another light cruiser and four destroyers were also lost, two cruisers and three destroyers badly damaged.

Japanese losses were one heavy cruiser, one light cruiser and one destroyer definitely sunk, and one battleship crippled. Two additional cruisers and at least three destroyers were left burning furiously and presumed sunk.

As usual when their preconceived plans were upset, the Japanese seemed incapable of adapting themselves to the altered situation. The bewildered task force limped off to the west to reorganize, their mission completely frustrated. Not a shell fell on Henderson Field that night. Our search planes, going up without hindrance the next morning, discovered the crippled battleship previously mentioned and summoned torpedo planes and dive bombers. These left her at dusk dead in the water and being abandoned by her crew; though they did not actually see her sink, next day only an oil slick remained where she had been.

The following night, however, a task force did get

through and shelled the field. Perhaps this was what remained of the same force, or perhaps another like it; so many enemy task forces were prowling the Solomons those days that it was hard to tell which was which. Again there was at least one battleship, plus cruisers and destroyers. Again the Japanese displayed that singular ineptness which characterized their operations throughout the Guadalcanal campaign. In October an intensive bombardment lasting an hour and twenty minutes had failed to knock out Henderson Field; now they shelled for only forty-five minutes and departed precipitately before the dire threat of a handful of PT boats which was all we could muster to throw against them.

One dive bomber and two fighters had been destroyed on the field. A few others had been damaged, none beyond prompt repair. There was no damage to the runway which could not be remedied in short order. The search planes were off with the dawn—and when they reported back, all hands knew that This Was It.

The Japanese transports were making their run for the island: twelve of them, crammed with troops and equipment, convoyed by five cruisers and six destroyers. Our air arm hit them with everything we had. Marine, Navy, Army: dive bombers, torpedo bombers, scout bombers, even B-17's; they attacked in swarms, in relays, shuttling from the scene of action back to Henderson Field to refuel and rearm, then back to the slaughter. They blasted everything that floated, concentrating on the transports. One after another sank or caught fire. Late afternoon found the survivors, abandoned by their protecting escort, still staggering forward.

Under cover of darkness, four of them actually made the run and beached near Tassafaronga. It was a brave but futile gesture. With the coming of daylight on 15 November, planes and long-range artillery destroyed them before they could unload. The number of bomb-happy soldiers who may have come ashore could not constitute more than a minor nuisance. The bulk of these two Japanese divisions had made their beachhead on the bottom of the Pacific.

But even as darkness was closing mercifully over the helpless transports, the Japanese Navy was rushing, hellbent, toward another major disaster. A strong task force was hastening down from the north, evidently intending to shell the airfield into helplessness in order to save the surviving troop ships. This included two battleships in addition to the usual heavy and light cruisers and destroyers. But coming up from the opposite direction were the two much more powerful U.S. battleships *South Dakota* and *Washington* escorted by four destroyers, under Rear Admiral Willis A. Lee.

The ensuing action did not last long. The Japanese lighter craft attempted to break through the thin destroyer screen in an effort to get at the big ships. They succeeded in sinking three of the destroyers, but that was all the good it did them. While the remaining destroyer was picking up the survivors from her sisters, the battlewagons opened up with radar-directed fire from their 16-inch guns. In the roaring half-hour before the enemy scattered and fled ignominiously the Japanese lost one battleship, three heavy cruisers and a destroyer sunk; another battleship, cruiser and destroyer, heavily damaged.

These three days of diverse but almost continuous action became known as the Naval Battle of Guadalcanal. Its effect on the Japanese was crippling; temporarily, at any rate: it left them without the ships to send more troops in to Guadalcanal, even if they had the troops to send after the terrible losses they had sustained in these attempts.[12]

And without these troops, Japanese offensive operations

---

[12] There were anxious days in the United States before this denouement became known. Certain of those self-appointed oracles, the news commentators, began writing off the whole Guadalcanal operation, to the great dismay of relatives of the men fighting there. The Navy, they declared, was unable either to reinforce or to evacuate the Marines ashore and had decided to abandon them to their fate rather than lose more lives and ships trying. A short-wave broadcast to this effect was picked up on the island where it caused much surprise and indignation. Apparently about the only people who refused to believe that the First Marine Division was licked were the men of the First Marine Division.

on the island itself came necessarily to a standstill. The decisive phase of the Guadalcanal campaign had closed.

As far as Guadalcanal was concerned, the First Marine Division was through to all intents and purposes as November drew to a close. For four months they had fought in one of the foulest climates on earth; had been bombed, shelled and shot at between periods of actual fighting. Now, as American troops continued to pour in, and Japanese troops were unable to reach the island, it was possible to start relieving these units on the lines. Soon they would be able to leave the island altogether. It seemed an age ago that they had arrived, expecting a stay of three to four weeks. . . .

Among the newly arrived troops was one especially spectacular unit, commanded by a spectacular man: the 2nd Marine Raider Battalion, under Lieutenant Colonel Evans F. Carlson. These were the people who had made the hit-and-run attack on Makin in mid-August, landing from submarines. At Guadalcanal they wrote another brilliant entry in their, and their leader's, record.

All of the Raider battalions were specially picked, specially trained. By nature, they were light, swift-moving, hard-hitting troops, mentally alert and physically hardy. Much was expected of them in training and in combat, and in recompense they were accorded certain special privileges in camp. This occasionally irked the line troops beside whom they did most of their fighting, since occasions for the employment of their specialty were comparatively rare. But when such occasions did arise, the Raiders were magnificent.

Carlson's battalion had landed at Aola early in November. Immediately they set out in pursuit of those Japanese who had fled into the interior.

What followed was a month of strenuous campaigning, covering some of the most difficult terrain on the island. Relentlessly the Raiders tracked down the Japanese they were pursuing. Their course carried them farther inland than Marines had ever been. Here they encountered groups of stragglers, flotsam and jetsam of the many columns which had beaten their brains out against the Marine defense.

296

Swinging far south of the perimeter, they came upon the trail cut by the Japanese for their ill-fated October assault. Here they found well-organized detachments of the enemy occupying well-stocked bivouac areas. Moving with incredible speed for that type of country, striking with stunning surprise and annihilating power, the Raiders cleared out all the territory below the airfield position for a depth of many miles in every direction.

When they entered the perimeter on 4 December, they had destroyed more than four hundred Japanese troops in twelve separate engagements, with a total loss to themselves of seventeen killed.

Following the enemy's crushing naval defeat, the nature of ground operations underwent a marked change. This did not become apparent immediately. For nearly a month our activities were confined mainly to patrolling, punctuated by infrequent clashes with an enemy who, unable to attack, appeared to have withdrawn a considerable distance from our lines.

Within the perimeter, there was a wholesale realignment of units. The First Marine Division completed evacuation on 9 December.

On this date Major General Vandegrift turned over command to Major General Alexander Patch, USA, Commanding General of the Americal Division. This unit was at full strength now, following the arrival of the 132nd Infantry, and more troops of the XIV Corps were pouring in. With the Japanese clearly incapable of attacking, General Patch judged the time ripe to inaugurate the offensive which was destined to drive them forever from the island.

It proved painfully slow going. As became evident, the Japanese, abandoning hope of resuming the attack with the resources at hand, had utilized the breathing spell to dig in defensively. They attempted to establish no continuous lines of resistance, no organized defense in depth; instead, they prepared isolated strong points to take full advantage of the rugged, jungled ground: in ravines, on reverse slopes, in other areas in defilade from our artillery fire where often a single machine gun nest could pin down an entire battalion. The consummate skill of the Japanese in the utilization of terrain and camouflage, which was to feature all Pacific campaigns, now came conspicuously to the fore.

And with it went that dogged persistence which caused men, without hope of escape or of gaining anything more than a little time, to fight grimly to the death. With equal grimness the Marines and soldiers learned to contain the pockets of resistance and push on, leaving them for the reserve troops to clean out at leisure.

The Army's Twenty-fifth Infantry Division arrived in mid-January. Expecting that the enemy was planning a last desperate stand in prepared positions in the high, rugged ground of Cape Esperance, General Patch moved this fresh unit far inland to converge on the cape from the southeast in conjunction with the drive along the northern coast. New as they were to the jungle, the Twenty-fifth pushed on relentlessly through some of the worst campaigning terrain in the world, and reached Cape Esperance, to find—nothing much. A few miserable stragglers showed a semblance of fight or slunk off into the jungle. Of the high officers who were known to have been on the island, of the formidable force which it had been thought was assembling here for a last stand, there was no trace. Organized resistance on Guadalcanal had ceased.

What had happened? Radio Tokyo promptly announced that the Japanese High Command, deeming Guadalcanal of little value, anyway, had withdrawn their troops intact without interference from the badly beat-up Americans. The Americans, inured by now to the reliability of Japanese broadcasts, paid no more attention to this claim than to a dozen previous fatuous boasts.

It was not until the end of the war gave us access to official enemy reports that we found out exactly what had happened. For one of the very few times during the entire war, Tokyo had told the literal truth. The Japanese Navy had actually accomplished what hardly an American on Guadalcanal would have believed possible. Using submarines, destroyers, any swift craft available; taking full advantage of the moonless nights, which grounded our aircraft, to shuttle back and forth to the nearest islands still in their possession, they had successfully evacuated not only their high officers,

298

but some sixteen thousand troops: rather more than our Intelligence believed still existed on the island. Here was a truly brilliant achievement to crown as bungling and inept a campaign as was ever waged by a major power.

These reports unearthed after the war disclosed another interesting and somewhat sinister fact not known at the time. By late January, 1943, the Japanese had managed to concentrate at Rabaul some fifty thousand mobile troops, together with the ships to transport them and the war vessels to convoy them. They had been definitely earmarked for another all-out effort to recapture Guadalcanal when the unexpected successes of the Australian-American drive in northern New Guinea caught the enemy command on the horns of a dilemma. This Japanese expeditionary force might well prove decisive in either theater, but it could hardly be divided between the two with any prospect of success. After much soul searching, the High Command decided to evacuate the Guadalcanal garrison to reinforce the central Solomons in hopes of making a stand there and assigned the troops at Rabaul to New Guinea—where the great bulk of them were to meet a watery grave in the Battle of the Bismarck Sea in early March.

The Guadalcanal campaign was the longest in the entire Pacific war. Ground fighting lasted for six months. And even after this had ceased, the Japanese were still able to reach the island with occasional air strikes which inflicted damage and casualties.

It was far from being the bloodiest in point of actual battle casualties. Marine units listed 1,242 as killed in action, died of wounds and missing; wounded numbered 2,655. But if the number of men knocked out by sickness were counted, casualties would have been close to total. Very, very few of the Marines who fought there—and not many of the later-arriving soldiers—failed to contract at least malaria. And malaria incapacitated men as effectively as wounds, not once but recurrently, sometimes over a period of years.

The importance of the operation has a number of facets.

It marked our assumption of the offensive, which we were never to relinquish; and by the same token, the end of the Japanese offensive. The strategic and tactical gains were obvious: guaranteed safety for our supply line to Australia; an air base and advanced staging area from which to strike toward the heart of the enemy's gains. It taught us much; and as the first head-on meeting with the Japanese, it set the pattern in many respects for things to come.

It demonstrated clearly to the world at large that the Japanese soldier was something less than the superman he had been pictured on the strength of his early, easy conquests.

What was he, then?

A Marine sergeant, interviewed by an Army intelligence officer at the height of the fighting, stated the point of view of the men in the ranks with admirable succinctness. "Hell," he said, "they ain't supermen; they're just a bunch of tricky little bastards."

A more scholarly analysis, written by a staff officer long after the heat of battle had subsided, put it somewhat differently:

"He (the Japanese soldier) fought, as an individual, as well and as bravely as any warrior the world has ever seen; he bore privation and hardship that would have put out of action most of the troops of the Allied forces, and in spite of those hardships and that privation, he attacked with determined ferocity whenever he came in contact with the American troops. In attack he was single minded and reckless of his life; in defense he was bitterly tenacious. He was in all ways except intelligence a worthy enemy and one to be respected." [13]

The word "respected" is correct in the sense it is used here, but it is open to connotations which would not win widespread approval. The men who fought him respected the danger that the Japanese soldier represented; they did not, with very rare individual exceptions, respect him as a man.

[13] Captain J. L. Zimmerman, USMCR, in "The Guadalcanal Campaign," monograph published by Historical Division, U.S. Marine Corps.

It was often too difficult to differentiate his bravery from sheer stupidity. Too often his tenacity was without point, and his Banzai charges, which never in the course of the entire war achieved any results of importance, seemed plain silly.

In his willingness to die, he frequently let death become an end in itself, losing sight of the fact that by dying he was supposed to accomplish something for his country, not merely earn himself a one-way ticket to that odd oriental Valhalla reserved for men killed in battle. Indeed, so engrossed did he sometimes become with the death fixation that he did not wait to be killed. In the course of the war many thousands, high officers as well as men in the ranks, were to follow the illustrious example of Colonel Ichiki and take their own lives rather than die fighting. Whether the Japanese war gods allow full credit for this type of exit has never been clearly established.

The Japanese soldier possessed great endurance, patience and the ability to subsist on a minimum of nourishment, but man for man he was smaller and less powerful physically than the American. Though his publicists made a great to-do about the manly virtues of fighting hand to hand with cold steel, he seldom resorted to this in actual practice, and nearly always came out second best when he did. Contrary to early belief, he was no better adapted by nature to the jungle than were our people; he had simply been there longer and received more special training, an advantage which was soon overcome. Nor was he any less vulnerable to tropical diseases. His people had cornered the natural sources of quinine, then the only specific against that ubiquitous scourge, malaria, yet, before the war had progressed far, American medical science had developed repressives equal or superior.

He did possess at the outset one great advantage: complete lack of inhibiting battle ethics, as defined by modern civilization and the precepts of the Geneva Convention. He would as soon kill a chaplain administering the last rites to the dying as he would an active enemy. Nothing delighted him more than killing our wounded lying helpless between the lines, unless it was killing the doctors and hospital corps-

301

men who went out to attend them. For one thing, chaplains, doctors and corpsmen, under the terms of the Geneva Convention, were not armed—not at the beginning, anyway.[14]

What we did not realize at the outset was that we were fighting what was essentially a medieval nation, with the medieval conception of total war, total destruction. And it was this conception which carried Japan down to the most abject defeat ever suffered by a supposedly first-class power since the Middle Ages. For once they had showed us the way, there was nothing for it but to play the game the way they wanted it played.

The Japanese High Command was full of surprises and paradoxes. The officer class was thoroughly professional and had been for generations, yet they proved grossly negligent, or ignorant, in several matters which the armies of other nations considered military fundamentals.

One of these was combat intelligence. Although their prewar espionage system was a model of far-reaching thoroughness, their officers in the field were nearly always without accurate knowledge of their enemy's strength and intentions, and seemed quite incapable of devising means for gaining such knowledge. Some of the egregious errors into which this led them have already been seen. There were to be many more.

Security, both internal and external, was another glaring weakness. Troops went into combat carrying diaries, letters, maps showing their dispositions, and even orders outlining in detail the action in which they were participating. Literally tons of documents were captured in enemy command posts; it never seemed to occur to anyone that they should have been destroyed. Japanese prisoners of war talked freely about everything they knew, even guiding our troops upon occasion. They had never been taught differently; their officers, having ordered them to die rather than be captured, could not consistently instruct them on how they should behave as prisoners.

Troop security in the field was treated with equal negligence. Patrols were constantly being taken by surprise.

[14] Japan never signed the Geneva Convention.

302

Columns marched through unknown country, shouting and jabbering at the top of their lungs, without benefit of a point or flankers. Time after time, patrols of ours simply walked undetected into the midst of their bivouac areas.

Their staff work was spotty: there was nearly always either too little of it or too much. That is, their operations were either impromptu affairs without adequate preparation, or planned in such intricate and elaborate detail as to be unworkable under combat conditions. And they were completely without ability to improvise when things failed to work out as expected.

Their only tactical innovation was the development of infiltration on a wide scale. In this they appear to have had a childlike faith. To anyone fighting a war by the book, the presence of active enemy elements on his flanks or in his rear is a serious matter, and this tactic had caused the British some trouble in Malaya and Burma, and the Dutch in the Indies. But in the Pacific we threw the book overboard and came to recognize infiltration for what it was: a minor nuisance to be dealt with by troops in reserve.

Aside from this, their idea of winning battles was to achieve surprise if possible, otherwise to overwhelm by sheer weight of numbers and indifference to losses. These means failing, they became what the sergeant previously quoted had called them: they abandoned tactics for trickery.

This assumed an almost infinite variety of forms. Individuals would feign a desire to surrender in order to get close enough to blow their captors—and themselves—to kingdom come with concealed grenades. They booby-trapped our dead and even their own. English-speaking Japanese cut in on our radio frequencies and tapped field telephone lines in order to issue false orders or misleading reports, or they shouted such orders in the midst of battle. Whole companies memorized catch phrases of English which they would yell for one reason or another. Snipers in ambush simulated wounded Marines by calling "Corpsman! Corpsman!" in order to lure to their deaths men engaged in errands of mercy.

Officers up through the rank of colonel were generally

brave and conscientious, if unimaginative and unresourceful. Above that, the qualities varied amazingly. We were to encounter the case of one general who carried through an exceedingly clever operation for the sole purpose of assuring his own safety, then abandoned to its destruction the army which had made his escape possible. Another, after ordering his men to their death in an effulgent proclamation, proceeded to kill himself rather than lead them. Not until Iwo Jima were we to meet a Japanese commander to whom high Marine officers could accord genuine professional respect.

Officers and men alike were essentially attack minded. All of their manuals and field regulations heavily emphasized the offensive aspects of warfare. And despite its general nature, the Guadalcanal campaign, save for its opening and closing phases, had been basically a Japanese offensive, or at the very least, a counteroffensive. There was a widespread belief at this time that they were physically and temperamentally incapable of sustaining protracted action of a purely defensive character; that that curious phenomenon, the Banzai charge, was in reality a form of combat fatigue: the crack-up of men whose nerves could no longer stand being on the receiving end of battle.

How infinitely wide this was of the truth, we were soon to learn. For following Guadalcanal, we would be the ones on the offensive. It would be our men's flesh and blood that were pitted against the emplaced weapons of the enemy. It might be said, without too great risk of contradiction, that Japan's greatest military achievement of the war was the conversion of a fighting force imbued for generations with the philosophy of attack into what were quite likely the most stubborn defensive fighters in all military history.

For that, unfortunately for us, is precisely what the Japanese became as the war moved westward.

Guarding Australia

The enemy had failed to turn the corner of New Guinea by sea; now they were to try it by land. In the late months of spring and early summer, 1942, the Australians kept the Jap troops pinned down along the northern coast; except for minor land actions, the main battles had been fought in the air, with the Australians and Americans slowly but surely wresting control of the air from the Japs. However, in late July, the Japs landed 5,000 troops at Gona Mission. From there they drove the Australian forces back through the jungle to the Kokoda Trail, sixty miles south; this was the route over the Owen Stanley Range and down through the jungle to Port Moresby. The Australian defenders were outnumbered five to one, but they fought a stubborn withdrawing action as they retreated southward up the Owen Stanley Mountains.

Gen. MacArthur, then in Australia, was determined to hold Port Moresby; it was the base from which he would fight his way back to the Philippines. Gen. Kenney, his air commander, flew pursuit fighters in; he used bombers to bring up fresh troops and badly needed supplies to the Australians in the mountains, and, as the Aussies withdrew toward Port Moresby, the flying time shortened enough to let the air force hit the Japs in their front lines.

"The Japs covered the sixty miles of their advance from Buna in five days. To push ahead another thirty miles took fifty days, and the speed of their advance slackened every day." * The Japs got all the way to the village of Ioribaiwa, thirty-two miles from Port Moresby, but here the Australians held, and a counteroffensive was soon launched.

* George H. Johnston, *The Toughest Fighting in the World*, p. 138.

FIGHTING BACK IN NEW GUINEA

by George H. Johnston

The limit of the Japanese advance toward Port Moresby—the mountain ridge and village of Ioribaiwa—was captured today, Sept. 28, 1942, and our troops are pushing ahead through a heavy rainstorm toward the scattered villages that line the "Kokoda Trail."

The Japs offered little resistance, although they had built up a high timber palisade across the top of the ridge in front of an involved system of weapon pits and trenches. 25-pounders blew great holes in the palisade and the Australians went in with the bayonets and grenades. The Japs didn't wait for any more. They scuttled northward through the jungle, abandoning a stack of unburied dead, a great dump of equipment and ammunition, and leaving to us the steep ridge down which we retreated only a couple of weeks ago with the Japs rolling stones and grenades down on us and plastering our rearguard with fierce mortar and machine-gun fire.

The Japs have left a lot of graves on Ioribaiwa Ridge, and trampled in the mud between the bodies of the dead is an elaborate shirt of scarlet silk with a black dragon embroidered on it. Most of the corpses are emaciated. General Blamey, the Australian Field Commander, was right about letting the jungle beat the Japs. The evidence scattered everywhere along the track and through the jungle is that this Japanese army was at the point of starvation and riddled with scrub typhus and dysentery. The stench of the dead and the rotting vegetation and the foetid mud

Condensed from the author's *The Toughest Fighting in the World.*

is almost overpowering. One of our doctors carried out a couple of autopsies. Many of the Japs, he said, had died because hunger had forced them to eat the poisonous fruits and roots of the jungle. It's clear now that the enemy stopped at Ioribaiwa Ridge because he was humanly incapable of thrusting ahead any farther.

The Australians are pushing ahead very cautiously, profiting by these grim reminders of an advance that went too fast, building up store dumps and medical posts as they go, taking meticulous care about sanitation and hygiene, advancing in three prongs that are exploring every side track and cleansing every yard of jungle as they go.

In this dense terrain of matted vegetation and half-hidden native pad-pads and steep gorges there are the ever present threats of ambush, counter-infiltration and outflanking. But the Australians are climbing slowly and grimly up the southern flanks of the Owen Stanley's with the knowledge that the only Japanese behind their thrusting spearheads are dead ones.

VALLEY OF SILENCE

From the crest of Imita Ridge the vast valley of Ua-ule Creek lay like a bowl of tumbled green jungle held between the jagged purple peaks of the lower Owen Stanley's. The three-toothed ridge of Ioribaiwa guarded the other side of the valley with an almost unbroken wall of jungle, clear in the tropical light. Beyond the afternoon thunderheads were massing above and between the rising peaks of the range. The rolling clouds had beheaded the great bulk of Mount Urawa and scattered tufts and wisps of cotton-wool across the flanks of distant Maguli.

The valley below was silent. The only sound was the soft hiss and drip of rain among the great jungle trees of Imita Ridge. But no sound came from Ua-ule Valley for no man lived there—not even a native—and the only movement was the play of shadows across the matted trees.

Down the north wall of this valley came the Japanese one day last month. For three bitter weeks they had driven everything before them. They had fought courageously, fanatically, mercilessly. Ragged, exhausted, hungry Australians straggled through the silent valley on their retreat to Imita Ridge, while the rearguard fought to stem the yellow tide on the crest of Ioribaiwa. Just as the enemy was hidden by that silent blanket of jungle so were the countless deeds of heroism.

In one tiny clearing a young Australian lay wounded by a sniper's bullet. His patrol was coming up behind him unaware of the hidden ambush. He could have feigned death and escaped when darkness came. Instead he shouted warnings and directions to his comrades. The enraged Japanese pumped more bullets into him but the Australian continued to direct his patrol. He was dead when his comrades returned after having wiped out the Japanese.

On this same terrible slope six Victorians had squirmed to within six yards of the Japanese positions to silence a troublesome enemy gunpit and had killed every man in it. Across this mysterious valley had shrieked the 25-pounder shells from the Australian guns that held the Japanese and blasted them out of Ioribaiwa. For the Japanese never reached the foot of that valley of silence, never climbed the southern wall of Imita. Across this valley last week went the grim-faced green-uniformed Australians on the terrible march back to the crest of the path through the Owen Stanley's—and beyond.

The silence of centuries returned to the valley of Ua-ule. It was just as it had always been as we looked across to jagged Ioribaiwa, its edges softened by the veil of falling rain. That rain would be falling gently on those few crude crosses. Some would bear the crudely penciled names of Australians . . . one or two the simple words: "Unknown Australian Soldier."

No man can give more than life itself. These men had given that to the valley of silence that somehow seemed part of Australia itself. Their sacrifice was a heritage to their country's history.

By some freak of the valley and the lowering shroud of rain clouds a thin sound tinkled up from the silent green depths—the sound of biscuit tins clanking together. . . .

308

THEY FOUGHT UPHILL

Five days ago the Japanese began their resistance again—on the wide shallow plateau of the Gap, the pass through the forbidding spurs of the main range. The weather is bad, the terrain unbelievably terrible, and the enemy is resisting with a stubborn fury that is costing us many men and much time. Against the machine gun nests and mortar pits established on the ragged spurs and steep limestone ridges our advance each day now is measured in yards. Our troops are fighting in the cold mists of an altitude of 6,700 feet, fighting viciously because they have only a mile or two to go before they reach the peak of the pass and will be able to attack downhill—down the north flank of the Owen Stanley's. That means a lot to troops who have climbed every inch of that agonizing track, who have buried so many of their cobbers and who have seen so many more going back, weak with sickness or mauled by the mortar bombs and bullets and grenades of the enemy, men gone from their ranks simply to win back a few more hundred yards of this wild, unfriendly, and utterly untamed mountain. Tiny villages which were under Japanese domination a few weeks ago are back in our hands—Ioribaiwa, Nauro Creek, Menari, Efogi, Kagi, Myola—and we are fighting now for Templeton's Crossing.

Already a new language is springing up on this green and slimy trail. Whenever Australians are in an area for long enough they soon invent a new slang to describe it. They adapt themselves to discomforts, give them ironical names and laugh them off. A few weeks ago these troops were still talking the language of the Middle East, which has been their home for more than two years. They talk now like the men who have been in New Guinea for months. The curses of New Guinea are varied enough to provide troops with their main subjects of conversation but, in rough order, the worst are mosquitoes, mud, mountains, malaria and monotony. The "mozzies" and malaria are worst down near the coast, but they are speedily re-

309

placed by the mud and mountains as you go inland. The monotony, of course, is everywhere, except where the fighting provides something special to think about.

They love mosquito stories, and the more fantastic they are the better they like them.

There was one about a Jap airman who was found lying on a hill. The official explanation was that he had been shot down by our fighters, but the boys in the know say that he was picked up at Lae by a mozzy, who carried him over the Owen Stanley's, looking for a nice quiet place to eat him. He saw a flight of Fortresses heading north, and, mistaking them for his wife and kids, he dropped the Jap and fell into formation.

I heard another one on the same lines about an ack-ack gunner who caught a mosquito in his sights, and, mistaking it for a Zero, opened fire with a Bofors gun. The third shell chipped one wing, and the fourth exploded right under his tail. The boys raised a cheer as they saw him come down smoking, but instead of crashing he picked up a rock and threw it at them. They can show you the rock, too.

They all grew out of the old tale about the two mosquitoes who found a good, juicy-looking staff sergeant asleep under his net one night. One of them politely lifted the net for the other to fly in, and his friend returned the compliment by turning over his identity disc to see if he belonged to the right blood group.

"Well, he's okay," one of them said. "Shall we eat him here or take him down to the beach?"

"Don't be silly. If we take him down to the beach the big chaps will grab him."

I can't vouch for that one. I never met the staff sergeant.

Moresby's best mosquito joke, I think, is a perfectly authentic signboard that stands alongside a shallow pool on the main road in the garrison. It was erected by an anti-malaria squad which forgot to paint in the hyphen. The pool was filled with gamboesia, the little imported minnow that eats mosquito larvae, and the sign reads:

310

Warning. Do Not Spray. Mosquito Eating Fish.

And everybody who passes always makes the customary remark of awe that tradition dictates: " 'Struth, are they that big?"

On the Kokoda track, however, after you've been walking a few hours, you soon get above the mosquito country. As the troops toiled and grunted up they would often stop and gasp with amazement at the enormous butterflies that drifted to and fro, or alighted on their arms to drink the sweat. The insect life, from scorpions to butterflies, is impressive.

Only for a time though. You eventually reach a stage when flora and fauna, and even the Japs, gradually lose interest. Your mental processes allow you to be conscious of only one thing—"The Track," or, more usually, "The Bloody Track." You listen to your legs creaking and stare at the ground and think of the next stretch of mud, and you wonder if the hills will ever end. Up one almost perpendicular mountain face more than 2,000 steps have been cut out of the mud and built up with felled saplings inside which the packed earth has long since become black glue. Each step is two feet high. You slip on one in three. There are no resting places. Climbing it is the supreme agony of mind and spirit. The troops, with fine irony, have christened it "The Golden Staircase"!

Life changes as you push up the track. Standards of living deteriorate, sometimes below normally accepted standards even of primitive existence. Thoughts become somber, humor takes on a grim, almost macabre quality. When men reach the nadir of mental and physical agony there are times when sickness or injury and even death seem like things to be welcomed. Near Efogi, on a slimy section of the track that reeks with the stench of death, the remains of an enemy soldier lie on a crude stretcher, abandoned by the Japanese retreat. The flesh has gone from his bones, and a white, bony claw sticks out of a ragged uniform sleeve, stretching across the track. Every Australian who passes, plodding up the muddy rise that leads to the

311

pass, grasps the skeleton's grisly hand, shakes it fervently and says "Good on you, sport!" before moving wearily on.

In this territory the Japanese are fighting, with a stubborn tenacity that is almost unbelievable, from an elaborate system of prepared positions along every ridge and spur. Churned up by the troops of both armies, the track itself is now knee deep in thick, black mud. For the last ten days no man's clothing has been dry and they have slept—when sleep was possible—in pouring rain under sodden blankets. Each man carries all his personal equipment, firearms, ammunition supply and five days' rations. Every hour is a nightmare.

"BUT KOKODA WAS EMPTY"

The Australians have re-conquered the Owen Stanley Range. Today, on November 2, they marched into Kokoda unopposed, through lines of excited natives who brought them great baskets of fruit and decked them with flowers. They marched back to the little plateau where Colonel Owen had died so many weary weeks before. They marched downhill through Isurava and Deniki, where many of them had fought the bloody rearguard action of August. The Japs had fled. Patrols cautiously went ahead to scout, squirmed their way through the rubber trees to test out Kokoda's defenses. But Kokoda was empty. There was no sound but the droning of insects and the noise of the rain pattering through the trees. Kokoda, "key to the Owen Stanley's," had been abandoned by the Japanese without a fight. Their defense of Kokoda had been the pass through the range, and they had failed to hold that defense line.

Today Australian troops in ragged, mud-stained green uniforms, in charred steel helmets that had been used for cooking many a meal of bully beef on the Kokoda trail, stood in ranks round the flagpole in front of the administrative building while an Australian flag (dropped with typical courtesy, friendship and thoughtfulness by an American fighter pilot) was slowly hoisted in the still air. There was no cheering. There was no band playing. There

312

was merely the packed lines of these hundreds of weary Australians, haggard, half-starved, dishevelled, many wearing grimy, stained bandages, standing silently at attention in the rain. For weeks their muttered "Kokoda or bust!" had been the most quoted saying of the track. Well, here was Kokoda, and lost in the rain clouds behind was the great blue rampart of the Owen Stanley's, with the shaggy 13,600-foot crest of Mount Victoria hidden by the afternoon thunderheads.

The shadow of the Australian flag, hanging limply in the still, moist air, fell across the lines of Japanese graves sheltering beneath the shattered debris of what once had been the Government station buildings. Within 12 feet of the flagstaff was the tall, simple memorial erected by the Japanese "in memory of the many soldiers of Nippon who fell in the great battle for Kokoda." And near by was the grave of Colonel Owen.

Littered all over the area were discarded Japanese anti-aircraft shells, smashed boxes which had contained stores, wicker baskets in which food had been dropped by parachute. In a valley beyond was the Japanese cemetery, with its hundreds of neat graves.

Within an hour the Australian spearhead was snaking down the narrow track leading from the little plateau on to the flat, jungle-choked plain below. They were marching on to try to catch the fleeing enemy.

TWO MEN ARE SITTING

On an upturned packing case alongside an airstrip in the Kunai 20 miles behind Gona sat a blindfolded Japanese prisoner, awaiting the transport plane that would carry him back to Port Moresby. He had bitten off the end of his tongue to ensure that he wouldn't talk. He could hear the roar of powerful aircraft engines as our transports swept in with guns and ammunition and food. He could hear the fainter throbbing of our bombers and fighters streaking over toward Buna. His share of the war was over, but in the tangled swamps and kunai patches of the Buna

313

plain thousands of his fellow countrymen were facing up for the final battle of a tough campaign.

The allies were closing in from seven directions. The Americans had gone into action twenty-four hours before, and three columns of green-uniformed doughboys were even now assaulting the tough defense perimeter around Cape Endaiadere, Buna and Giropa Point. The Australians were pushing up the track to Sanananda Point and another force, advancing with staggering speed, had reached to within a mile of the north coast at Gona. The village of Soputa, south of Sanananda, had just fallen to Australians and Americans after tough fighting.

But the surly little Jap with the bristly hair and with the dried blood caked at the corner of his mouth didn't know anything about these things.

It's been a tense week for the senior officers. General Harding, of the American 32nd Division, had to swim two miles to the shore when the lugger in which he was moving along the north coast was strafed and sunk by Zeros. Australia's General Vasey and America's General MacNider have been strafed and sniped at.

Back at headquarters are the senior generals—MacArthur, Blamey and Kenney, all now established in New Guinea to direct operations on the spot. Blamey, who lives in a camouflaged tent lined with maps on which colored pins illustrate the inexorable advance of the troops under his command, is cautious, and wisely planning to meet the worst contingency that can happen.

The senior soldier of them all, General Douglas MacArthur, miraculously retains complete privacy in a garrison area where there has never been privacy before, where even American and Australian nurses have had to avert their eyes from the roadside spectacles of nude soldiers showering under roadside hydrants, and naked men wandering carelessly everywhere.

MacArthur is just as remote, just as mysterious as he has been ever since he reached Australia eight months ago. He lives with Kenney in a white-painted bungalow surrounded by a riotous tropical garden of frangipani and hibiscus and flametrees. He is rarely seen. I remember how

314

one American soldier came up to me in a state of great excitement because he had seen the great man. "I got a glimpse of him before breakfast," he said. "He was walking beneath the trees in a pink silk dressing gown with a black dragon on the back." Another man told me he had seen MacArthur in the afternoon with signal forms in one hand and a bunch of green lettuce which had been flown up from the mainland in the other. Between munches he doubtless analyzed the progress of the carefully prepared plan to take Papua back from the Japs.

That plan probably had its beginning at a special press conference in July which I had flown down to Melbourne to attend. That conference was—and unfortunately still is—off the record, but one remark of the general's can be told. "We suffer because our forces are split over many fronts," he said, "but so long as we can keep fighting on every one of those fronts we keep the enemy fighting there, too, and his forces are similarly split. We must attack, attack, attack!"

Well, that is what is happening in Papua today. The Japs, for the moment, are on the defensive everywhere. There are many problems that the three generals must overcome. The Australians call this a "Q War"—a quartermaster's war, in which supply and movement are everything that matters, except fighting courage. Those problems have been largely solved by the dynamic General Kenney who has built up his air transport organization to an enormous scale. Almost every foot of our advance from Ioribaiwa across the Owen Stanley's and across the northern plain to Buna has been made possible only by the endless job of innumerable young pilots—many of them American kids from flying schools who flew the great Douglases and Lockheeds across the Pacific and straight to New Guinea—who have dropped or landed thousands of tons of food, equipment, munitions and guns.

If this is a Q War we have just seen a perfect example of efficiency in fighting that sort of war. The Japs have been beaten in the air, beaten on supply, beaten in straight-out fighting ability. Today we can see the end of the picture in sight. The Japs have lost almost all that they

315

have struggled so hard for during the last one hundred and twenty-one days.

And today two men are sitting. They are many miles apart. One is a blindfolded Japanese prisoner. I wonder what he is thinking? The other is the mysterious, aloof American general from the Philippines sitting beneath the frangipani and munching Australian lettuce as he reads the reports coming in from the front, where allied troops are battering down the enemy's final Papuan resistance. Perhaps he sees in this little jungle campaign the first complete justification of his months old theory of "Attack, attack, attack!" But I'm not sure. Because, you see, I don't know what he is thinking either. . . .

TWENTY-FOUR MARCHED OUT

Along the narrow, winding Sanananda track, flanked by swamps and thick jungle, both sides had dug in in small pockets. Little isolated battles were raging to the noise of thudding mortars, chattering machine-gun fire, and the zip and whine of bullets.

Sometimes our men advanced with blood-curdling yells to rout out Japanese nests at the bayonet point or with grenades. But the progress generally was pitifully slow.

Soon after we had smashed through the Japanese defenses at Soputa village, the enemy had brought up a 75-millimeter mountain gun, and for two days its shelling of the allied forward positions had held up any appreciable advance.

An order was issued that the gun was to be silenced at all costs. The job was allotted to 90 men of an A.I.F. battalion which had been fighting with magnificent courage and determination in the slimy Papuan jungles for two and a half months.

Under the command of Captain Basil Catterns, of Sydney, the 90 mud-stained, heavily armed men crept into the flanking underbush at dawn one morning.

The enemy gun position was only two miles away, but

316

the Australians had to make a wide detour to get round the deep, evil smelling swamps.

For more than eight hours the men hacked and smashed their way through the entangling vines and rotten trees, their direction plotted and corrected by the noise of the enemy gun in action.

Just before dusk, Catterns saw ahead of him a Japanese camp with strong defenses all round, and the mountain gun firing from a pit in front of the camp and sending shells over the trees into the Australian positions two miles away.

After a few moments' consideration the Australians decided to launch their first assault on the camp to clean out the Japanese troops.

The Australians were drawn up in a wide, sweeping curve. Zero hour was fixed at sunset, and they crouched in the jungle until the order to charge was given.

The sun dropped swiftly behind the darkening trees. Catterns gave the order. Within a few seconds one of the most spectacular and bloody battles of the New Guinea war was raging in the tiny clearing.

The Australians tore their way through two barricades of plaited vines that the Japanese had erected, and swept across three lines of trenches with Bren guns and tommy guns blazing. Others lobbed showers of grenades into the Japanese posts.

The Japanese were taken completely by surprise as thousands of bullets whacked into native huts. Screaming, they came pouring from the huts, but within a few seconds every exit had been blocked by a pile of Japanese dead. More were blown to pieces by Australian grenades, and others were mown down like ripe corn as the Australians continued their terrorizing rush through the camp.

Grenades burst among the fires on which the Japanese evening meal was cooking, and in the great flash of flame some of the huts caught fire.

Some Australians had been killed and many wounded. The enemy had recovered from his surprise, and was hitting back hard. The Australians circled round their wounded with blazing guns, and slowly retreated into the

317

jungle, carrying their wounded with them, behind the screen of gunfire. In the darkness the Australians dug defense positions as best they could while the wounded were attended to, and half the men fought a defensive action against more than a hundred Japanese, who maintained a constant night-long fire. from machine guns, mortars, and grenades. Other Japanese were pouring from a second camp nearby.

By dawn the Australians were completely surrounded and there was no way of getting a message through to inform their unit of their plight.

"We were holding a sausage-shaped perimeter sixty yards long and thirty yards wide," said Captain Catterns. "We had stacked our wounded around a large tree in the center of our position, but as the Japanese counter-attacked throughout the day the wounded were systematically picked off one by one by snipers. The Japanese sniped at the slightest movement.

"Under the protection of heavy machine-gun fire, their grenade throwers would advance and concentrate on one of our weapon pits or trenches, and plaster it until they were satisfied it was wiped out.

"Then they would turn to another Australian position. It was evidently their intention to whittle our defenses away one by one until we were exterminated."

Lieutenant Stewart Blakiston, of Geelong, one of the few officers to survive, said: "When we first occupied our little defense position we were hemmed in by jungle. When we left it looked like a sports field. Every blade of grass had been levelled and all the scrub and trees had been cut down by machine-gun fire. Even six-inch trees had been levelled to the ground by Japanese heavy machine guns. The parapets of trenches had been blown in and flattened by the constant hail of bullets, and the sides of weapon pits were shot away. Sometimes the Japanese would circle our defenses with their gunfire like Red Indians attacking a wagon train in the old wild western films. How any of us survived throughout that day I still don't know.

"Some of us almost cried with relief when, just before sunset, we heard the rattle of musketry as an Australian

318

battalion advanced up the track towards us. Some of the Japanese who were around us sped through the jungle to meet the new threat. There were enough of them left to keep us busy until after dark, when we were able to retire a few hundred yards to better defenses behind."

When the tide of battle had rolled on, by dawn next day, only four officers and 20 other ranks of the gallant 90 lived to march out from that terrible jungle clearing. But near the bodies of the 66 brave Australians who had not died in vain were the bodies of more than 150 Japanese.

And the Australians had done their job. They had silenced a dangerous enemy pocket; they had paved the way for an almost bloodless advance of two miles by the troops behind them.

And buried in the mud beside the tangled jungle track was the 75-millimeter gun—abandoned by the Japanese— which the Australians had been ordered to put out of action.

"THE WILDEST, MADDEST, BLOODIEST FIGHTING"

The Japanese are trying desperately to reinforce their last garrison in Papua. Under cover of darkness and bad weather several destroyers have succeeded in running the allied air blockade and have landed reinforcements at Buna. Other formations of fresh enemy troops have been brought down the coast from Salamaua in small boats, landing barges and even native craft. Today they continued their plan of reinforcement with submarines, at least nineteen (including one big fellow of 3,000 tons) of which were sighted heading for Buna on the surface in convoy formation. They crash-dived within sixty seconds when our planes came over.

Nevertheless our forces are closing in everywhere. At Gona the Australians have cut their way through to the beach and are now trying to silence the immensely strong pillboxes and gunpits that the Japanese have established near Gona Mission. At Buna the Americans have driven a wedge to within 800 yards of Buna government build-

319

ings, where the Japanese apparently have their focal positions. But it's a tough job. Deep swamps of black mud in which a man would drown limit the terrain over which we can attack. Every logical and practical line of approach is covered by a network of fortifications which the Japs have been working on for months.

Every weapon pit is a fortress in miniature. Some are strengthened by great sheets of armor and by concrete, but the majority are merely huge dug-outs—several are 150 feet long—protected from our fire and bombs by sawn logs and felled trees which form a barrier six, ten, and sometimes 15 feet thick. The logs are held in place by great metal stakes, and filled in with earth in which the natural growth of the jungle has continued, providing perfect camouflage. Many of the pits are connected by subterranean tunnels or well protected communication trenches. The pits are heavily manned and each is filled with sufficient food, water and ammunition to enable the Japs to withstand a long siege. From every trench or pit or pillbox all approaches are covered by wide fields of sweeping fire along fixed lines.

At the moment the most desperate fighting is taking place on the Gona beach sector, where the A.I.F. is gradually whittling away the enemy's grip in a series of ferocious, but costly, bayonet charges. One private described a typical attack to me today:

"We'd been advancing for hours through stinking swamps up to our knees when we reached better country in the coconut groves, but when we pushed through the plantation to the beach we met heavy machine-gun fire from a strong Jap post on the beach. We attacked in a broad, sweeping line, charging across the sand with fixed bayonets and grenades, and stormed our way right into the position.

"It was the wildest, maddest, bloodiest fighting I have ever seen. Grenades were bursting among the Japs as we stabbed down at them with our bayonets from the parapets above. Some of our fellows were actually rolling on the sand with Japs locked against them in wrestling grips. It was all over within a few minutes. A few of the Japs had

320

escaped, but the bodies of 30 were tangled among their captured guns.

"A bayonet charge like that is a pretty terrible business when you see your cobbers falling, when you can only see ahead of you a tree. You can't even see the Japs hidden among the roots until you're right on top of them, and they are still firing and yelling as you plunge the bayonet down. But it's the only way to clean them out. Those bastards fight to the last. They keep fighting until your bayonet sinks into them."

Another incident yesterday provided a typical illustration of Japanese desperation. A brawny American tommy gunner, 6 feet 3 inches tall, was patrolling alone down a track near Gona when a completely unarmed Japanese, slightly built and not much more than five feet tall, leaped out of the undergrowth, seized the big American by the throat and brought him crashing to the ground. They wrestled wildly for a few minutes, but the American broke the grip of the Jap, scrambled to his feet and brought the butt of his gun crashing down on the head of his assailant. The Jap fell to the ground, but when the American stooped over, he was grabbed by the ankle and again brought down. In the end the American was forced to strangle the Jap to death with his bare hands.

BOTTCHER'S SALIENT

Today the greatest individual act of heroism among the American forces in New Guinea came to an end when a grimy party of twelve men under the leadership of a tough sergeant who can scarcely speak English were relieved in the salient on Buna beach that they held against an overwhelming force of Japanese for seven days and nights. The establishment of that tiny salient and the holding of it might well prove one of the vital factors in breaking the Japanese grip on the entire Buna sector. Sergeant Herman Bottcher, of "Bottcher's Salient," richly deserves the D.S.C. he's going to be awarded, and also

321

the promotion to commissioned rank which is being rushed through the "usual channels."

Bottcher is 37 and he comes from San Francisco. He is German-born, from Landsberg, near Berlin, worked in Australia for some years in the late twenties, and then went to the United States to try his luck. He knows modern war, because soon after he received United States citizenship he lost it when he enlisted with the International Brigade to fight against the Axis in Spain. He was a good soldier and a brave fighter for the Republicans, in whose army he rose from the rank of private to that of captain. He enlisted later with the United States Army and found himself in Papua, fighting his second war against the Axis.

Bottcher is of medium size, wears a magnificent black beard, looks at you with fierce eyes, and speaks almost unrecognizable English with a thick German accent.

On December 5 the Americans were hammering in vain at the strongly defended Japanese posts outside Buna. The enemy held the village on one side and the Government station on the other. There had been a disheartening series of failures by the Americans to breach the defenses. Bottcher was in the thick of it. He came back to get a pail of water for some of his wounded and saw two or three American officers sitting on the ground trying to work out ways and means of assaulting the enemy line. Bottcher glared at them as he filled the bucket. "If you guys would get up off your goddam tails and start fightin' maybe we'd get something done!" he snarled and strode back to the forward positions.

Bottcher decided to do something himself. He called for volunteers to drive a wedge right into the Japanese positions and through to the beach. It was a tough job. Many men volunteered and Bottcher picked twelve of them.

They squirmed through the swamps and coconut palms toward their objectives through a hail of heavy fire, but the tommy guns and grenades of Bottcher and his men cleaned up enemy machine-gun posts, and brought snipers toppling from trees. After several hours of heavy fighting the little force reached its objective, where Bottcher ordered his men to dig in on the beach and stay there.

Trenches and weapon pits were dug. At dawn the Japanese attacked from both flanks, one force rushing from the village and one from the Government station. Both attacks were repulsed by fierce machine-gun fire, and the Japanese retired, dragging some wounded with them, and leaving forty dead on the beach. A few hours later a Japanese machine-gun post brought harassing fire to bear on the American post, so Bottcher crawled out with a pocketful of grenades, squirmed across the bullet-torn sand, and blew the post to pieces with grenades. He crawled back to his little garrison.

That night the watchful doughboys saw enemy barges moving offshore, and opened up on them with heavy machine-gun fire. One barge was set on fire, and Japanese could be seen scrambling from it on to the other, which escaped at full speed to the northward.

Next day a party of Japanese was seen sneaking across a bridge over Buna Creek, and Bottcher's guns brought down six of them before the others fled.

All this time the little beachhead was constantly under fire from strong enemy positions on both sides, but the thought of retiring never occurred to the German-born sergeant who had been wounded several times. The American post was causing great concern to the Japanese, and on the night of December 9 another double attack was made from both sides. Again the Japanese were driven back in confusion.

Next morning Bottcher and a few of his men crawled out of their trenches into no-man's-land. They counted seven more Japanese dead added to the pile of corpses in front of their weapon pits, and found two abandoned Japanese machine guns with ammunition. These were dragged back to the post to increase its armament.

Once or twice Bottcher had visitors. On one occasion the American commanding officer—General Eichelberger, a brave man and a fine soldier—crawled along to Bottcher's Salient, and did a bit of useful sniping while he was there! But most of the time the thirteen men were alone, with hundreds of Japanese all round them.

Today a stronger party of fresh troops went in to relieve them. But before he came out Bottcher was able to get a final crack at the Japs. For some hours they had watched the Japanese building a heavy timber barricade leading from Buna Village toward the American post. It was obviously their intention to launch an attack from behind the barricade. Bottcher got his mortars ranged and waited until the palisade was almost completed. Then he sent over a string of bombs and blew the timber wall and all the Japanese working on it to pieces. Since then the Japanese haven't attempted to begin the job again.

By a conservative count it is believed that Bottcher and his twelve men have killed more than 120 Japs from this little salient.

MASSACRE AT MAMBARE

The Japanese lost one north coast beachhead today, with the fall of Buna Village, and gained another at tremendous cost well up the coast near the Mambare Delta, 53 miles away. Attacking in force from Bottcher's Salient, the Americans smashed right through Buna Village to the coast, completely cleaned up the area, which is littered with the bodies of hundreds of Japanese, and effectively isolated the enemy's Sanananda force from the main garrison which holds a strong line from Giropa Point to Cape Endaiadere. General Eichelberger practically led his troops into the attack. This is every man's war up here. Senior officers will be found in the trenches with the troops, and right in the front line you will see commanding generals directing machine-gun and mortar fire and blazing away with tommy guns at Japanese snipers in the tree-tops!

I was just behind the front line at Gona, crouched down in the kunai grass with a party of 21 A.I.F. infantrymen from South Australia. They had been in action almost constantly for two months. They were thin, haggard, undernourished, insect-bitten, grimy, and physically near the end of their tether. They were fighting on fighting spirit alone.

324

And because that spirit was good they were still superlative troops.

They were talking among themselves about a Japanese weapon pit which was concealed in the butt of a huge jungle tree at the end of a clearing which lay beyond the kunai patch. The pit had held them up for two hours. Two of their number had been killed and five wounded when they first pushed through the kunai and ran into a scythelike sweep of fire from the Japanese positions. A twenty-three-year-old subaltern from Glen Osmond was talking quietly to the men.

"No use sitting round, I guess. We might as well get stuck into it!"

The men grinned. The lieutenant—who wore no badges of rank and was clad in the same green jungle uniform as the troops—turned to a lanky sergeant. "How much of that grass do you reckon they've cleared away between the post and the edge of the kunai?"

"Seventy or 80 yards, I'd say," replied the sergeant. A couple of privates nodded and a lance-corporal estimated it as "nearer a hundred."

"Well, there are 21 of us now," said a stocky little private from Renmark. "Once we get up to the bloody pit it would only take about six of us to dig the little blighters out."

He tossed a hand grenade a few inches into the air and caught it nonchalantly.

"You ought to be one of the six, sport," interjected another private, lolling on his back with his net-covered steel helmet over his eyes, and a piece of yellow grass moving up and down rhythmically to the slow champing of his jaws. "You're so bloody short, Tojo'll never be able to get a sight on yer!" A soft ripple of laughter ran round the little group.

But even that little burst of laughter was heard. From the Japanese post came the *pap-pap-pap* of a short machine-gun burst. The bullets zipped harmlessly high overhead. The man who was chewing grass tipped his helmet back and looked in the direction of the enemy post, invis-

325

ible behind the screen of kunai. "Use 'em up, Tojo," he muttered. "You ain't got much longer to go."

The lieutenant buckled his belt and looked round at his men. They grinned and reached for their rifles and Brens and tommy guns. "According to Shorty here, this job's going to mean 15 of us won't get through," he said, as if it were a grand joke.

"Wouldn't count on that," said the lanky man, spitting out the well-chewed piece of grass. "He always was an optimist!"

Another ripple of laughter. "Well, some come back, they say," grinned the lieutenant. He motioned to the men. They took a final look at their weapons, saw the grenades were ready, and began to squirm slowly toward the edge of the long grass. As he moved past the lanky man winked at me. "Give us a good write-up," he said.

The movement of the 21 men made little movement in the grass and the occasional shaking of the thick blades might have been only the wind blowing in from the beach. They reached the edge of the kunai. A few yards out in the cleared area were the twisted bodies of their comrades killed a couple of hours before. There was a sudden flash of steel as the Australians sprang to their feet and started running. They were yelling like madmen. For a split second there was no sound from the enemy position. Then it started. The wild *brrrrrpppppp-brrrrrop* of machine guns firing with fingers tight on the triggers, the crack of grenades, once the scream of a man.

The Australians were running in a straight line. It's no use swerving or dodging when you're charging into machine-gun fire. Their bayonets were at the high port. Men were falling. One threw up his hands, stopped dead, and stumbled to one side. Another fell as he was running, rolling over and over like a rabbit hit on the run. Another was spun around like a top before he crumpled up and slid to the ground. The little man who had predicted that six would get through had almost reached the Japanese pit when he fell. He went over backwards as if somebody had delivered a terrific uppercut.

He didn't live to find out, but his estimate was wrong.

326

Nine of the Australians got through. They wiped out the post, killing every one of the 19 Japs inside.

That is the meaning of morale. I saw that happen. I saw many other incidents just as expressive of the fighting spirit that makes these young Australians and Americans the world's best assault troops. These men, after the endless weeks of short rations, the gruelling fight across the Owen Stanley's, the sight of their comrades killed or wounded or evacuated with the mysterious malady known generally as "jungle fever," would not have been condemned had their spirit wilted, their morale weakened in the final bitter struggle that preceded the fall of Gona and Buna. But that morale had been tempered in the flame of hardship, adversity, and peril. It did not wilt.

"OF HUMAN THINGS"

The show is over. It is January 23, 1943. The last Japanese soldier in Papua has been killed or captured. Buna station, Giropa Point and Cape Endaiadere, where the Japanese resisted stubbornly from their foxholes for two bitter months, were crushed by Australian and American infantry charging behind Australian-manned and American-built light tanks. On the Sanananda track the last pockets, which had held out longer than any others, were crushed. Some of the Japanese gave themselves up. Others stayed in their foxholes to be killed or to die of starvation and disease. Yesterday fighting ceased.

It was on this date twelve months ago that the war in New Guinea began, when Rabaul succumbed to the furious onslaught of the men of Nippon. Much has happened since then. The 16,000 men that General Horii threw into the attempt to conquer Papua have been killed or wounded or captured. Mostly they have been killed. And General Horii himself is dead. So are many other uncounted Japanese, destroyed in their planes and destroyed in the scores of ships that have become twisted junk on the sea floor for the sake of Japanese aggression in the South Seas.

The Secret War

In any war there are men who are unwilling to wait for the main offensive operations to be organized; they are restless under the mass training methods necessary to develop a major fighting force. Such men often work out schemes for raids on the enemy, usually at great risk to themselves, which are fashioned to strike a telling blow at an enemy strong point. This sort of raid not only causes damage but, if publicized, earns psychological advantages for the raiders and their country.

During the early part of the Pacific war, raids were necessarily long-range operations to make contact with the enemy and were launched from ships, submarines or aircraft.

Captain Ivan Lyon, who had escaped from Singapore, was such a man as described above. He had a burning passion to get back at the Japs because he had been compelled to leave his wife and child in Singapore when that city fell. After a long struggle with Allied Command officers, he got their approval for a raid on the shipping in Singapore.

In such operations all members of the raid were carefully chosen and then rigorously trained. "Jaywick," as the operation was known, would be carried out by three canoes, each manned by two commandos, launched as close to Singapore as safety permitted. After toughening their bodies, and mastering the art of handling the canoes, the members of Jaywick practiced working with a new explosive—the limpet mine.

"The limpets, which looked like rectangular chunks of rusty iron, measured 11 x 8 x 3 inches. They weighed fourteen pounds loaded and contained a powerful horseshoe magnet and ten pounds of P.E. (plastic explosive), which was enough to blow a hole about five feet square in the plates of a ship. Limpets had two holes at the top. The instantaneous fuse and time pencil, which could be set for explosion any time up to six hours, went into one hole. One end of a five-foot wooden pole, like a broomstick, fitted into the other.

328

"The technique of fixing limpets was simple. As a two-man Folboat came alongside a ship at night, the bowman clamped a small magnetic 'holdfast,' with a line attached to it, to the ship's side, and held the 'anchored' canoe steady. The other canoeman, his limpet fused and timed, then fitted his 'broomstick' into the other hole and lowered the limpet into the water between canoe and ship, getting it as deep as possible before carefully easing it onto the ship's plates. Limpets could be fixed without noise, but if carelessly applied, they gripped too quickly and clanged against the plates, a sound that could easily be heard inside the ship and lead to discovery. Once the limpet was applied, the canoeman worked the stick out of the hole, the bowman released the holdfast, and the canoe was paddled or allowed to drift to the next limpet position." *

By August 1943, Captain Lyon's group was ready. An old Japanese fishing boat, the *Krait*, was especially fitted out to take them through the Jap-infested waters to Singapore, but first they had to sail from Cairns on the northeast coast across the top of Australia to Exmouth Gulf on the west coast. From here they would pick up new canoes and make final ready. On September 2, 1943, the *Krait* set sail for Singapore.

RAID ON SINGAPORE

by Brian Connell

At half past five they cast off, with everything ship-shape and ready for sea. Exactly one minute later, the shaft extension piece on the engine broke. Paddy McDowell's imprecations shook the engine room more than the broken shaft, but even his loving care could not achieve the impossible. *Krait* was immobilised and had to anchor. It looked as if the whole expedition would have to be called off. Only a long tow down to Fremantle and a week in

*Ronald McKie, *The Heroes*, p. 31. Harcourt, Brace & Co.

BIAK / JAYWICK / BALIKPAPAN

CHINA

FORMOSA

PHILIPPINE
ISLANDS

SOUTH CHINA SEA

PALAWAN

BALIKPAPAN STRIKE,
SEPT 30, 1944

BIAK LANDING
MAY 27, 1944

SINGAPORE

BORNEO

BALIKPAPAN

NOEMFOOR

JAVA SEA

CELEBES

NEW
GUINEA

JAVA

BALI

TIMOR

JAYWICK RAID, 1943

AUSTRALIA

EX-MOUTH GULF

the dockyards would put the damage right and by that time their time-table would start to overlap the monsoon. Lyon and Davidson were drafting the unpleasant wireless messages telling of their plight when, three hours later, the *U.S.S. Chanticleer,* the submarine-repair ship, entered the bay. This was too good to be true. Lyon had himself rowed across in the dinghy, and in no time *Chanticleer* sent a motorboat to tow *Krait* alongside. The broken shaft was taken out and by the following morning brazed together again, although the American mechanics insisted that it was only a temporary job and might perhaps get them back to Fremantle for a proper replacement.

Lyon, who had come to trust Paddy McDowell completely, asked him what he thought. "I think it will hold," the tough old Scot replied imperturbably—and that with 4,000 miles ahead of them in enemy waters and no spare. Lyon did not hesitate. At two o'clock in the afternoon of September 2 they put to sea—and three hours later nearly foundered.

As they cleared North West Cape, the full force of the wind hit them. With a wicked tide-rip running, *Krait* was beam on to the Force 7 westerly seas. They knew she could roll, but this was outside all their previous experience. Badly overloaded, she lurched drunkenly from side to side, with great green seas pouring inboard and crashing on the afterdeck. The wheelhouse looked like the conning tower of a submarine, completely awash. The hatches to the cabin and the engine room were battened down, but the men off watch in the cramped space under the awning had to hang on for their lives to the nearest stanchion, often waist-deep in swirling water.

It seemed as if one particularly large wave had finally put them under. Nothing of *Krait* was visible forward of the wheelhouse. She trembled, shuddered, almost on her beam ends, and then, just as it seemed as if they were going down, slowly shook herself free. Lyon himself was at the helm and slowly, with the help of Carse, managed to fight *Krait* round to port, head on to the murderous sea. For the faithful Morris, clinging desperately to the rails by the engine house, it was the worst moment of the whole voyage.

The tough Welsh miner had really thought that his last moment had come.

Within an hour they were out of the coastal tide-rip and in relatively calmer water. Course was once more set to the north.

The third day out, with only a gentle swell, white cloud flecks in the blue sky and a warm breeze presaging the hot days that lay ahead, Lyon called the crew together under the awning: "It's time you knew where we are really going," he told them. "It is not Surabaya, it's Singapore. I am sorry I couldn't tell you before, but we had to keep it completely dark for security reasons."

Singapore—more than a thousand miles inside the new Japanese empire—was a very different proposition from Surabaya, just round the corner once they were through the Lombok Straits, but the men were absolutely exhilarated at the prospect.

Later that day they started blackening themselves with the skin dye they had brought with them. It was a sticky, evil-smelling mixture, thinned with spirit. It stuck to everything better than it did to their own bodies. They had to leave white rings round their eyes because of the spirit and another white patch round their private parts, although the native sarongs they donned put that right. Sweat, water, and oil brought it off again, and however often they applied the dye, they never presented anything better than a curiously mottled appearance. It might serve to confuse the Japanese and natives from a distance, but, close to, the blue eyes of most of the party would give them away.

If challenged, the plan was for Jones, Berryman, and Huston, the three darkest of them, to run on to the foredeck, gesticulating innocently and pointing at the Japanese flag they were going to hoist at the stern. None of the others would bear close scrutiny. McDowell looked like a stringy fakir, Carse vaguely Burmese, and Lyon might pass under a cursory glance for a Malay—except for those green eyes. But Poppa Falls was definitely ginger and Young quite fair and if they put the dye in their hair it stood up as if electrified, with patches of the original colour showing through where the scalp sweated. The only real defence was some-how to dodge all shipping.

Carse, his logbook looking more like a Scotland Yard fingerprint record with its black smudges, thought little of the experiment: "It proved a rank failure," he wrote, "more black everywhere than on the person after an hour or two. The crew now resemble blackamoors. A more desperate looking crowd I have never seen. The sea remains calm and glory be praised the scattered clouds of this morning are becoming more and more numerous, showing every indi-cation of poor to bad visibility for the day of days, or rather night of nights."

He was thinking four days ahead to the dangerous pas-sage of the closely guarded straits between the islands of Lombok and Bali, the gantlet *Krait* would have to run to break through into the South China Sea. The following day, the sixth, with the sky clouding up nicely, they hauled down their blue ensign and hoisted in its place the poached egg of Japan. The flag they had brought with them was far too clean and new for its purpose, so they scuffed it round the deck with their feet until it looked sufficiently grubby and weather-beaten. Paddy McDowell also switched his engine over to the silencer and the powerful chug-chug-chug of the exhaust died away to a reassuring purr. It cut a little off their speed and they never reached seven knots again.

With the look-outs' eyes peeled for enemy aircraft, they held course to the north. The Admiralty pilot book for the eastern archipelago informed them that at this time of year weather conditions would be hazy, with visibility down to 6,000 yards, but to their consternation the weather during the seventh was as bright, clear, and sunny as a spring day. The eighth dawned the same, and, to add to their troubles, the engine started coughing on a faulty feed pipe, but this was repaired during the morning.

They were now well within range of Japanese air patrols, and they knew there was a large air base at Den Pasar on Bali. Shortly after midday they sighted the mountain peaks of Lombok and Bali to the north. They needed night for the dash through the straits between them, so they throttled down to four knots and even spent a couple of hours going back on their tracks to gain time. After they had turned again in the late afternoon they passed within twenty feet of a large floating log, surrounded by a school of huge sharks which seemed to be trying to bite it. It was not a pleasant sight and considerably doused their spirits. It was not only Japanese air and naval patrol craft they had to fear.

By dusk, the massive island volcanoes, Gunong Agoeng, 10,000 feet on Bali, and Gunong Rindjani, 12,000 feet on Lombok, seemed to fill half the sky. Nusa Besar Island, in the middle of the entrance to the straits, was about fourteen miles distant. As the light faded, a powerful searchlight started to sweep from the high land on the south-eastern corner of Bali off their port bow.

Lyon and Davidson were in the wheelhouse with Ted Carse. "What do you think, Don? Can we make it?" Lyon asked. Davidson gave a slight shrug of his shoulders. Carse had been watching the sweep of the light intently. "If we keep well over to the Lombok side," he said, "the flash should pass over the top of our mast. We are so low in the water that I think we shall be below their horizon." Paddy McDowell was told to subject his faulty bearing to maximum revolutions, a glorious six and a half knots, and, heading slightly to the north-east, *Krait* started to force the fifty-mile passage.

Misled again by the pilot book, they had underestimated the southerly tidal set in the narrows. Once a day the whole of the Java Sea tries to pour through this narrow funnel into the Indian Ocean, and they had caught this tremendous rip at its height. By 9 o'clock they were barely abeam of Nusa Besar Island. An hour later, as a fixed steady light became visible on its highest point, probably an observation post, they were barely a mile further ahead. At eleven o'clock they had actually lost ground and were back in the same position as they had been two hours earlier. The tide was running faster than the straining diesel could push the overloaded craft.

Between midnight and four in the morning they made about six miles. They had passed innumerable flickering lights, some of which might be bush-clearing fires, but sev-

334

eral of which looked like the headlights of motor cars. They had assumed Nusa Besar to be uninhabited—it had been, under the Dutch—but there was so much activity that they were thankful they had not carried out their original intention of lying up under its lee during the day and attempting the passage on the second night.

With every man on look-out, they peered into the darkness. Tired eyes can play curious tricks. Once, Lyon, who seemed to have a cat's vision at night, thought he saw a cruiser closing them, with three masts and a huge bow wave. After a few tense minutes, with arms at the ready, the bow wave resolved itself into a tide-rip and the masts into three tall trees on the top of a distant hill. Another naval patrol craft seen through their night-glasses turned out to be a sailing junk, beating laboriously against the current.

Although *Krait* was taking several minutes to thump through the worst of the tide-rips, the force of the current was now slackening, and Carse was reasonably sanguine about their being safely clear by the morning.

Their hopes were rudely shattered. As dawn broke they were still in the northern narrows, with Nusa Besar just visible astern. Daybreak was so spectacular that for a moment they forgot their danger. As the sun struck the top of the towering volcano, Gunong Agoeng, on Bali and the morning mists started to roll down the sides, the light caught the prismatic colours on the pinnacles and outcrops, cascading down, like a torch shone on mosaic. As the clouds cleared, the coast was left clear with perfect visibility. To the east, on the Lombok side, a merciful haze persisted, which should shield them from being sighted from Ampenan, the only known Japanese base in the area.

Apart from sighting a few coastal sailing *prahus,* no alarm was raised. At ten in the morning Carse wrote in his log: "Fixed position 8° 5′ South, 115° 55′ East. Thank Christ we are through the Strait, steering for Sekala, 68 miles distant. After a clear early morning the haze now at 1020 is increasing, although the island of Bali is still clearly visible. Lombok is almost totally obscured. . . . This war is certainly hard on the nervous system."

If all went well the next part of their journey should be

335

less eventful. Keeping to the east of the Kangean Islands, north of the Lombok Straits, the plan was to turn northwest, skirting the coast of Borneo, and then strike across to the Lingga Archipelago, the most southerly group of the maze of islands extended up to Singapore.

On the tenth, the day after they had cleared Lombok, Ted Carse's log was much more cheerful and discursive: "The morale of the crew is excellent. Corporal Crilly is doing a marvellous job in making all meals tasty in spite of bad weather and worse conditions. . . . By dark tonight we will be across the main shipping routes from Surabaya and Batavia to Balik Papan, Timor and all ports using the Macassar Strait. Our look-outs are particularly keen and so far have always sighted any objects long before we could possibly be seen by them. We have ample supplies of everything needed except water, which is rationed to three cups of tea a day and a water bottle every three days. Most of them seem to have no difficulty in this but I have been praying for a good shower of rain ever since the days have become hot. In latitude 5° South, with the sun only 5° North, its heat as close to the water as we are is terrific. The decks become too hot to stand on in bare feet. To counteract this, our freeboard is so little that with even a calm sea our waist is continually awash."

By the fourteenth they were standing away from Borneo on the last lap of their sea journey. That evening Carse made another of his revealing log entries: "A heavy cloud bank surmounted by mare's tails is rising astern. It might presage a fairly heavy blow. No rain so far. I can visualise a small nudist colony when it does come and bad luck for the man at the wheel. Summing up this afternoon, I decided we had seven more really dangerous days with the ship. Namely, to-day and tomorrow, dropping and picking up operatives, two days for this passage on return and, last but not least, THE STRAIT. If we survive the next two days the operation should be carried out successfully and then for our return journey. All the ship's company are in the best of health and spirits and are thoroughly enjoying the trip. So far we have experienced the most wonderful weather. Right

336

from Cairns we had a following wind and sea (these are the conditions in which the ship behaves best) and no really bad weather. But the last three days we have seen no flying fish at all. This seems rather remarkable in these waters. One solitary turtle was seen to-day and countless jellyfish."

The next day they sighted a junk on a converging course and *Krait's* labouring engine was unable to shake her off. "The fact that we can't leave a junk behind, although she is beating slightly to windward, is causing quite a little merriment," Carse commented. The two ships remained within sight of each other most of the day, but as the wind shifted during the afternoon, *Krait* started to draw ahead, without any sign of suspicious activity on the junk. Just to make sure, everyone had rubbed on another coat of their foul-smelling, sticky dye and Carse's logbook was covered again with his smudged fingerprints. There was also a more worrying note: "My eyes have been giving trouble lately," he wrote. "I can't read the sextant now by artificial light and this will mean working by sun and dead reckoning. Sun sights at present are rather unsatisfactory. Probably with a fortnight's rest away from this constant glare, they will improve sufficiently for the run home. I sincerely hope so."

They were now within a hundred miles of their target. Arms were inspected, their camouflage renewed, and every man, except for look-outs, told to remain under the awning with the minimum of movement.

At ten o'clock of the morning of September 16 they saw their first aircraft, apparently heading north for Singapore on a steady course, and then two sailing ships coming down the Strait towards them. One was a European-type yacht, probably captured at the fall of Singapore, but they both ignored *Krait* and, to everyone's delight, a cloud bank started building up from Sumatra, reducing visibility drastically and threatening a violent storm. The heavy black cloud formations came boiling up from the west, blotting out the sky. Lyon, Davidson, and Morris had seen this phenomenon before. It heralded a dreaded "Sumatra," a violent cyclonic storm which has wise seamen running for

337

harbour. *Krait* had weather conditions as bad when clearing Exmouth Gulf and if they could hold course they might be able to get through the Strait without detection.

Suddenly Davidson gave the order for action stations, each man taking up his Sten or Bren gun and going to his loophole post under the awning. Not 400 yards ahead, a 10,000-ton freighter emerged from the murk on their port side and cut across their bows. They reduced speed immediately, but the ship held on course and gave no evidence of having sighted them. Minutes later the storm struck and everything was blotted out. The wind hit *Krait* as if she had collided head on with a solid rock. The sea was lashed inboard, lifting spindrift twenty or thirty feet high. Then came the torrential rain lasting nearly three quarters of an hour.

The more inexperienced members of the crew had been warned what to expect, and once the first shock was over, busied themselves carrying a large sail forward to catch the precious fresh water. Hanging on grimly to rails and stanchions, they ferried every container they possessed past the wheelhouse to fill up the water tanks. Drenched, shouting, and happy, revelling in their first bath for a fortnight, the tension of half an hour earlier was completely forgotten.

The storm cleared as quickly as it had come, and they found that they were through the Strait and already north of Pompong Island, the first Lyon had decided to reconnoitre as their rear base for the pick-up and get-away. They were now in the almost land-girt sea, some 60 miles from east to west and 150 miles from north to south, which lies between the coast of Sumatra and the convex sweep of the islands of the Rhio and Lingga archipelagoes. To the north, within a score of miles of Singapore, the islands curve round towards Sumatra to form a natural barrier, with only half a dozen narrow channels between them. *Krait* had avoided the wide and well-guarded Singapore Straits, which lead into the port from the east, but was safely within the inner barrier to the south. Her outward task was largely done. Almost any of the islands in the northern part of this inland sea were within canoe range of their target.

They run very much to a pattern. Humps of dark-green

338

jungle, heavy with ficus palm and knotted undergrowth, vibrate in the heat haze, with mud flats and mangrove swamp on the shore, interspersed with rocky outcrops and small sandy beaches. Most of the inhabitants live in fishing villages, either built on stilts along the shoreline or clustered on some rare stretch of level land with a clearing for their primitive agriculture behind. Except for the occasional plantation, everything else is jungle, teeming with animal life. If they chose their hides carefully, the canoe teams were unlikely to be discovered even by the occasional hunter. The villagers are nearly all fishermen, their means of communication the *kolek* and the *prahu*. To these men *Krait* would be an object of no interest, provided her movements were not suspicious. But the canoes—that was another matter. They were unlike anything to be found in these waters and the merest sight of one of them would cause a buzz of *kampong* gossip.

Reducing speed, *Krait* turned south and slowly ran past Pompong Island. There seemed far too many native huts and fishing stakes along the shores for comfort and as they stood in to round a point they had another bad scare. Carse suddenly sighted a long straight mast with crosstrees about a mile and a half away, its structure unmistakably that of a naval patrol craft. Clamping on full speed and swinging the helm over, he turned through 180 degrees and sent little Berryman, with his keen eyes, scurrying up *Krait's* own mast to report.

The look-out soon had reassuring news. Only the mast was visible sticking out of the water and it must belong to a wreck.

Krait then stood over to the eastwards to see if Bengku Island offered any better shelter, but they found it surrounded by a seemingly impassable reef. They launched the dinghy to take soundings, and Davidson was just about to cast off when they heard the sound of an aircraft. It was coming in so low that for a moment they could not see it. With quick presence of mind, Lyon snatched up one of the conical coolie straw hats they were carrying on board, tossed it down to Davidson, quickly donned one himself, and as the plane roared over at not more than a hundred feet, looked up at it and waved in the most natural manner in the world. He could actually see the Japanese pilot looking down at them. He gave no sign of surprise, continued straight on, and was soon out of sight. It had been a bad moment. Lyon blew out his cheeks in relief and blessed the foresight which had made him have everyone blacken themselves with the dye as soon as the storm was over. Curious as they looked, it obviously worked.

Bengku proved useless, and towards evening they moved back to Pompong, where they had spotted one sheltered and uninhabited bay. They christened it Fisherman's Bay and dropped anchor for the night. The four officers held a conference. In spite of the scares of the day, Lyon had made up his mind that patrol activity was limited and that the best thing for *Krait* to do was to cruise gently northwards and then strike west to Pulau Durian, to arrive at dusk the following day.

"I don't know how the day is going to end," Carse was writing in his log, voicing the feelings of them all. "We have been zig-zagging and zig-zagging all day long from one deserted spot to another, only to find that we are approaching a worse one. Out of the frying pan into the fire would be appropriate, but it does the system no good. We have been looking for a place to anchor but the population is against us. As long as we keep moving, no matter how aimlessly, we don't seem to excite suspicion, but I don't think we could do it for long. We are within about 30 odd miles of Singapore and still getting closer by means of a staggered course, waiting and praying for dark. No lovers ever longed for darkness as we do, although it will probably show us the lights of Singapore. One thing about it is that we should be able to pick up all searchlights and observation post positions guarding the city."

Lyon had always hoped that *Krait* would be able to lie up in some deep cove, camouflaged with branches against the shore, to await the return of the attack party. This plan had now been abandoned. No suitable cover had been found, and in the eighteen months since he was last in these

340

waters, the Japanese had clearly organised extensive patrol activity. He would have to take the risk of sending *Krait* on an innocent-appearing run to Borneo, returning for the rendezvous. She was safer in the uninhabited sea lanes, off the main shipping routes, than in this congested litter of islands.

At four o'clock in the afternoon they passed along the small island of Panjang. A dark-green hump of hill and jungle, it appeared entirely uninhabited and offered several good beaches and sandy coves. Lyon made up his mind at once. This would be the base for the canoes, but they dare not land and reconnoitre in daylight, still within view of the observation post on Galang Baru, so they carried on northwards towards the Bulan Strait approach to Singapore to waste the three remaining hours of daylight.

It would be half past seven before it was dark enough for them to turn about. As the tropical night fell, a diffused glow seemed to fill the northern sky, even individual specks of light appeared. Lyon grabbed Davidson by the elbow. "There she is, Donald," he said. They were looking at the reflection of the lights of Singapore, twinkling a mere twenty-two miles ahead. They called the rest of the crew up into the bows. There was no mistaking the elation in Lyon's usually calm voice as he told them what they were looking at. The tension suddenly seemed to lift. The voyage was half over, they were safe, and they now knew the full extent of what was required of them. Slapping each other on the back, pointing, wrestling, panting in their excitement, it was several minutes before they took up their stations again.

Lyon whispered an order and Carse turned *Krait* round for her run back to Panjang. They started to get out the rest of the attack stores on the forward deck. Lyon, Davidson, and Page watched their every move to make sure that there was no last-minute confusion, while Carse's bad eyes peered ahead to con their position.

"As we turned, we noticed a searchlight coming from the Galang Baru O.P.," he wrote later in his log. "Then a violent rain squall accompanied by heavy, gusty winds struck us, obscuring everything. Suddenly out of the darkness ahead, our fishing *pagar* showed a lovely bright light. As we were at that time surrounded by reefs, with a strong ebb tide and no vision, it appeared God sent. If we return from this trip I am thinking of setting up a monument to their glory."

They arrived off Panjang at ten o'clock and anchored, but the sea was too rough and the wind too high to risk landing. At midnight the weather showed no signs of abating, so they weighed anchor to see if they could find a lee shore on the opposite side of the island. No sooner had they got under way than the wind dropped. They moved inshore again and Davidson and Jones paddled to the beach in the dinghy to reconnoitre. Within half an hour Jones was back, to say that the beach was perfect for the purpose.

The crew had practised transporting the canoes and loading the stores so often that they could do it blindfolded. Quickly Lyon ran through the final check: arms, knives, charts, binoculars, rations and water for a month, protective clothing, and, last but not least, the mines and spares that went with them. *Krait's* freeboard was so low that loading the dinghy presented no difficulty. Paddy McDowell came up from the engine room, and Young from his wireless set, to see them off. It was now half past four in the morning. Morris shouldered his way forward and leant over to shake Lyon by the hand: "The very best of luck, sir, and may we be seeing you again soon," he said. "Thank you, Morris, I hope so indeed," replied Lyon to his oldest companion.

Light-hearted as it all was, those left on *Krait* had the nagging thought that they might be seeing their six companions for the last time. The pick-up was to be at Pompong after dusk on October 1. If anything went wrong, *Krait* was not to wait beyond the rendezvous date, but to return to Exmouth Gulf without the operatives. There was no point in risking the whole party, and Lyon was confident that if the six of them survived they would be able to capture a junk and find their own way home.

For the six men of the attack teams, the parting from

Krait had been an even greater wrench. Although the vital stage of the expedition lay ahead of them, they felt very lonely, deposited a thousand miles inside the enemy lines, faced by a fortnight abandoned to their own slender resources. Lyon was worried as he stood on the sandy beach and watched *Krait's* familiar, ridiculous outline fade into the night—worried about Carse's eyes being able to stand up to the strain of the pin-point navigation which must bring them back to Pompong at the end of the month, worried about *Krait's* ability to give an account of herself now that her firepower had been reduced by half, worried that the only other two men with real knowledge of local lore and jungle survival, Davidson and Page, were standing beside him and that there was no one left aboard to hold the youngsters together should anything go wrong.

His other five companions gave him no qualms. They were fighting fit in spite of the fatigues of the voyage and the unbearable strain of the last forty-eight hours. Davidson, with his inexhaustible energy and inventiveness, tough as oak; Page, intelligent, resourceful, and utterly reliable; Falls, the young Greek god, powerful, tireless, ever alert; Jones, with his power-packed, thickset body and ready smile; and Huston, the "Baby" of the party, dogged, endlessly willing and making up in will power and determination for his lack of years. If they could not get to Singapore and back, then no one could.

For the moment they felt safe enough. In his quick reconnaissance from the dinghy into the jungle earlier in the night, Davidson had found nothing to indicate that this part of Panjang was in any way frequented. The folboats and the stores had been dragged up into the undergrowth and all was quiet, the breathless hush which even in the tropics precedes the dawn. Around and above them the huge ficus trees were whispering in the light airs. Beyond the horse-shoe of rocks that hemmed in their little haven, the treetops were etched in sharp profile against the glittering slate grey of the night sky, with the clouds slowly building up for the morning overcast.

It was an idyllic, peaceful scene. After the sour smell of diesel oil, hot tar, and timbers and the lingering fish stench

343

from *Krait's* ancient bilges, the jungle scents were almost overpowering in their sweetness. Ground lilies and a flowering tree with white midnight blossoms made the air round them almost tangible. They breathed it deeply, gathering strength for the trial that lay ahead.

There was nothing further they could do that night. Their muscles ached from the unloading and their brains were tired. Ducking back into the bush a few yards under cover, each of them burrowed out a hip hole under his groundsheet, wrapped himself in a blanket, and to the soothing rustle of the jungle insects was on the instant asleep.

The respite only lasted three hours, but was infinitely refreshing. As they sat round their first breakfast of emergency rations they held a council of war. The drop had been carried out ahead of schedule and they could afford to take the next two days resting, getting their land legs—each of them still swayed on solid ground with the inbuilt movement of *Krait*—building up their dump, and sorting out their stores. Davidson, the best silent tracker, moved off into the jungle to see how safe their hide-out was. Huston, sent down with a rake to remove all traces of their landing, was soon back with the encouraging report that the tide had obliterated everything up to the high-water mark and that a legion of bustling little land crabs had made his work quite unnecessary.

Davidson was equally reassuring. There was a native fishing village about a quarter of a mile away on the other side of the spit of land, but no sign of any tracks leading in their direction.

The forty-eight hours that followed were the best of the whole trip. They lazed around, wallowed in the fresh water, scrubbing off the filth of the voyage and enjoying the unspeakable luxury of cleaning their teeth in something other than pure brine. There was the occasional scare. For a tense half hour the shrilling of birds up the hill made them think that some native was after all making his way over from the village, but the noises in the undergrowth resolved themselves into a troop of monkeys, who surveyed the party with chirpy curiosity and then gradually leapfrogged away again. During the evening, they heard the disturbing plop-plop of a diesel. Clearly there was a patrol boat making an irregular inspection of the area. They heard it again on the second night, but at a different time, and it was obviously an inquisitive adversary of whom they would have to beware.

The evening of September 20 found them in magnificent trim. The stores and equipment for the three folboats were checked and rechecked—food and water for at least eight days, charts and the Admiralty register of enemy shipping, arms greased and ammunition inspected for mildew, and, above all, the precious limpet mines themselves. Here Page was the expert. The rods down which they were slid to be clipped on the side of ships with their magnets were cleaned and oiled until they ran like silk. The detonators, the hinges for the magnets, every working part was inspected.

They represented the last stage in the long haul across from Sydney and nothing could be allowed to impede their successful functioning. Three sets of them went into each canoe, together with the magnetic hold-fast which enabled them to hold steady in the tide as the canoe came alongside its target and each successive mine was fixed. Everything was in order and they were replaced inside their watertight containers. Then came the boats themselves. Every bamboo strut, every inch of the rubberised canvas, was run over by keen eyes and probing fingers for the slightest snag or flaw. The waist bands which fastened round the operators and prevented a single drop of water reaching the inside of the boat were checked for the slightest puncture; so were their hoods and protective clothing. Everything had survived the pitching and tossing of *Krait's* hot hold without a mark. They were ready to go.

Fully loaded, with its two operatives, the seaman in front and the officer to correct the course and speed behind, each canoe weighed some 800 pounds. They were low and sluggish in the water, but to ensure success they could not carry less. Once the mines and half the rations had gone, it would be a very different matter and even tired paddlers should be able to make them bounce back on the return journey.

After a last survey of the hide, with Page giving the natural camouflage a few final touches, the canoes were launched.

For their final hide and attack base, Lyon had selected Pulau Dongas, a small island lying just off the north coast of Batam and due south-east of Singapore, just behind Pulau Sambu. Paddling evenly now, with the west-east tide, they reached it just after midnight on the 22nd. Lyon had remembered it from his pre-war sailing days as entirely uninhabited, with an all-important supply of fresh water. There was an extensive swamp on the south side and a sandy spit at its northern head which should provide an excellent landing place. So indeed it proved to be. The canoes ran past its jungle-covered hump, and Davidson, in his usual role of scout, went in ahead. He returned full of enthusiasm. The sand beach ran in under mangroves, providing perfect cover and a much more extensive and comfortable hide even than on Bulat. The canoes were hauled up, with some difficulty as the tide was low, and, with one of their number, as always, on watch, the other five collapsed into sleep.

They had touched the limit of human endurance. In the three days since leaving Panjang none of them had had more than half a dozen hours' sleep. Lyon was the worst hit. For him the physical strain was compounded by the responsibility and concentration of leadership. This was the testing time for his plan. Davidson was a superb foil, but only Lyon could supply the detailed, instinctive knowledge of the terrain, the snap decision on tactics, choice and change of hide, and, with his knowledge of the Malay language, any hint from the overheard conversation of fishermen and villagers that their plan needed to be modified. He had lost weight and was looking gaunt and hollow-cheeked. Reading his mood, his companions redoubled their efforts, taking the minor details off the shoulders of the one man on whom everything depended.

They could afford to spend the next day resting. A detailed search of the island revealed not a single sign of human habitation or movement. Their sole companions were a colony of large black- and yellow-striped sea iguanas and

346

a couple of small crocodiles. While the others remained in the hide to check their canoes and equipment, Lyon and Davidson climbed to the highest point of the island to begin their watch on the Roads and work out their plan of attack.

Once a suitable observation point had been chosen, constant watch was kept by the six men in turn, plotting the position of the various ships at anchor and endeavouring to identify them with the help of the Admiralty Register they had brought with them. This went on for forty-eight hours.

"The Dongas observation post was opposite and eight miles distant from Kallang," Lyon noted in his report. "In conditions of good visibility it was possible to see into Keppel Harbour. A night watch was kept until 2300 hours on September 23, revealing no signs of any defensive activity. There was no black-out in Singapore and the lights of cars driving down Beach Road could be clearly seen. No harbour or navigation lights were burning and all shipping was stationary.

"The following day we were well rested and maintained a keen watch, during which we carefully scrutinised both shore and shipping. There was no change to be seen in the general outline of the city. A row of five to seven tall wireless masts have been constructed on the site of the former Paya Lebar station and there is a single mast on the roof of the Cathay Building. On the southernmost point of St. John's Island there is now a small signal station. At Sambu, three miles from our observation post, all visible oil tanks were still as left by the Dutch. There was tremendous activity on the western side of the island. The hammering of plates and drone of engines by day and night suggested either ship repair or building.

"In the harbour and Roads of Singapore there was considerable movement of shipping. At no time was there less than 100,000 tons at the same time."

That afternoon they plotted their targets, identifying and noting for the intelligence files back in Melbourne every ship they could see. The tankers they would ignore. It was the one type of vessel against which the limpet mine was least effective. Their main target was merchant ships. Three

347

limpets laid along the side against the main holds would blow a hole four or five feet in diameter and the ship must inevitably sink. Davidson and Falls, in the No. 2 canoe, were to take the group of ships lying in the Singapore Roads proper, to the east of Keppel Harbour. Of the other two, Page was to concentrate on the ships lying alongside the wharves on the island of Pulau Bukum, to the south-west of Singapore, and Lyon was to deal with the other group of ships lying in the examination anchorage between Bukum and the main island.

With the precious mines checked and double-checked again, they launched the canoes for the attack about eight o'clock at night. Everyone knew his role and there was no need for long farewells. Each man gripped the others' hand, they wished each other good luck and started off in company in their usual arrowhead formation. Readily accessible, each man carried a small rubber pellet filled with lethal cyanide. If any of them should be caught one bite brought instant death. If the attack failed, the Japanese would at least be denied the triumph of exhibiting their captives— and the crew of *Krait* would be safe.

They skirted warily past the glare of Sambu and, to their relief, as the night advanced, the lights of Singapore started to dim. Halfway to the target area, a searchlight was suddenly switched on from some high point, probably the top of the Cathay Building, swung slowly round, and then came to rest on the three folboats for a full half minute. They flicked their canoes bow on and sat transfixed. Then it continued its sweep and was as suddenly switched off. They expected every searchlight in the harbour to open up, but nothing happened. At moments of such heightened danger, every fear is justified, but it really seemed as if they had not been spotted.

They resumed their course, only to find that the increasing force of the tide started to take its toll. They turned the bows of the canoes further east to meet it, but they were barely making headway. They had now been paddling for more than three hours. Practised canoe operatives can continue for much longer without excessive fatigue, but it

348

was becoming clear that they were rooted in mid-channel and time was running out on them. They were nowhere near any ships yet and, even in the most favourable conditions, they would have to allow at least an hour for the actual attack. At all costs they must be back in their hide by daybreak. By one o'clock in the morning the attempt had become hopeless. At Lyon's careful hail, the three canoes drew together and the bitter decision was taken to break off the attack and run for safety. They would have to try from a point further west two nights later.

The tide was an equal enemy on the return journey. It carried them well to the east of Dongas and when it started to slacken they decided to race for the hide individually. Davidson and Falls, Page and Jones, the two stronger couples, reached the mangrove swamp in time, but there was no sign of Lyon and Huston. Wrestling with their lop-sided canoe, they had lost contact.

The strain was beginning to tell on Lyon by now. All the planning, all the responsibility, and most of the worry had been his and the physical effort was starting to wrack his frail frame. He might have done better to change partners with Davidson, as Poppa Falls could paddle for two all day, but this was not Lyon's way. The make-up of the crews had long since been determined and it was essential to have a pair of fast paddlers for emergencies and spying out the land ahead.

Lyon and Huston were safe. They had battled on until they could hardly see from exhaustion and had mistaken their bearings. They landed on the wrong side of Dongas just as dawn was breaking and spent an unhappy, sleepless day in pouring rain, hiding in an outcrop of boulders.

At seven o'clock that evening, having recovered sufficiently to discover where they were, they paddled round the point to rejoin the main party, to be greeted with cries of relief. "Lieutenant Davidson had anticipated our arrival and organised a much needed hot meal," Lyon was to report tersely but gratefully. "He had also made plans for an immediate change to an alternative hide, whence an attack could be launched the following night of the 26th/

349

27th, under favourable conditions. His prompt action on this occasion contributed greatly to the success of the expedition."

The new base, which both Lyon and Davidson had noted from their observation post on the previous day, was the island of Subar, lying due west from them on the other side of the Bulan Strait. As soon as Lyon and Huston had rested a little they set off, with Davidson and Falls in the slow folboat, and managed to beat the tide, which ran less strongly along the northern coast of Batam, quite comfortably. Subar had no beach and no water but was mercifully uninhabited. Dawn caught them still manhandling stores and canoes over the boulders, but they managed to hide everything under bushes and behind rocks and this time slept the whole morning.

By the afternoon they were sufficiently recovered to climb up for another look at their target. There had been little change in the moored ships and they had a much better view, straight into the examination anchorage, than had been possible from Dongas. The target areas were not changed, but the plan was altered to permit Davidson and Falls to take off separately, due north, to Keppel Harbour, while the other two canoes headed in a more north-westerly direction for Pulau Bukum. That evening, the twenty-sixth, found them faced by the sixth night of eight hours' paddling out of the last seven. They were still in relatively good shape, although their legs were suffering from a curiously rubbery feeling that came from long hours spent in an unnatural position in a canoe. But they had the spur of the actual attack to keep them going.

This time the final farewells were real. They were now two days behind schedule. Some check would have to be made on the results of the attack and, although Davidson was the expedition's photographer, he and Falls, as the strongest pair, in their original boat, were to ride the easterly set of the tide on their return journey and make their way down the Rhio Strait to the east of Batam Island, doubling back thence to Panjang and then making a bee-line for Pompong to hold *Krait*. The others should be able to make Dongas again from the examination anchorage and after confirming the effects of the raid, would rejoin the rendezvous down the Bulan Strait, the way they had come.

"Cheerio, Ivan, best of luck," said Donald Davidson, looking a little worriedly at Lyon's hollow-cheeked face, with the sleepless shadows under his eyes and the short stubble of his beard.

"The same to you, Donald. And thank you for everything. See you back at Pompong."

The others were more light-hearted, but their hand-grips were not less fervent. They manhandled their slate-grey canoes over the rocks, checked the fastenings on their skin-tight black vests and hoods, climbed in to the narrow circular opening which sealed the inside of their folboats from the sea, and with a last salute of their paddles set off.

The more northerly course made possible by the change of base had made things very much easier. Davidson and Falls were across the Straits in a couple of hours, and although they kept a wary eye on a searchlight which opened up on Blakang Mati Island off to port, encountered no serious difficulties. The two men had developed a warm understanding and chatted easily, with Davidson pointing out the main buildings and sights of Singapore to his fascinated companion. It hardly seemed possible that they could be passing unobserved right across the inner harbour of this Japanese bastion. As they drew closer in, they muffled their voices until Davidson pointed out the unmistakable triad pylons of the Keppel Harbour boom ahead of them.

Just as they altered course slightly, Falls spotted a set of navigation lights moving out at them from the night. They proved to be on a large steam tug turning into the same channel. It headed straight for them until it seemed impossible that they should not be either sighted or run down. Then, at the last moment, it turned towards Blakang Mati and they were left safe but badly shaken.

As soon as they had regained their composure they forged ahead again and to their surprise found the Tanjong Pagar end of the boom opened. The temptation was too strong for Davidson. Two days earlier, from Dongas, two large freighters had been sighted tied up alongside the wharves. If these could be sunk, they would block the

351

entire dock for months. Unhesitatingly, Davidson turned hard aport right into Keppel Harbour. It was a mad gamble to take, as the harbour was little more than five hundred yards wide, but the tug had not succeeded in spotting them from a mere fifty yards away and Davidson was so confident of the efficacy of their camouflage that he ploughed straight in. They paddled the whole length of the wharves, but their targets had gone. The vessels in the Empire Docks behind were too brightly illuminated and too small to justify the risk involved.

As they turned and made their way out again they found two small freighters against the east wharf, but considered that they were not worthy of their attention, compared with the large ships lying out in the Roads which were their original targets. Apart from the busy unloading going on in the Empire Docks under the arc lights, there was little sign of movement in the main harbour. Davidson could scarcely credit that the Japanese had become so lax in their security, but then, as he considered ruefully, perhaps they had very little to worry about—apart from enemy folboats loaded with limpet mines. But they had obviously not thought of that.

Out through the boom again they continued due east towards the shipping in the Roads. Here it was merely a question of taking their choice. The look-outs must have been unbelievably slack, as the operation went like clockwork. They might just as well have been attacking abandoned hulks in Sydney Harbour. Swinging at their anchors, the bows of all the ships were pointed towards Singapore in the current and, as the canoe drifted down the port side of each, they were nicely in the shadow from the lights of Singapore. The tide was running at about half a knot, perfect for their purpose.

Firm-fingered, they went through the drill. Out with the hold-fast and, as Davidson steadied the canoe, Falls set the fuse, slipped a mine down on its placing stick, and snapped the magnets against the hull well under water. It was as easy as that. Release the hold-fast, drift down the length of cordtex to the side of the next hold, and plant another mine. Three times and that was the ration. Slowly

352

and silently they drifted down to the next victim, which they had identified as the *Taisyo Maru,* which they had seen from Dongas. Ignoring a 10,000-ton tanker, they carefully chose three substantial cargo vessels of at least 6,000 tons' displacement. The third one had arc lights burning on deck, illuminating the surrounding water, but so confident were they now that nothing could deter them. As they worked, they could hear the chiming clock on Singapore's Victoria Hall counting out the quarter hours.

By half past one it was all over. The placing stick and hold-fast were dropped silently over the side. The mines were timed to blow at five o'clock. They had less than three hours in which to cross the Straits again and find a hide on the north shore of Batam Island. Confident, triumphant, swinging easily on their paddles, they set off to the southeast.

Eight miles to the west of them, the two other canoes had remained in company to within a mile of Pulau Bukum. The time was nine o'clock, just as Davidson and Falls were slipping into Keppel Harbour. Page and Jones continued straight on to the Pulau Bukum wharves, and Lyon and Huston turned a little north to the examination anchorage. They had both had an even easier passage than the third canoe, apart from the sweep of the searchlight on Blakang Mati which had bothered Davidson and Falls.

Page and Jones found that the wharves were brightly lit, with sentries on guard at the ships' gangways. They paddled the whole length of the docks, keeping fairly well out to sea, but only saw one suitable target, an old freighter of the *Tone Maru* class. A large tanker was too heavily laden to make any attack worth while, and the third vessel, a small freighter, had a barge alongside on which a number of dockers appeared to be working under arc lights against a background of what looked like cauldrons of steam. They both watched curiously this odd spectacle for some time but could not make up their minds what the men were doing.

They drifted down to the *Tone Maru*-class freighter and slipped down their first three limpets. They could hear the Japanese crew and workmen chatting away, completely unaware of the destruction which was in store for them. Num-

353

ber 3 canoe then made off again to the north towards the examination anchorage. Their second target was reasonably easy to identify, with its three sets of goal-post masts. They had marked it from the Admiralty list on Subar as the *Nasusan Maru*. This whole group of ships was blacked out and, as the lights of Singapore round the corner of the mainland to the east were greatly dimmed, they had some difficulty in finding their third target, an older 6,000-ton freighter. However, the tide carried them right down to it and they bumped the bow quite heavily as its dark mass emerged from the night. There can have been no look-outs on duty at all, as they heard no movement, fixed their mines without the least interruption, and immediately set off, in their turn, south-east, to the original Dongas hide.

Lyon and Huston had the most alarming experience. They were due to attack the more northerly group of ships, lying right up against Singapore Island itself. On the way they passed the *Nasusan Maru* with its three goal-post masts, but recognising that this "belonged to Page," carried on to the north.

The lights of Singapore were now hidden behind a spit of land and the two men found it completely impossible to distinguish the outlines of their targets against the background of hills. They paddled to and fro, losing a lot of time, until finally, in desperation, Lyon decided to return to the examination anchorage proper. All the ships there were blacked out, but two large tankers they had noted earlier were showing their obligatory red riding light, and rather than waste further time, he decided to attack one of these.

They had fixed one limpet on the propeller shaft and were just lowering a second, beside the engine room, when Lyon saw Huston looking upwards. He glanced up himself, and there, not ten feet above their heads, a man was watching them intently out of a porthole.

He made no sign or sound and, with an inspired reflex action, Lyon gestured impatiently to his partner to get on with the work.

There is no rational explanation for the man's com-

354

plete inactivity. Whether he thought they were starving Malays picking off barnacles for the family pot there is no way of telling. He continued to watch them earnestly as they fixed the last limpet and then, with Lyon willing Huston to remain calm, withdrew his head and lighted the lamp in his cabin as they pushed off. If he lived to tell the tale, he must have been a very surprised man three hours later. "He'll soon be dead," Lyon whispered to his partner with relish.

Nevertheless, he had upset their plans and they could not risk dallying in the anchorage any longer. For all they knew the alarm would be raised at any moment. Grim with anxiety at the thought that the whole purpose of the expedition was about to be wrecked by a general alarm, they bent their backs to their paddles and fairly skimmed the swell in a straight line for Dongas.

Both western canoes reached the island safely within a few minutes of each other shortly before five o'clock. Hauling up their folboats into the mangrove hide, Page had just given Lyon an excited account of their successful attack and Lyon was just telling the other two of the extraordinary incident with the tanker when the first booming explosion was heard. It came from over on the Keppel Harbour side and was their first indication that Davidson too had been successful. Listening intently, they counted two, three, from the Keppel Harbour direction and another four from their own area. So Davidson had successfully laid all his limpets, and unless he had had as unpleasant an experience as Lyon, must be on his way to safety.

The thunder of the explosions reverberated round the Straits and echoed back from the surrounding hills. No flashes were to be seen as the charges were all well under water. This was fantastic. They danced up and down, slapping each other on the back, whispering hoarsely and incoherently with delight, their rigid discipline not letting them down even in this moment of triumph.

The eastern sky was beginning to lighten. Within minutes of the last explosion every ship's siren in the Roads started to howl and a quarter of an hour later Singapore

355

and Sambu Island were suddenly blacked out.

Leaving Page and Jones to see to the safety of the boats, Lyon and Huston fought their way up through the trees in the direction of the observation post. By the time they had panted and clawed their way up the hill there was just enough light for them to find their vantage point.

As dawn came up, they could see that most of the ships in the anchorage had got under way and were starting to cruise aimlessly up and down. This made it very difficult to determine what had been sunk and what had not. One ship was definitely half submerged, with her bows sticking up out of the water, over in the examination anchorage, and the big tanker, the *Sinkoku Maru,* which had given Lyon and Huston such a fright, was burning fiercely and belching out thick black smoke which covered the whole area. This left five to be accounted for and, for the time being, they had to be entered as "certainly damaged, probably sunk."

The sirens and commotion continued most of the morning. At a quarter past six a flight of twin-engined aircraft took off from Kallang airfield and roared westwards towards the Malacca Strait. They returned bout two hours later and, after putting down again briefly at Kallang, took off individually and started to scour the southern approaches. One of them passed right over the Dongas hide and could be clearly identified as a twin-engined medium bomber.

By this time Page had joined the other two, leaving Jones to watch, bringing a welcome sackful of rations. They were too excited and intent on the activity in the Roads to eat very much, but nibbled absent-mindedly and thankfully at a few bars of chocolate.

At half past two another flight of nine medium bombers took off from Kallang and headed north. These they did not see return. The harbour area was patrolled throughout the day by Zero fighters and miscellaneous light aircraft, but the whole weight of the search was clearly concentrated to the north-west, the Japanese having assumed, quite reasonably, that the attack must have been launched down the Malacca Straits. Apart from the few perfunctory pa-

356

trols to the south in the forenoon, no special flights were made in that direction again, an excellent omen for the party's escape.

A mass of small motor sampans and other various craft started to congregate in the two roadsteads where the ships had been sunk, but it was very difficult to determine through the glasses whether they were engaged in salvage work or not. No ban seemed to have been placed on the movement of shipping. Native craft continued to move across the Straits all day, while the flights of civil aircraft in and out of Kallang appeared to follow the normal pattern of the previous four days of observation.

Innumerable patrol craft and launches criss-crossed the harbour throughout the day without any apparent purpose becoming discernible in their movements. Ships continued to arrive from the north-west and appeared to pass into the inner Keppel Harbour and, as the day advanced, most of those which had been out in the Roads either joined them or steamed off towards the north.

The Japanese were completely baffled and infuriated to the point of frenzy, as much by the loss of "face" as by their shipping sunk. They turned savagely on the Allied prisoners in their hands in their search for suspects and scapegoats. One British civilian under sentence for supposed espionage activities was interrogated, beaten, starved, and tortured when he failed to admit authorship of the sabotage raid. The internees in Changi gaol suffered a murderous period. Malays and Chinese were arrested in their hundreds on suspicion of possible complicity. For months, Singapore was subjected to a wave of terror which included the infamous "Double Tenth" massacre on October 10. For this the perpetrators paid with their heads when the Allied war crimes tribunals reckoned with them after Japan had surrendered.

The high command in Singapore never did learn how the attack had been organised or from whence it came. The confidential report which was dispatched in due course to Tokyo, and extracted from the files after the war was over by the Allies, read in part: "Singapore shipping espionage has been carried out by natives under European in-

357

structions. . . . An enemy espionage affair developed early in the morning of 27th September 1943 at Singapore. It was commanded by Europeans hiding in the neighbourhood of Palai in Johore. It was carried out by Malayan criminals through a Malayan village chief and the party was composed of ten or more persons, all of them Malayans. As a result of the raid, seven ships were sunk by bombs due to a clever plan."

Although it took weeks for the information to filter through, confirmation of the success of the operation slowly found its way through the Chinese guerrillas in Malaya to Chungking and thence to London and Washington. There was no doubt about it. All seven ships had been sunk, a total of nearly 38,000 tons, hundreds of miles within the Japanese perimeter. Surely it is one of the most astonishing exploits of the whole war.

For the "Jaywick" party on the spot, the most encouraging reaction came from the Malay villagers themselves. Three hundred yards south of Dongas was the village of Patam on the northern coast of Batam Island. Soon after it was light, Lyon and Huston heard so much shouting and noise coming from this direction that they swung round and focused their glasses on the village. The Malays could be seen running up and down, slapping each other on the back in high glee, imitating the noises of the explosions and raising both hands upwards and outwards in illustration of their effect. It must have been the first time that they had heard such reverberations since the fall of Singapore and it could only mean one thing. The Allies had struck back. Scores of *koleks* started pulling out from points along the shore and paddling into the Straits to see the fire and the pall of smoke hanging over the harbour.

One such *kolek* caught Davidson and Falls unawares. They had made their way across the harbour unscathed, but the tide had started to turn against them and they were still about six miles short of Pulo Nongsa, a little island off the north-east tip of Batam, which they had hoped to use as their hide, when the imminence of dawn obliged them to duck for cover immediately. They found an adequate hide behind a strip of beach under some rocks and dropped off to sleep. Half an hour later they were awakened by the explosions. They were by now some fifteen miles from Singapore, and although they ran down to the beach, could see very little of the commotion in the haze.

They, too, counted clearly up to seven and wondered why the other two canoes had only accounted for four ships between them. Did it mean that someone had run into trouble? The fact that there had been any explosions at all seemed to rule that out. They considered every combination of possibilities but realised they would have to wait four days until they met at Pompong before finding out the truth.

It was while they were standing there that the native canoe came round the point and caught them in full view. It was their first bad security lapse and entirely their own fault. In their excitement they had forgotten all the prescribed precautions, and if the natives had been hostile, might have had to pay dearly for it.

The sight of two bearded white men with their hands on their pistols was altogether too much for the simple villagers. It did not require much deduction for them to associate these two interlopers with the uproar in the Roads. Spinning round in their *kolek,* they paddled back like furies round the point again.

The question now was what to do. Should they risk a day passage to a new hide and probably run into further trouble or should they assume that the obviously terrified Malays would consider discretion the better part of valour and take no direct action? Their hide was in a fairly desolate part of Batam Island and it was extremely unlikely that there would be telephones or any such modern devices by which to report their presence to the garrison. The nearest centre of consequence was probably several hours' paddling away, so Davidson and Falls decided to stick it out. They spent an uneasy day at the alert among the boulders and, as night fell again, thankfully launched their folboat and started on their "forced march" south.

Hugging the eastern shore of Batam down the five-mile-wide Rhio Strait, they reached Tanjongsaoe Island, in the centre of the Strait, after nine and a half hours' steady paddling. The shore was uncomfortably congested with fishing huts and *pagars,* but they managed to find a serviceable hide.

The next night, that of September 28–29, they weaved through the maze of islands, keeping to the north of Pulau Lepang and Pulau Anak Mati, and then squeezing down the narrow channel between Pulau Rempang and Pulau Setoko until they reached the southern entrance of the Bulan Strait, a dozen miles from Panjang.

In relatively open water again, they were paddling on their last lap past the point of Tanjong Klinking when they heard again the threatening plop-plop of the diesel patrol boat which had harried them round Panjang. Edging into the shallows to avoid pursuit, they watched the launch pass within fifty yards. They could see the glow of light in the wheelhouse and could hear the crew talking. It passed on beyond the point, missing them again. Keeping close to the shore for the last five miles, they pulled safely into Otter Bay about four o'clock in the morning. The dump was intact, but there was no sign of the other canoes. At the end of their tether, they lay down to sleep.

The other canoes had still not joined them by the evening of the twenty-ninth, so, leaving a note describing their experiences and movements with the stores, where they knew it would be found, they pressed on. It was thirty miles to Pompong and they intended to stage halfway on the island of Abang Besar, on the far side of Dempu Strait. It meant passing dangerously near to the observation post and searchlight on Galang Baru, but this particular problem was solved by an even worse hazard.

The sky was already full of scurrying clouds when they set off. They could see the great black pall of a "Sumatra" building up, and just as they were about to draw abeam of Galang Baru it hit them. The wind, waves, and spindrift had been bad enough in *Krait.* In a tiny cockle-shell canoe in the open sea it was terrifying. The only thing they could do was to turn the folboat's bows into the wind and sea, close their eyes against the battering rain and flying spume, and judge their direction by the force of the hurricane on their cheeks.

The hermetically sealed canoe rode the mountainous seas like a porpoise, sliding up and down the immense waves without once threatening to overturn. The battle lasted two hours, when the storm dropped as suddenly as it had come. They just made Abang Besar before daylight, slept off their leaden tiredness during the day, and by one o'clock in the morning of October 1 had the canoe safely hidden under the trees in Fisherman's Bay on Pompong.

They spent the day drying out, resting, and sorting the new supply of rations they had picked up at Panjang. If all had gone well, *Krait* was to pick them up that evening.

From dusk onwards they kept uneasy watch. The hours ticked slowly past as their hopes sank. By midnight *Krait* was well overdue. There was no sign of the other canoe crews and the iron-nerved Davidson was just about to settle down on his groundsheet for a few hours' sleep, leaving Falls to continue the watch, when his sharp-eyed companion shook him awake again. "There's something moving in over there, sir," he whispered. "Can't hear a thing though."

With hope clutching fiercely through their infinite weariness, they tried to focus on this shadow within a shadow. It drifted nearer and suddenly there was no doubt. That long, low shape with the deckhouse covering the whole stern could only be *Krait*. She had come back and they were safe.[1]

[1] The other two crews made the rendezvous October 1st and the *Krait* got back safely to Australia on October 19. They had been away 48 days, traveling more than 4,000 miles to Singapore and back.—Ed. note.

Strategy for Attack

Early in the war, the Joint Chiefs of Staff in Washington had given Gen. MacArthur command of all operations in the southwest Pacific; Adm. Nimitz had been given command in the south, north and central Pacific. As the Japs were pushed back in both theaters, it was natural for both commanders to argue for priorities; each wanted the main attack route on Japan to be staged in his area. MacArthur argued for the New Guinea-Mindanao route, liberating the Philippines and then hitting the Japanese mainland. Nimitz, and his superior on the JCS, Adm. King, favored the island-hopping route through the central Pacific to Formosa and perhaps the China coast, invading Japan from there. A compromise was finally reached, with each commander given his head in his own theater, once his strategy was approved by the Joint Chiefs of Staff.

For example, Nimitz had agreed with MacArthur that Adm. Halsey's offensive in the Solomons would cover only Guadalcanal and Tulagi; but after the Japs had been driven off Guadalcanal, more airfields were needed to mount attacks farther north, and Halsey was given the task of pushing the Japs out of New Georgia, Bougainville and eventually New Britain. MacArthur was still involved in New Guinea; by the terms of the compromise, Halsey's operations were subject to MacArthur's approval. Rabaul, on New Britain, was to be neutralized or destroyed, whichever suited the strategic purpose when the time arrived.

New Georgia was invaded on June 30, 1943, by the 37th and 45th U.S. Infantry Divisions, together with several Marine battalions. Five new airfields had been captured by August 9th, from which U.S. planes could now stage operations against the Japs farther up the Slot.

In the New Georgia campaign, four PT squadrons, totaling about fifty boats, sank and harassed Jap troop barges sent down the Slot. One such action involving Jap destroyers occurred in the beginning of

August, in which Lt. John Kennedy, USNR (now U.S. Senator from Massachusetts), commanded one of the PT's.

The account of that action is written by John Hersey, then a war correspondent.

PT BOATS IN THE SLOT

by John Hersey

Our men in the South Pacific fight nature, when they are pitted against her, with a greater fierceness than they could ever expend on a human enemy. Lieutenant John F. Kennedy, the ex-Ambassador's son and lately a PT skipper in the Solomons, came through town the other day and told me the story of his survival in the South Pacific. I asked Kennedy if I might write the story down. He asked me if I wouldn't talk first with some of his crew, so I went up to the Motor Torpedo Boat Training Centre at Melville, Rhode Island, and there, under the curving iron of a Quonset hut, three enlisted men named Johnston, McMahon, and McGuire filled in the gaps.

It seems that Kennedy's PT, the 109, was out one night with a squadron patrolling Blackett Strait, in mid-Solomons. Blackett Strait is a patch of water bounded on the northeast by the volcano called Kolombangara, on the west by the island of Vella Lavella, on the south by the island of Gizo and a string of coral-fringed islets, and on the east by the bulk of New Georgia. The boats were working about forty miles away from their base on the island of Rendova, on the south side of New Georgia. They had entered Blackett Strait, as was their habit, through Ferguson Passage, between the coral islets and New Georgia.

The night was a starless black and Japanese destroyers were around. It was about two-thirty. The 109, with three officers and ten enlisted men aboard, was leading three

363

boats on a sweep for a target. An officer named George Ross was up on the bow, magnifying the void with binoculars. Kennedy was at the wheel and he saw Ross turn and point into the darkness. The man in the forward machine-gun turret shouted, "Ship at two o'clock!" Kennedy saw a shape and spun the wheel to turn for an attack, but the 109 answered sluggishly. She was running slowly on only one of her three engines, so as to make a minimum wake and avoid detection from the air. The shape became a Japanese destroyer, cutting through the night at forty knots and heading straight for the 109. The thirteen men on the PT hardly had time to brace themselves. Those who saw the Japanese ship coming were paralyzed by fear in a curious way: they could move their hands but not their feet. Kennedy whirled the wheel to the left, but again the 109 did not respond. Ross went through the gallant but futile motions of slamming a shell into the breach of the 37-millimetre anti-tank gun which had been temporarily mounted that very day, wheels and all, on the foredeck. The urge to bolt and dive over the side was terribly strong, but still no one was able to move; all hands froze to their battle stations. Then the Japanese crashed into the 109 and cut her right in two. The sharp enemy forefoot struck the PT on the starboard side about fifteen feet from the bow and crunched diagonally across with a racking noise. The PT's wooden hull hardly even delayed the destroyer. Kennedy was thrown hard to the left in the cockpit, and he thought, "This is how it feels to be killed." In a moment he found himself on his back on the deck, looking up at the destroyer as it passed through his boat. There was another loud noise and a huge flash of yellow-red light, and the destroyer glowed. Its peculiar, raked, inverted-Y stack stood out in the brilliant light and, later, in Kennedy's memory.

There was only one man below decks at the moment of collision. That was McMahon, engineer. He had no idea what was up. He was just reaching forward to slam the starboard engine into gear when a ship came into his engine room. He was lifted from the narrow passage between two of the engines and thrown painfully against the starboard bulkhead aft of the boat's auxiliary generator. He landed in a sitting position. A tremendous burst of flame came back at him from the day room, where some of the gas tanks were. He put his hands over his face, drew his legs up tight, and waited to die. But he felt water hit him after the fire, and he was sucked far downward as his half of the PT sank. He began to struggle upward through the water. He had held his breath since the impact, so his lungs were tight and they hurt. He looked up through the water. Over his head he saw a yellow glow—gasoline burning on the water. He broke the surface and was in fire again. He splashed hard to keep a little island of water around him.

Johnston, another engineer, had been asleep on deck when the collision came. It lifted him and dropped him overboard. He saw the flame and the destroyer for a moment. Then a huge propeller pounded by near him and the awful turbulence of the destroyer's wake took him down, turned him over and over, held him down, shook him, and drubbed on his ribs. He hung on and came up in water that was like a river rapids. The next day his body turned black and blue from the beating.

Kennedy's half of the PT stayed afloat. The bulkheads were sealed, so the undamaged watertight compartments up forward kept the half hull floating. The destroyer rushed off into the dark. There was an awful quiet: only the sound of gasoline burning.

Kennedy shouted, "Who's aboard?"

Feeble answers came from three of the enlisted men, McGuire, Mauer, and Albert; and from one of the officers, Thom.

Kennedy saw the fire only ten feet from the boat. He thought it might reach her and explode the remaining gas tanks, so he shouted, "Over the side!"

The five men slid into the water. But the wake of the destroyer swept the fire away from the PT, so after a few minutes, Kennedy and the others crawled back aboard. Kennedy shouted for survivors in the water. One by one they answered: Ross, the third officer; Harris, McMahon, Johnston, Zinsser, Starkey, enlisted men. Two did not answer: Kirksey and Marney, enlisted men. Since the last bombing at base, Kirksey had been sure he would die. He had huddled at his battle station by the fantail gun, with his kapok life jacket tied tight up to his cheeks. No one knows what happened to him or to Marney.

Harris shouted from the darkness, "Mr. Kennedy! Mr. Kennedy! McMahon is badly hurt." Kennedy took his shoes, his shirt, and his sidearms off, told Mauer to blink a light so that the men in the water would know where the half hull was, then dived in and swam toward the voice. The survivors were widely scattered. McMahon and Harris were a hundred yards away.

When Kennedy reached McMahon, he asked, "How are you, Mac?"

McMahon said, "I'm all right. I'm kind of burnt."

Kennedy shouted out, "How are the others?"

Harris said softly, "I hurt my leg."

Kennedy, who had been on the Harvard swimming team five years before, took McMahon in tow and headed for the PT. A gentle breeze kept blowing the boat away from the swimmers. It took forty-five minutes to make what had been an easy hundred yards. On the way in, Harris said, "I can't go any farther." Kennedy, of the Boston Kennedys, said to Harris, of the same home town, "For a guy from Boston, you're certainly putting up a great exhibition out here, Harris." Harris made it all right and didn't complain any more. Then Kennedy swam from man to man, to see how they were doing. All who had survived the crash were able to stay afloat, since they were wearing life preservers— kapok jackets shaped like overstuffed vests, aviators' yellow Mae Wests, or air-filled belts like small inner tubes. But those who couldn't swim had to be towed back to the wreckage by those who could. One of the men screamed for help. When Ross reached him, he found that the screaming man had two life jackets on. Johnston was treading water in a film of gasoline which did not catch fire. The fumes filled his lungs and he fainted. Thom towed him in. The others got in under their own power. It was now after 5 a.m., but still dark. It had taken nearly three hours to get everyone aboard.

The men stretched out on the tilted deck of the PT. Johnston, McMahon, and Ross collapsed into sleep. The

366

men talked about how wonderful it was to be alive and speculated on when the other PT's would come back to rescue them. Mauer kept blinking the light to point their way. But the other boats had no idea of coming back. They had seen a collision, a sheet of flame, and a slow burning on the water. When the skipper of one of the boats saw the sight, he put his hands over his face and sobbed, "My God! My God!" He and the others turned away. Back at the base, after a couple of days, the squadron held services for the souls of the thirteen men, and one of the officers wrote his mother, "George Ross lost his life for a cause that he believed in stronger than any one of us, because he was an idealist in the purest sense. Jack Kennedy, the Ambassador's son, was on the same boat and also lost his life. The man that said the cream of a nation is lost in war can never be accused of making an overstatement of a very cruel fact. . . ."

When day broke, the men on the remains of the 109 stirred and looked around. To the northeast, three miles off, they saw the monumental cone of Kolombangara; there, the men knew, ten thousand Japanese swarmed. To the west, five miles away, they saw Vella Lavella; more Japs. To the south, only a mile or so away, they actually could see a Japanese camp on Gizo. Kennedy ordered his men to keep as low as possible, so that no moving silhouettes would show against the sky. The listing hulk was gurgling and gradually settling. Kennedy said, "What do you want to do if the Japs come out? Fight or surrender?" One said, "Fight with what?" So they took an inventory of their armament. The 37-millimetre gun had flopped over the side and was hanging there by a chain. They had one tommy gun, six 45-calibre automatics, and one .38. Not much.

"Well," Kennedy said, "what do you want to do?"

One said, "Anything you say, Mr. Kennedy. You're the boss."

Kennedy said, "There's nothing in the book about a situation like this. Seems to me we're not a military organization any more. Let's just talk this over."

They talked it over, and pretty soon they argued, and

Kennedy could see that they would never survive in anarchy. So he took command again.

It was vital that McMahon and Johnston should have room to lie down. McMahon's face, neck, hands, wrists, and feet were horribly burned. Johnston was pale and he coughed continually. There was scarcely space for everyone, so Kennedy ordered the other men into the water to make room, and went in himself. All morning they clung to the hulk and talked about how incredible it was that no one had come to rescue them. All morning they watched for the plane which they thought would be looking for them. They cursed war in general and PT's in particular. At about ten o'clock the hulk heaved a moist sigh and turned turtle. McMahon and Johnston had to hang on as best they could. It was clear that the remains of the 109 would soon sink. When the sun had passed the meridian, Kennedy said, "We will swim to that small island," pointing to one of a group three miles to the southeast. "We have less chance of making it than some of these other islands here, but there'll be less chance of Japs, too." Those who could not swim well grouped themselves around a long two-by-six timber with which carpenters had braced the 37-millimetre cannon on deck and which had been knocked overboard by the force of the collision. They tied several pairs of shoes to the timber, as well as the ship's lantern, wrapped in a life jacket to keep it afloat. Thom took charge of this unwieldy group. Kennedy took McMahon in tow again. He cut loose one end of a long strap on McMahon's Mae West and took the end in his teeth. He swam breast stroke, pulling the helpless McMahon along on his back. It took over five hours to reach the island. Water lapped into Kennedy's mouth through his clenched teeth, and he swallowed a lot. The salt water cut into McMahon's awful burns, but he did not complain. Every few minutes, when Kennedy stopped to rest, taking the strap out of his mouth and holding it in his hand, McMahon would simply say, "How far do we have to go?"

Kennedy would reply, "We're going good." Then he would ask, "How do you feel, Mac?"

McMahon always answered, "I'm O.K., Mr. Kennedy. How about you?"

In spite of his burden, Kennedy beat the other men to the reef that surrounded the island. He left McMahon on the reef and told him to keep low, so as not to be spotted by Japs. Kennedy went ahead and explored the island. It was only a hundred yards in diameter; coconuts on the trees but none on the ground; no visible Japs. Just as the others reached the island, one of them spotted a Japanese barge chugging along close to shore. They all lay low. The barge went on. Johnston, who was very pale and weak and who was still coughing a lot, said, "They wouldn't come here. What'd they be walking around here for? It's too small." Kennedy lay in some bushes, exhausted by his effort, his stomach heavy with the water he had swallowed. He had been in the sea, except for short intervals on the hulk, for fifteen and a half hours. Now he started thinking. Every night for several nights the PT's had cut through Ferguson Passage on their way to action. Ferguson Passage was just beyond the next little island. Maybe . . .

He stood up. He took one of the pairs of shoes. He put one of the rubber life belts around his waist. He hung the .38 around his neck on a lanyard. He took his pants off. He picked up the ship's lantern, a heavy battery affair ten inches by ten inches, still wrapped in the kapok jacket. He said, "If I find a boat, I'll flash the lantern twice. The password will be 'Roger,' the answer will be 'Willco.'" He walked toward the water. After fifteen paces he was dizzy, but in the water he felt all right.

It was early evening. It took half an hour to swim to the reef around the next island. Just as he planted his feet on the reef, which lay about four feet under the surface, he saw the shape of a very big fish in the clear water. He flashed the light at it and splashed hard. The fish went away. Kennedy remembered what one of his men had said a few days before, "These barracuda will come up under a swimming man and eat his testicles." He had many occasions to think of that remark in the next few hours.

Now it was dark. Kennedy blundered along the uneven reef in water up to his waist. Sometimes he would reach forward with his leg and cut one of his shins or ankles on sharp coral. Other times he would step forward onto emptiness. He made his way like a slow-motion drunk, hugging the lantern. At about nine o'clock he came to the end of the reef, alongside Ferguson Passage. He took his shoes off and tied them to the life jacket, then struck out into open water. He swam about an hour, until he felt he was far enough out to intercept the PT's. Treading water, he listened for the muffled roar of motors, getting chilled, waiting, holding the lamp. Once he looked west and saw flares and the false gaiety of an action. The lights were far beyond the little islands, even beyond Gizo, ten miles away. Kennedy realized that the PT boats had chosen, for the first night in many, to go around Gizo instead of through Ferguson Passage. There was no hope. He started back. He made the same painful promenade of the reef and struck out for the tiny island where his friends were. But this swim was different. He was very tired and now the current was running fast, carrying him to the right. He saw that he could not make the island, so he flashed the light once and shouted "Roger! Roger!" to identify himself.

On the beach the men were hopefully vigilant. They saw the light and heard the shouts. They were very happy, because they thought that Kennedy had found a PT. They walked out onto the reef, sometimes up to their waists in water, and waited. It was very painful for those who had no shoes. The men shouted, but not much, because they were afraid of Japanese.

One said, "There's another flash."

A few minutes later a second said, "There's a light over there."

A third said, "We're seeing things in this dark."

They waited a long time, but they saw nothing except phosphorescence and heard nothing but the sound of waves. They went back, very discouraged.

One said despairingly, "We're going to die."

Johnston said, "Aw, shut up. You can't die. Only the good die young."

Kennedy had drifted right by the little island. He thought he had never known such deep trouble, but something he

370

did shows that unconsciously he had not given up hope. He dropped his shoes, but he held onto the heavy lantern, his symbol of contact with his fellows. He stopped trying to swim. He seemed to stop caring. His body drifted through the wet hours, and he was very cold. His mind was a jumble. A few hours before he had wanted desperately to get to the base at Rendova. Now he only wanted to get back to the little island he had left that night, but he didn't try to get there; he just wanted to. His mind seemed to float away from his body. Darkness and time took the place of a mind in his skull. For a long time he slept, or was crazy, or floated in a chill trance.

The currents of the Solomon Islands are queer. The tide shoves and sucks through the islands and makes the currents curl in odd patterns. It was a fateful pattern into which Jack Kennedy drifted. He drifted in it all night. His mind was blank, but his fist was tightly clenched on the kapok around the lantern. The current moved in a huge circle—west past Gizo, then north and east past Kolombangara, then south into Ferguson Passage. Early in the morning the sky turned from black to gray, and so did Kennedy's mind. Light came to both at about six. Kennedy looked around and saw that he was exactly where he had been the night before when he saw the flares beyond Gizo. For a second time, he started home. He thought for a while that he had lost his mind and that he only imagined that he was repeating his attempt to reach the island. But the chill of the water was real enough, the lantern was real, his progress was measurable. He made the reef, crossed the lagoon, and got to the first island. He lay on the beach awhile. He found that his lantern did not work any more, so he left it and started back to the next island, where his men were. This time the trip along the reef was awful. He had discarded his shoes, and every step on the coral was painful. This time the swim across the gap where the current had caught him the night before seemed endless. But the current had changed; he made the island. He crawled up on the beach. He was vomiting when his men came up to him. He said, "Ross, you try it tonight." Then he passed out.

Ross, seeing Kennedy so sick, did not look forward to the execution of the order. He distracted himself by complaining about his hunger. There were a few coconuts on the trees, but the men were too weak to climb up for them. One of the men thought of sea food, stirred his tired body, and found a snail on the beach. He said, "If we were desperate, we could eat these." Ross said, "Desperate, hell. Give me that. I'll eat that." He took it in his hand and looked at it. The snail put its head out and looked at him. Ross was startled, but he shelled the snail and ate it, making faces because it was bitter.

In the afternoon, Ross swam across to the next island. He took a pistol to signal with, and he spent the night watching Ferguson Passage from the reef around the island. Nothing came through. Kennedy slept badly that night; he was cold and sick.

The next morning everyone felt wretched. Planes which the men were unable to identify flew overhead and there were dogfights. That meant Japs as well as friends, so the men dragged themselves into the bushes and lay low. Some prayed. Johnston said, "You guys make me sore. You didn't spend ten cents in church in ten years, then all of a sudden you're in trouble and you see the light." Kennedy felt a little better now. When Ross came back, Kennedy decided that the group should move to another, larger island to the southeast, where there seemed to be more coconut trees and where the party would be nearer Ferguson Passage. Again Kennedy took McMahon in tow with the strap in his teeth, and the nine others grouped themselves around the timber.

This swim took three hours. The nine around the timber were caught by the current and barely made the far tip of the island. Kennedy found walking the quarter mile across to them much harder than the three-hour swim. The cuts on his bare feet were festered and looked like small balloons. The men were suffering most from thirst, and they broke open some coconuts lying on the ground and avidly drank the milk. Kennedy and McMahon, the first to drink, were sickened, and Thom told the others to drink sparingly. In the middle of the night it rained, and someone suggested moving into the underbrush and licking water off the leaves. Ross and McMahon kept contact at first by touching feet as they licked. Somehow they got separated, and, being uncertain whether there were any Japs on the island, they became frightened. McMahon, trying to make his way back to the beach, bumped into someone and froze. It turned out to be Johnston, licking leaves on his own. In the morning the group saw that all the leaves were covered with droppings. Bitterly, they named the place Bird Island.

On this fourth day, the men were low. Even Johnston was low. He had changed his mind about praying. McGuire had a rosary around his neck, and Johnston said, "McGuire, give that necklace a working over." McGuire said quietly, "Yes, I'll take care of all you fellows." Kennedy was still unwilling to admit that things were hopeless. He asked Ross if he would swim with him to an island called Nauru, to the southeast and even nearer Ferguson Passage. They were very weak indeed by now, but after an hour's swim they made it.

They walked painfully across Nauru to the Ferguson Passage side, where they saw a Japanese barge aground on the reef. There were two men by the barge—possibly Japs. They apparently spotted Kennedy and Ross, for they got into a dugout canoe and hurriedly paddled to the other side of the island. Kennedy and Ross moved up the beach. They came upon an unopened rope-bound box and, back in the trees, a little shelter containing a keg of water, a Japanese gas mask, and a crude wooden fetish shaped like a fish. There were Japanese hardtack and candy in the box and the two had a wary feast. Down by the water they found a one-man canoe. They hid from imagined Japs all day. When night fell, Kennedy left Ross and took the canoe, with some hardtack and a can of water from the keg, out into Ferguson Passage. But no PT's came, so he paddled to Bird Island. The men there told him that the two men he had spotted by the barge that morning were natives, who had paddled to Bird Island. The natives had said that there were Japs on Nauru and the men had given Kennedy and Ross up for lost. Then the natives had gone

373

away. Kennedy gave out small rations of crackers and water, and the men went to sleep. During the night, one man, who kept himself awake until the rest were asleep, drank all the water in the can Kennedy had brought back. In the morning the others figured out that he was the guilty one. They swore at him and found it hard to forgive him.

Before dawn, Kennedy started out in the canoe to rejoin Ross on Nauru, but when day broke a wind arose and the canoe was swamped. Some natives appeared from nowhere in a canoe, rescued Kennedy, and took him to Nauru. There they showed him where a two-man canoe was cached. Kennedy picked up a coconut with a smooth shell and scratched a message on it with a jackknife: "ELEVEN ALIVE NATIVE KNOWS POSIT AND REEFS NAURU ISLAND KENNEDY." Then he said to the natives, "Rendova, Rendova."

One of the natives seemed to understand. They took the coconut and paddled off.

Ross and Kennedy lay in a sickly daze all day. Toward evening it rained and they crawled under a bush. When it got dark, conscience took hold of Kennedy and he persuaded Ross to go out into Ferguson Passage with him in the two-man canoe. Ross argued against it. Kennedy insisted. The two started out in the canoe. They had shaped paddles from the boards of the Japanese box, and they took a coconut shell to bail with. As they got out into the Passage, the wind rose again and the water became choppy. The canoe began to fill. Ross bailed and Kennedy kept the bow into the wind. The waves grew until they were five or six feet high. Kennedy shouted, "Better turn around and go back!" As soon as the canoe was broadside to the waves, the water poured in and the dugout was swamped. The two clung to it, Kennedy at the bow, Ross at the stern. The tide carried them southward toward the open sea, so they kicked and tugged the canoe, aiming northwest. They struggled that way for two hours, not knowing whether they would hit the small island or drift into the endless open.

The weather got worse; rain poured down and they couldn't see more than ten feet. Kennedy shouted, "Sorry

374

I got you out here, Barney!" Ross shouted back, "This would be a great time to say I told you so, but I won't!"

Soon the two could see a white line ahead and could hear a frightening roar—waves crashing on a reef. They had got out of the tidal current and were approaching the island all right, but now they realized that the wind and the waves were carrying them toward the reef. But it was too late to do anything, now that their canoe was swamped, except hang on and wait.

When they were near the reef, a wave broke Kennedy's hold, ripped him away from the canoe, turned him head over heels, and spun him in a violent rush. His ears roared and his eyes pinwheeled, and for the third time since the collision he thought he was dying. Somehow he was not thrown against the coral but floated into a kind of eddy. Suddenly he felt the reef under his feet. Steadying himself so that he would not be swept off it, he shouted, "Barney!" There was no reply. Kennedy thought of how he had insisted on going out in the canoe, and he screamed, "Barney!" This time Ross answered. He, too, had been thrown on the reef. He had not been as lucky as Kennedy; his right arm and shoulder had been cruelly lacerated by the coral, and his feet, which were already infected from earlier wounds, were cut some more.

The procession of Kennedy and Ross from reef to beach was a crazy one. Ross's feet hurt so much that Kennedy would hold one paddle on the bottom while Ross put a foot on it, then the other paddle forward for another step, then the first paddle forward again, until they reached sand. They fell on the beach and slept.

Kennedy and Ross were wakened early in the morning by a noise. They looked up and saw four husky natives. One walked up to them and said in an excellent English accent, "I have a letter for you, sir." Kennedy tore the note open. It said, "On His Majesty's Service. To the Senior Officer, Nauru Island. I have just learned of your presence on Nauru Is. I am in command of a New Zealand infantry patrol operating in conjunction with U.S. Army troops on New Georgia. I strongly advise that you come

375

with these natives to me. Meanwhile I shall be in radio communication with your authorities at Rendova, and we can finalize plans to collect balance of your party. Lt. Wincote. P. S. Will warn aviation of your crossing Ferguson Passage."

Everyone shook hands and the four natives took Ross and Kennedy in their war canoe across to Bird Island to tell the others the good news. There the natives broke out a spirit stove and cooked a feast of yams and C ration. Then they built a leanto for McMahon, whose burns had begun to rot and stink, and for Ross, whose arm had swelled to the size of a thigh because of the coral cuts. The natives put Kennedy in the bottom of their canoe and covered him with sacking and palm fronds, in case Japanese planes should buzz them. The long trip was fun for the natives. They stopped once to try to grab a turtle, and laughed at the sport they were having. Thirty Japanese planes went over low toward Rendova, and the natives waved and shouted gaily. They rowed with a strange rhythm, pounding paddles on the gunwales between strokes. At last they reached a censored place. Lieutenant Wincote came to the water's edge and said formally, "How do you do. Leftenant Wincote."

Kennedy said, "Hello. I'm Kennedy."

Wincote said, "Come up to my tent and have a cup of tea."

In the middle of the night, after several radio conversations between Wincote's outfit and the PT base, Kennedy sat in the war canoe waiting at an arranged rendezvous for a PT. The moon went down at eleven-twenty. Shortly afterward Kennedy heard the signal he was waiting for— four shots. Kennedy fired four answering shots.

A voice shouted to him, "Hey, Jack!"

Kennedy said, "Where the hell you been?"

The voice said, "We got some food for you."

Kennedy said bitterly, "No, thanks, I just had a coconut."

A moment later a PT came alongside. Kennedy jumped onto it and hugged the men aboard—his friends. In the

American tradition, Kennedy held under his arm a couple of souvenirs: one of the improvised paddles and the Japanese gas mask.

With the help of the natives, the PT made its way to Bird Island. A skiff went in and picked up the men. In the deep of the night, the PT and its happy cargo roared back toward base. The squadron medic had sent some brandy along to revive the weakened men. Johnston felt the need of a little revival. In fact, he felt he needed quite a bit of revival. After taking care of that, he retired topside and sat with his arms around a couple of roly-poly, mission-trained natives. And in the fresh breeze on the way home they sang together a hymn all three happened to know:

> Jesus loves me, this I know,
> For the Bible tells me so;
> Little ones to him belong,
> They are weak, but He is strong.
> Yes, Jesus loves me; yes, Jesus loves me . . .

Atoll War

Bougainville was the next objective; it was on the way to New Britain, where the Jap stronghold of Rabaul supplied the enemy in both New Guinea and the Solomons. Assault forces, made up of the 3rd Marine Division, the 37th Infantry Division, a Marine raider regiment, several Marine battalions, and the 8th New Zealand Brigade Group, landed November 1, 1943, in swampy terrain at the center of the island, where the Japs least expected them. The assault forces secured their landings against little opposition, but they had long, hard fighting ahead of them, with the miserable terrain giving them as much trouble as the Japs. Bougainville was not officially secured until the end of March.

Quite another kind of battle was fought that same November, by the 2nd Marine Division on Tarawa. It had fought at Guadalcanal and Tulagi, where "they had learned much about Jap fighting methods. Practice had made them one of the finest jungle outfits in the world. But when it came to atoll fighting they had nearly as much to learn as the totally green 27th Division.* At Tarawa they learned." **

Tarawa was an atoll in the Gilbert Islands which had been a British possession before the war began. The Japs had occupied it and Makin, a near-by atoll, and fortified them. Betio Island, in the Tarawa atoll, had a three-strip airfield; its capture would be the first step toward the powerful Jap naval base of Truk in the Carolines.

On the 21st of November, after three days of shelling and bombing by both navy ships and carrier-based bombers, the first landing waves were waiting for the final shelling, which was supposed to give the coup de grâce to the Japs on shore. To the astonishment of the Marines,

---

* Simultaneously, the 27th Infantry Division was to assault Makin Island close by. Compared to Tarawa, Makin was lightly held, but the 27th had had no combat experience at all.

** Maj. Frank Hough, The Island War, p. 126.

378

the enemy answered this last concentration of fire, and H-Hour was postponed several times before the first wave was sent in.

"Naval gunfire ceased,* and the dive bombers returned to give the island a final pasting. As the amphibious tractors carrying the first assault waves entering the lagoon left the line of departure and waddled forward . . . they soon came under mortar, machine-gun and anti-boat fire. This was scattered and poorly controlled at first, showing the enemy were still dazed by the heavy bombing and shelling they'd received. The first three waves, all in amphtracks, got ashore without serious losses. But the Japanese were recovering rapidly. As the boats carrying the fourth wave (these were not amphtracks, but cargo carriers) piled up on the reef hundreds of yards from shore, there began a terrible carnage which will always be associated with the name Tarawa.

"The position (of the first three waves) was precarious in the extreme. The beach averaged only about twenty feet in width, bounded on the landward side by a four-foot revetment of logs forming a sea wall. This provided fair cover for men crouching close to it, but it was a major obstacle for any advance inland. And until they could establish a beachhead in depth and wipe out some of the weapons which were raking the reef and the top of the sea wall, they could not hope for substantial reinforcements or supplies.

"Wading 700 yards of coral reef is a slow laborious process under the best of circumstances. You trip over jagged boulders, climb hummocks, sprawl into sudden deep depressions where a heavily armed man can drown unless rescued. Now a storm of assorted shells threw geysers from the shallow water, and machine-gun bursts marched their precise ranks across it. Some of the men landed on the pier [this ran out 500 yards from shore to the end of the fringing reef, built partly on pilings, partly on coral] and made their way along that open, narrow, fire-swept roadway. Others crept through the water close along the pier's side. But to most, even this scant cover was denied. They came in straight across the reef, through the tortured water that was turning red around them. Tiny black dots of men, holding their weapons high above their heads, moving at snail's pace, never faltering. Some of them, miraculously, made it. Many others did not.

"At last, to stop the hopeless slaughter, the order was passed that

* Maj. Frank Hough, *The Island War*, pp. 133-139.

379

no more waves were to go in unless some of those guns could be silenced, or arrival of darkness would cover the landings.

"There was no jungle on this portion of Betio; only scattered coconut palms badly shattered by shell fire, and the open airstrips, most of their visible installations in ruins. Yet nothing moved about the ground. Few live Japanese were seen during all of the three days of intensive fighting. For, in a sense, the enemy had created their own 'jungle.' Their emplacements had become virtually integral parts of the island.

"Mostly they were below ground, dug deeply and sometimes reinforced with concrete. They were roofed with thick logs and steel beams or rails, on top of which coral rock was piled in considerable depth, sometimes sand.

"The small size of the firing apertures enhanced this concealment feature. It is characteristic of Japanese defense tactics to emphasize concealment, relying upon interlocking and overlapping lanes of fire rather than wide traverse of individual weapons. That is, the narrow firing opening limited the sweep of the gun to a lane directly to its front. Within that lane it was deadly; to either side it was helpless and dependent for protection upon the next gun whose fire lane was laid to tie in with that of the first gun, upon which, in turn, it was dependent for flank protection. And so on, until the defense sector became actually a series of separate mutually protective pillboxes, further defended by strategically placed riflemen in trenches, trees and camouflaged rifle pits.

"Such a position was deadly from the front and extremely difficult to flank. The individual components were all but impervious to small-arms fire and must be destroyed by close-up work with grenades, demolition charges and flame throwers. To get close enough, the attackers had to neutralize at least temporarily not only their immediate objective but the pillboxes and riflemen which covered its flanks.

"Such a system had the disadvantage of inflexibility: once one pillbox was taken, the problem of taking the rest was greatly simplified. But it remained to the end a case of destroying individual installations and individual Japanese who fought in concealment to the death.

"The situation was grim as evening drew on. . . . The men were ordered to dig in and hold what they had regardless.

"They did not have very much. The entire extent of shore line held amounted only to some 300 yards. Fractions of four battered battal-

380

ions held a perimeter line which ran inland about fifty yards to the edge of the airfield on the east, circled the base of the pier, and reached a maximum depth of 150 yards on a narrow front behind Red 2.*

"No artillery had been brought ashore. There was no room to set it up. All the Marines ashore had to depend on for fire support was naval gunfire and carrier-borne aircraft, neither of which could be very effective in the darkness against the sort of counterattack which was almost inevitable should the Japanese react according to precedent.

"But now events proved that the shelling and bombing, so disappointing on the whole, had been extraordinarily effective in an unexpected way. However slight the vital damage to the enemy's major installations, their communications had been completely destroyed, and harassing fire throughout the night kept them inoperative. Japanese in pillboxes, blockhouses and dugouts remained isolated from their command post and from each other, quite incapable of massing for any concerted action. There was no important counterattack and only a few ineffectual efforts at infiltration.

"The troops of the later waves still crouched in their landing boats beyond range outside the reef. During the night a number of these tried to make it ashore under cover of the darkness. But the darkness supplied little cover that night. Gasoline and supply dumps were burning all over Betio, adding their lurid glare to that of a small but tropically bright quarter moon. The white coral of the pier stood out starkly against the dark water. Black figures moved along it, antlike, to and fro: members of the shore party carrying in vital supplies of ammunition, water, food. The Japanese shelled them mercilessly. The Navy shelled the Japanese. Combat engineers repaired the pier as fast as the enemy blasted it. The shore party took their losses and carried on.

"All in all, it was quite a night. But when daylight found that thin perimeter still intact, a new feeling began to imbue the weary, hungry, thirsty men who held it: a conviction, tacit but implicit, that the crisis had passed. Although ninety percent of Betio smoked and smoldered in front of them, although enemy fire rose in frenzy and volume from every side, and there was no sign of weakening resistance anywhere,

* Designation of an assault beach. (Ed.)

all hands knew now that the issue was no longer in doubt—if it ever had been really."

The story of the second day on Tarawa is taken from Robert Sherrod's memorable *Tarawa.*

TARAWA: THE SECOND DAY

by Robert Sherrod

This is how things stood at dawn of the second day: the three assault battalions held their precarious footholds—Major Crowe's was about midway of the island's north beach, just east of the pier; Lieutenant Colonel Jordan's held a portion of the beach a couple of hundred yards west of Crowe, on the other side of the pier; and the third assault battalion, I learned, had landed on the strongly fortified western tip of the island. This last-named battalion, although separated from its staff and part of its troops, actually had been more successful than the first two. Under the leadership of one of its company commanders, Major Mike Ryan, who took over when the battalion c.o. landed in another pocket, it had fought its way inland until it held a seventy-yard beachhead before dark of the first day. The naval gunfire had been particularly effective on this western end of the island, knocking out all the big guns which had been the chief defense, and Major Ryan's men, had, in the words of Colonel Shoup, proved themselves "a bunch of fighting fools." The battalion, of course, was isolated from the rest of the Marines on the island.

During the first night the Japs, apparently because their communications had been disrupted and many of their men undoubtedly had been stunned, had not counterattacked. Probably as many as three hundred Japs, we learned later, had committed suicide under the fierce pounding of our naval guns and bombs.

382

Meanwhile, the Marines had landed Colonel Shoup's combat team reserve battalion, the first battalion of the Second Regiment. During the night considerable quantities of ammunition, some artillery, some tanks (light and medium), and other supplies had also been brought in.

General Julian Smith had sent a message from his battleship headquarters: "Attack at dawn; division reserve will start landing at 0600." The division reserve was the first and third battalions of the Eighth Marines.

Our casualties had been heavy on the first day, but well over half the dead, and practically all of the wounded, had been shot, not in the water, but after they had reached land and climbed the seawall. Those wounded more than lightly in the water had little chance of reaching shore. The amphibious operation up to that point, therefore, could have been called better than successful. The hell lay in the unexpectedly strong fortifications we had found after we landed.

It was not possible—and never will be possible—to know just how many casualties the three assault battalions had suffered D Day. Most officers agreed afterward that thirty-five to forty percent was as good a guess as any. Organization was ripped to pieces. The percentage of casualties among officers had been heavier than among the men, and key men such as platoon sergeants, virtually irreplaceable, had been killed or wounded. Therefore, we had to have more men quickly, and General Smith had said they were on the way.

Because the second day was even more critical than the first, and because it was the day the tide finally turned in our favor, I have written a play-by-play chronology (as I saw it) from my notes:

0530: The coral flats in front of us present a sad sight at low tide. A half dozen Marines lie exposed, now that the water has receded. They are hunched over, rifles in hand, just as they fell. They are already one-quarter covered by sand that the high tide left. Further out on the flats and to the left I can see at least fifty other bodies. I had thought yesterday, however, that low tide would reveal many more than that. The smell of death, that sweetly sick odor of decaying human flesh, is already oppressive.

Now that it is light, the wounded go walking by, on the beach. Some are supported by corpsmen; others, like this one coming now, walk alone, limping badly, their faces contorted with pain. Some have bloodless faces, some bloody faces, others only pieces of faces. Two corpsmen pass, carrying a Marine on a stretcher who is lying face down. He has a great hole in his side, another smaller hole in his shoulder. This scene, set against the background of the dead on the coral flats, is horrible. It is war. I wish it could be seen by the silken-voiced, radio-announcing pollyannas back home, who, by their very inflections, nightly lull the people into a false sense of all-is-well.

0600: One of the fresh battalions is coming in. Its Higgins boats are being hit before they pass the old hulk of a freighter seven hundred yards from shore. One boat blows up, then another. The survivors start swimming for shore, but machine-gun bullets dot the water all around them. Back of us the Marines have started an offensive to clean out the Jap machine guns which are now firing at our men in the water. They evidently do not have much success, because there is no diminution of the fire that rips into the two dozen or more Higgins boats. The *ratatatatat* of the machine guns increases, and the high *pi-i-ing* of the Jap sniper bullet sings overhead incessantly. The Japs still have some mortars, too, and at least one 40- or 77-mm. gun. Our destroyers begin booming their five-inch shells on the Jap positions near the end of the airfield back of us.

Some of the fresh troops get within two hundred yards of shore, while others from later waves are unloading further out. One man falls, writhing in the water. He is the first man I have seen actually hit, though many thousands of bullets cut into the water. Now some reach the shore, maybe only a dozen at first. They are calm, even disdainful of death. Having come this far, slowly, through the water, they show no disposition to hurry. They collect in pairs and walk up the beach, with snipers still shooting at them.

Now one of our mortars discovers one of the machine
384

guns that has been shooting at the Marines. It is not back of us, but is a couple of hundred yards west, out in one of the wooden privies the dysentery-fearing Japs built out over the water. The mortar gets the range, smashes the privy, and there is no more firing from there.

But the machine guns continue to tear into the on-coming Marines. Within five minutes I see six men killed. But the others keep coming. One rifleman walks slowly ashore, his left arm a bloody mess from the shoulder down. The casualties become heavier. Within a few minutes more I can count at least a hundred Marines lying on the flats.

0730: The Marines continue unloading from the Higgins boats, but fewer of them are making the shore now. Many lie down behind the pyramidal concrete barriers the Japs had erected to stop tanks. Others make it as far as the dis-abled tanks and amphtracks, then lie behind them to size up the chances of making the last hundred yards to shore. There are at least two hundred bodies which do not move at all on the dry flats, or in the shallow water partially cov-ering them. This is worse, far worse than it was yesterday.

Now four of our carrier-based fighters appear over the water. The first makes a glide and strafes the rusty freighter hulk, then the second, third, and fourth. Thousands of their fifty-caliber bullets tear into the old ship, each plane leaving a dotted, blue-gray line behind each wing. "The god-damn Japs must have swum out there last night and mounted a machine gun in that freighter," says an officer beside me. "I thought I saw some bullets coming this way."

Three more Hellcats appear. These carry small bombs under their bellies. The first dives for the freighter and misses by at least fifty yards. The second does likewise. But the third gets a direct hit and the old freighter gushes a flame fifty feet into the air. But the flame apparently is from the bomb explosion alone, because it dies out imme-diately. "May kill some of our own men out there with that bombing and strafing," observes the officer, "but we've got to do it. That Jap machine gun is killing our men in the water." A dozen more bomber-fighters appear in the sky. One after another they glide gracefully to within a few hundred feet of the freighter, drop their bombs, and sail away. But only one of the twelve gets a hit on the freighter. I am surprised at their inaccuracy—one bomb is two hundred yards beyond the target. These fighter-bombers are less accurate than the more experienced dive bombers.

0800: Back at Colonel Jordan's command post nobody is happy. Things are still going badly. Colonel Jordan is talking to Major Crowe: "Are there many snipers behind your front lines? Uh, huh, we have a hell of a lot, too."

"Where is my little runner? Where is Paredes?" asks Colonel Jordan.

"He is dead, Colonel. He was killed right over there," a Marine answers. Corporal Osbaldo R. Paredes of Los Angeles was a brave Marine. All during the first day he had carried messages through intense fire, never hesitating to accept the most dangerous mission. "Oh, hell!" says the misty-eyed colonel. What a fine boy! I'll certainly see that his family gets the Navy Cross." He stops suddenly. The Navy Cross seems quite inadequate now, only a few minutes after Paredes has been killed.

By now all the coconut trees from which snipers had been shot yesterday are filled again with more snipers. The sniper fire seems more frequent than ever and nobody can stick his head out of the battalion shellhole without getting shot at. The hell of it is that they are in trees only a few yards away, and they are hard to spot. They are not dangerous at any respectable range, but from their nearby positions they can kill a lot of Marines. A Marine comes by headquarters grinning. "I just got one," he says. "He dropped his rifle on the third shot, and it fell at my feet. But I swear I haven't seen him yet. I guess they tie themselves to trees just like they did at Guadalcanal."

0830: By now most of the Marines have arrived who will ever get ashore from those waves that were hit so badly early this morning. Those lying behind the tank blocks and the disabled boats get up once in a while and dash for shore. But I'm afraid we lost two hundred of them this morning, maybe more.

A captain comes by and reports that one of his men has

single-handedly knocked out eight machine-gun nests—five yesterday and three this morning. Another unattached officer, whose normal duty is a desk job, not combat, drops in and reports that he finally killed a sniper. He had been out looking all morning—"How can you kill the bastards if you can't see them?"—and he finally had fired a burst into a coconut palm. Out dropped a Jap, wearing a coconut-husk cap. We feel that we are eliminating a lot of Jap machine gunners and snipers now. As the last men come ashore, there is only one machine gun firing at them, and it hits nobody.

0940: Now the high explosives are really being poured on the Jap positions toward the tail end of the island. Our 75-mm. pack howitzers are firing several rounds a minute. The strafing planes are coming over by the dozens, and the dive bombers by the half-dozens. Now we have many 81-mm. mortars joining the deathly orchestra. Betio trembles like a leaf, but I ask myself, "Are we knocking out many of those pillboxes?"

We know the Japs are still killing and wounding a lot of men. The stretchers are passing along the beach again, carrying their jungle-cloth-covered burdens. One Marine on a stretcher is bandaged around the head, both arms, and both legs. One of the walking wounded, his left arm in a white sling, walks slowly along the beach in utter contempt of the sniper who fires at him.

1100: Finally at Colonel Shoup's headquarters. And what a headquarters! Fifteen yards inland from the beach, it is a hole dug in the sand back of a huge pillbox that probably was some kind of Japanese headquarters. The pillbox is forty feet long, eight feet wide, and ten feet high. It is constructed of heavy coconut logs, six and eight inches in diameter. The walls of the pillbox are two tiers of coconut logs, about three feet apart. The logs are joined together by eight-inch steel spikes, shaped like a block letter C. In between the two tiers of logs are three feet of sand, and covering the whole pillbox several more feet of sand are heaped. No wonder our bombs and shells hadn't destroyed these pillboxes! Two-thousand-pound bombs hitting directly on them might have partially destroyed them,

387

but bombing is not that accurate—not even dive bombing—on as many pillboxes as the Japs have on Betio. And when bombs hit beside such structures they only throw up more sand on top of them.

Colonel Shoup is nervous. The telephone shakes in his hand. "We are in a mighty tight spot," he is saying. Then he lays down the phone and turns to me, "Division has just asked me whether we've got enough troops to do the job. I told them no. They are sending the Sixth Marines, who will start landing right away." Says a nearby officer: "That damned Sixth is cocky enough already. Now they'll come in and claim they won the battle." [1]

From his battalion commanders Colonel Shoup receives regular telephone reports. One of them is now asking for air bombardment on a Jap strongpoint on the other side of the airfield, which we can see a few hundred feet from regimental headquarters. "All right," says the colonel, putting down the telephone. "Air liaison officer!" he calls, "tell them to drop some bombs on the southwest edge of 229 and the southeast edge of 231. There's some Japs in there giving us hell." The numbers refer to the keyed blocks on the map of the island. It seems less than ten minutes before four dive bombers appear overhead, then scream toward the earth with their bombs, which explode gruffly: *ka-whump, ka-whump, ka-whump, ka-whump*. Even nearer than the bombs, destroyer shells in salvos of four are bursting within ten minutes after a naval liaison officer has sent directions by radio.

Next to regimental quarters rises a big, uncompleted barracks building, which withstood our bombing and shell-

---

[1] The Sixth is one of the two Marine regiments which fought so bravely and brilliantly in France in World War I. But other regiments are jealous of the Sixth's honors. Examples: (1) in Shanghai it used to be said that the "pogey-bait" Sixth ordered $40,000 worth of post-exchange supplies—one dollar's worth of soap, the rest in candy ("pogey-bait"); (2) in New Zealand other Marines spread the rumor that the *fourragère* which the Sixth's men wore on their shoulders indicated that the wearer had a venereal disease.

ing very well. There are only a few small holes in the roof and wooden sides of the building. Five-foot tiers of coconut logs surround the building, to protect it against shrapnel. I run the thirty feet from Colonel Shoup's command post eastward to the tier and leap over it. Some Marines are in the unfloored building, lying on the ground, returning a Jap sniper's fire which comes from we know not where. Says a Marine: "That god-damn smokeless powder they've got beats anything we ever had." Then I cross the interior of the building, go through a hole in the wall and sit down beside some Marines who are in the alleyway between the wooden building and the tier of coconut logs.

"This gets monotonous," says a Marine as a bullet whistles through the alley. We are comparatively safe, sitting here, because we are leaning against the inside of the log tier, and the vertical logs that act as braces are big enough for us to squeeze behind. The problem is to flatten one's legs against the ground so that they are not exposed to the sniper's fire.

1130: These Marines are from H Company, the heavy-weapons company of the battalion I came with. "We've already had fifteen men killed, more in twenty-four hours than we had on Guadalcanal in six months," said the Marine sitting next to me, "and I don't know how many wounded.

"We started in in one amphib, and it got so hot the driver drove off before he had unloaded all of us. Then the amphib sank—it had been hit—and another one picked us up and brought us ashore."

Where had they landed? "Right over there by that pillbox with the four Japs in it," he replies. "You know who killed those Japs? Lieutenant Doyle of G Company did it— that's P. J. Doyle from Neola, Iowa—he just tossed a grenade in, then he jumped in with the Japs and shot them all with his carbine before they could shoot him."

By now it is fairly raining sniper bullets through our alley, as if the sniper is desperate because he isn't hitting anybody. The sniper is evidently a couple of hundred yards away, because there is a clear space that is far back from the open end of the alley. Japs can hide behind a coconut log without being seen all day, but nobody ever heard of one hiding behind a grain of sand.

A bullet ricochets off the side of the barracks building and hits the leg of the private who is second down the line. "I'm glad that one was spent," he says, picking up the .303-caliber copper bullet, which is bent near the end of the nose. I reach out for the bullet and he hands it to me. I drop it quickly because it is almost as hot as a live coal. The Marines all laugh.

These Marines calmly accept being shot at. They've grown used to it by now, and I suddenly realize that it is to me no longer the novelty it was. It seems quite comfortable here, just bulling. But I am careful to stay behind the upright coconut log which is my protection against the sniper.

Into the alleyway walks a Marine who doesn't bother to seek the protection of the coconut logs. He is the dirtiest man I have seen on the island—men get dirty very quickly in battle, but this one has a good quarter inch of gray-black dust on his beardless face and his dungarees are caked. A lock of blond hair sticks out from under his helmet.

"Somebody gimme some cigarettes," he says. "That machine-gun crew is out there in a shellhole across the airfield and there's not a cigarette in the crowd." One of the Marines throws him a pack of Camels.

The new arrival grins. "I just got me another sniper. That's six today, and me a cripple." I ask if he has been shot. "Hell, no," he says, "I busted my ankle stepping into a shellhole yesterday." His name? "Pfc. Adrian Strange." His home? "Knox City, Texas." Age? "Twenty."

Pfc. Adrian Strange stands for a few minutes, fully exposed to the sniper who has been pecking at us. Then the sniper opens up again, the bullets rattling against the coconut logs.

Pfc. Strang sings out, "Shoot me down, you son-of-a-bitch." Then he leisurely turns around and walks back across the airfield, carrying his carbine and the pack of cigarettes.

"That boy Strange," says the Marine next to me, "he just don't give a damn."

390

1200: Colonel Shoup has good news. Major Ryan's shorthanded battalion has crossed the western end of the island and the entire eight-hundred-yard beach up there is now ours. There are plenty of Japs just inside the beach, and the fortifications on the third of the island between Shoup's command post and Ryan's beach are very strong. And the entire south shore of the island, where there are even stronger pillboxes than there were on the north, remains to be cleaned out. That is the job of the Sixth Regiment, which will land this afternoon.

A young major comes up to the colonel in tears. "Colonel, my men can't advance. They are being held up by a machine gun." Shoup spits, "Goddlemighty, one machine gun."

1215: Here the Marines have been sitting in back of this pillbox (Shoup's headquarters) for twenty-four hours. And a Jap just reached out from an air vent near the top and shot Corporal Oliver in the leg. In other words, there have been Japs within three feet—the thickness of the wall—of the Marines' island commander all that time. Three Japs had been killed in the pillbox yesterday, and we thought that was all there were.

There is very bad news about Lieutenant Hawkins. He may die from his three wounds. He didn't pay much attention to the shrapnel wound he got yesterday, but he has been shot twice this morning. He wouldn't be evacuated when he got a bullet through one shoulder. "I came here to kill Japs; I didn't come here to be evacuated," he said. But a while ago he got a bullet through the other shoulder, and lower down. He lost a lot of blood from both wounds.

Said the corporal who told me this, "I think the Scout and Sniper platoon has got more guts than anybody else on the island. We were out front and Morgan (Sergeant Francis P. Morgan of Salem, Oregon) was shot in the throat. He was bleeding like hell, and saying in a low voice, 'Help me, help me.' I had to turn my head."

Lieutenant Paine, who had been nicked in the rear as he stood talking to us—"I'll be damned. I stay out front four hours, then I come back to the command post and get shot"—has more news about Hawkins. "He is a madman," says Paine. "He cleaned out six machine-gun nests, with two to six Japs in each nest. I'll never forget the picture of him standing on that amphtrack, riding around with a million bullets a minute whistling by his ears, just shooting Japs. I never saw such a man in my life."

The young major whose men were held up by a single machine gun was back again. "Colonel, there are a thousand goddamn Marines out there on that beach, and not one will follow me across to the air strip," he cries, desperately. Colonel Jordan, who by this time was back at his old job as observer, our battalion having been merged with Major Wood Kyle's reinforcing first battalion, speaks up, "I had the same trouble. Most of them are brave men, but some are yellow." I recall something a very wise general once told me, "In any battle you'll find the fighting men up front. Then you'll find others who will linger behind, or find some excuse to come back. It has always been that way, and it always will. The hell of it is that in any battle you lose a high percentage of your best men."

Says Colonel Shoup, "You've got to say, 'Who'll follow me?' And if only ten follow you, that's the best you can do, but it's better than nothing."

1300: Now they are bringing up the dead for burial near the command post. There are seven laid out about ten yards from where I sit. They are covered with green and brown ponchos, only their feet sticking out. I think: what big feet most American soldiers and Marines have! None of those looks smaller than a size eleven. The stench of the dead, as the burial detail brings them past and lines them up on the ground, is very heavy now.

Somebody brings in the story of a Jap sniper whose palm-tree roost was sprayed repeatedly. But he kept on firing, somehow. Finally, in disgust, a sergeant took a machine gun and fired it until he had cut the tree in two, near the top. The fall is supposed to have killed the Jap.

1430: Things look better now. The amphtracks—those that are left—are bringing stuff ashore and carrying the wounded regularly, and they get shot at only occasionally when they head back into the water. Major Ryan and his crowd are doing very well at the western end of the island,

392

and the Sixth Marines are about to land there and start down the south shore. We've got another company of light tanks ashore, and they are going up as close as possible to the Jap pillboxes and firing high explosives into the slits. The improved situation is reflected in everyone's face around headquarters.

1600: Bill Hipple and I head east along the beach to Major Crowe's headquarters. By this time we are so confident that the battle is running in our favor that we do not even crouch down, as we walk four feet apart, one ahead of another. After we cross the base of the pier the inevitable sniper's bullet sings by. "Jesus," says Hipple, "do you know that damned bullet went between us?" We crouch down under the protection of the seawall during the rest of the journey.

That tough, old-time Marine, Jim Crowe, is having a tough time yet, but he is still as cool as icebox lettuce. "We kill 'em and more come filtering up from the tail of the island," he says. I ask him about his casualties. "Already had about three hundred in my battalion," he says.

A young tank officer, Lieutenant L. E. Larbey, reports to the major as we are talking to him. "I just killed a Marine, Major Crowe," he says bitterly. "Fragments from my 75 splintered against a tree and ricocheted off. God damn, I hated for that to happen."

"Too bad," mutters Crowe, "but it sometimes happens. Fortunes of war."

The heavy tanks are being used against the pillboxes. They have tried crushing them, but even a thirty-two-ton tank is not very effective against these fortifications. "We got a prisoner last night," said Crowe, "and we have four more, temporarily, sealed up in a pillbox. I suppose they'll kill themselves before we get 'em out."

The strafing planes are coming overhead in waves now and the grease-popping sound of their guns is long and steady. "Don't know how much good they do," says Crowe, "but we know their bullets will kill men if they hit anything. One fifty-caliber slug hit one of my men—went through his shoulder, on down through his lung and liver. He lived about four minutes. Well, anyway, if a Jap ever

393

sticks his head out of his pillbox the planes may kill him."

1630: Crowe is talking on the phone, apparently to Colonel Shoup: "I suggest we hold a line across from the pier tonight." That means his men have advanced about two hundred yards to the east of the island, and he believes they can hold a line all the way across the island, which is about six hundred yards wide at that point. Meantime, my old battalion, plus the reinforcements, are cleaning out the center of the island, Major Ryan's battalion is holding the western end, and a battalion of the Sixth Marines is landing to start down the southern shore.

1700: Hipple and I are surprised to see two more correspondents—we had long since decided that none of the others was alive. But Dick Johnston, a young, pencil-thin U.P. man, and Frank ("Fearless") Filan, A.P. photographer, had also managed to land with the assault waves. "Filan, here," says Johnston, "is a hero. The Marine next to him was shot as they waded in. Filan started helping him back to the boat. But then a sniper opened up on the boat from the side. The Marine beat Filan to the shore. And Filan ruined all his cameras and equipment helping the Marine." The two correspondents report that at least one more correspondent arrived this morning. Don Senick, the newsreelman. "His boat was turned back yesterday," says Johnston, "but they got ashore this morning. Senick ought to get the Purple Heart. He was sitting under a coconut tree. A bullet hit above his head and dropped on his leg. It bruised him."

Lieutenant Larbey sits down beside us. "Were you ever inside a tank when it got hit?" he asks. "The spot inside the tank where the shell hits turns a bright yellow, like a sunrise. My tank got two hits a while ago." Larbey walks back to his iron horse. Says Johnston, "That guy is a genius at keeping his tanks running. He repairs the guns, refuels them somehow, and reloads them with ammunition."

A tall, grinning Marine is here at headquarters getting ammunition. He has a bandage on his arm, and a casualty tag around his neck like those the corpsmen put on every man they treat—in case he collapses later from his wound.

"Get shot in the arm?" asks Jim Crowe.

394

"Yes, sir," says Morgan.

"What'd you do, stick your arm out of a foxhole, eh?"

"No, sir, I was walking alongside a tank." And Morgan goes on about his business, gathering ammunition. Crowe looks up at the sky, which is full of planes. "Look at them goddamn strafing planes. They haven't killed fifty Japs in two days," he growls.

A grimy Marine seated alongside us muses: "I wonder what our transport did with those sixteen hundred half pints of ice cream that was to be sent ashore yesterday after the battle was over."

An officer comes in and reports to Major Crowe that a sniper is raising hell with the people working on supplies at the end of the pier. By this time we are stacking great piles of supplies on the end of the pier. The officer thinks the fire is coming, not from the beach, but from a light tank that is half sunk in the water. It is the same tank that I saw the naked figure dive into as I came ashore. These devilish Japs!

A destroyer standing so close to shore that it must be scraping bottom has been ordered to fire at a big concrete blockhouse a couple of hundred yards away from us. First, it fires single rounds—five or six of them. Then, when the range is found, it opens up with four guns at a time and to us it seems that all bedlam has broken loose. After about eighty rounds it stops. "They never hit it squarely," says Major Crowe, "but almost."

1803: Now, at three minutes past six, the first two American jeeps roll down the pier, towing 37-mm. guns. "If a sign of certain victory were needed," I note, "this is it. The jeeps have arrived."

1900: Back at regimental headquarters, Colonel Shoup wipes his red forehead with his grimy sleeve and says, "Well, I think we are winning, but the bastards have got a lot of bullets left." I ask him how much longer it would last. "I believe we'll clean up the entire western end of the island tomorrow, maybe more. It will take a day or two more to root them all out of the tail end of the island."

A surgeon grunts and rises from where he has been working feverishly over a dozen wounded Marines who lie on the beach. His blood-plasma containers hang from a line strung between a pole and a bayoneted rifle stuck upright into the ground. Four deathly pale Marines are receiving the plasma through tubes in their arms. "These four will be all right," the doctor thinks, "but there are a lot more up the beach that we probably can't save." He continues, "This battle has been hell on the medical profession. I've got only three doctors out of the whole regiment. The rest are casualties, or they have been lost or isolated. By now nearly all the corpsmen have been shot, it seems to me."

Lieutenant Colonel Presley M. Rixey, a blue-eyed, mustachioed Virginian who commands the artillery attached to Colonel Shoup's regimental combat team, is the first man I have heard pick the turning point of the battle, "I thought up until one o'clock today it was touch and go. Then I knew we would win. It's not over yet, but we've got 'em." Supplies are beginning to flow over the pier in quantity now. The last of Colonel Rixey's 37's and 75's are being landed, "At long last," he says.

"You know what," says Colonel Rixey, "I'll bet these are the heaviest casualties in Marine Corps history. I believe we've already lost more than ten percent of the division and we haven't landed all of it." Until now I haven't considered Tarawa in the light of history. It has only seemed like a brawl—which it is—that we might easily have lost, but for the superb courage of the Marines. But, I conclude, Colonel Rixey may have something there. Maybe this is history.[2]

1930: Hipple and I begin digging our foxhole for the night—this time a hundred yards further up the beach, next to Amphtrack No. 10. "This one came in on the first wave," says a nearby Marine, "there were twenty men in it, and all but three of them were killed."

As we dig deeper, the smell from our foxhole becomes oppressive. "Not all the Japs used those privies over the

[2] At Soissons July 19, 1918, the Marines suffered 1,303 casualties. They probably took more the first day on Tarawa, and the ratio of dead to wounded was 1 to 2 instead of 1 to 10.

water," I commented. Hipple has finished digging with the shovel, and now he begins smoothing the foxhole with his hands—all foxholes should be finished by hand. The smell is so oppressive we throw a few shovelfuls of sand back into the hole to cover at least some of the odor.

Then we lie down to sleep. It has been more than sixty hours since we closed our eyes and the danger of a night attack has been all but eliminated, so we sleep soundly.

2400: We are rudely awakened after three hours' sleep. The tide has come up and flooded our foxhole. This is unusual, because the tide has not been this high since we reached the island. We sit on a bank of sand, wide-awake and knowing that there will be no more sleep tonight. Besides, Washing Machine Charley will be due soon and nobody can sleep while being bombed.

0500: Washing Machine Charley was over at four o'clock. He dropped eight bombs in his two runs over the island. Said Keith Wheeler, later, "He was absolutely impartial; he dropped half his bombs on us and half on the Japs." Water or no water, we lay face down in our foxhole as he came over. As the bombs hit, there was a blinding flash a couple of hundred yards up the beach, to the west. A few minutes later a Marine came running up the beach, shouting, "There are a lot of men hurt bad up here. Where are the corpsmen and the stretchers?" He was directed to a pile of stretchers nearby. Soon the stretcher bearers returned, silhouetted by the bright half-moon as they walked along the beach. Washing Machine Charley had killed one man, had wounded seven or eight.

0530: At first sight, Bill Hipple looks at what had been our foxhole. Then he learns that the odor was caused, not by Jap excrement, but by the body of a dead man who had been buried beside the foxhole. Bill had been clawing the face of a dead man as he put the finishing touches on the foxhole.

Jungle War

On November 23, 1943, Tarawa was secured. The 2nd Marine Division had lost approximately 3,000 casualties, with less than 1,000 dead; but the enemy had lost almost every man on the island. Out of 4,000 Japanese, hardly more than 100 were taken alive as prisoners.

On December 26, 1943, the 1st Marine Division landed on Cape Gloucester, at the northwestern end of New Britain. While the landings here were comparatively unopposed, there would be at least three months of hard jungle fighting. With the western third of New Britain in U.S. hands, Rabaul would be effectively neutralized for the duration.

The fighting at Cape Gloucester was "a jungle slugging match,* where flame throwers were useless, it was often impossible to throw a grenade more than ten feet ahead, and the bazooka usually failed to detonate upon striking the soft earth of the Jap field works.

"The terrain was as rugged and treacherous as the Japanese. The direction of the advance necessitated what is known technically as cross compartment fighting; i.e., moving at right angles to the natural watershed. This meant that instead of following valleys and ridges, an interminable succession of these had to be crossed. Men would scale one ridge, wiping out the prepared positions, which cluttered both the forward and reverse slopes, then plunge down into another valley where they might or might not find a river which showed on none of their crude maps, with the enemy entrenched on the far bank. One such stream had to be crossed nine times before a bridge-head could be secured. Or perhaps there would be a swamp, neck-deep or worse. Then another fortified ridge, another unknown valley. . . .

"And always the rain and the mud, torrid heat and teeming insect life, the stink of rotten jungle and rotting dead; malaria burning the body and fungus infection eating away the feet, and no hot chow

* Maj. Frank Hough, *The Island War*, p. 168.

398

for weeks. And fury by day and terror by night and utter weariness all the time. And death."

In the following narrative, T/Sgt. Asa Bordages describes a small but bitterly fought action at one of the creeks—aptly called Suicide Creek—which held up the advance on Cape Gloucester for a time.

SUICIDE CREEK AT NEW BRITAIN

by T/Sgt. Asa Bordages

They came to "Suicide Creek." It had no name and it was not on the map, but that is what the Marines called it after they had fought two days in vain to win a crossing. The creek is swift, two or three feet deep, perhaps twenty feet across at the widest, twisting between steep banks. It flows over rocks that make footing difficult, and here and there a tree had fallen into the stream. The banks rise steeply from ten to twenty feet, up to little ridges in the jungle of Cape Gloucester.

The Marines didn't know the creek was a moat before an enemy strong point. They couldn't see that the heavy growth across the creek was salted with pillboxes—machine-gun emplacements armored with dirt and logs, some of them dug several stories deep, all carefully spotted so they could sweep the slope and both banks of the stream with interlacing fire.

Only snipers shot at the Marine scouts who crossed the creek, feeling their way through the thickets. More Marines followed, down into the creek, up the steep bank, on into the jungle. Then they got it. The jungle exploded in their faces. They hit the deck, trying to deploy in the bullet-lashed brush and strike back. Marines died there, firing blindly. Snipers picked off some of them as they lay there. It's perfect for snipers when machine guns are firing; you can't

399

hear the single pop above the heavier fire. You don't know you're a target until you're hit.

From the American side of Suicide Creek, Marines gave the trapped platoon overhead fire. The idea is to fling such a volume of fire at the enemy's position that he must hug cover and slacken his fire. The overhead fire spread an umbrella of bullets above the pinned-down platoon, enabling them to crawl out and crawl back across the creek, pulling out their wounded.

That's how it went all day as Marine detachments felt for a gap or a soft spot in the enemy's positions along the creek. They would be hit and pull back, and then detachments would push across the creek at other points. They'd be blasted by invisible machine guns, and leave a few more Marines dead in the brush as they fell back across the creek. Then they'd do it all over again.

There was nothing else they could do. There is no other way to fight a jungle battle—not in such terrain, when the enemy is dug in and your orders are to advance. You don't know where the enemy is. His pillboxes are so camouflaged that you can usually find them only when they fire on you. So you push out scouts and small patrols, until they're fired on. Then you push out patrols from different directions until they too draw fire. Thus you locate the enemy. Then you have to take the emplacements, the pillboxes, one by one in desperate little battles.

Private First Class Calvin B. King, of Pen Mar, Pennsylvania, remembers his platoon crossed the creek four times in a single day and four times had to stumble back under enemy fire. And not until the last time did they see a Jap.

"That time we got maybe a hundred and fifty feet into the brush and then we saw them coming at us," he said. "They had slipped around and were coming in from our flank to wipe us out. There were a lot of 'em. I don't know how many. It looked like they was everywhere.

"They didn't make a sound. They were just coming at us through the trees. We were firing, but they kept coming at us. There were too many of them to stop. We had to pull out. Machine guns were shooting at us from everywhere. And all them Japs coming. We'd pull back a little way and stop and fire, and then we'd fall back a little more.

"Somebody was saying, 'Steady . . . Steady there . . .' But I don't know who it was. I just kept firing. You don't think about nothing. You just shoot. Guys were getting hit. We had to pull them along with us. You can't leave a guy for the Japs. The things they do to 'em . . ."

There was a private first class from Oakland, California. He was blinded by powder burns. He couldn't know it was only temporary. All he knew was that he was blind in the middle of a battle. He was saying, "I can't see." He was fumbling around, trying to feel his way in the brush. The bullets were cutting all around, but he didn't ask anybody to stop fighting to help him. He just hung onto his rifle, like they tell you to, and tried to crawl out, though he couldn't see where to crawl. Corporal Lawrence E. Oliveria, of Fall River, Massachusetts, grabbed the blind boy by the arm, pulling him along as they withdrew. He'd pause to fire, and the blind Marine would wait beside him, and then Corporal Oliveria would lead him back a little farther. "The boy didn't moan or pray or nothing. He just kept saying, every now and then, 'I can't see.' "

By the time they got back to the creek, the Japanese were close on them, charging now. But the Marines had machine guns at the creek. They piled the Jap dead in the brush and broke the charge.

Another platoon tried crossing the creek at another point. Near the head of the line was "the Swede," a private first class from some place out west. He was a big guy, built like a truck, the last man in the world you'd ever suspect of being sentimental. His big ambition was to send his kid sister through college. It took some doing, but he was doing it on his service pay. The Swede was just stepping into the creek when he got it.

"You could hear the bullet hit him in the stomach," said Platoon Sergeant John M. White. "He just stood there a minute. He said, 'Them dirty bastards!' Then he fell down. He was dead.

"When we got across the creek, the fire was so hot we couldn't do a thing. You couldn't see a single Jap. All you could see was where the bullets were hitting around us. And men getting hit. But no matter how bad it got, I never saw one of the boys pass up a wounded man."

Private First Class Charles Conger, of Ventura, California, was one of those hit. A machine gun cut his legs from under him. Nobody saw him. Nobody could have heard him if he'd yelled—the firing was too heavy. He was as alone as a man can be. It was slow, painful, dragging through the brush, crawling head first down the bank, dragging limp legs. He had to pull himself on by inches, then belly down the bank sprayed with bullets as thick as rice thrown at a bride. He tumbled into the creek. The rocks were sharp. He was gasping in the swift water, struggling across against the force of the stream. It was only blind luck that White saw him. White was too far away to help, but he stopped and waved his arms to attract attention, ignoring cover until two Marines who were nearer saw the wounded man in the creek. Those Marines were almost across. Safety lay just ahead. They didn't have to stop. But they went sloshing through the water to the wounded man. They half carried, half dragged him with them.

The battalion tried all day to win a crossing at the creek. In the end, they could only withdraw to the ridge on the American side and dig in for the night. It was getting dusk as one machine-gun platoon finished its gun emplacements. Then the men began digging their foxholes. Most of them were stripped to the waist and they laid aside their weapons as they dug.

That was the moment the enemy chose to charge. They must have slipped across the stream and up the slope and watched the digging. They must have seen that if they could reach those emplacements and get those machine guns, they could swing them and smash the infantry company holding the next section of the line. That is why the Japanese, perhaps fifty of them, did not yell and did not fire a shot. They rushed with bayonets.

Down among his infantrymen, Captain Andrew A. Haldane, of Methuen, Massachusetts, was talking with First Lieutenant Andrew Chisick, of Newark, New Jersey. They heard a Marine yell. They looked up and saw the Japs racing toward the emplacements, and weaponless Marines scattering out of the way. Some had no chance of getting to their weapons. The Japs were hardly thirty yards from the nearest gun and closing fast.

Then more Marines were firing, but it wasn't enough to stop the charge. The nearest Japs were hardly ten feet from the guns. Captain Haldane ran toward the guns, firing as he ran. Lieutenant Chisick ran with him. Others joined the charge, some with bare hands, some with clubs or entrenching tools snatched up from the ground. The Japs reached one gun and swung it to enfilade the line. A Jap was in the gunner's seat. The Marines' charge hit the gun before he could fire a shot. He got a bayonet through the chest. The enemy broke, and the Marines cut them down. More than twenty dead Japs were scattered in the brush by the time it was quiet again.

The Marines were bombed that night. Dive bombers. The enemy set up a heavy fire of tracer bullets to show the bombers where their own lines were and where they should drop their bombs in the dark. Nobody will ever be able to describe a bombing. You can't describe hell. You can only go through it.

The Marines had to take the bombing after a day of battle, without any way of hitting back. The next morning, January 3, they attacked again. The enemy threw mortar shells. Sergeant White saw a shell explode, and ducked down the line to see if anyone was hit. "A kid was sitting there in his foxhole. He didn't have any head. He just had a neck with dog tags on it."

All through that second day, the Marines pushed small units across the creek at different points, still trying to find a soft spot in the Japanese defenses. Each time they were hit. They knocked out some of the machine guns, but each time, in the end, they had to fall back across the creek.

There was a boy firing from behind a log. His face was gray. He stopped firing and looked around. His eyes were dull, without hope.

"It don't do any good," he said. His voice was flat. He

403

wasn't speaking to anybody. He was just saying it. "I got three of 'em, but it don't do any good."

Platoon Sergeant Casimir Polakowski—known as Ski—said, "What the hell are you beefing about? You get paid for it, don't you?"

The kid managed a grin. As Ski crawled on down the line, the boy was fighting again, squeezing them off.

A platoon was pinned down in the jungle on their flank. They could neither go forward nor withdraw. They could only lie in the brush, held there by a crisscross net of machine-gun fire, while snipers took pot shots at them. Ski's platoon was ordered to lend a hand. They were bone-tired, but Ski said, "Let's get going," and they got.

Three of them were Denham, Melville, and O'Grady. Private Harry Denham, of Nashville, Tennessee, was called "Pee Wee" because he was so small. They say he went to "some fancy military school." But he didn't ask favors of anybody and he wouldn't back down before the biggest man in the regiment. Just a bantam rooster of a kid who'd take on anything that walked. Private First Class John O'Grady, of Ogdensburg, New York, left the talking for the trio to Denham and Melville. He was a quiet guy who never had much to say to anybody, but he seemed to talk plenty when the three of them were off by themselves. Maybe he told them what he wanted to be after the war. The kids all think about that. It's something to look forward to—and a guy needs something to look forward to. Private First Class John William Melville was called "Pete," but nobody seemed to know why. His home was Lynn, Massachusetts. He was twenty-six, almost an old man. He quit a white-collar job with the General Electric Company in Boston to join the Marine Corps.

Denham, Melville, and O'Grady—and Levy, Jones, and Brown—flung themselves at the enemy's flank so he'd have to break the fire that had the other platoon caught. Men dropped, but they kept going forward, fighting from tree to tree. They pushed the enemy back and held him long enough for the trapped platoon to pull out. That was long enough for the Marines to form a line so they couldn't be rolled up by counterattack.

Another lull then. The jungle was still. First Sergeant Selvitelle asked Ski how it was going. Ski was smoking a cigarette. His voice sounded tired.

"They got Denham, Melville, and O'Grady," he said. They were lying out there in the brush somewhere and he was smoking a cigarette.

The word came to move up. There was firing ahead. Maybe an hour later Ski was behind a tree when he saw a wounded Marine lying in the open. A sniper was shooting at the boy. Ski could see the dirt flung up when the bullets hit. The boy was trying to crawl away, but he couldn't.

Ski ran from cover and pulled him to a tree. The sniper saw him. All the sniper had to do was wait until Ski started to return to his post. Then he shot Ski in the back.

That was about the time Tommy Harvard's platoon crossed Suicide Creek, lugging their heavy machine guns. "Tommy Harvard" was the code name for First Lieutenant Elisha Atkins, who played football at Harvard, belonged to the Dekes and the Owls, and got his B.A. in 1942. "Very quiet and polite as hell" is the way a sergeant described him.

The enemy let First Lieutenant Atkins and about half his men cross the creek before they opened up. Six automatic weapons blasted them at point-blank range. There were at least three machine guns with perfect fields of fire. It happened too quickly for anybody to duck.

Sergeant Wills says, "I saw a man ahead of us and just as I saw he wasn't a Marine they all let fly."

Marines were hit. Somebody was screaming. Corporal John R. Hyland of Greenwich, Connecticut, was frowning as he tried to knock out the nearest machine-gun nest with rifle fire. The screaming man stopped.

Corporal Hyland said, "We ought to get the hell out of here." But he didn't move to go. He kept his place, still shooting at the spot of jungle where he guessed the gunport was, until the order was passed to withdraw.

The machine guns swept the brush just higher than a man lying flat. The trapped Marines rolled down the bank or pushed backward on their bellies until they could tumble into the creek. The screening bush was their only protection against the snipers perched in trees. As they rolled into the stream, they hunkered down as low as they could in the water. Some got down so only their faces showed above the water. All of them pressed against the Japanese bank as bullets slashed through the undergrowth above them, splattering the creek and the American bank beyond.

Two of the Marines had fallen on a big log lying in the creek. One of them was hit in the leg and couldn't move, but he was near enough for Sergeant Wills to pull him into the creek. Other Marines dragged him up against the brush-choked bank; but they couldn't reach the other boy on the log. He lay too far out in the field of fire. He'd caught a full machine-gun burst. He must have had twenty holes in him, but he was still alive. He was hung over the log, partly in the water. He was calling weakly, "Here I am, Wills . . . over here . . ."

They couldn't help him. They could only listen to him.

"Wills . . . I'm here . . . Wills . . ."

There were other wounded in the creek above them. They couldn't help them either. Most of those crouching in the bushes against the bank were wounded, too. The kid on the log was getting weaker. Just listening was harder than anything Sergeant Wills ever had to take.

"He was calling me, and I couldn't help him. All of them were guys we knew, but we couldn't do a thing. We had to lay in the water and listen to them. It was the coldest damn water I ever saw. Their blood kept flowing into our faces."

Their only chance was to creep downstream close against the bank and then make a dash, one by one, for the American shore. A little way down the twisting stream there was a spot where a man would have a chance to make it. Most places, he would have to stop to climb the bank. Only a man who wanted to commit suicide would try that.

It was slow work for the men in the creek, crawling downstream in the racing water, hampered by the thick tangles of vines and brush. Men caught in the vines struggled helplessly.

"Everybody had to cut everybody else loose as we went

along," says Private First Class Luther J. Raschke, of Harvard, Illinois.

He found young Tommy Harvard tangled in the vines and cut him loose. "I tried to help him along, but he wouldn't come. He'd been hit three times. A slug had smashed his shoulder. He was losing blood pretty fast. But he wouldn't leave. He was trying to see that everybody got out first. He told me, 'Go on, go on!' He wouldn't let anybody stop for him. He said, 'Keep the line moving!' He made us leave him there."

They made their dash; got safely out and reached the line of foxholes to which the battalion had fallen back again after that second day.

But Raschke couldn't forget the wounded officer they'd left in the creek. He said, "I guess everybody else is out."

"Yeah," said Corporal Alexander Caldwell, of Nashville, Tennessee.

"Well . . ."

"Yeah," said Corporal Caldwell.

So they got permission to go back into no man's land to hunt for their platoon leader. Corporal Caldwell took along two more volunteers, for they might have to carry Lieutenant Atkins, if they found him, and they might have to fight their way out. They were Louis J. Sievers, of Johnstown, Pennsylvania, and Joseph V. Brown, of Middletown, New York, both privates first class.

It was getting hard to see when they crawled down to the creek. Raschke stopped. They lay listening, but they could hear nothing except the rushing stream and, now and then, the sound of the Japanese talking. They had to make their choice then. They could go back without the lieutenant. Or they could risk calling. Nobody would blame them if they went back. Nobody would know they hadn't done everything they could do to find him.

Raschke lay on the edge of the stream and he remembers clearer than anything else how close the water was under his nose. The others were in the bush, rifles ready to fire if the enemy discovered him. Not that it would do any good. He'd be dead. For that matter, if the machine guns opened up, they'd all be dead.

"I was scared stiff," Raschke says. "I called as softly as I could, 'Tommy Harvard . . . Tommy Harvard . . .'

"A voice said, 'I'm down here.'

"It sounded weak, but we figured it might be a trap. So I said, 'What's your real name?'

"The voice said, 'Elisha Atkins.' So we knew it was him. We crawled down and pulled him out. He said, 'God! Am I glad to see you!' "

He was shaking from hours in the chill water, weak from loss of blood, but still calmly Harvard as they carried him to the rear.

During the two days the 3rd Battalion had been fighting vainly to win the crossing of Suicide Creek, the outfit on its left had been trying as stubbornly and as vainly to get across its segment of the stream.

During those two days, Marine Pioneers were toiling to build a corduroy road through the swamp in their rear so that tanks could be moved up to the line. The tanks finally reached the outfit on the 3rd Battalion's left, but they found the banks of the creek too steep for crossing. The gully formed a natural tank trap. So a Marine bulldozer was called to cut down the banks of the creek and make a fill in the stream so that the tanks could cross against the enemy.

The Japanese saw their danger. They concentrated fire on the bulldozer. Man after man was shot from the driver's seat—some killed, some wounded. But there was always a Marine to jump in the seat. He had no shield, no protection at all. He sat up in the open like a shooting-gallery target for all the enemy's fire. But the Marine bulldozer kept on till the fill was made and the tanks were rolling across the creek.

The advance of the tanks made the positions of the enemy opposing the 3rd Battalion untenable. If they tried to hold against the frontal attack of the 3rd Battalion, they would be hit by tanks and infantry from the flank. They'd be a nut in a nutcracker. They had to retreat or be crushed, and they retreated. The crossing of Suicide Creek had been won.

Operation Flintlock

After the Coral Sea battle and the defeat of the Japanese carrier forces before Midway in May and June of 1942, the U.S. took the initiative in the Pacific, never to lose it. From here on, our tactics followed a pattern: soften up the next group of enemy-held islands with air strikes; bombard enemy installations from offshore naval ships; then assault the beaches with the Marines and, when help was needed, the infantry. Thus, in the Central Pacific, the strategy of "island-hopping" developed; it was destined to keep the Japanese off balance throughout the rest of the war.

Some people called it "going up the ladder" to Japan, for the islands stretched out in the direction of Japan like a spider's web, effectively neutralizing Jap naval and air attacks on General Mac-Arthur's campaign in New Guinea. Then the Navy swung northeast and assaulted Tarawa in the Gilbert Islands in the first move to outflank Truk, Jap naval stronghold in the Carolines. After fierce fighting* the Gilberts were secured; air fields were rebuilt and supplies landed to provide a base for the continuing flanking movement around the Carolines.

The Marshall Islands were the next objective. As the operation took shape, air strikes were made on all the important islands in the Marshall group to keep the Japs guessing where the main blow would fall. Their planes and air strips were destroyed, eliminating Japanese air reconnaissance so that our attacking force achieved complete surprise.

Kwajalein atoll, largest island atoll in the world, was selected as the target. Our reconnaissance had discovered the Japs at work building a strip long enough to handle bombers. Two assaults were to be launched within the atoll itself: at Roi-Namur, the northern tip of the atoll, and forty miles to the southeast, Kwajalein Island, which supplied the name of the atoll.

The northern attack force consisted of the 4th Marine Division and 15th Marine Defense Battalion; the southern attack force was all Army—the 7th Infantry Division, plus 3rd and 4th Defense Battalions. The 7th Infantry Division had seen action in the capture of Attu in the Aleutians; the 4th Marine Division was new to combat, although they had undergone intensive training in Hawaii for the assault.

The Marines went ashore at Roi-Namur on February 1, 1944, meeting fierce resistance, but they succeeded in overwhelming the smaller forces and the island was declared secured on February 2.

Simultaneously, the infantry landed on Kwajalein. According to Captain Frank Hough, "the nearest island to the northwest, Enubuj, was seized with no great difficulty on the 31st of January, but Ebeye, the only island within practicable artillery range of the opposite end of Kwajalein, was so strongly held that its seizure was postponed until more troops could be made available."*

Meanwhile, because of the narrow front on Kwajalein, only two battalions were able to "operate abreast in contrast to four in line on Roi-Namur ... [and] since the distance traversed was considerably greater, the securing of Kwajalein Island required somewhat more time."* It was not declared secured until February 4.

"In the meanwhile, the 17th Infantry had opened the assault on the smaller strongly held island of Ebeye, directly north of the Eastern end of Kwajalein, abetted by naval and air support, plus artillery from the main island. The 1st Battalion landed on February 3 on the southern end and drove northward over badly battered terrain, against stubborn resistance." *

A close-up view of part of that action follows.

*Capt. Frank Hough, *The Island War*, p. 199.

410

ACTION AT THE PIGPEN*

by Lt. Col. S. L. A. Marshall

The 1st Battalion, 17th Infantry, passed the day of February 2 (D plus 2 day) on Ennylobegan Island, cleaning equipment, sunbathing, and hunting for souvenirs. The quest for souvenirs brought grief to two men, one of them a staff sergeant named Deini. In fooling with a Jap pistol, he shot a comrade in the stomach. It seemed as if the man would probably die.

Meanwhile the battalion commander, Lieutenant Colonel Albert V. Hartl, had received orders: The 1st Battalion would attack Ebeye Island the next morning. It was certain not to be a snap assignment like Ennylobegan Island. Ebeye, the third island north of Kwajalein Island on the eastern side of the atoll, held a Jap seaplane base. It was known to be strongly garrisoned.

So Hartl thought the case of Sergeant Deini over and figured that having lost one man, he couldn't afford to lose two. He called Deini and he said to him: "I'm not going to do anything about you. That man may die. In any case, we can't use him this time. That's your fault. You can square it by doing enough fighting for two men." Deini, who is a stevedore on the San Francisco docks in normal times, took it pretty grimly. He said he would do his best.

The mile-long, 250-yard wide target island was battered throughout that day by naval gunfire and air strikes. In the afternoon, Hartl's executive officer, Major Maynard E. Weaver, reconnoitered it first from the deck of a destroyer and then from a naval observation plane. He was over the island for two hours. Most of the buildings seemed to have

*From *Island Victory* published by The Infantry Journal 1945.

been leveled by the bombardment, but Weaver noticed that there were heavy concrete structures and fire trenches still in good condition at the north end of the island on the ocean side. Since the landing was to be made at the south end on the lagoon side, it seemed probable that the American right wing would carry the heaviest burden during the attack.

Hartl's battalion went ashore at 0930 on February 3 (D plus 3 day) after a preparatory hour-long bombardment by cruisers and destroyers. The Ebeye Island plan called for an even distribution of force across the island, with both flanks evenly weighted with arms and personnel. As it worked out, however, the enemy was by no means evenly distributed. Weaver had seen from the air that the heaviest buildings were on the ocean side of the island, where Company A was to operate.

That seemed significant; on Kwajalein Island, where the fighting was still in progress, the heaviest fighting occurred always where the enemy could make most use of his walls and cellars. But on Ebeye Island there were no pillboxes, fire trenches or underground works of any kind in between the shattered buildings. Thus there was little reason for Japanese to cling to the built-up area as it had no special strength. It seems probable that a large-scale redistribution of the garrison took place as a result of fire concentrations on the outer side of the island, and that they chose to defend most heavily on the lagoon side because it provided better ground cover. Company C carried the fight on the first day. One platoon did most of the fighting for the company.

The landing was unopposed. The 3d Platoon, which was to be in support position for the company during the advance up the island, landed in the first wave with the engineer detachment. It had come ashore in Alligators. Two of them stopped on the reef instead of going to the beach, and the men had to wade ashore through waist-deep water. One man fell into a shell hole and lost his BAR in the water. Private First Class Angelo Ciccotti stepped into another shell hole with the SCR-536 and drowned it out. The platoon pivoted on its left, while the right made the swing around, keeping contact with the platoon from Company A.

412

LVTs [1] kept their machine guns going from 300 yards out until they hit the beaches. Buffalos blazed away at the foliage line. The scene grew deathly quiet as the line formed and its right swung around the southern tip of the island. It came up even. The line then went ahead a few yards and halted. The 3d Platoon had completed its initial task.

The 1st and 2d Platoons, which had followed the 3d in by just a few minutes, halted and took cover at the beach only long enough to get their bearings. Then they came on through the 3d Platoon—the 1st on the right, the 2d on the left. For about 100 yards, the line stalked quietly through the underbrush, the men picking their way around uprooted trees and piles of debris.

The Buffalos had gone on up the beach, ahead of the left. Perhaps twenty minutes after the advance started, they broke the stillness by volleying inland, some distance ahead of the American line. Whether or not this fire did any damage to the enemy, it had one effect on our own forces. It made so much noise that when the first enemy fire crackled above our infantry line, the men did not sense it as a body. There was no sudden, sharp hail of bullets. By squads and by little groups, they heard the warning zing-zing-zing overhead or saw something rip through the foliage above them. This noise was doing them no harm, but by squads and by little groups they flattened as they heard the danger mount. It was a characteristic action, typical of the manner in which infantry so often loses momentum in attacking through brush-covered country. The faults that produce such stagnation are partly tactical and partly rooted in human nature.

That was true of Company C on this particular day. When the men went to earth, they could not see one another. No man knew where the next man lay on his right and left. To each man came a sense of loneliness. Yet the desire to cling close to the protecting earth was stronger than the desire to move and find one's fellows. It was not instilled in the squad and platoon leaders that their first duty on going

[1] Landing vehicle, tracked.

413

to earth was to check the whereabouts of their men so that group unity would develop group action. There was no SOP on this point. So they, too, waited until some grew tired of waiting and began calling to their men. Others stayed prone, doing nothing, "waiting for something to happen."

It also seems to be true of the infantry soldier that his feeling of insecurity rises according to the rate of fire which is coming against him, even when the fire is general and inaccurate. His confidence lifts with the lifting or ceasing of the fire. But let him then advance into the area from which the fire has come, and it will require, unless the fire picks up again, all of the driving diligence of his superiors to make him be wary and thorough. He can quickly convince himself that all is secure. Many of the infantry studies from the Pacific confirm this point. Company C was to prove it over and over on this particular day.

A few yards beyond where the center of the line first felt the fire passing overhead, there was a deep and wide storage bay running toward the lagoon from the left side of the road. It looked like a tank ditch. To the right of the road, some yards on beyond, was a second bay. A large enemy blockhouse and an air-raid shelter were on the far side of it. This was the source of the enemy fire though our men did not recognize it as such at the time.

The 1st Platoon was on the right of the road. Some of them saw the storage bay on the right of the road and figured that if they could get up to it, they would have a good breastwork. But automatic fire lowered and closed in on them and they had to take refuge in a shell crater. The two light machine guns were then brought up and fire was put on the bay. One squad bounded ahead to the bay and fired on the shelter. From the bay it moved off to the right of the shelter, took cover behind some palm stumps, and resumed fire.

The second squad was still some distance back and doing no good there. Sergeant Richard Maples went back to rally it and was hit by a bullet while talking to Lieutenant Isadore I. Feinstein. The squad came on up to the bay. As the men jumped down into it, heavy automatic fire poured in on them from the left rear. They had to hug the back walls

414

of the bay to get away from it, thereby exposing themselves to the fire of the enemy. One gunner had the presence of mind to put his panel on a rifle and wave it high in the air. The fire stopped. The men believed then that the fire had come from one of our own Buffalos on the lagoon shore.

The company line was already sagging backward, bow-shaped. The 1st Platoon was moving on the right. Its men were checked periodically by bursts of enemy fire and the forward movement was sustained through forward rushes by three or four men at a time. There was no real pressure against them, but the circumstances of fire and cover were such that they no longer worked in close co-operation one with the other.

Along the lagoon, a half-squad advancing up the beach had also speeded ahead with no interruption to its progress. This sector of the beach was clear; there were no Japs using the first fringe of cover inshore. So the half-squad went on and outdistanced the men on its right. The other half became echeloned [2] toward the rear as enemy machine-gun fire, coming from the blockhouse on the right of the road, developed against the right flank of the platoon. They went to earth man by man just inside the treeline. It was a fateful pause, for there the Jap artillery found them. Technical Sergeant Walter Feil and Sergeant Carl Swanson were hard hit. The wounded were soon carried out, but the shock of the artillery fire coupled with the effect of the machine-gun fire kept them pinned to the ground. They stayed there doing nothing.

These things contributed to the stretching of the line. The center was still well behind, retarded by automatic fire which was ranging across both sides of the road. Technical Sergeant Manford B. Lauderdale, Staff Sergeant John I. Inseth, and Private First Class Clay Vanwinkle, with a BAR, worked up under this fire, trying to get to the left-hand storage bay. They saw three Japs running from the forward shelter—the first enemy soldiers seen by the company.

[2] Bent or stepped back.

Sergeant Seth Stear yelled: "There they go. Get 'em, Rip!" But before Vanwinkle could fire the BAR, the Japs ducked into the bush. The group then threw grenades in their direction.

Over on the far right, Private Percy Johnson, the contact man with Company A, saw four Japs standing in a clearing about seventy-five yards ahead, and slightly left. He yelled to Lieutenant Erwin Desmonde, his platoon leader: "Come here! I see Japs."

Lieutenant Desmonde looked through his field glasses and exclaimed: "By God, they are Japs!" They fired and so did Private First Class Ballard T. Cogar with his BAR. The four went down—the first men hit by the company.

The reports of contact with the enemy by the 1st and 2d Platoons reached Lieutenant Charles E. Murphy at the company CP within seconds of each other. Lieutenant George E. Linebaugh, who commanded Company C, then took the extra precaution of ordering a Buffalo to advance up the left flank, take station, and stay in readiness to fire at any enemy force coming down the beach. He was worried about the half-squad on the extreme left which was up by itself and in position to be cut off. The Buffalo went forward, stopped thirty-five yards short of the men on the extreme left and began an indiscriminate fire inland which fell among the men who had been checked by the artillery. Sergeant Manuel Mendez yelled: "Cut out that goddam fire!" The Buffalo heard him and drew off.

As the stretching of the line continued owing to the advance of the right, men from the center pulled off in that direction and a gap appeared. Sergeant Gilbert Montenegro and his squad moved up automatically into this breach from the support, and, reaching the storage bay to the left of the road, found themselves in the front line. It was a good spot from which to get a clear view of the ground ahead. Montenegro saw that the automatic fire which had been harassing the center came from the blockhouse to the right of the road. The squad stayed there for a few minutes doing nothing about it. Then the tanks came up.

They had been ashore quite a while but did not move up into the action until Linebaugh phoned Murphy to send them along—two tanks on each side of the road so that two tanks would arrive in each platoon sector. The pair that came up on the left found the ground difficult and veered to the road. On the right, one tank got stuck in soft ground just short of the front line and the other didn't want to come along until its mate was free. Montenegro went to one of the tanks on the left and told the crew over the telephone that he wanted the tank to advance against the shelter to right of the road.

The tankers replied that they were taking orders only from the battalion commander. Lieutenant Charles E. Elliott, Jr., tried it and got the same reply. The tanks remained in place while there was hot argument back and forth as to whose authority the tanks were moving under. This added to the heat of a day already made oppressive by large fires which were throwing a choking smoke over the whole area. The tanks then told the battalion commander that they couldn't proceed because they were being fired upon.

Colonel Hartl replied: "The infantry is even farther forward and it's receiving fire." About forty minutes were lost during this futile interlude. Co-operation flagged because the men in the fire fight thought they had the authority to assign targets to the tank crews and the tankers had understood otherwise.

During the argument, Privates First Class Gerald D. Draughn and Edward Hodge, who were handling the bazooka, were ordered by Lieutenant Elliott to move up to an advanced position on the right of the road and fire at the shelter beyond the blockhouse. Covered by Private First Class Emmett Mull with a BAR, who came along behind them, they moved sixty yards out in front of the company, having to go that far before the bazooka could bear on the shelter door. Draughn couldn't see his first rocket because the discharge blew sand back in his eyes. But he thought it was a dud. The second hit fair on the entrance. He was ready to fire a third when he saw two Japs charging him from out the shelter. He yelled: "Get 'em, Hodge!" and Hodge shot one man with his M1. The other had already gone down. Private First Class Jack Winn, from the storage bay, had winged him with a snap shot. The third rocket was fired into the target. By that time the other men of the squad had come up to the two men and they stayed there under cover.

The deadlock between tanks and infantry was ended by a direct order from Battalion. One tank moved forward to attack the blockhouse. It had been told by the Infantry commander to engage with its artillery but it opened the attack with machine guns. The slugs had no effect. At fifty-yard range, the tank then shelled the entrance with its 75mm. gun. The infantry went along with the tank, and with this forward surge, the company line again became fairly straight.

The 2d Platoon's 1st Squad came under automatic fire while moving up the right side of the road toward the blockhouse. Two men were hit. Others in the squad saw Japs taking cover near a burned truck which lay ahead. Then two more men were hit. These things happened just like that—one, two, three—a matter of split seconds. The survivors figured the fire had come from the Japs hidden around the truck and they grenaded the ground all about it. The fire ceased. They thought the grenades might have done it. But what had happened was that a Jap machine gun far over on our left was firing across the front into our right. The half-squad moving along the beach put the blocks to the machine gun and its crew and could see that it had been working against the men moving up to the block-house.

Private First Class Wilbert Jackson had taken cover where he had a good view of the shelter which had been attacked by the bazooka. He saw a Jap rifleman come out of the rear entrance and shot him with his BAR.

The tank, having blasted the entrance, started on toward the blockhouse. Four Japs rushed it from the doorway as it got even with their position. One threw a grenade in the tracks. It bounced from the tank and the four Japs were cut down by fire from all along the 1st Platoon's position.

Such were the incidents developing from the first brush with the enemy, the defeat of his forward positions and the restoration of some mobility to the company. From the

418

rear the 60mm. mortars had barraged the area of the enemy shelters within a few minutes after the line stopped moving. The fire was at 400-yard range, and it was ranging about 200 yards over, on the right of the road. At least one burst was seen by the men of the 1st Platoon to hit Japs crouching in a foxhole. That was the only firing done by the company's light mortars. When the 2d Platoon came in check, it asked Lieutenant Linebaugh to have 81mm. fire put down just ahead of its lines. He refused. He figured that the left was so badly strung out at the time that any fire which could be put down safely would also be ineffective insofar as the enemy immediately engaged was concerned.

One BAR man, Private First Class James H. Gatlin, had carried on a one-man mop-up campaign during the first phase of the fighting, working over every debris pile at a close range with his weapon. He had been thoughtfully regarding one pile of palm and broken foliage when he saw it move. He fired into it, then lifted the branches and found two dead Japs, their wounds oozing blood. He then went on, firing into other piles, holding the BAR over sideways so that instead of climbing it went forward, and then turning it over and sweeping it back across again.[8] In one other pile he collected three dead Japs after giving it a burst of fire.

As the platoon had come forward it had received a few rounds of sniper fire. When this happened, one or two men began firing at the tops of the few palms that were still standing. This was contagious. More men fired at the tree tops, meanwhile paying little regard to the rubble piles and broken foliage through which they passed. If no fire came from such a spot, they assumed it was safe. It was only when our men began to drop from rifle fire well back of their lines, and the spraying of the tree tops yielded noth-

[8] When fired automatically the BAR tends to rise at the muzzle. This is controllable when the firer is shooting prone, but not in firing while standing. Private Gatlin, by turning his BAR half over as he fired it, obtained a horizontal movement of the gun and distribution of his fire along the ground, instead of a vertical distribution.

ing, that our men learned to prowl everything they came to, either by dosing it with rifle fire or tossing a grenade into it. The BAR proved an excellent weapon for this kind of work.

The 1st Platoon, having freed itself with the aid of the tanks, couldn't understand why the 2d Platoon wasn't going ahead. Neither could Company A, which had been moving along easily on the ocean side of the island. The advancing line was supposed to keep roughly straight. The units on the right, although no great distance from the men who had been checked on the lagoon side, were as remote from them in sympathy and in situation as if they had been on another island.

Derisive calls drifted over from the right flank. "You can't win a war sitting on your ass." That galled the men on the left even more than the invidious comparisons made by the battalion staff over the telephone. "If Company A is able to get forward, why can't the left flank of Company C go ahead?" The 2d Platoon had no ready answer to any of these critics. Engaged as it was, it had no way of knowing that it was carrying the big load for the battalion and that the other outfits were comparatively unengaged. The command in the rear couldn't get this view of the situation.

On the other flank, things were going ahead so leisurely that when water in the canteens began to run low, the men had time to cut up coconuts which littered the ground when the artillery ceased mauling the trees. That flank moved ahead by slow, easy stages to avoid getting too far beyond the 2d Platoon's position. Its experiences were in ironic contrast to what had been going on on the left.

The blockhouse by the road was well-battered when the tank ceased firing upon it. There were several gaping holes by the doorway, through which a dead Jap lay sprawled. One of the men from 1st Platoon tossed a couple of grenades inside and then the line passed on. Before the support got up to it, Staff Sergeant Otis Lasswell, Jr., saw a man from Company D shoot a second Jap as he stuck his head out the door. This made Lasswell wonder if anyone had cleaned out the shelter. He asked Lieutenant Daniel A. Blue if anything had been done to follow up the work of the tank. Blue didn't know. A bulldozer was then brought up to seal the entrance. The driver looked the place over, said: "It's too hot for me," and turned back toward the rear.

Lasswell went after a flame thrower. The flame was shot into all three entrances. The operator then climbed on top of the shelter and shot the flame through a six-inch vent on the roof. "There's no one in there now," he said to Lasswell when he got down. Lasswell agreed. They started to walk away.

Five Japs came out of the shelter with their hands up. One had been hit by a shell and died shortly after. Another had a slight burn on the arm. The other three hadn't been touched.

While they were collecting the Japs, a kitten walked out of the shelter. The troops played with it long enough to discover that it was shell-shocked. When put in any position, it would stay just that way and blink at them. Lieutenant Desmonde left them playing with the kitten and trying to stand it on its head. He went on over to the left to see what was holding up the 2d Platoon. He wanted to get his own 1st Platoon forward and he figured maybe the units on the other end of the line needed a little prodding.

The 1st Platoon's 2d and 3d Squads had moved up to the shelter on the right. During the approach, a couple of Japs were seen sitting in the doorway. They ducked back inside. But these Japs having disappeared, the men took no immediate steps to finish them. They stretched out on the ground around the shelter, resting and waiting for the company's left to get in motion. Half an hour passed. Private First Class Elmer Powell leaned against one end of the shelter, eating a candy bar. At the other end of it, a Jap machine gun fired periodic wild bursts toward Company A. The 1st Platoon's men saw the Jap was just wasting ammunition so they let him have his fun. On the ocean side of the shelter, around the corner from Powell, was another low entryway. A second Jap popped out of it, carrying a machine gun. He stumbled on the steps and the gun went off, alerting the Americans near by.

Private First Class Hjalmar Pederson lay in a shell hole opposite the entrance. Without raising his voice, he said to the man next to him: "My Got, de're cooming oudt." His second shot crumpled the Jap. Powell dropped his candy bar and leaped for the nearest cover, ten yards off. Private Cogar threw a grenade. It dropped fair into the far opening and exploded right under the Jap who had been shooting toward Company A. There was quiet for a minute or two. Then five distinct explosions were heard inside the shelter.

The men figured that that number of Japs had blown themselves up. Under the sudden excitement, their mood changed instantly from extreme carelessness to pronounced caution. They stood at a respectful distance and heaved ten grenades at the doorway. Then they improvised a satchel charge by wiring six blocks of TNT together with a detonator and tossed it in the door. It exploded with a loud report and blew dirt and timber from the building. Right after that the platoon advanced to a position beyond the shelter. Sergeant Romaine Kitcheon, spotter for the mortars, took up a post behind some sand-filled oil drums which protected the entrance to the shelter. He heard a noise, looked up, saw a Jap emerging and shot him through the head.

As the day wore on past noon, the battle lost its sweat for the men of 1st Platoon. The fires still blazed about the island but a strong wind from the eastward was whipping the smoke to the lagoon side. The men saw no sign of the enemy. They were through shooting for the day. They idled behind the palm stumps and in small shell craters and if they snoozed now and then in the strong sunlight, the enemy took no action to rouse them from their slumber. They knew that the left must be having some trouble because they could hear the rattle of automatic fire and snort of grenades exploding on that flank. But that was someone else's fight and the sounds signified little more to them than did the distant rumble of the artillery breaking over Kwajalein Island where the battle of the 32d and 184th Infantry was wearing into its third day. That one hundred yards of mangled palm forest which separated the two platoons made all the difference and their imaginations could not bridge the distance. It was as well so. They could do nothing to help the 2d Platoon and rest is good for weary feet wherever it is to be had. They marked time and they enjoyed the afternoon.

A stray chicken wandered into the 1st Platoon area. Three of the men ran it down. Then came a pig—a 150-pound pig, one of the farm boys present estimated. The pig seemed unconcerned but was straying back from somewhere up in the battle area. Lieutenant Feinstein had found a grass rope among some Jap stores and was carrying it around for a souvenir. He suggested to Kitcheon that they capture the pig, in lieu of anything better to capture. "And I will tie it by the neck," Feinstein said.

"It won't work," said Kitcheon. "You can't hold pigs that way." But he and Private First Class Raymond Cochran ran the pig down. Cochran caught it by the hind leg. The pig squealed and dragged him along the ground and everyone yelled. He and Kitcheon then roped it around the hind legs. In a few minutes it broke away and ran grunting toward the rear. The men kidded Kitcheon. They wondered where the pig had come from. The men of the 2d Platoon could have told them.

While the 2d Platoon had stayed pinned to the ground in the hour-long lapse which followed its buffeting by the artillery, two medium tanks stood steady in the ground occupied by the support squad. They took no part in the action. The platoon leader tried to talk with the crews. But they didn't respond to the telephone and they wouldn't open up when he hammered on the armor. The foot soldiers saw all this and the reaction upon their own spirits was characteristic.

The records of the Central Pacific operation show consistently that whenever tanks and infantry are supposed to be working in close combination and the tanks won't move, the infantry is always reluctant to go forward. The presence of immobilized tanks is a discouragement. They can stall the movement of an infantry that on its own might be quite willing. The 2d Platoon got hung on this rock. Motion was at last restored when on direct order from Colonel Hartl over the radio, the tanks came on up into the ground held by the assault line.

The scattered groups of the platoon responded immediately, and without orders. As the tanks came through, they got up from their cover and moved toward the enemy, even though a wild, harassing fire from rifles and automatic weapons continued to break over the front. Twenty-five yards farther along one tank threw a track on a coconut log and went out of the action. The other tank kept going. It stayed buttoned up and there was no communication. The tank would lurch forward fifteen or twenty yards, the infantry going along with it or a little behind it. Then the tank would stop; the crew wanted to be sure that the infantry was still with them. The infantry would flow on around the sides of it. When the tank again saw the infantry on ahead, it would come through and take the lead for another score of yards.

It was a crazy, jerky advance, continued like a game of leapfrog. But it was appropriate to the situation. For the moment, both arms needed the assurance which came from the presence of the other. As for the infantry movement, some of the men moved ahead at a walking gait with weapons at high port and others moved from cover to cover by short rushes. They advanced, not on orders, but according to their own initiative. If the first man in a group spurted for cover, the others in the group did the same. If two or three in another group started walking out, the whole group moved out the same way. Gradually the rest of the line moved up abreast of the half-squad which had held the advanced position on the beach.

They advanced perhaps 125 yards when the squad moving just within the line of cover along the shoulder of the beach saw a Jap caliber .50 air-cooled gun off to its left about twenty feet. The gun was pointed in the direction of the morning landings and is presumed to be the weapon which hit three men in the headquarters group when they came in on a later wave. The tank had passed on beyond the gun after firing a machine-gun burst down into the pit.

Sergeant Roger Horning crawled up to within about ten feet of the gun and fired one round from his M1 into the magazine. The gun blew up. Some of his men covered him as he crawled up to the pit and looked in. He was face to

424

face with a live Jap who blinked at him; they were so close that they could have bumped heads. It "scared the living hell" out of Horning. He flopped back into a shell hole just at the edge of the pit, a grenade in his right hand and a rifle in his left. As he recoiled, he threw the grenade. It came right back to him, rolling down the sand and settling at his feet.

He looked at it and kept on looking at it; he didn't think either of touching it or moving away from it. His thought and his body were paralyzed. The grenade was a dud. Seconds passed and he realized that the grenade wasn't going to explode. He jumped up and ran back to the squad, yelling for grenades. There were none at hand. He ran farther back, yelling for a flame thrower. Someone signalled him that the flame thrower was out of order.

Returning to the pit, he found that Sergeant Robert Genung had come up with an improvised satchel charge. Horning threw it at the pit, but he was excited and the cast was wild. The charge exploded across the surface, spinning the ground around. The two BAR men who had been covering Horning walked up to the pit, firing as they went. As they reached the edge, one BAR ran out of ammunition and the other jammed. They scurried back to make the necessary readjustments.

"This time," said Horning, "one of you fire during the advance and the other hold fire until you reach the pit." That was what they did. As they pumped lead into the pit, they saw one Jap fall but they could not see what was beyond him.

The spider holes began just beyond this gun position. The beach proper, which had been unoccupied during the first stage of the advance, had been organized from this point on with small pits just large enough to hold one man and in such juxtaposition to holes on beyond it that the occupant could move in either direction to quick cover. The holes had been covered with tin sheeting, palm fronds or other camouflage material, and could not be seen from a ten-foot distance. Amid these nests of small and rude individual positions were a number of redoubts built solidly of logs and bulwarked with oil drums or iron

425

sheeting, so that along the beach the enemy ground was much like a crude trench system organized in depth. Flanking the lagoon, railroad iron had been cabled to the coconut trees to repel tanks or other vehicles coming ashore. The 2d Platoon was approaching the area generally from the flank, but the detailed defenses of the ground were such that there was menace in every direction.

As Horning crawled on beyond the flank of the machine-gun pit, he saw a layer of palm fronds on the ground twenty yards to the fore. Quite suddenly the palms moved, as if from pressure below, and he knew there was a Jap there. He told Lieutenant Elliott what he had seen, and Elliott ordered him to go forward and prowl the spot.

He crawled on, five, six yards, then he yelled back to Elliott: "I won't go on until I'm sure there's no one in that pit." Elliott threw three grenades in the pit. Horning heard them explode and he crawled on. He got up to the fronds and under the edges he saw a black pit and something moving within. He pulled the pins of two grenades and rolled them over the edge. Both exploded. The Jap inside the hole took death sitting down.

Private First Class Robert Everett had crawled up to Horning while he was working. He then crawled on around the hole. Horning, preoccupied with the grenades, didn't see Everett rise up and stand with his back to another patch of fronds just beyond the first hole. When his gaze rose, there was just time to yell: "Watch it!" A Jap from out of the second hole was making a flying tackle at Everett's knees. Everett spun out of it, and as he twisted, he jammed the muzzle of his BAR against the Jap's head and pulled the trigger. They went down together, but only Everett got up.

That was the way it went. The holes were everywhere. Each one had to be searched from close up. Every spot where a man might be hiding had to be stabbed out. So greatly was the beach littered with broken foliage that it was like looking through a haystack for a few poisoned needles.

Before the 1st and 3d Squads gave over this kind of duty for the day, two men had been killed and eight wounded by fire from the spider holes. The attention of all hands had to

426

be focused on the foreground. The fire which cut the men down came from the spider holes farther up the line. It was the kind of bitter going that made it necessary for the junior leaders to prod their men constantly. The leader of the 3d Squad had been trying to get his men forward against the fire. Private First Class John Treager got up, rushed forward about ten yards, hit the dirt, fired a few shots with his BAR and crumpled with a bullet in his head.

Somewhat farther along, a bayonet was seen sticking up through a patch of fronds. The Jap crouched within it hadn't room to draw in the whole length of the weapon. Private First Class Edward Fiske fired his BAR at the hole; the dried fronds caught fire from the tracers. At that point Fiske ran out of ammunition.

Private First Class Julian Guterrez then took up the fire with his M1. He stood directly above the hole and fired down into it. Then the hole exploded; the Jap inside had turned a grenade on himself. A man's shattered arm came flying out of the hole and hit Guterrez on the shoulder, splattering blood all over his face and clothing. The arm bounced off and fell to the side. As Guterrez looked at it, fascinated and horror-stricken, he saw another bayonet rising out of a patch of fronds just beyond the outstretched and still-quivering fingers. He yelled to a man behind him. The man relayed a grenade and Guterrez pitched it with all of his might into the patch of fronds. It erupted a shower of palm leaves and blood and flesh.

Guterrez reeled over toward the lagoon to cleanse himself of the blood. Before he could reach the water, in sight of all the other men, he vomited all over the beach. Minutes passed before he could gather himself together again.

By this time 2d Platoon, officers and men, had lost all sense of time. They had come along for several hours, clearing the frond coverings from the spider holes with their bayonets, where they did not first blast them after detecting some sign of the enemy. They were dog tired. Their losses had been fairly heavy. Yet oddly enough, most of them thought it was late morning though the day had worn into late afternoon. Lieutenant Linebaugh had given battalion headquarters a report on casualties. He then talked to Lieutenant Elliott about a relief. Elliott went around to his men and told them to halt in place until the 3d Platoon came through.

Lieutenant Blue told his men to drop packs and gas masks and the 3d moved up, two squads on the line. Each squad had two scouts out front, the leading scout moving about fifteen to twenty yards ahead of the platoon and the second splitting the distance back to the line. No tanks went forward with the men; it wasn't the kind of fight in which tanks could do much good. However, the situation was quiet for the moment. When the 3d reached the front, the men of the 2d were sitting around tight-mouthed. There was no fire.

The platoon advanced at a walk in squad column and kept going. As they passed the 2d, Genung said to Blue: "Tell your men that they must watch out for the spider holes. They must search every one of them." Lieutenant Blue then saw for the first time what 2d Platoon had been up against. As far as he could see up the beach, there was a reticulation of the palm frond patches which meant danger to his men. He passed the word to them: "Go at every patch with fire first and then with your bayonet." He kept telling them that that was what they must do.

They moved on twenty-five, thirty, forty yards. There was no enemy fire. The men searched the first few lines of holes diligently, ripping the fronds off with their bayonets. They found nothing. Lieutenant Blue noticed that they had already begun to ease up, hitting a hole and then skipping a hole. They went on another twenty-five yards. The man ahead of Blue stepped across a frond patch and kept on moving.

Blue yelled: "Godammit, what are you doing—stepping across a hole you're supposed to search. There may be a Jap in there." A Jap rifle lay across the hole. From underneath, a hand reached up for it before Blue could close the distance. Blue saw the hand; saw, also, that five of his men were beyond it. He took the chance and fired at the hand. The bullet split the hand at the knuckles. The Jap had started to rise, but Blue's rifle was so close that the blast knocked him back again and the helmet flew from his head. Blue fired two slugs into the back of the Jap's head.

"Start looking into every hole or we'll all be killed," Blue shouted to his men.

It was then that Staff Sergeant Pete Deini, who had accidentally shot a man on Ennylobegan Island, came to the fight. Deini had been walking along like the others, but had been doing a lot of thinking. He knew there was something wrong with the platoon. He could feel it. He knew the men were afraid. He felt fear in himself. But he wondered how he could feel it in the others. Then he got it. The sergeants had clammed up. The men were accustomed to hearing them bark. When they didn't, the men knew the sergeants were fearful, and they could not rally their own confidence.

He found what to him was the obvious answer: Somebody had to talk it up and keep talking it up; it wasn't enough simply to act or to bark an order after things had gone wrong. He saw his duty and throughout the rest of the afternoon he spark-plugged the whole operation. Moving from group to group, he showed them how the thing had to be done, and he talked as he worked. When he saw men hesitate in front of a spider hole, he went through them, ripped the fronds away, and used the bayonet, if the bayonet was needed.

As he worked, he talked without ceasing: "Come on. You can do the same thing. Watch me. There are more of them. Keep busy. Keep moving. Keep your eyes open." Then he moved on to another hole. It was Lieutenant Blue's estimate that Deini in person cleared out at least fifty per cent of the positions covered by the platoon and that the thoroughness of the other men was due almost wholly to him. The other men acknowledged it, only they said their lieutenant shot too low when he credited Deini with only half of the work. The man does not talk well. He has an impediment in his speech. But his was the clearest voice sounded by a junior leader during the invasion of Kwajalein Atoll.

Spider holes in large number still confronted the left of the platoon when the right came up to an obstacle of a

429

different kind. Between the road and the shoulder of the beach the ground fell away into a deep swale which had been cleared for about seventy-five feet in both directions. Within the swale was a shelter for pigs. Vines grew all around and over it and tin sheeting had blown down around the sides so that it was impossible to see clearly what lay within. Forward of this penned area was another small structure—a shed or feed house—lying close to the road.

The left flank, moving along the beach, was about abreast of the pen but had not yet seen it, when Private First Class Vern Howell, the front scout of the right-hand squad, came alongside it. He stepped up to the nearest corner and the second scout, Private Clifford Hahn, caught up with him. Howell was puzzled. It was his first time in the lines.

"What is the front line like?" he asked Hahn.

"You're it," said Hahn. "Didn't you know it?"

"But what do you do?"

Hahn replied: "You just keep going until you see someone shooting at you. And you keep looking all around."

Howell kept going. The squad had come on up even with him and the two scouts continued on, Howell some feet ahead. He paused for a minute and squatted at the forward corner of the inclosure. Then he began to straighten up. As he came half-erect, fire from the pen and the little building riddled him. Then men of the squad saw his body jerk, but he did not fall. He sagged over against the side of the inclosure.

There was no recoil in the platoon. They knew where the fire had come from. They weren't sure whether Howell was dead. But the sight of him standing there galvanized them. The squad from the beach moved up to the left side of the inclosure. The right squad pressed up against the rear. They could not lie prone and fire. To bear upon the pen at all, they had to stand erect and shoot down into it. But they gave it everything they had—BAR and rifle fire, grenades and finally satchel charges.

Private First Class Edwin Jeffers, a BAR man, ran up to within reaching distance of where Howell stood, put his BAR on the hole through which the Jap volley had poured, and kept on firing until he was called back by his platoon

430

leader, who figured that Jeffers would get it if he stayed there. The fire was still hot. A first-aid man got up to the men who were firing along the rear of the pen. Howell was pointed out to him. The men figured if he could stand he must still be alive.

"Do you think I can get up there?" the aid man asked Sergeant Lasswell.

"That's up to you," Lasswell answered. "I can't tell you to go."

He asked another man and got the same answer.

The aid man didn't say anything. He took one more look forward and then ran toward Howell. That was too much for Private First Class Jeffers. He couldn't stand the idea of the man going out alone, and he too went running forward to cover the aid man with his BAR. They reached Howell. The aid man took hold of his shoulder. The figure fell over, and from the manner of the fall, the men of the squad knew he was dead. Jeffers and the aid man tore back for cover.

The fight went on. Lasswell, looking through the rails of the pen saw a wounded Jap lifting a rifle. He fired three slugs into him. At each hit, the Jap shook all over but kept crawling toward Lasswell, pulling himself with his elbows. Lasswell gave him four more bullets and the man died.

Deini had grenaded the pen from the right and had heard men scream as the grenades went off. He then ran around to the left of the pen. Sergeant Steinkamp saw a Jap moving toward the rails on the left and killed him with his first bullet. A rifle poked up through the vines in the center. Deini saw it, realized that it was pointed straight at him, ducked instantly.

Private First Class Nick E. Eloff was standing right behind Deini and the bullet hit him in the wrist. Deini saw that he couldn't get the Jap marksman from that side, and he whipped back to the right where there was a good opening. He shot the Jap with his rifle. Then he ran out of ammunition, reached for more and found that a Jap grenade had cut away his ammunition belt and half of one trouser. He had felt the burst but hadn't believed it was that close. He called for a satchel charge, and he heaved

431

it far over the rail at the spot where he had seen the grenade thrower's hand come up from above the timber. There was a terrific explosion which shook down the building inside the pen. Private First Class Thomas Burrescia brought up his flame thrower on the beach side and tried to reach the mass of wreckage with it. But the wind was too strong and the flame blew back on our men.

All of this time battalion headquarters was prodding the company commander to get the platoon forward, and he in turn was prodding Lieutenant Blue. He was told to leave the pigpen to Company B which would do the mop-up job, and to get on with the advance. But Blue figured that the commanders were much too remote from his situation to judge of it. As the pen grew quiet and it appeared that the Jap detachment which had driven the pigs out of their cover was pretty well liquidated, he still did not wish to leave the safety of his rear in Company B's hands. He couldn't see the support force and wanted to be sure.

So the 1st Squad moved around the pigpen by way of the beach and took position in front of the pen. The support squad came up to the line on the left and the platoon continued forward. A medium tank came along a few minutes later and after the covering squad had moved out of muzzle-blast range, the tank fired three rounds of 75 HE into the pen. Still, a live Jap was caught crawling from the pen on the following morning.

Spider holes confronted the left of the line for another 150 yards. Deini again led the way through them, working four times as hard as any other and talking to the men all of the time. They reached another Jap air-raid shelter then. A medium tank was sent against it. The tank was still pumping 75 shells into it when Company B came through and Lieutenant Blue's men fell back to the mop-up position.

As for the soldier Deini had accidentally wounded by a bullet from a Jap pistol on Ennylobegan Island, the Medical Corps managed to save him to fight in other battles.

END ON SAIPAN

by Maj. Frank Hough

The seizure of the Marshalls * and MacArthur's drive along northern New Guinea had effectively flanked Truk; had provided us with bases from which it could be kept neutralized and from which we could mount an attack against it should we so desire. But it had not been cut off from the homeland and its intermediate bases. Troops and supplies could still be poured in. This was an expensive process now, but we had reason to believe that it was being done, and with some success. Truk, a tough nut to begin with, was getting no softer fast, despite the knocking out of its air power.

The same applied to a number of other places. Our swift conquest of Tarawa had startled the Japanese. Seriously alarmed by the success of our operations in the Marshalls, they set about a hurried modification of their basic strategy. So long as their outer defense line held, their intermediate defenses had been of secondary importance. Now, in a kind of frenzy, they began pouring troops, equipment and sup-

* Maj. Frank Hough, *The Island War,* p. 211: Resistance on Kwajalein Atoll was crushed completely by February 7, 1944. One week later, an assault force moved out to invade Eniwetok, another atoll in the Marshalls, with two good airfields only 669 miles from Truk. The Marshall Islands conquest gave the Allies bases for new air and sea operations, fanning out over a radius of 2,000 miles to the Marianas and Palau. Airfields on the Marshalls, once in operation, effectively neutralized Truk. "Island-hopping had evolved into island-leapfrogging. In the process tens of thousands of soldiers on whom Japan had depended to retard the progress of the U.S. sat impotently on their arms without firing a shot from the beginning to the end of the war."

plies into the Marianas and western Carolines at an unprecedented rate.

Experience had proved that there was no foretelling with any certainty where we would strike next; therefore, they were obliged to reinforce all of their garrisons in this area, giving such priorities as they could to those spots which, to their minds, appeared our most probable objectives. As usual, when they had any leeway at all for their calculations, they guessed wrong.

The strain on their resources was severe, aggravated as it was by the brilliant work of the U.S. submarines in the waters which their convoys must traverse. How many thousands of lives and tons of supplies and shipping were lost during this period probably never will be known.

To obtain the necessary troops, they were obliged to draw upon armies in the homeland, China, and Manchuria. One aspect of the long-range effect of this was brought out dramatically more than a year later. When the Russians attacked in Manchuria on the eve of the war's end, they, and the world in general, were somewhat astonished to discover that the vaunted Kwantung Army was only an ineffective hollow shell of its former self. But the men who had fought their way across the Pacific were not surprised; they knew that the cream of that army had died long since, out there in the islands.

But all this is second-guessing; utilizing knowledge obtained during and after the operation in question. At the time the Marianas campaign was determined upon, we knew only enough to convince the planners that, while this would constitute a bold stroke, the indications were that it would not be a rash one. The threefold advantage to be gained in the shortest possible time was the determining factor: (1) Truk would be absolutely and irrevocably cut off; (2) we would be established firmly in the enemy's intermediate defense line; (3) we would have air bases within heavy-bomber range of Tokyo itself.

Reliable intelligence had been exceedingly difficult to obtain. We had some fair estimates of the respective garrison strengths at the time of the Marshalls operation and we knew that these had been heavily reinforced since, but

434

whether they had been doubled, tripled or even quadrupled we had no sure way of estimating. This was especially the case with the main Japanese base, Saipan, which also served as a staging point for the entire area, as well as for Truk, Woleai and other strong points in the central and western Carolines. Any attack here would be certain to encounter an inestimable number of transient troops standing by for shipment elsewhere, over and above the greatly augmented garrison.

Second only to Saipan in strength and importance was Guam, our former possession which had been lost in the early days of the war. Guam was the southernmost of the Marianas and the largest of the group—indeed, the largest island in the Central Pacific between the Hawaiians and the Philippines. Of lesser importance but known to contain garrisons and airfields were: Rota, thirty-two miles northeast of Guam; Tinian, two and one half miles southwest of Saipan and within easy artillery range of that island; and Pagan, 172 miles north of Saipan.

To strike this vital blow against what was, in many respects, an unknown quantity, the High Command mustered the most powerful force to operate in the Pacific up to this time; the largest force ever to operate under Marine command. This included both Amphibious Corps, embracing three Marine divisions and one Marine brigade, all reinforced, and two reinforced Army Infantry divisions, plus Corps and miscellaneous supporting troops. Here was every assault unit the Marine Corps had in the Pacific at the time, with the sole exception of the First Division, as yet unrecuperated from the protracted New Britain campaign.

The chain-of-command was unique and somewhat confusing, although it worked out excellently. The plan called for division of the whole force into two groups under single over-all command: the Northern Group [1] (V Amphibious Corps, Lieutenant General Holland M. Smith) to attack Saipan, and, when the situation warranted, to stage a shore-to-

---

[1] For official purposes this group was given the unwieldy title: Northern Troops and Landing Force (NTLF). Southern Group was similarly designated STLF.

shore assault on Tinian; and the Southern Group (III Amphibious Corps, Major General Roy S. Geiger) to attack Guam. The Marine Corps at this time had no echelon in the field higher than an amphibious corps; yet here was a situation where two amphibious corps must operate together under a single over-all command which, according to book, simply did not exist.

The troops assigned to the Northern operation numbered altogether about 77,413, not all of them, of course, strictly assault troops. The combat units included the Second Marine Division, veterans of Guadalcanal and Tarawa; the Fourth Marine Division, veterans of the Marshalls; and the Twenty-seventh Infantry Division (Army), one regiment of which had fought at Makin, another at Eniwetok. Supporting these were various corps troops, notably artillery, both Army and Marine, the 7th Field Depot, four Marine and four Army Amphibian Tractor battalions operating a total of 722 vehicles, and one Army DUKW (amphibious truck) battalion plus one separate company.

Also brought along was an odd orphan battalion whose somewhat enigmatic status might better be cleared up at the outset. This was made up of men, many of them combat veterans, who had been crowded out of the divisions by the revision of the Tables of Organization. Known originally as the 2nd Marine Provisional Battalion, on the eve of sailing for Saipan it was designated 1st Battalion, 29th Marines, the remainder of that regiment being currently in training at New River, North Carolina, and due overseas shortly. Throughout this operation 1/29 was attached to the 8th Marines, Second Division, forming in effect a fourth battalion of that regiment and proving a very useful addition.

Just what strength the Japanese could muster against this array was not known with any certainty. Estimates ranged from twenty thousand to twenty-five thousand combat troops, which would seem to give us fair assurance of having the minimum three-to-one numerical superiority deemed necessary to success in an amphibious assault against a strongly held position. This proved a remarkably shrewd estimate for all practical purposes. Later studies, during and after the operation, indicated that actually there were

436

29,662 enemy troops on Saipan on D-Day, but the discrepancy was largely compensated for by the fact that the most recently arrived were virtually unarmed as a result of U.S. submarine attacks on their convoy on the way out.

The Marine divisions assigned to this operation had had combat experience, but not in terrain even approximately resembling this. Here was no small, flat atoll island to be overrun in a matter of hours of concentrated, savage fighting: like Tarawa, where the Second Division had fought, or Roi-Namur, where the Fourth Division had received its baptism of fire. Nor was it, by any stretch of the imagination, another Guadalcanal. There the Second Division had mastered the close-in bitterness of jungle fighting; here they would be mostly in the open, against a dug-in enemy strongly supported by artillery.

Another novel feature was provided by the civilian inhabitants of the place. Hitherto, the only natives encountered on target areas in the Pacific had been scattered handfuls of Melanesians and Micronesians, semisavages who had no special stake in the outcome and were interested only in keeping out of the way until the issue was settled. But Saipan, as a result of Japanese development and immigration, had attained a reasonably high degree of civilization and boasted a civilian population reliably estimated to number in the vicinity of twenty thousand persons.

The attack on Saipan achieved tactical surprise, to a greater degree, perhaps, than the planners had dared to hope. Although repeated air strikes had neutralized the airfields, so had similar strikes neutralized all the other islands within reach. It was not until the intensive two-day prelanding naval bombardment was well under way that the Japanese High Command on Saipan became convinced that their island, not any one of a dozen others, was to be our true objective.

There was a reason for this. In spite of the urgency of strengthening their intermediate defense line, the Japanese were physically incapable of strengthening all these islands simultaneously; hence, had been obliged to work out a system of priorities. In their infinite wisdom, they reached the conclusion that MacArthur's drive along the New

437

Guinea coast would outrun the drive across the Central Pacific and therefore assigned to the Palaus, far to the southwest, top priority on men, armament, building materials. The Marianas' elaborately planned defenses were not scheduled for completion until November.

But this was all to the good on 15 June, 1944: beaches and reefs were unmined, heavy coast defense guns lay unmounted beside their half-finished emplacements, permanent defense positions were makeshift or negligible, and there was no organized system of defense in depth on all of Saipan.

Once they had determined our intentions, however, the Japanese command reacted with their customary vigor, and somewhat unaccustomed acumen. They picked our landing beaches accurately and refused to be fooled by any feints elsewhere, although a last-minute demonstration by the floating reserve off Tanapag Harbor did delay transfer of one regiment temporarily. Already they had considerable artillery in position to defend the threatened area, and more was rushed to the scene with all possible expediency. Unfortunately for them, the ferocity of the naval gunfire and air strikes caused such heavy casualties that they were obliged to move the guns to the reverse slopes of the low ridges in that neighborhood where their full effectiveness could not be brought to bear until the landings were well under way.

As in the Gilberts and Marshalls, the landing had to be made over coral, the fringing reef here extending seaward a distance of eight to twelve hundred yards. There was a narrow deep-water passage through to the docks at Charan Kanoa, but enemy artillery had this so well zeroed-in that it proved unusable until these guns could be put out of action. So it was over the reef that the Marines came, and so well had the technique been developed as a result of previous operations that seven hundred-odd amphtracks landed some eight thousand men in the first twenty minutes.

But such are the complications of any ship-to-shore movement that even an unopposed landing is bound to be fouled-up in one way or another. And enemy artillery, mortar and anti-boat gunfire made the Saipan landing a grim and bloody business, for all the expedition with which it was

438

carried off. The amphibious tanks, which were supposed to support the assault waves across the reef and then spearhead the drive inland, proved so slow and clumsy that they were soon outstripped by the LVT's, thus losing much of their effectiveness.

The invasion began as a toe-to-toe slugging match and continued that way throughout the first two days. The Japanese were supremely confident. They had an unusual proportion of heavy weapons and tanks. Despite the fact that they had not really expected to be attacked· until the last minute, they had managed to get plenty of troops to the scene; even though these did not have permanent prepared positions of the sort they might have liked, terrain features were all in their favor. And, as so often happened, they underestimated the strength of the attackers.

The evening of D-Day found the 10,000-yard beachhead pushed inland to a maximum depth of about 1,500 yards. Artillery was set up and firing, tanks and the Division command posts were ashore. But the situation was far from good. The Japanese still held dominating heights in front of the Marine positions, still had plenty of artillery and heavy mortars. Our lines were not integrated in places, units being out of direct contact with their neighbors. The largest and most serious gap was the one which had existed all day between the two divisions. In an effort to close this, 1/29 (the orphan battalion previously described) had been landed during the afternoon on the right of the 8th Marines, to which regiment they remained attached throughout the campaign. But the gap still remained at nightfall, and the two divisions dug in with their inner flanks deeply refused (bent backward).

There was artillery fire all night; heavier artillery fire than troops of ours had ever before received from the Japanese.

The second day saw a continuation of the dogged slugging match, and again the situation at nightfall was one to cause concern. We still lacked possession of the ridge which marked the O-1 Phase Line. The 165th Infantry, of the Twenty-seventh Infantry Division, had been thrown in on the left of the 23rd Marines in another attempt to close the gap between the divisions; another futile effort. Casualties for the two days already ran over 3,500—twenty per cent of those to be sustained during the entire campaign. Tanks had proved largely useless in the face of so much enemy artillery. With all Marine reserve troops ashore and committed, there was real danger of losing the initiative should fighting continue on such a scale, a serious business at this stage of an operation.

One puzzling feature of those first two days was the small number of enemy dead found in the overrun positions. Past experience indicated that, with such heavy shelling and intensive fighting, heavy casualties to the defending side were inevitable. Yet few indications were found that this was the case here. Not until later, when the advance began to discover concentrations of Japanese bodies well behind the former lines, was it definitely established that the enemy had been carrying off their own dead. This was a new wrinkle with them, and it fooled, or partially fooled, a number of our people. It was to recur repeatedly, however, in subsequent operations.

With the swinging of the main drive toward the north, clearing the southeastern corner of the island was assigned to the Twenty-seventh Infantry Division, two regiments of which were now ashore. The 165th Infantry secured Aslito airfield on D + 3 and drove on to the eastern shore. Here they wheeled southward, with the 105th on their right, gradually driving the enemy back to the narrowing confines of Nafutan Point. The terrain here was rugged and heavily jungled, making progress slow and difficult. After several days of strenuous work, however, the surviving Japanese were penned into a small pocket on high ground near the tip of the point, where the 2nd Battalion, 105th Infantry, was left to contain them while the 165th and 106th, which had landed on D + 5, were transferred northward to join the main drive.

The dual aftermaths of this move did not occur until some days later and will be discussed here in their chronological relation to the campaign as a whole.

D + 3 definitely marked the conclusion of the initial phase of the Saipan operation. Matters had not worked out strictly in accordance with expectations. Casualties had been higher than anticipated, for one thing: 4,856 altogether, including six battalion commanders, some of the assault units sustaining up to sixty per cent. Somewhat makeshift means had to be devised for evacuation of the wounded. These were taken offshore by such craft as happened to be available for the purpose and transshipped to such transports as had the means to care for them, often before adequate records could be made. Since these transports were departing from time to time for widely divergent ports, men carried on the casualty lists as missing in action often turned up weeks and even months later in hospitals in such unexpected places as the Admiralty Islands, Guadalcanal, even Nouméa.

Another difficulty was caused by the civilian population. Civil Affairs officers were included on both Division and Corps T/O's (Table of Organization), but this was the first time they had been called upon to cope with the problem on anything but the smallest scale. They were wholly unable to obtain adequate personnel for the job, or to get priorities on food, transportation or gear necessary for caring for their charges.

Although the island's second town lay directly in the zone of the initial assault, it was assumed for some obscure reason that few, if any, civilians would be taken during the first few days. Actually there were some four hundred in our hands on D-Day, 1,500 by the end of D + 2; wretched, homeless creatures for whom we had no food, no clothes, no guards and not even the beginnings of a stockade where they might be secured and sheltered. Fortunately they proved patient, docile people, and soon supplies of Japanese food were captured which proved sufficient for their immediate needs, although the conditions under which they were obliged to exist for some time reflected little credit upon their captors.

There were three other features of the Japanese defensive effort during those first four days which, although their effect on the outcome was negligible, deserve mention here.

Early on the morning of D + 3, the Japanese injected an element of novelty into the proceedings by attempting an amphibious operation of their own. Intelligence had been aware for some time that the enemy had organized special units whose object was to effect landings behind our lines,

441

on the not wholly ridiculous theory that, once the assault troops were well engaged some distance inland, the beaches would be exceedingly vulnerable. These special units had, on paper, well worked-out T/O's and quite elaborate tactical instructions, which we had never had the opportunity of seeing them attempt to carry out until that morning of 18 June. Then, in the first light of dawn, thirty-five landing barges were discovered making their way out of Tanapag Harbor, heading south with bland disregard for the powerful naval force standing by some distance to seaward. Not that this force was necessary; with the aid of a lone destroyer, the LCI gunboats blew the whole flotilla out of the water in a matter of minutes.

Another feature was air attack. The first Condition Red sounded early in the night of D-Day, and because the enemy air potential in the area was known to be considerable, caused the transport convoy to put to sea. They might as well have saved themselves the trouble. Only two to six planes came over, dropped a few poorly directed bombs and departed hurriedly. Such raids became almost nightly features throughout the campaign, with never anything resembling a serious attack in force. In the course of twenty-six small raids during fourteen nights, fourteen of the raiders were shot down by AA fire, and after the captured airfield had been made operational for our own planes the danger was still further lessened.

Long-range artillery fire from neighboring Tinian, five thousand yards to the southwest, also proved an occasional nuisance, nothing more. Some of our own 155's were assigned to deal with this. Time after time they seemed to have knocked out the enemy emplacements, only to have the guns open up again a day or so later. It was merely harassing fire, however, poorly directed and in the main ineffective.

By now the Japanese failure must have been evident even to themselves. Far from driving the invaders into the sea, they themselves had been driven from their strong positions, forced back all along the line. Their communications had been so disrupted that, although this was not immediately apparent, they lacked the means to organize major counter-

442

attacks with sufficient promptness to cope with changing situations. Yet their morale remained unimpaired, as it would for many days to come before the bitter, desperate end.

One reason for this was their extraordinary powers of self-deception. A complete log of incoming and outgoing radio messages, captured later, illustrated this graphically. Abject failure did nothing to diminish the confident boastfulness of the island command. Over the air waves, the battle they fought was terrific indeed, with every retreat a brilliant victory inflicting fantastic losses upon the rash invaders. No one reading through those dispatches, without knowledge of what was actually happening, could avoid the conviction that the Japanese were winning, and handsomely. And that, apparently, is just what the people at home believed. Not until the last suicide-bent straggler leaped into the sea from Marpi Point did the Government have any real inkling that the battle was going against them, that Saipan had been irrevocably doomed for three weeks, and the blow hit with such stunning force as to bring the Tojo Cabinet down with a crash that shook the whole Greater East Asia Co-Prosperity Sphere.

But the home Government had been practicing precisely the same sort of mumbo jumbo on its own part. For encouragement of the brave boys at the front, it cooked up a series of smashing victories all over the Pacific and sank the whole U.S. Navy two or three times more. And the fighting men seemed to accept all this as no more than the literal truth. What if a considerable portion of the "sunken" enemy fleet lay in plain sight offshore shelling the daylights out of them at leisure, and the skies were dark with the invaders' planes from carriers and the captured airfield? The mighty Navy of Nippon would soon take care of those interlopers, sink them as many times more as might be necessary.

On D + 4 (19 June) realignments for the northward drive had been completed, and the advance began. The going was slow and produced some hard though unspectacular fighting. The southern portion of the island, low and comparatively level, with canefields and much cleared land, had

443

been mostly secured by now, and the advance lay across rising ground, increasingly brush covered, toward the dominating height of Mount Tapotchau.

Here were encountered with increasing frequency those geological phenomena common to such formations, which were to play such an important part in all operations in the western islands: coral-limestone caves, occurring naturally as a result of the upward pressure of volcanic forces which had created the island and broken its surface into sharp ridges and ravines. These caves furnished splendid defensive positions, particularly to a people with the naturally underground tendencies and endless patience of the Japanese. They occurred usually in the faces of cliffs, in defilade from artillery or naval gunfire and all but invulnerable to aerial bombing. They were susceptible to man-made improvements, but fortunately on Saipan there had been little time or materials available for such work. Here were few of the reinforced concrete bulkheads, steel doors, elaborate galleries which would be encountered in some later operations. Nor had many of the natural positions been developed to obtain scientifically interlocking fields of fire for mutual protection.

The caves on Saipan could usually be by-passed, and this was precisely what was done. The assault troops pushed on, keeping unrelenting pressure on the enemy, leaving the reduction of the caves and their immobilized occupants to special mopping-up details from the reserve, liberally equipped with flame throwers and demolition charges.

The movement pivoted on the 2nd Marines, holding the extreme left, on the island's western shore. This unit had seized its sector of the designated final beachhead line and held there, making no advance at all until D + 9, when they moved to the outskirts of Garapan. They had received special training in town fighting, hitherto unknown in the Pacific, and had as one of their principal objects the capture of the island capital.

The 6th Marines, on the right of the 2nd, did not do much advancing either during the early stages but patrolled extensively to their front. On their right the 8th (with 1/29

444

attached) faced exceedingly difficult terrain, rising ruggedly to Tapotchau itself.

At the beginning of the drive, the Fourth Division adjoined the Second Division on the right, with the 23rd and 24th Marines in line, the 25th in reserve, though these regimental positions were shifted from time to time. This was comparatively simple while they were traversing the narrow waist of the island where Magicienne Bay cut deeply inland. By the evening of D + 7, however, they had reached the upper end of the bay where the broad, blunt projection of the Kagman Peninsula adds another two miles, approximately, to the island's width. To cope with this suddenly expanded front, it was necessary to bring the Twenty-seventh Infantry Division forward to take over the center of the lines while the Fourth took over the new sector on the right, thereby giving rise to one of the most unfortunate incidents in the whole Pacific war.

For a fair understanding of this controversial subject, it may be well to consider the position in which the members of the Twenty-seventh Division found themselves when they were moved into the front lines on D + 8.

Although the 165th Infantry had seen action on Makin and the 106th on Eniwetok, this had been of brief duration and fought under utterly different conditions than those encountered on Saipan. Furthermore, the Army's training differed in several essentials from that of the Marines, as did certain tactical conceptions of its leaders. Yet now three infantry regiments (less 2/105) were placed between two veteran Marine divisions to advance across naturally difficult terrain contested by a determined enemy.

The result was that not only did they fail to keep pace with the advance of the elements on either flank, but for the first two days they failed to achieve any essential advance at all.

They had been trained to conserve their strength; to rely upon artillery and air strikes to knock out major obstacles in their path before committing the infantry to assault, regardless of how long this might take. The Marine hypothesis, on the other hand, held time to be of the essence. An amphibious operation against a sizable land mass was utterly dependent upon the uninterrupted flow of supplies across the landing beaches: the offensive must be sustained and the enemy kept off balance until a final beachhead line is established beyond artillery range of these beaches and deep enough to insure against a sudden breakthrough in force to the rear areas, otherwise the beaches cannot be considered secure and the whole operation remains in jeopardy. This had been the main tactical consideration at Guadalcanal, Bougainville and Cape Gloucester.

Cut from the same cloth was a difference in tactical method which contributed further to slowing down the advance in the center. With the object of keeping unremitting pressure on the enemy, the Marine units continued advancing until dusk, when they dug in on a continuous line of double foxholes, either with no flanks or with the flanks deeply refused. The Army units, on the other hand, halted an hour or more before dark and established a series of mutually supporting strong points: ideally, two companies of a battalion forward, each dug in on a full perimeter defense, and the third some distance behind and covering the gap between them.

Each method had its characteristic advantages—and disadvantages. The Marines claimed that theirs, in addition to maintaining the utmost pressure on the enemy, provided the greatest possible protection against that Japanese tactical specialty, infiltration. It was, however, much harder on the men and might have proved a serious weakness in the event of a major breakthrough since nothing remained behind the front line except for the mortars and the command posts. They contended further that the Army method was a setup for infiltration, especially since the early hour of digging-in gave the enemy plenty of time to scout the position by daylight and form their plans accordingly.

That the Army method constituted a stronger defense in depth was undeniable, but this appeared a minor point in view of the enemy's apparent inability, since D + 2, to attack in force. And even this argument was weakened subsequently when the only two major breakthroughs achieved by the Japanese during the campaign were effected at the expense of the ill-starred 105th Infantry.

446

There were other minor differences, all stemming from the same root, notably methods of using artillery and the Army's refusal to by-pass enemy pockets of resistance, however ineffectual and immobilized these might be. The difference in theory was, at this stage, a fundamental one. The Army contended that Marine methods were reckless of human life; unnecessarily so. The Marines held the Army to be overcautious to the point of timidity; that securing with all possible speed was all important in an amphibious operation, and that the smaller number of initial casualties incurred by the Army method was more than counterbalanced in the end owing to the necessarily longer duration of the campaign.

What it all added up to was that, on this first attempt at a unified operation, the two theories were not readily reconciled. When the Twenty-seventh Division could not, or would not, keep pace with the two Marine divisions, the inside flanks of those units were left dangerously exposed, to the peril of the entire effort. And when, after two days, Major General Ralph Smith, Commanding General of the Twenty-seventh, could not (or, again, would not) take the steps necessary to remedy the situation, Lieutenant General Holland M. Smith, Commanding General of the V Amphibious Corps and Northern Marianas Attack Group, arbitrarily relieved him of his command.

There is nothing novel about an officer being relieved of his command in the field. It has occurred in every major war which has ever been fought. It occurred numerous times in this war; in the Army, Navy and Marine Corps. What raised the hue and cry in the case of Smith vs. Smith was the fact that the two officers involved belonged to different branches of the service; that a general in the senior and vastly larger branch had been removed by a general in the junior and much smaller service, regardless of the fact that the Marine Corps held the command and responsibility for this particular operation, and furnished the bulk of the troops.

But the Saipan affair did not involve arbitrary imposition of Marine command upon an Army division, as many were led to believe from the heated and none-too-clear debate in the press, and elsewhere. The officer succeeding to the command of the Twenty-seventh Division was Major General Sanford Jarman, U.S. Army, who had been brought along to be Commanding General of Saipan garrison forces once the island was secure. Under General Jarman and his successor, the Twenty-seventh gradually pulled itself together, rectified its tactical position, and carried on successfully against the enemy until close to the end of the campaign.

The change in command of the Twenty-seventh Division took place on D + 9 (24 June). In the meanwhile, the advance had continued steadily, inexorably but slowly, against stubborn opposition, complicated by difficulties in getting supplies forward over the rugged, jungle-choked terrain.

On D + 7 the 6th Marines cleared the way for an assault by the adjoining 8th Marines upon Mount Tapotchau by capturing the hill known as Tipo Pale, dominating the strongly held valley which flanked the main elevation. For the next two days the 8th Marines and their attached elements fought their way stubbornly upward. On D + 10, supported by a heavy mortar barrage, elements of 1/29 and the Second Division Reconnaissance Company executed a brilliant encircling movement behind the Japanese troops dug in on the forward slope and occupied the summit, nearly surprising the enemy CP located in a tunnel dug all the way through the narrow crest.

A strong counterattack was beaten off during the night, but the hill was not really secured until the remaining elements of the 8th Marines had cleared the enemy entirely from the reverse and flanking slopes, a job which took the better part of the next two days. This accomplished, all units with any excuse for doing so proceeded to establish observation posts up there, affording them a remarkably clear view of the entire northern half of the island.

With the fall of Tipo Pale, which dominated Garapan, the 2nd Marines had advanced along the western shore to the lower edge of that town, where they dug in to await straightening of the whole front line. On the extreme right the Fourth Division completed mopping up of the entire Kagman Peninsula in three days and anchored their flank firmly on the shore again. Early in the morning of D + 11, the 2nd Battalion, 25th Marines, from the reserve, was moved

448

into the gap on the left of the 8th Marines caused by the clearing of the Tapotchau slopes, tying in with the Twenty-seventh Division, in the center, which was still in the process of getting straightened out under its new commanding general. Thus, by D + 12 (27 June) a firm and well-integrated line had been established across the full width of the island, firmly securing dominant Mount Tapotchau and somewhat more than the entire southern half of Saipan.

About this time occurred a novel incident which, though it had no effect upon the outcome of the campaign, brought some passing excitement to the people in the rear areas who had begun to believe themselves pretty remote from the war.

As previously related, a Japanese detachment of undetermined size had been cut off in the south when the 25th Marines had reached the eastern shore. The Twenty-seventh Division, taking over this sector, had driven them gradually into a corner on Nafutan Point, the southeastern tip of the island, where 2/105 had been left to contain them and finish them off at leisure. During the night of D + 11 (26 June) a sizable group of these broke out of the trap and started hellbent for the airfield where our planes were now freely operating.

The effort was unusually well organized as such things go, complete with written orders, a chain-of-command and a slogan deemed fitting for the occasion: "Seven lives to repay our country"—meaning, evidently, that each man was supposed to kill seven Americans before going to join his ancestors. In addition, they were to do as much damage as possible to installations and equipment, and try to get through to their own lines to the north.

Exactly how many started out on this fantastic sortie it would be impossible to say. Some five hundred bodies were counted in the morning, and it is quite possible that some got through to their own lines, or at least to the cover of the hilly jungle.

They were singularly unsuccessful in all respects. Not only did they fail to kill "seven for one"; it is improbable that they killed much more than seven for the whole five hundred. They got as far as the edge of the airfield where they destroyed one parked plane and damaged two others before being driven off by an aroused crowd of Seabees and aviation ground personnel. The survivors then struck out toward the north where presently they came up against the CP of the 25th Marines, currently in reserve. There, to all intents and purposes, the effort ended, though irritated Marines from artillery and other infantry units were still blasting stragglers out of bushes and holes well into the morning.

On the front the next few days were spent in minor advances and consolidating positions. Then on D + 17 (2 July) the whole line surged forward. On the left the 2nd Marines, specially trained in town fighting, occupied the high ground behind Garapan and fought their way about halfway through the rubble of the town itself. Farther inland the remainder of the Second Division scored substantial advances against diminishing opposition, the rejuvenated Twenty-seventh Division in the center keeping pace. The Fourth Division also moved with alacrity, except on the extreme right, along the shore, where strong Japanese concentrations in prepared positions were encountered.

The advance continued in much the same manner for the next three days. On the left the 2nd Marines completed the occupation of Garapan on D + 18, and the 6th pushed on to Tanapag Harbor, by-passing enemy strong points on swampy Mutcho Point. On the following day they advanced another 1,500 yards, securing the important dock area, and the 8th Marines took the sea plane base. The center, too, scored steady, substantial gains, but the extreme right continued to encounter difficulties, causing that flank to bend backward rather sharply. No substantial advance was made there until D + 19; then on D + 20 (5 July) the 23rd Marines broke through crumbling resistance to straighten out the line.

The narrowing of the island meanwhile had pinched the Second Division out of the line, their sector being taken over by the Twenty-seventh. The 105th Infantry, now holding the extreme left flank, advanced to a point near the lower edge of Tanapag town and dug in there to serve as pivot for a new turning movement. It had become clear that such Japanese resistance as remained was concentrated along the western shore. The decision was, therefore, to swing the

450

right around until the line roughly paralleled the island's axis and attack downward from the high ground.

This maneuver took most of the next two days. The 105th stood fast, as did the 165th on its right, consolidating positions on the high ground behind Tanapag. The Fourth Division, meanwhile, continued to drive northward on a front about two thousand yards wide, pivoting on the right of the Twenty-seventh Division. The 2nd Marines had been attached to the Fourth Division for this phase of the operation, so that they now had four regiments in the line; the line itself, as a result of this turning movement, running roughly northeast to southwest, facing the western shore except at the extreme north and extreme south where the flanks bent to face northward.

That, then, was the tactical situation on the critical night of D + 22 (7 July), when the initiative on Saipan passed briefly to the Japanese.

General Saito, an elderly man rendered more infirm by the rigors he had gone through, had recognized the handwriting on the wall for some time. Extravagant promises from the homeland of naval and air relief could no longer blind him to reality. General Saito was a brave man, brought up under the code of Bushido, indoctrinated with the standard of battle ethics known as "senjinkun." His thoughts on the matter are incorporated in his remarkable last message to his troops, one paragraph of which will suffice for present purposes:

> *The barbarous attack of the enemy is being continued. . . . We are dying without avail under the violent shelling and bombing. Whether we attack or whether we stay where we are, there is only death. However, in death there is life. We must utilize this opportunity to exalt true Japanese manhood. I will advance with those who remain to deliver still another blow to the American Devils, and leave my bones on Saipan as a bulwark of the Pacific.*

What Saito planned was, in short, a Banzai in the grand manner. It was to be frankly suicidal, dedicated to the "Seven lives to repay our country" slogan which had motivated the Nafutan Point breakthrough, but without even the tactical objective of those men: to rejoin their own main force. This was their main force.

To insure its being the largest mass suicide yet staged in the Pacific, Saito laid his plans sufficiently far in advance to allow for concentrating such troops as he had left. With his communications so thoroughly disrupted, he had to rely entirely upon runners. He figured on a minimum of three days, and the orders were issued accordingly: all units still functioning as such, and all other personnel still able to navigate under their own power were to rendezvous at a designated spot near the village of Makunsho by the night of 6 July.

The runners had to do most of their work at night, under constant harassing fire. It was impossible for them to reach all of the elements concerned in the time allowed, inevitable that some of their dispatches should fall into American hands. Our people were aware well in advance that something on a large scale was coming up, and all hands were alerted accordingly. What they could not predict with any certainty was exactly when it would break or what direction it would take.

General Saito issued his "Last Message" at 0800 on the morning of 6 July, even as his troops were beginning their rendezvous. He had decided by that time that he was too old and weak to be of any use in such an operation. His closing words: "I advance to seek out the enemy. Follow me!" were not intended to be taken literally. Actually he proposed to depart this world ahead of his troops, to meet them later on in the place all of them were going.

The message issued, the old general sat down to the most sumptuous meal his attendants could prepare from what was left of their food supplies: saki, canned crab meat, etc. Then, after the traditional goings on associated with such a ceremony, he repaired to the mouth of the cave which served him as a CP, bade farewell to his staff and seated himself crosslegged, facing in the general direction of the emperor's palace. A ceremonial dagger was handed to him. Perhaps his hand trembled as he went through the motions of drawing his own blood. The instant that blood flowed,

452

his adjutant, acting upon well-rehearsed orders, shot him in the right temple. His body was subsequently recovered by the Marines and buried with military honors.

It is believed that Admiral Nagumo [2] followed a similar procedure in his own CP at about the same time. From the best evidence available, it appears that command of the actual attack devolved upon Colonel Suzuki of the 135th Infantry.

Exactly how many participated in this attack, the Japanese themselves could never be sure. From the best available evidence, bodies subsequently buried, it appears that the number ran upward of three thousand. The advance elements, at least, were well organized. They started southward from Makunsho about 0400 on the morning of 8 July, moving in formation, following in general the right-of-way of the narrow-gauge railway near the shore. They scattered the American outposts and slammed head on into the 1st and 2nd Battalions of the 105th Infantry at 0510. And broke through; there was no stopping that many men whose only thought was to kill and be killed. Our artillery pounded furiously the area from which the attack was developing, but was necessarily ineffective at the point of contact for fear of hitting our own people.

Dawn revealed a situation of chaotic confusion. 1/105 and 2/105 had been shattered. Savage fighting swirled about a dozen isolated American pockets of resistance. Some were overrun; some held out. Some battleshocked soldiers escaped into the hills. Those nearest the shore were driven into the sea. Wading, swimming, they fled across the reef, with machine-gun bullets cutting the water around them and mortar shells dropping in their midst, to be picked up by naval craft at the reef's edge.

The Japanese drove on. Marine observers in the hills, watching proceedings through glasses, now glimpsed a strange phenomenon. Behind the enemy assault formations

[2] An obscure end for a conspicuous career. It was Nagumo who commanded the task force which attacked Pearl Harbor with such disastrous results, and also that other task force which sought to attack Midway—with the disaster in reverse.

moved a weird, almost unbelievable procession: the lame, the halt and the blind, literally. The sick and wounded from the hospitals had come forth to die. Bandage-swathed men, amputees, men on crutches, walking wounded helping each other along. Some were armed, some carried only a bayonet lashed to a long pole or a few grenades, many had no weapons of any sort. If they could manage to kill a few Americans, that would be all to the good. But it was not important; theirs was not to reason why but to die in battle. Later it was discovered that some three hundred patients too weak to move had been killed in the hospital by their own people. This was IT: the end, the works, everything.

About one thousand yards behind the infantry positions, Batteries "H" and "I" of the 10th Marines (Second Division Artillery) were working their 105's furiously. As the enemy broke through and surged toward them, they lowered to point-blank range. The Japanese kept coming. The artillerymen cut their fuses to burst the shells at 150 yards, at 100 yards, and fired straight into the seething mass of their assailants. Many Japanese died here; the survivors kept coming. Hastily the Marines removed the firing blocks to make the guns useless and fell back fighting as infantry, and the enemy overran the emplacements.

But the end was at hand. Men from the other batteries of the 10th Marines hurried to their comrades' aid with rifles, carbines, machine guns, BAR's. Clerks, messmen, CP personnel, came in with whatever weapons they could lay their hands on. Roaring in over the heaped bodies of enemy dead, they recaptured the guns and put them into operation again. The greatest of all Banzais was over, as such.

The rest of the day was devoted to mopping up the remnants. The 6th and 8th Marines, which had gone into reserve a few days earlier upon being pinched out of the line, were moved forward again for this messy work. The 165th Infantry and the 23rd Marines attacked westward from the high ground. Thus died those Japanese who had survived their madness up until then. Nightfall found only two pockets of stubborn resistance pinned against the shore, and these were cleaned out the following day.

The carnage had been ghastly beyond belief. Burial par-

454

ties needed days to deal with the great number of dead. One observer visiting the scene described exhausted soldiers and Marines lying down to sleep amid already rotting corpses for the simple reason that no spot in the area was free of corpses. One single space about an acre in extent was entirely covered with them. As regards its only conceivable object, suicide, General Saito's Banzai had been an unqualified success.

The campaign was soon over after that. On D + 23, while mopping up of the Banzai remnants was still going on, the Fourth Division swung its line around to face northward again, extending the width of the island. With the 2nd Marines (temporarily attached) on the left, the 24th in the center and the 25th on the right, they drove northward against trifling resistance. Here and there a handful of Japanese who had missed the Banzai for one reason or another tried to fight and died miserably in their holes. Others fled before the advance; fled to the edge of the cliffs that dropped away from the plateau to the low shelf of the rocky beaches. More died here, by their own hands or those of the Marines. Some struggled down the cliffs to the shore.

Here was enacted the crowning horror of the whole campaign. Some hundreds of fleeing civilians had taken refuge on the northern shore and in the caves in the cliffs which faced it. Now, believing themselves to have reached the last extremity, they set about a veritable orgy of self-destruction. Mothers and fathers stabbed, strangled or shot their screaming children; hurled them into the sea and leaped in after them, all in plain view of the Marines atop the cliffs or trying to get to the beach. Men hardened in one of the bloodiest campaigns of the Pacific turned away from the sight, sick at heart and physically ill.

Surrender pleas were largely in vain. These people had been told repeatedly that the Americans would kill them, preferably by torture. Now when a few of the miserable creatures showed a disposition to tempt this fate, they were shot down by Japanese soldiers in their midst or others still holed up in the caves in the cliff faces. LCI gunboats lay offshore while Japanese language interpreters exhorted surrender through loudspeakers. Japanese soldiers, using the

455

helpless civilians for cover, fired upon them. One such character was seen to shoot, one by one, a group of about fifteen, mostly women and children, pausing systematically to reload his rifle when necessary, capping the performance by blowing himself up with a hand grenade.

Unable to accomplish their humanitarian mission, the LCI's finally turned their guns against the caves from which the sniping was coming. When the Marines were able finally to occupy the beach, their prisoners totalled a bare handful, most of these badly wounded children whose parents had failed to finish them off before taking their own lives.

Saipan was formally declared secure at 1615 on D + 24 (9 July). All this meant was that organized resistance had ceased and the entire island had been overrun. At long last the artillery was silent, having no areas left in which to fire. But actually some thousands of armed Japanese still lurked in the jungles, hills and caves. For weeks afterward they were being hunted out and killed, often at the rate of more than a hundred a day, in one of the biggest mopping-up operations in history. More than a year later, when final peace came to the Pacific, there were still Japanese soldiers at large on Saipan.

But for all practical purposes the campaign, as such, ended on 9 July. Americans, to the number of 3,143, had died there, 13,208 had been wounded and 335 were still carried as missing on the casualty report dated 12 August. Against this, were 23,811 known Japanese dead and 1,810 military prisoners, the largest number taken in any campaign to date. How many civilians died could not be estimated. There were 14,735 interned in the stockades.

The price had been high, but no one disputed that the purchase had been worth it. The Marines on Saipan had little time to think about that matter, however. They could only lick their wounds, get such rest as was possible and try to absorb in the minimum time the new blood which had come to them in the form of fresh replacements from the States.

456

TURKEY SHOOT

While the Marines were fighting on Saipan, Adm. Spruance had a huge naval force drawn up west of the Marianas to ward off expected Japanese sea strikes; Task Force 58 comprised fifteen carriers, seven battleships, eight heavy cruisers, thirteen light cruisers and sixty-nine destroyers, under the tactical command of Adm. Marc Mitscher.

The Japanese had hoped to entice the U.S. naval forces into battle farther southwest, in waters within range of their land-based planes, to offset U.S. numerical superiority in carrier aircraft. But once news of the Marianas invasion reached Adm. Toyoda, commander of the Japanese Combined Fleet, he ordered a rendezvous of his forces in the Philippine Sea to attack the U.S. fleet. His tactical commander, Adm. Ozawa, had forces inferior to Mitscher's in every category except heavy cruisers—nine carriers to Mitscher's fifteen, five battleships to Mitscher's seven, etc.—and the plane disparity was even more striking—in everything but float planes, the U.S. outnumbered Ozawa's forces two to one.

However, once the battle began, Ozawa expected major support from planes based in the Marianas and at Truk, where reinforcements had been ordered before the action began. And his search planes had a greater range, giving him the chance to spot the enemy's position before his own forces were detected.*

Ozawa's planes did discover Task Force 58 on June 18, 1944, the day before the battle. Mitscher's task force was drawn up in five circles, four carrier groups approximately four miles in diameter, with perimeters of battleships, cruisers and destroyers to provide fire screen; to the west of the carriers a battle line (circular) of six battleships, four cruis-

---

* S. E. Morison, *New Guinea and the Marianas*, p. 233: Jap planes could search in a radius of 560 miles, while the more heavily armored U.S. planes' range was only 325-350 miles; also, Jap attacks could be launched from 300 miles, U.S. attacks from about 200.

ers and a dozen destroyers to engage enemy strikes, with two picket destroyers further west to warn of their approach.

Adm. Spruance wanted the fleet to remain close to Saipan, fearing the Japs might feint to the center, then attempt an end run around the U.S. fleet to get at the Marianas invasion forces. He "ordered the fleet to advance westward during the daylight and retire eastward at night —until information of the enemy requires other action." *

This tactic would forestall the discovery of the Jap fleet until the second day of battle, too late to enable Task Force 58 to close for decisive action.

The next day, June 19th, Ozawa's carrier planes launched four separate raids. But their approaches were plotted by radar on the U.S. carriers in time for intercepting planes to meet them. What few planes got through to the fleet were destroyed by anti-aircraft fire or driven off.

The Japanese lost about 315 planes that day, in such a slaughter that the June 19th action became known as "The Great Marianas Turkey Shoot." In the meantime U.S. submarines sank two big Jap carriers— the *Shokaku* and *Taiho*.

The next day Air Search gave Mitscher the correct position of the Jap forces, approximately 275 miles away; the range was risky for the U.S. carrier planes, and their return would require night landings on the flight decks, but the air groups were launched. They met resistance from the remnants of the Jap planes, but sank an enemy carrier, *Hiyo*, destroying two-thirds of Ozawa's remaining aircraft. American losses from the action were only twenty planes.

Adm. Ozawa had 35 planes left out of 430. He turned his fleet homeward, beaten in the greatest carrier battle of the war. His failure can be attributed to the inexperience of his carrier pilots (their training hadn't been completed before they were sent into battle), and his dependence on land-based aircraft, which he'd expected to operate from the Marianas and Truk; unknown to him, the reinforcements he'd asked for had been diverted at the last moment to hit MacArthur's invasion of Biak.

The Battle of the Philippine Sea stirred up much argument among the U.S. naval commanders. Adm. Spruance was charged with being too cautious, not allowing the ships of Task Force 58 to steam westward on the 19th to make contact with the Jap fleet (subs had signaled their approximate position). If they had, they would have been in position, early on

* S. E. Morison, *New Guinea and the Marianas*, p. 251.

June 20th, for day-long strikes at the Japs, and the toll of ships could have been much greater.

Two weeks after Saipan fell, Tinian was assaulted; on July 24th, the 4th Marine Division and two regiments of the 2nd Marine Division landed, the remainder of the 2nd Marine Division being brought over the next day. Tinian was declared secured on August 1st, and, together with Saipan, would soon be turned into a base for bombing attacks on Japan itself by the new long-ranging B-29's.

Guam was to have been assaulted during the middle of June, but when Saipan turned out to be a tougher nut than expected, Adm. Spruance held up the Guam attack. D-Day was set for July 21st. The 3rd Marine Division were aboard the transports seven weeks, waiting.*

Two separate landings were made on Guam; because of the long delay prior to the actual assault, the U.S. Navy conducted the longest bombardment of any of the Pacific Island campaigns. The beaches were softened up as never before, and the landings went off as close to perfection as one could hope for, with the tanks and artillery being put ashore on D-Day.

"The story of the next four days is one of dogged, bitter fighting. The 3rd Marines battled their way inch by inch up the Chonito Cliff, suffering heavily from casualties and exhaustion. The 21st Marines moved toward the higher ground across successive ridges only to find beyond each, another jungle-packed ravine filled with Japs covered by mortar and artillery concentration, on the reverse slopes of higher ridges beyond." **

The battle for Guam was reported by Sgt. Alvin M. Josephy, then a Marine Corps Combat Correspondent.

* Hough says, *The Island War,* "No one who has never traveled to combat aboard an overcrowded assault transport in the tropics, can comprehend what those men went through during the 48 to 52 days the various elements were at sea" (p. 264).

** Maj. Frank Hough, *The Island War,* p. 270.

BANZAI ON GUAM

by Alvin M. Josephy, Jr.

The battle for Guam was, from the news perspective back home, just a battle for "another little island"—good for a few days' headlines.

On Guam, however, it was another story. Some of the fiercest moments of the struggle were still ahead of us. Our Division CP was in an amphitheater near the shore, in an area that lay beyond the right flank of our original beachhead. The amphitheater was formed by towering hills and coral bluffs. The open (or shore) side was bounded by a road. It was a fairly secure spot, guarded by rings of MPs and free from Jap mortar fire. Here, General Turnage and his staff set up tents from which to direct the deepening of our beachhead.

Our line was now many thousand yards long, and that it was a thin line was no secret. We were only one division, and we had no reinforcements. We had to push and keep pushing; and the more we pushed, the wider our perimeter became and the more men we needed to hold it. We looked forward to the day when we would join the Provisional Brigade on the other beachhead. They had elements of the 77th Army Division with them as reinforcements. The 77th had begun landing its men late on D-Day on that beachhead. As soon as we all joined, we could possibly count on reinforcements from the Army. Until then, however, we had to hold and deepen our perimeter alone.

During the night of July 25—D plus four—it rained. Toward morning we noticed the sound of gunfire coming closer to our Division CP. Then the guards up on the hills that formed the amphitheater began to shoot. At first there were just sporadic shots—a rifle or a carbine shot into the night. Then they came oftener. There were hand-grenade blasts, and the sudden bursts of BARs and machine guns.

Wheaton and I could hear men stirring in the holes around our foxhole. Occasionally a shot rang out very near to us. Then a hand grenade popped, so close that it might have been thrown by a man in a nearby hole. We peered cautiously over the lip of our foxhole and waited for a form to show itself.

Nothing happened, but by dawn the woods on top of the hills above us were resounding with shots. We got out of our holes carefully. Soon the word spread: the Japs had broken through. Several thousand of the enemy were behind our front lines, threatening all our rear units.

Things occurred then with terrible speed. Our artillery CP was overrun. Japs, carrying land mines and picric-acid charges around their belts, emerged from a draw and, throwing grenades, hit the artillery unit to which Wheaton and I had originally been attached. Our men fought back with rifles and hand grenades from the foxholes in which they had been sleeping. The Japs screamed in English (Staff Sergeant Jim Hague, one of our combat correspondents who was caught in the middle of the battle in his foxhole, reported that men that day heard Japs cry, "One, two, three, you can't catch me!") and charged into one of our machine-gun positions, taking the gun away from the crew. The Marines fought back with another machine gun and drove the Japs back up the draw. Lieutenant Rodgers, with whom we had sailed to Guam, collected a squad of men and boldly led it after the Japs. A flurry of shots from among some rocks stopped the group. One shot hit Rodgers, and he fell. The next moment there was an explosion; a hand grenade or a stick of dynamite—no one knew which—had hit the Lieutenant, and his body blew apart. Several other Marines were killed there, men who had been in our hold sailing to Guam.

While the artillerymen were fighting off the Japs, a second band of enemy rushed down another draw to appear suddenly at our Division hospital. The corpsmen and patients could hear firing coming nearer but thought nothing of it until a wounded man appeared, running at top speed and yelling: "The Japs are coming! The Japs are coming!"

There was no time to wonder how the Japs had broken so deeply into our rear. The corpsmen grabbed rifles and carbines and flung themselves behind cots and cartons of plasma and dressings. Some of the ambulatory patients hopped out of bed and ran for the beach. A cook, whose foot had been wounded the night before when he had been carrying ammunition, scrambled from his cot without a stitch of clothing on and hobbled as fast as he could to the shore. The Japs soon appeared at the hospital, screaming and throwing grenades. The corpsmen fired at them and tried to stop them. One corpsman killed seven Japs with a carbine. Patients inside the ward tents grabbed their weapons and joined the fight as hand-grenade fragments ripped into the canvas flaps. A doctor, in the middle of an operation, paused an instant, trying to decide what to do. The next moment two mortar bursts shredded the top of the surgery tent. The doctor ordered corpsmen to take up positions around the tent. Then he finished the operation.

It was a wild, swirling fight, but it was soon over. Reinforcements arrived from the Division CP and helped the corpsmen wipe out the Japs. Every enemy in sight was killed. But no one knew how many more were still behind our lines and out of sight. Reports from the front lines estimated that at least two thousand Japs had broken through during the night. There must still be almost that number wandering through the brush and hiding temporarily in caves behind our perimeter—a menace, since at any moment groups of them might attack other units, as they had attacked our artillery CP and the Division hospital.

Every Marine and Seabee on our beachhead was mobilized. Squads were formed to look for and attack the enemy that had broken through. All normal activity behind our front lines ceased. Cooks, drivers, clerks, telephone operators, unloaders on the reef—everyone available—went into the hills that morning to eliminate the threat to our beachhead.

Meanwhile we wondered what had happened. How had

462

so many Japs gotten through, and when? The story, when it came down to us from the front lines, was the story of the first banzai charge our Division had ever met: a vicious, drunken, night counterattack designed to hurl us off of Guam and back into the sea.

The Japs' preparations for it had begun two nights before. That evening two of our PFC's, Joseph Basso and Russell Elushik, had been in an advanced foxhole in front of B Company, the 21st Marines. Basso, a husky former machinist, had been trying to get to sleep when Elushik, who was on guard, fired into the night with his automatic rifle. Basso leaped to his feet, to find the ground around the foxhole swarming with Japs. The two men stood back to back and fired as fast as they could at the enemy forms. The Japs, however, quickly overwhelmed them. The two men were dragged out of the foxhole and across the ground toward the Japanese lines. They struggled and yelled, but they were too far away from other Marines to make themselves heard.

At last Elushik, who weighed about two hundred pounds, twisted himself free and broke away. The Japs dragging Basso let go and chased after Elushik. Basso scrambled breathlessly back to his foxhole and retrieved his automatic rifle. He saw the Japs overtake Elushik and knock the big man down. At the same moment, Basso emptied his rifle at the Japs, trying not to hit the form on the ground. Several of the enemy fell. There was a sudden silence. A few Japs crawled stealthily away. Basso utilized the pause to scramble back to his own lines, get a man to cover him, and go back after Elushik. When he reached Elushik, the big man was still alive, despite the fact that his left hand had been cut off by a Jap saber, both his arms and legs had been broken, and he had a bayonet wound through his neck and back. Elushik and Basso were both evacuated that night. Elushik later died, but Basso, suffering from severe shock, recovered and rejoined his unit.

Nothing more was thought of the episode until two nights later when it became evident that the Jap raiding party had tried to take our men prisoners in order to obtain information. The enemy had chosen to hit the 21st Marines' sector in a counterattack and had needed an appraisal of our strength. Although they failed to secure information from Basso and Elushik, the Japs by themselves estimated our situation correctly. They narrowed the main force of their attack down to our weakest unit— the 1st Battalion of 21st Marines. Here, in the very center of our whole beachhead line, no more than 250 men manned a position that ran for more than two thousand yards—a frontage normally requiring about 600 men. Company B, in the center of the 1st Battalion zone, was down to approximately 75 men out of an original landing strength of 217. The Marines, dug in on a ridge top a couple of miles from the shore, were organized in small knots to cover areas around them—islands of resistance, so to speak.

On the night of July 25 the Japs prepared to strike this sector.

That night, unaware of what lay ahead, our men on the ridge ate a dinner of cold K rations. The hours passed, and it began to pour and drizzle alternately. The Marines tucked ponchos around themselves and squirmed sleepily in the mud. Toward midnight one of the men on watch noticed that the Japs were throwing a lot of grenades. On both sides of him, other Marines were hurling their own grenades back into the night. Many of these burst five and ten feet above the ground, the fragments showering on the wet dirt.

At about three a.m. a rifleman named Martinez heard a swishing of grass out ahead of him, like men moving about. Then he noticed the *pang* of pieces of metal hitting each other and a busy stirring in the darkness that made him uneasy. He peered into the mist but was unable to see anything. Then, as he listened, other things happened. A barrage of hand grenades flew through the darkness and exploded behind him. They kept coming, and he noticed mortar shells beginning to crash more frequently on the ridge.

He woke the other two men in his foxhole. They had been curled in their ponchos, and they got to their feet uncertainly. At the same moment an orange signal flare shot up from the Japanese lines. A singsong voice shouted into the night, and an avalanche of screaming forms bounded suddenly into view. With their bayonets gleaming in the light of sudden flares, they charged toward the Marine foxholes, throwing grenades and howling: *"Ban-zai-ai!"* like a pack of animals.

The Marines awoke with a start. Along the ridge, wet, groggy men bolted to their feet and grabbed their weapons. Grenades exploded like a crashing curtain against the onrushing Japs. A man on a telephone yelled for uninterrupted flares, and flickering lights began to hang in the air like giant overhead fires.

All along the line the enemy attack was on. Red tracer bullets flashed through the blackness. Japanese orange signal flares and American white illumination shells lit up the night like the Fourth of July, silhouetting the running forms of the enemy. On the right and the left the attack was stopped cold. As fast as the Japs came, they were mowed down by automatic rifles and machine guns. The enemy assault gradually focused on a draw where some American tanks were parked. The tanks fired their 75s at the charging masses. At first the Japs attacked the steel monsters like swarms of ants, firing their rifles at the metal sides and clambering up and over the tanks in a vain attempt to get at the crews inside. They screamed and pounded drunkenly on the turrets and locked hatches, but in their excitement they failed to damage a single tank. Finally, as if engaged in a wild game of follow-the-leader, many of them streamed past the tanks, down the draw toward the beach.

The rest, cringing before the tank fire, moved to the left, hoping to break through our lines and get to the draw farther down the slope of the ridge, behind the tanks. The front they now charged was that of B Company. Here, against the 75 men, the full force of the Japanese attack broke.

In their three-man foxhole, the rifleman Martinez and his two companions had maintained steady fire directly ahead, diverting the first rush of Japs to other sections of the line. During a pause in the fighting, one man left the hole to go back for more hand grenades. Martinez and a Marine named Wimmer were left alone. Around them they saw some of the other Marines withdrawing, sliding down the ridge to a secondary line of foxholes about ten yards to the rear. Here and there, in the light of the flares, they could see them pulling back wounded men.

Trying to decide whether to withdraw themselves, Martinez and Wimmer were confronted suddenly by the first wave of Japs. With bayonets fixed, the enemy came more slowly, throwing grenades and then falling to the ground to wait for the bursts. The first grenades exploded around the Marines without harming them. Then one shattered Wimmer's rifle, and the two men decided it was time to withdraw.

As they crawled out of their foxhole and ran and slid down the slope of the ridge, they noticed a group of screaming figures pour over the crest farther to the right and run headlong down the hill. It was the first indication that the enemy were breaking through. Now the Japs would be in our rear, and it would no longer be easy to tell friend from foe.

Martinez and Wimmer reached their platoon command post—an old shellhole ten yards from the top of the ridge, held by Second Lieutenant Edward W. Mulcahy. When the two Marines reached him, Mulcahy was trying desperately to make his field telephone work; but the wires to the rear had already been cut by mortar shells.

Wimmer slid into the hole beside the Lieutenant, and Martinez lay on the forward lip of earth as protection with his rifle. The night was hideous with explosions, lights, screaming enemy, and the odor of *sake*. Against the skyline a handful of Japs appeared. Martinez fired at them, and they backed out of sight. A moment later a string of hand grenades rolled down toward the Marines. Though most of them bounced harmlessly by to explode behind them, one blew up in front of Wimmer's face. Fragments shattered Mulcahy's carbine and struck him on the left side of the head and body. It felt as if he had been slammed with a two-by-four plank.

When he regained his breath, he saw Wimmer holding out his pistol.

"You take it, Lieutenant," Wimmer said in a strange voice.

466

The Lieutenant protested. The enlisted man would need the weapon for himself.

Wimmer raised his head and smiled. "That's all right, sir," he breathed. "I can't see any more."

The shocked Lieutenant tried to bandage Wimmer's splintered face. The noise from the top of the ridge showed that Marines were still up there, fighting back. It gave the three men hope. The Lieutenant began to shout in the night, like a football coach, "Hold that line, men! You can do it!"

The Marine line on the crest, however, had by now disintegrated into a handful of desperate knots of men, fighting together with the fury of human beings trying not to be killed.

Action around two heavy machine guns was typical of what was occurring. A Jap grenade hit one gun, temporarily putting it out of action. The crew members fixed it quickly and started firing again. A second grenade hit the gun's jacket and exploded, knocking off the cover and putting it completely out of the fight. The same blast wounded one of the men. His three companions moved him to a foxhole ten yards behind the shattered gun. One man jumped in beside him, and the other two ran back to the machine-gun foxhole with their carbines. Heaving grenades like wild men, they managed to stall any Jap frontal charge for the moment.

Meanwhile, the other gun was also silenced. Riflemen in foxholes near by heard a sudden unearthly screaming from the gun position. By the wavering light of flares, they saw one of the crew members trying to pull a Japanese bayonet out of another Marine's body. The same instant a wave of Japs appeared from nowhere and swept over both men. Three of the enemy, stopping at the silent machine gun, tried to turn it around to fire at the Marines. In their hysteria, one of them pulled the trigger before the gun was turned, and the bullets sprayed a group of Japs racing across the top of the ridge. Finally the Japs tried to lift the entire gun on its mount and turn the whole thing. A Marine automatic rifleman blasted them with his BAR, and the Japs dropped the gun. Two of them fell over the bodies of the Marine crew. A third pulled out a grenade and, holding it

467

to his head, blew himself up. A moment later another band of Japs appeared. Again, several paused at the gun and tried to swing the heavy weapon around. They had almost succeeded, when from the darkness a lone, drunken Jap raced headlong at them, tripped several feet away over a body, and flew through the air. There was a blinding flash as he literally blew apart. He had been a human bomb, carrying a land mine and a blast charge on his waist.

Other units all along the line had equally serious moments during the night. Though none had been overrun like B Company, several withdrawals occurred. On the left of B Company, however, A Company also stood firm, inspired by Captain William G. Shoemaker, one of the most popular officers in the 3d Division. As wave after wave of Japs rushed A Company's lines, only to be hurled back, Captain Shoemaker made his way calmly among his men, exhorting them to hold.

"If we go, the whole beachhead goes," he explained. "It's up to us to stay here."

Once a rumor swept along the line that the order had been given to withdraw. Men looked around wildly for confirmation. Captain Shoemaker heard the rumor. He leaped to his feet—a hulk of a man, wrapped in a captured Jap trenchcoat—and roared into the night: "By God, we hold here! The beachhead depends on us!"

His men held.

At about 0600, three hours after the enemy attack had begun, a last wave of Japs charged over the top of the hill. It was the wildest, most drunken group of all, bunched together, howling, stumbling and waving swords, bayonets, and long poles. Some were already wounded and were swathed in gory bandages. The Marines yelled back at them and chopped them down in their mad rush. In a moment it was over. The last wave of the three-hour attack died to a man.

But daylight revealed in all their seriousness how successful the earlier charges had been. It was then that the furious, pellmell Jap attacks had begun to hit our rear units.

Immediately behind the punctured 21st Marine line, engineers, artillerymen, and 21st CP personnel formed a sec-

468

ondary line of defense. Other groups, armed with grenades and automatic weapons, moved through the wooded draws and valleys behind our front, in a roving attempt to find the Japs.

The prompt action saved a potentially serious situation. The Jap plan had counted on driving our Marine line straight back into the sea, first piercing it so that the remnants would have to withdraw, and then fanning out in the rear, disrupting our communications and disorganizing the elements on the beach. The attacking enemy, never well organized and from the start under the influence of alcohol, disintegrated once it got through our lines until it became a hodge-podge of wandering bands and individuals without leadership, communications, or well-defined aims. Some of them managed to do damage, like the group that hit our artillery CP. Others caused temporary disruptions, like the mob that stumbled on our Division hospital. But they were only small groups without tactical coordination, and they became easy prey for our mopping-up bands. By noon we had wiped out most of them. The rest of the enemy took to caves to hide and—like bewildered, sick animals—to puzzle over their fate.

As our units re-formed their lines, it was found that Company B had almost been wiped out during the night. Only 18 men remained out of the 75 who had dug in the evening before. The survivors were put into another company, and B Company temporarily ceased to exist.

Many more of our men were killed or wounded that morning mopping up the scattered Jap bands behind our lines. What happened at the artillery CP, where Lieutenant Rodgers and some of our shipboard comrades lost their lives, occurred also around other units. One of our most tragic losses was that of Captain William O'Brien, the 3d Division's Legal Officer, who was liked by everyone who knew him. Although a staff officer, he voluntarily led a squad through the hills above the Division CP looking for Japs. Somehow the other men lost sight of him, and they came back without him. One of his closest friends was our adjutant, Major Bob Kriendler, who had been busy keeping tabs on our casualties as they piled up during the night. It had been a sad job for him, for many of the dead and wounded had been his friends. Then someone came in to say that Bill O'Brien was missing. Major Kriendler couldn't believe that anything had happened to the Legal Officer. He kept his fingers crossed and assured everyone that his friend would turn up during the day. But just after noon, a man came into Kriendler's tent on some other business. "Say, it's too bad about Bill O'Brien, isn't it?" he said to the Major.

Kriendler thought the newcomer was merely repeating the rumor. "He'll turn up," he replied.

But the newcomer leaned forward. "I don't think you understand," he went on. "I just saw Bill down at the cemetery —they brought him in. No one saw him get killed. They just found his body."

The banzai charge on Guam was never fully reported by the civilian press. Most of the civilian correspondents at the time were on the other beachhead with the 1st Brigade and the Army. In front of our lines our bulldozers and burial squads found some eight hundred Japs. Behind our lines we killed or sealed in caves about two thousand more. The newspapers in the United States put it simply: an enemy counterattack was repulsed with severe losses to the Japanese. Such reporting could not convey the terror of the night attack or the businesslike devotion to duty of our men. Because the eighteen survivors of B Company and the others who stood all along the line that night failed to give way, the beachhead was saved, as Captain Shoemaker had said it would be. By maintaining their line, our men were able to close the gaps, trap the enemy in the rear, and the following day launch a new attack of their own.

The Jap charge had wasted the cream of the enemy troops on the island. After the failure of the charge they had nothing more to oppose us with. They continued to hurl smaller attacks against us at night—some of them drunken assaults—and retreat before us by day; but their offensive power was broken.

As we pushed inland, some of our units continued to have desperate moments among the wooded hills and valleys. In many places the hills were steep coral formations that afforded the Japs numerous caves in which to hide. Many of

470

these caves were neutralized by "Slug" Marvin's flame-throwing team. Once a company commander sent for Marvin and told him that he had seen a Jap duck into a cave. He asked Marvin to get him to surrender or seal him up. So Marvin climbed on top of the cave and hollered: "Nipponese, take off your clothes, come out with your hands up, and we'll take you prisoner and treat you well."

Instead of one voice replying from inside the cave, several called back: "Go to hell!"

Marvin then threw in three thermite grenades and listened. With the hiss of the grenades quieted, he still heard jabbering inside. He ordered a flame-thrower used. A thirty-foot stream of fire flashed into the cave and licked the walls and floor. The jabbering continued.

"TNT!" Marvin yelled.

They threw in twenty-five pound TNT charges, used the flame-throwers again, and then sprayed the inside with an automatic rifle. At last everything was still. Marvin pushed impatiently into the cave's mouth. Inside he counted thirty dead Japs. Later, when rear elements came up and made a thorough check of the cave, they found sixty-three dead enemy. The cave, which the company commander had seen *one* Jap enter, was big enough to hold five hundred men at a time!

Marvin's team eventually got worn out. Of twenty-one men who had landed with him, only six were left on their feet. Marvin sent the survivors back for a rest and volunteered to take over a rifle platoon whose commanding officer had been a casualty. Leading the platoon forward one day, "Slug," in his usual fashion, got far out ahead.

He turned and yelled back. "Come on up here, you men! I'm not a scout!"

Just then something hit his cartridge belt: a Jap hand grenade, a rifle shot—no one ever knew. "Slug's" ammunition exploded into him and around him like a fireworks display. Litter bearers carried him back to the beach, and he died a few days later on a ship. He was awarded the Navy Cross posthumously.

Close-range fighting and sudden death from small arms and occasional artillery shells characterized the remainder

471

of the battle for Guam. By D plus 8, we seemed to be well in control of the situation, although we were still suffering casualties. Our Division line swung around, joined the Brigade and the 77th Division who had pushed inland from the other beachhead, and established a line of attack clear across the island. Then we moved abreast, heading for the northern coast of Guam.

About this time, I left Wheaton and went to the 9th Marines, whose three combat correspondents had all been casualties on D-day. The 9th Marines were pushing the attack in the center of our line and meeting little resistance. We entered Agana, the capital city of Guam, and found nothing there. The town in which our men had looked forward to having their first liberty in a year was a complete shambles and deserted. The Japs did not choose to defend it, possibly because by then their communications and command were thoroughly disrupted. It would have made an excellent site for defense, however. Our naval and aerial shelling had turned it into a jungle of ruins.

Moving quickly, we left Agana and occupied the Japanese Tiyan airfield on the other side of town. The field looked like a country airport back home, though not so good. A few scattered buildings had been smashed to ruins. About twenty-five shattered Jap planes lay in the bushes and among trees along the strip. The area was deserted, and we pushed on, entering the jungle of the northern half of Guam.

It was impossible to see more than a few feet ahead through the thick foliage. We moved in skirmish lines but knew that we were leaving enemy stragglers behind. They were cut off and leaderless and were mostly wandering around in the jungle trying to stay out of our sight. They hid in caves during the day and came out to try to find other Japs at night. We were leaving them to rear elements for mopping up. Our commanding officers wanted the rifle units to keep going and wipe out any large band of Japs they found, so that no sizeable enemy group could get its breath and reorganize.

What happened when the Japs got a chance to reorganize was made grimly evident to us soon after we passed the Tiyan airfield. We had emerged on a narrow jungle road, leading to a village called Finegayan. It was about noon, and I was helping to guide a member of an artillery forward observing team up to our front-line company. A radioman, he was relieving someone who had been with us five days. The FO team members each worked five days with the forward companies, then rested in reserve a couple of days.

Along the road Jap snipers took potshots at us. We clung to the side of the trail beneath the protection of tall grass and bushes. We passed many Jap bodies, lying on the road and in the brush. They had just been killed, their skin was loose and wrinkled, and the blood was still red on their clothes.

We noted an unusual amount of firing ahead of us. Rifle and machine-gun shots cracked through the grass. Mortar shells crashed among the trees, sending up columns of black smoke. Overhead one of our observation planes was whirring back and forth. Going on, we reached a green wooden house by the side of the road. About thirty Marines lay on stretchers in front—it was an aid station. Doctors and corpsmen were working over a line of men. Two jeep ambulances were being filled with wounded. It looked like the biggest battle since we had left the ridges above the beachhead.

We found the company CP to which the radioman had been ordered to report. The Marines were crouched in shellholes and newly dug foxholes. The dirt—red and moist, almost like mud—covered the men's clothes and faces and hands. We were ordered to get down and stay down. The firing ahead was sharp. Bullets were striking trees around us. Men scurried back and forth through the grass, hunched over, the way they had moved along the beach on D-Day.

"This war ain't over yet," a sergeant said, chewing on a wad of tobacco. "I guess you know they got a lot of our guys here just now." He waved his arm around at the grass. "We got over a hundred Nips in the past half-hour, I reckon."

Although the sounds of battle were all around us, we couldn't see anything. After some time we could reconstruct what had happened. It had been an enemy ambush. The

473

Japs had had two road blocks in parallel lines across the road, about a hundred yards apart. There were mines in the roads, then antitank and heavier guns on both sides of the road, and, stretching inland, round spider pits dug into the ground to keep the tanks from going around the traps. The pits had been filled with Japs ordered to halt the tanks.

Somehow the tanks got through, but the infantry didn't. The first row of Japs let most of our men through, then opened fire on their backs. At the same moment the second row of Japs opened fire in our men's faces. The rear line of Japs were eliminated in bloody, hand-to-hand fighting. Some of the Japs jumped out of their pits to run. Our men cut them down. One Marine, PFC Francis P. Witek, killed fourteen Japs with his BAR, fearlessly standing up in the open to get a good aim at them. Then he was killed by a Jap hand grenade. (Witek received the Congressional Medal of Honor posthumously for this gallantry.)

The battle ended almost as suddenly as it had begun. A short time after the radioman and I arrived, the firing slackened and then ceased. Men lifted themselves warily and poked around in the grass. We went forward along the road about fifty yards and saw the road block that had trapped our men. A Jap 77, with big wooden wheels, stood silently against the trunk of a breadfruit tree; around it sprawled dead Japs. In from the road was a line of spider pits—round holes about two feet across and three feet deep. In each one there were two dead Japs, mashed and gory. Some had been hit with grenades, other looked as if tanks had run over them. Around the lips of their holes lay unused ammunition, black and red hand grenades, and Molotov cocktails— green *sake* bottles filled with gasoline. None of the bottles had been used. Some of our men poked for souvenirs, using their bayonets to cut the belts and buttons of the dead Japs so as to see whether they were wearing flags underneath their clothes. One Jap had a battle flag wrapped around his leg beneath a puttee. The white of the flag was covered with characters in black ink—good-luck messages from his friends and family back home. One of our interpreters, glancing at the flag, pointed to one set of characters. "That," he said, "reads: 'Death to the Anglo-American devils.'"

The man who had gotten the flag grinned. "Now ain't that sweet?" he muttered.

The road was open now, and I left the radioman and went back to the aid station. Somebody there said we had killed one hundred and nine Japs and had had almost as many casualties ourselves. Stretcher bearers were still looking around through the tall grass for our dead. A jeep came up, pulling a trailer full of new shoes and dungarees.

"Them's for my boys," the driver shouted gleefully. "I never forget them. Tonight I'm bringing up hot soup and doughnuts!"

He unhitched the trailer and took me back in the jeep. The smell along the road was growing stronger. The dead were turning ivory-colored. We passed a Marine lying on his back just off the road.

"Keep low," the driver said. "A sniper just winged that poor guy while I was coming up."

We got back without incident, and I returned to the Division CP. Some of the civilian correspondents were there. They had brought mimeographed copies of the day's news from one of the transports off shore—news that had been picked up by radio from San Francisco. One of the items said that the battle of Guam was almost over. I felt a little bitter when I went to bed that night.

The next day Captain Shoemaker of A Company, the 21st Marines—the officer who had gallantly exhorted his men to hold the line on the ridge the night of the banzai charge—was killed. Ironically, he was doing nothing at the time but resting. His men were taking a breather, lying along both sides of the same road on which we had been ambushed. Suddenly an enemy 77 shell swooshed through the air from somewhere up north and crashed with a burst of smoke. Fragments ripped into the Captain, and he died almost immediately. The men gathered around his body while they waited for a jeep ambulance, and many of them cried. One man with tears staining his dusty face turned away. "All the good ones go," he said.

On the 11th of August we reached the cliffs along the northern shore of Guam and looked down at the surf

475

breaking on the reef six hundred feet below. We sent patrols down the cliffside and out to the breakers. Then we announced that Guam had been secured.

That night I went back to the Division CP that had been moved into the jungle about halfway up the island. We had set up a fly tent and slept on top of the ground beneath the canvas. In the middle of the night somebody in a foxhole on one side of us began shooting—past us. Someone on the other side returned the fire. Others joined in, and the bullets flew back and forth. Suddenly a grenade hissed through the night and exploded. The fragments rattled against our fly tent. We pressed ourselves as flat against the ground as we could, praying that nothing would hit us. Suddenly in the darkness one of the other men in our tent yelled: "God damn it, don't you know this rock is secured!"

It would be a nice ending to the story to say that this stopped the senseless firing around us, but it didn't. And it would also be nice to say that the island at that time was *really* secured, but it wasn't. There was still a lot of fighting on Guam ahead of us.

476

MacArthur in the Southwest Pacific

While the Navy "island-hopped," General MacArthur, Allied Commander in the Southwest Pacific, drove up the northeastern coast of New Guinea, on his way back to the Philippines. He had a dirty job. His supply lines were halfway round the world, and his priority for ships and supplies was generally second to the Navy's.

MacArthur developed his own style of island-hopping. Army assault units of American and Australian troops were put ashore up the coast to surround and wipe out Jap strong points; in this manner, Salamaua, Finschhaven, and Lae were taken, and then, by-passing the big Jap stronghold at Wewak, Aitape and Hollandia were assaulted.

Walter Karig says, "Although several airfields had been acquired with the Hollandia occupation, none could be used by the Army's heavy bombers which had to use the strips near Lae or those in the Admiralties, 440 miles to the east. It was of strategic urgency to obtain heavy bomber fields closer to the operating area.* There was nothing suitable short of Biak, where the Japanese had three excellent strips along the south coast." **

On the morning of May 27, 1944, Major General Horace Fuller's 41st Division hit the beaches. There they would find a garrison of 10,000 Japs and when the island was taken, the last major target in New Guinea would be secured. But Biak was not an easy nut to crack. The terrain, as General Eichelberger describes it, "was scarred and pitted by the accidents of Nature's past, and some of the cliffs and limestone terraces along its southern shore seemed as barren as the mountains of the moon.

"[There were] caves with the dimensions of a narrow dark hallway, caves as deep and large as five-story tenement buildings and with as many levels of connecting galleries, caves with weird stalactite and

*For the campaign in the Philippines.
**The End of an Empire, pp. 204-205. Rinehart & Co.

stalagmite formations reminiscent of the Carlsbad Caves of New Mexico. It is also an island of subterranean streams, and scarce (and evil-tasting) surface water. Soldiers fought for the precious water-holes, and more than one American died as he crawled forward in the night to replenish his water-bottle.

"It was plain that Biak could not belong to us before we had captured the caves. The first riddle—no one had solved it before 1 Corps arrived—was to find the main caves. Where were they? Where were the entrances and exits? Aerial photographs were of no help in locating them. Our maps told us nothing."*

The following selection about the caves of Biak is written by Colonel Harold Riegelman, Chemical Officer to the Corps Commander, General Eichelberger. As such, one of Col. Riegelman's duties in chemical warfare was, if called for, to direct the use of the flame thrower. The experience with this weapon in the early days of the war was disappointing, to say the least. He tells of one such experience during the attack on Buna in New Guinea:

"On December 8, early morning, Lieutenant Emory of E Company reconnoitered, crawling slowly through the kunai grass and circling toward the breastworks. Corporal Giglio of the Engineers, one of the flame thrower operators, followed close behind. They reached the breastworks. Giglio could not see the grass-screened gun embrasure. Emory removed his helmet, raised it on the muzzle of his carbine ever so little above the crest of the breastworks. A spate of fire bent the grasses in front of the bunker but the helmet was just outside the arc. Giglio thus located the embrasure. The two returned to E Company lines.

"The sun was high and cooking when Giglio moved again on hands and knees through the steaming kunai. His 60 pound fuel tank covered with burlap weighed heavily on his back. The flame gun and hose snagged the base of the tall grass. Sweat poured over his face and body. The alternate operator followed to take on where Giglio left off if Giglio was hit. Then came Emory, Sergeant Niese of the Division's Chemical Section laden with grenades and a wrench for the flame thrower, and four riflemen.

"At the same time, three automatic riflemen circled through the kunai toward the left flank of the bunker. They hoped to get to its

*From *Jungle Road to Tokyo* by Lt. Gen. R. L. Eichelberger. Viking Press.

478

rear and fire into it to divert the occupants and the snipers from the flame thrower party.

"Emory's team reached the breastworks without drawing a shot. Giglio slid along the shallow trench to its far end. He was not hot now. He was cold as ice. The three automatic riflemen on the opposite flank opened diverting fire as planned. Giglio left the trench. He crawled eight yards. He started his ignition and pressed the fuel release. A searing flame billowed toward the bunker. Something wrong with the pressure. The burst rolled only fifteen yards—seven yards short. The four riflemen charged from behind the breastworks. One was hit in the shoulder and dragged himself back to cover. The other three were pinned to the ground. Giglio crouched low and moved forward. He repeatedly released bursts, which were shorter and shorter as the pressure grew weaker. Yard by yard he drew closer to the bunker. Yard by yard the range of his weapon faded. Giglio knew he was licked. But he was so close to the gun port. He could see it plainly enough. Too plainly. A magnet that drew him onward. If only the goddamned gun would work! He was only fifteen yards away now. A set up. A perfect set up. If only the goddamned gun.

"Emory was desperate. He ordered the alternate operator to stay under cover. What else to do? The flame gun was no damn good. The whole business was a flop. The goddamned.... Blackness. Niese ordered the men back. Giglio was motionless. The wounded rifleman had stemmed the trickle from his shoulder. The lieutenant was dead. The sniper had got him between the eyes. Somehow the wounded and the well crawled back to our lines. Two of the automatic riflemen did not return.

"And there was Giglio. The sun was low when his eyes fluttered open, and consciousness emerged from the black depths. The lead which had crashed through the top of his helmet had knocked him out cold, but left him untouched. He lay quiet in the short twilight. His head throbbed. His mouth was very dry. As darkness fell he slowly, very, very slowly disengaged the straps which supported the fuel tank. He inched back almost imperceptibly to the shallow trench, to the breastworks, through the kunai. As he approached his lines he whispered hoarsely, "I'm Giglio. Don't shoot. I'm Giglio."

"There was indeed plenty wrong with these weapons. There was the low pressure in the nitrogen, hydrogen, and fuel cylinders. Many cylinders had pin holes through which gas was lost. Batteries for the ignition were not protected against New Guinea heat and humidity. The permeating moisture corroded the ignition system.

"The pin holes had to be welded. The flame throwers were rebuilt and thoroughly waterproofed so that they could be fired after twenty hours immersion in water. These things were not done in the States. They were done by our 10th Chemical Maintenance Company in Brisbane.

"The weapon was still not entirely dependable. Four times out of five it would perform. That was a lot better than at Buna. But there was still the question of tactical employment. That remained to be worked out.

"Also I learned that the Japs had flame throwers, better indeed than the model with which we were then equipped. But the Japs had not used their flame throwers. This fact gave point to reports of the almost pathological dread of fire by the Japanese. I had heard that from early childhood they are warned against fire and forbidden to use it under any circumstances likely to endanger the flimsy houses in which they lived. Evidently the lesson was well learned and was carried into battle to such a degree that they even dreaded to use their own very efficient flame throwers. It was, of course, possible that the development of the weapon was not accompanied by development of techniques to use it. But that would not prevent unsuccessful attempts to use it, resulting in the death of the operator—a cost these Japs did not used their flame throwers. This fact gave point to reports of the reported to me.

"All men fear fire. But there are degrees of fear. And if as I began to believe, the Japanese fear was beyond normal, certainly the possibilities of using flame with minimum risk to our own personnel were well worth exploring." *

Flame throwers were used on Biak against the caves but, according to General Eichelberger, with only limited success. Other means were necessary, and as usual it was at the risk of soldiers' lives. Colonel Riegelman arrived on the island about the middle of June at the time General Fuller was being relieved of command because of "not sufficient progress."

*Colonel Harold Riegelman, *Caves of Biak,* pp. 67, 68, 69. Dial Press.

THE CAVES OF BIAK

by Colonel Harold Riegelman

In the afternoon came the call from Sixth Army Headquarters, now bivouacked on the east shore of Humboldt Bay. General Eichelberger hurried over by jeep and boat. General Krueger ordered him and his staff to take over the "Hurricane" Task Force at Biak. Krueger said that despite the communiqués and press stories to the contrary, things were not going well. Severe fighting, incredibly rough terrain, and heat and scarcity of water were rapidly wearing down the 162nd, part of the 163rd, and the 186th Regiments of the 41st Infantry Division which made up the bulk of the task force. Krueger was not satisfied with the contradictory reports he had received. The airdromes had not yet been secured although it was nearly three weeks after the landing. Eichelberger and his Corps were to relieve General Horace H. Fuller and his staff as the Task Force Command, but Fuller was to remain as Division Commander. Eichelberger was to take with him, in addition to his own headquarters, the 34th Regimental Combat Team of the 24th Infantry Division.

On the evening of June 15 we were aboard LST 459 anchored in Humboldt Bay. We were to proceed west to Wakde, pick up a destroyer and two more LSTs, and then move on to Biak. Our small convoy carried Corps headquarters, Corps artillery, and the 34th Regimental Combat Team.

We left Hollandia in early afternoon of June 16 and made rendezvous with the rest of the convoy off Wakde. The sunny skies till mid-morning of the second day out gave way to rain and blessed overcast, screening our approach from air observation.

All I knew about Biak was that it was an island, a degree

south of the Equator, one of the Schouten group lying north of Geelvink Bay toward the western end of New Guinea. Biak was roughly triangular in shape. The south shore ran about 40 miles east-west; its west shore slightly shorter, ran north-south; its hypotenuse north-east with a shoreline of some 50 miles. Biak was 300 miles from Hollandia, less than 1,000 miles from the Philippines, and within fighter-plane range of that poisonous dot in the ocean, Palau, from which most of our air troubles were stemming. The northern portion was mountainous with ridges up to 2,000 feet. The altitude dropped toward the south but the country was broken throughout, except for the area of the three landing fields—Mokmer, Borokoe, and Sorido—on the flat, low, southern coastal fringe of Biak. There could be no assault on the Philippines from New Guinea unless Biak were secured on the east of the sea lane and Halmehara on the west.

I remembered now with gratitude that we had stripped everything at Hollandia in order to outfit the "Hurricane" Task Force for its mission. As of May 27, when it stormed Biak, it had no lack of munitions and supplies. I was troubled about General Fuller—a splendid officer, aggressive, resourceful, and worshipped by his Division. This must have been a terrific blow to him. Krueger was ruthless when it came to relieving commanders who did not deliver on Krueger's schedule.

Early morning of the third day, Sunday, June 19, we landed dry shod at the jetty and were transported along a soupy coral road westward to the half-evacuated headquarters of the 41st Division.

Lieutenant Colonel Frank Arthur's Division chemical section had just left its quarters in the skeleton of a former native church, its roof half off, its timber supports leaning drunkenly toward the road, as though it were a toothless, decrepit face leering out from under a thatched fringe. I directed Sergeant Harriman to set up a command post tent next to the church and pray that, if fall it must, it would collapse forward or backward and not sidewise. While our truck was on the way, I hurried off to General Fuller's tent.

I felt as though I were making a condolence call. Fuller's

482

face did not weaken the illusion. It showed the deepest distress. In repose, it was alert, sinewy, mobile. Direct grey eyes, tanned, taut skin. Now the lips were tight, the lines deep, the eyes moist.

"We're all sorry, General."

"I know. But what's done is done. I'm leaving the Division."

"General, don't do that. The Division idolizes you."

"No, Harold, I've been kicked out as Task Force Commander and the Division can't have the confidence in me it must have in its leader. . . . From the beginning I begged and pleaded for one more regiment. I know what this operation needs. With one more regiment we'd have had the airdromes in operation a week ago. Now, they send in another regiment—but not to me."

The grey eyes filled and a tear streaked the weathered cheek. Anger, frustration, humiliation.

He left the tent, mounted a jeep, and rode away from the Division he'd brought to Australia more than two years before, trained to razor edge at Rockhampton, commanded brilliantly from Buna to Hollandia, and landed at hot, cave-infested, waterless, stubborn Biak—with a smaller force than the mission required.

Now my section was set up. My bedding roll was taken over to my tent. All through the morning there had been intermittent small arms and mortar fire over the hill to the north. Our howitzers were growling west of us.

After noon mess, I was off to visit Frank Arthur at the new Division headquarters near the Mokmer drome. As my jeep moved west I began to appreciate Fuller's difficulties. The densely jungled strip between the road and the shore widened. Beyond the shore line the reef extended some 200 yards the length of the south shore and was now exposed by the low tide. On the land side of the road the brow of the high ridge came closer and rose higher. The jungle disappeared and revealed a steep slope of rotten coral rising eighty feet to the base of a sheer eighty-foot coral cliff. Near the base of the cliff a gallery was deeply etched; some twenty feet above this there was another gallery. We passed this stretch, crossed a polluted stream which emerged from

483

under the cliff. From this point the high cliff mass pushed the road out to the very shore line. This was the former village of Parai. Just past the abandoned hovels, the road was forced into the shallow sea, soon emerging as the hill mass fell back and swung in a wide arc behind Mokmer drome, which was commanded from the north by these receding heights.

This was the almost fatal route of the 162nd Infantry. It landed at Bosnek on May 27 against light opposition. The Japs took to high ground, held their fire except for occasional sniping, and did not use their planes. By that night the regiment had slogged eight miles up the coastal road and well past the narrow defile beyond Parai. There had been no fire from the cliff galleries as the regiment passed below, and came to a point less than a quarter mile from Mokmer Airdome. One battalion was further advanced than the rest. The troops moved too fast for their artillery and had none in support. Desultory sniping continued through the night.

At dawn the Jap trap was sprung. Artillery, machine gun, rifle fire, and mortars plastered our troops. The forward battalion was cut off by an invisible, deadly wall of steel and lead. Tanks bore down on that isolated force but for some mysterious reason failed to follow up their advantage.

Our destroyers came in close and, while not effective in causing casualties among the cave-protected Japs, discouraged an attack which might well have annihilated the regiment. The destroyers themselves took some punishment from Jap six-inch shells. The forward battalion managed at length to rejoin the main body, and this fell back under the protection of the cliffs where they overhung the sea west of Parai.

That noon a rescue party of amphibious engineers arrived with ten "buffaloes." These wriggled across the reef bearing ammunition and medical supplies. They delivered their precious cargoes and departed loaded with wounded. By some miracle the barrage of artillery and mortar fire laid upon the sea-going vehicles took no toll of them, their cargo, or their crews.

484

That night the 162nd was sealed off by the Japs at Parai and the cliff galleries which were no longer silent above the coastal road. At dawn the Japs attacked again and again and yet again. Seven of their tanks were destroyed by five of our Shermans. All attacks were repulsed with heavy losses on both sides. The night of the 28th, the fleet of buffaloes under cover of darkness evacuated the 162nd with its equipment. A bad licking. A near disaster which could have been a major calamity had the regiment fought less valiantly or the Japs followed up their early advantages more aggressively.

Nevertheless, here was Mokmer drome—ours, though not yet sufficiently secure from enemy fire for use by our planes. This feat had been accomplished by the 186th Infantry Regiment, reinforced by the 163rd when that Regiment was later brought in from Wakde. The 162nd had effectively demonstrated that the coastal road was an unprofitable approach to the drome. The 186th worked its way northward up the slopes of Bosnek and then westward through the broken rocky ground behind the heights overlooking the sea. This land was waterless save for one water hole which the Yanks won, lost, and won again. Water, ammunition, and supplies had to be man-packed. Every inch of the way was contested. Japs magically appeared and disappeared into their caves. They laid ambush after ambush. Much of the fighting was with pistols, knives, and bare fists. Jap artillery and mortars fired and were withdrawn into caves. The heat was unbearable. But the invaders were persistent and, at long last, overran Mokmer drome and held the nearest ridge to the north. But the Japs still controlled the higher ridges further north and northwest. Patrols reached Borokoe and Sorido, but these objectives had not yet been occupied in force. General Eichelberger had reorganized his forces, reconnoitered the contested areas, and was ready to move hard and fast.

I found Arthur in his shelter near the sea, somewhat leaner than at Hollandia and equally serious. Arthur was always serious unless something struck him as particularly funny. That brought a swift, brief guffaw, after which Arthur was serious again. It was quite evident that nothing

485

struck him as being particularly funny just then. He was manifestly glad to see me and I was certainly glad to see him. He was worried.

"How are things going, Frank?"

"Not too well, sir. These damned caves. If we could only use some of the Jap gas. We've captured a lot of it, mostly poison smoke candles. Just the thing for these caves."

"How about the flame throwers?"

"Fairly good. No good against the deep ones. The day after we landed we took heavy fire from a beach cave. We organized a flame thrower assault party. The riflemen deployed across the beach and neutralized the cave entrance while the flame-thrower operator advanced under cover of the embankment until he was within 20 feet of the cave entrance. Then he let go, obliquely into the entrance, and moved directly in front for a final burst. The flame flushed four Japs, all of whom were killed by the riflemen in the party.

"A number of beach caves got that treatment from the 186th Infantry. Right after the final burst, high explosives were thrust into the cave and detonated.

"We've used flame throwers against them in the hills, usually without sufficient reconnaissance and usually with too few flame throwers. There have been good exceptions. We found Japs dead in caves, their clothes burning. Some were dead with no marks on them, nothing to indicate the cause of death. Still others rush out, often with clothing aflame, and are picked off by rifles. And some few commit hara-kiri. Our tactical theory has proved itself. Where there have been failures it is because the doctrine has not been well applied. . . . We could use more flame throwers if we had them. The Jap planes have been nightly visitors at our old headquarters where you are. We spent a good part of the dark hours in the ground."

"I gathered as much. Damn near room for a battalion in the holes you dug at Headquarters."

"You'll be glad we dug 'em."

Arthur's Sergeant Roe called me to one side to say that

486

the Lieutenant Colonel was a bit sensitive on this subject. As Roe put it: "You see, sir, down Bosnek way we got strafed or bombed very frequent. The Lieutenant Colonel, he used to jump into an open ditch. And well, there was a latrine on one side of the ditch, a garbage dump on the other side. And well, a Nip bomber came over one night and dropped two eggs. Not in the ditch, sir. There was one in the garbage dump and most of the garbage landed on the Lieutenant Colonel. But you could still see who he was. The other landed in the latrine on the other side of his ditch. And after that you couldn't see the Lieutenant Colonel, sir. And for a long time you wouldn't want to see him. But, by Jesus, you could smell him a hell of a long way off."

We talked about our arrival and Fuller's departure. Arthur resented the replacement, but his resentment was directed at Sixth Army. I assumed this feeling was general. I hoped it was. It would not have helped this operation if it were directed against us.

I saw the disabled Jap tanks, inspected a nearby mortar platoon, talked to the men, noted their drawn, bearded faces and eyes, red from lack of sleep. They did not complain. "I guess they think we must be pretty good, sir, to have our company, just one company, support the whole goddam task force."

Evening mess at Corps. Long tables. General Eichelberger with his four Gs, Chief of Staff, and aides at one side of the tent. Chiefs of sections at the next table. There was a buzz of conversation.

Above it, Eichelberger's voice:

"How about it, Chemical Officer? What do you do with those caves?"

"We got a lot of Jap gas that isn't being used, sir."

That was a pretty weak topper for the General's little joke. The buzz of conversation stopped a moment and then resumed. Much to my relief the joke was dropped.

I picked my way gingerly toward my section tent. I felt superfluous. Arthur was the best division chemical officer in the Southwest Pacific. There was really nothing. . . . Good God! Maybe Eichelberger *wasn't* joking! I stopped dead in my tracks and hurried back through the maze of tent ropes and mantrap air shelters. The General was on his way to his tent. I overtook him at the flap.

"Sir, it just came to me that you might not have been joking when you popped the caves at me."

He looked at me gravely.

"Harold, I was never more serious in all my life."

"Very good, sir. That's all I wanted to know. Good night, sir."

"Good night. And be careful. I don't want to have to get a new chemical officer."

"Thanks! My sentiments exactly, sir."

The air alert wailed. A single Jap plane swooped over headquarters. There were bursts of strafing fire down the road toward Bosnek. It was over almost before the alarm ceased. And I was back in my C.P. tent and planning for the morrow.

Three days later, Wednesday, the 21st, I was ready to report to the General.

In the areas investigated Sergeant Harriman had always been with me along with two or three other enlisted men armed with grenades and carbines. On two patrols Arthur had joined us. We had uncovered a number of beach caves east of Bosnek. We took turns crawling into each cave; where possible, one man went directly behind and covered with a carbine the one whose turn it was to enter first. When in doubt whether the cave had been abandoned, we tossed in a grenade or two before entry. That would sterilize the caves, which were not large. I measured each cave, sketched it in plan and elevation, and indicated its field of fire and tactical use.

There were beach caves just west of Parai. Each was examined. I was climbing up the face of the cliff above the entrance of one of these caverns when my hand, groping for a hold on a narrow shelf, disturbed a smooth, round object. As I pulled myself up, a skull grinned at me from among a small pile of human bones. I had evidently uncovered the corpus delicti of an ancient crime.

With Arthur I crossed Mokmer drome by jeep to the first rise beyond. Our objective was one of the outlets of the

488

West Caves. These were still held in force by the enemy. The First Battalion of the 162nd Infantry had invested them. But the main and secondary entrances could not be approached without drawing fire.

We dismounted short of the rise and followed a rocky trail over the ridge into a hollow, up a steep incline to higher ground beyond. We stepped warily now for, while we claimed the ground as ours, the fact was still in dispute. Over to our right the smoke of battle rose from what appeared to be a wide crater. Rifle and machine-gun fire were intermittent. Occasionally a Jap "knee mortar" coughed and we looked skyward for the small black projectile which could be ducked if seasonably seen. We circled to the left and crawled forward through the brush to the edge of a hole a full sixty feet deep and 120 feet across, the sides perpendicular, the bottom strewn with broken rocks. We peered cautiously over the edge. In the opposite wall was a cave portal twenty feet high, the view within obstructed by large stalactites. This, Arthur explained, was the "funnel" or west "entrance" of the West Caves.

"We believe there is," he explained, "some sort of gallery with side chambers running about 300 feet easterly to another open fault or sump about twenty feet deep and seventy-five feet across. The main entrance is in the wall of that sump. And the sides of the sump are not so sheer as this. In fact, there is a trail from the cave entrance along one side of the sump leading to normal ground level. There are a couple of machine-gun emplacements on that side and on the opposite side of the sump. A hornet's nest if ever there was one. We call that the south sump. A narrow neck of ground separates this from the north sump, which is wider than the south sump and deeper. At the northwest corner of the north sump there is another entrance. I know all these connect because we lowered a half dozen 4.2 inch mortar shells filled with FS (sulphuric fumes) smoke into this funnel just inside the cave and detonated them electrically. We saw smoke rise from the north and south sumps. Also from several fissures between here and the south sump. We dumped several hundred gallons of gasoline into those fissures and then dropped phosphorus bombs through them.

The gasoline caught fire and set off a lot of ammunition within the cave net. You can still hear it popping."

I could. Deep in the cavern a sound as though of children's firecrackers in a neighbor's basement.

"We know there's a lot of Japs in there, but we don't know how many. We think they are very unhappy."

It was after Wednesday evening mess. I was putting the finishing touches on my recommendations for reduction of cave defenses, when a message arrived from Clovis Byers. "Dawn attack on the West Caves tomorrow." I told Perrini to stop typing. There might be changes in the text tomorrow. I went to bed.

Dawn, Thursday. Lieutenant Colonel Henry Antell, Cornell '17, lately of the *New York Times*, presently assistant G-1, was with me. He had asked me the night before to take him along. Sergeant Harriman drove the jeep. Before sun-up we were at the headquarters of the First Battalion, 162nd Infantry. The battalion commander, Major Benson, was waiting. He showed me his dispositions on the field map. The south sump of the West Caves was the main objective. The first platoon of Company C was in position there with two tanks. The rest of the company was engaged in neutralizing and sealing off egress from the north sump. The two other companies of the battalion were held in reserve, available as needed.

We started from battalion headquarters, Benson leading. I followed. Antell and Harriman, each with carbines, and three riflemen walked single-file through sparse woods. We passed over a flat area, odor of the dead heavy in the still, cool air, and worked our way into a fold below the south sump. The pop of the Jap knee mortars divided our attention between the treacherous, rocky footing and the sky. Off to the right a single bark of one of our own sixty-millimeter mortars evidently registering. There were occasional rifle shots and short bursts of machine gun fire. We crouched low as we moved ahead.

We reached a point below the sump and crawled up the steep embankment. Smoke haze hung over the crater. Two light tanks were maneuvering on the rim. They opened up with a succession of salvos from their seventy-fives. A splin-

490

tered tree stump was near one of the tanks. I wriggled on to the ridge behind the stump. The opposite side of the sump was a vertical wall. In this wall, the main entrance to the West Caves. Thick stalactites hung from the upper lip of the ten-foot mouth, giant tusks which extended to the lower lip and melted into it. Behind these columns the roof of the mouth and the floor sloped back and down into blackness. The seventy-fives made no impression upon the coral. I worked my way around the rim of the sump. Bodies of dead Japs were about. Not all the dead were Japs. Ahead was an American sergeant lying on his back, his young, thoughtful face placid, his black hair tousled, his body relaxed in last repose.

The sun was up. The seventy-fives were still firing. It was late in the morning. There had been no progress. The Japs were sitting it out, deep within their caverns. An idea had begun to come to life. It might be a wild one, but it could hardly be worse than what we were doing. I talked with Benson. He thought it worth trying and sent a request to the engineers. The plan was not complicated. It was apparent that the cave was impervious to all calibres we could bring to bear. Its entrance defied demolition. But if a large enough charge of TNT were exploded at the entrance, perhaps the concussion would stun if not kill the defenders. In either case we could get in and destroy them.

Across the sump at a point just above the cave entrance a party of engineers arrived with a quarter-ton trailer. They set up a winch and lowered 850 pounds of TNT with wires attached. It was now just past noon. I suggested to Benson that he pull his troops back a hundred yards and bring the tanks to lower ground. These orders were issued. We lay on our stomachs a safe distance from the sump. Firing had ceased in the area. Silence, so still one felt it. I had no idea what 850 pounds of TNT would do. I only knew it was a lot of TNT, a great deal more than I had ever seen used. A crack-brained idea. I wondered if we were far enough back. My speculations were cut short by an ear-splitting roar. A cloud of dust and smoke rose out of the sump, high in the air. The thud of falling rocks. A few landed about us. We came sharply to a squat in order to bring as much of us

491

as possible under the protection of our steel helmets. The platoon and the tanks were ordered back into position.

Benson and I proceeded to the sump. The coral columns screening the mouth had disappeared. They lay in broken pieces on the lower lip of the entrance. But then another problem occurred to me. I presumed that gases had been generated by the explosion, which might endanger an assault party. If this were true I had no idea how long it would take these gases to dissipate.

There seemed but one solution. It was as distasteful to me as it was obvious. I walked down the trail cut into the north side of the sump. Benson and Antell followed. Harriman trailed above and behind, his carbine ready for any movement within the cave. There was none. I advanced into the gaping mouth and peered down into the blackness. The blackness stared back. After a moment, I could see dim outlines of prostrate forms. Foul odors drifted up from the hole. But whether these were poisonous or the backdraft of decomposing flesh, I did not know. I suggested to Benson that he wait a minute or two and then send his men in to bayonet every Jap whether breathing or still. I had my battered folding camera in a leather case attached to my web belt. I took a closeup picture of the toothless yawning mouth.

My work seemed finished here, and I felt I could now complete my report. Antell, Harriman, and I left. We passed half-crouched around the rim of the north sump. Beyond was a large shell crater. Our guide explained that a party of seven Japs had collected there early that morning to eat breakfast preparatory to a sortie on some unknown mission. The crew of a sixty-millimeter mortar spotted them and fired a single shot, the shot we had heard on our way from battalion headquarters. It landed precisely in the center of the Jap patrol, and there were the seven bodies radiating from the point of impact symbolically like the rays of the rising sun.

My report was ready that evening, complete with sketches. Sergeant Sliger took it to the Chief of Staff.

"The techniques of reduction of cave nets are frontal and vertical attack, envelopment, isolation, siege, and assault.

492

The means include all ground fires capable of being laid on the target using high explosive and white phosphorous shell and grenades, air bombardment, strafing, flame throwers, gasoline demolition charges, and smoke. Tanks are employed to precede infantry, firing cannon and machine guns at point blank range.

"Clusters of FS-filled 4.2-inch chemical mortar shell are defused, No. six detonators being substituted, lowered in front of windward cave openings of cave nets and fired electrically. In addition to the harassing effect of FS in confined spaces, the drift of the smoke rising in plumes from remote openings reveals their precise location and they are promptly invested, thereby cutting off supply and escape without unnecessary risk of reconnaissance." I also recommended the introduction of HC smoke pots into windward entrances. This smoke is harmless in the open, but is lethal in enclosed spaces. Neither of these smokes was classified as a poison gas.

"When demolition proves impracticable due to the hardness of the coral rock, charges of TNT ranging up to 850 pounds are exploded at a cave entrance with telling concussion effect that kills or incapacitates the occupants. But this requires prompt assault by infantry shooting or bayoneting all bodies alive or dead."

There was further detail concerning concussion charges and a suggested ratio of these to the size of the cave net; also a note on the desirability of simultaneous detonation at several entrances to the same net. This section of the report also covered charges placed in holes drilled in the ground above caves to disrupt subsurface communications and lighting, produce casualties, and destroy stores.

I stressed the importance of thorough ground and air reconnaissance before any assault and the removal of screening foliage by searching high explosive and white phosphorous fires including rockets and bazookas. The report noted that otherwise bombardment and strafing had little physical effect except to pin the enemy within the cave and obstruct and limit his field of fire.

I discussed the portable flame thrower and how it should be used in attacking shallow caves to avoid back-blast; the use of mechanized flame throwers against cliff galleries. And gasoline poured into windward or depressed entrances and ignited by grenades to exhaust oxygen, harass the defenders, and explode their ammunition.

I skeptically retained a suggestion which occurred earlier in my investigations and had become less and less attractive: the employment of well-trained war dogs to carry time charges into caves. We had several of these dogs with us in Biak. They were invaluable in alerting our patrols against ambush.

Meanwhile G-1, with the help of prisoners taken during the day, had pieced together events which preceded the previous day's attack.

The commanding officer of some 10,000 troops defending Biak was Colonel Kuzume. The West Caves were his last stand. These accommodated 900 men, were equipped with electric light, radio, and fresh water and well supplied with food and ammunition. By Wednesday, June 21, the force was reduced to about 235 men. Colonel Kuzume assembled these in the large chamber between the south sump and the funnel. The officers, who occupied the more elaborately improved connecting cave which opened into the north sump, were present. Colonel Kuzume stated that further organized defense was useless. He suggested that the remnant of his command still in the West Caves could remain and continue to resist or make a banzai suicide attack or escape into mountains in the northern part of the island with the possibility of ultimate rescue. Then he burnt all his documents, placed the regimental colors upon the pyre, and, as these were reduced to ashes, disemboweled himself in traditional fashion. At the end of that night, while the moon was high, 109 of his officers and men elected the banzai attack and were wiped out. This left 125 in the caves when the First Battalion attacked next day. A number of these were wounded and others were in bad physical and mental condition as a result of the harassing technique preceding the attack.

Kuzume's tactics were plain enough and were well suited to the cave-pocked terrain. His men were in detachments of varying sizes depending upon the size of the caves and cave

494

nets to which they were anchored. They broke out of these shelters for surprise attacks and then returned to their warrens. Their mortars and artillery were kept under coral cover when not in use. These tactics were harassing and costly to us. But they suffered from a weakness which indicated that they might later prove fatal to the Japs. They precluded the massing of a co-ordinated, effective striking force and invited isolation and piecemeal destruction. Judging from the evidence of plentiful stores along the coast, the caves were abundantly supplied with food, equipment, ordnance, and ammunition. Also, with radio communications. So the key to securing the airdromes was the reduction of the caves within striking distance of the coast. With these cleaned out the main fighting force could be destroyed, and the southern coastal strip which was all that was tactically usable on the Island would be safe, save perhaps for occasional and decreasingly effective raids by diminishing numbers of wasting remnants unable or unwilling to chance the forbidding areas to the north.

Night. A message to report to Clovis Byers' tent.

The floor of Clovis' tent was three feet below the surrounding ground. Two feet more of sand bags fairly secured the interior from air bomb fragments and sniping. The flaps and sides were sealed to black out the lantern light within. General Eichelberger was seated at Clovis' field table. Clovis, the four Gs, and the Artillery Officer were seated in a horseshoe facing the General. All were grave. I sensed some sort of disagreement and this was confirmed by the General's first question: "How much Jap gas do you have?"

"Plenty, sir. We have taken great quantities, mostly poison smoke."

"Could this be used against the remaining caves?"

"Yes, sir."

"With what effect?"

"It would reduce them in half the time, with possibly one-third fewer casualties to us."

"Harold, there is a disagreement between me and my staff. I believe we should use that gas. My staff differs. I shall follow your judgment."

"Sir, in my opinion the staff is right. And I believe you'd be relieved in twenty-four hours after you used gas. In the end that would cost us more in time and casualties than if we keep on as we are."

"Thank you. That is all."

I returned to my tent and went to bed. I never thought I should see the day when I would oppose the use of gas against the Jap, especially his own gas. Yet I could not think I had been wrong in this.

On the fifth day after the attack on the West Caves I returned to inspect the north sump and was not surprised to hear that the West Caves were no longer a threat, but was shocked to learn that our troops had not yet occupied the cave net. It was clear that if I was over-cautious in respect to the accumulation of lethal gases from the explosion, Major Benson went me one better and held his men out long enough for a small number of the defenders to recover from the effect of the concussion. These were sufficient to keep one rifle company in the cave area for five days. I had been the first and last American in the net in that period. The lesson was clear. The gases from the explosion dissipated within a few minutes. I had expected that, having gone in and come out myself without drawing fire, on the heels of the first day's attack, patrols would quickly follow. But they did not. A twenty-minute delay spoiled that opportunity. Since then a half-dozen Japs had been shot from time to time attempting to escape from their fateful tomb.

At long last a patrol was about to undertake the mopping up of the main cave net. Meanwhile, I wished to explore the north sump. All was silent there. No Jap had shown himself in that sump for several days. I organized a small party and prepared to enter. The north sump was almost forty paces across and forty feet deep. A small cave opened off one side. I placed an enlisted man there with orders to shoot ·if there was any movement within which did not identify itself as of our party, and I proceeded to the larger entrance across the sump. Within the mouth I followed an incline ending somewhat below the floor of the sump, at a cavern which appeared to have been used as a kitchen. One side of the cavern showed a drop of ten feet to a shelf. I disposed of the party so that the first men down were covered from the kitchen and these in turn covered the next group to descend. From the shelf we peered into a large pit, the floor of which, twenty feet below, was covered with wood planks. A ladder led to that level. Down it a grizzled, bearded enlisted man climbed with pistol and flashlight, searching out the dark crannies with his beam as he paused from rung to rung, our own carbines and pistols cocked to nail any sign of life. Once down, he became the security detail, and we rapidly followed. The chamber in which we found ourselves was large, dark, unbearably hot, fetid, and swarming with flies. All of us were dripping perspiration. A third of the area of about 500 square feet was occupied by a palm-thatched hut, evidently an officers' billet. Another third was covered by a tarpaulin for junior officers or, more likely, orderlies. The center, where the ladder was located, was open.

I found in the hut a treasure house of equipment, sketches, and diaries. I carefully bundled the sketches and diaries for G-2. Among the sketches I found a map of the West Caves and was relieved to note that it conformed closely to the sketch appended to my report, save for two additional chambers in the main net. The map showed a passage connecting the officers' cave with the net, as expected.

I found the passage at the point indicated by the map. It was barely wide enough for one man to squeeze through. I worked my way along this damp, foul corridor, feeling for a precarious footing on the slimy, jagged rock floor, until a breath of cooler air warned me that I was about to enter the main net. I went no further. If our patrols had entered as planned, a movement on my part in the dark might well end a promising career. I returned. The party climbed up and out of the pit.

The patrols had in fact entered the south sump cave mouth and had finished their round of the net. A hellish tour. More than a hundred bodies in various stages of decomposition. One live Jap who was promptly shot. The stench was weighted to suffocation with filth, death, and corruption. And this ended the story of the West Caves—

longer by five days than it needed have been. But fruitful in result and in the clue it had given to the reduction of similar nets. The one mistake which postponed the end would not be repeated. It was not a costly mistake, for the explosion permanently paralyzed the striking power of the defenders, and they caused no further casualties among our troops. Yet these same troops might have been more usefully employed elsewhere.

We left Biak to return to Lake Sentani on June 29, less than a fortnight after Corps arrived. Mokmer, Boridoe, Sorido were all secure and in use. There were still some caves to be cleaned out, notably the East Caves in the pocket above Ibdi near Parai. But these were isolated and did not retard the development of the airdrome.

Long Strike in the Pacific

In early September, 1944, General George C. Kenney, Commander of the Allied Air Forces in the Southwest Pacific met General MacArthur at Hollandia. He proposed a series of attacks on the Japanese oil refineries at Balikpapan (Borneo). Most of the aviation fuel used by the Japanese air forces was produced at Balikpapan; if the refineries were destroyed, the enemy would suffer fuel shortages to an extent that many of their planes might be grounded.

General MacArthur was scheduled to invade the Philippines only weeks away and gave the plan of attack his approval. The missions were to be flown just as soon as the bomber strips could be readied on newly won Biak and Noemfoor.

On September 30th, October 3rd and 5th, B-24 Liberator bombers blasted the refineries with 1,000-pound bombs. The Japanese rushed reinforcements from their air fields in the Philippines but General Kenney, informed of the move, drew on all available bombers in the area to increase his strength.

On October 10th, 106 Liberators, escorted by P-38s picked up along the way, had "one of the toughest fights of the war" to quote General Kenney. But this strike, plus another on the 14th, put the Balikpapan refineries out of commission for the rest of the war.

The preparations for the first raid were unusual because the round trip of 2,500 miles to Balikpapan taxed the flying capacity of the B-24 to the utmost. Until the B-29s with their longer range began to operate from Saipan this was the longest strike of the war. It could be said to be the most daring.

499

RAID ON BALIKPAPAN*

by Captain Elliott Arnold
and Captain Donald Hough

On a blistering hot day in September, 1944, a few officers were called together at the headquarters of the Far East Air Forces in the Southwest Pacific and were told to make plans for a bombing mission: the target was to be the Dutch oil refinery at Balikpapan on the east coast of Borneo.

The officers went to a map. They put their fingers on the island of Noemfoor, in the Netherlands East Indies, from which the B-24s would take off. They found Balikpapan. They measured. It made a round trip of twenty-five hundred miles.

Now the heavy bombers in the Southwest Pacific were not unused to flying big distances. Planes in groups of twos and threes had flown that far in the early days, and once some thirteen B-24s made a round trip of about that same length.

But there was one vital factor in the distance involved in this new mission that none of the earlier strikes had encountered: there were to be no less than seventy-two airplanes involved, and for the bulk of the run they had to fly in formation for protection in attacking the most heavily guarded target in the Southwest Pacific.

And airplanes flying in formation have to jockey endlessly to keep their positions—and in this slipping back and forth burn up gasoline.

For size of attack and for the mission involved there was only one other place in the world they could look for comparison: at the bombing of the Ploesti oil refinery in

*From *Big Distance*. Duell, Sloane and Pearce, 1945.

500

Rumania on August 1, 1943. That didn't help much. That added up to a little over two thousand miles, and that was considered a milestone in long distance B-24 bombing at the time.

This mission, as it was outlined to the officers on that summer afternoon, would take the formation from Noemfoor—which was the closest we could get our Liberators to Balikpapan at that time—across the northeast tip of New Guinea, across the Ceram Sea, past the Soela Islands, across Molukka Sea, across the Celebes, and finally across the Makassar Strait to the target. The planes would be in the air for more than sixteen hours.

Stretched across the face of Europe it would be the approximate equivalent of bombing Leningrad from London and return.

And the trip would have to be made without fighter protection, because no fighters could fly the distances from the bases we then had available. And from the moment the big four-engined bombers left their bases they would be in enemy-controlled territory every inch of the way. It was known there were many enemy bases en route, all of them operational, many of them with clusters of fighter planes. And it also was known that Balikpapan itself was defended by the newest and deadliest of the Japanese anti-aircraft guns.

For a target they had a dilly. Balikpapan, with its two main plants and its paraffin works, was Japan's largest refinery in the Netherlands East Indies, with a capacity of four million barrels of crude oil. It was estimated that Balikpapan, discovered originally by American oil men and developed with their skill, was supplying Japan with thirty-five per cent of her war fuel requirements.

The men got down to work.

The order specified that each plane was to carry three thousand pounds of bombs and full ammunition for the gunners to protect themselves. Best striking time would be just after eight o'clock in the morning, when atmospheric conditions should be most helpful. That meant a night take-off.

The seventy-two airplanes were to be flown by two groups

of the Thirteenth Air Force and one group of the Fifth Air Force, and men from all three groups co-operated in laying down the plans.

In view of the distances to be flown in formation, the planners decided to forget most of the flight characteristics of a B-24 over long distances, and to pretend they were starting out with a brand new airplane. The problems of loading each plane would be so utterly different from anything attempted before that for all practical purposes the Liberator might well have been a new type aircraft.

The first thing the men did was to get out all the data on weights and balances and figure out just what the airplane would weigh when fully loaded and gassed for the trip. The figure added up to the total of almost seventy thousand pounds. Now the B-24 was originally designed to carry a maximum gross of forty-eight thousand pounds, and with the knowledge gained over the years, normal overloading was up to sixty thousand pounds. And that was for "normal" missions—the fifteen- and eighteen-hundred-mile strikes.

They went over the ship inch by inch and threw out what they thought could be spared. Little things—bomb hoists, extra bomb shackles, radio frequency tuning meters, tool kits, personal equipment. They finally got down to rock bottom: sixty-eight thousand five hundred pounds. They were more than four tons over normal overloading and they could lighten the plane no more.

Somebody remembered the Truk and Yap missions of which the boys still spoke dreamily as long missions, long and heavily loaded missions. They looked up figures. Each plane would weigh over a ton more than any plane that had bombed Truk and Yap.

Gasoline was the next problem. The exact amount of fuel used in these missions is a secret, but it can be revealed that more than seven hundred gallons of gasoline above the normal load was needed for each plane. A gallon of gasoline weighs six pounds.

To get the most mileage from the gas it was necessary to put the center of gravity at a place where the ship would fly the easiest. The factory-determined center of gravity, with normal gasoline load, was useless under these new con-

502

ditions with the additional weight distributions. To add to that problem was the fact that an instrument night take-off and instrument flying for the first few hours of the trip would be necessary.

Still working on the theory that as far as all previous specifications went they were going to handle what would be tantamount to a new airplane, the airmen next called in the civilian factory representatives from Consolidated, the builders of the B-24, and conferred with them. Every scrap of information from the factory now was carefully studied with the representatives on hand.

The center of gravity decided upon could not be constant, because, as the airplane burned up its gasoline, as the gunners fired their ammunition, the load would lighten and the weight would become redistributed. Especially as the gas tanks in the different parts of the ship emptied.

Individual airplanes were loaded as they would be for the mission and flown in test runs. It was found necessary after exhaustive experiments that a special series of directions be contrived, taking into consideration each hour of flight and the changing conditions attendant on each hour. Instead, for instance, of each man wearing from the start his parachute, his emergency ration belt, his medicine kit, flak suit, helmet—even his canteen—a special and definite place in the ship was chosen to place these things. Even the men themselves were redistributed in the airplane, away from their normal stations.

Then the factory representatives were called upon again, together with the most experienced pilots in the theater, along with engineering personnel, to figure out the best power settings to get maximum mileage. Flying an airplane is not a mechanical job—some pilots get much more mileage out of their gasoline than others because of their more expert handling of the controls and for this mission no such latitude could be permitted because the gasoline leeway was too critical to permit it.

The speed of the airplane was set at one hundred and fifty miles an hour and the planners figured out a theoretical chart of power settings to get maximum range. Taken into consideration were the take-off, conditions of climb, cruising, approach to target, breakaway, descent and cruise home, and for each hour of the trip a chart of changing settings was set up to allow for the changing weight of the plane as the heavy gasoline was consumed.

These weight-distribution and power-setting charts were printed for each pilot who was to take part in the mission.

Some odd things were discovered. For instance, flaps normally are used to slow up an airplane. With the load carried, however, it was found that for the first couple of hours of flight five degrees of flaps increased the air speed three miles an hour. This fact was noted.

With a working plan to go by, the men outfitted six airplanes and loaded them as the new specifications called for. Six average crews were chosen—men who were not distinguished either for their excellence or their lack of skill. A flight plan was drawn up which would duplicate the projected Balikpapan mission in mileage and route— except that it was flown over territory that was either friendly or neutral. The planes were sent out, with a daylight take-off, to test the theories.

The airmen who planned the show sweated out that mission. It would tell them whether they had been right or wrong, whether the show was feasible or not. The mission would have to be undertaken in any case, but this test flight would indicate whether there was going to be an inevitable bail-out or a chance for home.

The planners were exhausted. They had received word of the Balikpapan mission-to-be just nine days before the day designated for the strike. During that time some of the planes were changing from one base to another—from one island to another—in the general strategic shifting of air bases in the Southwest Pacific. Only the flight echelon had moved to its new base, forward, and the water echelon was still behind. Not all the equipment had arrived. The men had to plan for and work on the Balikpapan show in the midst of this move, a move which always entails a great amount of confusion and difficulty.

The six planes returned to base. All of them had made the flight successfully. They had carried the extra heavy loads of gasoline. In the planning, each plane was allowed

504

a surplus of four hundred gallons. So close was the planning that the plane which returned furthest off schedule had burned just seventy-five gallons more than estimated. The closest of the six planes was just two gallons off estimate.

The airmen breathed easier. The mission, at least on logistics, was feasible.

Then the navigators sat down to plan the route. There were high mountains in New Guinea and they couldn't fly the planes straight across. They decided that the planes would take off individually, just after midnight, fly individually all night, and then rendezvous at daybreak at a selected assembly point. Formation flying at night was ruled out—it would tire the men too much and burn up too much gas.

Rendezvous was pinpointed over the middle of the Celebes. Daybreak was the hour. Celebes was entirely enemy-held and the rendezvous was within forty miles of a Jap airdrome known to be operational.

The rendezvous was about ten hundred and thirty-five miles from the point of take-off. It was about two hundred and twenty miles from the target. The first twelve planes were given just twenty-four minutes to assemble at rendezvous and start out in formation to the target. The sections that followed were given similarly rigid schedules. That meant that individual navigators had to navigate for almost one thousand miles at night and reach a given point within twenty-four minutes of each other.

It was arranged that the leader of the first section, Colonel Thomas C. Musgrave, Jr., would circle the assembly point, fire a red flare, flash an Aldis lamp, and that would be a signal for the others to gather for the remainder of the trip to the target. For formation over the target a javelin step-down was selected. This called for three-plane elements, each element slightly lower than the one in front of it.

The formation made for a beautiful bomb run, keeping the pattern tight and neat, but it was more dangerous than other kinds would have been as far as protection against enemy fighters was concerned. In that formation, planes cannot give each other maximum protection.

The weather officer, nicknamed Thunderhead in honor of the stuff he usually reported, was called in for a preview of the weather to be expected. He went into a huddle and emerged with the following prediction: a series of high towering cumulus—the dreaded cloud monuments that airmen fear and avoid. These would continue through the night. There would also be thunderstorms. However, over a ten-year range, the weather, it was estimated, would be better that time than at any other time in the year, and from the weather angle also, the mission was feasible.

The men who would have to fly the mission were getting so they winced every time they heard the word "feasible." It sounded so damned weak. . . .

Last-minute preparations were perfected. One of the groups was based elsewhere than on Noemfoor. The planes from that group were to collect on the Noemfoor strip with the others and all would take off from there. Each plane had to be airborne exactly sixty seconds after the one ahead of it. While planes were taking off, the ones which preceded them would be en route to rendezvous. Delays in take-off would add up at the end of the night flight and if the schedule were not maintained, planes would have to circle pointlessly over rendezvous, burning precious gasoline. With seventy-two planes taking off from the same strip, if there were an average delay of only thirty seconds a plane that would add up perhaps to a delay of more than a half an hour over assembly point.

Crash trucks, derricks, bulldozers, all were brought down to the strip. So heavily were the planes overloaded it was feared that one or more might crack up on the night take-off. Orders were issued that if a plane cracked up it was to be hauled off the strip immediately so as not to delay the others. Planes that got into trouble after take-off had to keep in the air until the last plane got away before landing again. Ambulances were stationed near the field. Medics went to the line to wait for emergencies.

At two o'clock on the afternoon of September 29th the first briefing of all aerial engineers was undertaken. Then the pilots and co-pilots were called in. The printed long-range distribution and weight charts were explained. The

506

reasons for every item of change in them were analyzed. This was not the usual "poop" which might be conveniently disregarded once the airplanes were aloft. A parachute *had* to be moved from here to there at exactly this time—this had to be shifted there and a man must move from this point to that point. This all had to be done, or a gallon of gasoline, ten gallons, maybe more, would be wasted. The tiniest deviation from the charts might mean the difference between a safe return and a bail-out over enemy-held territory.

The engineers were given refresher courses in transferring fuel. The ordinary wing and wing-tip tanks were to be augmented by bomb-bay tanks holding several hundred gallons each and tests had disclosed that a few of the airplanes flew nose heavy, at a slight angle; it was thought there might be some difficulty in transferring gasoline with the planes pitched at that angle.

At seven-thirty that evening the main briefing took place. Everybody who was going on the mission was told officially for the first time what the target would be. There had been a lot of rumors but this was the first official announcement. The men opened their eyes slightly, sighed, some of them, and said nothing.

They were told exactly what lighting facilities would be available for take-off. In the event the Nips came over to strafe and bomb during take-off the enemy was to be ignored as far as possible and take-off to proceed on schedule. Planes were to circle in a definite pattern before relanding if they developed mechanical trouble. If the mechanical trouble was so serious the planes couldn't stay aloft until the last plane took off, the pilot was to run his faulty ship over the water, bail out with his crew and let the ship crash. Nothing, nothing at all, must interfere with the mission. There was only one strip for this particular show and top priority for all movement on it was for planes taking off.

The men were told that from the moment they were airborne they would be over enemy territory one hundred per cent of the way. They were given dictionaries of native words in case of forced landings.

The first plane was ordered to take off at 0030—just thirty minutes after midnight on the morning of September 30, 1944.

Meanwhile the strip itself had been readied for the show. Palm trees at the far end of the strip had been cut down, tops had been removed, so the weighted planes would have plenty of clearance. A field hospital was taken down and moved away from the end of the strip. Final instructions were given: twenty minutes before each individual time of take-off the planes were to start engines, crews check for combat readiness, and then the pilots to taxi into position.

It was a beautiful night. There was a moon. The palm trees were silhouetted against the light sky. You could see clearly and plainly. The men liked the moon. They would have it only for a few hours but what there was of it was welcome. There was tension in the air. Rumors spread. From all over Noemfoor—or at least from the portion of it that we owned—men gathered. The linemen, looking over their airplanes, patting them, stroking them gently. Other flying men. The ground personnel. Men from other branches of the service. They were all there looking at the long line of airplanes. Most of the airplanes were unpainted, shining silver in the moonlight. Some still had the old camouflage.

Then at the right moment the first airplane rolled up to the head of the strip and the motors roared until the island itself seemed to quiver and then the giant lumbering craft moved on down the strip and gathered speed and then was airborne and climbing slowly. The mission was started.

The first twenty-four airplanes were airborne in exactly twenty-four minutes. Despite the load there was no accident. The last plane of the seventy-two got off safely. There was a long-drawn sigh from the men on the ground. So far so good. Then, a little later, two airplanes returned with mechanical failures. They climbed out of the planes almost in tears. Seventy airplanes were off on the show.

In the air it was a long night. Frequently the navigators figured when they had crossed their tiny points of land by the towering cumulus clouds which usually stack up

508

over land. The navigators sweated. The men moved like clockwork inside the planes deftly moving things from place to place—often a matter only of inches—as the charts required.

Dawn broke over the Celebes. It was one of those incredibly beautiful mornings that occur only in the tropics, thousands of feet in the air. The morning was purple and red and the clouds tinted with pastels; then the sun rose above the clouds. The men blinked their eyes. With the first light they were crossing the Celebes, on schedule.

The first section of twelve planes was collected at rendezvous point within thirteen minutes. The navigators had flown nine hundred miles in the dark and had reached their pinpoint within thirteen minutes of each other. It was the kind of navigating that brought lumps to the throats of pilots and men scattered throughout the ships.

Then suddenly Musgrave, in the lead ship, found he had unexpected company. Two Jap twin-engined airplanes began to parallel the formation, just out of gun range. The men knew why they were there and why they made no attempt to attack the bombers. They were flying along, radioing course and speed and altitude for the Jap antiaircraft at Balikpapan.

The Americans watched them bemused. There was nothing they could do.

A Jap airdrome, Mangar, was to be used as a checkpoint. It was an ironic thing to choose as a checkpoint but there was nothing else. The field was just thirty miles north of the target. Shortly after the turn on Mangar the lead plane was to be turned over to its bombardier to fly over the target for the bomb run. The other planes were to follow in formation. When the formation got to Mangar it ran into unexpected weather.

The clouds were closed in ten-tenths below them. That means total coverage. The clouds were packed together until they looked like the top of a soap bucket. You couldn't see anything through them. The planes flew the prescribed course to the target. So far the enemy had made no attempt to stop them. The element of surprise had been more successful than anyone had dared to hope.

But then, just before the formation got five miles from the target, when it was already settled into the long bomb run, into the climax of the mission, into the job for which the airplanes were made and the men trained, the Jap fighters came up in droves, like specks of hailstorm, and hit them.

It was an attack that dry military parlance calls determined and sustained. The men call it eager. The Nips were eager beyond anything that anyone had ever before experienced. They came to within twenty-five feet of the big bombers, blazing away with all their guns. They flew into and through the formation. They got above the bombers and went into an almost vertical dive, every gun shooting as they came down. It seemed as though they had been sent up with orders to stop the raid, to turn it away, at all costs. Balikpapan was vital to the Jap war and the Japs knew it.

The planes plodded on. The gunners were shooting away. A Jap plane here and there went down. Finally, the planes came to the target area itself and to the bullets and cannon shells of the enemy airplanes now were added the shells from the anti-aircraft on the ground. The flak was thick and heavy and the Jap fighters ignored it and kept attacking through it. That in itself was unusual. It is more normal for fighters to break away when their flak takes over, but the Nips disregarded their own ground fire and pressed in.

Then came a heart-break. When the bombers finally arrived over the target itself, it was almost completely covered with clouds.

Musgrave saw a small hole in the clouds and through it a portion of the target. The Nip was throwing up shells from his new 120-mm ack-ack guns and each time a shell exploded it crashed open with a terrific noise and if it came close enough the concussion rocked the ships back and forth. The air was filled with phosphorus bombs, incendiaries.

The easy thing to do was to drop the bombs in the general target area. The hole had closed in but the men knew roughly where the target was and could have dropped their

510

bombs, sure of hitting something, then got the hell away. That would have been the easy thing to do.

But the men had been briefed on pinpoint targets within the refinery, on the small vital nuclei which would put the whole thing out of business for a while. The mission had been planned too laboriously, the trip had been too long and too hard to sacrifice accuracy and deadliness at the last minute.

Musgrave ordered the bombardier to hold his bombs. He swung the formation in a great arc to the east. He would try to come in at a new angle. It didn't matter if the new attempt gave the Nip fighters a field day, if it gave the ack-ack just that much more time to try to shoot them down.

A few minutes later the formation approached from a new angle. The planes and flak had followed it all the way. Following Musgrave, the formation circled for forty-five minutes until they could see exactly what they had been told to bomb, and then, and only then, did Musgrave give the word and the bombs were released.

Later reconnaissance pictures showed that the bombing had done just what it was supposed to do. In that mission— and in the three that were to follow in short order—almost half of the Balikpapan refinery was destroyed and the remainder was put out of action for more than six months.

Their bombs away, the planes turned and started for home. The Jap fighters were remorseless. They attacked for one solid hour without let-up. Now that the bomb run was over the bombers could devote themselves entirely to scrapping with the enemy fighters. The boys shot down seven of the Nip planes and counted nine probables. We lost two Liberators, and many others were damaged. Some were damaged so badly they had to make forced landings en route, but when the mission was ended only one crew and half of another crew were missing. The rest were rescued.

The furious Nips swarmed all around. The stories some of the men told when they returned have become sagas among our flying men in the Southwest Pacific. The planes had been over the target, in all, for more than an hour. Time over target, normally, is counted in minutes. . . .

Over the target a lead ship of one of the elements got it and nose-dived into Balikpapan town before anyone could bail out. First Lieutenant Oliver L. Adair, pilot of another ship, pulled into the lead to take the missing ship's position. At the same time Adair's ship was hit in an inboard engine and the wing and tail and fuselage were hit. Oil spurted over the red hot cylinders and started to burn. Flames were blazing in a fifty-foot tail behind the airplane. Despite this, Adair shoved up the power on his three remaining engines and moved into the lead.

His right-waist gunner, Staff Sergeant Charles F. Held, had his gun shot out of his hands. The mount was destroyed and the ring site knocked off and the back end of the gun broken apart. He rigged up his parachute for a cushion. He held the loose gun against the chute pack and grabbed the hot barrel with his other hand and fired bursts at the attackers.

"I couldn't aim, but my tracers were coming close enough so the Nip knew the gun was still working."

He could only fire a few bursts at a time. The recoil would jolt him back against the other side of the plane and when he returned home finally his chest was black and blue, covered with bruises from the pounding and the hand that held the barrel of the gun was burned through the glove that he wore.

Everybody on that ship prayed. Once the boys heard the co-pilot, Second Lieutenant Raphael F. Baird, try to wisecrack in his throat mike to cheer up the men, and then give up the attempt, and instead, whisper, "Oh, my God, let me get out of here, please God, let me get out of here. . . ."

The top-turret man, Staff Sergeant Wilbur L. Bowen, said later, "Half the time I was praying hard enough to save half the people in the United States. And half the time I was cursing hard enough to put a good bishop in hell. When I saw three planes coming in at once with their wing edges sparkling I just prayed they wouldn't hit us. And then when one of my guns jammed I would pound on the magazine and cuss in the worst way I know how."

512

On the way home they had to chop out the ball turret and the top turret to lighten weight. Working with axes and a machete they chopped the top turret into small pieces and threw it out. Then they worked for three hours on the ball turret. They got nearly everything out but some braces and armor which the ax wouldn't cut. One of the men pulled his automatic pistol and shot away the rivets that held the metal together.

The main gas tanks were full of small leaks. The men stopped them up with bits of candle, rags, a pencil, a broken screwdriver. There were holes in the hydraulic brake line they couldn't see.

The pilot figured he could make a normal landing. He ordered seven of the crew on the flight deck. The ship went in to land on Morotai. It settled for a perfect landing. The brakes held long enough to slow the ship down to eighty-five miles an hour and then the left brake broke its line and the right brake locked and the ship jerked to one side toward a bank.

It ploughed through palm trees. One stump flew into the bomb bay and hit Held in the leg. One of the props on the ship cut through a parked truck as the driver raced for cover. The nose wheel buckled and flew back into the bomb bay to hit Held in the other leg.

Twelve seconds after the ship had buried its nose in a sand bank every man was out of the ship. Held got out of the top escape hatch, hit the top of the ship, and did a complete flip-over into the dirt.

And from a latrine in the path of the bomber a first sergeant ran out—his trousers still below his knees. . . .

One of the waist gunners in another ship began to pass out ammunition to the other gunners and had to leave his own gun abandoned. Staff Sergeant John W. Clarry, the other waist gunner, began to fire both guns simultaneously, standing in the middle of the airplane, his arms outstretched.

"I saw one coming in at the right and I fired until he went out of sight," he said later. "Then out of the corner of my eye I saw an attacker coming in from the left. I fired at him and then they were coming in fast and thick from both sides. I started to fire both guns at once. Of course I couldn't do any aiming but I managed to turn a couple away with my tracers. The guns were shaking me to pieces. I could hardly hold on to them with one hand. For a while I could fire with one gun for a second and then turn and fire the other. I never was so busy in my life."

Flak tore apart one of the big airplanes, ripping the belly from nose to tail. The first burst crashed through the bombsight and sent powdered glass spraying into the eyes of the bombardier, Second Lieutenant Gordon G. Schimke. This was before the bomb run, and Schimke knew he still had a job to do. He was almost unconscious from shock and the pain was excruciating, but he felt his way back, temporarily blinded, and salvoed his bombs. Other men on the ship were knocked unconscious from the concussion.

Two engines went out. The electric system was shattered. The fuel lines were cut so fuel could not be transferred. Shells burst into the bomb bay and metal fragments tore into the flak suits the men were wearing. The rudder and the tail assembly were riddled and the pilot, First Lieutenant Richard G. Egelston, had to trim the ship to hard right rudder to keep it going straight.

They couldn't keep on. The pilot ordered the men to bail out. Another B-24 stayed close to help in whatever way it could. Then a Navy flying boat hove in sight. The co-pilot of the B-24, Second Lieutenant Ralph L. Krueger, saw it. Everyone bailed out except the pilot and co-pilot. With Egelston still fighting the controls, Krueger crawled through the ship to make sure every man was out. Then pilot and co-pilot bailed out together.

Within two hours the flying boat had gathered every man out of the sea. The boat made six attempts to get off the choppy waters before it could get itself airborne. Then finally aloft again, all the men looked at the ball gunner from the B-24, Staff Sergeant Richard B. Page, who was accounted a very calm man ordinarily. While descending in his chute he had been seen to uncork his canteen and drink a long swig of water.

"I suddenly felt thirsty," he explained simply.

514

The flying boat proceeded to base. The troubles were not yet over. The ship came in during an alert. Trigger-happy ack-ack gunners fired several salvos at it before it was recognized.

Did you ever hear how the infantry, sometimes after a bitter fight, after the long march back, straightens out its ranks, gets into parade order, its ranks depleted but the heads of the remaining men high and proud?

Well, on the way back Musgrave found four ships near him. They all seemed to have the same idea. They closed into perfect formation.

On the ground at Noemfoor men were sweating out the mission. There were thousands of them packed among the palm trees. Pilots from a nearby night-fighter squadron were there. They said the bomber boys had sweated them out time and time again and now they were there to help sweat out the bomber boys.

And then the planes came in. The first five planes in their perfect formation. Riddled with holes. Parts of the tails and wings and turrets gone. But in perfect formation.

Captain William J. Stuart, Jr., Operations Officer for one of the groups, burst into tears as he recognized his own ships. He stood there rigid, the tears pouring down his face.

"I'm not ashamed of it," he said. "God damn it, I'm not ashamed of it."

Peleliu

General MacArthur was now in position to invade the Philippines, but first he had to secure final approval from the Joint Chiefs of Staff, and priority for naval support for the landing operation. Admirals King and Nimitz were promoting a different strategy that would by-pass the Philippines, or at most occupy Mindanao in the Philippines for its airfields. While these two points of view, among others, were debated in the councils of the JCS, there was concurrence on the necessity for the invasion of the Palau Islands, on the southern flank of Truk, the Jap naval base. The airfields on Peleliu and the bomber strip on Anguar were deemed necessary for the invasion of the Philippines.

At the last minute Admiral Halsey suggested to Admiral Nimitz that the Palaus be by-passed; in the first days of September 1944 he had led carrier strikes on Yap, the Palaus, and Mindanao, and met almost no opposition from enemy planes. He deduced that the Jap air forces in these areas could be written off as a threat to the Philippines invasion, particularly if his carriers were attached to MacArthur for air support.

S. E. Morison says, "Admiral Nimitz did not accept this suggestion. He felt Peleliu and the Kossal Passage (to the north) were needed as staging points for Leyte." * Furthermore, the Peleliu expedition was only two sailing days away from their scheduled D-Day.

This force was III Amphibious Corps, commanded by Major General Roy S. Geiger. The assault troops for Peleliu were the 1st Marine Division, under Major General William H. Rupertus. The 81st Infantry Division, under Major General Paul J. Mueller, had as its main target the island of Anguar, although they were to stand by to help with Peleliu if needed.

"Naval bombardment blew off most of the scrubby jungle growth

---

*S. E. Morison, *Leyte*, p. 33. Little Brown & Co. Copyright 1958 by Samuel Eliot Morison.

behind the airstrip and beaches [on Peleliu] revealing numerous caves; but few gave them a thought. Admiral Oldendorf was so pleased with the results of his three-day bombardment that on the evening of 14 September, over voice radio to Admiral Fort, he made a very unfortunate remark: 'We have run out of targets.' And General Rupertus rashly predicted to news correspondents that Peleliu would be secured within four days." *

The men gathered in the troopships hoped the brass were right. The bombardment of Kwajalein had so stunned the Japs that the landing waves had a comparatively easy time in the early hours of the invasion. But such was not to be at Peleliu. Even after the first waves were in, there was still havoc on the beaches; Captain Frank Hough describes the scene:

"These later waves crossed the reef amid the debris of those which had preceded them: wreckage of gear and vehicles, bodies bobbing sluggishly in the shallow water or draped grotesquely across protruding coral heads. Shells still fell among them, and some were hit. Ashore, they found the beach and a stretch extending up to a hundred yards inland heavily mined. . . . They found pillboxes dug into the raw coral, roofed with coral chunks set in, and piled on . . . blending in so well with the natural terrain that a man had to walk practically up to the narrow firing apertures before recognizing them for what they were. They saw a few Japanese dead, some of them wearing gas masks, for reasons best known to themselves; but they saw a lot more dead Marines." **

At the extreme left of the assault beaches, the 3rd Battalion 1st Marines hit a coral ridge, 30 feet high, which was filled with spider trenches and pillboxes, and which enfiladed their part of the 3,000-yard landing beach. The story of this action follows.

*Leyte, p. 35.
**Hough, The Island War, p. 293. J. B. Lippincott.

517

CORAL COMES HIGH

by Captain George P. Hunt

After running as hard as I could for about seventy-five yards I slid into a shell hole out of breath, my lips and tongue as dry as sandpaper. Black vapor and the pungent odor of gunpowder which was seeping from the earth helped to clog my throat. Sweat was running off the end of my nose. I rolled a swig of water around in my mouth. Looking behind I saw that Kelly and Blackburn, my runners, and the radio operator and Stramel were in the hole with me. Schmittou was just over the edge of the hole flattened behind a bush. A bullet snapped into the dirt right next to me. I heard vicious rattlings of shots and earth-shaking bursts of mortar shells which fell in a relentless pattern, closer and closer, to the right, to the left, straddling our position. Shrapnel whistled and plunked into the trees.

I could not see my platoons, but I thought I heard the sound of their firing on my right and left.

"Corpsman up here!" Schmittou was calling. "Burton's hit." Delbarter, big, muscular, crawled out of the hole.

"Hello, control, this is five; hello, control, this is five. Do you hear me? Over." That was the radio; Sellers calling. He should be about fifty yards down the beach.

"Send up stretchers. We're getting casualties," I told him.

"Comin' right up," his drawl blurred over the air.

I was trying to get in with my platoons on the radio; I had to know how they were doing. "Hello, one, hello, two, hello, three: This is control. Do you hear me? Over," the radio operator droned on. No word.

Colonel Ross from Regiment jumped into the hole. Good God! What was he doing here? He must have landed too far to the left.

"What outfit is this?"

"K Company. Like a cigarette?" I offered him one.

"No thanks. I've got to be moving. Take care of my radio operator; he's been hit."

"No, he's dead, Colonel," said Delbarter.

"Oh," he paused: "Good luck." He scrambled out of the hole.

I heard a scuffling behind me. Blackburn was wounded in the arm. His young face turned very white, and his lips curled up with the pain. I got Sellers on the radio again.

"Where in hell are the stretchers?"

"I sent 'em up fifteen minutes ago. They should be there by now. There's Japs all around us back here."

A few minutes later Dempsey and Hooker appeared with a stretcher. They laid Burton on it and carried him off. A mortar shell struck just then, very near. I saw Dempsey standing up, raising a hand which was dripping with blood. He pointed to his fingers.

"Two of 'em gone," he shouted, and damned if he wasn't smiling!

The radio operator was still calling the platoons. Still no answer. The uncertainty became agonizing. I heard the heavy throbbing of big stuff, the unmistakable persistence of Jap machine guns from the vicinity of the Point. I saw flame and smoke rising from our beach, heard the sizzling of burning Alligators, and the mortars were pounding about us with more intensity. The Jap fire was building up.

Suddenly I heard the call I had been waiting for. It came slurred and crackling at first, then clear as a bell.

"Hello, control, this is one, hello, control, this is one, do you hear me? Over."

"Yeah, Willis, I hear you, what's the dope?"

"Hello, old man, I'm up just behind the third platoon. Estey and Koval were hit. They've had a hell of a lot of casualties and need stretcher bearers badly. I'm seein' what I can do up here."

"Do you have contact with the second on your right?"

"No, nothing in there but Japs."

"Well, push through and take the Point," I told him, "I'm coming right up."

"OK, OK," he answered, "that's what I figured."

519

I called Major McNulty at Battalion on the radio. "We're pretty well shot up and there's a gap between my two assault platoons. I'm throwing the first platoon in to take the Point. The goddam naval gunfire didn't faze the Japs! We need stretcher bearers!"

"All right, Bub, I'll have L Company fill in the gap. I'll send up everybody I can spare with stretchers."

But there was still no word from the second platoon.

Kelly, whom I had sent up to find Estey and the third platoon, returned with a bullet hole through his shin. Pantingly he told me:

"Jese, there are K Company guys dead and wounded lyin' all around. Mr. Estey got it twice in the arm. He's lyin' in a hole and looks pretty bad. They're askin' for you. They got shot up when they were goin' up the beach toward that Point. Yeah, and they think Koval's dead, and McNeel, and Webber took over. I got hit up here about ten yards." Just then a bullet clipped off the radio antenna.

The decision was made now; I had committed my whole company.

I told the radioman to follow me, rolled out of the hole and, running from tree to tree, headed toward the Point.

The human wreckage I saw was a grim and tragic sight. First it was bewildering; then it made me hot with anger; but finally my feelings cooled to accepting a gruesome inevitable fact. There was Gasser, whose face, always pale, was as white as the sand on which he lay. Shrapnel had shattered his rifle and a piece had penetrated his neck. It was an effort for him to grin, but he did. I saw Culjak, very tall and dark, with a bloody bandage around his arm. Kneeling in a hole in the sand I asked him what had happened to him. He was in the second platoon.

"I was on the left with Bandy and Dolan trying to keep contact with the third platoon. But I got separated from my outfit. I don't know what happened to them. Then I ran into a Jap and killed him with a grenade, but he got me in the arm."

I saw McMatt lying on his side with a small hole in his stomach which oozed purple blood. Someone had taken off his clothes. Slowly he turned his head toward me, and

I saw that his blue eyes were glassy. He opened his mouth, and his white lips formed a word, but no sound came forth. Exhausted by the effort he let his head slump back, and blood was drooling from his mouth. The corpsman who was squatting next to him shook his head.

These were only three of the wounded and dying which littered the edge of the coconut grove from where we had landed to the Point. As I ran up the beach I saw them lying nearly shoulder to shoulder; some of them mine; others from outfits which landed immediately behind us. I saw a ghastly mixture of bandages, bloody and mutilated skin; men gritting their teeth, resigned to their wounds; men groaning and writhing in their agonies; men outstretched or twisted or grotesquely transfixed in the attitudes of death; men with their entrails exposed or whole chunks of body ripped out of them. There was Graham, snuffed out a hero, lying with four dead Japs around him; and Windsor, flat on his face, with his head riddled by bullets and his arms pointed toward a pillbox where five Japs slumped over a machine gun; and Sharp, curled up on his side, still holding his automatic rifle which pointed to a huddle of dead Japs thirty yards away. His aim had been good. Stieferman was alive, his face and body peppered by shrapnel. His words came slowly and raspingly.

"Hello, Captain. Sorry I had to get it like this, but I saw those three Japs, and as soon as I threw a grenade at 'em I got one in return. It cut me up a little bit, but I got all three of them. I know I did."

I saw McNeel, his eyes turned up in death, a yellow pallor on his rugged face. He was lying directly in front of a forty millimeter gun lodged in a pillbox of reinforced concrete. The gun was scarred and wrenched from its base. Inside dead Japs sprawled on top of each other. An open, half-empty canteen and a Tommy gun lay next to McNeel's head.

No wonder the Japs had done such damage. The Point, rising thirty feet above the water's edge, was of solid, jagged coral, a rocky mass of sharp pinnacles, deep crevasses, tremendous boulders. Pillboxes, reinforced with steel and concrete, had been dug or blasted in the base of the perpendicular drop to the beach. Others, with coral and concrete piled six feet on top were constructed above, and spider holes were blasted around them for protecting infantry. It surpassed by far anything we had conceived of when we studied the aerial photographs.

Willis had moved swiftly and had already assaulted the Point; the sound of sporadic firing came from the other side. Jap dead fringed the base of the rise to the Point and filled up the niches and holes in the coral. They were big healthy men, and had new equipment. I climbed up the rocks and saw Willis' muscular, bowlegged figure.

"Good going, Will," I congratulated him, "you've done a wonderful job."

"It wasn't me, it was these men," he answered, waving his arm in a wide sweeping gesture.

"We've got to hold this place now," I said, "how many men do you have left?"

"About thirty, all that's left of my platoon and Estey's. What happened to the second? There's nobody on our right."

"I don't know," I answered, "I think they've had a hell of a rough time. It looks like we're isolated up here."

The men were in a line behind boulders forming a circular, all-around defense of the Point. They were resting, occasionally rising up to shoot at a stray Jap. Otherwise it was quiet, except for the steady thumping of mortar shells on the beach and the reef behind us, and the distant chattering of machine guns far off to our right. The immediate silence seemed ominous. Standing on the rocks I looked back and could see gray files of troops moving inland from the beach, through the debris of the coconut grove. They would push on the right and overrun the airfield. I wondered how the fight was progressing over there, but there was no way of knowing now. The entire beach was swarming with tractors, men evacuating wounded and unloading supplies, aid stations which had been hurriedly set up to meet the sudden rush of casualties. The sands were black with milling men.

"What a target!" I exclaimed to Willis. "No wonder the Japs are raising so much hell!"

522

It was ten-thirty. I called Major McNulty on the radio and told him that the Point was secured.

"That's fine," he answered, "what supplies do you need?"

"We need water, grenades, ammunition and barbed wire, and as many reinforcements as you can scrape together. I've only got about thirty men up here. We must have machine guns! Mine were nearly all shot up when they landed."

"OK, Bub," he answered, "I'll get the stuff up to you as soon as I can by tractor along the reef. Be on the lookout for L Company moving into the gap on the right. They will make contact with you."

There was nothing to do but wait, rest and strengthen our line. The men had already started to build foxholes of rocks and fallen logs. The clouds had broken overhead, and the sun was relentlessly beating down on us, reflecting from the coral rocks with doubled intensity. As the men worked the sweat drenched their clothes and skin. In the bay the warships were firing far inland, and even where we were we could feel the concussion. The Point seemed almost unscarred by the terrific bombardment we had seen before the landing. I was amazed that the pillboxes had weathered it untouched. Few trees had grown in the coral, and what ones were there were short and crooked and gnarled. Our shelling had reduced most of them to jagged stumps. We had paid dearly for the Point, but there was compensation in the fact that we had counted 110 dead Japs and that we now held a very strategic position. There was no possible way of knowing how many out of my entire company had been killed or wounded. I knew there were a lot, nearly two-thirds I estimated, figuring that the second platoon over on the right had suffered as heavily as the first and third. Stramel radioed that most of my machine-gun platoon had been mowed down on the beach and there were no more than eight men left and all the guns had been knocked out. Hanson radioed me that the mortar section was still intact down the beach where Sellers was, but there was no wire communication available to the Point. We would have to rely on the radio to direct mortar fire, but the batteries were fading fast and would probably be entirely dead by nightfall. Sellers was dangerously straddled by Jap mortars.

I walked along the line and met Webber and Hahn. What was left of their third platoon was in position on the line, and the three of us had time to sit down on the baked rocks for a few minutes and have a sweaty cigarette. We were dripping with perspiration, and our wet fingers soaked and spoiled our smokes before we really had time to enjoy them. They were anxious to talk about the fight. Hahn's gray eyes were bright with excitement, and a half grin crooked the thin line of his mouth. He pointed to a rise in the coral behind me. "Right there," he said, "Humplik and I walked right into three Japs who were setting up a heavy machine gun. We came barging around these big boulders like two damn fools and were on top of them before we knew it. They looked up at us and started jabbering excitedly and reaching for hand grenades. Luckily I had one in my hand which I threw just in time. It went off in the middle of them and killed two. The other one took off at a dead run after tossing a grenade at us, and Humplik drilled him. The grenade hit directly between us. It was a dud. We set the Jap gun on the line, up there by those high rocks."

"I saw it," I said. "Have you got plenty of ammunition for it?"

"Sure, there's stacks of it in some of these pillboxes."

Jap mortars began to drop shells on the beach, close to our lines. We ducked behind the rocks and waited for them to pound in our positions. But fortunately they stopped just below the Point and started back down the shore line in a rapid series of explosions.

"God!" exclaimed Webber, "that's murder for all those people crowded together on that beach!"

"Yeah," added Hahn, "and they could certainly raise hell with us if they dropped a concentration in here."

"You know, Captain," said Webber, changing the subject, "I wonder what the Japs thought when we hit the beach. We were all striped up with camouflage paint and poured out of the tractors hollering like a bunch of Indians and charging at the Japs full speed. Several guys were shouting 'Gung Ho!' but most of them had their own war cry. We ran smack into the Japs as they were running out of their pillboxes to their spider holes."

"Damn right," I said, "if you hadn't moved in so fast we would never have had the momentum to take this Point." Webber flicked away his cigarette and leaned forward with his elbows on his knees. He was as unruffled as though he were riding in a streetcar. "And you should have seen Rowe," he went on, grinning broadly, showing straight teeth. "He has these white workman's gloves, and every once in a while as he moved up with his BAR under his arm, which is almost as big as he is, he would stop right in the middle of all the shooting, pull off his gloves, take a nail file from his pocket and file his nails. Then he would twirl his mustache. And Lindsey Jones was just as funny. When the Japs were all around us below the Point, Lindsey sat in a bush picking them off, sayin' all the time in his southern accent, 'Mah, mah, theah suah a' lot of Japs around heah.' "

"The Japs didn't seem to bother him much," commented Hahn, smiling. Sweat rolling down Hahn's face left streaks in the camouflage paint and the gray coral dirt smudged across the top of his cheeks. He took off his helmet and rubbed the perspiration from the back of his neck.

"Nothing can bother that guy," replied Webber, "he's as rugged as an ox. When Carter was hit, Lindsey went over to help him. He was putting a bandage on Carter's chest when he saw a Jap sneakin' up on him. He waved his arm at the Jap and yelled at him, 'Git away from heah, you Jap, can't you see I'm fixin' a man?' The Jap got behind a tree and all Lindsey could see of him was the edge of his helmet sticking out on either side of the tree. So Lindsey put aside the bandage, took up his BAR and fired a shot which went right through the tree and into the Jap's head."

I told Hahn and Webber what I knew of our situation and to keep a sharp lookout for L Company which was to close the gap on our right, then continued along the line which in total length could not have been over a hundred yards. I saw Sovik, Willis' platoon sergeant, who told me about a Jap who wanted to surrender and come

525

into our lines just after we had seized the Point. His words tumbled out quickly.

"The Jap had his pack on and was carrying his weapon, so we shot him, just to be on the safe side, and damned if he didn't blow up. He must have been loaded down with dynamite and grenades."

"Yeah," drawled Lees, who had come up while Sovik was talking and whose sallow, hardened face bore a casual expression, "they're tricky little bastards. You've got to watch 'em. There are lots of 'em running around out there with our helmets on."

The men were asking for water; their canteens were dry. There were only a few grenades left and what ammunition each man had in his belt. We looked expectantly toward the beach for the Alligator which would bring us supplies, and to our right for signs of L Company moving up.

I was sitting behind a white boulder trying to enjoy a cigarette. I felt as though I was in an oven, and the rocks were hot to the touch. My thoughts wandered to the dead men lying on the slope of the Point. So many lives had been snuffed out so quickly that it seemed impossible and incredible. Once again I thought of a fantastic dream with no logic, only a pattern of grotesque, lugubrious shapes and a background of tuneless music and uncontrolled rhythms.

The explosion of a mortar shell startled me— Then more—they were dropping in our midst. Shrapnel whined through the rocks, ricocheting and clipping the tree stumps. I heard a voice say very calmly, "Looks like I'm hit." A chunk of steel smashed into the rocks on my left, throwing chips of stone. Again the voice, "Yes, I'm hit all right; in the leg. Feels like the bone's broken." The barrage stopped. There was silence, and I waited for the cry "Corpsman!" None came. One more round fell on the edge of the cliff. I looked around; yes, it was Duncan who was wounded in the leg, and he was as cool as ice. His face had turned as gray as the rocks around him. They carried him to the water's edge to wait for the tractor. If the Japs continued

526

those concentrations soon there would be none of us left. But perhaps they did not know—

Then I saw Sergeant Bandy of the second platoon scrambling over the rocks toward me. He had lost contact in the area of the gap and had just found our positions. I was certainly glad to see him. "What happened to the second platoon?" I asked him. He waited until he got his breath back before answering, and he wiped the sweat out of his eyes with the sleeve of his jacket. About a hundred and fifty yards in from the beach most of the second platoon had been caught in a tank trap and on trying to assault out of it had been terribly shot up. The trap was nearly fifteen yards wide, ten feet deep and extended parallel to the shore line for several hundred yards. It was a mammoth trench with sloping sides of loose coral sand, hidden in the torn and uprooted underbrush of the coconut grove. It was raked by machine guns from the sides and from the precipitous coral ridge to its front where pillboxes had been blasted in the rock. Woodyard was dead and Macek, his platoon sergeant, had been hit in the arm as soon as they had landed. Good God! I called Sellers on the radio and told him the information.

"We just got the same word down here," he said. "We're going to try to evacuate what's left of the second platoon as soon as we can. Battalion is bringing up tanks."

Dusk was approaching fast. The tractor with the supplies had just arrived, and we had to work quickly unloading it so that it could get back to the beach before night. Case after case of hand grenades and ammunition, cans of water which tasted of oil and had grown hot under the sun, rolls of barbed wire, crates of "C" rations, we piled on the coral ledge at the foot of the cliff and by chain gang lugged it up the rocks to the top of the rise where it was distributed to the men. The crew of the tractor gave us two of their machine guns which strengthened our scanty line considerably. Parties moved out in front of the positions to lay the barbed wire. Snipers harassed them, and a bullet lodged in the heart of a redheaded kid with freckles who had

527

just been talking to me. "Gosh, Captain," he had said, "I never expected it to be as rough as this. If I live through it, I sure hope I never see another one like it." He had walked away with a broad smile on his grimy face. The tractor left and rolled down the reef. Mortar shells began to drop near it, following it all the way back but miraculously never scoring a hit.

Sniper fire had increased, popping from every direction outside of our perimeter. Occasionally a mortar shell would burst dangerously near. Two squads of L Company's machine-gun platoon had worked their way up to us during the afternoon, but no troops had appeared on our right where the gap was. Haggerty with his eighty-one millimeter mortar observation group had joined us, but he had no communication with his guns two thousand yards behind us. So he and his four men reinforced our line, manning a machine gun. Over his carrot-red hair he was wearing a blue baseball cap.

My radio was on its last legs. I had heard Sellers say that they had successfully evacuated what was left of the second platoon from the tank trap under the cover of tanks and that an estimated 150 Japs had moved in the gap. Then the radio faded out. I called him loudly for more information, but there was no answer.

It was almost dark. I was talking over our situation with Willis when Monk Meyer and Dolan appeared over the edge of the cliff from battalion headquarters. They had stolen through the coconut grove behind us and said it was lousy with Japs. Battalion had established a provisional line about two hundred yards back after the second platoon had been withdrawn from the tank trap.

"You're isolated up here," he said, looking at me, "and surrounded by Japanese."

"Yes, I know that," I replied. "Nobody has made contact with us."

"A Company and L Company have been trying to all afternoon. They had the hell shot out of 'em attempting to move into the gap which must be over two hundred yards wide," he said; then after a pause: "Do you think you can hold out?"

528

"Sure we can. Looks like we'll have to."

"Well, I must get going now. I think I'll swim back outside the reef. Take it easy and good luck." He disappeared over the rocks, and we sat silently for a few moments absorbing his information. I heard the water lapping against the rocks at the foot of the cliff. The evening was quiet and breathless.

"Anyway," said Willis, suddenly, "there's one thing to be said for our situation. We'll be able to kill some more of the bastards!"

As blackness crept up and completely enveloped us, we were subdued to an eerie silence. Even the clicking sounds of a small stone falling from the rough surface of a rock, probably brushed off by the sweep of a man's elbow, seemed a harsh disturbance. Though there was no moon, the sky, massed by thick and voluminous clouds, was just light enough to reveal the weird and grotesque silhouettes of knotted trees and stumps. The jagged, pinnacled rocks rose like witches' fingers, and the bald, cracked humps of boulders, appearing indiscriminately and catching the merest reflection of light, seemed like tremendous human pates which had been brutally clubbed to submissiveness. Surrounding us were the woods which had become dark and impenetrable in the night.

When one lies in a hole peering intently into the black, listening, smelling, hearing only the sound of one's breathing, waiting, expecting, the stillness may become appalling, dead objects may rise slowly and live, the motionless may move, sounds of leaves stirred by the breeze may become the sneaking movements of human feet, a friend may be an enemy, an enemy a friend, until, unless controlled by toughness of mind, one's imagination may become haunted by the unseen and the unheard. One may panic under this strain, jump up, screaming hoarsely and firing his weapon blindly all around him until shot dead by his friends because he is endangering their lives and might have already shot one of them. One may suddenly see incredible sights in the trees such as a shining yellow airplane, hung there,

529

swarming with Japs and belching fire and bullets, and whisper what he sees to his buddy who then gets a friend and carries the raving one off the line. Another may be merely nervous and fire shots at nothing, giving away his position to Japanese scouts who are silently watching from the underbrush. Still another, feeling no alertness and allowing himself to be overcome with fatigue and being a slouch of a man, may fall asleep and meet a dreadful end on the point of an enemy bayonet. That man betrays himself as well as his friends.

I wanted to catch some sleep during the early hours of darkness as the Japs would probably attack later on. I lay down on the ground which was strewn with stones and stiff, prickling growth and found myself wedged between two rocks. I raised up and tried to rake the stones out from under me with my fingers but found that most of them were firmly embedded. In spite of the fact that I was extremely tired, the immediate concern of trying to twist my body into a position which would ease the prodding of the stones kept me awake. Alternately, each of my legs would go to sleep, requiring a painful shift to wake them up, and periodically the small of my right foot would develop a cramp. My body finally became used to these discomforts, and I was able to lie still, drifting into that drowsy state of mind when thoughts of the past flow swiftly and easily.

I dimly heard the occasional crack of a grenade being thrown, then the explosion, and the shrapnel humming through the air—a few Japs sneaking around in front of our lines—that's the way to keep 'em off, use grenades— good—the men knew their stuff—don't fire your rifles and machine guns until you can hear the Japs distinctly and know that they are attacking—don't let 'em know where our guns are located—wait until they hang up on our barbed wire—goddam these crabs. I thought I felt a slight breeze relieving the closeness of the night. It was a shame about Woody—I wonder if he knew he'd get it—no, I was just reading into him—it was strange that he should have instructed Stramel back in the states when he was a corporal and Stramel only a private then—the two were certainly glad to see each other—and now—well, I hope Stramel's OK. And I had heard a rumor along the line that Schmittou had been stuck with a bayonet—couldn't believe it—not Schmittou who was pretty good with his Tommy gun. Another explosion and whine—hope that one got a couple of 'em—I had seen Bennett very solemnly sitting in a shell hole looking at a picture while bullets were clipping the brush around him.

"What are you doin'?" I asked him.

"Lookin' at my wife's picture, wonderin' if I'll ever see her again."

The crack of a rifle made me rise up, fully awake. There was long silence. I listened very intently but heard no sound. I screwed my helmet around on my head and lay back once more on the bed of stones. I looked at my watch; the luminous dial showed eleven thirty-five. I noticed that here and there the clouds had broken and stars were blinking through the openings.

LaCoy was calling Sellers softly over the radio, hoping that it would work in a possible change of atmosphere. But all that the batteries could pick up was martial music. It was the second time the Japanese had jammed the air, the first having occurred in the morning when Sellers was trying to call the second platoon. A woman had broken in, jabbering incessantly, drowning out his call. He bellowed through the mouthpiece.

"F— you, you bitch! Git off the air!"

The woman continued to jabber.

LaCoy remarked to me several weeks after we left Peleliu that during battle when he found himself stationery for any length of time he frequently felt a warning from nowhere to move. He always obeyed that feeling. In one instance he was sitting behind a rock on the Point and suddenly felt this urge. No sooner had he jumped to another spot when a bullet snapped into the rock exactly where his back had been resting. I have experienced the same thing several times. I was on the Point in a hole among the rocks, and for no reason at all other than a

531

quick hunch I moved thirty yards away to another one. Immediately a mortar shell burst about five feet from where I had left. The shrapnel flew alarmingly near to my new position but did not touch me.

Premonition of danger is a definite thing. When all your senses are alert you can feel its approach. On patrol through jungle trails where you are liable to meet Japs head-on, where they wait in ambush, where they bivouac, you can feel when they are near. A sharp, prickling sensation runs up your back, you slow down your patrol and approach with infinite caution and silence. It is similar to that feeling when you are sure that someone is looking at you but you cannot see him. Something happened to Hahn on the Point which is like it. He came up to two friends who were resting by a Jap pillbox. He sat down to talk with them when he suddenly felt himself alerted by this premonitive feeling. He stood up quietly and approached the exit of the pillbox. Inside he saw five Japs dressing wounds on their legs. He sprayed them with his Tommy gun.

Hand grenades were bursting in rapid succession. The explosions were muffled in the woods where there were gullies and small miscellaneous ridges. Then much louder bursts—approaching our lines—closer—and I heard the cry "Corpsman!" Jap mortars, big stuff, were pounding in the middle of us. Shrapnel was clinking across the rocks. We could only hold and take it, and there was nothing to fire at but the impenetrable black of the woods. The Japs were probably trying to soften us up for the attack. If we could live through the barrage we would be waiting for them. Wham, Wham, Wham, awful thumping along our lines.

"I'll be damned!" Jarvi was muttering, "that one got me in the thigh." He put on a bandage.

"Cut me in the arm too," Sovik was swearing, "it's hot as hell."

The fury increased. Flares swished up from the rear. Sellers was shooting blind—I followed the cometlike streaks through the sky, and as they passed over my head I prayed they wouldn't break over our own positions and light us up like a Christmas tree. But they burst into flaming sparks well in front of us, flooding the woods with orange light—good work, Bull!—he had hit the range on the button.

"There they are. I see 'em, I see 'em!"

"Well, plug the bastards, don't look at 'em!"

A machine gun fired a burst, another one—it opened up with a vibrating roar, BARs and rifles and grenades chattered in a wild medley.

Then it was dark. White muzzle flashes spit into the black. The noise increased as the Japs answered and their bullets spattered on the rocks and ricocheted in every direction and their mortar shells thundered into the coral, raising a stink of gunpowder. Sellers was shooting more flares. They would keep the Japs down. The roar of the fight gathered new strength. Our tracers cut flaming trails through the woods, and then suddenly the Jap mortar shells stopped falling; were they closing in for the assault? And as quickly our fire ceased on the left, on the right; in the center it continued for a moment. There was utter silence. The smell of powder smoke hung over the rocks.

The woods were grim and ominous, and sometimes we could hear faint scuffling in the rocks and the underbrush. Flares revealed nothing. We fired short bursts and threw grenades at the sounds. Except for that and the pleading, sometimes angry cry, "Corpsman!" the night remained quiet.

At the first sign of daylight the Japanese suddenly renewed their activities with such intensity that an assault seemed almost certain, and we soon understood the sounds that we had heard during the night. Snipers swarmed in the trees and bushes all around us, and from a long dip in the ground about thirty yards in front of us came barrage after barrage of grenades and mortars. We could see the Japs bob up quickly, catch the fling of their arms as they hurled. Below in the rocks we presented excellent targets for the Japs in the treetops. Almost before I knew it we were engaged in a blistering fire, fighting with our backs to the ocean.

A larger gun opened up, and the shells spread pink smoke as well as shrapnel. We were spraying the trees. The fight became a vicious melee of countless explosions, whining

533

bullets, shrapnel whirring overhead or clinking off the rocks, hoarse shouts, shrill-screaming Japanese. Faces were gray with coral dirt and the smeared remains of the camouflage paint. Hibbard ran by to pick up a BAR from a man who had slumped over with a bullet in his chest. I caught a glimpse of his face—chalked with dust, blue eyes almost turned black, dark circles under them, creases around his mouth. Knight was smiling—dark, roughly chiseled, Indian face—Hunter standing over Kuld's body just for a moment, strangely meditative, I remember—Kuld, big and red-headed and freckled, as calm in death as he had been in life with blood at the corners of his mouth—Beazley, his side ripped open by a grenade—our trousers torn by the sharp coral—water supply low, our lips and tongues parched.

"Hello, five, this is control. Hello, five, this is control. Do you hear me, over?" LaCoy was trying to get Sellers. If he did I would holler for reinforcements—they could bring them up by tractor. We needed them—badly—no answer —the air was as dead as a morgue. Then Haggerty was volunteering; his red hair had turned sandy with dust—eyes like black needle-heads.

"Yes, Hag," I shouted, "go ahead. Get through. Bring some more people up here—anybody, I don't give a damn. Hurry and take care of yourself!"

"I'll bring 'em up!" he yelled, and climbed down the rocks to the beach.

Casualties were mounting fast. They ran past me down to the shelter of the beach shelf, holding bloody arms, with red dripping down their legs, cursing their luck and the Japs. Some were carried down on sagging stretchers. I smelled the powder vapor, acrid, choking, could see it swirling white—sweat in my eyes, stinging—jacket was wet on my back—rock chips spattering at my feet. Jap stuff kept coming—Jesus! why didn't they assault?—then we could knock them down like tenpins. They were dodging in and around the rocks in front of us—closer now—wiry little bastards—bandy-legged. I saw Hunter standing up throwing a grenade. As his arm swung forward he ducked and bullets crackled on the rocks over him. He stood up

534

with his rifle at his shoulder and fired three shots. Suddenly he whirled around, his rifle flew up, and his helmet was rolling on the rocks. I saw blood streaming down his face.

"Hell of a lot of 'em out there," he was saying. "I got that mortar with my last grenade, but I missed the bastard that hit me. Just a graze on the head; I was lucky." He ran down below the cliff. I saw Willis and Lees next to me, crouching behind a rock.

"The line's getting awful thin," Willis observed, "looks like we'll have to draw in and tighten up."

"But that'll mean pulling back about twenty yards, and the Japs will move in on us covered by these boulders. We would be worse off then than we are now."

"Yeah, once they get in among these rocks here we're through." A Jap grenade struck a boulder, rolled and clinked down to within three yards of us.

"Another dud," Lees remarked casually, "we've been getting a lot of 'em."

Roderick, white as a ghost, jumped behind the rock with a shrapnel hole in his back which pumped up blood in spurts. "Take it easy," Lees told him, "turn around and I'll fix you up." He placed a bandage on the wound tying it firmly across the shoulders. The blood seeped through the bandage. Willis was shouting: "We must get these wounded boys out of here! Where in hell is the tractor?"

More and heavier stuff throwing pink vapor—the din was increasing—I was wondering if we'd get out of this alive—we were surrounded—we must hold the Point— even if we—

I looked down the beach. There were no troops coming our way, no tractor. Mortar shells were crashing on the sand and the reef just below the cliff, spreading shrapnel dangerously near to the wounded men who were lying there.

"Get in closer to the rocks!" I bellowed.

Over on the right McComas was gazing intently at a rocky rise about a hundred yards in front of him. His eyes were coal black and his muscular body was alertly straining forward. I remembered his immobility, strangely noticeable in the turmoil of the fight. A grenade was fixed on his rifle which rested lightly in his hands. With a catlike movement he suddenly disappeared from my view behind the boulders.

I heard Webber's voice, calm—Boston accent—saw his face, hawk-nosed and gray-eyed and smiling through dirt smears.

"McComas just knocked out the big mortar that's been hittin' us so hard. I think we've nearly cleaned 'em out on the right; there's a slew of dead Japs out there on the rocks."

I saw Devlin on the left standing upright on the line throwing grenade after grenade. His jacket was unbuttoned and flying out with his motions.

"There he goes!" he yelled, pointing with a long arm towards the woods. Hoffman, his face smudged with dirt and powder grime, stood up beside him, and his BAR vibrating and spitting flashes. Then other men stood up on the rocks. Then more, in the center, on the right, firing faster, hurling barrages of grenades that hammered a resounding note of finality. I saw the backs of running Japanese.

I turned around and there was Haggerty coming toward me with his rolling gait and his baseball cap low over his eyes. He pushed the visor back. An unlighted cigarette was hanging from the left corner of his mouth, "I've got some men, extras from other outfits I found on the beach, and we laid a phone wire along the reef from Battalion."

"Good work, Red. Get 'em on the line. The Japs are falling back."

Fifteen men were piling out of the Alligator onto the coral edge, and our wounded were taking their places. Stacked on the beach were cans of water and more grenades and bandages and sulfa drugs and morphine and stretchers. I picked up the phone and rang Battalion, but heard no rasping sound. The wire had snapped already.

Now, just after the Japs had pulled back, the line was quiet except for the occasional crack of a rifle. Powder smoke clung low on the rocks and curled in and out among the niches. The men were watchful, haggard; some had stubble under their chins, many had shed their jackets and were

536

trying to cool themselves. The dirt mixed with sweat had ground into the skin, and several had scorching red rashes under their arms. Dark circles were prominent under their eyes which were bloodshot. They were talking in low, calm tones. I heard no bravado, no complaining, no hysterics, no irritable arguments. Every face seemed older than it should have been, more hard-bitten.

Rowe was sitting on top of a rock with his knees crossed. He wore his helmet cocked on the right side of his head as though it were a Stetson. He fingered his thin mustache musingly as he watched the woods and the rocks in front of him where dead Japs lay in brown heaps.

"Hello, Rowe," I accosted him, "how have you been doing?"

"Pretty well, Captain, pretty well," his voice was razor-edged, "except that I'm wonderin' how O'Brien is—whether he kicked off or not. A-a-a-ah," he spat, "when you see your buddy stiff on the deck with foam droolin' out of his mouth, his eyes poppin' out and his hands clutchin' at the air you feel like you could kill every livin' son of a bitch of a Jap from here to Tokyo. I got a few of those bastards out there but that's not enough. I wouldn't stake a hundred of 'em against Obie. Yeah, Captain, and it all starts you wondering —whether—well, that's war I guess."

Through every mind ran the same thoughts; we had lost too many good men; how long could it keep up? The Jap had laid off for a while, but he would hit us again; we were still out on a limb; would we get relief so we could sleep? would we die?—so what—and we were bitter mad at the Japs. We hated them, and we would kill them and keep killing them or we would be killed. If it hadn't been for him we would never have been on this goddam island in the middle of no place with all these rocks, the blasted heat and no water or chow.

War Under Water

There was always speculation as to what motivated the Banzai attacks; at Guam, it was obvious that most of the Japs had revved up their courage with hard liquor. American troops came upon huge stores of Scotch and American whisky, sake and beer on Guam, which led to the discovery that the Japanese apparently had their main liquor supply dump there for the whole central Pacific area.*

For all the comprehensive planning that went into these island operations, there was frequently a scarcity of good maps. Oddly enough this was so at Guam; even though Guam was an American possession before the war, there wasn't a single good map the planners could depend on. Reconnaissance of the islands to be assaulted was therefore doubly important; most of it was in the capable hands of the air forces. But submarines were also used, particularly in the first island campaigns, when airfields weren't within range. Submarines surfaced offshore to look over the fortifications on the beaches, the underwater demolition problems that had to be solved before the troops could go in, etc. This was a minor part of their job, of course; the submarine was an immensely important assault weapon in the Pacific Theater. In 1943, American submarines sank Japanese merchant tonnage of 1,335,000 gross tons, plus 22 warships. In the first months of 1944, well over a million and a half gross tons were sunk.

By the end of 1944, the total tonnage of the Jap merchant marine fell to less than 2,000,000 tons, a crippling drop from 5,500,000 tons two years earlier.

The submarine service did not encourage publicity during World War II. Of the publications since the war, Samuel Morison's histories of naval operations are excellent sources for the accomplishments of the submarine. And Battle Submerged, by Adm. Harley Cope and Capt. Walter Karig, offers a good one-volume account of the sub campaigns in the Pacific; the following chapter is taken from it.

* Maj. Frank Hough, *The Island War*, p. 260.

538

SUBMARINE VS. DESTROYER

by Adm. Harley Cope and Capt. Walter Karig

Destroyers are the prime enemy of submarines. One of their essential duties is to screen larger vessels from submarine attacks, wherefore they are of shallow draft; light, fast and agile; hard to hit with a torpedo and quickly maneuverable to avoid attack. They can "spin around on a dime." They all carry depth charges and the newest listening gear. At the beginning of the war there wasn't a Jap destroyer afloat that didn't consider herself more than a match for any number of submarines, and, by all the rules except the incalculable factor of human intelligence, they should have been. But this confidence began to ooze a bit after the hunted turned hunter and we started cutting them down.

Of fifty-two American subs lost during the war, Japanese surface forces definitely only accounted for sixteen. Counting all the "possibles," they certainly did not sink more than twenty-four, mines probably accounting for most of the balance. On the other side of the ledger, Japanese anti-submarine forces lost forty-two destroyers and approximately one hundred lesser escort vessels to our submarines. The light vessels of the Japanese Navy not only failed fully to protect the heavy ships and the convoys, but they themselves took disproportionate losses in their war with the submarines.

They were worthy adversaries. The Japanese ships were good, and their crews brave and well-trained, by Japanese standards. They just weren't smart enough. They fought an orthodox war, whereas the Americans used ingenuity and initiative. It was the old story of the Indian fighter versus the classically trained Redcoat.

539

The duty of the submarine was to slip past escorting destroyers and, undetected, get to the valuable tankers and cargo ships. Normally, a sub didn't even consider attacking a destroyer unless it was found alone, or the submarine was backed into a corner and had to fight her way out. There were a few cases when the submarine, having been balked in an effort to reach the convoy, picked off the destroyers just to get even, but this was very rare. A tanker sunk meant that more than one ship couldn't go to sea for lack of the fuel of which Japan had to import every drop. Better to save a torpedo for a second chance at an oiler or munitions ship than to sink an escort.

There came a time, though, when the old feeling about destroyers was reversed. By April, 1944, when Jap tankers were rarer than destroyers and the mobility of the Japanese fleet was threatened, the Joint Chiefs in Washington decreed that, to maintain this condition and aggravate it, submarines were to give enemy destroyers high priority. They were made number two on the list, right after the much sought-for but by now rarer tankers.

Only one Jap destroyer, the *Sagiri*, was sunk by subs in 1941, and she was torpedoed off Borneo by a Dutch submarine. It was not until February 8, 1942, that an American submarine started the ball rolling and then only out of necessity. The ancient S-37, commanded by Lieutenant John C. Dempsey, was completing an eventless daylight submerged patrol off eastern Borneo and was just preparing to surface for the night to charge batteries when several ships were sighted through the periscope. Gearing the S-37's croupy Diesels into high to wring out her full ten and a half knots, Dempsey followed in the darkness. It was almost eight o'clock, when he had drawn close enough to see that hopes were partially realized in that it really was a Japanese convoy, but a column formation of four enemy destroyers was interposed between the S-37 and the cargo ships. Breaking through this tight defense posed a problem for which there was no satisfactory answer. A run around end by the plodding S-boat was as out of the question as a Percheron coming from behind to win the Derby. After pondering the situation for a few minutes vainly

540

hoping for an inspirational angle of attack on the convoy, Dempsey decided to take on all four destroyers!

Later submarines were equipped with from four to six tubes forward, and four aft. What Dempsey proposed to do was rather like hunting a herd of lions with a single-barreled shotgun.

With four targets and four torpedoes he simply parceled one out to each destroyer in the column. That he got one out of the four was almost a seagoing miracle.

The third destroyer in the column caught its torpedo in the solar plexus. The amidships section rose twenty feet above the bow and stern ends and the *Natushio* went down, first of the two score plus that finally fell to American submarines.

This attack brings into sharp focus the prewar concept of submarine attacks on destroyers. Dempsey wouldn't have considered using a single torpedo on any larger type ship, but a destroyer was not thought to be worth a full salvo. A submarine that had fired four torpedoes at a single destroyer then, even though sinking it, would have been more likely to receive censure for wastefulness than praise for sinking an enemy ship. In 1944, almost any sub would pick one ship and let fly a four-torpedo salvo if presented with the same target.

In 1941 an average of 1.8 torpedoes were fired at each destroyer target. In 1944 it was 3.3 per attack. Of course the scarcity of torpedoes in 1941, as compared to the unlimited number available in 1944, probably had considerable bearing on this trend.

The directive from the Commander in Chief for the subs to bear down on destroyers came long after Sam Dealey had given the *Harder* her baptism of blood and a reputation that made her name a most descriptive one. The short, cheerful, tooth-brush-mustached officer was the second of six submarine skippers to receive the Congressional Medal of Honor. The Service, the whole Naval Service, suffered one of its heaviest and most saddening losses when the *Harder* failed to return from her sixth patrol. The long string of vicious depth-charge attacks that had all but

541

blasted the *Harder* out of the water during five previous patrols finally caught up with her off western Luzon.

Sam Dealey arrived at Pearl Harbor on May 23, 1943, to take the *Harder* out for his first war patrol in command. Optimistically maybe, realistically as it proved eventually, Rising Sun stencils had surreptitiously been taken aboard to ornament the conning tower with the symbols of her kills. She looked far too bare among the grizzled veterans that were returning to the Base with a broom at the yard-arm.

The operating area for her first patrol was in Empire waters south of Honshu. On the night of June 22, the *Harder* made her first tackle and brought down a large freighter. Three well-placed torpedoes insured the first Rising Sun a place on her conning tower. She also received her baptismal depth-charge attack, prolonged and savage.

Now the *Harder* was a veteran too! When she arrived at Midway on July 7, returning to Pearl Harbor, there was a new light in the eyes of every man aboard, and a new swagger and jauntiness in their walk. For there was more than one scalp depicted on the conning tower and one stood for the ex-seaplane tender *Sagara Maru*. Sam Dealey had become a "hot" skipper on his first patrol.

On August 24 *Harder* headed back to her old area south of Honshu on her second patrol, to take up where she had left off. The hunting was still good, and the stenciled flags now accounted for an additional four cargo ships and one tanker.

On October 30, 1943, she started her third patrol as a member of Commander Freddie Warder's (of *Seawolf* fame) pack, accompanied by the *Snook* and *Pargo*. The hunting this time was conducted in the Marianas area. On this cruise the *Harder*'s torpedoes bagged three big freighters, insuring that some 20,000 tons of stores and supplies would never reach their destination on Saipan except as litter on the beaches.

When she returned from this patrol the *Harder* was sent to the coast for a "face lifting" treatment during a month at the Mare Island Navy Yard, and a well-earned shore leave for the crew.

Early in March, 1944, she was back at Pearl Harbor, ready, as the skipper phrased it, to "ride the Pacific merry-go-round again." And on March 16 she took off for her new area of operations in the western Carolines, in the immediate vicinity of Woleai Island 500 miles west of Truk. It was there that she intercepted the new directive making enemy destroyers a primary target.

It may have been coincidence, but she had no sooner received the changed order of things than the *Harder* showed strict compliance by summarily removing a destroyer from the Imperial Navy. The target obligingly provided was the *Ikazuchi,* of the 1,850 ton *Fubuki* class.

To fit the *Harder* for her fifth and most memorable war patrol she was sent alongside the tender at Fremantle, Australia. In addition to the usual refurbishing there was always a little extra patching up required when this submarine hit port. She always seemed to undergo more than her share of depth-charge attacks.

The *Harder* left Fremantle on May 26, 1944. Her assigned area was in the Celebes Sea off the northeast coast of Borneo, in the Sulu Sea, and in addition to sinking ships, she had two other assignments. One was to remove some Intelligence operators from the northeast coast of Borneo. A couple of other subs had failed in their attempts to rescue them, but success was mandatory for the *Harder* because the increasingly desperate Japs were closing in on our people. Evidence of the mission's importance was the presence of the Australian Ace Commando, Major William Jinkins, loaned to give aid in this rescue attempt.

Their other assignment was extremely important too. The heavy naval forces of the Japanese were known to be concentrated at Tawi Tawi anchorage in the Sulu Archipelago (northeast of Borneo). When we delivered our first blow at the gates of what the Japs considered their inner defense line, the Marianas, our High Command expected the reaction at Tawi Tawi to resemble a disturbed hornets' nest. So the *Harder* and *Redfin* (Lieutenant Commander Marshall H. Austin) were sent to hang around that vicinity and catch the first movement of the enemy. They were given permission to do any damage they could but they were especially directed to find out in which direction the Japs would jump.

Captain Murray Tichenor, operations officer for Submarines Southwest Pacific, went along on the *Harder* as an observer. He wanted to see at first hand how practicable the operation orders were that he had been scribbling for the boats. It's sometimes difficult to understand every facet of an operation from a seat on the tender. Furthermore, he also wished to observe at first hand the conditions under which the subs operated. Finally, and perhaps compellingly, he loved the submarine service and when a man attains four stripes it is rare that he gets a chance to see the enemy through a periscope. He certainly got an eyeful on this trip. In fact, there were times when he even hinted that Sam Dealey was putting on a show for his special benefit.

After doing considerable broken field running through fleets of fishing boats the *Harder* arrived off Cape Mangkalibat, which thrusts from eastern Borneo into the Strait of Makassar, at dawn on June 5.

The skipper strongly suspected by their actions that some of the sailboats were a little out of character for fishing vessels. They behaved more like wolves in sheep's clothing —spotters for the Japs, but Dealey's tight schedule didn't permit time to prove it. Anyway, it didn't matter too much if the boats were on picket duty because the enemy already had the grimmest sort of evidence that United States subs continually haunted those waters. It wasn't their presence, which they were impotent to prevent, but catching them that bothered the Japs most.

Rain squalls are often a great nuisance and source of discomfort but those the *Harder* encountered this cruise were an undisguised blessing. They permitted her to arrive undetected at the southern entrance of Sibutu Passage. This is the channel that lies between Sibutu Island on Borneo's northeast coast, and Tawi Tawi, the Japanese anchorage between Borneo and the Philippines.

Inasmuch as this is the only deep-water channel between the Celebes and Sulu Seas, the Japs knew that our subs had to use the passage, and they had no intention of letting any go through.

544

The *Harder* waited until after darkness before giving the Japanese the opportunity to try and stop her. As the affair turned out, it would have been a lot cheaper for them if they had given the submarine a safe conduct passage—including personal escorts.

Just as the *Harder* was getting all wound up to start her dash the radar operator brought the proceedings to a halt by reporting that a convoy was barging down the pass.

"We're not in such a big hurry after all," grinned the skipper. "Besides, this is business that can't wait. The other job can, within reason."

Sam described this first encounter thus: "The moon was full, brilliant, and almost overhead during the latter part of the run, but was shielded intermittently by low cumulus clouds. Our intent was to dive ahead of the convoy and to maneuver into a position between the flank escorts and the tankers from which an almost simultaneous attack could be made on the destroyer and the three closely grouped ships of the convoy. This optimistic intention was later frustrated."

And for a very good reason. The moon suddenly broke through the clouds, floodlighted the surfaced sub and made all on deck feel as self-consciously prominent as Lady Godiva at a ball game. The nearest destroyer wasn't slow to take advantage.

"It was immediately apparent," said Sam Dealey, "that he was headed hellbent for the *Harder*, smoking heavily and showing a prominent bow wave."

Two choices remained. She could dive or—

"We turned tail toward the destroyer, made flank speed and hoped the Jap would get discouraged and return to his convoy but he had other intentions (none of them friendly). His speed increased to 24 knots and the range was gradually whittled down to 9,000 yards as he followed down our wake. (At 19 knots we left a wake that looked like a broad avenue for five miles astern.)

"It was painfully evident that our business with the convoy would have to wait until the destroyer was taken care of."

The *Harder* decided she had run far enough. Now, she

had only one thing in mind: Get that fellow! She submerged to periscope depth, twisted around to bring the stern tubes to bear, and waited for the destroyer, racing down her wake, to come within torpedo range. And at twenty-four knots it couldn't take long! The Japanese was steering a straight course, charging after the sub which he apparently thought was still fleeing on the surface. It was a poor guess.

"At a range of 1,150 yards," related the skipper, "we sent a triple dose of torpex (referring to the war-head explosive) toward the Jap. The first shot missed ahead, the second and third shots were observed to hit near the bow and under the bridge respectively. The target was immediately enveloped in flame and smoke, the tail rose straight in the air, a half a dozen of his depth charges going off.

"Surfaced at 1,000 yards distant, watched the destroyer go under, and headed back toward the spot where it had been. One Franklin buoy (or one of similar design) burned lonesomely over a large oil slick—but there was no ship and there were no survivors to be seen. The last moments of the destroyer were observed by the commanding officer, most of the fire control party, by Captain Tichenor and the bridge lookouts."

Japanese records indicate that this was the destroyer *Minatsuki*.

The first pressing problem had been disposed of handily. Now to take the convoy under consideration. Full speed ahead on four engines! "From here," observed the skipper, "it would be a race to see who could get to Tarakan first."

But another destroyer popped into sight to offer strenuous opposition to any attempted liberties with the three precious tankers. Again the *Harder* prepared to square away for a passage at arms, but this time the target was wide awake and watchful. When the submarine let fly with her punch, the destroyer neatly sidestepped and countered savagely with heavy depth charges that battered and buffeted the *Harder* for the next hour and a half. As Sam Dealey admitted, "That fellow was on their varsity!"

546

When the weary destroyer drew away from her rather groggy opponent, the *Harder* took cognizance of the time element that had inexorably crept into the problem. It was too late to try for another pass at the fast-stepping convoy, so the submarine headed for Sibutu and rescue for the trapped observation party.

At dawn the *Harder* sighted what was believed to be the mast of a ship, and the submarine slithered down for an attack position from well below the surface—just in case a plane happened to be sitting around overhead. After an hour and a half Sam figured that it was about time to take a look at the traffic and tried to come up to periscope depth. Then the most sickening sensation a submariner can feel, more dismaying than the jolt of depth charges, jarred all hands—the grate of the keel on a submerged obstacle. No one had suspected that the heavy set of the uncharted current during the night had taken them near the reef on which they were now in danger of being hung. Dealey gave the immediate order to blow main ballast tanks, then backed full speed and miraculously managed to clear the reef without apparent damage. But all hands sprouted goose bumps at the thought of what might have happened, if the skipper hadn't had the hunch to plane up for a look-see when he did. The Jap base was much too close for any Americans to be stranded on a reef, if they were lucky enough to get that much fresh air before extinction.

But the target? To top it all off, the "ship" was still where it had first been seen, and where it still is—a small island!

Shortly before noon the *Harder* submerged again to wait out an aircraft contact when a destroyer suddenly loomed up on the periscope, coming at a fast clip and only about 4,000 yards away. No one suggested that this might be an island when the *Harder* turned toward her. A minute later the two killers were headed for each other and closing fast. The Jap had seen the periscope. That was made as plain by his belligerent approach as if he had flown a flag hoist.

"Stood by with four tubes forward to fire down his throat, if necessary," related Sam in his war diary later.

"At that stage there wasn't much choice. Angle on the bow changed from zero to 10 degrees starboard, then quickly back to 15 degrees port." The situation was growing more tense every second. What would the destroyer do next? If he would only stay on a steady course for just a few minutes! At this rate it looked as though it might surely have to be a head-on "down the throat" shot, with the target practically crawling over the submarine the next moment.

At a range of 650 yards the angle on the bow had opened to 20 degrees port. The skipper filled his lungs to expel a sigh of relief, and then the destroyer perversely but cannily began to swing back. Sam Dealey, his forehead bathed in sweat, waited no longer; he couldn't, unless he wanted the fellow coming through his conning tower.

"Fired one-two-three in rapid succession. Number four wasn't necessary. Fifteen seconds after the first shot was fired it struck the destroyer squarely amidships. Number two hit just aft—number three missed ahead. Ordered right full rudder and ahead full to get clear. At range of 300 yards we were rocked by a terrific explosion believed to have been the destroyer magazine. Less than one minute after the first hit, and nine minutes after it was sighted, the destroyer (later identified as the *Hayananmi*) sank tail first, observed by the Commanding Officer, Executive Officer, and, of course, Captain Tichenor."

But a lot of other equally interested persons had seen it go down. Sound reported fast screws racing up from all directions. So the sub went deep and philosophically rigged for depth charging, while the yeoman broke out the forms on which to record each explosion.

They weren't long in coming—and continued for two gruelling hours.

At 3:30 that afternoon the *Harder* had crawled from under and was again at periscope depth, tubes reloaded, looking for trouble. Two *Fubuki*-class destroyers came steaming up—and the *Harder* prepared to make someone pay for the depth-charge drubbing, but at 4,000 yards the destroyers suddenly wheeled about and quit the neighborhood.

However, it was still a busy area. Later in the afternoon an investigating committee of six destroyers headed for the submarine.

"Looked as though the *Harder* had worn out her welcome here," observed Sam. "We felt as if we had a monopoly on the whole Pacific war this date. (Such popularity must be preserved.)" The temptation was to further deplete the Imperial Navy's dwindling forces but the skipper—

"Made a quick review of the whole picture and decided that discretion here was definitely the better part of valor. The battery was low, air in the boat was none too good, the crew was fatigued, and our navigational position in a narrow strait, with strong and variable currents, was not well known. I really believe that we might have gotten one or two of the enemy ships, but under the above listed conditions, a persistent and already humiliated enemy (after two sinkings within twenty-four hours just off a fleet base) would probably have developed an attack from which the *Harder* might not have pulled through. No apologies are made for my withdrawal. The gamble would have been taken at too great a risk."

The skipper having made his decision, the *Harder* began evading to the north to lose the destroyers and get on with her assigned task. The navigator was unable to fix the ship's position due to a "fuzzy" horizon, but it appeared they were headed up the center of Sibutu Passage. A tiny blip suddenly blossomed on the radar screen, dead ahead at 1,500 yards. It was sighted immediately from the bridge by moonlight, a small boat by all appearances. At 1,200 yards it was discovered to be a low rock pinnacle sticking straight up out of the sea, with white foam breaking around it. Dealey ordered full right rudder, and "within 400 yards of grounding on this pinnacle as we reversed course," he noted in his diary. "Special credit is due Wilbur Lee Clark RT (radio technician) 3c, USNR, for his alert watchstanding. He undoubtedly prevented a grounding which might well have been disastrous."

The navigator was able to check his position a little later on Sibutu Island light and by midnight the submarine was heading north again. At ten o'clock on the morning of

June 8 the *Harder* was submerged off the northeast tip of Borneo below Cape Unsang. She was two days late for the rendezvous; Sam apologetically explained later that the compulsory sinking of two destroyers had delayed them.

Late that night the submarine crept in to keep her rendezvous with the Intelligence operators. With nothing to break the stillness of the night except the muffled paddling of the rubber boat, Major Jinkins pulled off his little miracle and got the operators aboard safely. There was a silent hand shake and a low murmur of thanks before they disappeared down the hatch.

Sam lost no time clearing the neighborhood. The Japs had been ready to spring their trap on the operators at dawn, and when it became obvious that the prey had escaped, they wouldn't have any trouble guessing how it had been managed. Sam wanted deep water under him before the investigating planes inevitably arrived.

At 5:32 a.m. the expected snooper came diving in. The Japs hadn't waited until dawn to find out that the agents they had hunted so long and persistently had been snatched away.

"Bridge lookout sighted float-type plane—close," related the skipper. "Made quick dive. Bomb exploded as we passed 75 feet—also close! The sub was thoroughly shaken and resulted in an early and prompt reveille for all hands, but no damage of a serious nature was sustained."

The new passengers were already getting a quick initiation into routine life aboard the *Harder*. One of them vowed later that if he had suspected what they were going to have to go through before he reached Australia nothing could have dragged him off Borneo. He would have insisted upon waiting for the next boat.

The skipper didn't doubt that the plane had sent a hurry call to the destroyers at Tawi Tawi. They could be expected to come swarming out in a few hours, looking for trouble— and the *Harder*. Conditions to receive them properly were not auspicious from the *Harder*'s point of view.

"The smooth glassy sea," explained Sam, "with aircraft overhead precluded a successful attack at periscope depth, so it was decided to swing to the northeast and not attempt

550

a southward transit of Sibutu until nightfall. However, the longer we remained undetected, the more convinced that Jap aviator would be that his bomb hit the mark. Such an assumption wouldn't have been far wrong."

At 11:00 a.m. "sound picked up propeller noises of two destroyers approaching from the westward (direction of Tawi Tawi. The advance guard!). A periscope attack in the glassy sea against alerted destroyers with air support was not considered to be 'good ball.' Increased depth and rigged for silent running. Both destroyers passed overhead and nearby several times."

By early afternoon the searchers had been shaken off. Sam returned to periscope depth to find that the seas had picked up enough to ruffle the surface, so now they could make a periscope attack. He headed directly for the northern entrance to Sibutu, ready to do battle once more.

Soon after sunset the *Harder* was on the surface speeding down the pass. Radar picked up a few patrol vessels but they were far enough abaft the beam for the *Harder* to show them her heels. Nevertheless it indicated that the enemy was going to make his best attempt to prevent the submarine from going through.

At 9:00 p.m. the skipper recorded, "Entered northern bottleneck of Sibutu Passage with the Jap fleet base at Tawi Tawi just six miles away on port beam. Trouble was expected here and did we find it!"

Just a minute later radar reported a destroyer ahead. Sam saw it at the same time. It didn't worry him because by now he felt competent to handle the destroyer situation. Another was sighted almost immediately near the first, but Dealey still felt confident that he would be able to handle both of them.

The actions of the destroyers seemed to indicate that they were simply patrolling the narrows, and had no suspicion that a stranger was entering their midst. If they could just be kept in ignorance a few minutes longer! Sam picked out the logical one to "gun" first—the larger one.

"At 3,000 yards both destroyers zigged 30 degrees to their right (with the first presenting a 30 degree port track) and the picture became 'just what the doctor ordered.' At a range of 1,000 yards on the nearest target, both destroyers were overlapping, with a 100 degree track showing, so without further delay commenced firing the bow tubes. No. 1 appeared to pass just ahead of the first destroyer, No. 2 struck it near the bow, No. 3 hit just under the destroyer bridge, and No. 4 passed astern of the near target. The sub was swinging hard right to avoid hitting the first destroyer and fire was withheld on remaining tubes until a new setup could be put into the T.D.C. (target data computer) for an attack on the second destroyer. About 30 seconds after turning the second destroyer came into view just astern of what was left of the first one which was burning furiously. Just then No. 4 torpedo, which had passed astern of the first target, was heard and observed to hit the second target (no more torpedoes were needed for either).

"Meanwhile, a heavy explosion, believed to be caused by an exploding boiler on the first destroyer, went off and the sub (then about 400 yards away) was heeled over by the concussion. At almost the same time a blinding explosion took place on the second destroyer (probably the ammunition going off) and it took a quick nose dive. When last observed by the Commanding Officer and Executive Officer (and the eager Captain Tichenor, naturally) the tail of the second destroyer was straight in the air. And the first destroyer had disappeared."

The *Harder*, so far in her one-ship war, had whittled down Admiral Ozawa's badly needed light forces by four destroyers and the patrol wasn't even over.

The submarine surfaced to see the damage and to make a rapid shift to a more quiet neighborhood. Only a large cloud of steam and heavy vapor hung over the spot where the first destroyer had been. A lighted buoy marked the spot where the second ship had taken her last plunge.

At flank speed the *Harder* tore along to the south before the night flyers could arrive. Half an hour later she had to duck under for a while to let one go by, but she was soon up and off again.

At 11:05, however, things weren't so simple. "Sighted aircraft float-type plane, flying at height of 100 feet, coming in off our starboard quarter and almost on top of us. It is believed that he sighted us just as the rudder was shifted hard left. He whizzed by the starboard beam at a range of 100 yards! Submerged. First aerial bomb not so close, second aerial bomb damned close! Increased depth."

Then the bombs became more distant.

"Sound contact on approaching ship. Rigged for silent running. Remained deep for remainder of night to rest a weary crew."

At 0445, "Surfaced to change air in the boat before another all day dive, and to cram more 'amps' in the battery."

Before dawn she was once more submerged and heading for a point south of Tawi Tawi for her reconnoitering duty.

Destroyers were observed on apparently routine patrol but none came close to the lurking submarine. The passengers became wistful for the comparatively quiet life of dodging Jap patrols in the jungle.

At 5:00 p.m. the next afternoon, June 10, excitement surged through the *Harder* like a tidal wave when Sound reported a large movement of ships, light and heavy screws. The very thing they had come to witness! The passengers now began to ask, "Is this trip necessary?"

A quick periscope observation disclosed a large task force—three battleships, four or more cruisers, and six or eight destroyers. Float-type planes circled overhead. The first movement of Ozawa's force was coming out!

The skipper describes what happened: "Sea was glassy smooth and events which followed quickly showed that our periscope was sighted.

"While watching and identifying the nearest of the battleships (which was definitely of the *Musashi* class) it was suddenly enveloped in a heavy black smoke and Sound reported hearing three positive explosions. The first assumption (and hope still remained) was another of our subs had put three torpedoes in the battleship, but a reconstructed version of the affray shows that the following was more likely.

"Immediately after the smoke and explosions around the battleship, a destroyer, which until then had blended in with the big ship, headed directly for us belching black

553

smoke. It is believed that one of the float-type planes had spotted our periscope and dropped a smoke float near it. Whereupon the battleship's escorting destroyer laid down a quick smoke screen between us and the battleship and dropped three 'scare' charges as he headed our way." But there was no guessing about the destroyer that was heading for the *Harder* with a bone in his teeth and fire in his eyes. "The sound man obtained a 'turn count' for 35 knots on the destroyer. His bow wave and rapidly closing range verified it!

"With the idea that we were now scheduled for another working over anyhow, it was decided to have a crack at the destroyer first. The bow was swung toward him for another 'down the throat' shot. (Maybe recent events have just gotten us too much in the habit of shooting destroyers anyhow?) At a range of 4,000 yards . . . the angle on the bow still zero and the destroyer echo ranging right on us steadily! The picture had reached the stage where we had to hit him or else."

When the range was 1,500 yards Sam calmly fired three torpedoes. With the destroyer knifing directly down on them the "fish" wouldn't have far to run—that is, to hit.

"Sound had now picked up other fast screws moving in from the starboard beam but this was no time to look; the *Harder* went deep.

"Fifty-five and sixty seconds respectively after the first shot, two torpedoes struck with a detonation that was far worse than depth charging. By this time we were just passing 80 feet and were soon beneath the destroyer. Then all Hell broke loose! It was not from his depth charges for if they had been dropped at that time this report would not have been completed, but a deafening series of progressive rumblings that seemed to blend with each other. Either his boilers or magazines, or both, had exploded and it's a lucky thing that ship explosions are vented upward and not down.

"The previously reported sound on the starboard beam was now reported moving in for his share of the fun and started laying his barrages as we were going deep. It is believed that they fell astern. They were loud and close and added their bit to the jolting around but none com-

554

pared in intensity to the exploding destroyer we had just passed beneath.

"Other explosions, believed to be aerial bombs, began to land nearby, and all added up to make the most uncomfortable five minutes yet experienced during the *Harder's* five war patrols. Something between twenty or thirty distinct depth charges or bombs were counted but no one was interested in numbers at the time."

Finally the *Harder* pulled clear of the bombed area and once more all hands, including the passengers, drew a deep breath. When they again raised their periscope in the darkness, a lone lighted buoy was burning forlornly over the spot where the attack had taken place. For the extraordinary exploit of sinking five destroyers in a matter of almost four days, Sam Dealey was awarded the Congressional Medal of Honor.

After surfacing, the *Harder* sent a contact report by radio announcing that the first of the heavy forces had left Tawi Tawi anchorage. At dawn she was back counting noses in the anchorage.

After a few days more the *Harder* returned to Australia to discharge her thankful passengers and to get a few more torpedoes so she could continue her patrol.

She never returned from the sixth patrol.

Burma and the Ledo Road

The Japanese had moved into lower Burma early in 1942, pushing the British-Indian 17th Division ahead of them as they advanced on Rangoon. In March, they drove the last British troops out of Rangoon, and scattered the Chinese divisions Chiang Kai-Shek had sent in to help. The retreating British were joined by remnants of the Chinese who were led by American General "Vinegar Joe" Stilwell. Still, the onrushing Japanese never gave them time to organize for a concerted front. By the end of May, what was left of Burma Corps had retreated across the Burmese border into India.

General Slim, commanding the Burma Corps, described the last days of the retreat: "Ploughing their way up slopes, over a track inches deep in slippery mud, soaked to the skin, rotten with fever, ill-fed and shivering as the air grew cooler, the troops went on, hour after hour, day after day. Their only rest at night was to lie on the sodden ground under the dripping trees, without even a blanket to cover them. Yet the monsoon which so nearly destroyed us and whose rain beat so mercilessly on our bodies did us one good turn—it stopped dead the Japanese pursuit. As the clouds closed down over the hills, even their air attacks became rare.

"On the last day of that nine hundred mile retreat I stood on the bank beside the road and watched the rear guard march into India. All of them, British, Indian, and Gurkha, were gaunt and ragged as scarecrows. Yet as they trudged behind their surviving officers in groups pitifully small, they still carried their arms and kept their ranks. . . . They might look like scarecrows, but they looked like soldiers, too." *

Throughout the remainder of 1942 and for most of 1943 there was not a large-scale land campaign on the India-Burma front, although the British sent the 14th Division probing into Arakan to capture a limited objective but were thrown back. In the meantime the Burma Road had

*Field Marshal the Viscount William Slim *Defeat into Victory*, p. 87. David McKay Co.

been cut and American bomber crews flying out of the Chinese mainland could not be supplied, nor could vital war supplies be given to the Chinese armies. But by building air bases in Assam and flying transport planes over the Himalayas to China the lifeline was kept intact. Meanwhile, work would be rushed to build a new road to China —the Ledo.

The strategy behind the decision to rush work on the Ledo Road and open the campaign in northern Burma was pressed on the British by President Roosevelt and his Chiefs of Staff. In a letter to Prime Minister Churchill in early February, 1944, the President stressed the need to build up air power in China which could be used against Japanese shipping and in raids on Japan itself. He wrote, "I have always advocated the development of China as a base for the support of our Pacific advances.... It is mandatory that we make every effort to increase the flow of supplies into China. This can only be done by increasing the air tonnage or by opening a road through Burma. Our occupation of Myitkyina will enable us immediately to increase the air-lift to China by providing an intermediate air-transport base as well as by increasing the protection of the air route.... The continued build-up of Japanese strength in Burma requires us to undertake the most aggressive action within our power to retain the initiative and prevent them from launching an offensive that may carry them over the borders into India.... I most urgently hope therefore that you back to the maximum a vigorous and immediate campaign in Upper Burma." *

Churchill, on the other hand, felt that North Burma was the worst place to fight the Japanese. The country was "the most forbidding fighting country imaginable" and land advances had to be undertaken with tenuous lines of communications. He preferred "to contain the Japanese in Burma, and break into or through the great arc of islands forming the outer fringe of the Dutch East Indies ... but we never succeeded in deflecting the Americans from their purpose." *

Against these conflicting viewpoints, one should keep in mind that all parties still believed the Japanese homeland would have to be invaded. The atomic bomb was not then a part of the strategic planning.

To General Slim, commanding the 14th Army, fell the task of driving the Japanese back in North Burma. In the following selection, he

*Closing the Ring, pp. 561, 562. Houghton Mifflin. Copyright 1951 by Houghton Mifflin Co.

recounts his opinion of the strategy, and the story of part of the resulting campaign, dealing specifically with Stilwell's drive on Myitkyina and Orde Wingate's Chindits operation behind the Japanese lines.

THE NORTHERN FRONT IN BURMA*

by Field Marshal The Viscount William Slim

The northern was the most isolated of the Burma fronts. To reach it by rail—there was no road—you left Dimapur and continued your seemingly interminable journey through the tea-garden area of Assam. As you crept northward, it was impossible to avoid a growing feeling of loneliness, which even the sight of the increasingly busy airfields of the Hump route, strung along the line, failed to dissipate. At last Tinsukia, the junction for the Assam oil fields, was reached, and your train turned wearily into the branch for Ledo. Ledo, in December 1943, seemed rather like the end of the world. Instead, it was the start of the road to China, the road that, if it ever were built, would replace the one from Rangoon, so effectively closed in early 1942.

Many people at this time, Americans no less than British doubted if the Ledo road *could* be built. They doubted if the Chinese divisions would ever be able to drive back the Japanese and clear the route. They doubted if the Ledo railway would carry and maintain the troops, labour, equipment, and material required. They doubted if any road builders could overcome the monsoon climate combined with the extreme difficulty of the terrain. Many, even of those who believed it possible, did not think that the Ledo road would ever repay the expenditure in men and resources that would have to be devoted to it. Indeed, at this time Stilwell was almost alone in his faith that, not only could the road be built, but that it would be the most potent

*Condensed from *Defeat into Victory*, Chapter 12.

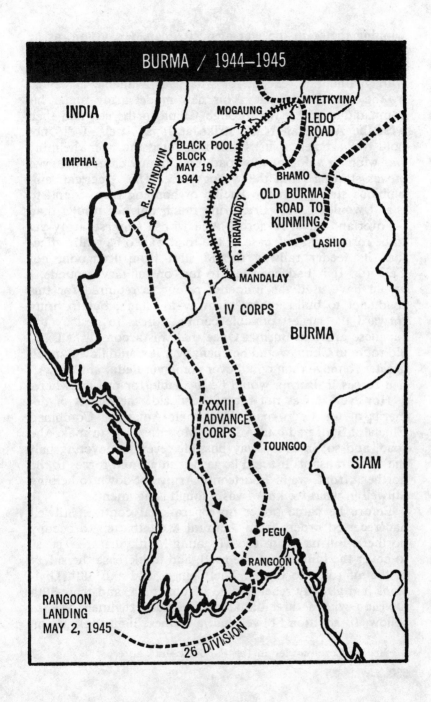

winning factor in the war against Japan. His vision, as he expounded it to me, was of an American-trained and -equipped Chinese force, of some thirty divisions to begin with, maintained, except for what was available in China, by the road from Ledo. This new model army under his command would drive through China to the sea and then with the American Navy strike at Japan itself. I did not hold two articles of his faith. I doubted the overwhelming war-winning value of this road, and, in any case, I believed it was starting from the wrong place. The American amphibious strategy in the Pacific of hopping from island to island would, I was sure, bring much quicker results than an overland advance across Asia with a Chinese army yet to be formed. In any case, if the road was to be really effective, its feeder railway should start from Rangoon, not Calcutta. If it had been left to me, on military grounds, I would have used the immense resources required for this road, not to build a new highway to China, but to bring forward the largest possible combat forces to destroy the Japanese army in Burma. Once that was accomplished, the old route to China would be open; over it would flow a much greater tonnage than could ever come via Ledo, and the Allied forces in Burma would be available for use elsewhere.

However, it was not for me to decide the merits or demerits of the Ledo road. The Anglo-American Combined Chiefs of Staff had told Admiral Mountbatten [1] to make the road, and so, in every way possible, even to devoting half the total transport lift and large British ground forces to the northern front, we in Fourteenth Army got down to helping Stilwell in what we knew was a tough assignment.

Before he came under my operational control, Stilwell had received orders from Admiral Mountbatten to occupy northern Burma up to the Mogaung-Myitkyina area, so as to cover the building of the road, and to increase the safety of the air route to China. The Chinese 22d and 38th Divisions had already reached Ledo from India, and their 30th Division with a three-battalion American regiment was to follow. In addition Stilwell had a Chinese light tank group,

---

[1] British Commander in the Far East.—Ed. note.

560

an irregular force of American-officered Kachin tribesmen, and I had given him the Fort Hertz detachment of a battalion of Burma Rifles with local levies. For air support he had the considerable American Northern Sector Air Force. The whole of this Chinese-American-British force was known, rather clumsily, as Northern Combat Area Command. Further, Wingate's Special Force of several brigades was to be put, mainly by air, in rear of the Japanese opposing Stilwell to cut their communications.

By February 1 the 38th Chinese Division had, after a series of small actions, occupied Thipha Ga, while a regiment of the 22d Division, moving wide on the right flank, cleared the Japanese from the Taro Valley, which lay on the east bank of the Chindwin River, separated from the Ledo road in the Hukawng Valley by a range of rugged jungle hills. This was the 22d Division's entry into the campaign, and they did well. In all these actions Stilwell had kept a close hand on the Chinese troops, steadying them when they faltered, prodding them when they hesitated, even finding their battalions for them himself when they lost them. He was one of the Allied commanders who had learned in the hard school of the 1942 retreat. His tactics were to press the Japanese frontally while the real attacks came in through the jungle from the flank, with probably a road block well behind the enemy. In this way, by a series of hooks around and behind the Japanese, he pushed forward. He also was an advocate of the sledge hammer to crack a walnut at this stage. He saw to it that if a Japanese company was to be liquidated, it was attacked by a Chinese regiment.

At the beginning of March I visited Stilwell at Thipha Ga just as he was launching up to then his biggest attack for the capture of Maingkwan, a large village and the capital of the Hukawng Valley. Besides his two Chinese divisions, he now had with him the American Long-Range Penetration Regiment. Stilwell had changed its original commander for Brigadier General Merrill, whom I had known well and liked. After him, the regiment was christened "Merrill's Marauders." Merrill was a fine, courageous leader who inspired confidence, and I congratulated myself that

I had restrained my Gurkha orderly, that day in 1942, when he would have tommy-gunned a jeepload of men wearing unfamiliar helmets. If he had, the Marauders would have had another commander, and that would have been a pity.

The fly-in of Wingate's Special [2] Force, due to commence on March 5, was intended primarily to help the American-Chinese advance, and I wanted to make sure he was completely familiar with the final arrangements.

Stilwell was always rather prickly about Wingate's force. To begin with, Mountbatten and Wingate between them had persuaded the American Chiefs of Staff to send United States troops, even if only a regiment, to the Burma front, when he himself had failed to get them. Further, he felt passionately that all American troops in the theatre should be under his direct command, and had been angered when they were allotted to Wingate. Stilwell had pressed for them to be transferred to him, and confessed quite frankly to me that he had been very surprised when Mountbatten yielded to his request. Nevertheless, he did not seem particularly grateful to the Supreme Commander and some bitterness remained. Nor did he approve of Wingate's long-range penetration methods; he preferred the short-hook tactics.

On the morning of Sunday, March 5, I circled the landing ground at Hailakandi. Below me, at the end of the wide brown air strip, was parked a great flock of squat, clumsy gliders, their square wing tips almost touching; around the edges of the field stood the more graceful Dakotas that were to lift them into the sky. Men swarmed about the aircraft, loading them, laying out towropes, leading mules,

[2] Wingate's Long-Range Penetration Force was known as the Chindits. Gen. Slim describes it as "the old cavalry raid on enemy communications which, to be effective . . . must be made in tactical coordination with a main attack elsewhere." Gen. Wavell had made Wingate commander of all guerrilla operations in Burma in early 1942. In early 1943, Wingate had conducted his first raid into Burma, penetrating some 200 miles behind Japanese lines, but according to Gen. Slim "gave little tangible return for the losses it had suffered and the resources absorbed."—Ed. note.

humping packs, and moving endlessly in dusty columns, for all the world like busy ants around captive moths.

I landed and met Wingate at his temporary headquarters near the air strip. Everything was going well. There had been no serious hitch in the assembly or preparation for the fly-in, which was due to begin at dusk that evening. For some days previously our diversionary air attacks had been almost continuous on Japanese airfields and communication centres to keep his air force occupied. Meanwhile, ostentatious air reconnaissances over the Mandalay district had been carried out in the hope of convincing the enemy that any airborne expedition would be directed against that area. The attacks on airfields were useful in keeping Japanese aircraft out of the sky, but the false reconnaissances, as far as I ever discovered, had little effect.

Just a month earlier, on February 4, Stratemeyer, the American commander of the Eastern Air Command, and I had issued a joint directive to Wingate and Cochrane, the American commander of No. 1 Air Commando. In this, Wingate's force was ordered to march and fly in to the Rail Indaw area (*Rail* Indaw to distinguish it from another Indaw not on the Mandalay-Myitkyina railway), and from there to operate under direct command of Fourteenth Army, with the objects of:

(1) Helping the advance of Stilwell's Ledo force on Myitkyina by cutting the communications of the Japanese 18th Division, harassing its rear, and preventing its reinforcement.

(2) Creating a favourable situation for the Yunnan Chinese forces to cross the Salween and enter Burma.

(3) Inflicting the greatest possible damage and confusion on the enemy in North Burma.

The tactical plan for getting the force into position behind the enemy was based on four assembly places:

"Aberdeen," 27 miles northwest of Indaw.
"Piccadilly," 40 miles northeast of Indaw.
"Broadway," 35 miles east-northeast of Indaw.
"Chowringhee," 35 miles east of Indaw.

These places were all away from roads and uninhabited. They were selected because there was enough flat ground to make the building of an air strip possible in a short time and because there was water in the immediate vicinity. They were, in fact, fancy names written on the map within striking distance of Indaw.

It was intended that in the first wave 16 Brigade should march to Aberdeen, 77 Brigade fly in two halves to Piccadilly and Broadway, and 111 Brigade land at Chowringhee. The remaining three brigades, 14, 23, and 3 West African, were to be held for the second wave, which it was expected would be required to relieve the first in two or three months.

As the afternoon wore on the atmosphere of excitement and suspense at Hailakandi grew—the old, familiar feeling of waiting to go over the top, intensified by the strangeness and magnitude of this operation. Everyone, even the mules, moved about calmly, quietly, and purposefully. Except perhaps for those patient beasts, it was, all the same, obvious that everyone realized that what was, up to this time, the biggest and most hazardous airborne operation of the war was about to begin.

During the morning the gliders had been loaded with supplies, ammunition, engineer equipment, signalling stores, and men's kits. In the late afternoon the first wave, 77 Brigade Headquarters, the leading British and Gurkha infantry, and a small detachment of American airfield engineers emplaned. Each Dakota was to take two gliders. This was a heavy load, and, as far as I know, never before had these aircraft towed more than one. There had been a clash of opinion among the airmen themselves on its practicability. Cochrane, in charge of the gliders, was confident it could be done; Old, whose Combat Cargo planes would provide the tugs, maintained it was unsound. Various airmen, British and American, took sides, and argument was heated. Eventually, after experiments, Wingate agreed with Cochrane, and then Baldwin and I accepted the double tow. Now as I watched the last preparations I was assailed by no doubts on that score. The Dakotas taxied into position. The towropes were fixed. Everyone was very quiet as the roar of engines died down and we waited for zero hour.

564

I was standing on the air strip with Wingate, Baldwin, and one or two more, when we saw a jeep driving furiously toward us. A couple of American airmen jumped out and confronted us with an air photograph, still wet from the developing tent. It was a picture of Piccadilly landing ground, taken two hours previously. It showed almost the whole level space, on which the gliders were to land that night, obstructed by great tree trunks. It would be impossible to put down even one glider safely. To avoid suspicion no aircraft had reconnoitered the landing grounds for some days before the fly-in, so this photo was a complete shock to us. We looked at one another in dismay.

Wingate, though obviously feeling the mounting strain, had been quiet and controlled. Now, not unnaturally perhaps, he became very moved. His immediate reaction was to declare emphatically to me that the whole plan had been betrayed—probably by the Chinese—and that it would be dangerous to go on with it. I asked if Broadway and Chowringhee, the other proposed landing places, had been photographed at the same time. I was told they had been, and that both appeared vacant and unobstructed.

Wingate was now in a very emotional state, and to avoid discussion with him before an audience, I drew him on one side. I said I did not think the Chinese had betrayed him as they certainly had no knowledge of actual landing grounds, or, as far as I knew, of the operation at all; but he reiterated that someone had betrayed the plan and that the fly-in should be cancelled. I pointed out that only one of the three landing grounds had been obstructed, and that it was the one which he had used in 1943 and of which a picture with a Dakota on it had appeared in an American magazine. We knew the Japanese were nervous of air landing and were blocking many possible landing sites in North and Central Burma; what more likely than they should include a known one we had already used, such as Piccadilly? He replied that, even if Broadway and Chowringhee were not physically obstructed, it was most probable that Japanese troops were concealed in the surrounding jungle ready to destroy our gliders as they landed. With great feeling he said it would be "murder." I told him I doubted if these places

565

were ambushed. Had the Japanese known of the plan I was sure they would either have ambushed or obstructed all three landing grounds. Wingate was by now calmer and much more in control of himself. After thinking for a moment, he said there would be great risk. I agreed. He paused, then looked at me. "The responsibility is yours," he said.

I knew it was. Not for the first time I felt the weight of decision crushing in on me with an almost physical pressure. The gliders, if they were to take off that night, must do so within the hour. There was no time for prolonged inquiry or discussion. On my answer would depend not only the possibility of a disaster with wide implications on the whole Burma campaign and beyond, but the lives of these splendid men, tense and waiting in and around their aircraft. At that moment I would have given a great deal if Wingate or anybody else could have relieved me of the duty of decision. But that is a burden the commander himself must bear.

I knew that if I canceled the fly-in or even postponed it, when the men were keyed to the highest pitch, there would be a terrible reaction; we would never get their morale to the same peak again. The whole plan of campaign, too, would be thrown out. I had promised Stilwell we would cut the communications of the enemy opposing him, and he was relying on our doing it. I had to consider also that one Chindit brigade had already marched into the area; we could hardly desert it. I was, in addition, very nervous that if we kept the aircraft crowded on the airfields as they were, the Japanese would discover them, with disastrous consequences. I knew at this time that a major Japanese offensive was about to break on the Assam front, and I calculated on Wingate's operation to confuse and hamper it. Above all, somehow I did not believe that the Japanese knew of our plan or that the obstruction of Piccadilly was evidence that they did. There was a risk, a grave risk, but not a certainty of disaster. "The operation will go on," I said.[8]

[8] In an account of this incident written shortly afterward, but which I did not see until after his death, Wingate reversed his role and mine. In it he stated that he used these arguments to

566

Wingate accepted my decision with, I think, relief. He had by now recovered from his first shock and had realized that the obstruction of one landing site need not hold all the implications he had imagined. We walked back to the group of officers and, with Baldwin's concurrence, I announced that the fly-in would proceed, adding that as Piccadilly was obviously out, it was for Wingate as the tactical commander to decide what changes should be made. He stated the case for continuing the operation clearly and calmly, and directed that the troops allotted to Piccadilly were to be diverted to Chowringhee. Although this was strictly Wingate's business and not mine, I very much doubted the wisdom of this. Chowringhee was on the east of the Irrawaddy; the railway and road to be cut were on the west. Before the troops could be effective, therefore, they had to cross the river, and I questioned if this could be done as quickly or as easily as Wingate thought. I asked Calvert, the commander of 77 Brigade, and I found him strongly against Chowringhee. Cochrane also opposed it for the very sound reason that the layout there was quite ·different from Piccadilly and Broadway and there was little time to rebrief pilots. Baldwin, who as commander of the Third Tactical Air Force, had the over-all responsibility for the air side of the operation, was emphatic that Chowringhee could not be used by Piccadilly air crews, and that settled it. Wingate saw the force of these opinions and accepted that the fly-in would take place as originally planned, except that the troops for Piccadilly would go to Broadway.

Cochrane collected the Piccadilly Dakota and glider pilots, whose destination was now changed, to rebrief them. Curious to see how he would break the news of the alteration and a little anxious lest so obvious a hitch at the start

---

urge that the fly-in should go on and that I accepted them and agreed. That is not my recollection of his first reactions, nor in accordance with my notes made nearer the time. In any case, the point is of little consequence, as whether Wingate persuaded me, or I him, the responsibility for ordering the operation to continue and for all its consequences could not be his, but must be Baldwin's and mine.

might have a rather depressing effect of them, I followed to listen. Cochrane sprang on to the bonnet of a jeep. "Say, fellers," he announced, "we've got a better place to go to!"

The leading Dakota, with its two gliders trailing behind, roared down the runway just after six o'clock, only a few minutes behind scheduled time. The moment one was clear the next followed at about half-a-minute intervals. The gliders took the air first, one or two wobbling nervously before they took station behind, and a little above, the towing aircraft. More than once I feared a Dakota would overrun the strip before the gliders were up, but all took off safely and began the long climb to gain height to cross the hills. The darkening sky was full of these queer triangles of aircraft labouring slowly higher and higher into the distance. Eventually even the drone of engines faded and we were left waiting.

And an unpleasant wait it was. Sixty-one gliders had set off. The full complement for Broadway and Piccadilly had been eighty, but we had agreed that sixty was about the most we could hope to land on one strip in the hours of darkness, so the rest had been held back. I sat in the control tent, at the end of the air strip, to which all messages and signals came. At the rough table with its field telephones was Tullock, Wingate's chief staff officer, who proved himself quick, reliable, and cool in crisis, and Rome, another admirable staff officer. As the moon came up, in spite of hurricane lanterns and one electric lamp, it was almost lighter outside than within. There was a pause. Then came a report of red flares, fired from the air a few miles away. That meant a tow in distress—ominous if difficulties were beginning so soon. I took a turn outside and thought I saw a red Very light fired high up in the distance. I returned to the tent to find more rumours of gliders down or tows returning before they had crossed our lines. Not so good. Then another long wait. We looked at our watches. The leading aircraft should be over Broadway now with the gliders going in. We ought to get the first wireless message any minute. Still it did not come. Wingate prowled in and out, speaking to no one, his eyes smouldering in a pallid face. Tullock sat calmly at the phones. A garbled re-

568

port over the telephone from another airfield told us that a tow pilot had seen what looked like firing on the Broadway strip. It was the time when doubts grow strongest and fears loom largest. Then, just after four o'clock in the morning, the first signal from Broadway, sent by Calvert, came in plain language, brief, mutilated, but conveying its message of disaster clearly enough—"Soya Link." The name of the most disliked article in the rations had been chosen in grim humour as the code word for failure. So the Japanese *had* ambushed Broadway! Wingate was right and I had been wrong. He gave me one long, bitter look and walked away. I had no answer for him.

Then more signals, broken, hard to decipher, but gradually making the picture clearer. Gliders had crashed, men had been killed, there were injured and dying lying where they had been dragged to the edge of the strip—but there was no enemy. There had been no ambush. A great weight lifted from me as I realized that this was going to be like every other attack, neither so good nor so bad as the first reports of excited men would have you believe. We had to recall the last flight, as Broadway was too obstructed by smashed gliders to accept them. The situation was still far from clear to us as I left the control tent after dawn, but I was confident that if only the Japanese did not locate them for the next twelve hours, the Chindits would have the strip ready for reinforcements by nightfall.

Of the sixty-one gliders dispatched only thirty-five reached Broadway. The airmen who said that one Dakota could not tow two gliders had been right. In practice the steep climb to cross the mountains, so close to the start, put too great a drag on the nylon ropes and many parted. It also caused overheating in the aircraft engines and unexpected fuel consumption, with dire results. Many gliders and a few aircraft force landed, some in our territory, nine in Japanese. There was a brisk battle near Imphal between the Chindits of a crashed glider, convinced they were behind the enemy lines and determined to sell their lives dearly, and our own troops rushing to their rescue. Gliders by chance came down near a Japanese divisional headquarters and others beside a regimental headquarters far from

Broadway. These landings confused the enemy as to our intentions and led to a general alert for gliders and parachutists through all his units.

Long afterward we discovered that it was not the Japanese who had obstructed Piccadilly but Burmese tree fellers, who had, in the course of their work, dragged teak logs out of the jungle to dry in the clearing. The firing reported at Broadway was a nervous burst from a shaken glider pilot.

Even without the enemy, that night at Broadway was tragic and macabre enough. One or two of the leading gliders, circling down to a half-seen gap in the jungle, had crashed on landing. The ground-control equipment and its crew were in a glider that failed to arrive so that, until a makeshift control could be improvised, it was impossible to time landings. Some gliders hurtled into the wrecks, others ran off the strip to smash into the trees or were somersaulted to ruin by uneven ground concealed under the grass. Twenty-three men were killed and many injured, but more than four hundred, with some stores, and Calvert, the brigade commander, landed intact. Most of the engineering equipment did not arrive, but the small party of American engineers, helped by every man who could be spared from patrolling, set to work with what tools they could muster to drag the wreckage clear and prepare the ground. Never have men worked harder, and by evening a strip was fit— but only just fit—to take a Dakota.

Next night the fly-in continued. Fifty-five Dakotas landed at Broadway and the first flights reached Chowringhee, where also there was no sign of enemy. By March 11 the whole of Calvert's 77 Brigade and half Lentaigne's 111 Brigade were at Broadway. Lentaigne's Brigade Headquarters and the other half with "Dah-force," a body of Kachins with British officers for use in raising the local tribes, were safely at Chowringhee. Between March 5 and 10 one hundred glider and almost six hundred Dakota sorties flew in nine thousand troops and eleven hundred animals. In addition, Ferguson's 16 Brigade had reached Aberdeen after its long march, so that Wingate now had nearly twelve thousand troops well placed, as he put it, "in the enemy's guts."

No sooner had these decisions been taken than Special

570

Force suffered a tragic loss. Wingate, flying from Imphal to his new headquarters at Lalaghat in a Mitchell bomber, crashed by night in the wild tangle of hills west of Imphal. He, and all with him, were instantly killed. The cause of the accident cannot be definitely stated. The wreckage was eventually found on the reverse side of a ridge, so it was unlikely that the aircraft had flown into the hill. The most probable explanation is that it had suddenly entered one of those local storms of extreme turbulence so frequent in the area. These were difficult to avoid at night, and once in them an aeroplane might be flung out of control or even have its wings torn off.

I was at Comilla when the signal came in that Wingate was missing. As the hours passed and no news of any sort arrived, gloom descended upon us. We could ill spare him at the start of his greatest attempt. The immediate sense of loss that struck, like a blow, even those who had differed most from him—and I was not one of these—was a measure of the impact he had made. He had stirred up everyone with whom he had come in contact. With him, contact had too often been collision, for few could meet so stark a character without being either violently attracted or repelled. To most he was either prophet or adventurer. Very few could regard him dispassionately; nor did he care to be so regarded. I once likened him to Peter the Hermit preaching his crusade. I am sure that many of the knights and princes that Peter so fiercely exhorted did not like him very much—but they went crusading all the same. The trouble was, I think, that Wingate regarded *himself* as a prophet, and that always leads to a single centredness that verges on fanaticism, with all its faults. Yet had he not done so, his leadership could not have been so dynamic, nor his personal magnetism so striking.

While all this was going on the Chindits had not slackened their activity. Ferguson's 16 Brigade from Aberdeen attempted to seize Rail Indaw by surprise, but was compelled to abandon the attempt and fall back. Exhausted by this abortive effort after their long march, there was nothing for it but to fly them out. However, Lentaigne still had three mobile brigades, considerable numbers of

571

"stronghold" troops, and the Japanese communications both road and rail to their 18th Division were effectively cut. Meanwhile, Stilwell to the north of them had been pushing his Chinese southward.

While Stilwell struck for Myitkyina, the Chindits at Blackpool [4] had continued to block Japanese communications, and 111 Brigade with the Kachin Irregulars closed on Myitkyina. It was obvious that, as they thus approached one another, daily tactical co-ordination between Stilwell's and Lentaigne's forces was becoming urgent. On May 17 I therefore placed Special Force under Stilwell's direct orders. He now had an American brigade, five Chinese divisions, three mobile Chindit brigades, and their stronghold troops, a great superiority over the battered Japanese 18th Division, Take Force, and the odds and ends of their 56th Division pulled in from the quiet Yunnan front.

Then that front, so quiescent for two years, sprang into violent activity. On the night of May 10-11, forty thousand Chinese crossed the Salween on a two hundred mile front at three points between Hpimaw and Kunlong. Within a few days twelve Chinese divisions, seventy-two thousand men, under General Wei Li Huang, were on the west bank. The Japanese 56th Division, about twelve thousand strong, outnumbered and without air support, fought skillfully and tenaciously to hold the mountain passes against them. During May and early June the Japanese were pushed slowly back toward Lungling, but a battalion and some detachments were surrounded in Tengchung. The garrison held out with fanatical valour until September 21, when the town fell to assault and every Japanese in it died.

The battle around Lungling between the Japanese 56th Division and six Chinese divisions raged until the end of August. The Japanese Lieutenant-General Matsuyama with great skill and resolution defeated every attempt at encirclement and kept open his communications to the south. He had one stroke of luck. A Chinese plane, mistaking Tengchung for a friendly airfield, landed there with three Chinese staff officers, carrying not only complete details of the of-

[4] A stronghold-block established in May.—Ed. note.

572

fensive but the new cipher of their army. Matsuyama was, after that, the only commander in Burma who had reliable advanced information of his enemy's intentions and moves. He made good use of it. The Japanese hurried up reinforcements and then, with the bulk of their 2d Division and a regiment of their 49th, put in a fierce counterattack which for a time stopped the Chinese dead and reduced their subsequent advance to a crawl. The Chinese losses were heavy, not only from disease and privation, but because their training, armament, and leadership, which were much below those of Stilwell's troops, made them no match for the Japanese. Nor were their losses being replaced from China. Wei Li Huang had no easy task. His only real advantages were numbers and air support from American fighters and medium bombers which lost much of its value in these wild mountains.

Still, this mass, pressing in on their right flank, however slowly it moved, was a menace to the Japanese front in North Burma. Indeed, even toward the end of May their whole position there was rapidly becoming precarious. The 18th Division was beginning to crack. Stilwell's main force was closing in on Kamaing. In addition to the large Chinese force attacking Myitkyina, the Fort Hertz detachment was approaching from Sumprabum and Morrisforce was operating against the town from the east of the Irrawaddy. The fall of Myitkyina, although it no longer seemed imminent, could be only a matter of time.

A brigade of Lentaigne's Special Force held Blackpool, near Hopin, against constant attack for three weeks, cutting the enemy's main line of communication at a critical time. The Japanese concentrated most of Take Force, including a regiment of the 53d Division, against the Chindits here and bombarded them heavily with field and medium artillery. Worst of all, they established anti-aircraft guns in range of the landing ground. In spite of that, the British and American Dakota pilots, unable to land as the strip was under direct fire, continued to drop their loads, but supply was intermittent and there was no evacuation of wounded. Then the weather broke badly and, as the Japanese closed in, so did the clouds. Air supply and air support both ceased. On May 25 the Chindits, carrying their wounded, broke out of Blackpool and plodded northwest toward the Indawgyi Lake around which other columns of Lentaigne's men were collecting. The rain had made it impossible to keep earth air strips in action and there seemed little hope of getting out the increasing number of sick and wounded that were being laboriously brought in by their comrades. The R.A.F. found the answer in two Sunderland flying boats, which, as a change from submarine hunting in the Indian Ocean, flew from Colombo to this fifteen-by-five miles stretch of water in the heart of Burma. Working throughout some of the worst monsoon weather, they flew out nearly six hundred casualties.

During the first weeks of June Stilwell's Chinese had kept up their drive down the Mogaung Valley. Fighting with increasing confidence and boldness, they destroyed the Japanese who tried to bar their way at Shaduzup and Laban. Then on June 16 the Chinese 22d Division took Kamaing, and on the 20th Calvert's 77 Brigade of Lentaigne's force stormed Mogaung, just ahead of the Chinese 38th Division coming from the north. By this time, too, the great battles around Imphal had definitely turned against the Japanese. Such reinforcements as he could scrape up, Kawabe, the enemy commander in chief, was sending there to cover his withdrawal. His two northern fronts were crumbling and there was little he could do to bolster them up. He was by now plainly reduced to fighting merely a delaying campaign in North Burma.

Negotiations had been going on between Admiral Mountbatten and Generalissimo Chiang Kai-shek for Wei Li Huang's Yunnan armies to come under Southeast Asia Command when they crossed the Burma border. As seemed inevitable, however, where Chinese were concerned, there was considerable mystification about the command of these troops. To begin with, the Sino-Burmese frontier was not marked in these outlandish hills. British maps showed it in one place, the Chinese several miles farther west. In any case, whatever the line, it was likely that at times some parts of the same Chinese formation would be on each side of it—a hopeless complication. The Generalissimo kept a

574

tight hand on these Yunnan troops, and Stilwell's control, exercised through an American mission, was, I gathered from him, pretty nebulous. Still, whether he commanded them or not, Stilwell's own force now amounted to about seven divisions and the agreement had been that when Kamaing was taken he should pass from my command. It was only logical to regard him as an army commander on the same footing as myself and place him, like me, under Eleventh Army Group, but once again Stilwell refused to serve under General Giffard. He insisted on coming directly under Admiral Mountbatten, although there was no organization at Southeast Asia Command Headquarters to deal direct with an army. When I visited Stilwell on his passing from my command he said, with his frosty twinkle, "Well, General, I've been a good subordinate to you. I've obeyed all your orders!" That was true enough, but so was my retort, "Yes, you old devil, but only because the few I did give you were the ones you wanted!"

The long-drawn-out siege of Myitkyina was a great disappointment to Stilwell, and it was at this period that he really lived up to his nickname, Vinegar Joe. He was extremely caustic about his unfortunate American commanders, accusing them of not fighting, and of killing the same Japanese over and over again in their reports. He was equally bitter against the Chindits, complaining that they did not obey his orders, had abandoned the block at Hopin unnecessarily, and had thus let strong Japanese reinforcements into the Kamaing-Myitkyina area. He asked for British parachute troops to restore the situation, but, apart from the fact that the small parachute formation available was already in the thick of the fighting at Imphal and could not have been extricated, there was no doubt he took a much too alarmist view of the position on his front. Lentaigne retaliated to the accusations hurled at him by complaining that Stilwell was demanding the impossible and that, by continually setting simultaneous tasks for all his columns, was making it impossible to give any part of his force the time essential for reorganization and evacuation of casualties without which they could not operate effectively. Relations between the two commanders became strained, and

575

finally, at the end of May, Stilwell asked Admiral Mountbatten to withdraw Special Force. As a result, early in June, although I was no longer in command of this front, I was sent to N.C.A.C. to adjudicate between Stilwell and Lentaigne and to attempt to heal the breach.

I found Stilwell bitter and Lentaigne indignant, both obviously and very understandably suffering from prolonged strain. One of the troubles was that Stilwell, in his then mood, would not meet Lentaigne and really discuss things with him. There was too much of the Siege of Troy atmosphere, with commanders sulking in their tents. However, with me, Stilwell, after one or two outbursts, was reasonable and explained his charges against the Chindits. I had already seen Lentaigne and heard his version. Stilwell's orders on the face of it were sound enough and it was quite obvious that the Chindits had not carried out all of them. It was equally clear that in their present state of exhaustion, after the casualties they had suffered and in the rain which made movement so difficult, unless given some chance of reorganization they were physically incapable of doing so. Stilwell replied to this by pointing to his Marauders who, he said, were still operating effectively. Without belittling their efforts, I pointed out that Lentaigne's men had endured the strain of being actually behind the enemy's lines for longer periods than Merrill's and that their incidence of battle casualties, as compared with sick, was much higher. As far as his complaints against Morrisforce on the east of the river were concerned, I told him I thought it was a bit hard to reproach a few hundred men for not doing what thirty thousand had failed to do on the other bank. Finally, looking at me over the top of his glasses, he said, "What do you want me to do?" I said, "See Lentaigne, talk things over with him, give his columns a chance to get out their casualties and reorganize, and keep his force on until Myitkyina falls." He agreed, and I returned to headquarters.

I had hoped that Myitkyina would fall by the middle of June, but at the end of the month it was still apparently as far from capture as ever. It then became obvious that the remains of Special Force were not fit to continue operating throughout the monsoon. Admiral Mountbatten himself

576

this time visited Stilwell and an arrangement was made by which two of Lentaigne's brigades that had been longest in the field should be medically examined and all unfit men flown out at once—the remainder to operate for a short time further and then follow them. The last of Special Force would remain until the 36th British Division, which was refitting at Shillong in Assam, began to come into Stilwell's command, when they, too, would be taken out.

Actually it would have been wiser to take the whole of the Chindits out then; they had shot their bolt. So, too, for that matter had the Marauders, who a little later packed in completely. Both forces, Chindits and Marauders, had been subjected to intense strain, both had unwisely been promised that their ordeal would be short, and both were asked to do more than was possible.

On the afternoon of August 3, after a siege of two and a half months, Myitkyina fell. Some days before Mizukami, the Japanese commander, had ordered what was left of the garrison to break out. He had then committed suicide. Maruyama, the original commander, had again taken over, and under his leadership the Japanese attempted to escape by night on rafts down the river. Most of them were intercepted and killed, but Maruyama himself and a couple of hundred did get away.

The capture of Myitkyina, so long delayed, marked the complete success of the first stage of Stilwell's campaign. It was also the largest seizure of enemy-held territory that had yet occurred. Throughout the operations on the northern front the Allied forces, Chinese, British, and American, had been vastly superior to the Japanese on the ground and in the air, even without including the Chinese Yunnan armies. This superiority was achieved only because the main Japanese forces were held locked in the vital Imphal battle, and any reinforcements they could rake up were fed into that furnace. The Japanese had the advantage of position and communications, but even their desperate courage and defensive skill could not hold back such a numerical preponderance. Yet, when all was said and done, the success of this northern offensive was in the main owing to the Ledo Chinese divisions—and that was Stilwell.

Behind the Japanese Lines

A dissenting opinion of "Old Vinegar Joe" Stilwell is expressed in the following selection by Major John Masters who commanded the Chindits III Brigade at the Blackpool Block. He received orders in late April to move out of the Aberdeen stronghold, where the Chindits had operated behind the Japanese lines since March, move north toward Stilwell's forces, and establish a block north of Hopin.

Masters felt that setting up these stronghold-blocks were "a waste of the Chindits' greatest asset, jungle mobility." Further, the block would bring him too close to the Jap lines where their "forward commanders" could give the Chindits a rough time. They had been in action a number of weeks and furthermore, as he says, they were primarily a raiding group, not intended for permanent defense fighting.

On May 7th, Masters chose the location of the block in a complex of ridges in view of the village of Namkwin. It was necessary to select a terrain that not only could be defended against attack, but which also provided room for an air strip for the purpose of receiving supplies and additional arms, and big enough to handle the C-47 transport planes.

Just before dusk on the 7th, Masters marched his men into the block.

"First the brigade defense platoon and Burma Rifles under Macpherson, then myself and a small command group, then the two battalions, with main Brigade Headquarters sandwiched between them. As I reached the spine of the block site, a single, long burst of light automatic fire roared in the Namkwin Chaung below, or among the dark hills beyond. Dreadful surmises flashed through my mind. We had been seen reconnoitering this morning! An entire Japanese regiment lay concealed under our feet, ready to spring the ambush! The steady advance continued. No one ever did find out who fired that burst or why; but it was a Japanese, because the fire was the extra-quick light crackle of his gun, not our Brens.

"An hour after dark the tail of the brigade entered the block. Now, barring more serious disturbance, we had the night to dig ourselves in.

"No one slept that night. Sweating, weary, we dug our trenches, we stacked our ammunition, we worked, in hundreds, to level the paddy bunds for the gliders, which I had already requested for the following night. The gliders would bring bulldozers, wire, mortar ammunition, and extra tools. On the hill, in a northward facing re-entrant, Brigade Headquarters dug in. Briggs set up his radios, and established communication with Mokso Sakan, Air Base, and Force Headquarters. III Brigade's block was in position: code name—Blackpool." *

BLACKPOOL BLOCK

by Major John Masters

The Blackpool hill looked something like a sharp-spined animal, say a boar, lying with head down, forearms and legs extended sideways, and short tail outstretched. There were other minor features and cross ridges, but that is the general outline. The area between outstretched members constituted defilade (shelter) from enemy fire, from three directions in each case. The Namkwin curved in round the animal's left forefoot and then on past its nose. Our water point was sheltered just inside that forefoot. The airstrip extended along the animal's right side, the near edge about one hundred yards away from the tips of right forefoot and right hind leg. The tail joined another hill feature, which was not part of the block. To left and straight ahead were tangled hills, split by streams and gorges and folds, all heavily forested.

To every part of the position I gave a code name. I might have used the animal simile, calling the points Neck, Right Fore, and so on; but all my men were cricket players and

*Major John Masters, *The Road Past Mandalay,* pp. 225-226. Harper & Brothers.

579

I named the positions as on a cricket field—Cover Point, Midwicket, Deep, etc. I wondered whether these names might displease Mr. Churchill if he ever came to hear about them. He fulminated, rightly, about soldiers who lost their lives in operations called Lollipop; if they were to die, let them die in Crusade and Armageddon. But Tommy, who knew British troops better than I did, assured me that the small, familiar names gave comfort and familiarity to the foreign field, so they stuck. . . .

While the battalions filed into the block I gave orders for the evacuation of the animals. I had seen the effects of shell-fire on the beasts, which could not be adequately protected. Nor did I have room for them in Blackpool. I kept only twenty-five, for emergency, to go out with patrols, and to help carry stores up from the strip. The rest I sent back, under Macpherson, over the hills to the Mokso Sakan base.

At first light I went round the perimeter with the battalion commanders and arranged the junction points, exact siting of reserves and headquarters, mortar defensive fire and SOS tasks, and the usual other details. The rest of the day I spent between the paddy fields, which would become the airstrip, and the block itself. I had pushed strong detachments across the paddy into the dense thickets the other side, and toward Namkwin village. The mortars began to range on their defensive tasks. On the strip, under the merciless sun, two hundred men worked stripped to the waist, with rifles slung. Now, certainly, the Japanese knew we had arrived.

One by one the paddy bunds disappeared, and early in the afternoon Chesty Jennings told me that gliders could land on the northern half. If they landed too far down they would have a roller-coaster ascent up the five-foot bank, on which we had not made much impression, to the southern half of our split-level field.

The gliders must have been waiting, ready for take-off. The first arrived in the twilight. Our mortars put down smoke bombs in front of Namkwin—they could not quite reach it—while the glider circled out over the valley. I heard the stutter and pop of small-arms fire from Namkwin, and our Vickers machine guns began firing slowly at it. The glider came on in a long, graceful approach. He picked up his line, steadied, came on. Quarter of a mile short and two or three hundred feet up, his tail flicked and he dived vertically into the ground just the other side of the Namkwin Chaung. The heavy crash reverberated across the fields and echoed back from the block. Beside me Chesty spoke urgently to the pilot of the second tow plane, even then circling high above us. "Bring him in from the hills, right-hand turn!" Chesty said. They heard and obeyed. The second glider turned over the hills, and came in faster. He landed safely, followed soon by four more. (I sent out a patrol to the crashed glider. The three men in it were dead, but none appeared to have been hit by bullets. Chesty thought that the glider had stalled. I don't know, but I shall not forget the sudden lurch in my own stomach, and the bitten-off cry I gave as the tail went up and the nose straight down.)

The tired soldiers pushed the gliders to the edge of the strip and unloaded them. Within half an hour two small bulldozers and a grader began work, and Chesty had taken over one of the gliders as control tower for the field, and began to put down the strip lights. Working parties, some with mules, began the long slow carry of wire, ammunition, and tools up into the block.

All night and all next day work continued at a frenzied pace—inside the block, digging and wiring and laying of cable, ranging mortars, cutting of fields of fire—on the paddy, the tremendous task of making the five-foot bank into a slope which a loaded C-47 could take at 50 or 60 mph in the middle of its landing run.

About four o'clock in the afternoon I went down to the strip to make the final decision. Was it ready? We walked up and down the hump. "It's not good," Chesty said, "but it ought to do." He looked at me, "How urgent is it that they should come in tonight?"

"Very urgent," I said.

The Japanese had used tanks against the White City, and I wanted field guns in, quickly. Nor had we so far received anything like enough wire, mortar ammunition, or medical supplies. Even as I spoke a shell, coming from the north, sighed lazily over the block and burst on the hills behind us. It was soon followed by another, which fell short. "Desultory shelling," an innocent might have said; but it was ranging. The Japanese were preparing to attack.

I told Chesty not to conceal the state of the strip but to make it quite clear to the air forces that I expected them to make the attempt that night.

That night they came. The lead plane circled over the valley, a dark triangle in a dark sky. Chesty pulled the switch that lit the thinly spaced rim of lights round the field. A few rifle shots went off from Namkwin out there in the valley and the droning sound of the motors came closer. Chesty talked quietly to the pilot. His headlights stabbed out above the northern jungle.

"You're high," Chesty said sharply. "Put her down."

The pilot put her down, she hit just short of the step in the middle, bounced high over it, landed out of control, swung sharply left and roared off the runway into the bushes, making a long, loud noise. After a short interval flames rose. By their light I saw men jumping out of the door, and the silhouetted black figures of Cameronians, who were on close guard that side, running to help. A few seconds later the flames went out.

Chesty called down the second plane. This one landed well, rose twenty feet into the air as she went over the hump, bounced, and taxied to a halt off the runway at the far end, where control officers and unloading parties waited.

The third plane landed smoothly, but did not stop in time. The last paddy bund ripped off its undercarriage and it slid on its nose into the bushes. The fourth landed safely. I heard rifle fire from somewhere in the block behind me; it would have to wait.

By now I had another brigade major, "Baron" Henfry, late of the Indian Cavalry, retired to Kenya, returned to battle. Geoffrey Birt, whom I urgently needed as an engineer officer, had returned to his own job. At this moment he was at the far end of the strip with a squad of sappers, waiting to unload explosives and other engineer stores from the planes. He went to examine the third plane, the one that had lost its undercarriage.

582

It lay dark and deserted, doors open. He stooped to have a look under the wing. From immediately behind him someone threw a grenade. Geoffrey saw it by the strip lights, and dived flat. The grenade exploded under the wing of the plane a few feet from him. The plane caught fire. A patrol of Cameronians rushed into the scrub, Tommy guns crackling. The fifth plane came in to land. But the burning C-47 lay across the wire that linked the field lights, and all the lights went out.

The plane now landing opened up its engines with a great roar and climbed away. The crew of plane No. 4, who had just opened the doors, saw No. 3 burst into flames, heard the grenade, the clatter of Tommy guns. They felt something must be amiss, and I don't blame them. Their doors slammed shut, the engines groaned, and the plane tore off down the strip in the dark. Before it reached high speed its wing caught the only other undamaged plane, No. 2. It slewed and skidded to a halt. That made two C-47s written off and two damaged as the price of the night's work. I could think of nothing but Beatty's remark at Jutland— "I don't know what's the matter with our bloody ships today. Steer two points closer to the enemy."

Chesty said, "The strip's not that bad. They're jittery."

"Can you get the lights fixed?"

"In half an hour. But there are only two more to come in for tonight and I think we'd better send them back. By tomorrow they'll know what asses they've made of themselves, and they'll do it right."

I didn't agree with Chesty's harsh judgment on his fellow airmen. It was a difficult strip and no pilot can feel encouraged, when lumbering in low over enemy territory in a C-47 to see the plane ahead of him burst into flames on landing. He can't know that there are no casualties or, if he does, guarantee that the same will apply to his own plane. But neither we nor 14th Army could afford to lose any more C-47s, and, after confirming that the planes already down contained some stores that I regarded as vital, I told Chesty the rest of the flight could go home.

A messenger arrived, panting: "The enemy are attacking the Deep, sir. Seems like probing, Colonel Thompson says." The Deep was the tip of the boar's nose, the extreme north point of the block. I climbed back into Blackpool, joined Tommy, and listened to a desultory battle going on down the ridge below. The shooting, never very strong, died down about one o'clock in the morning, and I returned to my headquarters.

Unless I were a bloody fool or, far worse to think about, unless the Japanese had changed their tactical doctrine, the night's attack was designed to locate our strong points and machine-gun posts in the Deep sector. That, in turn, meant that the Japanese would make a serious assault on the same sector the following night. The Japanese had not learned much, though, because Tommy knew his stuff perfectly well and only Bren guns and rifles, and mortars from the central keep, had fired. The queens of the battlefield, the machine guns, had kept quiet.

Before I got to sleep John Hedley limped in, his knee heavily bandaged. I had sent him out, with a small reconnoitering patrol, to find what use the enemy were making of the road and railway. He had found out (during four hours of darkness the enemy had used neither), but he had run into a similar Japanese patrol, killed some of them, and got a grenade splinter in the knee. Doc Whyte came and said, "He'll have to go out." I swore, and John pleaded; but he had to go.

The next morning the Japanese began harassing fire with 105-mm. guns from up the valley, the guns they had ranged in the previous afternoon. I had a lump of homogenized ham and egg halfway to my mouth when I heard the distant *boom boom* in the north. I dived, map in one hand and egg in the other, for the slit trench behind me. Baron Henfry was as quick; Pat Boyle (the new Intelligence officer) a shade slower. The shells whistled with a sudden rising shriek and burst ten feet away, one behind and one in front of the trench.

I returned to my study of the map, and my breakfast. The Baron said, "I think Pat's been hit, sir." (The Baron, a wise, amusing, and extraordinarily brave man, was some fifteen years older than I and so always very punctilious to pay me all the due forms of respect.) I looked down and

584

saw that Pat, crouched in the bottom of the trench between the Baron and me, seemed to be unconscious. Actually, a shell splinter had creased his skull, temporarily paralyzing him but not depriving him of his senses. He has recorded as the most pungent memory of his life those moments when he lay in the bottom of the trench, with more shells bursting far and near, unable to speak or move, and hearing the Baron's remark and my reply, "Oh. Is he dead?" And then the Baron: "I think so."

Until then Pat had been pretty sure he was alive, but now he had doubts. It wasn't until the Baron's saturnine face approached his that he managed to roll his eyes. Even now, he says, he can feel the welling up of joy as he heard the Baron's surprised, "No, he's alive."

Before the shelling ended we suffered several casualties in the area immediately around my headquarters, including the artillery major who had arrived only ten hours earlier, in one of the C-47s, to command the troop of field guns that would soon follow. A shell splinter in the spine killed him instantly.

After a couple of hours the shelling stopped. I had not liked it. I remembered Willy outside Deir-es-Zor—"Wait till you've really been shelled." There would be worse to come. Meanwhile, now that I knew where the Japanese had put their artillery—in the north—I could at least move headquarters and the main dressing station from their northward facing re-entrant to a more sheltered spot. This I did at once. My new command post lay high up behind the boar's left armpit.

Like a flywheel, a noisy flywheel worked by a rackety motor, the battle gathered momentum.

An hour before dusk shelling began again, on the Deep and on the sectors supporting it to left and right. After dark the assaults began with screams and yells and the Very lights shining on bared teeth, pot helmets, long bayonets— then sudden darkness and the clatter of bullets. An hour later the C-47s came. They made their last turn exactly over the spot where I calculated the Japanese officer directing the attacks would have his command post. I did not go down to the strip that night but alternated between my own and Tommy's command post, the latter on the crest of the ridge overlooking the sectors being attacked. By two o'clock the attacks faded, having lasted seven hours, almost continuously.

I got a little sleep and at daylight went down to the strip. Work was going slowly as the men's exhaustion grew on them. The guns had come in, with the gunners, and the dozers were moving them into position. Tons of stores and ammunition had come, but there were not enough men, with the battle going on and reserve companies standing to their alarm posts, to do the carrying. Everyone had been up most of the night, and now we had to carry the stores up from the strip, put down more wire, dig some positions deeper, repair others, bury the dead, patrol the jungles, protect the airstrip. I decided to remove all three-inch mortars from the battalions' control and use them as a single battery, so that I could bring the fire of all eight of them down on any sector with no delay. That meant more cable laying, more ranging. The field guns, no sooner in position, began to range on Namkwin. I sent an urgent message for sound-ranging and flash-spotting equipment so that we could find and engage the enemy artillery. The monsoon was building, the sky was seldom clear, and our fighters had not come over as frequently as earlier. Partly this was due to the demands of Stilwell, in action north of Kamaing, and to the great Imphal battle, then reaching its climax. The result was the same—the enemy artillery grew increasingly bold, and used plenty of ammunition. They were probably sited close to ammunition dumps. They were certainly not short of shells.

We buried our dead, treated our wounded. Shelling continued. Baron Henfry chose the heaviest shelling to stroll around, thumb-stick in hand, talking to the soldiers.

Tommy reported that during the night assaults some Japanese had dug in ten to twenty yards from his wire, with snipers up trees, who could look almost directly into his forward weapon pits. Over a part of his sector no one could move without being shot at. I crept up with him to the ridge crest to look. Enemy field guns began firing on

586

some of the rear positions. King's Own snipers lurked among shattered trees, Bren guns ready, watching the tattered forest below. Single shots rang out, Bren guns stammered, leaves whispered, boughs cracked. "Got him!" Another shot.

We crept back. The forward company would have a very unpleasant day, but would suffer few casualties as long as they sat low and tight. The snipers in the trees dominated them, but from higher up the ridge we dominated the snipers. All the same it was an unpleasant development and I ought to have foreseen it. At the White City the Japanese had withdrawn a considerable distance during the day. At that distance our mortars and—above all—our aircraft could get at them. They had learned the lesson, and now were leaning up against our wire, so close that to attack them with aircraft would be very dangerous to us.

Tommy arranged to relieve his forward troops with a reserve company after dark. Meanwhile two platoons, heavily supported, went out by the Water Point and attempted to clear the Deep sector, sweeping right-handed around the block, their right on our wire.

The attempt failed, the force losing several killed, including its leader, a really brave and excellent young officer. It was a bad moment for me, rather different from the permanent knowledge that war is a bloody business, because I had emphasized to Tommy that this was an important job and he had better send his best man. He had agreed. Those words are the aching refrain of command. They beat without cease in the mind and over the heart: *Send your best man. . . .*

That evening, with more planes coming in and the monsoon liable to break any day, I knew I had to do something drastic to complete our defensive preparations. I had to have the absolute maximum possible number of men carrying up stores from the field. Eight mortars, going fast use up sixteen hundred pounds of ammunition in a minute, and there were hundreds of Bren guns, rifles, and Tommy guns also eating it up, besides grenades; and food; and now the field guns. The Japanese had, so far, concentrated on the Deep, and they had left detachments there to harass us during the hours of daylight. Surely they would continue attacking that sector?

I decided to take the risk. I ordered the whole of the perimeter, except the Deep, to be stripped down to one section per platoon front, with no battalion reserves. The Deep, and a brigade reserve of one rifle company, I kept at full strength.

The Japanese continued their attacks—on the Deep. The actions for the next five nights defy description or reasonable analysis. At the northeast corner of the block, around the Deep, a furious battle raged from dusk till an hour or two before dawn, fought at ten yards' range with Brens, grenades, rifles, Tommy guns, two-inch and three-inch mortars and some machine guns. Three hundred yards to the left of the attacking Japanese, and in full view of them, C-47s landed with glaring headlights on the by now brilliantly lighted strip. From the hills behind, and from anywhere in the valley, they could see the aircraft being unloaded, our casualties carried into them, hundreds of men walking up and down between the strip and the block. Between the strip and the attacking Japanese I had no troops at all, though the area was thoroughly covered by machine gun and mortar emergency tasks; and the far side of the strip was only thinly protected. From my usual nightly position near the ridge top, or with the reserve company, I listened to the roar of battle from ahead and the roar of aircraft from the right. The Japanese never came anywhere but at the same place, the Deep, and head on.

The weight of this frenzied offensive fell on His Majesty's 4th Regiment of Foot, the King's Own Royal Regiment, who fought back with grim ardor. The long battle reached three crises. The climate caused the first.

Before entering the block I had thought of burning the jungles around it, partly to remove cover which the enemy could use (our own cover would, I knew, soon be removed by their shell fire), partly to ensure that the Japanese could not set fire to it at a moment opportune to them. I decided against it because a fire, once started, is not easy to control. But, on the fourth day of the Deep battle we

588

saw movement on the ridge to the west of the block, about one thousand yards away. The ridge overlooked both the Namyung and Namkwin Chaungs, and also gave a fair view of the reverse slopes of the Deep position. We began to mortar it. After ten minutes I saw smoke rising and thickening over there. The jungle scrub had caught fire. The Japanese put it out, while we mortared them some more. Almost immediately, on the other side of the block, enemy shells or mortars set fire to the dense lantana scrub in front of the positions held by the Cameronians to protect the field guns. (This was roughly around the boar's right forefoot.)

I did not think the Japanese had done this on purpose, any more than we had in the other direction. The dryness of the air, and of the foliage, had reached their hot weather peak, and the jungle was like tinder. The heat was close, stifling, and very severe; it, more than the enemy, had caused the failure of patrols I had sent out to pinpoint and call down air strikes against the enemy artillery positions. But I had to treat this fire as part of an attack plan. I called an immediate stand-to and ordered the mortars to begin a heavy shelling with smoke bombs on and beyond the forward edge of the new fire. Smoke bombs have a fair incendiary action and I wanted to set fire to the rearward lantana, where the Japanese would be forming up if they intended to attack. Henning held a company ready to counterattack. The field guns, already half-hidden in drifting smoke, swung round to fire muzzle-burst over the positions we might have to vacate if the fire came on. Crouched on top of the ridge, looking in both directions, praying that the Japanese would not now start their daily harassing fire, Henning and I passed a taut twenty minutes.

I did not notice that the sky had darkened over. As the flames took full hold of the lantana, it began to rain.

Trembling, I returned to my headquarters and lit a cigarette. Every wonderful drop falling on my burning face and arms was like a gift from God; but every drop sparkled with new problems. The monsoon had broken. The weapon pits, in which men must lie and fight and try to rest, would fill with water. I could not now rely on the airfield, and that would delay our evacuation of casualties. One of

589

the reasons why morale remained high was that the wounded received such prompt attention. Some badly wounded men had been on their way to hospital, in an aircraft, ten minutes after being hit. Worse, I would not be able to replenish ammunition, for we were using a great deal of it. Why the Japanese had been such incredible fools as not to shell the field and make it unusable, I did not know. Now the rains would do it for them. . . . And where in the name of God were the floater brigades? The White City had been evacuated thirteen days earlier, and 14 Brigade was supposed to come straight up here. My brigade had marched 140 route miles in fourteen days to establish this block. Surely those bloody nitwits could cover 120 route miles in thirteen days? Where the *hell* were they? Where were the West Africans?

I gave myself up to despair and anger. The enemy guns ought to have been silenced two days ago. The opportunities being missed! What use were field guns to me? They were here, inside my bastion, to support the floater brigades as they rampaged up and across the valley. The floater brigades weren't here. My men were being worked and fought into the ground while twenty bloody battalions, forty flaming columns of Chindit bullshit, sat on their arses and drank tea and wondered how we were getting on.

But soft, we are observed. A strange officer is coming to report to me. I learn that he is Major Douglas de Hochepied Larpent of the 5th Fusiliers. God knows how he got here. He just wants to fight.

(Douglas reports: *The officer in charge of the unloading party told us we must doss down on the edge of the strip and report to the Brigadier in the morning. I tried to get some sleep at the foot of a large tree. There were others sleeping nearby but I seemed to be the only one at all concerned at the prospect of being hit. It struck me as odd. At about the same time I became aware of a highly unpleasant smell which I was then too green to recognize. In the morning I found I had been sleeping in the mortuary. I was not a little relieved to get up and with the other new arrivals set out to find the Brigadier's Command Post and report to him. As we were soon to realize the situation was far from*

590

healthy but my chief impression of Jack was of his complete confidence. He seemed to be on top of the world, thoroughly enjoying himself and ready to cope with anything. . . .)

. . . Command doth make actors of us all. Or as one might say, liars. But I recovered myself. We were holding the enemy, and would hold him. The floaters *must* arrive soon.

The second crisis came when the close-quarter fighting at the Deep reached the limit of human tolerance. I decided I must force the Japanese farther away, at any cost. First, we removed the secondary charges from the three-inch mortars and fired them with primaries only. The bombs, fired from the middle of the block, arched high and fell five or ten yards from our forward positions. Next, I called for a heavy air strike, and told the air force to use 250-pound bombs. I expected to kill twenty of my own men if they bombed accurately, forty if they didn't.

Six fighter-bombers came. Chesty, standing with a radio in a trench above the Deep, brought them down on successive east-west runs across the foot of the sector, their target being the outer limit of our wire. They raced down from the sky, one behind the other, the great bombs slipped loose and whistled, shining, down. All my mortars opened rapid fire, all the machine guns opened rapid fire. The hill quaked and heaved, the noise beat in huge waves against my eardrums, steel splinters whined and droned over the hill and far out across the valley, trees crashed and fell, raw white wounds gaping, all the leaves vanished and hung in the boiling smoke and dirt. The aircraft dived lower, firing their multiple .50-caliber machine guns. For long moments the monstrous tearing roar filled earth and sky and being.

When they flew away, no one moved for a long time, and no one fired. We went down to remove and replace our casualties. There were none.

One enemy sniper lived, and fired a few shots during the rest of the day, and the usual attack followed that night, but the following day no Japanese were within two hundred yards of our wire. I bombed them again, this time with B-25s.

The enemy began to use his heavy mortar. Its shell weighed sixty pounds (the shell of our heaviest, the three-inch, weighed ten pounds), and when it landed on a weapon pit it saved the need for burying parties. Every day Tommy and his padre moved about across the Deep sector, under sniping, speaking to the men in the trenches, pausing here and there to pick up a handful of yellow-stained earth and sprinkle it over the torn "grave," and say a short prayer.

The rain now fell steadily. The Deep sector looked like Passchendaele—blasted trees, feet and twisted hands sticking up out of the earth, bloody shirts, ammunition clips, holes half-full of water, each containing two pale, huge-eyed men, trying to keep their rifles out of the mud, and over all the heavy, sweet stench of death, from our own bodies ahd entrails lying unknown in the shattered ground, from Japanese corpses on the wire, or fastened, dead and rotting, in the trees. At night the rain hissed down in total darkness, the trees ran with water and, beyond the devastation, the jungle dripped and crackled.

A Japanese light machine gun chatters hysterically, and bullets clack and clap overhead. Two Very lights float up, burst in brilliant whiteness. *Click, click, click—boom, crash, boom,* three mortar bombs burst in red-yellow flashes on the wire.

The third crisis came on May 17. On that day our Lightnings (P-38s) patrolled the valley for several hours, searching for the guns which had done us so much damage. They did not find them. Toward evening the P-38s left and I went down to the water point, as I usually did, to wash, shave, and brush up for the night's battle. While I was shaving, the enemy began to shell the block with 105s and 155s. Twelve guns or more were firing. Soap all over my face, I looked across at the ridge to the west, where the enemy had once put a mortar, and saw movement there. Mortar bombs from the ridge whistled into the block. The shelling grew more urgent and I walked quickly up to my command post —I tried never to run.

The shelling concentrated on the Deep and became a violent, continuous drumfire. My stomach felt empty and I was ready to vomit. I should have relieved the King's Own.

This was more than human flesh could stand. Nothing to do now though. The attack would come in immediately after the bombardment.

The shelling increased again. For ten minutes an absolute fury fell on the Deep.

Major Heap, the second-in-command of the King's Own, tumbled in, his face streaked and bloody and working with extreme strain. "We've had it, sir," he said. "They're destroying all the posts, direct hits all the time . . . all machine guns knocked out, crews killed . . . I don't think we can hold them if . . . the men are . . ."

I didn't wait to hear what the men were. I knew. They were dead, wounded, or stunned.

I took the telephone and called Tim Brennan, commanding 26 Column of the Cameronians, and told him to bring his whole column to the ridge crest at once, with all weapons and ammunition, manhandled, ready to take over the Deep. "Yes, sir," he said pleasantly. I had time to call Henning and order him to spread out to occupy Brennan's positions as well as his own, before going quickly, my breath short, to the hill crest.

The shelling stopped as I reached it. Tim arrived. Johnny Boden, the mortar officer, arrived. *Now, now, the Japanese must come.* I told Boden to stand by with smoke and H.E. to cover the Cameronians. 26 Column arrived, at the double. Still no assault. Tim ran down the forward slope, his men behind him. I waited, crouched on the ridge top. Ordered Boden to open up with his mortars. The enemy must have this blasted slope covered by machine guns. I knew they had. They didn't fire. It was twilight, but down the slope in the smoke, I could clearly see Cameronians jumping into the waterlogged trenches, King's Own struggling out and up toward me. The Cameronian machine guns arrived, men bent double under the ninety-pound loads of barrel and tripod. Bombs burst, smoke rose in dense white clouds. I told the officer to move the machine guns again, after full dark, if he could. "Of course, sir," he said impatiently.

The men of the King's Own passed by, very slowly, to be gathered by Heap into reserve. They staggered, many were wounded, others carried wounded men, their eyes wandered, their mouths drooped open. I wanted to cry, but dared not, could only mutter, "Well done, well done," as they passed.

The minutes crawled, each one a gift more precious than the first rain. I sent wire down, and ammunition, and took two machine guns from Henning's 90 Column, and put them in trenches on the crest, ready to sweep the whole slope. Full darkness came, with rain. An hour had passed, a whole hour since the enemy bombardment ended. In our own attacks we reckoned a thirty-second delay as fatal.

With a crash of machine guns and mortars the battle began. All night the Cameronians and the Japanese 53rd Division fought it out. Our machine guns ripped them from the new positions. Twice the Japanese forced into the barbed wire with Bangalore torpedoes, and the blasting rain of the mortars wiped them out. At four a.m., when they launched their final assault to recover their bodies, we had defeated them.

The next morning, as the rain fell more heavily, our patrols found the enemy had gone altogether. They had left the Deep sector and the hills across the Namkwin. They had abandoned the mortar post on the westward ridge. They had all gone. The forest was full of blood and flesh, and mass graves, and bodies fallen into stream beds, and bomb craters, and thousands of cartridge cases.

I have no means of knowing how many casualties we inflicted during the first phase of the Blackpool battle, except a postwar Intelligence interrogation, when a Japanese officer said, "Fifty-three Division had little fighting against the Chindits except on one occasion only, when one regiment was annihilated near Hopin." This was us. A guess would be eight hundred to a thousand casualties. We suffered nearly two hundred, mostly in the King's Own.

We were now in sole ownership of the block, and all terrain for at least a mile around. I began to send urgent messages: 14 Brigade *must* get a move on; 77 Brigade now moving northward the other side of the railway valley, should come across to us. Obviously the Japanese would attack us again, and so give us a wonderful opportunity to sandwich the attackers between the block and another bri-

594

gade. A decisive victory lay to hand. . . . But the rain continued to fall, and movement would soon be difficult. The battle must be fought before that happened. Then *we* would be in possession, and the Japanese line of communication totally cut, for the valley here was much narrower than at the White City, and he would have no chance of slipping even small parties past us.

If the floater brigades did not come, on the other hand, our situation would be precarious. And one particular sound I listened for above all others, for when I heard it the jig would be up—unless the floater brigades had arrived.

Meanwhile my two battalions were out on their feet, having marched hard for fourteen days, and worked and fought like maniacs for ten more, without cease. I should be surprised to learn that anyone averaged as much as five hours' sleep a day. My own figure was closer to three.

Two battalions, which had been holding the Broadway stronghold, did manage to cross the valley, and came under my command—the 2nd Battalion the King's Regiment (Liverpool) under Lieutenant Colonel Scott, and the 3rd Battalion 9th Gurkha Rifles, under Lieutenant Colonel Alec Harper. The King's did not arrive in top condition. One of their two columns ran into the enemy in the valley at night, and turned back. Mike Calvert sent them out again, but that column's morale was shaken when it finally arrived, and both were tired. The appearance of Blackpool, and the smell hanging over it, and the thin, determined ghosts who met them, cannot have reassured them. I sent the King's out at once—for they were less tired than my original two battalions—on a battalion sweep of the hills to the north, again in an effort to locate and destroy the enemy artillery. The attempt failed. The 3/9th Gurkhas I put onto the perimeter, withdrawing all the King's Own into reserve. The rain had not yet put the strip out of commission and a large daylight fly-in of C-47s, under fighter cover, evacuated all our casualties.

We heard that Merrill's Marauders had taken Myitkyina. This was most cheering news, and the brigade burst into a collective smile of joy and appreciation. (*"Will this burn up the limeys!"* Stilwell wrote in his diary.) But Myitkyina

595

was seventy miles away and the key bastion of Mogaung, between it and us, had not yet been taken. Even if the American-Chinese advance started southward from Myitkyina immediately, no one could reach us for at least two weeks. In that time enemy pressure would build up relentlessly against me. By God, those floater brigades had *got* to come, at once.

I learned that Myitkyina itself had not fallen—only the airfield. Joe Lentaigne ordered me to meet him at Shaduzup on the Ledo Road, a hundred miles due north of Blackpool, and report to General Stilwell. I handed over command to Tommy and flew out in an L-5. After an hour or so I saw the great ribbon of the Ledo Road, looking like a trench cut through the dense forest, and landed near Stilwell's headquarters.

Joe Lentaigne met me and took me to the hut allotted to him. He was in good shape and full of his usual energy, but not very happy about the relations between Stilwell, himself, and the Chindits. Old Vinegar Joe, he thought, was basically rather a volatile chap. When things were going well for him, he didn't hate everyone; when they weren't, he did. Joe saw trouble ahead.

Then he took me in to meet the general. Stilwell wasn't hating everybody that day—the Marauders' successful march to Myitkyina was the reason—but otherwise he looked just as the press photographs showed him. He asked me if I was stopping all traffic in the railway valley. I said I had stopped all traffic on the main road and railway, by shelling and by what patrols I could find, but that some enemy were certainly sidling past on the farther side, near the Namyin Chaung, and would continue to do so until the floater brigades arrived.

I asked him when Myitkyina would fall and, I think, suggested that he fly the Marauders at once from the Myitkyina strip onto my own at Blackpool, where they could take over the block and release me to attack; or, perhaps, themselves go against Mogaung. (I know that this plan was in my mind at the time, but I cannot remember whether I put it to Stilwell, or only to Joe in our private talks.) Stilwell answered my question about Myitkyina by saying, "Soon."

That was all. Joe and I saluted and went out. In his hut again we talked some more. I told him I thought the Marauders were the key to future relations between Joe Stilwell and ourselves. They were fighting infantry, they had killed a lot of Japanese, they could march, and I was certain we would get on well with each other. *("Stilwell's staff!"* Joe burst out. *"He's difficult enough, but they're impossible. There's one chap who keeps whispering in Stilwell's ear that the Chindits do nothing but march away from the enemy and drink tea, by Jove, eh, what?")* I told him that in my bad moments I shared the man's opinion, about some at least of my fellow Chindits. Joe said sharply, "Fourteen Brigade's doing its best, Jack," and I apologized. We got back to the Marauders. Stilwell was flying large numbers of Chinese into Myitkyina to capture the town itself—all we owned so far was the airstrip; couldn't the Marauders be flown to Blackpool? I would willingly put myself under their commander. Joe didn't believe Stilwell would consider it, but he'd think it over.

(It was all a waste of breath. Stilwell and his devoted staff had destroyed Galahad [code name for the Marauders] by treating them like dirt, by running them into the ground, and by breaking every promise he made them. *"I had him in my rifle sights,"* an American soldier said. *"No one woulda known it wasn't a Jap that got the son-of-a-bitch."* Merrill had suffered a heart attack. The men's morale had faded with their last physical reserves of strength. Within a week of this meeting between myself and Stilwell, the Marauder's Colonel Hunter met Stilwell outside Myitkyina and handed him a document detailing the charges against Stilwell and his staff. Two days later Hunter declared that the Marauders were no longer fit for action and must be relieved. Stilwell left Hunter in front of Myitkyina with the troops who replaced the Marauders [Galahad II], then relieved him and sent him back to the U.S.A.—by ship, by special order; so that he could not reach Washington ahead of Stilwell's own whitewashing. Stilwell and his stuffed baboons (a Marauder's phrase), having disposed of their American infantry, their best fighting force, turned their attention to us. *"Galahad is shot,"* Stilwell had noted in his diary, with understandable triumph. His next target was not hard to guess.)

Neither Joe Lentaigne nor I knew anything of this, thank God, when I returned that evening to Blackpool.

There was a letter from Barbara. She was well, my baby was well. They'd be off to Kashmir soon. Oh, yes, there'd been a terrific explosion in the middle of April, when an ammunition ship blew up in Bombay Harbor and set off other ships, and large pieces of human body sailed through windows a mile from the docks.

Damn it, I thought irritably, this is too much. But I had many men under me who had lost wives and mothers in the German bombings of 1940 and 1941. Fold the letter carefully away, write a reply on a message pad. Fold that whole world away, and passion and love, so that they couldn't be hurt; yet of course they were there, in what I felt whenever I saw a man, any man, reading a letter; for we were all human.

Three more peaceful days followed. We patrolled, and worked hard to repair the damage and prepare for more assaults. On May 22 enemy forces began to push forward from the southeast. Four artillery pieces, from the same direction, shelled the airfield. Two light planes and a C-47, which were on it, took off immediately. The third phase of the Blackpool battle began.

I sent the Cameronians out toward the enemy, to delay his advance. I debated long and anxiously whether I should send out another battalion to lie in wait on the hill feature to the south (adjoining our boar's tail), where they would be on the flank of the Japanese advance—if it continued in the direction it seemed to be taking. I decided against it, and I think I was wrong. The grim, set-teeth, bulldog struggle to hold the Deep had had its effect on me, and I was incapable of repeating the stroke (bold to the point of rashness) which had stripped the defenses of Blackpool to concentrate on the vital area. I should have done it again, trusting to my knowledge of the Japanese in battle, but there was a purposeful and professional air about this new assault which I did not like. He was pushing in my patrols and outposts; he was shelling the field; he was not coming

598

on like a mad dog, and I did not think I could trust him to do the obvious.

I held everyone, except the slowly retreating, overpowered Cameronians, inside the block. But, oh, God, let 14 Brigade come! The greatest opportunity of the entire Chindit campaign lay there, then, before my eyes. I sent out signals which passed from urgency to frenzy. Hurry, hurry, kill yourselves, but come!

Late in the afternoon C-47s came for a daylight supply drop, escorted by P-38s. From down the valley, behind the advancing Japanese, above the intermittent pop and crackle of small-arms fire, I heard the one sound I had been expecting, and fearing, the sharp double crack of heavy anti-aircraft guns. Puffs of yellow-black smoke appeared behind one of the C-47s. They turned for home. The P-38s searched and dived, but the A.A. guns did not fire again.

With a heavy heart I sent a Most Immediate signal to Joe asking for permission to abandon the block at my discretion. The direction of the new Japanese attack would prevent night supply drops on the airfield, and, with the A.A. guns, only night drops were now possible. Night drops on the block, or on the jungle to the west, could never keep us supplied with ammunition in heavy battle. It would take too many men, too long, to find and bring in the boxes.

The prospects were grim. Had my orders been more flexible I would have moved the brigade out of the block there and then, withdrawn a short distance into the jungle, and hung about there, ready to emerge and establish a new block when 14 Brigade and the West Africans appeared. But I had no discretion, and when my request reached Joe Lentaigne he had to take it to Stilwell.

It could not have come at a worse moment, for the attacks on Myitkyina had failed, the Marauders had reported their condition, and Stilwell's misanthropy was at its strongest. He told Joe Lentaigne we were a bunch of lily-livered Limey popinjays. Joe replied hotly. Every minute of argument, accusation, and counter-accusation at Shaduzup cost my men more lives, saw the expenditure of more irreplaceable ammunition, and locked us more closely into an action which could only have one end, and from which, minute by minute, it became more difficult for me to extricate my brigade if permission eventually were granted.

I was near despair, but apparently maintained a front of unbroken optimism. (I find this hard to credit, but there are witnesses. Douglas Larpent and Desmond Whyte noticed it and wondered whether recent strain had unhinged me. The Cameronians' padre went in a kind of horrified awe to Tim Brennan and told him he'd heard me telling Johnny Boden to "drop a few bombs over the wire," with no more feeling than if I'd been asking him to lob a couple of tennis balls.) But I was not commanding a bunch of children, or starry-eyed hero worshipers. Our work had been so successful because every man knew what I was doing and why, which means that he understood tactics. All officers and men understood the situation as well as I, and the superb courage which had fought the enemy to a standstill while we had an attainable purpose now lost some of its fire. The only battle my brigade really wanted to fight at that moment was against 14 Brigade and I told all battalion commanders to see that such bitter talk stopped at once. None of us could know the circumstances of the other brigades, and we must, in the old Rifle phrase, "Look to our front."

The battle marched slowly on. Slowly the enemy forced the Cameronians back. Our field gunners fired over open sights at large masses of Japanese advancing beyond the shell-pitted airstrip. The enemy shelling set fire to the wrecked aircraft and abandoned gliders. Our Bofors light antiaircraft guns depressed their barrels and joined in.

Night fell. Shelling caused slight casualties, except that a direct hit killed many wounded men in the main dressing station. Probing attacks reached the perimeter along most of the eastern face. The enemy held the airfield. We were using ammunition at a tremendous rate. We had to.

In the morning the enemy withdrew a little from our wire and ten Zeros bombed us. The bursting bombs and the tearing roar of machine guns sounded like the end of the world, but they didn't kill many of us and the soldiers treated the raid as a half-hour of relaxation, for during it the shelling and mortaring stopped. Soon afterward they began again. The Japanese were now using, in addition to

600

battalion guns, regimental guns, 105- and 155-mm. guns, all types of mortar, including the six-inch coal scuttle, and, of course, all types of rifle, machine gun, and grenade.

I had called for a supply drop of ammunition, particularly grenades and mortar bombs. The C-47s came in the afternoon, through rainy skies and scattered cloud. I believe they were originally escorted by P-38s, which were drawn off by Zeros. All our planes were of the Royal Air Force. It was not night, but they came in from the west, low, twisting and turning over the steaming, forested mountains. At the last they straightened and flew on a level, straight course. The boxes and crates dropped from the open doors, the parachutes opened. Hundreds of enemy rifles and machine guns glazed up at them through the irregular, drifting smoke of our mortar bombs. Then, clear as a knell, I heard from across the valley, the sharp coughing *bom-bom-bom* of heavy antiaircraft guns. Directly over me the port engine vanished from a C-47's wing; he swung down, the other engine frantically roaring. On, a wing whirled away, he hung, fell, turning like a maple seed. Another came on among the hills, only fifty feet above the jungle, twisting frantically, another crossed his bows, they were over the loads shooting out, swinging, drifting, but oh, Christ, the waste of love and life, for some fell among the Japanese, and some we could never reach, and what we did would only last a few hours. The crashed plane burned opposite the Deep, with tall orange flames and black, black smoke. I ground my teeth, and waited, and watched. My infantry were dying, too.

The Royal Air Force never did anything more gallant. I believe only four out of eight aircraft returned to base. We received, and gathered, half of one aircraft load of ammunition.

Tim Brennan brought Sergeant Donald to my command post to tell me about a successful counterattack by which he had cleared the Japanese off a small feature outside the airstrip entrance. Sergeant Donald (who got a Distinguished Conduct Medal for this action) had been wounded and as I held out a cigarette to him I saw that he was shaking violently in reaction from the close-quarter bayonet and grenade fight. He took the cigarette and said, "Thank you, sir—" and then, strongly and in a broader Scots—"Ma han's trrembling, but Ah'm no' a wee bit frightened, sirr!" Once again, I nearly burst into tears. It wasn't the responsibility, or the battle that created the strain, it was the love and pride.

The night of May 23-24 passed in some confusion. Shells kept cutting the telephone lines and I felt, at moments, that I did not have full control over my own forces. Before dawn an enormous bombardment began and in the earliest light, under incessant rain, I learned that the Japanese had got inside the perimeter, overrunning a post held by the 3/9th Gurkhas. How it had happened, no one knew. Alec Harper at once began to try to regain the position.

The telephone buzzed. It was Henning. He began to say something but after a few words the connection was suddenly changed and a young frantic voice shouted, "They're all round! I can see them! They're in everywhere, I can't hold—"

I interrupted him. "This is the brigade commander. Who's speaking?" It was that uncomfortable facility for sounding calm when I am not, for the young officer's voice changed as though by a miracle—actually, by a tremendous effort of self-control. He gave me his name and post, reported that the Japanese had broken through in such and such places, and asked for orders. I told him to prevent the enemy from moving about, and to keep his head (keep his head, by God!). He said, "Yes, sir. Thank you, sir."

The battle spread all over the eastern half of the block. Desmond Whyte reported forty-five helpless casualties in the M.D.S., all space full, and more coming. Minutes later two direct shell hits solved some of those problems with murderous thoroughness.

The 3/9th Gurkhas could not dislodge the Japanese from the hillock they occupied. From it they swept the whole of the east side with light machine guns and mortars. We blasted them with mortar bombs and at the same time tried to clear other Japanese out of the forward areas around the field gun and Bofors pits, whence the young officer had spoken to me. We failed. I ordered all troops

602

to withdraw from that sector, the guns to be spiked and abandoned. The men withdrew, suffering few losses under smoke and high-explosive cover from mortars and machine guns.

I saw, in the middle of the block, a line of men moving very slowly across a slope fifty yards from me. They looked like Japanese and I raised my carbine. The men trudged on in the drifting mist and rain and, just in time, I saw that they were my own men. But everyone moved like that, in a kind of cosmic slow motion. The Cameronians and gunners coming out of the forward eastern sector moved like sleepwalkers, so did the Japanese wandering about among them. A Cameronian lieutenant fell head-first into a weapon pit and two Japanese soldiers five yards away leaned weakly on their rifles and laughed, slowly, while the officer struggled to his feet, slowly, and trudged up the slope. The shells fell slowly and burst with long, slow detonations, and the men collapsed slowly to the ground, blood flowing in gentle gouts into the mud.

Johnny Boden reported that he was almost out of mortar ammunition. I went to the ridge crest, the center of the block. When I was fifty feet away a coal-scuttle bomb burst on a big tree there, and killed fourteen artillerymen, just arrived and coming into reserve under Douglas Larpent. The artillery lieutenant, closest to the blast, totally vanished.

I ordered Thompson and Scott, the commanders of the King's Own and the King's respectively, to attack the Japanese-held hillock in the southeast corner of the block, meanwhile trying to group the remnants of the gunners and the somewhat disorganized Gurkhas into a new reserve. The whole eastern half of the block blazed with fire and confused movement. One more Japanese breakthrough would cut us in two.

The supporting fire for the big counterattack failed and the attack failed, in spite of Tommy Thompson's personal heroism. When he came back, a severe wound in his shoulder, near the neck, I turned away from them all and lit a cigarette.

A signal giving me discretion to leave the block was probably on its way. After what happened to the C-47s yesterday any other order was lunacy, unless the floater brigades were at this very minute preparing to attack the enemy in the rear. And they weren't. But no signal had come yet. Bombs burst round me, bullets clacked by. I was therefore bound by the original orders to hold the position to the last man and the last round. The last bullet was not quite shot. After another hour of this, it would be. The last man . . . I had plenty of men left, far too many to see killed upholding my honor and military reputation. In any case they could only court-martial me, and I would be happy to have that chance to tell what we had done. Above all, my military knowledge told me that, unless Slim and Stilwell had gone mad, the discretionary order *must* be on its way.

I decided to withdraw from the block while we still had enough ammunition to use it in the difficult task of breaking contact. This is never easy to do in daylight, between forces as large as those engaged here. And we had, at a guess, about ninety men who could not walk unaided, and another thirty or forty who could not walk at all. The mechanics of the task I knew. I had learned them on the North West Frontier. The commander thins out the forces in actual contact and, with the men so obtained, sets up a series of covering positions, one behind the other and any suitable distance apart, depending on the ground. Finally the screen in contact breaks and runs for it, covered by fire from the first layback, as the successive positions are called. When they are well clear, Layback No. 1 withdraws, covered by Layback No. 2; and so on, leapfrogging continuously. It sounds easy but it can only be carried out by troops in full control of themselves. Once you turn your backs to the enemy, strong psychological pressures urge you to keep moving, faster and faster.

I gave the orders: Henning to establish the first and strongest layback astride the water point; Harper the second and third; withdrawal along the Namkwin Chaung to the *chaung* and track junction at 227105, about four miles away; Scott and some of his battalion to go there direct and prepare the area for defense; next day, if possible, further withdrawal up the track to Pumkrawng. I sent two last radio messages, one to Force telling them that I intended to withdraw from Blackpool immediately, and by what route, the other to 30 Column at Mokso Sakan, ordering them to march at once to meet us, bringing all horses, mules, rations, and ammunition. A hundred other details I should have settled—how the wounded were to go, who was to control them, covering fire between laybacks, action in case of meeting opposition from behind—but there was no time. I had to rely on the discipline and training of my brigade.

But one matter I must decide personally—the use of animals remaining in the block. Having suffered surprisingly little at first, shells and bombs had killed many these last two days. Only three or four horses and perhaps ten mules were fit to move. It did not take me long to decide that two radio sets and a charging engine, together with the cipher chest, must have absolute priority. I think I ordered that the remaining mules should carry Vickers machine guns and ammunition, the horses severely wounded men. All animals were to be loaded to the limit of their strength. These decisions, and the hard circumstances, meant that men must carry picks and shovels, grenades, some two-inch mortars and ammunition, many wounded, and anything else necessary for our survival, in addition to their personal weapons and what rations they had left.

The orders given, men began to drift back past me almost at once—Scott and some of the King's; I went down with them, found our own barbed wire blocking the stream. Henning and I shot it away, strand by strand, with our carbines. Back up to my command post. Henning and 90 Column moving fast to the water point.

Battered, sleepwalking soldiers passed, here two fit men, here two more supporting a third with a shattered foot, then a man with a head wound, then half a dozen unwounded, each with rifle and pick or shovel. Some wore shirts and trousers, some wore one or the other, some neither. Many men had no packs, for theirs had been buried or destroyed by shellfire. Now came a group, with an officer, struggling under a three-inch mortar. These, I had specifically ordered, could be abandoned, for the barrel and base plate constituted very heavy loads, and the bombs weighed ten pounds each, but this mortar platoon was determined to hold on to at least one of its weapons, and I did not try to interfere. It rained, it stopped raining. For ten days none of us had felt any awareness of rain, or knew whether we were wet or dry, except as it affected our job, made the rifle slippery in the hand, caused the Bren-gun barrel to hiss and steam.

Men trudged on in a thickening stream down the muddy, slippery path past my command post. Shells and mortar bombs continued to burst all round. From the eastern ridge the thinning lines of our forward troops increased their fire. A soldier of the King's Own limped by, looked up at me and said, "We did our best, didn't we, sir?" I could not stop to think, to accuse myself of being unworthy of him and his like, I could only face the problems as they came, give answers, and try to keep awake.

A Cameronian lay near the ridge top, near death from many wounds. "Give me a Bren," he whispered to his lieutenant. "Leave me. I'll take a dozen wi' me."

I went to the mule lines and saw Maggy quietly eating bamboo, a red gash in her belly and her entrails hanging out of it. She seemed to be in no pain and I hugged her neck, then Briggs shot her for me. Henning reported 90 Column in position astride the water point. I looked through my binoculars at the westward ridge, which the Japanese had occupied during the first battles. If they held it now we would have a bad time, as it dominated the Namkwin for at least a mile. Mortaring from it we would have to grit our teeth and bear as we trudged past. No, I could cover it with machine guns, for a time at least. I sent a man back with a message to Alec Harper, to be sure to put strong protection on that flank of his layback.

The men passed and passed, walking, limping, hopping, supporting others, carrying them. Tim Brennan reported that he thought he could break contact when I ordered. The Japanese were not pressing their advantage, and at the moment seemed to be under shellfire from their own artillery.

A doctor spoke to me. "Will you come with me, sir?" I followed him down the path. It was clear of moving men.

The whole block was clear, except for a part of 26 Column. A little way down the path we came to forty or fifty ragged men, many slightly wounded, who had carried stretchers and improvised blanket litters from the main dressing station as far as this. Here they had set down their burdens, and now waited, huddled in the streaming bamboo, above and below the path. I noticed at once that none of them looked at me as I stopped among them with the doctor.

The stretchers lay in the path itself, and in each stretcher lay a soldier of 111 Brigade. The first man was quite naked and a shell had removed the entire contents of his stomach. Between his chest and pelvis there was a bloody hollow, behind it his spine. Another had no legs and no hips, his trunk ending just below the waist. A third had no left arm, shoulder, or breast, all torn away in one piece. A fourth had no face and whitish liquid was trickling out of his head into the mud. A fifth seemed to have been torn in pieces by a mad giant, and his lips bubbled gently.

Nineteen men lay there. A few were conscious. At least, their eyes moved, but without light in them.

The doctor said, "I've got another thirty on ahead, who can be saved, if we can carry them." The rain clattered so loud on the bamboo that I could hardly hear what he said. "These men have no chance. They're full of morphia. Most of them have bullet and splinter wounds beside what you can see. Not one chance at all, sir, I give you my word of honor. Look, this man's died already, and that one. None can last another two hours, at the outside."

Very well. I have two thousand lives in my hand, besides these. One small mistake, one little moment of hesitation and I will kill five times these nineteen.

I said aloud, "Very well. I don't want them to see any Japanese." I was trying to smile down into the flat white face below me, that had no belly, but there was no sign of recognition, or hearing, or feeling. Shells and bombs burst on the slope above and bullets clattered and whined overhead.

"Do you think I want to do it?" the doctor cried in helpless anger. "We've been fighting to save that man for twenty-four hours and then just now, in the M.D.S., he was hit

607

in the same place." His voice changed. "We can't spare any more morphia."

"Give it to those whose eyes are open," I said. "Get the stretcher bearers on at once. Five minutes."

He nodded and I went back up to the ridge, for the last time. One by one, carbine shots exploded curtly behind me. I put my hands over my ears but nothing could shut out the sound.

I found Titch Hurst of the Cameronians on the ridge, and Douglas Larpent, the latter commanding the rear party. I said, "Retire in five minutes. I shall be with the first lay-back at the water point."

We looked across the shallow valley where the forward sections were engaging the Japanese with a sharp fire. The fire strengthened, under Douglas' orders. I walked down the path, looking, but the bodies had been well hidden in the bamboo and the path was quite empty. I muttered, "I'm sorry," and "Forgive me," and hurried on, and reached the water point. There, with Henning, I waited.

Soon 26 Column started coming down, some running, some walking. Up ahead I could see that the slow trail of the severely wounded had already passed the second layback. I waited, growing very tired, with Henning, until the last of 26 Column was upon us. Now was the most dangerous moment. We stared up the path, waiting for the Japanese to come on. But they did not come, and at about noon, fifty minutes after giving the first order, after seventeen days, having been defeated, I left the Blackpool block in the rain.

Philippine Victory

The next Marine beachhead was on Peleliu in the Palau Islands, a little more than 500 miles southeast of the Philippines. "In our hands, a pistol pointed at the enemy stronghold. In Jap hands, a potent threat to any invasion we might aim in that direction." *

As it happened, we were aiming an invasion in that direction. "MacArthur [had taken] a long hop up the northern New Guinea coast, landing on the 22nd of April to seize air strips at Hollandia and Aitape, by-passing Jap strongpoints at Wewak and Hansa Bay. . . . On the 30th of July, a week after the Marines had landed on Guam, MacArthur's troops seized Cape Sasanpor near the extreme western end of New Guinea.

"MacArthur's threat was aimed at the Philippines. A simultaneous seizure of Moratai by the Army and Peleliu by the Marine Corps on the 15th of September secured the gateway for his reconquest." **

On October 21, 1944, the 6th Army landed two corps under MacArthur on the beaches of Leyte Gulf; MacArthur had returned to the Philippines, after not quite three years. He could announce that Leyte was secured on December 26th; on January 9th, he invaded Luzon, reentering Manila on February 4, 1945. The worst threat to American recovery of the island had already been beaten off; one of the greatest naval engagements in world history, certainly the largest, had taken place on October 23rd to the 26th.

* Maj. Frank Hough, *The Island War*, p. 294.
** Maj. Frank Hough, *The Island War*, p. 212.

THE BATTLE FOR LEYTE GULF

by Hanson Baldwin

The greatest sea fight in history—perhaps the world's last great fleet action—broke the naval power of Japan and spelled the beginning of the end of the war in the Pacific. The Battle for Leyte Gulf, fought off the Philippine Archipelago, sprawled across an area of almost 500,000 square miles, about twice the size of Texas. Unlike most of the actions of World War II, it included every element of naval power from submarines to planes. It was as decisive as Salamis. It dwarfed the Battle of Jutland in distances, tonnages, casualties. But, unlike Jutland, there was no dispute about the outcome. After Leyte Gulf, the Japanese Fleet was finished. Yet it was a battle of controversy. . . .

The Empire was dying, and there were some who faced the fact. The long retreat was over, the great spaces of the Pacific had been bridged by the countless ships of the American "barbarians," and the enemy was knocking upon the inner strongholds of the Samurai. For Japan it was now the desperate gamble, the all-out stroke—to conquer or to die.

And so, the Shō ("To Conquer") plans were drawn; if the inner citadel—the Philippines, Formosa, the Ryukyus, the main islands—were penetrated by the U.S. Fleet all the remaining Japanese naval power that could steam or fly would be mobilized for a desperate assault.

From August 31 to September 24 the fast carriers supported by the battleships of Admiral William F. Halsey's Third Fleet had raked over Japanese bases from Mindanao to Luzon, and on the twenty-first while Radio Manila was

610

playing "Music for Your Morning Moods," naval pilots combed Manila Bay. The bag throughout the islands was large, the enemy opposition was surprisingly feeble, and Admiral Halsey reported to Admiral Chester W. Nimitz, commander-in-chief, Pacific:

". . . no damage to our surface forces and nothing on the screen but Hedy Lamar."

The weak Japanese reaction led to a change in American strategy.[a] The planned capture of Yap and step-by-step moves to Mindanao in the southern Philippines and then northward were eliminated; the amphibious assault upon the island of Leyte in the central Philippines was advanced by two months to October 20, 1944. . . .

It started, according to plan. A great armada of more than 700 U.S. ships steamed into Leyte Gulf at dawn on the twentieth; a lone Jap plane braved the skies. Initial Japanese opposition was weak; the vast American armada —the greatest of the Pacific war, with some 151 LST's, 58 transports, 221 LCT's, 79 LCI's, and hundreds of other vessels, may have overawed the defenders. By the end of A plus 2—October 21—103,000 American troops had been landed on Leyte with few casualties, and only three warships had been damaged.

Four hours after the first landing on Leyte, General Douglas MacArthur waded ashore; later Colonel Carlos Romulo, the little Filipino, who was with him, was to quip:

"There was the tall MacArthur, with the waters reaching up to his knees, and behind him there was little Romulo, trying to keep his head above water."

In front of a Signal Corps microphone on the beach just won and beneath rain-dripping skies MacArthur recalled the bloody epic of Bataan:

"This is the Voice of Freedom, General MacArthur speaking. People of the Philippines: I have returned. . . ."

[a] This and succeeding letters and numerals refer to comments on this account by Admirals Kinkaid and Halsey, which are printed at the end of Mr. Baldwin's report.

But the Japs had not been fooled. At 0809, October 17, just nine minutes after U.S. Rangers had made preliminary landings on one of the smaller islands in the mouth of Leyte Gulf, Japanese forces had been alerted to carry out the *Shō* I plan. Admiral Soemu Toyoda, commander-in-chief of the Japanese Combined Fleet and leader of what he knew was a forlorn hope, had his last chance to "destroy the enemy who enjoys the luxury of material resources." From his headquarters at the Naval War College just outside Tokyo, he sent the word "To Conquer" to his widely scattered units.

The *Shō* plan was daring and desperate—fitted to the last months of an empire strained beyond its capabilities. The Japanese Fleet had not recovered from its cumulative losses, particularly from the heavy blow it had suffered four months earlier in the Battle of the Philippine Sea,[b] when Admiral Raymond W. Spruance, covering our Marianas landings, had destroyed more than 400 Japanese planes, sunk three Japanese carriers, and broken the back of Japanese naval aviation. In mid-October, when Halsey—in a preliminary to the Leyte Gulf landing—struck heavily at Formosa, Toyoda had utilized his land-based planes and had also thrown his hastily trained carrier replacement pilots into the fight. The gamble failed. But the "pathology of fear" and the curious propensity of the Japanese for transforming defeats into victories in their official reports magnified the normally highly inflated claims of enemy aviators; Tokyo declared the Third Fleet had "ceased to be an organized striking force."

An enemy plane dropped leaflets over recently captured Peleliu:

FOR RECKLESS YANKEE DOODLE:

Do you know about the naval battle done by the American 58th [sic] Fleet at the sea near Taiwan [Formosa] and Philippine? Japanese powerful Air Force had sunk their 19 aeroplane carriers, 4 battleships, 10 several cruisers and destroyers, along with sending 1,261 ship aeroplanes into the sea. . . .

Actually only two cruisers—*Canberra* and *Houston*—were damaged; less than 100 U.S. planes lost; the Japanese were to have a rude awakening as the great invasion [1] armada neared Leyte Gulf.

But for Toyoda, the Battle of the Philippine Sea and his futile gamble in defense of Formosa had left the Japanese Fleet naked to air attack. Toyoda had carriers,[c] but with few planes and half-trained pilots. *Shō* I, therefore, must be dependent upon stealth and cunning, night operations, and what air cover could be provided chiefly by land-based planes operating from Philippine bases and working in close conjunction with the fleet.

Toyoda also confronted another handicap—a fleet widely separated by distance. He exercised command—from his land headquarters—over a theoretically "Combined Fleet," but Vice-Admiral Jisaburo Ozawa, who flew his flag from carrier *Zuikaku,* and who commanded the crippled carriers and some cruisers and destroyers, was still based in the Inland Sea in Japanese home waters. The bulk of the fleet's heavy units—Vice-Admiral Takeo Kurita's First Diversion Attack Force, of battleships, cruisers, and destroyers—was based on Lingga Anchorage near Singapore, close to its fuel sources. The Japanese Fleet was divided in the face of a superior naval force; it could not be concentrated prior to battle.

These deficiencies, plus the geography of the Philippines, dictated the enemy plan, which was hastily modified at the last minute, partially because of the Japanese weaknesses in carrier aviation. Two principal straits—San Bernardino, north of the island of Samar; and Surigao, between Mindanao and Dinagat and Leyte and Panaon—lead from the South China Sea to Leyte Gulf, where the great armada of MacArthur was committed to the invasion. The Japanese ships based near Singapore—the so-called First Diversion Attack Force—were to steam north toward Leyte, with a stop at Brunei Bay, Borneo, to refuel. There the force would split; the Central Group, Vice-Admiral Takeo Kurita, flying his flag in the heavy cruiser *Atago,* with a total of five battleships, ten heavy cruisers, two light cruisers, and fifteen destroyers, would transit San Bernardino

Strait at night; the Southern Group, Vice-Admiral Shōji Nishimura,[2] with two battleships, one heavy cruiser, and four destroyers, was to be augmented at Surigao Strait by an ancillary force of three more cruisers and four destroyers under Vice-Admiral Kiyohide Shima, which was to steam through Formosa Strait, with a stop in the Pescadores, all the way from its bases in the home islands. All these forces were to strike the great American armada in Leyte Gulf almost simultaneously at dawn of the 25th of October and wreak havoc among the thin-skinned amphibious ships like a hawk among chickens.

But the key to the operation was the emasculated Japanese carriers, operating under Vice-Admiral Jisaburo Ozawa from their bases in Japan's Inland Sea. These ships —one heavy carrier and three light carriers, with less than 100 planes aboard—"all that remained of the enemy's once-great carrier forces"—were to steam south toward Luzon and to act as deliberate decoys or "lures" for Admiral Halsey's great Third Fleet, which was "covering" the amphibious invasion of Leyte. The northern decoy force was to be accompanied by two hermaphrodites—battleship-carriers, the *Ise* and *Hyuga,* with the after-turrets replaced by short flight decks, but with no planes, and by three cruisers and ten destroyers. Ozawa was to lure Halsey's Third Fleet to the north, away from Leyte, and open the way for Kurita and Nishimura to break into Leyte Gulf.

At the same time all three forces were to be aided—not with direct air cover, but by intensive attacks by Japanese land-based planes upon American carriers and shipping. As a last-minute "spur-of-the-moment" decision, the Japanese "Special Attack Groups" were activated, and the Kamikaze (Divine Wind) fliers commenced their suicidal attacks upon U.S. ships. As early as October 15, Rear Admiral Masabumi Arima, a subordinate naval air commander, flying from a Philippine field, had made a suicide dive and had "lit the fuse of the ardent wishes of his men."[d] All of these far-flung forces were under the common command of Admiral Toyoda far away in Tokyo.

Such was the desperate *Shō* I—perhaps the greatest

614

gamble, the most daring and unorthodox plan in the history of naval war.

It committed to action virtually all that was left of the operational forces—afloat and in the air—of Japan's Navy —four carriers, two battleship-carriers, seven battleships, nineteen cruisers, thirty-three destroyers, and perhaps 500 to 700 Japanese aircraft—mostly land-based.

But the opposing American forces were far more powerful. Like the Japanese forces which had no common commander closer than Tokyo, the U.S. Fleet operated under divided command. General MacArthur, as theater commander of the Southwest Pacific area, was in over-all charge of the Leyte invasion, and through Admiral Thomas C. Kinkaid, he commanded the Seventh Fleet, which was in direct charge of the amphibious operation. But Admiral Halsey's powerful covering force of the Third Fleet—the strongest fleet in the world—was not under MacArthur's command; it was a part of Admiral Chester W. Nimitz's Pacific Command forces, and Nimitz had his headquarters in Hawaii. And above Nimitz and MacArthur, the only unified command was in Washington.

The gun power of Kinkaid's Seventh Fleet was provided by six old battleships—five of them raised from the mud of Pearl Harbor, but he had sixteen escort carriers [3]—small, slow-speed vessels, converted from merchant hulls—eight cruisers and scores of destroyers and destroyer escorts, frigates, motor torpedo boats, and other types. Kinkaid's job was to provide shore bombardment and close air support for the Army and anti-submarine and air defense for the amphibious forces.

Halsey, with eight large attack carriers, eight light carriers, six fast new battleships, fifteen cruisers, and fifty-eight destroyers, was ordered to "cover and support forces of the Southwest Pacific [MacArthur's command] in order to assist in the seizure and occupation of objectives in the Central Philippines." [e] He was to destroy enemy naval and air forces threatening the invasion. He was to remain responsible to Admiral Nimitz, but "necessary measures for detailed coordination of operations between the . . . [Third

Fleet] . . . and . . . the [Seventh Fleet] will be arranged by their . . . commanders." [1]

It opened with first blood for the submarines. At dawn on October 23 the U.S. submarines *Darter* and *Dace,* patrolling Palawan Passage, intercepted Admiral Kurita, bound for his rendezvous with destiny. The *Darter* put five torpedoes into Kurita's flagship, heavy cruiser *Atago,* at 1,000 yards range; damaged the cruiser *Takao. Dace* [4] hit the cruiser *Maya* with four torpedoes. The *Atago* sank in nineteen minutes as Kurita shifted his flag to the destroyer *Kishinani* and later to the battleship *Yamato.* The *Maya* blew up and sank in four minutes; *Takao*—burning and low in the water—was sent back to Brunei, escorted by two destroyers. Kurita steamed on, shaken but implacable, toward San Bernardino Strait.

October 24 Aboard battleship *New Jersey,* flying "Bull" Halsey's flag, the plans are ready for this day as the sun quickly burns away the morning haze. In the carriers, bowing to the swell, the bull horns sound on the flight decks— "Pilots, man your planes."

At 6 a.m. the Third Fleet launches search planes to sweep a wide arc of sea covering the approaches to San Bernardino and Surigao straits. Submarine reports from *Darter, Dace,* and *Guitarro* have alerted the Americans— but not in time to halt the detachment of Third Fleet's largest task group—Task Group 38.1 commanded by Vice-Admiral John S. ("Slew") McCain with orders to retire to Ulithi for rest and supplies. The fleet's three other task groups are spread out over 300 miles of ocean to the east of the Philippines from central Luzon to southern Samar; one of them—to the north—has been tracked doggedly all night by enemy "snoopers." As the planes take off to search the reef-studded waters of the Sibuyan and Sulu seas and the approaches to San Bernardino and Surigao, Kinkaid's old battleships and little carriers off Leyte are supporting the "G.I.'s" ashore.

At 0746, Lieutenant (j.g.) Max Adams, flying a Helldiver above the magnificent volcanic crags, the palm-grown islands, and startling blue sea of the archipelago, reports a radar contact, and a few minutes later Admiral Kurita's First Diversion Attack Force lies spread out like toy ships upon a painted sea—the pagoda masts unmistakable in the sunlight.

The tension of action grips flag plot in the *New Jersey* as the contact report comes in; the radio crackles "Urgent" and "Top Secret" messages—to Washington, to Nimitz, to Kinkaid, to all task-group commanders. McCain, 600 miles to the eastward, enroute to Ulithi and rest, is recalled and Third Fleet is ordered to concentrate off San Bernardino to launch strikes against the enemy.

But at 8:20 far to the south, the southern arm of the Japanese pincer is sighted for the first time; Vice-Admiral Nishimura—with battleships *Fuso* and *Yamashiro*, heavy cruiser *Mogami*, and four destroyers—steaming toward Surigao. *Enterprise* search-attack planes attack[5] through heavy AA fire; *Fuso*'s catapult is hit, her planes destroyed, and a fire rages; a gun mount in destroyer *Shiguro* is knocked out—but Nishimura steams on to the east, his speed undiminished. And Halsey continues the concentration of his fleet near San Bernardino to strike the Japanese Central Force.

There has been no morning search to the north and northeast, and Ozawa's decoy carriers, steaming southward toward Luzon, are still undiscovered.

The *Shō* plan now moves toward its dramatic denouement. Japanese planes flying from Philippine bases commence the most furious assault since the landing upon the Seventh and Third Fleets. To the north off Luzon, carriers *Langley*, *Princeton*, *Essex*, and *Lexington* face the brunt of the winged fury. Seven Hellcats from the *Essex*, led by Commander David McCampbell, intercept sixty Japanese planes—half of them Zeke fighters—and after a melee of an hour and thirty-five minutes of combat the Americans knock down twenty-four Japs with no losses. *Princeton* claims thirty-four enemy from another large raid; the *Lexington*'s and *Langley*'s "fly-boys" are also busy; over the air come the exultant "Tally-hos," and "Splash one Betty— Splash two Zekes" of the pilots.

But the Japs draw blood. At about 0938, as Third Fleet

starts converging toward San Bernardino and the carriers prepare to launch deckloads to strike the enemy's center force, a Jap Judy dives unseen and unrecorded on the radar screen out of a low cloud. She drops a 550-pound bomb square on *Princeton*'s flight deck; the bomb penetrates to the hangar deck, ignites gasoline in six torpedo planes, starts raging fires. The fight to save her starts, but at 1002 a series of terrific explosions split open the flight deck like the rind of a dropped melon, throw the after plane elevator high into the air, and by 1020 *Princeton*'s fire mains have failed and she is dead in the water, with a 1,000-foot pall of smoke above her and hundreds of her crew in the water. The task group steams on southward to the San Bernardino rendezvous, while cruisers *Birmingham* and *Reno* and destroyers *Gatling, Irwin,* and *Cassin Young* hover about wounded *Princeton* in a day-long fight to save her.

But as *Princeton* flames and staggers, Kurita's Central Force of five battleships, accompanied by cruisers and destroyers, is running the gantlet. Carrier strikes start coming in against Japan's First Diversion Attack Force about 10:25 a.m., and the exultant U.S. pilots concentrate against targets none of them had ever seen before—the largest battleships in the world. *Yamato* and *Musashi,* long the mysterious focus of intelligence reports, lie beneath the wings of naval air power—their 69,500-ton bulk, 18-inch guns, 27.5-knot speed—dwarfing their sisters. *Musashi* is wounded early; oil smears trail on the blue water from her lacerated flank as a torpedo strikes home. But she is strong; her speed is undiminished. Not so *Myoko*'s. This heavy cruiser is badly hurt in the first attack; she drops to fifteen knots and is left astern to limp alone into port; Kurita has lost four out of the ten heavy cruisers that sortied so gallantly from Brunei.

But he has no respite. At three minutes past noon another strike comes out of the sun. The Jap AA fire blossoms in pink and purple bursts; even the battleships' main batteries are firing. Several American planes are hit; one goes down flaming—but *Musashi* takes two bombs and two torpedoes; she loses speed and drops back slowly out of formation.

618

An hour and a half later *Yamato* takes two hits forward of her Number 1 turret, which start a fire—but her thick hide minimizes damages; the fire is extinguished. But *Musashi* is now sore-wounded; she takes four bomb hits in this attack and three more torpedoes; her upper works are a shambles, her bow almost under water, her speed down first to sixteen and then to twelve knots.

But Kurita's slow agony drags on during this long and sunlit day. He hopes in vain for air cover. *Yamato* is hit again in the fourth attack and the older battleship *Nagato* damaged.

At six bells in the afternoon watch (3 p.m.) Kurita orders the limping *Musashi* to withdraw from the fight. But not in time.

The final and largest attack of the day seeks her out as she turns heavily to find sanctuary. In fifteen minutes *Musashi* receives the *coup de grâce*—ten more bombs, four more torpedoes; she's down to six knots now, her bow is under water, and she lists steeply to port—a dying gladiator.

Kurita is shaken. He has had no air cover; he has been subjected to intense attack; his original strength of five battleships, twelve cruisers, and fifteen destroyers has been reduced to four battleships, eight cruisers, and eleven destroyers; all of his remaining battleships have been damaged; fleet speed is limited to twenty-two knots. There is no sign that Ozawa's northern decoy force is succeeding in luring the Third Fleet away from San Bernardino. At 1530 Kurita reverses course and steams away toward the west. And American pilots report the "retreat" to Admiral Halsey aboard *New Jersey*. . . .

To Admiral Halsey there is "one piece missing in the puzzle—the [Japanese] carriers."

The northern task group of Third Fleet has been under attack by enemy carrier-type planes, which might have been land-based—but none of the sightings has reported enemy carriers. Where are they?

At 1405 (2:05 p.m.), as Kurita's central force is pounded in the Sibuyan Sea, *Lexington*'s planes take off to find out.[6] They are under orders to search to the north and northeast in the open seas untouched by the morning search.

The search planes fly through a cloud-speckled sky and intermittent rain squalls, leaving behind them a task group harassed by fierce, though intermittent Jap air attacks.

The flaming *Princeton,* billowing clouds of fire and smoke, is still afloat, with her covey of rescue ships around her. Despite intermittent explosions and singeing heat, cruisers *Birmingham* and *Reno,* destroyers *Morrison, Irwin,* and *Cassin Young* have clustered alongside, pouring water from their pumps on the blazing carrier. Submarine contacts and enemy air attacks interrupt the fire fighting; the rescue ships pull off. At 1523 (3:23 p.m.), about the time Kurita, 300 miles away, reverses course and heads to the westward in the Sibuyan Sea, cruiser *Birmingham* comes alongside *Princeton*'s blazing port side again. The cruiser's open decks are thick with men—fire fighters, line handlers, antiaircraft gunners, medical personnel, fire and rescue squads, watch-standers. There is fifty feet of open water between blazing *Princeton* and her salvor, *Birmingham;* a spring line is out forward between carrier and cruiser.

Suddenly a "tremendous blast" rips off Princeton's stern and flight deck; steel plates as big "as a house" fly through the air; jagged bits of steel, broken gun barrels, shrapnel, helmets, debris rake *Birmingham*'s bridge, upper works, and crowded decks like grapeshot; in a fraction of a second the cruiser is a charnel house, her decks literally flowing blood—229 dead, 420 mangled and wounded—the ship's superstructure sieved.

Aboard *Princeton* all the skeleton fire-fighting crew are wounded. Captain John M. Hoskins, who had been scheduled to take command of *Princeton* shortly and had remained aboard with the skipper he was relieving, puts a rope tourniquet around his leg, as his right foot hangs by a shred of flesh and tendon. The surviving medical officer cuts off the foot with a sheath knife, dusts the wound with sulfa powder, injects morphine. . . . Hoskins lives to become the Navy's first "peg-leg" admiral of modern times.

But still *Princeton* floats on even keel, flaming like a volcano, manned by a crew of bloody specters. . . .

At 1640 the search to the north pays off. U.S. planes sight Ozawa's decoy force of carriers. The contact reports electrify Third Fleet, but mislead it, too; Ozawa's northern group of ships, which were sighted about 130 miles east of the northern tip of Luzon, includes two hermaphrodite battleships but our fliers mistakenly report four.[7] Nor do our fliers know Ozawa's carriers are virtually without planes.

The contact reports decide *Princeton*'s fate; her weary crew of fire fighters are removed, the day-long struggle is ended, and at 4:49 *Reno* puts two torpedoes into the flaming hulk and the carrier blows up, breaks in two, and sinks. Mangled *Birmingham*, which lost far more men than the ship she was trying to save, steams with her dead and dying to Ulithi—out of the fight. . . .

Two hours later, near Sibuyan Island, the giant *Musashi*, pride of Kurita's Central Force, loses her long fight. Fatally wounded, she settles slowly deeper and deeper in the calm sea, and as the evening closes down, the greatest battleship in the world capsizes and takes with her to the depths half of her crew. But no American sees her passing. . . . And no American has seen Kurita, earlier in the afternoon, alter his course once more and at 1714 head once again with his battered but still powerful Central Force back toward San Bernardino Strait. . . .

At 1950, with the tropic dusk, "Bull" Halsey makes his decision and informs Kinkaid, commanding Seventh Fleet:

"Central force heavily damaged according to strike reports. Am proceeding north with three groups to attack carrier force at dawn." [8]

Third Fleet concentrates and steams hard to the north in what irreverent historians of the future are to call "Bull's Run." Night snoopers from *Independence* shadow the Jap northern force, and orders go to the carriers to launch planes at sunrise.[g] San Bernardino Strait is left uncovered—not even a submarine [h] patrols its waters; Kinkaid and

621

Seventh Fleet, protecting the Leyte invasion, believe it is barred by Halsey; Halsey, banking too heavily on exaggerated claims from his pilots,[i] thinks Kurita's central force has been stopped by the day's air attacks and the battered Jap survivors can be left safely to Kinkaid. On such misunderstandings rest the course of history and the fate of nations.[j]

Surigao Strait is dark under the loom of the land. Since the morning there have been no sightings of the Japanese southern force; even its exact composition is not known. But Kinkaid and the Seventh Fleet have no doubts; the Japs will try to break through this night. Kinkaid and Rear Admiral Jesse B. Oldendorf, his "O.T.C." (officer in tactical command) have made dispositions for a night surface battle. They have provided a suitable reception committee, including PT boats deep in the strait and covering its southern approaches, three destroyer squadrons near the center, and at the mouth—where the strait debouches into Leyte Gulf—six old battleships and eight cruisers.[9]

Into this trap the Japanese southern force blunders in two divisions—each independent of the other. Nishimura, with battleships *Fuso* and *Yamashiro,* cruiser *Mogami,* and four destroyers, lead the way. Cruising twenty miles behind Nishimura is Vice-Admiral Shima with three cruisers and four destroyers from Jap home bases. The two Jap forces attack piecemeal and uncoordinated; neither knows much of the other's plans. Shima and Nishimura were classmates at the Japanese Naval Academy; their careers have bred rivalry; Nishimura, formerly the senior, has been passed in the processes of promotion by Shima, who commands the smaller force but is now six months senior in rank to Nishimura. But Nishimura, a sea-going admiral, has seen more war. Neither seems anxious to serve with the other; there is no common command.

Radars on the PT boats pick up the enemy about 11 p.m. as "sheet lightning dim[s] the hazy blur of the setting moon and thunder echo[es] from the islands' hills."

Thirty-nine PT boats, motors muffled, head for Nishimura and attack in successive "waves" as the enemy ad-

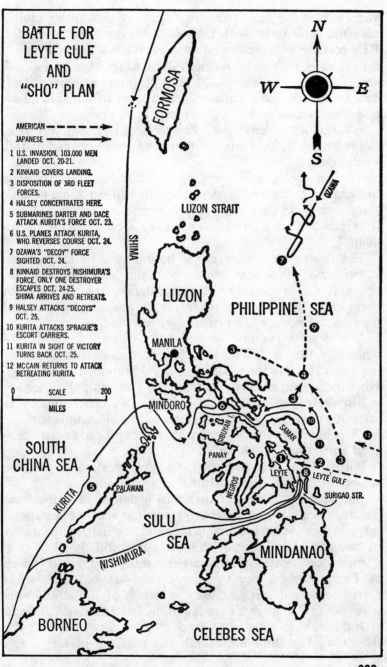

BATTLE FOR LEYTE GULF AND "SHO" PLAN

AMERICAN - - - →
JAPANESE ────→

1 U.S. INVASION, 103,000 MEN LANDED OCT. 20-21.

2 KINKAID COVERS LANDING.

3 DISPOSITION OF 3RD FLEET FORCES.

4 HALSEY CONCENTRATES HERE.

5 SUBMARINES DARTER AND DACE ATTACK KURITA'S FORCE OCT. 23.

6 U.S. PLANES ATTACK KURITA, WHO REVERSES COURSE OCT. 24.

7 OZAWA'S "DECOY" FORCE SIGHTED OCT. 24.

8 KINKAID DESTROYS NISHIMURA'S FORCE. ONLY ONE DESTROYER ESCAPES OCT. 24-25. SHIMA ARRIVES AND RETREATS.

9 HALSEY ATTACKS "DECOYS" OCT. 25.

10 KURITA ATTACKS SPRAGUE'S ESCORT CARRIERS.

11 KURITA IN SIGHT OF VICTORY TURNS BACK OCT. 25.

12 McCAIN RETURNS TO ATTACK RETREATING KURITA.

0   SCALE   200

MILES

FORMOSA

N / W / E / S

OZAWA

LUZON STRAIT

SHIMA

LUZON

PHILIPPINE SEA

MANILA

7

9

3

4

3

10

SOUTH CHINA SEA

MINDORO

6

SIBUYAN I.

SAMAR

11

12

3

2

PANAY

1

LEYTE

8 LEYTE GULF

KURITA

5

PALAWAN

NEGROS

SURIGAO STR.

SULU SEA

NISHIMURA

MINDANAO

BORNEO

CELEBES SEA

vances. But the Japs score first. Enemy destroyers illuminate the little boats with their searchlights long before the PT's reach good torpedo range; a hit starts a fire in *PT 152;* a near miss with its spout of water extinguishes it; *PT 130* and *PT 132* are also hit.[10] But Nishimura is identified; course, speed, and formation are radioed to Kinkaid's fleet and the harassing PT attacks continue.

Aboard destroyer *Remey,* flag of Destroyer Squadron 54, Commander R. P. Fiala turns on the loud-speaker to talk to the crew:

"This is the captain speaking. Tonight our ship has been designated to make the first torpedo run on the Jap task force that is on its way to stop our landings in Leyte Gulf. It is our job to stop the Japs. May God be with us tonight."

The destroyers attack along both flanks of the narrow strait; their silhouettes merge with the land; the Japs, in the middle, can scarcely distinguish dark shape of ship from dark loom of land; the radar fuzzes and the luminescent pips on the screen are lost in a vague blur.

It is deep in the mid-watch—0301 of the twenty-fifth— when the first destroyer-launched torpedoes streak across the strait. In less than half an hour Nishimura is crippled. His slow and lumbering flagship, the battleship *Yamashiro,* is hit; destroyer *Yamagumo* is sunk; two other destroyers are out of control. Nishimura issues his last command:

"We have received a torpedo attack. You are to proceed and attack all ships."

Battleship *Fuso,* cruiser *Mogami,* destroyer *Shigure* steam on toward Leyte Gulf.

But before 4 a.m. a tremendous eruption of flames and pyrotechnics marks *Yamashiro's* passing; another American torpedo has found her magazine, and the battleship breaks in two and sinks, with Nishimura's flag still flying.

Fuso does not long outlive her sister. Up from the mud of Pearl Harbor, the avengers wait—six old battleships patrol back and forth across the mouth of the strait. This is an admiral's dream. Like Togo at Tsushima and Jellicoe at Jutland, Kinkaid and Oldendorf have capped the T; the remaining Jap ships are blundering head on in single column against a column of American ships at right angles to the Jap course. The concentrated broadsides of six battleships can be focused against the leading Jap, and only his forward turrets can bear against the Americans.

Climax of battle. As the last and heaviest destroyer attack goes home in answer to the command—"Get the big boys" —the battle line and the cruisers open up; the night is streaked with flare of crimson.

Fuso and *Mogami* flame and shudder as the "rain of shells" strikes home; *Fuso* soon drifts helplessly, racked by great explosions, wreathed in a fiery pall. She dies before the dawn, and *Mogami,* on fire, is finished later with the other cripples. Only destroyer *Shigure* escapes at thirty knots.

Into this mad melee, with the dying remnants of his classmate's fleet around him, steams Vice-Admiral Shima— "fat, dumb, and happy." He knows nothing of what has gone before; he has no cogent plan of battle. *Abukuma,* Shima's only light cruiser, is struck by a PT torpedo [11] even before she is deep in the strait; she is left behind, speed dwindling, as the two heavy cruisers and four destroyers steam onward toward the gun flashes on the horizon. About 4 a.m. Shima encounters destroyer *Shigure,* sole survivor of Nishimura's fleet, retiring down the strait.

Shigure tells Shima nothing of the debacle; she simply signals:

"I am the *Shigure;* I have rudder difficulties."

The rest is almost comic anticlimax. Shima pushes deeper into the strait, sees a group of dark shadows; fires torpedoes and manages an amazing collision between his flagship, the *Nachi,* and the burning stricken *Mogami,* which looms up flaming out of the dark waters of the strait like the Empire State Building. And that is all for futile Shima; discretion is the better part of valor; dying for the Emperor is forgotten and Shima reverses course and heads back into the Mindanao Sea and the obscurity of history.

The Battle of Surigao Strait ends with the dawn—debacle for the Japanese. One PT boat destroyed; one destroyer damaged for the Americans. The southern pincer toward Leyte Gulf is broken.[k]

October 25 Dawn of the twenty-fifth of October finds
Admiral Ozawa with his decoy force [1] eastward of Cape
Engano (fortuitous name: Engano is Spanish for "lure" or
"hoax"), prepared to die for the Emperor. At 0712, when
the first American planes appear from the southeast, Ozawa
knows he has at last succeeded in his luring mission. The
day before he has at times despaired; some seventy to
eighty of his carrier planes—all he has save for a small
combat air patrol—have joined Japanese land-based planes
in attacks upon Halsey's northern task group. But his
planes have not come back; many have been lost, others
have flown on to Philippine bases. This day twenty aircraft—token remnants of Japan's once great flying fleets—
are all that Ozawa commands. A few are in the air—to die
quickly beneath American guns, as the first heavy attacks
from Halsey's carriers come in.

The American carrier pilots have a field day; the air
is full of the jabberwock of the fliers.

"Pick one out, boys, and let 'em have it."

The Jap formation throws up a beautiful carpet of anti-
aircraft fire; the colored bursts and tracers frame the sky-
sea battle. The Japanese ships twist and turn, maneuver
violently in eccentric patterns to avoid the bombs and torpedoes—but their time has come. Before 8:30, with the
day still young, some 150 U.S. carrier planes have wrought
havoc. Carrier *Chiyoda* is hit; carrier *Chitose*, billowing
clouds of smoke and fatally hurt, is stopped and listing
heavily; the light cruiser *Tama*, torpedoed, is limping astern;
destroyer *Akitsuki* has blown up; light carrier *Zuiho* is hit,
and Ozawa's flagship, the *Zuikaku*, has taken a torpedo aft,
which has wrecked the steering engine; she is steered by
hand.

A second strike at 10 cripples *Chiyoda*, which dies a slow
death, to be finished off later by U.S. surface ships. In early
afternoon a third strike sinks carrier *Zuikaku*, the last survivor of the Japanese attack upon Pearl Harbor. She rolls
over slowly and sinks, "flying a battle flag of tremendous
size." At 1527 carrier *Zuiho* "follows her down." The hermaphrodite battleships, with flight decks aft—*Hyuga* and
Ise, "fattest of the remaining targets"—are bombed re-

626

peatedly, their bulges are perforated, their decks inundated with tons of water from near misses; *Ise*'s port catapult is hit—but they bear charmed lives. Admiral Ozawa, his flag transferred to cruiser *Oyodo,* his work of "luring" done, straggles northward with his cripples from the battle off Cape Engano. Throughout the day he is subject to incessant air attack, and in late afternoon and in the dark of the night of the twenty-fifth U.S. cruisers and destroyers, detached from the Third Fleet finish off the cripples.

The price of success for Admiral Ozawa's decoy force is high; all four carriers, one of his three cruisers, and two of his eight destroyers are gone. But he has accomplished his mission; Halsey has been lured, San Bernardino Strait is unguarded, and the hawk Kurita is down among the chickens.

Off Samar that morning of the twenty-fifth, the sea is calm at sunup, the wind gentle, the sky overcast with spotted cumulus; occasional rain squalls dapple the surface. Aboard the sixteen escort carriers of Seventh Fleet and their escorting "small boys" (destroyers and destroyer escorts) the dawn alert has ended. The early missions have taken off (though not the search planes for the northern sectors). Many of the carriers' planes are already over Leyte, supporting the ground troops—the combat air patrol and ASW patrols are launched, and on the bridge of carrier *Fanshaw Bay,* Rear Admiral C. A. F. Sprague is having a second cup of coffee.

The coming day will be busy; the little escort carriers have support missions to fly for the troops ashore on Leyte, air defense and anti-submarine patrols, and a large strike scheduled to mop up the cripples and fleeing remnants of the Japanese force defeated in the night surface battle of Surigao Strait. The escort-carrier groups are spread out off the east coast of the Philippines from Mindanao to Samar; Sprague's northern group of six escort carriers, three destroyers, and four destroyer escorts is steaming northward at fourteen knots fifty miles off Samar and halfway up the island's coast.

The escort carriers, designated CVE's in naval abbreviation, are tin-clads-unarmored, converted from merchant ship or tanker hulls, slow, carrying eighteen to thirty-six planes. They are known by many uncomplimentary descriptives—"baby flat-tops," "tomato cans," "jeep carriers," and new recruits "coming aboard for the first time were told by the old hands that CVE stood for Combustible, Vulnerable, Expendable!" Their maximum of eighteen knots speed (made all-out) is too slow to give them safety in flight; their thin skins and "pop-guns"—five-inchers and under—do not fit them for surface slugging; they are ships of limited utility—intended for air support of ground operations ashore, anti-submarine and air defense missions—never for fleet action.

Yet they are to fight this morning a battle of jeeps against giants.

Admiral Sprague has scarcely finished his coffee when a contact report comes over the squawk-box. An ASW pilot reports enemy battleships, cruisers, destroyers twenty miles away and closing fast.

". . . check that identification," the admiral says, thinking some green pilot has mistaken Halsey's fast battleships for the enemy.

The answer is sharp and brief, the tension obvious: "Identification confirmed," the pilot's voice comes strained through the static. "Ships have pagoda masts."

Almost simultaneously radiomen hear Japanese chatter over the air; the northern CVE group sees antiaircraft bursts blossoming in the air to the northwest; blips of unidentified ships appear on the radar screens, and before 7 a.m. a signalman with a long glass has picked up the many-storied superstructures and the typical pagoda masts of Japanese ships.

Disbelief, amazement, and consternation struggle for supremacy; the escort carriers, Admiral Kinkaid himself—in fact, most of the Seventh Fleet—had been convinced the Japanese center force was still west of the Philippines [12] and that, in any case, Halsey's fast battleships—now far away to the north with the carriers in the battle for Cape Engano—were guarding San Bernardino Strait. But Kurita has arrived. . . . And about all that stands between him

628

and the transports, supply ships, and amphibious craft in Leyte Gulf and Army headquarters and supply dumps on the beach are the "baby flat-tops" and their accompanying "small boys."

There's no time for planning; within five minutes of visual sighting Japanese heavy stuff—18-inch shells from *Yamato,* sister ship of the foundered *Musashi*—are whistling overhead. Sprague, giving his orders over the voice radio, turns his ships to the east into the wind, steps up speed to maximum, orders all planes scrambled. By 7:05 a.m. escort carrier *White Plains*, launching aircraft as fast as she can get them off, is straddled several times, with red, yellow, green, and blue spouts of water from the dye-marked shells foaming across her bridge, shaking the ship violently, damaging the starboard engine room, smashing electrical circuits, and throwing a fighter plane out of its chocks on the flight deck.

White Plains makes smoke and the Japs shift fire to the *St. Lô,* which takes near misses and casualties from fragments. The "small boys" make smoke—and the carriers, their boiler casings panting from maximum effort—pour out viscous clouds of oily black smoke from their stacks, which veils the sea. . . . There is a moment of surcease; the planes are launched, most of them armed with small-size or anti-personnel or general-purpose bombs or depth charges—no good against armored ships. But there has been no time to rearm. . . .

The air waves sound alarm. Sprague broadcasts danger in plain language; at 0724 Admiral Kinkaid, aboard his flagship *Wasatch* in Leyte Gulf, hears the worst has happened; the Jap fleet is three hours' steaming from the beachhead; the little escort carriers may be wiped out. Just five minutes before, Kinkaid has learned that his assumption that a Third Fleet cork was in the bottle of San Bernardino Strait was incorrect; in answer to a radioed query sent at 0412 Halsey informs him that Task Force 34—modern fast battleships—is with Third Fleet's carriers off Cape Engano far to the north.

Kinkaid in "urgent and priority" messages asks for fast battleships, for carrier strikes, for immediate action. . . .

629

Even Admiral Nimitz, in far-off Hawaii, sends a message to Halsey:

"All the world wants to know where is Task Force 34 [13] [the fast battleships]?" [m]

But in Leyte Gulf and Surigao Strait the tocsin of alarm sounded via the radio waves puts Seventh Fleet—red-eyed [n] from days of shore bombardment and nights of battle— into frenetic action. Some of the old battleships and cruisers are recalled from Surigao Strait, formed into a task unit, and they prepare feverishly to ammunition and refuel. Seventh Fleet's heavy ships are in none too good shape for surface action; their ammunition is dangerously low from five days of shore bombardment, many of their armor-piercing projectiles were used in the night battle; destroyers are low on torpedoes, many ships short of fuel. . . .[o]

And in the battle off Samar, Sprague is fighting for his life.

Within twenty minutes, as the baby carriers steam to the east, launching planes, the range to the enemy has decreased to 25,000 yards—easy shooting for the big guns of the Japs, far beyond the effective reach of the American five-inchers. . . .

Destroyer *Johnston,* Commander Ernest E. Evans, commanding, sees her duty and does it. Without orders she dashes in at thirty knots to launch a spread of ten torpedoes against an enemy cruiser working up along a flank of the pounding carriers. She spouts smoke and fire as she charges—her five-inchers firing continuously as she closes the range. She escapes damage until she turns to retire; then a salvo of three 14-inchers, followed by three six-inch shells, hole her, wound her captain, wreck the steering engine, the after fire room and engine room, knock out her after guns and gyro compass, maim many of her crew and leave her limping at sixteen knots.

Sprague and his carriers, veiled in part by smoke, find brief sanctuary in a heavy rain squall; the curtain of water saves temporarily wounded *Johnston.* But well before 8 a.m. Kurita has sent some of his faster ships seaward to head off and flank the escort carriers; gradually Sprague

630

turns southward, the enemy coming hard on both his flanks and astern. . . .

"Small boys, launch torpedo attack," Sprague orders over the TBS circuit (talk-between-ships voice radio).

Destroyers *Heermann* and *Hoel* and wounded *Johnston*, her torpedoes already expended but her guns speaking in support, answer the command—three destroyers in a daylight attack against [14] the heaviest ships of the Japanese fleet, three tin-clads against four battleships, eight cruisers, and eleven destroyers.

"Buck," Commander Amos T. Hathaway, skipper of the *Heermann*, remarks coolly to his officer of the deck: "Buck, what we need is a bugler to sound the charge."

Hoel and *Heermann*, followed by limping *Johnston*, sally forth to their naval immortality.

In and out of rain squalls, wreathed in the black and oily smoke from the stacks and the white chemical smoke from the smoke generators on the fantails, the destroyers charge, backing violently to avoid collisions, closing the range. They hear the "express-train" roar of the 14-inchers going over; they fire spreads at a heavy cruiser, rake the superstructure of a battleship with their five-inchers, launch their last torpedoes at 4,400 yards range. Then Hathaway of the *Heermann* walks calmly into his pilothouse, calls Admiral Sprague on the TBS, and reports:

"Exercise completed."

But the destroyers are finished. *Hoel* has lost her port engine; she is steered manually; her decks are a holocaust of blood and wreckage; fire control and power are off; No. 3 gun, wreathed in white-hot steam venting from the burst steam pipes, is inoperable; No. 5 is frozen in train by a near miss; half the barrel of No. 4 is blown off—but Nos. 1 and 2 guns continue to fire.

By 8:30 p.m. power is lost on the starboard engine; all engineering spaces are flooding; the ship slows to dead in the water and, burning furiously, is raked by enemy guns. At 0840, with a twenty-degree list, the order is given to "abandon ship." Fifteen minutes later she rolls on her port side and sinks stern first—holed repeatedly by scores of major-caliber shells.

In *Heermann,* the crimson dye from enemy shell splashes mixes with the blood of men to daub bridge and super-structure reddish hues. A shell strikes a bean locker and spreads a brown paste across the decks. *Heermann* takes hits, but, fishtailing and chasing salvos, she manages to live.

Not so, wounded *Johnston.* Spitting fire to the end, and virtually surrounded by the entire Jap fleet, she is over-whelmed under an avalanche of shells, to sink about an hour after *Hoel.*

The four smaller and slower destroyer escorts make the second torpedo attack. *Raymond* and *John C. Butler* live to tell about it; *Dennis* has her guns knocked out, but *Samuel B. Roberts,* deep in the smoke and framed by shell splashes, comes to her end in a mad melee. She is hit by many heavy-caliber projectiles, her speed reduced, and by 9 a.m. a salvo of 14-inch shells rips open her port side like a can opener, wrecks an engine room, starts raging fires. The *Roberts,* abaft her stack, looks like "an inert mass of battered metal"; she has no power; she is dead in the water.

But the crew of No. 2 gun load, ram, aim, and fire by hand. They know the chance they take; without compressed air to clear the bore of the burning bits of fragments from the previous charge, the silken powder bags may "cook off" and explode before the breach can be closed. But they fire six rounds, despite the risk. The seventh "cooks off" and kills instantly most of the gun crew; the breach is blown into a twisted inoperable mass of steel. But Gunner's Mate 3/c Paul Henry Carr, the gun captain—his body ripped open from neck to groin—still cradles the last 54-pound shell in his arms, and his last gasping words before he dies are pleas for aid to load the gun.

But smoke screens, rain squalls, and torpedo attacks have not saved the slow and lumbering baby flat-tops. Kurita has sent his cruisers curving seaward; slowly the fight swerves round from south to southwest; Sprague's carriers, strung out over miles of ocean, steam wounded toward Leyte Gulf, with the enemy destroyers coming hard on their landward flank, battleships astern and Jap cruisers to seaward.

632

The flat-tops dodge in and out of the 150-foot water-spouts from the major-caliber Japanese shells; they chase salvos and fire their five-inchers defiantly. *Fanshaw Bay* takes six hits from eight-inch shells, which wreck the catapult, knock holes in the hull, start fires. *Kalinin Bay* takes fifteen hits; *White Plains* is racked from stem to stern by straddles. But their thin skins save them; most of the huge armor-piercing projectiles pass clean through the unarmored carriers without exploding. *Gambier Bay,* trailing and on an exposed windward flank where the smoke screens do not shield her, takes a hit on the flight deck, a near miss close alongside, loses an engine, drops to eleven knots, then loses all power—and is doomed. For an hour, far behind the chase, she dies in agony, hit about once a minute by enemy fire. She sinks about 9 a.m., flaming brightly, gasoline exploding, a Jap cruiser still riddling her from only 2,000 yards away.

Well before 9:30 the chase which is drawing closer and closer to crowded Leyte Gulf, where frantic preparations are in progress, has enveloped the northern group of escort carriers; the central group is now under fire, and the sixteen jeep flat-tops have lost 105 planes.

". . . it seemed only a matter of time until the entire Northern Group would be wiped out and the Middle Group overtaken . . ."

Two destroyers, a destroyer escort, and a carrier are sunk or sinking; two carriers, a destroyer, and a destroyer escort are badly hurt.

Aboard *Kitkun Bay,* an officer quips:

"It won't be long now, boys; we're sucking 'em into 40-mm. range."

Suddenly at 0925, Vice-Admiral Kurita, with victory in his grasp, breaks off the action, turns his ships to the north, and ends the surface phase of the battle off Samar.

"Damn it," a sailor says. "They got away."

Kurita's action, inexplicable at the time, has some, though incomplete, justification. The charge of the American "small boys"—one of the most stirring episodes in the long history of naval war—and the desperate gallantr of the uncoordinated and improvised air strikes by the pilots of the escort carriers have had their effect. During the early action off Samar, U.S. carrier pilots—from the little CVE's—have harassed Kurita constantly, have shot down more than 100 enemy planes, dropped 191 tons of bombs and 83 torpedoes. The enemy ships have turned and maneuvered violently to avoid torpedoes. Effective smoke screens have confused the Japanese. The air attacks have been mounting in intensity and effectiveness as planes have been launched from the center and southern group of escort carriers and have been diverted from ground-support missions on Leyte to the new emergency. Pilots have strafed the Japanese ships recklessly, have dropped depth charges and anti-personnel bombs, have zoomed above Japanese mastheads with no ammunition and no weapons to win time and to divert and to distract.

The torpedo attacks by surface ships and aircraft had damaged enemy ships, and Kurita's fleet—composed of units now capable of widely differing speeds—is strung out over miles of ocean. Cruiser *Kumano,* torpedoed, is down to sixteen knots; cruisers *Chikuma* and *Chokai* are crippled; superstructures, charthouses, and communication equipment in other ships are damaged by five-inch shell fire and aircraft strafing; the Japs are shaken. Kurita, who has lost close tactical control of his command, [15] does not comprehend his closeness to victory; he thinks he has engaged some of the big, fast carriers of Third Fleet instead of merely the escort carriers of Seventh Fleet. Intercepted U.S. radio traffic convinces him—erroneously—that Leyte airstrips are operational.[p] He believes the rest of Halsey's powerful forces are nearby; he knows that Nishimura's southern pincer has been defeated in Surigao Strait; he has never received messages from Ozawa, far to the north, reporting the success of his decoy mission. So Kurita recalls his ships and assembles his scattered forces—and his chance has gone.

Admiral Sprague notes his thankful bewilderment: ". . . the failure of the enemy . . . to completely wipe out all vessels of this Task Unit can be attributed to our successful smoke screen, our torpedo counterattack . . . and the definite partiality of Almighty God."

The rest was anticlimax.

Kurita's irresolution was reinforced by mounting American attacks. Only two hours from the soft-skinned amphibious shipping in Leyte Gulf—his original goal—Kurita wasted time assembling his scattered forces and aiding cripples, and his fleet milled around in much the same waters, steering varying courses. *Suzuya*, cruiser, was fatally damaged by air attack, and at 10:30 a.m., two to three hours' flying time to the eastward, Admiral "Slew" Mc-Cain's Task Group 38.1 (which had been sent to Ulithi for rest, hastily recalled, and was steaming hard to the rescue) launched a strike. The bell has tolled for Kurita, and Japan's rising sun has passed the zenith. And far to the north, "Bull" Halsey, striking at Ozawa's decoy force, was alarmed at length by Kinkaid's frantic appeals for help; his fleet reversed course when within forty miles of decisive surface action, and Halsey detached some of his fast battleships to steam southward at high speed—but too late to intervene.[16]

The rest of that day, the twenty-fifth, and all of the next—the twenty-sixth—was mop-up and fierce stab, as the Japanese survivors fled and Jap land-based aircraft struck hard in angry futility. Japanese Kamikaze planes, attacking after the crescendo of battle, hit the escort carriers—damaged three and broke the back of *St. Lô*, which had survived the 18-inch guns of *Yamato*. But Kurita, who reached so closely to the verge of fame, paid heavily for the luxury of indecision. Air attacks struck him again and again during the afternoon of the twenty-fifth. Three of his damaged cruisers, crippled and on fire, had to be sunk. *Tone*, one of his two remaining heavy cruisers, was hit aft and damaged, and during the night of the twenty-fifth, as Kurita took his battered survivors back through San Bernardino Strait, U.S. surface forces caught and sank destroyer *Nowake*. At midnight of the twenty-fifth only one of Kurita's ships, a destroyer, was wholly undamaged.

On the twenty-sixth there was more slow dying as Halsey's and Kinkaid's fliers, augmented by some Army Air Force land-based bombers, chivvied and attacked the retreating Japs; and the First Diversion Attack Force, "which had already undergone more air attacks than any other force in naval history, once again braced itself for the final ordeal." Destroyer *Noshiro* was sunk; *Yamato*, with its gigantic but futile 18-inches, was hit twice and its superstructure sieved with splinters, and other cripples of the battle off Samar and the Battle of Surigao Strait, including cruiser *Abukuma* and destroyer *Hayashimo*, were finished off. And there still remained the gantlet of U.S. submarines. . . .

At 2130, October 28, "what remained of the Japanese Battle Fleet re-entered Brunei Bay."

The *Shō* plan—the great gamble—had failed completely. In the sprawling battle for Leyte Gulf, Japan had lost one large and three light aircraft carriers, three battleships, including one of the two largest warships in the world, six heavy cruisers, four light cruisers, and eleven destroyers; most of the rest of her engaged ships were damaged severely or lightly; hundreds of planes had been shot down, and between 7,475 and 10,000 Japanese seamen died. The Japanese Navy as a fighting fleet had ceased to exist; Leyte Gulf was a blow from which the enemy never recovered.

But for the United States it was, nevertheless, incomplete victory when we might have swept the boards. The penalty of divided command,[17] of failure to "fix definite areas of responsibility," and unwarranted assumptions by both Kinkaid and Halsey [q] led to the surprise of our jeep carriers and to the escape of Kurita with his battered survivors, including four battleships, and of Ozawa with ten of his original seventeen vessels. Admiral Halsey ran to the north, leaving behind a force (the Seventh Fleet) inadequate in strength and speed to insure Kurita's destruction, and then just at the time when he was about to destroy all of Ozawa's force, he turned about and ran to the south in answer to Kinkaid's urgent calls for help.[r] The Japanese "lure" worked, but the *Shō* plan, which depended funda-

636

mentally upon good communications, split-second co-ordination, and bold leadership, foundered in complete and fatal failure.

To the United States the cost of overwhelming victory was 2,803 lives, several hundred aircraft, one light carrier, two escort carriers, and the "small boys" who had helped turn the tide of battle—destroyers *Johnston* and *Hoel* and destroyer escort *Samuel B. Roberts,* fought by "well-trained crews in an inspired manner in accordance with the highest traditions of the Navy."

NOTES The battle for Leyte Gulf will be, forever, a source of some controversy, comparable to—though in no way as bitter as—the Sampson-Schley controversy after the Spanish-American War, or the Jellicoe-Beatty differences after Jutland. [18] Admiral Halsey and Admiral Kinkaid to this day believe their judgments were justified; each feels the other could—and should—have covered San Bernardino Strait.[8]

Leyte Gulf is a case history of the importance of communications to victory. Grossly inadequate communications made the co-ordination essential to Japanese success impossible; Kurita, for instance, never received Ozawa's messages. [19] But in the U.S. forces too many messages—and some messages improperly phrased [20]—led to the assumptions which made possible Kurita's surprise of Sprague's jeep carriers.

On October 24, while Third Fleet was launching its air attacks against Kurita, who was then in the Sibuyan Sea, Halsey sent out "a preparatory dispatch" [t] to his principal Third Fleet commanders designating four of his six fast battleships, with supporting units, as Task Force 34.[8] This task group was to be detached from the main fleet and used as a surface battle line against the Japanese surface ships if developments warranted. Halsey did not actually form this task force; he merely informed his own commanders that this was a "battle plan" to be executed when directed. However, Kinkaid, Nimitz and Vice-Admiral Marc A. Mitscher intercepted this message, though it was not directed to any of them, and later in the battle—and partly because of subsequent messages—all misconstrued it.

When Halsey made his decision late in the evening of the twenty-fourth to steam north with all his available fleet and attack Ozawa, he informed Kinkaid that he was "proceeding north with three groups." Kinkaid, having intercepted the earlier message about Task Force 34, thought Halsey was taking his three carrier groups to the north and was leaving four of his six fast battleships to guard San Bernardino Strait. But Kinkaid, busy with preparations for the night action of Surigao Strait, did not specifically ask Halsey whether or not Task Force 34 was guarding San Bernardino Strait until 0412, October 25, and he did not get a negative reply from Halsey until just about the time Kurita burst out of the morning mists upon the surprised Sprague.

If Kinkaid had tried to clarify the situation earlier; if he had *not* intercepted the Task Force 34 message, or if Halsey had reported to him that he was "proceeding north with all my available forces," instead of "proceeding north with three groups," the surprise would not have occurred.[u]

There was one other factor that contributed to surprise. Kinkaid *did* send one or two aircraft to scout southward of San Bernardino Strait along the coast of Samar on the night of the twenty-fourth–twenty-fifth and the morning of the twenty-fifth. There was no report from the night search plane—a lumbering PBY "Black Cat," and the dawn search did not start until about the time Kurita's top hamper appeared over the horizon.[21] Halsey's fleet also sent out night "snoopers" and one report was received by Third Fleet on the night of the twenty-fourth indicating Kurita had turned east again toward San Bernardino.

The fact remains, however, that there had been no clear understanding, prior to the event, between Seventh and Third Fleets about San Bernardino Strait; the "coordination" required by Admiral Halsey's orders was defective, and he himself has written (in the *U.S. Naval Institute Pro-*

638

ceedings) [22] that Leyte Gulf "illustrates the necessity for a single naval command in a combat area responsible for and in full control of all combat units involved.*

"Division of operational control in a combat area leads at the least to confusion, lack of coordination, and overloaded communications (a fault which was pronounced during the battle on the American side), and could result in disaster."

In Third Fleet's after-action report of January 25, 1945, Admiral Halsey's reasoning which led him to take all of his available forces to the north in answer to Ozawa's "lure" is phrased as follows:

"Admiral Kinkaid appeared to have every advantage of position and power with which to cope with the Southern (Japanese) force. The Center force might plod on through San Bernardino Strait toward Leyte, but good damage assessment reports, carefully evaluated, convinced Commander Third Fleet, that even if Center Force did sortie from San Bernardino Strait, its fighting efficiency had been too greatly impaired to be able to win a decision against the Leyte forces (Seventh Fleet). The Northern force (Ozawa) was powerful, dangerous, undamaged, and as yet unhampered. Commander Third Fleet decided to (a) strike the Northern force suddenly and in full force; (b) keep all his forces concentrated; and (c) trust to his judgment as to the fatally weakened condition of the Center force—judgment which happily was vindicated by the Japs' inability to deal with the CVE's and small fry which stood toe-to-toe with them and stopped them in their tracks." [23]

Admiral Kinkaid's position, as stated in *Battle Report,* obviously does not agree completely with these conclusions:

". . . one must keep in mind the *missions* of the forces," Admiral Kinkaid is quoted. "The key to the Battle for Leyte Gulf lies in the missions of the two fleets.

"The mission must be clearly understood. The mission of the Seventh Fleet was to land and support the invasion force. My title was Commander of the Central Philippines Attack Force. Our job was to land troops and keep them ashore. The ships were armed accordingly with a very low percentage of armor-piercing projectiles.[w] The CVE's carried anti-personnel bombs instead of torpedoes and heavy bombs. We were not prepared to fight a naval action. . . .

"The only thing I can think of that I would have done differently if I had known Kurita was definitely coming through San Bernardino unopposed is that I would have moved the northern CVE group more to the south and I would have had a striking group from the escort carriers up looking for him at dawn.

"What mistakes were made during the battle were *not* due to lack of plans. Any errors made were errors of judgment, not errors of organization. The two areas coming together—the Central Pacific and the Southwest Pacific— posed a difficult problem of command, but one head would not have altered things." [24] [x]

Despite errors of omission and commission and initially exaggerated reports of damage by our fliers, Leyte Gulf was indubitably a major American victory. But the Japanese, who had a gambling chance—never of all-out victory —but at the best of causing the United States sufficient losses to extend the war, contributed to their own decisive defeat—by their communications failure,[y] their lack of air cover, the unco-ordinated nature of their air and surface operations, amazing deficiencies in timing, and the irresolution or blundering ineptitude of three of their four principal commanders. Only Admiral Ozawa, the "bait," really carried out his mission.

Luck, as well as judgment, obviously played a major part in the battle. But luck lay, in the final analysis, with the larger fleet and the more skilled commanders. The Japanese took their "eye off the ball," abandoned their fundamental objective—the thin-skinned amphibious shipping in Leyte Gulf—in the midst of battle, and thereby violated a cardinal military principle.

And the Americans—Third and Seventh Fleets—as Admiral Halsey radioed to Hawaii and Washington, broke "the back" of the Japanese Fleet "in the course of protecting our Leyte landings."

SPECIAL NOTES BY
ADMIRAL THOMAS C. KINKAID, USN (RET.)

The notes are keyed to numerals or letters in text.
Explanatory material in brackets inserted by author.

1. The invasion armada was "MacArthur's armada" in the sense that it came from his area, S.W.P.A. [Southwest Pacific Area], and might well be called the "great armada from Down Under" [or from MacArthur's area, or S.W. P.A.]. MacArthur derived his authority from the Combined Chiefs of Staff. He was designated "Supreme Commander" in S.W.P.A. and was specifically prohibited from taking personal command of any of his forces. He was required to exercise command through his three major commanders for land, sea, and air, Blamey [General Sir George Blamey, Australian Army general commanding land forces]; Kinkaid, and Kenney [General George C. Kenney, U.S. Army Air Forces, commanding air forces].

From the time we departed from ports in the Admiralties and New Guinea to invade the Philippines, I had direct command of the "armada," including the Army forces embarked, until I turned over command of the Army forces ashore in Leyte to Krueger [Lt. Gen. Walter Krueger, commanding Sixth Army]. MacArthur was present as a passenger in his capacity as Supreme Commander, Southwest Pacific Area. I exercised direct command, as witness the fact that I decided to go ahead with the operation without referring to MacArthur when Halsey sent a despatch, received when we were a few hours out from Hollandia, stating that he was concentrating his forces to attack the Japanese Fleet and would not be able to give the planned support to our landing at Leyte. When MacArthur joined our convoy, I sent him a bridge signal: "Welcome to our city." He replied with a gracious message referring to the fact that this was the first time he had sailed under my command and ending with: "Believe it or not we are on our way."

2. Nishimura was due in Leyte one hour before Kurita. He was ahead of schedule without reason—a serious error

641

in a coordinated effort. Kurita was late for good and sufficient reasons.

3. The Seventh Fleet had eighteen CVE's. Two had been sent to Halmahera for replacement planes and only sixteen were present during the action. The Seventh Fleet had a few PBY's, tender-based. Counting eighteen CVE's, the total number of [U.S.] carriers was thirty-four.

4. It is interesting that the *Darter* and *Dace* paced Kurita through the night in Palawan Passage and attacked at dawn—a good job. An extremely important fact, from the operations point of view, is that Kurita was separated from most of his communication personnel in the transfer from *Atago* to *Kishanani* to *Yamato*. Any naval commander will sympathize with him in that situation.

5. Only one strike was made on Nishimura and that only by small search-attack scouting groups. Davison [Rear Admiral Ralph E. Davison, commanding Task Group 38.4 of the Third Fleet] reported that the move to concentrate was taking him out of range of the enemy southern force, but Halsey continued the concentration. In the Seventh Fleet we felt well able to take care of the [enemy] southern force and had all day to make plans for its reception. I was not informed directly by Halsey that he was leaving Nishimura to me.

6. Halsey had ordered a morning search to northward by the northern group, but Jap attacks prevented it from getting off until the afternoon.

7. In the Seventh Fleet we had counted noses carefully and had come to the conclusion that only two BB's [battleships]—*Ise* and *Hyuga*—could be with Ozawa in the [enemy] northern force.

8. Halsey had four groups of carriers and had given preparatory orders to form TF [Task Force] 34. ". . . proceeding north with three groups" is phraseology which failed to give information of vital import not only to me and to Nimitz but to many others. Mitscher [Vice-Admiral

Marc A. Mitscher, commanding Task Force 38—the four carrier task groups and their supporting combat ships of the Third Fleet] actually sent instructions for the employment of the two BB's which were to stay with him, believing that TF 34 would be left behind to guard San Bernardino. It was impossible to believe anything else. The proposed composition of TF 34 was exactly correct in the circumstances.

Even though Halsey banked "too heavily" on the exaggerated claims of his pilots, he knew from the *Independence* night search planes that Kurita was headed for San Bernardino and he should have realized:

a. That the composition of the Seventh Fleet was designed to provide support for the amphibious landing and the troops ashore—not for major combat. Slow speed of the old battleships and a high proportion of high-capacity projectiles in their magazines made them an inadequate adversary for the Japanese central force, even if they had been available and were filled with fuel and ammunition.

b. That the Seventh Fleet would be engaged through the night with surface forces in Surigao Strait and, in any case, could not leave Leyte Gulf unguarded and take station off San Bernardino.

c. That the three CVE groups of the Seventh Fleet would be on station at daylight 25 Oct. carrying out their mission and would need cover.

d. That my destroyers would have expended their torpedoes in Surigao Strait and that the battleships would be low in AP ammunition and even in HC ammunition, having rendered gunfire support to forces ashore for several days.

9. Rarely has a commander had all day to stay quietly (except for the antics of Jap planes) in port and prepare without serious interruption for a night action. The tactical dispositions and plans of the Seventh Fleet were checked and counterchecked by all concerned.

10. I believe contact was made about 2215 [10:15 p.m.] a few miles south of Bohol Island. All three PT's of that

group were damaged by gunfire and unable to report the contact, but one of them (using his head) managed to make contact with the next PT group to eastward which sent through a message, which was received by Oldendorf [Rear Admiral J. B. Oldendorf, who was in tactical or direct command at Surigao Strait] about twenty-six minutes after midnight.

11. Fired by *PT 137*. The PT fired at a destroyer, missed, but hit and badly damaged the cruiser [*Abukuma*].

12. No, we did not think that the Jap central force was west of the Philippines, but we did think that TF 34 was guarding San Bernardino.

Also, it is of interest that in Leyte Gulf the temporary headquarters of the Army commanders were only a few yards from the water's edge and the beaches were piled high with food and supplies and ammunition for immediate use. Destruction of those supply dumps would have left our forces ashore without food and ammunition. Halsey has said that Kurita could only have "harassed" our forces in Leyte Gulf.

13. I think it should be pointed out that the first six words of Nimitz's despatch was "padding" [inserted by the communications officer for code security]. The despatch was first brought to me without padding, as it should have been. Later I was told of the "padding." [Halsey originally took this phrase, "All the world wants to know . . ." as tacit criticism of him and was irritated.]

14. The attack of the DD's [destroyers] and DE's [destroyer escorts] against the Jap heavy ships was the most courageous and also the most effective incident brought to my attention during the war.

15. Kurita committed a grave error in losing tactical control of his force. He had lost most of his communication personnel. He had been seriously damaged by torpedo hits from Seventh Fleet planes and surface ships and by bomb hits from Seventh Fleet planes, and the upper works of his

644

ships, charthouse, radio, etc., suffered from five-inch shell-fire and from strafing. His ships sheered out of formation to dodge torpedo attacks, real or dummy, made by planes and escort vessels. Soon his individual units became widely separated, which he should not have permitted, and he could not see his forces, or the enemy's, because of the heavy smoke laid by the CVE's and their escorts. He was confused and his subordinates did not help him by reporting the nature of the enemy they were attacking. Ozawa had failed to inform him of his success in drawing Halsey away. Also, I have no doubt that Kurita was physically exhausted after three grueling days.

16. McCain sensed what was going on long before Halsey did and he launched his strike beyond range for a return flight—340 miles.

The following paragraphs constitute my analysis of what occurred:

Halsey had done exactly what the Japs wanted him to do. He had left San Bernardino unguarded, permitting Kurita to pass through the strait unopposed. Having taken all six of his BB's 300 miles to the north, when two would have been adequate and four were needed at San Bernardino, he belatedly at 11:15 turned south in response to my appeals and to the despatch from Nimitz, again taking all six BB's with him and leaving Mitscher without any. Mitscher urgently needed two BB's. By that time, 11:15, Mitscher's planes had developed Ozawa's force and the *Ise* and *Hyuga* were known to be with him, but Halsey took all six BB's south. Later Mitscher sent DuBose [Rear Admiral Laurence T. DuBose] to mop up the cripples (with four cruisers and twelve destroyers). Ozawa was informed of the actions of DuBose, and sent the *Ise* and *Hyuga* south to look for him. Fortunately the Jap BB's passed to eastward of our cruisers on their way south and again on their return course to northward.

Halsey informed me that he would arrive off San Bernardino at 0800 26 Oct. Too late! Later, at 1600 [4 p.m.], after fueling, he decided to speed up and took two of his fastest BB's, *Iowa* and *New Jersey*, with three cruisers and eight DD's, south at 28 knots. He missed Kurita entering the strait by two hours. Suppose he had intercepted him? Were two BB's enough?

Suppose Halsey had turned south at top speed immediately upon receipt of my first urgent message at 0825. He would have been about five hours closer to San Bernardino. Actually he steamed north for two and three quarters hours at 25 knots—69 miles—whereas if he had steamed south at 28 knots—77 miles—there would have been a total of 146 miles difference in his 11:15 position.

The net result of all of this was that the six strongest battleships in the world—except the *Yamato* and *Musashi*—steamed about 300 miles north and 300 miles south during the "greatest naval battle of the Second World War and the largest engagement ever fought upon the high seas"—and they did not fire a single shot. I can well imagine the feelings of my classmate, Lee [Rear Admiral Willis A. Lee, commanding the battleships of Third Fleet].

Even today Halsey believes it was not a mistake to take the whole Third Fleet north and he apparently overlooks the fact that the absence of TF 34 from San Bernardino Strait precluded the total destruction of Kurita's force on the spot, to say nothing of the loss of American lives and ships of the CVE force. The threat to our invasion of the Philippines seems not to have come to his mind. Halsey has stated that I should have sent CVE planes to scout the Sibuyan Sea and San Bernardino Strait during the night of 24-25 Oct. As is evident, I believed that TF 34 was guarding San Bernardino and that Lee was being kept informed by the night-flying planes from the *Independence*. Actually, I did order a search to the northward during the night by PBY's and a search toward San Bernardino at daylight by CVE planes, mostly out of curiosity to find out what was going on.

Even if I had known that San Bernardino was wide open, I did not have the force to meet Kurita. You have quoted me correctly from *Battle Report*. I would not have denuded Leyte Gulf of a defense force. I would have moved the CVE's clear of direct contact with Kurita's surface forces. And, of course, I would have sent planes from the CVE's to

646

keep track of Kurita, although none were equipped or trained for night search.

In that case would Kurita have reached Leyte? It is interesting to speculate. It is very possible. His direct contact with the northern group of CVE's, though painful to us, delayed his progress, seriously damaged his forces, and so confused him that he turned back within two hours of his goal.

17. "Divided command" is, of course, not sound procedure. The hard, cold fact is, however, that despite the divided command both Halsey and I had what appeared to me to be clear-cut, definite missions. Had Halsey been mindful of his covering mission when Ozawa beckoned him to come north, he never would have left San Bernardino wide open. Also, he would have told me in a clearly worded despatch just what he was going to do about it.

The "unwarranted assumption" which you attribute to me probably refers to my assumption that TF 34 was guarding San Bernardino. Perhaps that was unwarranted, but, to my not unprejudiced mind, all logic seems to point the other way. Halsey's mission included covering our amphibious operation from interruption by the Japanese Fleet. His preparatory order to form TF 34, which I intercepted, set up a plan to guard San Bernardino against the passage of Kurita's forces which was perfect in concept and perfect in composition of the forces assigned to TF 34. I did not intercept further modifying messages regarding TF 34. Had I done so, I most certainly would not have remained silent.

It was inconceivable that Halsey could have scrapped a perfect plan. His message, "going north with three groups," meant to me that TF 34 plus a carrier group was being left behind—entirely sound. Not only did I and my staff believe it, and Nimitz and, presumably, his staff believe it, but Mitscher and his staff believed it also. As I have already pointed out, Mitscher actually gave orders for utilization of the two battleships which were to accompany him on the northern trek [four of the Third Fleet's six battleships were to have been left behind in TF 34 to guard San Bernardino; two were to have gone north with Mitscher's carriers after

Ozawa]. When Mitscher and his staff found out that TF 34 was not being left to guard the strait, his chief of staff— [Captain] Arleigh Burke, tried to get Mitscher to send a message to Halsey on the subject, but Mitscher declined on the ground that Halsey probably had information not known to him.

Later in your notes you point out that I did not specifically ask Halsey whether or not TF 34 was guarding San Bernardino until 0412, 25 Oct. That is correct. In the absence of information to the contrary from Halsey, anything else was unthinkable. Early in the morning of 25 Oct. a meeting of the staff was held in my cabin to check for errors of commission or of omission. It broke up about 0400 and my operations officer, Dick Cruzen [Captain Richard H. Cruzen], came back into the cabin and said, "Admiral, I can think of only one other thing. We have never directly asked Halsey if TF 34 is guarding San Bernardino." I told him to send the message.

18. The controversy has not been bitter for the simple and sole reason that I refused to take part in it. I have not publicly stated my side of the case but have kept quiet for ten years—not so Halsey. He has published several articles or interviews in addition to his book endeavoring to justify his actions at Leyte, sometimes at my expense.

19. I believe that the radio on Ozawa's flagship went out with the first bomb hit, but other ships could have sent a message to Kurita for him.

20. Only Halsey's strangely phrased message led to Kurita's surprise of Sprague's carriers.

In the early morning some important messages from me to Halsey were delayed in transmission and that should not have been.

21. Actually one or two PBY's took off from a tender in Surigao Strait to make the northern night search. They were ill equipped for that sort of mission. They had quite a hell of a time because every U.S. ship they came near fired at them. I imagine that their greatest concern was to avoid U.S. ships rather than to find Jap ships.

648

The dawn search ordered from the CVE's should have gotten off much earlier.

22. Halsey's writings in the *Naval Institute Proceedings* were subjective. If he had been mindful of his covering mission, and had no other distractions, the question of "a single naval command" would be purely academic.

23. Halsey's reasoning regarding the [enemy] center force falls short of the mark. His "careful evaluation" of the damage reports was not shared by everyone. Kurita's movements seemed to belie any such evaluation. We knew from our plot that Kurita was approaching San Bernardino at 22 knots. Some plodding! Halsey had a later report from the *Independence* plane which was not forwarded to me. Did he not plot Kurita's progress?

A count of noses by my staff showed that Ozawa's force could not have been as "powerful and dangerous" as Halsey seems to have thought. He took 119 ships north to deal with 19 ships in the [enemy] northern force. An intelligent *division* of his forces was in order. In setting up TF 34, he had actually made that intelligent division of forces but he failed to implement it.

Halsey's decisions (a) and (b) would have been sound if he had had no other obligations. His decision (c) can be described only as erroneous. I doubt if anyone will disagree with the statement that the only reason why Kurita did not reach Leyte Gulf, destroying the CVE's en route, was that he turned back when victory was within his grasp. His [Halsey's] judgment as to the "fatally weakened condition of the [enemy] center force" was definitely shown to be in error. Did his "judgment which was happily vindicated" include a forecast that Kurita would break off the action? If so, his crystal ball was certainly in fine working order. Does anyone believe in the "Japs' *inability* to deal with the CVE's and small fry"? They did not deal with them as they could have, but is that "inability"?

24. I am quoted correctly, but I did not have an opportunity to edit my remarks. In the last line "one head would

not have altered things" might have been reworded because it meant that "one head would not have produced a better end result if both Halsey and I had carried out our specific missions."

SPECIAL NOTES BY
FLEET ADMIRAL WILLIAM F. HALSEY, USN (RET.)

a. I do not remember what Radio Manila was playing. They were usually sending out lying propaganda from "Tokyo Rose" or some other renegade Japanese Nisei. We used Radio Manila as an alarm clock. As soon as we heard the air-raid alarm, we knew our pilots had been sighted.

The change in the American strategy was the direct result of a recommendation sent by me. I recommended that the taking of Yap and Palau be eliminated and that a landing be made in the central Philippines instead of Mindanao. I had once previously recommended that the seizure of Palau be dropped. Admiral Nimitz approved my recommendation, except that about Palau, and immediately forwarded it to the Combined Chiefs of Staff, then sitting in Quebec. General Sutherland, in Hollandia, General MacArthur's chief of staff, in MacArthur's temporary absence, approved the landing in the central Philippines instead of Mindanao. The Combined Chiefs of Staff approved, and it received almost immediate approval from President Roosevelt and Prime Minister Churchill. It was fortunate that the Quebec Conference was on at that time.

The 1st Marine Division had heavy losses on Peleliu (in the Palau group), in many ways comparable to Tarawa. One combat team from the Army 81st (Wildcat) Division also received many losses in the fighting on Peleliu, where they so ably assisted. We constructed airfields on Anguar, captured by the 81st Army Division, and on Peleliu Island, and a partial naval base in Kossol Roads. Kossol Roads was not occupied by the Japanese and we merely had to make arrangement for its defense from the Japanese on Babelthuap Island, the largest island of the Palau archipelago. I mention these actions and this timing to show that this was not a "Monday quarterback" estimate of the situation on my part. Ulithi was not recommended to be dropped, as I always considered this a necessity as a fleet anchorage. It was occupied without opposition. Peleliu, Anguar, and Kossol Roads were a great convenience, but I thought then, and I think now, not a necessity for the further campaign in the Pacific.

The beginning of the end of the war in the Pacific was evident before the Battle of Leyte Gulf. When our fleet obtained freedom of movement, practically anywhere in the Pacific, the Japanese were doomed to defeat.

The *Shō* plan was just another of the many plans the Japs devised. They all failed.

Toyoda had carriers, but with few planes and half-trained pilots. Now that it is the Monday after the Saturday game, everyone seemed to know this excepting my staff and me. We bore the responsibility. If the rest of the Navy did not then know it, we, in the Third Fleet, were thoroughly cognizant that the carrier had replaced the battleship, and was potentially the strongest and most dangerous naval weapon our opponents possessed. We had been fighting the Japs for several years. We did not know how many planes the Japs had, but we could not take a chance. We knew the *Princeton* had been attacked and it was reported they were carrier planes. As we stood northward on the morning of the twenty-sixth, we had a large "bogie" on our screen. We naturally thought they were carrier planes heading toward the Japanese carriers. They finally went off our screen heading toward Luzon. We had been "shuttle-bombed" many times by the Nips, and only once off Guadalcanal had succeeded in reversing this process.

My decision to go north was not based on pilots' reports solely. A possible battle with the Japanese Fleet had long been a matter of discussion and study by us. We had played it frequently on a game board constructed on the deck of the flag quarters. We had long since decided the carriers were potentially the most dangerous ships the Japs had, not only to ourselves, but to MacArthur and the Pacific campaign. We named them our primary targets. We knew Kurita's ships had suffered damage from our attacks, particularly to their upper works and probably to their fire-control instruments. This was borne out by their poor shooting against the baby carriers.

b. The "Turkey Shoot" in the Marianas (the Battle of the Philippine Sea) was a magnificent show. That it alone broke the back of Japanese naval aviation, despite its great success, I seriously doubt. I cannot and will not forget the wonderful American pilots in the South Pacific and Southwest Pacific who had knocked out so many Japanese naval air groups and squadrons based on Rabaul. This statement is based on Japanese answers to American interrogations after the war. The fliers who accomplished this were from the U.S. Army Air Force, U.S. Naval and Marine Aviation, the R.N.Z.A.F. and the R.A.A.F. The Japs made their usual mistake of feeding in these groups piecemeal and were thoroughly knocked out.

c. The Japanese Navy had a number of carriers nearing completion in the Inland Sea. I have a fairly good-sized circular plaque, presented to me after the war. In the middle is a U.S. ensign—around the U.S. ensign and near the periphery are the silhouettes of various Japanese ships representing carriers, battleships, a heavy cruiser, light cruisers, and submarines. On the periphery it bears the inscription: "Plaque made of metal obtained from these vessels sunk by U.S. Carrier planes, July 1945 at Kure Naval Base, Kure, Japan." The names and numbers are interesting. CV-ASO, CV-AMAGI, CVE-RYUHO, BB-ISE, BB-HYUGA, BB-HARUNA, CA-SETTSU, CL-TONE, CL-OYADA (fleet flagship), CL-AOBA, CL-IZUMA, CL-AWATE and 5 SS. (CV large carrier, CVE small or jeep carrier, BB battleship, CA heavy cruiser, CL light cruiser, and SS submarines.)

We had orders to get rid of the Japanese Navy so that they could not interfere with the Russians if they decided to invade Japan. I sometimes wonder, in view of present-day events! Of course these ships were sitting ducks, and even high-altitude bombing, with some luck, might have hit them.

There is one Japanese cruiser that I would have felt sorry

652

for, if I could have felt sorry for a Japanese man-of-war in those days. She had escaped from the Battle of Leyte Gulf, sorely wounded. The Japs had brought her into a bay or cove on the west side of Luzon, and heavily camouflaged her and made her almost invisible. They were working night and day to make her seaworthy to return her to the home land. In the meantime, our fliers were combing every nook and corner, looking for Jap ships. As one of our last flights was about to return, a lucky photograph was taken of this hideout. Our photographic interpreters made out this cruiser. A heavy strike was made on her the first thing next morning, and that was curtains for this cruiser.

d. A "Betty" tried to land among our parked planes on the *Enterprise* during our attack on the Marshall and Gilbert Islands on 1 Feb. 1942 (Eastern Time). Thanks to the masterly ship handling by then Captain, now Admiral (Retired), George D. Murray, U.S. Navy, the "Betty" was forced into a slip while coming up "the groove" and did only minor damage. The "Betty" hit the edge of the flight deck, broke her back, and went over the side. She was undoubtedly on fire when she hit us. She cut off a gasoline riser aft and set it on fire. She cut off another gasoline riser forward, but no fire resulted, and cut off the tail of one of our SBD planes. The fire from the gasoline riser was soon under control, and I remember no further damage, except some slight and easily repairable damage to the flight deck. This was my first encounter with a Kamikaze plane; I saw many later. I doubt if this Japanese even knew he was a Kamikaze. She had dropped all her bombs and fortunately, for us, missed the *Enterprise*. His intentions were very clear. He knew his plane was doomed, and determined to do us as much damage as possible. He tried to land among some thirty-five or forty of our planes, lately returned from a strike, refueling and awaiting the return of all planes for respotting. The quick thinking of the ship's captain prevented what might have been a catastrophe. I do not mean to detract from Rear Admiral Masabumi Arima's very brave, but very foolhardy, suicide dive. Apparently we fought to live, the Japanese to die.

e. My orders went further than the quoted "to cover and support forces in the Southwest Pacific, in order to assist in the seizure and occupation of objectives in the Central Philippines." This is being written from memory without the advantage of notes, so my overriding orders can only be vaguely quoted. They were that, other conditions notwithstanding, the destruction of the Japanese Fleet was my paramount objective.

f. "Necessary measures for detailed coordination of operations between the [Third Fleet] and the [Seventh Fleet] will be arranged by their commanders." These are just so many words and nothing more. They were impossible of accomplishment. Kinkaid and I had not seen each other since we met in Hollandia, just after the plans for the invasion of the Philippines had been changed. Some key members of my staff and I had flown from Saipan to Hollandia to discuss preliminary arrangements with Kinkaid and his staff and MacArthur's staff. Both Kinkaid and I had been too busily occupied to confer during the Philippine invasion. This illustrates, as nothing else can, the importance of a unified command in the combat zone. Had Kinkaid or I been in Supreme Command at the time of the Battle of Leyte Gulf, I am sure it would have been fought differently. Whether for better or for worse can never be answered.

g. Night snoopers not only scouted the northern force but also the Sibuyan Sea and made reports of Kurita turning once again to the eastward—heading toward San Bernardino Strait. A report of this was directed sent to Kinkaid around 2100 or 2130 that night.

h. I had no operational control of submarines, except those specifically assigned to us for some operation. I had no submarines assigned to me at that time.

i. I never thought Kurita's force had been stopped by the day's air attacks. I had received and directed transmittal of a report that his force was again heading toward San Bernardino Strait. I did not bank too heavily on so-called exag-

654

gerated claims from pilots. We had rather good evaluation of pilots' reports at this time. I did think Kurita had been rather badly mauled by our pilots, particularly in their upper works and that their fire control would be poor. Their poor shooting against the CVE's, destroyers, and destroyer escorts the next day tended to corroborate this. I did not expect them to be opposed by CVE's, destroyers, and destroyer escorts. Their thin skins probably saved them somewhat. After the Battle of Guadalcanal, in which Rear Admiral Callaghan and Rear Admiral Scott lost their lives, there were some thin-skinned ships that were holed by heavy-armor piercing shells with little damage. I remember one destroyer, I have forgotten her name, that I inspected later. As I remember it, she had fourteen 14-inch hits from a Jap battleship. Her commanding officer was Commander Coward. Never did a man have a name so inappropriate to fit with his actions in battle.

j. I object to the statement "that on such misunderstandings rest the course of history and the fate of nations." I had no misunderstandings, with the possible exception (if true) that the Jap carriers had no planes. I knew what I was doing at all times, and deliberately took the risks, in order to get rid of the Jap carriers. My estimate that the Seventh Fleet could take care of Kurita's battered forces was amply justified even against the CVE's and small fry during the action of Oct. 26. These brave American ships put up a fight that will be an epic for all time. My hat is off to them.

k. The battle of Surigao Strait, with Admiral Oldendorf in tactical command, was beautifully conceived and executed. Never has a T been so efficiently capped, and never has a force been so completely defeated and demoralized as was the Jap Surigao force.

l. I am still far from sure that Ozawa's force was intended solely as a lure. The Japs had continuously lied during the war, even to each other. Why believe them implicitly as soon as the war ends? They had plenty of time, before reciting them, to make their stories fit their needs. Despite

655

their "banzai" charges, their "Kamikaze" planes, their "foolish bombs" (men-driven), their one- and two-man submarines, built for the purpose of sacrificing their crew, and the many other foolish things they did, it is still difficult for me to believe that they would deliberately use their potentially most dangerous ships as deliberate sacrifices. This is partially borne out by reports from Americans who interviewed Admiral Kurita after the war. When asked why he turned away from Leyte Gulf, he stated that he intended to join forces with Ozawa and attack the Third Fleet.

m. Admiral Nimitz's despatch to me was "Where is Task Force 34?" The despatch as quoted is a gross violation of security regulations. [This despatch has been quoted in its entirety in numerous previous publications.]

n. I note the Seventh Fleet is described as red-eyed from days of shore bombardment and nights of battle. My fleet had been fighting almost continually since early September. When we finally reached Ulithi in late September, for rest and replenishment, we were chased out by a typhoon after a one-night stand. We were almost continually in combat, until some time after the Battle of Leyte Gulf. I wonder what color my splendid pilots' eyes were? I do not know, but I do know they were approaching a stage of exhaustion that kept me on edge. I dared not let up on the Japs when we were running them ragged. This goes for all my officers and men, manning battle stations, above and below decks. It was an almost unendurable strain. We fought no battle for Cape Engano—we fought to do away with the Jap carriers.

o. I knew what force Kinkaid had and believed them capable of taking on Kurita's damaged force. I did not know of Kinkaid's ammunition situation in his old battleships. I have since been told that one of these battleships in the Surigao Strait action did not fire a single shot from her main battery.

In moving north, I took a calculated risk. I figured then, and still believe, that if Kurita had arrived at Leyte Gulf he

could make nothing but a "hit-and-run bombardment."
While in command of the South Pacific, my forces in Guadalcanal had many times been bombarded by Japanese battleships, cruisers, and destroyers. The forces ashore caught un-
merciful hell, but these bombardments served to delay us
no more than a short time. Shipping put to sea, usually only
partly unloaded, and moved away from the bombardment
area. The troops ashore had to take it in such dugouts as
they had. On most occasions I had no heavy fighting ships
to oppose them, and they bombarded at their leisure. On
one occasion PT boats drove them away. On another, Dan
Callaghan and Norm Scott (both rear admirals) made the
supreme sacrifice, but with their few ships, cruisers, anti-
aircraft vessels and destroyers, they routed the Japanese
forces consisting of battleships, cruisers, and destroyers.
Their supreme sacrifice was not in vain. As a direct result
of this action, the Japanese lost the battleship *Hiyei*—left a
derelict and sunk by our planes the next day. During one of
their last bombardments, we had been able to fool them
and got two of our new battleships near Savo Island, the
South Dakota and the *Washington*, under command of Rear
Admiral, later Vice-Admiral, W. A. Lee, Jr., USN. As a result of the night action that followed, the Japs lost various
destroyers and one battleship. She was sunk that night.

p. A statement is made that Kurita's intercepted radio
traffic convinced him, erroneously, that Leyte airstrips were
operational. This was not entirely erroneous. Admiral Mc-
Cain flew his planes off at such a distance that it was impossible for them to return to their mother carriers. They were
directed to land on Leyte airstrips. They did, and for a few
days thereafter they operated from these fields until I was
directed to return them to Ulithi. This was done, via Palau
to Ulithi. Incidentally, I do not remember seeing a report of
the damage McCain's fliers inflicted on Kurita's force. It
must have been not inconsiderable.

q. I do not fully understand what the author means by
unwarranted assumptions by me. Possibly that I placed too
much credence in the pilots' reports; I do not believe that I

657

did. These reports were carefully evaluated, and after due consideration a calculated risk was taken. My estimate that the Seventh Fleet could take care of Kurita's battered forces was amply justified. "The proof of the pudding is in the eating." Remember this estimate was "Saturday quarterbacking" and not "Monday quarterbacking."

r. I am in agreement that I made a mistake in bowing to pressure and turning south. I consider this the gravest error I committed during the Battle of Leyte Gulf.

s. I have never stated, to my knowledge and remembrance, that Kinkaid could and should have covered San Bernardino Strait. I have stated that I felt that Kinkaid's force could have taken care of Kurita's battered force, and furthermore, that Kurita was only capable of a hit-and-run attack if he entered Leyte Gulf. Such an attack, by my experience in the South Pacific, would have little effect on the troops ashore and could cause only a slight delay in the over-all picture.

t. I did not send a preparatory despatch, but instead a "Battle Plan" addressed only to the Third Fleet. To insure that the Third Fleet did not misunderstand, I sent a further message saying this plan would not be executed until directed by me. As Commander Task Force 38, Vice-Admiral Mitscher should have received both messages.

u. The statement that, had I sent a despatch to Kinkaid that I was "proceeding north with all my available forces" instead of "proceeding north with three groups," the surprise would not have occurred is purely academic. I did not know that he had intercepted my battle plan and believed it had been executed. A carrier task group was well defined, and every naval commander in the area knew its composition. My despatch was a correct one. I had notified all interested parties when Admiral McCain's Carrier Task Group started for Ulithi. I am sure no one misconstrued that message.

658

v. I have explained before that orders requiring "coordination" were mere words and meant nothing. I still stand by what I have written about Leyte Gulf, that "it illustrates the necessity for a single naval command in a combat area, responsible for, and in full control of, all combat units involved."

w. I knew nothing of how the Seventh Fleet was armed. At that time I believe we were rearming the Third Fleet under way. I gave no thought to the Seventh Fleet's armament of shells.

x. I am in agreement with Admiral Kinkaid when he says any errors made were errors of judgment. I am in complete disagreement when he states, "The two areas coming together—the Central Pacific and the Southwest Pacific— posed a difficult problem of command, but one head would not have altered things." As I have previously stated, "had either Admiral Kinkaid or I been in supreme command, the battle would have been fought quite differently."

y. There is only one word to describe the communications on the American side during this battle, and that word is rotten. We sent in a long report describing the deficiencies and interference we encountered, also a recommendation for drastic changes. As I remember, our combat circuit was filled with long and relatively unimportant intelligence summaries that could and should have been deferred. Most of these were not Navy reports. As a consequence, there were long and intolerable delays in getting urgent messages through. This should never be permitted again.

These comments have been written almost entirely from memory and without the advantage of any notes or reports. I hope I am not trusting my memory too far; ten and a half years is a long time.

Japan's Doorstep

The Japanese Navy was destroyed. Adm. Ozawa admitted that, after this battle, their surface forces were strictly "auxiliary"; from now on, the war was carried on only by the land forces, land-based air power and special Kamikaze attacks.

But the U.S. Navy's job didn't end here; during 1945 there would be fierce fighting in the waters around Okinawa, primarily against the Kamikaze planes.

The naval war might be in its last stage, but some of the worst fighting was still to come. There was still Okinawa to be taken; and, before that, the Marines were to be tested once again—this time in the crucible of Iwo Jima, about eight hundred miles from Tokyo. Iwo was within P-51 range of Japan; as an American base, it could provide Japan-bound bombers with fighter escort to the target and back.

"The bulk of the defenses in central Iwo were strictly man-made. Except for Mount Suribachi and the rugged northern third of the island, the terrain provided few naturally strong positions. . . . The land, however, lent itself readily to preparation. The beaches and most of the soil consisted of a curious loose volcanic ash, variously described as a coarse sand and a fine gravel.

"Tunnels ran clear under the airfields, connecting positions hundreds of yards apart. One, explored for 800 yards, contained two battalion command posts, complete with electric lights and hooked up with all sectors by means of an elaborate communications system.

"The strange ash combined with cement to make a concrete of very superior quality, and this was everywhere. Artillery, mortars, anti-tank guns reposed in emplacements with reinforced walls four to eight feet thick, from which they were trundled out for firing through armor-plate doors or on rails, or were fired through fixed ports barely above ground level. Entire hills were hollowed out, to be reconstructed from within.

"Iwo had been pounded intermittently from the air ever since our capture of bases in the Marianas, and from the sea on several occa-

660

sions. In anticipation of a 20 January D-Day, American air power began what was to prove a record softening-up, Army, Navy and Marine Corps flyers working the island over in turn and in conjunction. For a while the most noticeable effect of this was increased resistance. Time after time the airfields were reported neutralized, only to have the next day's flight met by swarming enemy fighters and anti-aircraft fire of increased volume and accuracy. Involvement of the fleet in the Philippines necessitated postponing the landing until 3 February—but the air assault continued. It continued following the final postponement, until 19 February, by which time it had been sustained at full pitch for seventy-two days.

"H-Hour was set for 0900, 19 February.

"Everything seemed to work splendidly during that first hour. Resistance was scattered and sporadic, rated as slight to moderate. It began to look as though at last the long-sought-for result had been achieved: the neutralization of a fortified island by naval gunfire.

"But if the Japanese were giving little trouble at this particular stage, nature was giving plenty. The amphtracks hit the beach, only to find themselves in trouble immediately. Assault troops leaped to the ground to carry their rush forward—to find themselves up to their calves, or deeper, in that strange, loose volcanic ash which comprised the greater part of Iwo's soil. . . . Amphtracks, lurching and staggering across the beach, brought up short before a high terrace of the same material varying from five to eighteen feet, unscalable in most places because it afforded no traction. The forward rush of troops became a grim plodding. . . .

"Then all hell began to break loose. From Suribachi to the south, and the tangle of ridges to the north, artillery and mortars of all shapes and sizes commenced pounding the beach area and the water immediately offshore which the landing craft must traverse. That these weapons had been carefully ranged in beforehand for this particular purpose was all too apparent. The fire was deadly.

"The infantry, which had driven two hundred to three hundred yards inland with no great difficulty, found themselves suddenly pinned down. Harmless-appearing sand hummocks spat automatic weapons fire from narrow apertures only a few inches above ground level. Underground pillboxes and blockhouses, these proved to be reinforced concrete sunk deep in the shifting sand. The successive terraces leading up to the central table-land were studded with them. Tanks, lumbering up from the beach with great difficulty, ran into the fire of those deadly Japanese 47-mm. guns. Land mines were everywhere. The grim aspect

661

of Iwo Jima, which during the next three weeks was to make the bloodiest operation ever handled by the Marine Corps, had begun in earnest.

"The final breakthrough to Iwo's northeastern shore occurred early in the afternoon of D-plus eighteen (9 March), and it was the 3rd Division, in the center, which achieved it. Other divisions, claiming that the 3rd consisted of a pack of glory hunters, pointed out that in their hurry to be first they had by-passed many unconquered strongpoints which remained to plague them from the rear. Which was true, except that the same applied in varying degree to virtually every unit on the island. With the enemy dug so deeply into ridges and the sides of ravines, in caves connected by tortuous underground passageways, it was a literal impossibility to seal them all up during the initial advance." *

The following selection deals with this very problem; it is taken from "U.S. Marines on Iwo Jima," a report compiled by five Marine Corps Combat Correspondents.

IWO: JUNGLE OF STONE

by Marine Combat Writers **

The northern half of Iwo, beyond the Japs' cross-island defenses, was a desolate, broken area of smoking sulphuric sand and barren, jagged ridges. The tall masses of rock sprawled and tumbled without pattern, where a series of earthquakes had once pushed up millions of tons of volcanic stone and left them lying in craggy heights and bare, sharp-edged spines several hundred yards long.

The looming rocks and narrow chasms added new terrors to the advancing Marines. It was like going through a miniature Grand Canyon, with Japs hidden in hundreds of caves

* Maj. Frank Hough, *The Island War,* pp. 331, 337-39, 350.
** Capt. Raymond Henri, 1st Lt. Jim Lucas, T/Sgt. David Dempsey, T/Sgt. W. Keyes Beech, T/Sgt. Alvin Josephy, Jr.

and pillboxes among the rocks and boulders. Moreover, the ridges, which often rose to the height of three-story houses, were undermined and laced like other parts of the island with interconnecting tunnels in which the Japs could hide. The rocks could be painfully and methodically cleared of Japs again and again, but always the enemy managed to reappear from inner caverns and recesses to harass our rear.

The fighting from approximately D plus 16 to D plus 25, around one such ridge that lay in the 3rd Division's zone of action near the third airfield, was typical of the struggles waged for all of them—struggles characterized not only by close-in, bitter combat, but also by a seemingly endless series of tragic episodes and unexpected deaths.

We first saw this particular ridge during one of the many battles that had flamed among its peaks and gullies. Its tall, twisting mass—running almost ten city blocks in length— looked as if it had been hit by many heavy explosions. The rocks and boulders had tumbled down the ridge's slopes in chaotic landslides. You had to look closely to distinguish the black mouths of cave entrances and the carefully camouflaged pillbox positions that lay among the debris.

White clouds from American smoke grenades made the scene unearthly. It blew like steam across the ridge's stone walls. Three American tanks lay 50 yards away, firing their 75s point-blank at a concrete pillbox perched near the ridge's summit. The Marines attacking the ridge crawled among the stones and sandy shellholes, peering through the smoke for enemy movements.

A flamethrowing team, guarded by two automatic riflemen, worked its way cautiously up to an already-blackened hole. The air was filled with the noise of exploding grenades and with the smell of cordite and dead bodies.

The smoke blew away from one section of the section of the rocks. The exposed stones and caves looked like an ogre's face, showing broken black and brown teeth, ready to snap at the Marines attacking it. From behind one of the "teeth"—a black hole in the wall—a Nambu machine gun chattered. A Marine rifleman, caught upright, scrambled toward the protection of a boulder. He stopped abruptly, reached for his throat and fell to his his knees. The machine gun kept chattering. The Marine screamed and slowly dropped to his full length.

It was ironic that at the time this ridge of death was almost a mile behind our front lines. Elements of the 9th and 21st Marines had first seized it several days before and, thinking it secured, had gone on. When we had passed it earlier in the morning, on our way toward the front, it had still been peaceful and quiet. A radio jeep had been parked in the open, its driver unconcernedly eating a can of rations. The only other Marines in sight had been a group of engineers, probing on their hands and knees for mines and joking about the hot sand burning through the knees of their pants.

None of us suspected that there were still Japs in the desertlike area. The ridge had had its day already, and we assumed that its story was over. The Marines who had originally taken it on D plus 16 had clambered across it, first knocking out its gun positions with mortars, bazookas and tank fire, in the usual way, and then poking into every hole for surviving enemy. Some of the holes needed treatment with hand grenades and flamethrowers, while others were sealed with demolitions. But there had been little trouble, and soon the ridge had become quiet. The lines had gone on. Platoons had moved ahead, fighting through the lost world of the sulphur area, up to the third airfield. Support elements had followed, pausing near the ridge, then flowing on toward the northern end of the island. Finally an aid station had arrived and set up among the tumbled boulders. And that was when the fireworks, which we were now witnessing, had begun.

The ridge, like all the others on Iwo, had been thoroughly integrated into the Jap scheme of defenses. Fifteen-centimeter guns had sat on top of the humps commanding the view in all directions. They had been shattered by our naval and aerial bombardments. From the ridge's sides, antitank guns, mortars and machine guns had poked out at the dreary landscape. Their scores of hiding places ranged from small concrete pillboxes, set into the rock, to narrow cave entranceways, camouflaged with stones, sand and sticks.

664

The entrances led into the network of tunnels and caverns. They ran all through the ridge and allowed the defenders to dart its length, from hole to hole, without being seen.

The Marine aid station had set up in a small amphitheater formed by the rocks at one end of the ridge. A smashed Jap antiaircraft gun loomed overhead, its long pocked barrel pointing into the sky.

The corpsmen had been too busy to notice the rocks. A battle was in progress 1,500 yards ahead, and the stretcher bearers were bringing back a stream of wounded. They set the litters down tenderly and went back for more wounded. The doctors and corpsmen worked silently over the torn and bleeding men.

A heavy Jap machine gun had suddenly rattled from the side of the ridge, just as a man carrying a crate of ammunition was passing by. He dropped his load of mortar shells, looked startled, and crumpled in a heap in the sand. A group of Marines, idling across the open space, hit the dirt and wriggled behind rocks. Two automatic riflemen, attached to a rifle company in reserve, peeked over the lip of the shellhole in which they had been resting. They tried to see where the bullets were coming from. They spotted an opening in the rocks and fired at it. The Jap machine gun ceased rattling. The two Marines cautiously clambered out of the shellhole and crawled toward the ridge. Other Marines, sensing a fight, waved to each other and began to close in. They covered each other with carbines and rifles and edged slowly toward the rocky hole.

A blaze of enemy small-arms fire came from at least five different parts of the ridge. Three Marines toppled over and the others dived for cover. The bullets whistled past the men in the aid station. The corpsmen looked up bewildered, then dropped to their hands and knees and went on working over the wounded.

The Marines in front of the ridge huddled behind rocks and waited. A step into the open meant death or injury. They studied the wounded men lying out in the open and tried to figure how to pull them to shelter. Finally a little corporal from New York City licked his lips and handed his rifle to the man next to him.

"Here goes," he said. He crawled out to the wounded man lying nearest to him.

He had almost reached him when there was another burst of fire and he stiffened. The injured man was also hit. His body jerked and quivered. Blood flowed from underneath the corporal's head. Both men had been instantly killed.

One of the corpsmen, a lanky fellow from Texas, left the aid station and came around the ridge to see what all the shooting was about.

"Get down," a Marine yelled at him. The corpsman dropped behind a rock and pushed his helmet back on his head. His eyes were bloodshot and glassy from lack of sleep.

"Hey," he called, "knock it off. This here's a hospital."

The Marines didn't appreciate the humor. They pointed down the road behind him. The corpsman turned. There were four stretcher bearers stumbling along the road with a wounded man, hurrying to the aid station.

The corpsman cupped his hands over his mouth to try to warn the stretcher bearers. There was too much noise. They couldn't hear him. The Japs began to fire at them. They ran faster. The corpsman wanted to run out and knock them flat, but something held him spellbound.

A bullet hit one of the stretcher bearers in the leg. He looked around wildly and crashed to the ground. The stretcher spilled on top of him. The men in front tripped as they tried to hold on to the stretcher. The Japs kept shooting into the group. The bullets peppered the sand around them. The wounded stretcher bearer jumped up again and grabbed his end of the litter. He started to drag the stretcher along, but dropped it. The man on the stretcher hung half over it. His head and shoulders dragged along the ground.

The other men half-crawled and half-ran with the stretcher until they reached the rocks. The wounded stretcher bearer loped after them. When he reached the shelter, he fell again. It was a miracle that he had been able to stay on his feet. The bullet had laid open his calf as if it had been hit by a meat cleaver. The man on the stretcher was stone dead. One of the bullets from the ridge had hit him in the skull.

666

No one knew how many Japs were in the ridge or where they had come from, or when. A supply captain, coming up from the rear, saw what was going on and radioed for tanks and demolitions men. More Marines from neighboring units gathered. They inspected the ridge from safety points behind some rocks.

When the tanks arrived, the Marines had started the step-by-step of again cleaning out the ridge. The dangerous and tedious work that had originally been done on D plus 16 by the front-line troops had to be repeated. The Marines threw smoke bombs and phosphorous grenades against the rocks and moved in with bazookas and automatic weapons. When the smoke drifted away, they had to shoot fast, or a Jap would catch them from one of the many holes. The tanks hurled their 75s at every position their gunners could locate. Engineers tried to fling dynamite charges into the caves.

Despite their preponderance of weapons, the Marines found that there were too many holes. They would attack one only to be shot at from another one half a dozen feet away. Moreover, the ridge was not a straight wall but, in many places, curved like an S. Entranceways protected each other, so that Marines would be hit in the back from holes guarding the one they were assaulting. The interconnecting tunnels inside the ridge also allowed the Japs to play deadly tag with the Marines. They would shoot out of one hole. But by the time Marines got close enough to that hole, the Japs had left it and were shooting from another one twenty yards away and higher up in the wall. The Marines had to post guards at every hole they could see in order to attack any of them. The tunnel also curved and twisted inside the ridge. The Japs could escape the straight trajectory weapons and grenades thrown into the cave entrances, merely by running back into the interior.

Finally flamethrowers were called. They threw long jets of flaming liquid into the holes and along the curving walls of the tunnels. The roaring flames did the trick. The Marines heard the Japs howling. A few rushed out of the caves on fire. The Marines shot them or knocked them down and beat out the flames and took them prisoners. When the Marines began to hear muffled explosions inside the caves,

667

they guessed that some of the Japs were blowing themselves up with hand grenades.

The scene became wild and terrible. More Japs rushed screaming from the caves. They tumbled over the rocks, their clothes and bodies burning fiercely. Soon the flame-throwers paused. A Marine lifted himself cautiously into view. There were no shots from the caves. A Jap with his clothes in rags hunched himself out of one hole, his arms upraised. The Marines stood up behind the rocks and waved to him to come out. The Jap indicated that there were more who would like to surrender. The Marines motioned him to tell them to come out.

Almost forty scared and beaten men emerged from different holes. Some of them had round pudding faces. They grinned nervously and said they were Koreans. They had been forced by the Japs to stay in the caves. They said that everyone else in the caves had either been burned to death or had committed suicide.

The Marines sent them to the rear. Then they groped cautiously among the rocks from hole to hole, examining each entranceway. Dead bodies, some hit by bullets and grenade fragments, some burned into frightful black lumps, lay in the holes. The smell was overwhelming and men turned away in disgust.

The battle of the ridge seemed over. An officer made a note to bring up demolition crews as soon as they could be spared by the front-line companies. They would seal up the holes in this troublesome ridge. The Marines gathered their casualties and drifted away. The tanks shifted into reverse and backed out. Peacefulness settled once more over the area.

But it was not for long. The sudden death, which we had come on, was to strike again from the ridge, this time bitterly close.

That same day, several hours later, Sergeant Reid Chamberlain (El Cajon, Calif.) came up to the aid station. He was on his way to a front-line company. Chamberlain was a prominent figure in the Marine Corps. He had served with General MacArthur on Bataan and Corregidor early in the war. He had escaped from Corregidor to help organize Fili-

668

pino guerrilla bands. He had stayed in the Philippines a year and a half and had been commissioned a lieutenant in the U.S. Army. Finally he had returned to America and been awarded the Distinguished Service Cross. Then he had resigned his Army commission, re-enlisted as a sergeant in the Marines, and had come overseas again. He was now a battalion runner with the 21st Regiment. He was short and handsome and wore a brown mustache. Despite the publicity that had been given to his exploits as a guerrilla leader in the Philippines, he had stayed modest and unassuming and was one of the most popular men in the outfit.

A small group of us accompanied Chamberlain to the front-line company. We began to cross the clearing which we thought had been rid of Jap sniper fire. To escape occasional mortar shells that were dropping in the open, we clung perhaps too closely to the rocky walls of the ridge. We were picking our way among the stones and the burned Jap bodies when three shots rang out from the hillside. We scattered and tried to run behind some boulders. Chamberlain drew his pistol and looked frantically around. There was another shot. We heard a thud. We thought the bullet had struck the curving side of the ridge.

When we reached safe spots, we paused and looked back. Our hearts beat wildly. Chamberlain was nowhere in sight. An ambulance driver and an automatic rifleman were crouched behind nearby rocks, their teeth clenched, their hands gripping their weapons. They were trying to find the hole from which the shots had come. We called Chamberlain but received no answer. Slowly we tried to edge back. Rifle shots cracked at us from several holes, and we ducked again.

The long, rocky ridge was once more alive with enemy. Again Marines began to gather, coming up cautiously to help us. They dashed from rock to rock and slid among the boulders, trying to seek cover from the many caves that looked out at us. We told them about Chamberlain, lying somewhere among the rocks. We formed a team quickly and began crawling forward. When the Japs fired at us again, the men covering us saw where the shots were coming from. They sent a stream of automatic fire at the holes and "buttoned up" the Japs. One burly sergeant stood straight up without a helmet on and, gritting his teeth, fired his carbine from his hip, moving directly at a hole as he fired. The jeep ambulance driver finally reached Chamberlain's body and lifted his head. A trickle of blood flowed from behind his ear. His eyes were open, but he was dead.

There is nothing you can say or do when a good friend is suddenly killed in battle. You feel stunned, angry, sad and somewhat frustrated. We could have fired point-blank the rest of the day at those holes. The Japs would only have laughed at us. In an instant they had claimed one of our best men. Chamberlain's wonderful war record had ended abruptly. After so many heroic deeds, it seemed an added tragedy that he was killed while doing nothing but walking. There was nothing anybody could do about it.

We crawled back and sent for flamethrowers, only to find that we couldn't get any more that day. They were all busy up front. Meanwhile, an outfit of the 9th Marines was moving up and pitching its bivouac on top of the ridge, which had become silent again. We hunted up the commanding officer and told him there were still Japs inside the hill. We related to him all that had happened at the ridge that day. He listened concernedly but decided it was too late in the afternoon to try to root out the Japs still in the caves. He posted guards behind the rocks facing the ridge and gave them orders to keep all straggling Marines away from the holes.

Another combat correspondent, Technical Sergeant Francis Barr (Dallas, Texas), had come up with the new outfit and was digging in for the night. What happened that night was later revealed by Barr.

According to him, as soon as it got dark the Japs tried to come out of their holes. The Marine guards saw them slithering out among the rocks and opened fire, killing some and driving the others back in. The Japs screamed and cursed when they realized they were trapped. Some of them committed suicide inside their holes.

Corporal H. E. Duke (Cheyenne, Wyo.) heard the muffled sounds of hand grenades exploding underneath him in the ridge. He had been sitting in a blackout tent, making

670

out some operational reports on a typewriter. He looked at his watch. It was just before midnight.

Suddenly there was a terrific explosion that rocked the whole hill. A huge boulder flew through the tent and smashed Duke's typewriter into smithereens. Outside, Corporal Vincent M. Langa (Cleveland, Ohio) was blown out of his foxhole 20 feet into the air. Private John F. Muralt (Minneapolis, Minn.), a chaplain's assistant, was buried, as the explosion sent slides of hot sand into his hole.

A flash of flame shot into the air and there was a series of rumbles and more explosions. The ridge quivered and shook. Rocks, dirt and hunks of concrete showered among the dug-in Marines. Platoon Sergeant Rudolph Rott (Wonewoc, Wis.) thought the whole ridge was on fire.

By the light of the flames, the men dug each other out and scrambled down the ridge to safety. Stones cascaded after them in landslides that sealed up half the holes in the ridge's wall. The men took up positions behind the rocks and waited for the Japs to come out. Platoon Sergeant Waldo D. Humphrey (Kansas City, Kans.) saw two of them sitting among the stones in a dazed condition. They were carrying anti-personnel mines around their waists. He killed them as they tried to get up. Another man struggling down the slope saw other Japs trying to rush out from the holes, only to be buried in landslides. Their arms and legs protruded from the dirt and rocks. A group of five Japs, running along the wall of the ridge, were spotted by the light of the flames, and instantly killed.

"They looked like little devils running through Hell," a corporal said later on. "All they needed were pitchforks."

Slowly the Marines realized what had happened. The Japs had blown themselves up and, with them, the whole ridge. When dawn came, the Marines discovered that they had suffered only one serious casualty. Many men, like Private Muralt, had been completely buried by the rocks and sulphur ashes, but companions had dug them out before they had smothered. Scouts who poked into some of the remaining holes found that the Japs had used land mines and 125-pound aerial bombs to blow up the hill. They also discovered empty canteens on some of the torn Japanese bodies, indicating that the men who had tried to come out earlier in the night had probably been after water.

It was almost impossible and certainly foolhardy to try to trace the winding tunnels to their sources. The Marines instead decided to blow up all the holes still unsealed and trap whatever Japs might still be alive in the ridge's inner recesses.

It was a long and tedious job. The demolitions men worked all day, placing charges in the mouths of more than forty caves. When they were blown up, it was almost impossible to know whether tiny holes and cracks had not been left among the tumbled rocks through which hiding Japs could still fire. By nightfall, everyone felt a sense of frustration and further trouble. An officer in charge of a group of the engineers shook his head and said, "We ought to put up a sign here, 'Pass at your own risk.' "

The sign was not put up. If it had been, it would have made some of the men laugh. But the terrible ridge was still nothing to laugh at. It was still "hot." A supply unit for a 3rd Division regiment was the next outfit to run into the death that lurked among its rocks.

When the supply unit moved up, the area again looked secure. The unit pitched tents and galleys, built ration piles, parked jeeps and trailers and nonchalantly went about its business of shuttling hot food, ammunition and water to the battalions ahead.

Someone told the new arrivals about the ridge. But they looked at its silent, strewn rocks and shrugged. The fighting was now more than a mile ahead. A sniper or two this far back couldn't cause trouble.

But this time it wasn't a sniper.

A jeep and trailer, setting off one afternoon with hot coffee and doughnuts for the front lines, was fired at. The driver didn't wait to find out what kind of weapon was shooting at him. He knew it was something big. He stepped on the gas and raced out of the area. On the way back he was shot at again. Jeep ambulance drivers and other supply men reported similar attacks on them. Finally a tank, lumbering over the road, was hit. The crew jumped out and hid behind some rocks.

672

After a while, they came back and reported that an anti-tank gun was somewhere among the debris of the ridge. Some of the members of the supply unit armed themselves with rifles and carbines and went to have a look. A shower of small-arms bullets from the ridge drove them back.

They sent for help to an engineering outfit, but were told that demolitions men could not be spared at the moment. The drivers who had to take that road, moving back and forth to the front, called the route "Suicide Run." Every time they approached the rocks they stepped hard on the gas and raced past them as fast as they could go. The anti-tank gun hurled shells at them each time, but fortunately there were no hits. Finally, a tank was sent up. It waited behind some rocks till the Jap gun fired and showed its position. Then the tank blasted at it with its 75. In a few moments the Jap position was a pile of smoking rubble. Automatic riflemen who moved in to catch enemy survivors found the troublesome weapon to be a 47-mm. antitank gun. The Japs had kept it concealed during all the previous fighting around the ridge.

It would seem as if that might have ended the story of the ridge. But it didn't. As the battle for Iwo reached its conclusion in the northern cliffs, Jap riflemen and machine gunners continued to hang on inside the tunnels back here and fire out at passersby whenever a good shot was presented. The area soon became full of Marines. Rear camps pitched among the rocky heights dotting the landscape. And with the concentration of men to shoot at, the Japs meted out sudden death and injury to scores of unsuspecting Americans.

A wireman, stringing a telephone line between rear command posts, was shot through the head. Two cooks were winged in the arms. A whole mortar platoon was pinned down in its holes by a Jap machine gunner. A barber and an officer who was having his hair cut were sent running by a burst of rifle shots.

Whenever the Marines could spot exact positions from which Japs were firing, they attempted to knock them out. With automatic rifles and bazookas, they crept among the rocks and blasted at the small holes. Then they threw dynamite charges into the slits and hoped they would do the trick.

It was an almost hopeless task. The Marines soon realized that there was only one way to eliminate the Japs. That was to wait until they came out. And come out they eventually did, for food and water. One night near the end of the campaign five enemy emerged and crept up to a regimental headquarters unit. Automatic riflemen, in a circle of foxholes around the bivouac area, saw the Japs in the moonlight and opened fire. They killed all five.

In the same way, other Japanese stragglers were eliminated, one by one, group by group. But on D plus 25, the day the Marines overran the last bit of Iwo Jima and the island was declared secured, death was still coming from the ridge. A Jap sniper that day shot a passing corpsman through the ear.

We never knew just how many Japs were in that ridge or where they kept coming from. Some thought that the Japs moved around at night from one part of the island to the other, looking for water, and that at dawn they disappeared into the nearest ridges. Other men thought the Japs moved from ridge to ridge through underground tunnels. Only if we were someday to tear away from the sides of the ridges the tumbling rocks and debris which now cover the many holes would we ever be able to trace to their sources the tunnels that fill their dreadful interiors.

Last Stop Before Japan

By July 1944, the Japanese drive on Imphal and the plains of India beyond had been repulsed. The British 14th Army now gathered itself for a counterattack; their objective: push the Japanese back across the Chindwin River and burst out into Central Burma, linking up with Stilwell driving south.

Meanwhile Mountbatten hoped to launch an amphibious attack on Rangoon where, if he met with success, he could slice through the Jap communications to the north and divide their forces. He needed two or three new divisions and a sizable increase in the shipping then at his disposal. However, a series of events thwarted his plan: first, he had to postpone his attack date due to the prevailing demands for men and equipment in Europe as the German resistance continued to be stubborn through the fall of 1944; then, because the Japanese were threatening Chungking, the Chinese capital, and Kunming, the receiving base for all airborne supplies then being sent into China, Chiang Kai-shek insisted on the withdrawal of two Chinese divisions fighting in Burma under Mountbatten, recalling them to China; next, the U.S. was persuaded to shift three air transport squadrons then under Mountbatten over to help Chiang.

In spite of these frustrations at Mountbatten's command level, General Slim's 14th Army continued to push forward into Burma, while the remainder of Stilwell's forces, now under American General Sultan, fought their way south to the old Burma Road at Namkhan. These advances were won in the hardest kind of fighting in the Burmese hills and jungles under the most rugged conditions. It was this kind of attrition that Mountbatten had wanted to avoid by his Rangoon stroke.

By February 1945, Mountbatten decided to commit the 14th Army to strike directly for Rangoon. Despite Chiang's halting his Chinese troops at Mandalay, then drawing them off for his own use in China, and despite imminent monsoon weather, General Slim continued to drive forward. The Japanese fell back toward Toungoo and Rangoon. When in mid-April it looked as though the monsoon would stop the drive, Mountbatten sent his 26th Division round by sea in an amphibious landing at Rangoon. A few days later at Pegu, the 17th Division, rushing south, met the 26th Division striking north from Rangoon, and now the last escape route to the East for the Japanese was cut off.

The war in Burma was almost over. Plans were now made to invade the Malay Peninsula, but before the British could mount an attack the drive on the Japanese mainland itself reached a critical stage.

At a meeting in San Francisco in late September, 1944, certain members of the Joint Chiefs of Staff had agreed with Admiral Nimitz on the strategy for seizing the approaches to Japan itself. Prior to this meeting, arguments had been heard within the JCS for landings on Formosa and China, but these were put aside in September. It was decided that General MacArthur would invade Luzon, while Admiral Nimitz would invade the Bonin and the Ryukyu Island groups. The islands selected by Nimitz in the two groups for the assaults were: Iwo Jima in the Bonins because it would serve as an emergency landing base for crippled bombers on their way back from Japan to Saipan, and Okinawa in the Ryukyus because it would provide major air and naval facilities for the invasion of Japan itself.

The battle for Iwo Jima is told in *Combat: Pacific Theater*. While the mop-up of the last remnants of the Japs on Iwo was still progressing, invasion forces moved toward the beaches of Okinawa. D-Day would be April 1st, 1945.

The usual air strikes, mine sweeping and naval bombardment in preparation for the landings took place. In his volume, *Victory in the Pacific*, Morison describes the work of the Underwater Demolition Teams, known as the "Frogmen" whose job it was to reconnoiter the beaches, map them, and destroy obstacles placed in the way of landing craft.

"Each team proceeded to a point about 500 yards off its assigned beach in an LCVP. The landing craft then turned parallel to the reef, casting off a swimmer about every 50 yards. Each man, clad only in trunks, goggles and rubber feet, was festooned with the gear of his trade. He carried a reel of marked line knotted every 25 yards, the bitter end of which he secured to the edge of the reef. He then turned toward the beach, uncoiling the line as he swam, halting every time he felt a knot to take soundings with a small lead line; or, if the depth were one fathom or less, with his own body which was conveniently painted with black rings at 12-inch intervals. The swimmer recorded his soundings with a stylus on a sheet of sandpapered plexiglass wrapped around his left forearm. After an hour or more of recon-

676

naissance, depending on the width of the reef, each swimmer was picked up by his LCVP, which in the meantime had been planting little colored buoys on dangerous coral heads. The method of recovering swimmers was simple and effective. A sailor held out a stiff rope to the swimmer, who grasped the 'monkey's fist' at the rope's end, while the boat .was making three or four knots, and was hauled on board. Landing craft then returned to their APDs where the swimmers' data were correlated and entered on a chart. All this went on under gunfire support from destroyers and gunboats, and 'really beautiful air support,' as Commander Draper L. Kauffman USNR described it, from escort carrier planes. This kept the enemy so busy ashore that he never even fired on the underwater demolition teams." *

OKINAWA**

by Major Frank Hough

Everybody knew that the Okinawa operation was going to be tough. But exactly how tough, and in what peculiar respects, could not be foretold with any accuracy.

Nor could anyone foresee that this was to be in actuality the last act of the long-drawn-out and bloody drama which had been played across 3,200 miles of ocean. Before, during and immediately after the campaign, participants and military students alike regarded Okinawa rather as a rehearsal —a full-dress rehearsal and necessarily a costly one—for the grand finale to be staged on the big home islands to the north. On the basis of this preview, the ultimate prospect appeared grim indeed.

Although Okinawa produced a few surprises and possessed certain features which differentiated it from previous Pacific actions in which the Marines had participated, it was productive of few tactical innovations of importance.

*Victory in the Pacific, pp. 120-121. Little Brown & Co.
**From The Island War. J. B. Lippincott.

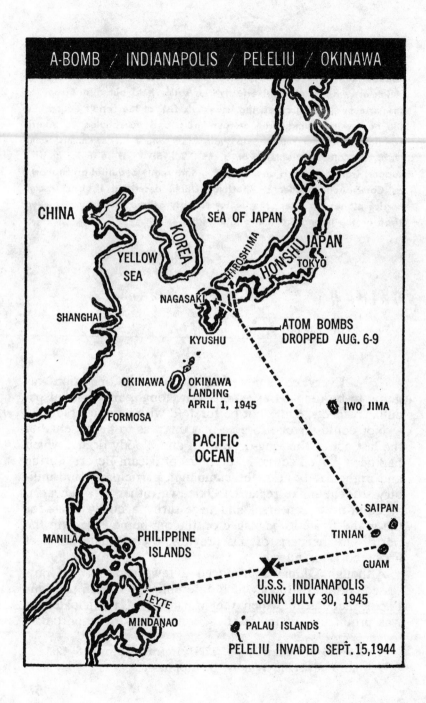

A-BOMB / INDIANAPOLIS / PELELIU / OKINAWA

CHINA

SEA OF JAPAN

KOREA

YELLOW SEA

HIROSHIMA

HONSHU JAPAN

TOKYO

NAGASAKI

SHANGHAI

KYUSHU

ATOM BOMBS DROPPED AUG. 6-9

OKINAWA

OKINAWA LANDING APRIL 1, 1945

IWO JIMA

FORMOSA

PACIFIC OCEAN

SAIPAN

MANILA

PHILIPPINE ISLANDS

TINIAN

GUAM

X

U.S.S. INDIANAPOLIS SUNK JULY 30, 1945

LEYTE

MINDANAO

PALAU ISLANDS

PELELIU INVADED SEPT. 15, 1944

The costly lessons of three years had been well learned; we knew the best methods of fighting the Japanese, and we had developed the weapons with which to fight them. That the fight proved protracted, bitter and bloody may be attributed to the fact that the Japanese, too, had learned much.

They fought well and skillfully on Okinawa, as they had on Peleliu and Iwo Jima, with little of the tactical blundering, the frittering away of their strength in fruitless missions, the useless dying-for-the-sake-of-dying which had marred so many of their earlier operations. That they lost in the end was due in part to a fallacy in the conception on which their defense strategy was based; this and the fact that, well as they fought, the Americans fought better.

Since the Japanese held the ground and could compel us to fight the way they wanted to fight, it might be well to examine this basic strategy at the outset. It was not, as many first assumed, an impromptu expedient forced upon the enemy. Intelligence subsequently obtained proved it to be a thoroughly studied play, worked out in detail to serve as a standard operating procedure, not only on Okinawa but on all islands within the Japanese inner-defense zone which we might attack, and presumably, in modified form, on Japan itself. Of course, all this was not known at the beginning, and Japanese behavior at the time of the landing took most of the invaders by complete surprise; very pleasant surprise at the outset, though it was to have its grim aspects later on.

This "Okinawa Defense Plan," as it was officially known, was based upon two factors U.S. troops had never encountered before: proximity to Japan proper, and reliance upon the destructive power of the newly developed Kamikaze weapons. Instead of scattering forces to attempt an all round defense of a very extensive coast line, these would be concentrated on the best defensive terrain the island afforded. There, in elaborately prepared positions arranged as a defense-in-depth, they would make the invaders come to them and fight a war of attrition, husbanding men and material against the happy day when the Kamikazes would destroy or drive off the supporting ships, thus enabling reinforcements to pour in from the near-by home islands to help with mopping up of the impudent invaders on shore. Except for the critical dependence placed upon a weapon as yet unproved, this reasoning was sound, and there is evidence to indicate that many of the defenders believed right up to the end that it was going to work.

Kamikaze tactics were something the Japanese mind could grasp—and perhaps only the Japanese mind. They constituted a logical step forward toward the goal for which Japan seemed hell bent at this period: national suicide. Kamikaze in its essence was simply large-scale organization of what had always been Japan's greatest military asset: the willingness of her men to die.

Although they boasted that every pilot was a potential Kamikaze, only a minority actually were. Had it been otherwise, the result might have been different, for there were a lot of Japanese planes over Okinawa and the offshore shipping during the campaign, often in very large flights. But most of these turned out to be ordinary bombers and fighters on routine attack missions with no more intention of crash-diving than our own people had when on similar missions.

Of the genuine Kamikazes, those who actually crash-dived their targets—or tried to—comparatively few achieved what they set out to do. Our planes intercepted many before they could attack. The accuracy and volume of our AA brought down most of them well short of their objectives. Of those who did get through to their targets, many simply missed and crashed into the sea, as a result of their own ineptness or the decrepitude of their planes, or both.

Actually, not a single major combat ship of the U.S. Navy was sunk at Okinawa, though several were damaged so seriously that they had to be withdrawn for repairs. The tremendous volume of AA fire our capital ships were capable of throwing prevented most of the attackers from getting through to the targets, and many hits were needed to sink the big ships, unless they were very lucky hits indeed. Especially during the later phases, the Kamikazes showed marked reluctance to approach these vessels at all, preferring to single out lone destroyers on patrol or outpost, or small convoys of lightly guarded auxiliaries.

680

But although it failed to influence the outcome of the Okinawa operation, or of the war itself, this sustained Kamikaze attack was a thoroughly grim business for all hands concerned. Ship and personnel losses, while absurdly small as compared with enemy claims, were nothing to be treated lightly. Yet the Navy never faltered in its support of the troops ashore.

These troops comprised the X Army (USA), commanded by Lieutenant General S. B. Buckner. The assault forces were made up of two corps: the III Amphibious Corps, Major General Roy S. Geiger, consisting of the First and Sixth Marine Divisions, both reinforced; and the XXIV (Army) Corps, Lieutenant General John R. Hodge, consisting originally of the Seventh and Ninety-sixth Infantry Divisions, both reinforced. (The Twenty-seventh and Seventy-seventh Infantry Divisions which later functioned as operational components of the XXIV Corps, were assigned initially to special missions and did not participate in the opening phases of the campaign. The Second Marine Division, which had been detached from III Amphibious Corps, was kept afloat as X Army reserve and did not participate as a division in the operations ashore.) Supporting and service troops were balanced heavily in favor of artillery, AA artillery, transport and engineers.

L-Day was set for 1 April, H-Hour for 0830. Following the conventional naval gunfire preparation and air strikes which had long since become standard operating procedure, the advance waves came in through the smoke, crossing the fringing reef in amphtracks. Beyond the line of demarcation, supporting troops bobbed about in landing craft, awaiting their turn. By 0840 the assault waves were all ashore. So far, everything had gone according to preliminary plans; from this point onward, however, practically nothing did.

Strong resistance had been anticipated; but there was no resistance, either during the landing or after the troops were safely in. Yontan Airfield, the securing of which it had been feared might require days of hard fighting, was completely overrun by 1130 of L-Day; taken almost intact, with many operational enemy planes still on the runways or in the revetments. The perimeter on which the troops dug in at nightfall embraced six thousand yards of shore line and ran inland to a depth of four thousand yards. Corps reserve and most of the tanks and artillery were safely ashore.

The Japanese defense plan was not known at this time, and all hands were inclined to regard this landing as a miracle of sorts. Had complete tactical surprise been achieved? The easy capture of the virtually undamaged airfield seemed so to indicate. The Japanese were not noted for giving away their airfields, certainly not intact airfields on islands known to be held in considerable strength. But whatever the explanation, the fact was that the troops were ashore and the supplies pouring in at a rate no one would have dared to anticipate in advance. One characteristic of American military leaders has always been their ability to adapt themselves quickly to unexpected situations; and the situation here appeared most propitious. Commanding generals and their staffs worked late into the night, amending their original plans to take advantage of it.

Actually, as subsequent intelligence proved, the Japanese command had had a very good idea of where we would attempt to land, and just about what troops we intended to put ashore. The easy fall of the airfield resulted from a slip-up on their part rather than any special acuteness on ours. They had not planned to defend it, but they had planned to destroy the planes and make the field unserviceable. For this purpose they had organized all the special and service troops in the region, together with many Okinawan conscripts, into what they designated a "Specially Established Brigade." These men proved pretty poor material: poorly organized, low in morale and so inadequately armed and equipped that they had earned the nickname within their own army as the "Bimo Butai," or poverty-stricken detachment. Under the prelanding naval bombardment, they had simply taken to their heels, in such haste that they had not paused to destroy anything and in such confusion that never thereafter were they able to function as a unit.

The region where the landing was effected lay a short

682

distance below the narrow Ishikawa Isthmus, roughly one third of the way up the island's long axis, which was to serve as the line of demarcation between the two operational phases contemplated in the original tactical plan. Phase I was to include seizure of all of the island south of Ishikawa by the XXIV Corps; Phase II all of the island to the north by the III Amphibious Corps. The two drives were to operate simultaneously and be mutually supporting as necessity dictated. Which phase would be completed first depended upon a number of unforeseeable factors and was a matter of no great importance.

Operation orders called for the two corps to land abreast, III on the left, XXIV on the right, each with two divisions in line. The left of the Marine sector, extreme left flank of the whole attack, was assigned to the Sixth Marine Division (less 29th Regiment which was in Corps reserve), with the First Marine Division on their right tying in with the Seventh Infantry Division, which, in turn, maintained contact with the Ninety-sixth Infantry Division, the extreme right flank of which had as part of its function acting as pivot for the southward turning movement of the XXIV Corps.

When resistance continued negligible on the second day (L + 1, or 2 April), it was decided to press the advance with all possible speed compatible with security. This led to a rapid widening of the front, necessitating movement of all division and corps reserve units into the line in order to maintain contact. So well did matters progress that the first arbitrary phase lines designated in the original plans were abandoned, and before nightfall of L + 1 permission had been given to push on beyond the line of L + 5 without pausing for further orders, should the situation warrant.

On L + 2 the First Marine Division Reconnaissance Company, pushing ahead of the 1st Marines on the III AC's extreme right reached the eastern shore. Pressing on from there, they proceeded to scout the long, narrow finger of the Katchin Peninsula, covering the entire area by nightfall without finding any enemy personnel or installations. In the center and left of the Corps area some scattered sniper fire was encountered, and rugged ground prevented these elements from completing the crossing. However, the

Sixth Division Reconnaissance Company had pushed sufficiently far ahead to scout the village of Ishikawa, on the eastern shore near the base of the isthmus.

By then the Tenth Army command had lifted all restrictions upon advances beyond the phase line L + 10. As a result, the First Marine Division secured the entire eastern shore line in its area by the end of the following day (4 April), thus reaching what had been designated originally as the L + 20 line, their final objective. In the left sector, the Sixth Marine Division reached the L + 15 line by 1250, across the base of the isthmus. Here the 4th Marines paused to reorganize while the 22nd pushed on to secure the whole of the narrow neck, moving in two columns up either shore. What the highly conservative initial plan had visualized as possibly taking nearly three weeks had been accomplished in four days. Two operational airfields (the Army had taken Kadena) were in our hands, and the island was cut cleanly in half.

For the remainder of Phase II, the activities of the First Division were confined to mopping up their area, seizing near-by offshore islands and patrolling the expanding area in the rear of the swiftly advancing Sixth Division. It was a period of rest and recuperation, though no one was quite certain what they were recuperating from. Veterans of malarial Guadalcanal, muddy Cape Gloucester and bloody Peleliu still rubbed their eyes in amazement and assured recently arrived replacements that it was never like this in the old Marine Corps. One officer summed up the feeling in a letter to a former comrade who had been transferred Stateside after Peleliu: "Peace—it's wonderful."

In the meanwhile, the Sixth Division drove on to the northward, advancing swiftly against negligible resistance. Now and again isolated riflemen or small groups sniped at them from caves or other concealment. Occasional mortar shells landed near by. In such instances the advance elements simply by-passed, leaving cleaning out of the small nests to their own reserve which, in turn, was backed up by patrols from the First Division. The enemy was considerably less of a problem than that of keeping their own supplies flowing forward in adequate quantity over a network of

684

roads which had never been designed to handle such traffic as poured over them now.

By 8 April the Sixth Division had passed the neck of the rugged Motobu Peninsula. Captured documents and POW interrogation indicated that a force of Japanese existed somewhere in the northern portion of the island, though intelligence estimates of its strength varied. Should this force choose to make a desperate late stand—which, being Japanese, it almost certainly would—as likely a place as any would be the mountainous interior of this large headland. Air observation, though it could not be too satisfactory in terrain of this nature, tended to bear out this supposition.

The Division, therefore, paused here to regroup. Combing the rest of the island to the north was assigned to the 22nd Marines, operating a series of strong patrols rather than a solid advance. The 4th Marines deployed across the base of the peninsula to seal it off from the rest of Okinawa, and the 29th, recently rejoined from Corps reserve, moved on to Motobu in three columns.

The two flank columns made satisfactory progress, encountering no resistance more formidable than increasingly difficult terrain. The Division Reconnaissance Company, pushing hard, reached Bise, at the peninsula's western tip, on 12 April, and it soon became clear that the entire coastal perimeter was free of the enemy.

In the center, however, the story was different. The battalion (1/29) operating here met scattered resistance almost from the outset of its advance, and on the night of 9/10 April found itself involved in a sizable fire fight in the midst of as fantastic a jumble of precipitous hills, ridges, cliffs and gorges as any organized military unit was ever called upon to operate in. Here, it became apparent, was the main enemy position and, being Japanese, he could be counted upon to defend it to the last. By 12 April constant probing had pretty well developed its nature and extent, but the result was not reassuring.

The defenses were of the type commonly used by the Japanese in hilly country: caves, natural and artificial, foxholes, dugouts, emplacements cunningly designed to be mutually protective with interlocking fields of fire and constructed to be proof against virtually anything but a direct hit from the artillery. As always in such a situation, the only way to oust the enemy was to go in and root him out with rifles, grenades, flame throwers. And what made this position particularly formidable was what appeared the virtual impossibility of getting in. Fifteen-hundred-foot hills, laced by cliffs and ravines barred the way for tanks. Indeed, from most directions the approaches were such as to test the skill of a professional mountain climber, even without the enemy in there shooting at him.

But here at last was an instance where no beachhead was at stake, security of which called for unremitting pressure on the enemy, regardless. Nothing threatened in the entire III Corps area, embracing about two thirds of the island. After all, this was by nature essentially an Army operation; the Division could take its time, concentrate on achieving its difficult objective at minimum cost.

More troops were brought in, and all available artillery. Naval gunfire and air strikes were called for, to no great avail in such terrain. Two battalions of the 4th Marines (the 1st and 2nd) were moved up to Suga on the west shore on 13 April, and 3/22, no longer needed for patrolling of the northern reaches of the island proper, came to Awa, to the south, in general support. 1/29 and 2/29 which had been operating generally to the north of the Japanese position, now concentrated on its eastern face. On 14 April, supported by artillery and air strikes, they assaulted from that direction, while the two battalions of the 4th together with 3/29 attacked from the west simultaneously in a pincers movement.

The action developed into a slow, deadly slugging match. Evacuation of the wounded became a major problem; bringing up supplies and ammunition was almost as difficult. On the eastern sector the terrain became so bad at length that the units operating there could advance no farther. But on the opposite side the 4th Marines, to which was attached 3/29, achieved a breakthrough in the southern portion of their sector on 17 April and, driving northward across the front of 1/29 and 2/29, overran the entire posi-

686

tion. After that it was just a matter of mopping up isolated nests of die-hards. The peninsula and adjacent small islands were declared secured on 20 April.

The Japanese force on Motobu Peninsula was not especially formidable as regards numbers. As in all cave fighting where men are blown to bits and sealed underground, a full count of enemy killed was impossible. Subsequent intelligence indicated that this was the so-called Udo Detachment: 2nd Battalion (Colonel Udo), Second Infantry Unit, of the Forty-fourth Independent Mixed Brigade, together with reinforcing troops mustering a total strength of about 1,200. They fought stubbornly and well, however, utilizing with great skill as fine a bit of naturally defensive terrain as ever soldiers were asked to hold. The commanding officer on the scene was believed to be Major Tomio Sato, though Colonel Udo himself was known to have been there at the time of the original landing.

The 1st Battalion of the same unit, similarly reinforced, was in garrison on Ie Shima, a sizable island of about seven square miles lying three and one half miles west of Motobu and containing a large airfield. Being within practicable artillery range of each other, these positions could be made mutually supporting, and there is evidence that the Japanese planned so to utilize them at one stage of the game. As events worked out, however, they had no opportunity. On 16 April, with the Marines strongly engaged in the tumbled hills of Motobu, the Seventy-seventh Infantry Division effected a landing on the western end of Ie Shima, drove the full length of the comparatively level island against spotty resistance, and secured on the twenty-first.

During the fighting on Motobu, the 22nd Marines had gone on with their extensive patrolling of all of Okinawa lying to the north of the peninsula. It was mountainous country, inhospitable and sparsely populated in normal times, though somewhat better filled now by an influx of refugees from the south. This had not been anticipated and taxed somewhat the capacity of our Civil Affairs units, but the people proved docile and co-operative on the whole, once their Japanese-fostered terror of Americans had been assuaged.

687

Because of the nature of the terrain, pre-invasion plans had allowed for the possibility of the enemy making a stand in force somewhere in the region. However, the largest force encountered numbered only some two hundred, and these were believed to have escaped from Motobu. Such other soldiers as were picked up proved to be stragglers and local conscripts with no stomach for a fight. The leading patrol reached the end of the island on 13 April, and the systematic combing of the region continued until the end of the month, patrols of varying size operating from fixed bases up and down both coasts and far inland.

On 30 April, while the Sixth was resting and regrouping, orders were issued by X Army detaching the First Marine Division from the III Amphibious Corps and attaching it operationally to the XXIV Corps. For things had been going very differently in the south. The northern two thirds of Okinawa was secure; Phase II was over.

But down in the Army sector, Phase I was just beginning.

As at Peleliu and Iwo Jima, Japanese were showing signs of having become security-conscious. Papers were being destroyed to prevent their capture; diaries were disappearing from the packs of officers and soldiers; situation maps ceased to be strewn around with the lavish hand to which we had become accustomed; in short, all the various material which had proved invaluable to our Intelligence in previous operations was found in decreasing quantities on the enemy dead and in overrun bivouac areas, when it was found at all. As a result, we knew a lot less about them than we would have liked. We knew that they were on Okinawa in force, but we did not know where or how deployed. This the XXIV Corps had to find out—the hard way.

For the few days immediately following the initial landing, the experiences of the XXIV Corps paralleled those of the III Amphibious. They crossed the island without difficulty and drove southward at their leisure against nothing more serious than scattered harassing fire. On 4 April they reported "resistance stiffening." On the eighth they were advancing slowly in the face of "greatly increased resist-

688

ance." On the eleventh they failed to register any gains at all and were taking a heavy pounding from the largest and best co-ordinated concentration of Japanese artillery yet encountered in the Pacific, and it took no clairvoyance to figure out that they were at least in the vicinity of the enemy's main defense position.

At this time the Corps had three divisions in line across the island: Seventh on the left, Ninety-sixth in the center, and Twenty-seventh, which had landed and been attached on 9 April after seizing some adjacent islands, on the right. They continued to operate in this formation for the remainder of the month, a stubborn slugging match in which advances were measured in yards, even feet, by which time the troops were badly in need of rest. Two minor airfields had been taken, Yonabaru on the east by the Seventh Division, and Machinato on the west by the Twenty-seventh, but there were no signs of any weakening in the fanatical resistance of the Japanese.

The first large-scale regrouping occurred on 30 April with the First Marine Division relieving the Twenty-seventh Division on the right. The Seventy-seventh, fresh from its quick conquest of Ie Shima, took over the center from the Ninety-sixth, which had encountered some exceedingly rugged going there. At this time both of the new divisions were attached to XXIV Corps, but in the case of the First Marine Division this proved only temporary. To provide more troops on the widening front, the entire western sector was assigned to III Amphibious Corps on 7 May, and the Sixth Marine Division began moving in on the right of the First the following day. Most of the Marine Artillery, which had been attached to XXIV Corps to support the drive southward, now reverted to III Amphibious control.

The next three days were spent in realigning: moving the elements of both corps forward abreast to a predetermined line of departure for a co-ordinated drive in force. The Japanese resisted with great strength, and torrential rains and the resulting mud further hampered the movement. Tanks, artillery and motor transport bogged down, and it was necessary to manhandle pack howitzers to the front lines to fire direct-support missions. Not all of the units were in position by 10 May, but the jump-off was made regardless.

The Japanese defense consisted of well-prepared positions arranged in great depth across terrain admirably suited to this purpose. They offered little in the way of novelty in the matter of construction, their outstanding features being the thoroughness with which they had been planned, the care with which they had been built, and the huge concentration of artillery which had been mustered in their support. The hard core of this resistance lay along a rough arc across the normally pleasant Okinawa hills, with their picturesque tombs which the enemy found so useful as machine gun nests: from the modern capital of Naha on the west, through ancient Shuri, to the village of Yonabaru on the east coast. It was not this main line which the soldiers and Marines faced when they jumped off on 10 May, only the outlying positions that covered it: a stretch of rough terrain some two miles in depth, packed solid with dug-in Japanese armed to the teeth.

There followed nearly two weeks of slow, bitterly contested progress. The Japanese fought with their customary tenacity; the Americans used the tactics and weapons developed through the experiences of three bloody years. As usual, every ridge and hill, every cave and pillbox, nearly every individual hole and rock had to be taken by assault. With the beachhead long since secured, the terrible urgency of most island operations was lacking. The attackers could take their time; utilize artillery, naval gunfire, and air strikes to save lives.

But the protracted struggle was terribly hard on the troops. Every effort was made to keep fresh men available —comparatively fresh, that is. The XXIV Corps, with a larger reservoir of manpower to draw on, relieved an entire division from time to time. The III Amphibious, however, had only the two Marine Divisions, the Second Marine Division having been detached from floating reserve and returned to Saipan. They solved the problem as best they could by keeping only two regiments of each Division in the lines, sometimes only one, sending the others back into reserve for a rest at as short intervals as practicable.

690

New place names began to find their way into the news accounts, and thence into Marine Corps lore: Dakeshi Ridge and Dakeshi Town, pocketed by the First Marine Division on 11 May; Sugar Loaf Hill, assaulted by the Sixth Marine Division on 14 May but so stubbornly defended and so fiercely counterattacked that they were able to get and retain a strong grip upon it only on the eighteenth by dint of some of the most desperate and courageous fighting in the entire war; Wana Ridge and the village of the same name, directly covering the enemy's key position at Shuri, where the First Marine Division fought from 15 to 22 May.

The Japanese dug deep into their bag of tricks and came up with a few new ones. They were conserving their manpower for once, intent on a war of attrition; nevertheless, they did not hesitate to counterattack when the tactical situation appeared to warrant, and, as at Peleliu and Iwo Jima, such operations were invariably well conceived and more or less efficiently executed. There had not been a stupid Banzai in the old-fashioned sense in the Central Pacific since Guam, and on Okinawa their ground troops enjoyed better co-ordination from the artillery and air force than had ever been achieved before. For here the Japanese had both supporting arms in formidable strength. Air attacks occurred frequently by day and sometimes almost continuously at night. Usually the main objective of these was the large fleet, necessary to supply an attack of such size, that lay continually offshore, but such strikes played a part in ground tactics, too. On 24 May they even attempted an airborne attack on Yontan Airfield in conjunction with an all-out bombing. The bulk of the attacking planes were shot down short of their objective, but one effected a belly landing within a hundred yards of the control tower and spewed forth a suicidal crew who managed to wreak considerable damage before the surprised defenders were able to liquidate them.

On several occasions they tried amphibious landings behind our lines. Alert Navy patrol craft broke up most of these en route. But on the night of 4 May during a two-day series of strongly supported counterattacks, a number of the enemy estimated between company and battalion strength contrived to get ashore in the rear of the First Marine Division, and died there. On the thirteenth and again on the fifteenth, after the Sixth Marine Division had taken over the extreme right, parties ranging from about forty to sixty men eluded the patrol craft long enough to get in, only to be eliminated with little damage to ourselves. On the east coast a similar attempt in some force was foiled by the Seventy-seventh Infantry Division.

By 22 May continuous rains and heavy traffic had made such quagmires of the inadequate roads that supply and evacuation problems stalled the drive in the center for the better part of a week.

But the sustained pounding had had its effect upon the Japanese as well. They were physically weary, their morale probably shaken by the inexorable advance which had penetrated deep into their organized defense zone. By now all of Shuri save the ancient castle was in American hands, with our line bent around it on either flank. Although we did not realize it fully at the time, this was the key to the entire situation: when it fell, so would the whole defensive position. Fully aware of this, and with the attackers in front of them too bogged down to sustain the constant heavy pressure, the Japanese seized the opportunity for an orderly withdrawal, depending upon the constantly lowering skies to veil them from aerial observation and leaving behind a strong force of die-hards to conceal their intentions and cover their retreat.

Our airmen, however, spotted the evacuation on 26 May and promptly attacked. Artillery, naval gunfire and strafing added to the enemy's discomfiture. An estimated three to four thousand were caught in this holocaust, but between the rain and mud and the suicide garrison left in the Shuri area, our ground troops were unable to pursue effectively.

Shuri Castle, strictly speaking, lay within the zone of the Seventy-seventh Division, near where its right flank tied in with the First Marine Division, but in that rugged region flanks often became mixed up. On 29 May a patrol from the 1st Battalion, 5th Marines, operating to the east of their sector, discovered the approaches unexpectedly open on this side. Receiving permission to attack, they drove westward,

692

overcame the weakened defenders and hoisted the flag over that troublesome citadel, thus ending the most bitter and protracted fighting of the campaign.

Meanwhile, on the extreme left the Seventh Infantry Division, operating over somewhat more favorable terrain, had smashed major resistance and penetrated some distance south of Yonabaru by 24 May. Their progress now was being held up less by the enemy than by weather conditions and the necessity of maintaining contact with the center, still bogged down in front of Shuri.

On the right the Sixth Marine Division was engaged against Naha, the island capital. After some bloody fighting, they had managed to seize and hold some high ground, dominating the city from the north. Beyond here, however, they were temporarily stymied by an important natural obstacle: the Asato Gawa (river). To negotiate a crossing, the Division stole a leaf from the Japanese's own book: infiltrating under cover of darkness on the morning of 23 May, most of the 1st and 3rd Battalions, 4th Marines, got safely across and by daybreak had secured a strong bridgehead. Bridging operations were commenced immediately and completed under considerable difficulties, but the rain and the Japanese combined to curtail its usefulness for some time.

Naha was a shambles, pounded to rubble by gunfire and bombing. Under the rubble were the Japanese. Promptly the Sixth Division set about the slow, dirty work of getting them out—or sealing them in permanently. By midmorning of 28 May they had taken all the area west of a canal running north and south through the city and secured a height dominating the west, making possible a large turning movement. They reached the Kokuba River on the thirty-first, and by 1 June had taken all the land lying north of Naha Harbor and cleared the entire Division sector.

The crucial phase of the Okinawa campaign was past. It had taken an even two months of as difficult fighting as the Pacific War had produced. More hard fighting and the better part of another month would be required to ring down the bloody curtain, once and for all.

General Buckner was killed early in the afternoon of 18 June. That was the day the 8th Marines had moved into the line to contribute their freshness and full strength to the slow, weary drive. The general had not come to the front especially to watch them, but by chance he found himself near their command post, on a hill which afforded an excellent view of what was going on up forward, and he paused to watch the attack for a few minutes. By this time the Japanese artillery had been reduced close to the vanishing point. No shells had fallen in this area all morning. Now, however, by some devious quirk of destiny, a lone gun somewhere in the shrinking enemy territory let go a few random rounds. The first one felled the general, though none of the several others near him was so much as scratched. He died before they could evacuate him.

The death of General Buckner at this late date had no effect on what remained of the campaign. The end was in sight, and General Geiger, succeeding to the command, simply carried through as his late chief would have done. This was, incidentally, the first instance of a Marine officer commanding an Army unit of comparable size, though in World War I, Major General Lejeune had commanded the Army's Second Division in several major operations.

With securing of the southern shore in both sectors, organized resistance ceased on Okinawa. But owing to the broken nature of the terrain and the elaborate defenses through which the drive had penetrated, a mopping-up job of colossal proportions remained to be done on the many hundreds of the enemy inevitably overlooked.

This was accomplished simply by throwing the direction of the drive into reverse. On 25 June, with the XXIV Corps now on the right, III Amphibious on the left, the X Army started back northward through the region they had just traversed so painfully, while the reserve regiments of both Corps established a tight block along the whole length of the Naha-Yonabaru highway to prevent escape of any Japanese from the trap. The movement was regulated by predetermined phase lines, the units moving in co-ordination and keeping abreast with little difficulty.

Now there became increasingly manifest a phenomenon

694

which had been observed first during the closing days of the southward drive: the Japanese began to surrender; not merely individuals and small groups, but in crowds. Throughout the campaign our propagandists had labored unremittingly toward this end by means of radio, loudspeakers, printed material dropped from the air, but it had required the bald fact of demonstrated conquest to bring conviction. By 30 June when the mopping up was completed, the whole region cleared out, the III Amphibious Corps had taken a total of 4,029 military prisoners of war, including fifty-one officers; yet up until 15 June, they had taken only 322. Those taken by XXIV Corps and miscellaneous units brought the grand total to 7,401.

This unprecedented situation included some odd features. Because of the difficulty in distinguishing the Japanese from the Okinawans, many enemy soldiers sought to avoid capture by donning civilian clothes and losing themselves among the native population. Of such, eleven hundred and seventy were apprehended and identified, but it is probable that many more got away with it—for a while at least. One young Japanese lieutenant, commanding officer of a machine gun company in the Sixty-second Division, was captured hiding in a cave with his Okinawan girl friend, too warsick and lovesick to care particularly what went on. He told a number of interesting things to our Intelligence officers, and subsequently the couple was treated to a Buddhist wedding with all the trimmings, newspaper accounts of which brought many indignant letters-to-the-editor from folks back home who had never seen a Jap, let alone seen one get married.

During the Okinawa campaign, too, occurred a strange "armed truce" on a near-by island. The commander of the small Japanese garrison here, called upon to cease his hopeless, pointless holdout, asked time to consult Tokyo by radio. This done, he met several American emissaries on his beach and announced regretfully that he had been forbidden to surrender, but that he would not fire on parties of our people visiting the island for recreational purposes, provided they did not molest his people. It was never like this in the old Pacific War! By the standards of what had gone before, this was degenerating into practically civilized warfare.

Of profound importance throughout the Okinawa campaign was the work of the Tactical Air Force, X Army, under Marine Major General F. P. Mulcahy, who was succeeded in this command on 11 June, 1945 by Major General L. E. Woods. During the crucial days of the ground fighting, this force was made up predominantly of elements of the Second Marine Aircraft Wing, its staff augmented by Army and Navy officers to provide a joint operational command. The advance echelons came ashore in the wake of the assault forces and began setting up for business on 4 April. MAG 31 and MAG 33 had the fighter planes of several of their squadrons in and operating from Yontan and Kadena airfields on 7 and 9 April. MAG's 22 and 14, also fighter units, arrived in May and early June respectively, and the torpedo bombers of VMTB 232 (22 April) and VMTB 131 (29 May).

Army fighters began appearing in May and had grown to formidable proportions by the end of the ground fighting. The Army Bomber Command was set up 2 June, but did not get into full-scale operation until July, following which it gave a very vivid account of itself indeed.

The fighter planes on Okinawa performed all the missions conventional for their type: interceptor patrol, far-reaching combat patrols, bomber escort, etc., but their activity which contributed most directly to the outcome of the campaign was the flying of close-support strikes for the ground forces. The terrain and nature of the enemy defenses made this particularly important, and all possible planes were made available for this work. Rockets, bombs and strafing were all employed liberally, and napalm was used whenever the tactical situation made this practical. And a somewhat less conventional phase of air support achieved unprecedented importance in this particular operation: parachute drops of supplies to troops isolated in the more remote regions through the breakdown of the road system under the torrential rains. The torpedo bombers proved most useful at this work, too. Altogether, 612,564 pounds of food, medical supplies and ammunition were delivered in this manner, and so efficiently was the system developed that recovery was estimated at ninety-eight per cent.

The persistent, large-scale Japanese air activity over Okinawa contributed to give the TAF fighter pilots a field day. During the early stages of the operation, the enemy were sending over attack missions of three hundred or more planes, and even as mounting destruction whittled down their strength, they were able as late as 22 June to mount an attack estimated to include 150 to two hundred aircraft. As many among the attackers were suicide-bent Kamikazes, inexperienced pilots in obsolete or second-rate planes, their destruction was all the simpler. Between 7 April when the first sortie was flown and 30 June, fighters of the TAF destroyed a verified 610 enemy aircraft, killing an estimated 1,054 crewmen, with a total loss to themselves, including all air and ground units, of 77 KIA, 54 MIA and 150 WIA.

These figures do not include enemy planes damaged or destroyed on the ground, or those shot down by AA. When it is considered that the Navy (planes and guns) had destroyed 2,604 enemy aircraft and damaged 352 others within five hundred miles of Okinawa by L + 33, some idea of the magnitude of the catastrophe to Japanese airpower can be realized.

But the most important aspect, so far as the Marine Corps was concerned, was that once more the air arm had justified brilliantly the basic reason for its existence: support of the ground forces on the field of battle.

June thirtieth marked the end of mopping up on Okinawa. The last feeble flicker of Japanese military activity had fizzled and gone out. *Finis* was written to three months of sustained blood and bitterness. Now the troops could rest, those who were not among 7,283 resting already and forever in the soil they had died to conquer, or the 31,398 wounded scattered among a score of island hospitals.

A vacation from mud and blood and horror—but for how long? It occurred to few of the weary men, plodding toward their new bivouac areas or preparing to re-embark for their bases, that there was the most remote possibility that they had heard shots fired in anger for the last time.

697

Kamikaze

In the Okinawa campaign, the Navy fought off ten mass attacks of Kamikaze planes, or "floating chrysanthemums" as the Japanese called them; each attack numbered 45 to 355 planes. There were hundreds of smaller Kamikaze strikes, plus the more conventional sorties by dive bombers and torpedo planes.

Among the measures Admiral Turner * took to provide protection for the expeditionary forces was the radar picket screen. This was a network of radar stations fifteen to one hundred miles from shore. In the beginning a destroyer or a minesweeper patrolled day and night within an area of 5,000 yards of the station. Later, when the pickets were taking their heaviest punishment, another destroyer and additional landing craft with anti-aircraft armament helped increase the firepower of the stations.

S. E. Morison says, "Radar picket stations were the premier posts of danger in the Okinawa operation. Destroyers and other vessels assigned to this duty suffered tremendous losses, and protected other ships around Okinawa from sustaining even greater losses. By giving early warning of approaching Kamikaze attacks, vectoring out C.A.P.** to intercept, and most of all bearing the brunt of these attacks, the pickets gave the finest kind of self-sacrificing service." ***

The following selection From Morison's *Victory in the Pacific* describes two battles at picket stations off Okinawa.

*Commander of the Joint Expeditionary Force at Okinawa.
**Combat Air Patrol—a patrol of escort carrier planes was maintained over each picket daily.
****Victory in the Pacific,* p. 235. Little, Brown & Co.

THE GALLANT FIGHT
OF THE RADAR PICKETS

by Admiral S. E. Morison

Admiral Deyo's night retirement disposition,[1] still short of four heavy ships and six destroyers which had not got the word, consisted of nine battleships and cruisers steaming in circles respectively of 5,000 and 12,000 yards' diameter, with a screen of seven destroyers 4,000 yards outside. The disposition turned away towards Ie Shima. At 1753 destroyer *Leutze,* which had already been damaged off Iwo Jima, sighted a plane coming in eight miles distant and at 1800 opened fire. Within a few moments the clear evening air was spotted with black bursts from 5-inch gunfire, almost every ship was spouting red balls from her 40-mm quads, and the water was laced with spray from shorts. About twelve Kates and Oscars came in so low over the water that lookouts saw them before radar did. *Leutze* and *Newcomb* [2] bore the brunt of this attack. In quick succession one kamikaze crashed *Newcomb's* after stack, a second was splashed, and at 1806 a third, carrying a large bomb or torpedo, crashed into her, amidships, gouging deep into the bowels of the ship with a tremendous explosion that cut off all remaining sources of power and blew "both engine rooms and the after fireroom into a mass of rubble." "With intentions of polishing us off," wrote Commander I. E. McMillian, "a fourth plane raced toward *Newcomb* from the port beam and although under fire by her forward batteries came through to crash into the forward stack, spraying the entire amidships section of

[1] April 6, 1945.—Ed. note.
[2] Also a destroyer.—Ed. note.

Newcomb, which was a raging conflagration, with a fresh supply of gasoline." Flames shot up hundreds of feet, followed by a thick pall of smoke and spray which so completely covered the destroyer that sailors in nearby battleships (including the present writer) thought that she had gone down.

Destroyer *Leutze*, closing rapidly to render antiaircraft assistance to *Newcomb*, also assumed that she was sinking and swung out boats in preparation for rescue; but when close aboard she observed that McMillian's ship was still holding together. A solid mass of flame swept from bridge to No. 3 gun, but her valiant crew showed no intention of abandoning ship. Lieutenant Leon Grabowsky (Naval Academy 1941), C. O. of *Leutze*, gallantly risked his ship to help her sister, closed her weather side at 1811 (only ten minutes after the first crash), passed hose lines on board to help fight fires; and then, at 1815, a fifth plane approached, heading for *Newcomb's* bridge. One of her 5-inch guns, fired in local control, made a hit which tilted the plane just enough so that it slid athwartship and on to *Leutze's* fantail, where it exploded.

Now *Leutze* too was in trouble. A fire sprang up in the after ammunition handling room. While one of her repair parties continued fighting fires on board *Newcomb*, the other two attempted to check flooding on their own ship and jettisoned topside weights. Steering control was lost with the rudder jammed hard right. Seventeen compartments laid open to the sea by the Japanese bomb let in so much water that *Leutze* began to settle. Destroyer *Beale*, with all fire hoses streaming, now closed the disengaged side of *Newcomb*; and not until then did *Leutze* signal "Am pulling away, in serious danger of sinking." At 1842 Lieutenant Grabowsky requested Admiral Deyo's permission to jettison torpedoes and depth charges. After permission had been granted *Leutze* signaled "Believe flooding under control." Minesweeper *Defense* (Lieutenant Commander Gordon Abbott USNR), which had been slightly damaged by two kamikaze hits shortly after 1800, took *Leutze* in tow at 2005. While making her slow way to Kerama Retto *De-*

700

fense sent this cocky message: "Sorry to be late, have scratched a kamikaze and taken two on board. Now have destroyer in tow." She arrived off Kerama Retto and cast off her tow at 0230.

Newcomb, one of the "fightingest" destroyers in the Navy (she had led a torpedo attack in Surigao Strait), lost nothing in comparison with *Leutze;* Nelson's accolade to his sailors, "They fought as one man, and that man a hero," could well be applied to her crew. The exec., Lieutenant A. G. Capps, after being pulled out from under the tail of a crashed kamikaze, directed the local-control fire of the forward gun and then handled the firefighting; the surgeon, Lieutenant J. J. McNeil USNR, carried several severely injured men to a place of safety, operated on surgical cases in the wardroom in the midst of the uproar, and so continued all the following night; Lieutenant (jg) D. W. Owens USNR "by his personal direction and fearless leadership" quenched a magazine fire. Two out of 78 enlisted men singled out for special commendation in the Action Report may also be mentioned here: fireman Francis J. Nemeth was securing steam lines when burned to death by the spreading fires and machinist's mate Richard C. Tacey was killed trying to reach some of the black gang who were trapped by the flames. All crews of guns that could shoot fired until they were blown overboard or killed.

Newcomb had all fires under control before fleet tug *Tekesta* towed her, too, into the calm waters of Kerama Retto. One marveled at the sight of them there next morning: scorched, scarred and half wrecked, *Leutze* alongside repair ship *Egeria,* with part of a kamikaze plane still resting on her fantail; *Newcomb* with No. 2 stack gone, No. 1 leaning crazily to starboard, her entire deck abaft the superstructure buckled into the contour of a roller coaster, and her fantail about six inches above the water. *Leutze* had lost only 7 men killed or missing and 34 wounded, but *Newcomb's* casualties were 40 killed or missing and 24 wounded. Both ships had to be beached or dry-docked and there was some question whether they were worth repairing, but repaired they were.

Two destroyers fared even worse that afternoon. *Bush* (Commander R. E. Westholm), on radar picket station No. 1, and *Colhoun* (Commander G. R. Wilson), on station No. 2, were the first to be encountered by "floating chrysanthemums" flying southwest along the Nansei Shoto. The ships had been out there since April 1 and 3 respectively, with "seldom a dull moment." Advance elements of the massed air attack heckled them all through the midwatch and *Colhoun* received eleven bombing attacks, all of which missed, between 0230 and 0600 April 6. The forenoon watch was fairly quiet. Around 1500, 40 to 50 planes flew down from the north, stacked at various altitudes between 500 and 20,000 feet, and began orbiting and attacking *Bush,* while about 12 others went after *Cassin Young* (Commander J. W. Artes) at station No. 3, next to the eastward.

Bush shot down two Vals and drove off two more, a few minutes before 1500. Thirteen minutes later a Jill was sighted heading low for her. Commander Westholm promptly swung ship to bring it abeam and unmask his main battery. Fire was opened at a range of 7,000 to 8,000 yards. The plane jinked and weaved at an altitude of 10 to 35 feet above the water, and although every gun on the destroyer was firing, it kept coming and crashed between the two stacks. The bomb exploded in the forward engine room, killing every man there, and most of those in the two fire rooms. Flooding started immediately and *Bush* took a 10-degree list, but escaping steam smothered the fires and power was regained as the auxiliary diesel generator cut in. Handy-billys were used to control the flooding, the wounded were treated on the fantail or in the wardroom and although the ship had gone dead, everyone expected to save her, and all hands cheered when a C.A.P. of four planes appeared overhead.

Colhoun at 1530, learning by radio that *Bush* was in need of help, began to close at 35 knots, bringing along her C.A.P. for the short time it could remain. The chief fighter-director commander in *Eldorado,* Admiral Turner's flagship, sent out another C.A.P. which encountered so many Japanese planes en route that a general melee devel-

702

oped some 15 miles south of *Colhoun's* course. This C.A.P. splashed bandits right and left, but ran out of fuel and ammunition before it could help the destroyers. At 1635 *Colhoun* closed *Bush*, then dead in the water, smoking badly and apparently sinking. She signaled a support craft, *LCS-64*, to rescue the crew and tried to interpose herself between the sinking ship and a flight of about 15 Japanese planes. They approached, and one went for *Bush* at 1700. Commander Westholm ordered about 150 of his men fighting fires topside to jump overboard for self-protection, and trailed knotted lines for them to climb on board again. All his 5-inch guns that would bear were jammed in train, but his 40-mm guns opened fire and frightened one Val away.

Colhoun in the meantime was shooting everything she had at an approaching Zeke, which missed and splashed midway between the two ships. "This left one down, eleven to go," remarked Commander Wilson. Another was hit by a 5-inch shell at 4,000 yards, and its port wing caught fire. *Colhoun's* guns Nos. 1, 2 and 3 were quickly trained on a third Zeke diving at her starboard bow, and the first salvo hit him square on the nose; he splashed 50 yards abeam. Just then Wilson received a report that a fourth Zeke was about to crash his port bow. Too late he ordered full left rudder. The plane, already aflame, hit *Colhoun's* main deck, killing the gun crews of two 40-mm mounts. Its bomb exploded in the after fire room, killing everyone there and rupturing the main steamline in the forward engine room. Lieutenant (jg) John A. Kasel, the engineer officer, opened the cross-connection valve before diving for the bilge, so the after engine room had steam and a speed of 15 knots was maintained.

Colhoun was already getting her fires under control (despite loss of all handy-billys) when, at 1717, commenced the fifth attack on her within 15 minutes, by two Vals and a Zeke. The gunnery officer had the presence of mind and found the time to assign target sectors to his five-inch guns. One Val was splashed 200 yards on the port quarter. One missed *Colhoun* and was shot down by fire from *Bush* and *LCS-84*. The third plane crashed the forward fire room,

703

where the bomb exploded, piercing both boilers, blowing a
4-by-20-foot hole below the waterline, and breaking the
keel. *Colhoun* went dead in the water; all power and communications were lost. The indefatigable damage control
party then applied CO_2 and foamite fire extinguisher. The
gunnery officer re-established communication with guns
1, 2 and 4 of the main battery. The wounded were treated,
fires brought under control; and the men had just begun to
get rid of depth charges and torpedoes when at 1725 the
sixth attack on *Colhoun* (and fourth on *Bush*) started.

Three planes dove on each bow and one on her quarter.
All *Colhoun's* guns were now manned in local control; and
it takes such strength and determination to point and train
a 5-inch 38 without power, that the strong young bluejackets
had to be relieved after two minutes. One Zeke was splashed
150 yards away. The other two were hit by 40-mm fire but
only slightly damaged. One, a Val, caught its wing in the
after stack, caromed on No. 3 gun, knocking off its gas
tank which burst into flames, and then bounced off main
deck into the water. There the bomb exploded, knocking
a 3-foot-square hole below the water line and so deluging
the after part of the ship with water that all fires were
extinguished and everyone on the fantail was washed overboard. The third plane missed *Colhoun,* pulled out and
started to dive on *Bush* against her 40-mm fire, the best
she could now deliver. It missed the bridge, and crashed
main deck between the stacks. The impact almost bisected
Bush; only the keel held her together. Her men already
overboard climbed back, the repair party threw water on the
fire and almost had it under control when, at 1740, a fourth
plane, a Zeke, made a weaving dive. *Colhoun's* No. 4 fired
at it but missed. For the last time the 20-mm and 40-mm
guns of *Bush* spoke. The kamikaze cleared her by five feet,
gained altitude, did a wingover, came in again, and crashed
her port side at 1745, starting a terrible fire and killing or
fatally burning all the wounded in the wardroom. A handy-
billy, shifted to this fire, was no better than a garden hose
on such a blaze; the entire forecastle was enveloped in
flames, and ready ammunition began to explode.

Still neither crew would give up its ship. *Colhoun,* with

704

only a bucket brigade operating, was taking water fast, but *Cassin Young* and a tug were coming in to assist. Commander Westholm counted on the fires in *Bush* above the main deck burning themselves out, as his ship was well buttoned up below; and although she could hardly fail to break in two in the heavy sea, he hoped that each half might be salvageable. Shortly before 1800 the bow began to settle. Suddenly a Hamp appeared "out of nowhere" and, evidently deciding that *Bush* was a goner, dived on *Colhoun*. Direct hits were scored on the plane at very close range. Already aflame, it hooked the pilothouse and crashed the port side. *Colhoun* was so badly damaged already that this additional hit did not make things much worse.

By that time daylight had begun to fade. Other Japanese planes were visible, but not another ship was within hailing distance. Damaged *LCS-64*, with many survivors on board, had cleared out. At 1830 a big swell rocked *Bush*. She caved in amidships, jackknifed until bow and stern sections were at a 135-degree angle, and quietly went down in a 350-fathom deep.

Commander Wilson of *Colhoun,* after consulting his exec. and heads of departments, decided to abandon ship. When *Cassin Young* closed at 1900, he begged her to search for *Bush* survivors. *LCS-84,* which also closed, commenced the arduous work of rescuing men in the rough sea. About 200 were transferred to *Cassin Young* between 2015 and 2100. *LCS-87* then came alongside and took over all who remained in *Colhoun* except a skeleton salvage crew of four officers and 17 men. Fires flared up again, and the men ran out of foamite and CO_2. When fleet tug *Pakana* arrived from Kerama Retto at 2320, *Colhoun* was listing 23 degrees and awash up to her No. 4 gun. The tug had no pumps to lend, so Commander Wilson ordered *LCS-87* to take off the skeleton crew, and, at his request, *Cassin Young* sank her by gunfire. She had lost 35 men killed or missing and 21 were wounded.

The plight of *Bush* survivors was desperate. To keep afloat they had one gig, a number of floater nets which were constantly breaking up and capsizing, and a few rubber life rafts inflated by CO_2, which were excellent—one supported 37 men. The seas were ten to twelve feet high and whitecapped. Both air and water were cold. The men had taken a beating in the successive attacks on their ship and were suffering agonies from their burns. Many could stand no more, slipped out of their life jackets and went down. The gig finally attracted the attention of *LCS-64*, which commenced rescue operations at 2130; a fleet tug from Kerama and a PC arrived shortly after. They had to work in complete darkness as Japanese planes were still about. As the rescue vessels approached survivors some became excited and tried to swim to them, and drowned from exhaustion; or when alongside were broken against the hull, or caught in the propellers. Other men died after being taken from the water. Seven officers out of 26, including Comdesdiv 98, Commander J. S. Willis, and 87 men out of 307, were lost.

The INDIANAPOLIS

The heavy cruiser *Indianapolis* had been damaged by a Kamikaze at Okinawa and in consequence had had to lay up for repairs at Mare Island in the States. Because of her chance presence on the California coast in July, she was given the task of transporting "the heart of the (atomic) bomb—a subcritical mass of Uranium 235"—to Tinian. After delivery, she was then ordered to Leyte, via Guam, to join Task Force 95. The second night out from Guam, the *Indianapolis* caught two torpedoes from a Jap lying directly in her path. She went down in 12 minutes with some 800 men awash in the sea as survivors.

"Without an escort possessing sound gear, the cruiser was dependent on radar and eyesight to detect a submarine. And she was not zigzagging when she encountered the underwater enemy. It was an overcast night and standing fleet instructions required ships to zigzag only in good visibility. Captain McVay's routing instructions directed him to zigzag "at discretion," which he did by day, but not at night. He did not appear to be disturbed that in his briefing there was a report of a submarine near his estimated position at 0800 next day, and of another 105 miles from his ship's track on 25 July. Nor was the ship 'buttoned up' above the second deck. Since these old heavy cruisers had no air conditioning, the Captain, to make sleep possible for his men in tropical waters, allowed all ventilation ducts and most of the bulkheads to remain open. The entire main deck was open, as well as all doors on the second deck, and all hatches to living spaces below." *

*S. E. Morison, *Victory in the Pacific*, p. 321.

ABANDON SHIP*

by Richard F. Newcomb

On the bridge, the watch began to settle down. Jack Orr checked his course and speed, Casey Moore strolled around the open navigation bridge and found all watch-standers on duty. The moon was appearing more often now, and was a little brighter, but at times it was difficult to make out faces on the bridge and impossible to see far out over the water. Just after midnight, the bugler of the watch, Donald F. Mack, went into the chart house to see the quartermaster, Jimmy French. French's striker, Seaman First Class William F. Emery, was also in there.

Suddenly, there was a tremendous blast forward, followed by a sheet of red-yellow flame and a giant column of water rising higher than the bridge. The ship shuddered and a few seconds later came a second blast, much nearer the bridge, much more violent, louder and more terrifying. For a split second after the second blast there was utter silence, except for the swish of water and the hum of turbines.

Nearly everyone on the bridge was thrown to the deck by the first blast, then dashed again to the deck or bulkhead by the second explosion. Within seconds, the ship roused to life in a massive reflex action. For an instant there was pandemonium, but no panic. There is always something unbelievable about your ship taking a hit. As in everyday life, things happen to the other fellow, not to you. The first reaction is one of sheer surprise, tinged with disbelief and perhaps resentment and the beginnings of anger.

*Condensed from *Abandon Ship,* pp. 64-101.

708

But—and here is where training pays off—most men snapped quickly to defense posture and began automatically to perform the tasks assigned for just such an emergency.

There was no panic on the bridge. Casey Moore raced to the splinter shield and peered forward in the murk. The bow seemed oddly down, and he could make out smoke and a few figures moving about on the deck. Orr steadied the helmsman, and the JL talker. Seaman First Class A. C. King picked himself up from a maze of wires and put his phones back on his head. The bosun's mate of the watch, Coxswain Edward H. Keyes, went mechanically to the public-address box, whistled a test pipe down it and found it dead. The blue lamp on the control panel would never glow again. King raised nobody on his phones, and Keyes told Orr, "Everything is dead on the sound system, sir."

"Go below and pass the word 'All hands topside,'" Orr shouted, drawing both consciously and subconsciously on his recent experience with the sinking destroyer in Ormoc Bay. The fatal thud of torpedoes was familiar to him now.

After his first look around, Casey Moore reacted like any good damage-control officer. He sprinted to the ladder and went below to have a look.

Captain McVay's emergency cabin was port side at the back of the house built on the navigation deck, with the door facing aft. He awoke with a start at the first blast, and it flashed through his mind that a second kamikaze had found the target.[1] The second blast threw him out of bed, and as he hit the deck it occurred to him that this was not kamikaze territory. Must be mines, or torpedoes, or internal explosion. Acrid white smoke was already seeping into his cabin, and as he went out on deck he noticed it there, too. Stark naked, he made his way around to the bridge.

"Do you have any reports?" he called to Orr.

"No, sir," the OOD replied. "I have lost all communications. I have tried to stop the engines. I don't know whether the order has ever gotten through to the engine room."

"I will send down word to get out a distress message,"

---

[1] The *Indianapolis* had stood duty off Okinawa.—Ed. note.

Captain McVay said. He was not alarmed. The ship had no list as yet, and this was not his first experience with battle damage. They had saved the ship before and they could do it again.

As he turned back to get his clothes, he told Orr, "See what information you can get."

McVay quickly picked up pants, shirt, and shoes and returned to the bridge, dressing as he went. As he reached the bridge, things began to happen pretty fast. For one thing, strange noises sounded from below, and strange noises on a ship usually mean trouble.

Casey Moore came back just then from his first quick look around, and reported the damage was severe.

"Most of the forward compartments are flooding fast," he said, "and there are no repair parties there. Do you want to abandon ship?"

"No," McVay replied, "our list is still slight. I think we can hold her. Go below and check again."

Moore left the bridge, but he never returned.

The whole ship was beginning to strain and groan in a way never intended.

"Have you any word from the radio room yet on whether they've gotten off a message?" the Captain asked Orr.

"No, sir, no word yet."

The ship was definitely slowing down, and the bow was low and acting queerly. It seemed to plunge head on into the seas instead of rising with them. The list was only about three degrees to starboard.

Jack Janney appeared from his cabin, on the starboard side, exactly opposite McVay's. Captain McVay sent him to the radio shack, to get the distress message out.

"Send a message saying we have been hit, give our latitude and longitude, say we are sinking rapidly and need immediate assistance," Captain McVay told him. Janney went down the ladder, never to return.

No sooner had he left the bridge than Commander Flynn came up the ladder.

"We've been badly damaged, Charlie," he said. "We're

710

taking water fast. The bow is down. I think we are finished. I recommend we abandon ship."

Captain McVay had been coming to the same conclusion himself. He could not see from the bridge, with flame and smoke pouring up from the foredeck, but there is a feel about a ship. She was acting most strangely, and she seemed to be almost totally without lights and power, a sure warning of mortal damage in the belly. All he needed was the opinion of a man of Joe Flynn's experience and judgment.

"Okay, pass the word to abandon ship," McVay said. Flynn left the bridge for the last time.

Not many skippers have to give the command "Abandon ship!" It is a fateful command, yet when it must be given there is no time for reflection. That time comes later, perhaps.

The captain's biggest worry was whether or not word had gotten out. Unescorted as they were, and 300 miles from the nearest land, it was vital that someone know of their plight. Not a single dispatch had been sent from the ship since she left Guam, nor had any been addressed to her, and it was another 36 hours before she was expected in Leyte. The potentialities for disaster were great, considering that the *Indianapolis* carried only two small boats.

Now that the command had been given, McVay wanted to be sure someone knew they were in trouble. None of his messengers had returned from the radio shack, so the captain decided to go himself. For all its benign look and air of tropical romance, it was not a friendly sea. Besides a probable enemy out there, who had been known to machine-gun helpless men, the ocean had its own perils. Shark, barracuda, and other strange and rapacious fish abounded, and sun and salt could be vicious enemies. Nor was there any hope of atolls or reefs, for the water here was some of the deepest in the world. It was imperative that someone know they were in serious trouble.

As McVay put his hand to the ladder leading down, the ship took a great lurch to starboard, going over to about 60 degrees. For a moment he clung to the ladder, then slid down to the signal bridge. The vessel paused for a moment in her roll, but it was obvious that McVay would never reach the radio room.

He looked to port and saw several men struggling to get to the lifelines.

"Don't go over the side unless you have a life jacket," he roared. "I think she may stay here a minute or two. Get the floater nets against the stack."

From above, Lieutenant Orr, still clinging to the splinter shield, cried, "That's the captain talking; get the floater nets."

But within thirty seconds the tired old ship rolled full 90 degrees to her starboard side. Now the bulkheads were horizontal and the decks vertical. McVay grabbed the communications deck lifelines, now above him, pulled himself up, walked across the bulkhead and pulled himself up another step to the side of the ship. There he stood for a moment, upright on her side, staring down at the vast expanse of red bottom.

He walked slowly aft, thinking she still might stay afloat. But he had gone only a few steps when the bow of the vessel began to sink. The water line advanced gently along the hull, and in a moment it washed him off. It was only twelve minutes since the first blast had ended his sleep.

Doc Haynes glanced into the warrant officers' mess as he passed and noticed a poker game. But it was nearly midnight, and he was tired. In his cabin he quickly undressed and stretched out on his bunk. He was already asleep when the impact of the first torpedo hurled him into the air and he landed on his desk. He had no sooner put his foot to the deck than the second one smacked home, directly under him. Flame swished down the passageway and singed him as he started out the door, a life jacket held in front of his face. Behind him, the room was now on fire, and forward the passageway was full of smoke and flame. The deck tilted crazily.

Haynes turned aft, hoping to get through the wardroom and onto the quarterdeck. Everywhere he turned there was fire, but he made it to the wardroom. Only a red haze illuminated it, and the heat was fierce. The doctor fell, and as his hands touched the deck they sizzled. He rose in shock and threw himself into an armchair. As he gasped for breath in this inferno, someone standing above him screamed "My God, I'm choking," and fell on him.

Haynes rose in fright, and across the wardroom someone yelled, "Open a porthole! Open a porthole!" The doctor struggled to the starboard side and reached for a port, only to find it had been blown open and was slapping against the hull. He hooked it up and leaned out, gulping in fresh air, and as he did so something kept slapping him in the face. It was a line, hanging from the deck above. Oblivious to the pain in his hands—a surgeon's hands—he grasped the line and yanked it. It held.

Scarcely knowing what he was doing, he eased himself through the porthole and pulled himself up to the main deck. The air was much better there, and he made his way across to the battle dressing station in the port hangar. He was still dressed as he had been in his bunk—pajama bottoms only. The ship was a shambles topside, and slowly Haynes' mind began developing the pictures his eyes had taken—papers and broken furniture in the water, fire-reddened decks and bulkheads, jagged metal, and an awful hole beneath his escape port. He had no time to draw conclusions yet, but in a mechanical daze turned to the scene before him in the hangar. Wounded men lay everywhere, singly and in bunches, limbs twisted, faces contorted. Some were quiet and alive, others just quiet. Chief Pharmacist's Mate Schmueck was already administering morphine in no set pattern, just to those closest and in the most violent agony.

Haynes pitched in, not as an officer but as a doctor, responding automatically to years of training. Once he collapsed across a man he was helping, and revived as the man pushed him away. For the first time he noted that his patients were beginning to slide away to starboard, and with this realization the whole picture fell into place—the gaping hole, the fire, the debris, the list, and down below those now-ominous sounds—the death rattle of a ship.

"Get some life jackets, John, we've got to get these

men ready," he told Schmueck. There was no question about it, the ship would soon sink.

Schmueck and another sailor returned with armloads of life jackets, but time was getting short. The starboard rail was already under water. They struggled as best they could, but some men shrieked and writhed in pain as they tried to get jackets around them.

"Don't touch me, don't touch me," screamed one horribly burned man, who somehow had escaped from the hell below. Escaped? He had only transferred the place of his death.

Those still able to move were given a choice. As the ship rolled on her beam, they could either drop into the water on the starboard side or scramble up to the high side. Doc Haynes and some others crawled up to port and walked out on the hull. Soon they were walking on red bottom paint, and then it was just water and thick black fuel oil in great waving blankets.

When Ensign Woolston arrived in the wardroom a few minutes after midnight for a cup of coffee after his watch, he had barely sat down at the mess table when flames from the first blast roared up the passageway and through the wardroom doors. A few seconds later, when the second fish cracked home just beneath him, the whole room burst into flame like the inside of a firecracker. Woolston instinctively rolled under the table, out the other side, and through the window into the pantry in one smooth continuous movement. As the flash flame died away, he picked himself up and returned to the wardroom. The steward's mate of the watch appeared and they began searching for a dog wrench in the reddening darkness, coughing and spitting from the smoke. Woolston felt himself slipping, growing faint from lack of air.

He shook himself and muttered out loud, "Wait a minute, Woolston, this is not the way to go."

His hand fell on the wrench, and he undogged two ports and thrust his head out into the blessed, cool air. The water was rising, even on the high side, indicating the vessel was both settling in the water and canting to starboard.

714

"I think I'll rest a minute," the steward's mate said, as Woolston slithered through the porthole. He may have gotten out of the wardroom later, but not one of the thirty-two stewards, steward's mates, or officers' cooks survived.

Woolston climbed to the communications deck to get a life jacket and stumbled across a crack in the deck. Glancing forward, it looked to him as if the bow was under water, at least on the starboard side, but it appeared to be still holding. Splintered wood and steel were thrown up from the main deck in several places, and flames licked up from below. As a damage-control officer, he realized that the ship was in a bad way, with fire below and the sea probably cascading into the hull from at least two holes. As he ranged back and forth on the port side, trying to find somewhere to help, he heard the word from above, "Abandon ship! Abandon ship!"

By the time Woolston reached the well deck, the list was increasing rapidly. Hands reached down to him from above, and a human chain pulled him up onto the port side of the hull. The men slithered into the water, and Woolston found another life jacket floating by him. He passed it to a steward's mate, who had none.

In Radio II, Woods [2] was no man to sit around waiting for orders that might never reach him (and never did). He sat down at a transmitter position and began sending on 500 kilocycles, the international distress frequency. Herbert J. Miner, Radio Technician Second Class, peered over Woods' shoulder and watched the antenna meter fluctuate. Woods was keying the simple SOS—three dots, three dashes, three dots—followed by the ship's position. Miner noted that the SOS was definitely going out—when that meter fluctuated it proved there was power in the antenna.

No one knew how many times it went out, but Miner told his buddies later, as they waited for rescue, that it was at least three times. In any event, Woods stuck at his key until the ship went so far over he told his men, "Get out

[2] Chief Radio Electrician L. T. Woods.—Ed. note.

of here as fast as you can." The men cleared the shack in a rush, just as the ship laid out flat on her side.

Every ship and shore station round the world is supposed to guard 500 kc. There was just a possibility—

When the *Indianapolis* departed Guam, she carried eighty-two officers (including the passenger, Captain Crouch) and 1,114 enlisted men. Around midnight on Sunday, perhaps sixty-five of the officers were in officers' country in the forward part of the ship. Most of them were asleep, but a few were still in the wardroom, or the showers, or reading in their rooms.

The two torpedoes cracking home, each carrying 1,210 pounds of high explosive, bracketed officers' country fore and aft. Well over a ton of explosive was delivered to the cruiser's tender belly within a space of 175 feet. The first hit at about Frame 7, or some twenty-eight feet back from the bow and, if she was running true to her depth setting, rammed smack into the chain locker. There is no telling exactly where she hit, but it was probably not aft of Frame 7. The two tanks for storage of high-octane aviation gas were at Frame 15. Only one was full, 3,500 gallons, but had it exploded the entire bow might have been blown off.

The second torpedo struck a telling blow. With this one shot alone, the *Indianapolis* was doomed. Besides opening a huge hole amidships, it wiped out all communications, lights, and power in the forward half of the ship, and with them went the fire mains, radio, radar, and fire control for the guns. Striking at Frame 50, directly below the bridge, the blast must certainly have opened the forward fire room to the sea, destroying any pretense of watertight integrity that the vessel might have had.

Within seconds of the two blasts, the forward half of the ship erupted into frenzied life, with men stumbling through darkened passageways, coughing and spitting from smoke and noxious fumes from dozens of sources. Some men floundered aimlessly, like beheaded chickens, others ran silently and swiftly with great purpose. Some screamed and bled, others merely bled, and some did not move at all.

On balance, officers and men did the best they could. As

716

the shattered bow plowed into the swells, no longer able to rise with them, the tremendous force of the sea against the exposed bulkheads was too much for man or ship. The transverse bulkhead at the chain locker leaked in a dozen places through split seams, sprung plates, and twisted doors. This alone could have been serious, but it was nothing compared to the amidships hit, which ripped the bottom open laterally—like a giant can opener. The men forward did not know the extent of the damage amidships, but they soon felt its effects. Water pouring in from starboard tipped the mighty ship to that side, and water cascading in forward pulled the bow down, as if to make it easier for her to slake a mortal thirst.

The scene on the fantail was fantastic. Within minutes it was peopled with men crawling everywhere, like flies on a piece of garbage. In the light of the intermittent moon, or flames from forward, they gathered there by instinct, droves of them, over five hundred in all. No one told them to go there, but after all instinct was invented long before thought. And once they arrived, there was no one to tell them what to do. The great bull voice of the PA system, representing the unseen presence on the bridge, was stilled. No orders, no instruction, no central direction would ever come from it again.

So they gathered and they waited. A few were wounded or burned, most of them were not, and many were naked or wore only the skivvies or shorts they had been sleeping in. Not one in a score had shoes on, or carried a knife, flashlight, or any of the dozen other items they had been instructed to have ready in case of just such an emergency. No one was figuring, even then, on abandoning ship. Some men had already gone over the side, to be sure—blown off the forecastle or driven over by panic—but they were not many. Most of the men were calm, if confused. It was inconceivable that this big ship would sink.

But as the bow slowly sank, and the stern began to rise, the feeling of impregnability gave way to a new thought. The seed of doubt matured rapidly as the list to the right developed. A few officers and leading PO's kept telling the men, "Get a life jacket, get a life jacket." Strange creakings, bangings, bubblings, and cracking sounds rose from below and the ship began to slew around, obviously out of control.

Men began to drop off the starboard lifeline, despite orders by some officers or in response to urging by others. It was all happening so quickly, and there was no word from above. Men acted individually, in response to their own natures. They were dribbling off the side now like peas from a planting machine. When the last great lurch came, there was no longer time for individual decisions. They could only get away from the ship in the best manner open to them. She was clearly going down.

Some were reluctant to go, for they feared the dark, oily void awaiting them more than the ship breaking up beneath them. By some miracle, it might stay afloat. Such things had been known to happen. Ensign Twible screamed for the men to go over the side, but no one moved. They waited until he himself went, then followed him in a rush, like sheep. Some men clung to guns, stanchions, lifelines, any projection, until it was let go or drown. Others, high in the superstructure, plotted it coolly and waited for a hole to drop through, taking no chances on getting tangled in the rigging or dropping into a swarm of debris or flailing men.

Hundreds fought their way up to the port railing, and walked or slid down the hull. Some waited too long and became fouled in the screws, as Nos. 3 and 4 rose from the water. No. 3 was still turning, a terrifying and relentless meat-grinder. In the minds of everyone was the fear of suction when the ship went down. True or not, everyone has heard that a sinking ship exerts terrible suction when it goes down, and can drag anyone near the hull down with it. So once in the water, every man struck out for safety, one thought only in mind—get away from the ship.

And the last ones off had little time, for the ship seemed anxious to go. As the head and midships, now filling rapidly, sank lower the final hundred feet or so of the giant hull raised straight up out of the water and seemed to stand there for a moment.

Hundreds of men, directly under it, watched in terror as

718

it hung there, fearing any moment it might topple on them. Captain McVay, now a shipwrecked sailor like the lowliest seaman, saw the screws above him and thought, "Well, this is the end of me."

But they were wrong. The *Indianapolis* waited but a moment, then slipped straight down, like a leadline, disappearing quickly and silently, without suction, without anguish. Thus ended her career of twelve years, eight months, and twenty-three days afloat—the last major vessel lost in World War II.

The time was 12:14 a.m., Monday, July 30, 1945, East Longitude date.

The nearest land was still some 250 miles away, directly south, the top end of the Palaus archipelago. Guam was 600 miles to the east, Leyte 550 miles west, and to the north there was nothing for nearly a thousand miles. The water at this point was probably 10,000 feet deep, give or take a couple of thousand.

Captain McVay was fortunate, though there were times later when he might question this. He struck out swimming, away from the menacing hulk above him. After only a few strokes, a wave of oil and water washed over his head, and he turned to look. The ship was gone.

The captain struck out again, and almost immediately ran into a crate of potatoes, late tenant of the fantail. He climbed astride this, reached out and grabbed a shattered desk floating by, and almost in the same instant saw two rafts not twenty feet away. Captain McVay quickly swam to them, and as he climbed in one he heard men calling for help.

He called back and soon Quartermaster Allard swam alongside, towing two shipmates who looked more dead than alive. Allard pushed Seaman Second Class Ralph D. Klappa toward the raft and Captain McVay reached out for him, saying, "You can make it the rest of the way."

"I can't do anything," Klappa said and started to slide. Only eighteen years old, he had been to sea just fifteen days. McVay pulled him aboard and the youngster lay in the raft,

719

vomiting oil and salt water. Meantime Allard helped Seaman Second Class Angelo Galante, 20, over the side and then pulled himself aboard. Galante joined Klappa in retching as they lay in the raft, recovering from fright and exhaustion.

McVay and Allard lashed the rafts together and spent the night investigating their new home. They quickly discovered the rafts had fallen into the water upside down. Paddles, rations, matches, flares, and other emergency gear were all secured to the bottom. By incredible chance, they saw and heard no one else throughout the night. A man low on the water can see practically nothing, even in daylight, and particularly with a twelve-foot swell running. But at dawn they discovered another raft and floater net nearby, with five more men on it. Captain McVay directed them to come over, and soon the three rafts were lashed together with fifteen feet of line between each. This kept the party from straying but allowed enough line so the rafts wouldn't bump.

As Captain McVay surveyed his command through one eye (the other was inflamed from fuel oil and nearly closed) he thought he was seeing about him the sole survivors of the 1,196 men aboard the *Indianapolis*.

He was greatly mistaken. There were hundreds of men within a few thousand yards, all struggling for their lives, and none as well off as the captain's group. There were a number of reasons why Captain McVay could not see them, or they him.

Men left the ship in a variety of ways over a period of 12 minutes, during most of which the ship was still under way. The first off were soon left far behind, mere heads bobbing in a blanket of fuel oil, virtually undiscernible even from a ship in broad daylight. Those who stayed till the last were split into groups determined by the point at which they had left the ship, the swirling and eddying of waters around the hull, their swimming strength, and the impedimenta thrown in their way from the foundering vessel.

And hardly were they in the water than the sea began inexorably to separate them. The swimmers, nearly totally

720

immersed, presented little surface to the wind and thus the prevailing current began carrying them to the southwest at about one knot. But those on rafts or debris felt the force of the ten-knot wind and were wafted off to the northeast at varying speeds. By daybreak, the groups were scattered over a line of several miles, on a generally southwest-northeast axis. A man with his eyes six inches above water can't see much in a moderately rough sea, even from the top of a twelve-foot swell. If his eyes are smarting from salt water and fuel oil, and partly blinded by a hot sun, he can see even less. Men on a raft have a better chance, but even on a crest you can't see into the troughs of other waves, and you may be scanning east when a head bobs up to the west, only to subside into a valley as you turn.

Monday dawned clear and the men welcomed the sun. It seemed at first to warm them spiritually after the cold night, and promise strength and help. They took heart and, as man seems to do in any circumstance, began organizing this new watery world. There was no question of over-all command, for already the groups were widely scattered. Indeed, in most cases each group knew only of its own existence and was fully occupied with its own problems. Some few small groups, finding themselves close together in the morning, did put their meager forces together. Almost from the start they fell into two large groups, and a dozen or more small, isolated clusters.

In perhaps the largest group—some three hundred men that first day—Lieutenant Commander Haynes was the senior surviving officer, and by virtue of rank, training, and force of personality he took charge. Strictly speaking, he was not the senior officer, for Commander Lipski, the gunnery officer, was there. But he was clearly dying. The flesh on his hands had been burned down to the tendons, and his eyes were burned closed. Shipmates gathered round him and tried to hold his tortured body out of the stinging sea and oil, and Doc Haynes looked on in anguish, unable to lessen his pain. From somewhere, a cork life ring appeared, and they used that for the severely injured. It knew more than one tenant. A long piece of line was formed into a large circle, and perhaps a hundred and fifty men clung around the per-

721

imeter. With only this flimsy line, they felt better. There were many other arrangements—one man clung to a toilet seat. Schecterle, just out of sick bay minus his appendix, latched onto a lard can, occasionally dipped into the contents to still the pangs, and alternately used the top as a heliograph. Plenty of ammunition cans were in evidence for a while, and the rubber-type, inflatable life belt was worn in several styles. Some put it around their middle, as indicated. Others wore it like a bandolier, lay across it side saddle, or sometimes floated—using it as a pillow. In any form, it was nearly useless, and the wise man watched for a kapok that might soon be vacated.

Off to the northwest, less than a thousand yards away at the start, was a second large group. Whatever it was at the start, by dawn Monday death had weeded it down to 120 men and perhaps eight to ten officers, senior of whom was Dick Redmayne. Now he found himself in command of three small rafts, one floater net, some 5-inch ammo cans and other flotsam. His force included one seasoned warrant officer, three or four green ensigns, and assorted enlisted men, fortunately including a couple of chiefs. Among them was Benton, whose courage would win him the Navy and Marine Corps medal.

To the northeast, capping the triangle, were the splendid isolationists: the men whose great good fortune it was to have nearly separate quarters on the rafts. Besides McVay's enclave of three rafts and nine men, the biggest single floating command fell to Ensign Rogers, a tall, rangy lad who had been to sea only two weeks. He had been aboard so briefly that though he was a junior officer of Turret IV, he still didn't know his duties or even how it worked. Only the night before, his roommate, the ever-efficient Ensign Woolston, had let him in on the open secret that a sub had been reported along their course. Rogers paid no more attention to this than anyone else. Anyway, he was busy writing a letter to his bride. It was their first anniversary (one month, that is), and he didn't want her to think he had forgotten it.

Rogers was one of the last to leave the ship, and when he hit the water he went down, down, down. He thought he would never come up, but he did and right in front of

722

him was a raft. He grabbed a hand rope on the side and hung on as the ship reared above him, hesitated a moment, and then plunged. It was unbelievable that anything as big and safe and solid could disappear in a moment, but she did. After the final waves washed over him, Rogers climbed into the raft and met his new "shipmates," a mountain boy named Willie Hatfield, Seaman Second Class, from Salt Lick, Kentucky, and Chief Ferguson. During the night they picked up another man. Ferguson was suffering from his leg wounds, and Rogers put a tourniquet around his thigh. Throughout the night, he periodically released the pressure, fearing gangrene, and when dawn came he carefully unwrapped the bandage made of the mess-cook's pants. There was a deep cut at the knee, and four or five inches of flesh gouged out below it, besides less serious cuts on the leg and foot. "Doc" Rogers rewrapped the wound as best he could, and cut the loss of blood to a slow ooze. Figuring rapidly, he reasoned that the ship would be missed Tuesday morning, when it failed to show off Leyte for target practice. Search would start immediately and they should be found by Wednesday morning. Ferguson could last that long, he figured. Ferguson never complained.

During the night, the McVay rafters became scavengers, snatching from the sea any interesting looking objects they passed. At first light, the captain began to take stock of his possessions. His wristwatch was working fine, and he decided to keep a log, using paper and a pencil stub disgorged from various pockets and wallets. The sun gave an approximate position, and a fish line streaming in the water indicated drift. In spite of the wind, the rafts drifted west, and a few degrees south. The inventory revealed a relatively secure position. There were ten twelve-ounce cans of Spam, two large tins of malted-milk tablets, seventeen cans of biscuits, but no water. At least the food would be ample for some days to come.

Paddles were retrieved from the underside of the rafts, and one carton yielded fifty small packages of Camels. Oh boy, all the comforts of home! Well, nearly. There wasn't a lighter in the crowd, and the matches from the emergency kits were soaked. Cigarettes and no way to light them; they cast the cigarettes back into the water, removing at least that form of small torture.

They also found a first-aid kit—unneeded—and, very reassuring, a can of Very flares and an emergency signaling mirror. In the can were a small pistol for firing the flares, and twelve flares in all, four each of red, green, and white. Captain McVay began to feel better. With his little convoy stretching out over seventy-five feet of water, and his signaling devices, he was confident they would be sighted by a plane on this heavily traveled track.

Life was becoming a little grim now. The men were tired, and they ached. All soon discovered that the designer of their rafts had never had to sit on them very long. The rounded top chafed on the buttocks and soon wore them sore. Hands blistered from paddling and every cut or abrasion began to develop salt-water ulcers. There seemed no way to keep dry, even in the rafts, and the constant salt-water dousing was irritating, physically and mentally. It was uncomfortable to sit down, but if you stood up and fell, you had a new cut to contend with. Elbows were turning raw from rubbing and the skin seemed tender and sensitive all over.

For the swimmers, the battle for survival began the instant they hit the water. First it was the struggle to get their heads above the water and out of the slimy, choking oil. They sputtered and coughed, some vomited for hours, spewing out the irritating substance, and many were blinded in one eye or both. Their noses, mouths, and throats smarted from the oil, and membranes became inflamed. And always there was the chop and splash of waves. By dawn, many were already seriously exhausted, but as the sun rose and they began to see others around them, the men took heart.

As the sun rose on Monday, the sea flattened out a little and the men felt better. The kapoks were holding them high, and the worst of the oil bath was over.

As the heat rose, thirst began to bother some men, particularly those who had dehydrated themselves with retch-

724

ing or coughing. But there was no deliberate drinking of sea water that day. The men warned one another about that, and they all knew it was bad for you. Potatoes, canned peanuts, onions, other bits of food floated on the surface in some places, but most of the men wouldn't eat anything. They were afraid of upsetting their stomachs further, or getting even thirstier. A few ate anything that came by, and even hid a surplus in their pockets for later, but hunger was not a real problem yet.

It was some hours before they began to realize that sharks and other rapacious fish were among them. Suddenly a man screamed, his head bobbed for a moment, and he began flailing the water with his arms. Blood welled to the surface, and other men took up the cry. They beat the water with their arms and legs and shouted and screeched in an effort to scare the intruders away. At first they thought only of sharks, because everyone knew about sharks, and the telltale dorsal fin was often in evidence on the fringes of their circles. Gradually word spread from the older men that these warm equatorial waters were also host to carnivorous fish that could not be so easily seen.

The injured who survived the first few hours were weakening now, with the sun high and hot, and the sea and the oil and their wounds all conspiring to sap their strength. It was pitiful to those around them not to be able to help, but there was nowhere to put them, nothing to give them, no way to protect them. They put some in the rafts, but there their bodies were fully exposed to the cruel sun. So they put them back in the water and tried to tie them to the rafts, if they were too weak to hold on. In these last hours of agony, those who had been spared injury gave unstintingly of their strength, their food, even their life jackets to help those who could not help themselves. But in most cases it was not enough. The burned and the maimed slipped away, one by one, and by Monday night nearly all of them were gone.

The strongest and the bravest tried to stay alert, even riding herd on the group like swimming cowpunchers, bringing back the strays and holding the men together. More than

725

one, in this way, used up the reserves that might have kept him alive in the final hours of agony. They were, in truth, laying down their lives for their friends.

For most men, the night was worse than the day. Man's spirit normally sinks at night, and during the long, dark hours they fell prey to fears forgotten by day. It was a grim band, indeed, that struggled through the first twenty-four hours in the water, and in the hours just before dawn a few men began to ask themselves why they fought on. A few, weak and dispirited, perhaps impelled by some previous purposelessness in their lives, may indeed have succumbed to the lassitude of despair. It was so easy just to slip down, to let go, to sink, and in a few moments it was all over. But the first streaks of morning light in the sky revived the great majority of them, and they prepared to meet the day of rescue. For surely help would come on Tuesday.

Tuesday was hot again, hotter than Monday, but nobody wished for night to come. Besides the fears of the dark, ships and planes couldn't see you at night. Night was a foe. But as the daylight hours passed, nothing happened. No plane passed overhead, and no ship came plowing down on them.

Almost from the first, men began discovering that life-jacket design was an art not yet mastered. The rubber life belts were the worst.

In the first place, many refused to inflate, for a variety of causes. Even if they did, they gave little support when worn around the waist, as intended. For one reason or another, perhaps because some were old or the sea water and oil affected them, many burst in a matter of hours. They were better than nothing, to be sure, but not much. The kapok jackets, of the so-called horse-collar type, gave good support, but the collars soon began to rub the men's necks and chins, increasing their suffering as the salt water and oil inflamed the irritated parts.

Thirst was more of a problem than hunger. As the sun rose higher and hotter on Monday, some men began thinking of schemes for making the sea water potable. At this stage, before dementia had set in on a large scale, and

726

their bellies began to hurt, they talked a little of "straining" the water, or "evaporating" it.

"How about it if you hold some water in your hands? Won't the sun evaporate the salt out?"

"What do you say we strain some water through this hat a couple of times? We can catch it in this handkerchief and squeeze it through again. That ought to do it."

"Knock it off, it'll still kill you," said the clearheaded around them. But pretty soon even the clearheaded had problems of their own, and they became less careful or less watchful. Then the men who could stand it no longer took first a little drink, then a bigger one, and a still bigger one. It is a horrible death, but soon over. During the last paroxysms, friends about them sought either to hold them or to escape from their wild thrashings, until at last the bodies subsided and became still. It was time then to salvage the life jacket and knife, mirror, or any other potentially useful object and let the body sink slowly out of sight.

Wednesday was a delightful day for the swimmers. It was the day they learned the *Indianapolis* had not sunk after all. She was lying just below the surface of the water, and the gedunk stand was open, featuring six flavors of ice cream, and the scuttlebutts were pouring forth pure, sweet water as usual. The first man to discover this was so delighted with the find that he urged all those around him to go down with him and slake the terrible thirst that was driving them mad. As the word passed, a sort of frenzy ran through the swimmers and in a short time many were diving like swans, using up the last resources of strength that might have saved their lives. Some men who had not yet passed fully into the world of fantasy tried to restrain them, but it was useless.

But Wednesday night was a night of terror. When darkness fell the demented men were the victims of stark fear, and every shape became an enemy.

"There's Japs on this line," someone screamed and a little knot of men would be plunged into a melee, fighting with fists, cans, cork, anything that came to hand. Now and then a knife blade flashed in the moonlight, followed by a groan

727

and then a struggle for a life jacket whose recent owner needed it no more.

"Here comes a Jap, he's trying to kill me," a sailor shouted. "Help! help!" The frenzied men took up the shout and began swinging wildly at anyone near. Two men climbed on Doc Haynes and dragged him under. When he struggled to the top again he tried to calm the men, but it was no use. They were too far gone for reason. Those who still possessed their senses could see the toll was terrible.

Toward morning, calm slowly returned and it was obvious the men were falling into the final stupor that precedes death. Haynes moved among the pitiful survivors, trying to rouse them for one last day's fight. He lifted head after head from the water, rolled back an eyelid and, in some, detected signs of life. These men he slapped and cajoled into consciousness, trying to pull them back from the brink.

Thursday began as a day of calm—the calm of death for the swimmers. With all strength gone, all emotion spent, they seemed nearer death than life, and indeed they were. There was little talk or movement, just a quiet waiting for the end to overtake them. Hanging in their waterlogged life jackets, their mouths and noses nearly in the water, they no longer wished nor hoped for anything, not even death. The inevitable sun rose, higher and hotter, and still no complaints. They were not capable of caring any more. A few, slightly stronger than the others, looked up occasionally or even strained to listen when they thought they heard a plane. A little before noon, with the sun still mounting, a few looked up when a plane droned by, high overhead. There was a scattering of muttered curses, even a doubled fist raised weakly out of the water. The plane passed over, to the north. They had known it would.

Then, here and there, a heart fluttered. The plane seemed to pause, to turn. Some thought it was starting down. It was, it was!

"He sees us, he sees us!" someone screamed. Others joined in, and arms and legs began to splash.

"They're coming, they're coming!" "He's turning, he's turning!" "Here he comes!"

728

Like sleepers roused from stupor the men began to come alive, joining in the chorus one by one. Where they got the strength no one can say, but soon the ocean was kicked into a froth, and cries echoed from many throats. Some men could only croak or grunt, their gullets swollen nearly shut, and some men didn't move or utter a sound. Too late, too late.

It was almost exactly three and a half days—eighty-four hours—since the *Indianapolis* had gone down.

The big, friendly plane circled slowly and then—over the southernmost knot of men—a raft, some life jackets, and other gear spewed from the plane and fell nearby. Grateful men swam out to get the raft, careful not to overtax their strength, and when they reached it clung to the sides, too weak to climb in. Others grabbed the fresh dry life jackets to replace their waterlogged ones. Men for miles around watched as the plane slowly climbed away from them, and held their breath until they saw that she was not going away. It was comforting to have her there, even though she could do them no immediate good. As long as she stayed they knew she was helping them, telling someone by radio where to look, calling others to their aid.

The second plane, a PBM, arrived from the northeast a little after noon. She didn't stay long, but she dropped three more life rafts and then hurried on to the west, toward Leyte. Hope was getting stronger now; other planes would be coming, and ships. Another plane, a Ventura like the first, arrived a half hour later, and also from the south. The two Venturas orbited overhead and seemed to be talking, or planning, and watching. Then the first Ventura, their friend, their savior, took off southward, obviously going back to base to get more help. The second Ventura remained overhead, but it wasn't until nearly four o'clock, with the sun already starting down, that the next plane arrived. This was a big amphibian from the south, and after a look around she began to drop things, like an elephant littering the track at the circus. Out came rafts, one after another, and cartons of rations, dye marker, life jackets, casks of water. Some of the water casks split on hitting the water, some of the gear sank, and some was useless, but it was all welcome, if only as a symbol that help was on the way.

But day was definitely waning, and the men in the water began to wonder if still another night in the water, their fourth, would be required of them. To make matters worse, the sea was beginning to make up again. Toward sunset those few left in the southernmost group, the Haynes group, watched in wonder as the PBY slowly glided down as if to make a landing run. It looked like suicide, with the swells running nearly twelve feet high by this time. But the giant plane kept coming down and suddenly pancaked into a trough, took three mightly bounces in a towering spray, and came safely to rest on the water.

Strangled cheers broke through sore and swollen lips and throats as the PBY began to taxi slowly around the periphery, pausing now and then to scoop a lone swimmer into its belly. Those who now had rafts, nets, or other means of support cursed at the plane as it passed them without stopping, but it was obvious what the pilot was doing—as darkness fell he was hurrying to pick up the lone swimmers, those with nothing to cling to.

It was very nearly dark now, and just as the last light began to fade a second PBY came in from the south, low and slow. This one, bearing Army markings, quickly came down to wave-top height, knifed through the tops of several swells and cut her power, disappearing in a trough. Soon she appeared on the crest of a wave, safely landed. She seemed quite a way off from any swimmers, but maybe some could find her in the dark. Those still in the water, and there were hundreds, were alone again now, but at least they had hope, and perhaps a raft, to sustain them through the darkness.

Eight or ten miles to the north, Captain McVay and the other raft parties could see the plane activity through the afternoon. McVay was greatly cheered, not only because rescue seemed near but because the concentration of activity far south indicated there might be many more survivors than he had believed. But as the afternoon waned and the

730

planes seemed to be working ever southward, the raft crews began to worry that they would not be seen.

Again at dusk, as he had each night, Captain McVay led the men in reciting "The Lord's Prayer." It seemed more helpful than usual this night.

But this was not to be a night like the others. About 9:30 some of the swimmers and rafters began to notice a light far to the south. At first it seemed it might be an illusion or a faint moon rising behind the clouds. As time passed, however, the light became stronger and within a half hour it seemed pretty definitely to be a searchlight, reflected off the clouds. By the time an hour had gone by, the light was unquestionably brighter, and coming closer, although still a long way off. By 11:00 they were sure—it was a ship coming at them, fast, and with all lights on.

Now that help was so near, they feared sleep more than ever and were less able to fight it, being on the outer edges of oblivion.

"I mustn't sleep, I mustn't sleep," they told themselves. Men who had not once slept in eighty hours, or so they believed, vowed they would not succumb now, with help so near, so near. But the sea was rougher Thursday night, security so close, and they were so tired—not every man kept his vow.

On the rafts to the north, the men could see the searchlights off to the south, first one, then several, and finally by dawn there was great activity. But it did not move north, or so it seemed.

For the swimmers, actual rescue in the form of help from surface vessels began shortly after midnight on Thursday, exactly four days, or ninety-six hours, from the sinking of the *Indianapolis*. By chance, the first vessel approached from the south. Had she come from the north, she might have seen the men on the rafts first—the men who could wait—and delayed long enough to cost even more lives, for with the swimmers minutes counted. But the planes on the water and the accident of approach led the ships directly to the men who needed help the most, and through the black hours from midnight to dawn the rescue vessels picked up one of the most pitiful bands of men ever to escape the sea. Men suffered from burns—sun or flame—fish bites, salt-water ulcers, inflammation of the nose and throat, acute dehydration, pneumonia, fractures, and cuts and bruises from a thousand sources. But hearts still pumped and blood still flowed and from now on it would be up to medical science.

At dawn the rescue vessels began to see what they had been doing and to realize the magnitude of the appalling tragedy before them. Command and planning took over from the frantic and haphazard methods of the dark hours. They began to take stock of how many men they had aboard, how many might still be in the sea, and how best to comb the area for the last remaining survivor. On orders now, the vessels spread out in search pattern sniffing for the living among this welter of oil, debris, and bodies.

Last to be rescued were the rafters, at the north of the group. Their most anxious moments came in the last hours of Friday morning darkness, when it seemed the ships were so near and yet would miss them. But at dawn they saw planes to the north and hope rose again. The planes were obviously on box search, and coming ever closer.

At 10:00 a.m. they saw ships, and suddenly someone shouted, "My God, ships bearing down on us! The hell with the planes, we know these guys will pick us up."

It was the end of one of the strangest, most dramatic battles of men against the sea.

Potsdam to Hiroshima

On July 26, 1945, while meeting in Germany during the Potsdam conference, President Truman and Prime Minister Churchill issued a proclamation calling for the surrender of Japan unconditionally. Nine days earlier the President had been notified that the first experimental atomic bomb explosion in New Mexico had been a success. He and the Prime Minister decided to use the bomb on Japan if their terms were not met. There was no direct reply from the Japanese Government, and on August 2nd, while President Truman was returning to Washington he issued the order to drop the bombs.

According to Churchill, "there never was a moment's discussion as to whether the atomic bomb should be used or not. To avert a vast, indefinite butchery, to bring the war to an end, to give peace to the world, to lay healing hands upon its tortured peoples by a manifestation of overwhelming power at the cost of a few explosions, seemed, after all our toils and perils, a miracle of deliverance." *

Over a million leaflets were dropped on eleven principal Japanese cities warning of bombing attacks to come. There was little effect upon the military rulers of Japan who still held full sway over the people; the die-hard militarists always managed to turn each reverse into a rationalization for eventual victory or an improvement of their strategic position. They were only too willing to commit the nation to a suicidal last stand.

Fortunately, the Emperor and certain other Japanese leaders chose to defy the militarists, but they were not able to do much until the atomic bombs were dropped. Even then, the military assessed the Hiroshima explosion as a "four ton block-buster," revising it a little later to "100 tons."

A meeting of the Japanese war cabinet was held in Tokyo on August 9. During the meeting, news of the Nagasaki bombing was reported.

*Winston Churchill, *Triumph and Tragedy*, p. 639. Houghton Mifflin.

The Japanese War Minister and his Chiefs of Staff still held out against unconditional surrender. "Finally the Emperor, who had neither constitutional nor traditional right to make a decision or even to express an opinion without Cabinet consent, took the issue in his own hands: 'To stop the war on this occasion is the only way to save the nation from destruction. . . . I decide this war shall be stopped.' " *

On August 10, the Japanese Government accepted the Potsdam terms. But it was too late to save the citizens of Hiroshima and Nagasaki.

THE GREAT WHITE LIGHT

by Major Gene Gurney

In the beginning, back in 1939, 1940, and 1941, the idea had been to develop a bomb as quickly as possible, and to use it. Gradually as the awesome nature of the new weapon became more apparent, some doubts were raised. The responsibility that went with the power of the bomb was great indeed, and it would trouble men forever.

President Truman assumed responsibility for the use of the atomic bomb almost as soon as he assumed the office of President of the United States. Immediately after he had taken the oath of office, Secretary of War Stimson told him of the new weapon soon to be ready for use against the enemy. A few weeks later, after the President had received a thorough technical explanation of the bomb, Stimson suggested that a committee be formed to work out just how it should be used.

Named to the Interim Committee, as it was called, were: Secretary Stimson, chairman; George L. Harrison, acting chairman in the absence of Stimson; James F. Byrnes, personal representative of the President; Undersecretary of the

*Walter Karig, *Battle Report: Victory in the Pacific,* pp. 508, 509. Rinehart & Co.

734

Navy Ralph A. Bard; Assistant Secretary of State William L. Clayton; and scientists Vannevar Bush, K. T. Compton, and J. B. Conant. These men were hand-picked by the Commander in Chief to deal with the most fearsome weapon ever developed by man. It was their task to recommend what was to be done with the top secret bomb which would be ready by August 1.

On June 1, after a series of conferences, the Interim Committee officially adopted a series of recommendations concerning this weapon and sent them along to the President. And with them went the blueprint of a new era of warfare.

The recommendations were:

1. The atom bomb should be used against Japan as soon as possible.

2. It should be used on a dual target—that is, a military installation or war plant surrounded by, or adjacent to, houses and other buildings most susceptible to damage.

3. It should be used without prior warning of the nature of the weapon.

The principal considerations in reaching these decisions were later disclosed by Mr. Stimson:

"As we understood it, there was a very strong possibility that the Japanese Government might determine upon resistance to the end in all areas of the Far East under its control. In such an event the Allies would be faced with the enormous task of destroying an armed force of 5,000,000 men and 5,000 suicide aircraft belonging to a race which had already amply demonstrated its ability to fight literally to the death.

"We estimated that if we should be forced to carry this task to its conclusion, the major fighting would not end until the latter part of 1946, at the earliest. I was informed that such operations might be expected to cost over a million casualties to American forces alone. Additional large losses might be expected among our Allies, and, of course, if our campaign were successful and if we could judge by previous experience, enemy casualties would be much larger than our own.

"My chief purpose was to end the war in victory with the

735

least possible cost in the lives of the men in the armies which I had helped to raise. In the light of the alternatives which, on a fair estimate, were open to us, I believe that no man, in our position and subject to our responsibilities, holding in his hands a weapon of such possibilities for accomplishing this purpose and saving those lives, could have failed to use it and afterwards looked his countrymen in the face."

Unaware of the momentous decisions being made in Washington, the combat crews of the 509th went through the week-long indoctrination course given to all new arrivals.[1] By the end of June they were ready to resume their flight training. First came three weeks of navigation training flights and bombing missions against Rota, Guguan, Truk, and Marcus with regular 500- or 1,000-pound bombs instead of the dummy bombs carried at Wendover. Then on July 20, training began to take the 509th to Japan. By the 29th they had made 12 strikes, each one a precision attack against a target near, but not actually in, one of the cities chosen for the atomic bomb.

A list of potential targets for the bomb had been drawn up after the Interim Committee had made its report. The Committee had pointed out the advisability of choosing a target that included a military installation plus a surrounding civilian area. The choice was further limited by the fact that the bomb's effectiveness could be measured only if it were dropped in an area still relatively undamaged. Weeks of intensive bombing by General LeMay's 21st Bomber Command had already destroyed the largest Japanese cities. Of those left, Kyoto was the largest, followed by Hiroshima, Niigata, and Kokura. This list met with the approval of General Arnold; on July 3 the Joint Chiefs of Staff ordered that there be no bombing of the four cities. Secretary Stimson, however, questioned the presence of Kyoto on the list. It was a religious and cultural center, and Stimson felt that its destruction would never be forgiven by the Japanese. With the approval of President Truman, Kyoto was removed from the list and replaced

[1] A new bombardment unit, designated the 509th Composite Group, especially organized for dropping the bomb.—Ed. note.

with Nagasaki at the suggestion of General LeMay's staff, although it was far from ideal as a target.

The four target cities were studied carefully so that the practice strikes of the 509th could be planned to give the crews as much experience as possible for the important mission they might someday have to fly. The navigation and bombing procedures used and the sharp turn away from the target were all similar to what would be the case if an atomic bomb were dropped. The bombs that were dropped were 10,000-pounders with ballistics similar to the atomic bomb.

The 509th was a highly trained outfit; its marksmanship on these training missions was impressive. But all its bombing reports and strike photos went straight to General LeMay, by-passing the usual lines of communication with higher headquarters, and so the other groups based in the Marianas wondered about the 509th. It had the very best of beautiful, new equipment, yet it didn't take part in the big fire raids on Japan. Its planes bore different markings— a black circle bisected by a black arrow. Its section of the base was full of restricted areas surrounded by barbed wire and guards, and there seemed to be numerous civilians about —the scientists and technicians who were to assemble the bomb.

If the rest of the Twentieth Air Force was in the dark about the mission of the 509th, the members of the unit didn't know much more about it. They all knew they were going to drop a special kind of bomb. Each of the men was working on his own part of the project, but security forbade discussion, even among themselves. They did not know what kind of bomb it was or how powerful it would be. They certainly hadn't seen it, because not until August 1, in one of the 509th's bomb huts where temperature and humidity could be carefully controlled, was the first bomb assembled.

The bomb lying in the air-conditioned hut on Tinian was the "Little Boy." It had never been tested, but the scientists were sure it would work. Since the 16th of July they had been sure that their second bomb, the "Fat Man," would work even better than the "Little Boy." At 5:30 a.m.

on the 16th the plutonium bomb had been exploded in the desert near Alamogordo, New Mexico, with results that exceeded the expectations of its designers.

President Truman and Secretary Stimson received the news of the successful test explosion while they were attending the Potsdam Conference. The President had agreed with the recommendations of the Interim Committee, and now he reaffirmed his earlier decision to use the powerful new weapon in the hope of saving the millions of lives that would be lost in an invasion of Japan. Japan was warned on July 26 to surrender unconditionally to avoid "inevitable and complete" destruction. Two days later the Potsdam Declaration was rejected by Premier Suzuki.

The chain of command that extended from President Truman down to the crew of the "Enola Gay" had already started to function. On July 25, General Carl A. Spaatz, commander of the United States Army Strategic Air Forces, had been given a directive which ordered the 509th Composite Group to drop the first atomic bomb as soon after August 3 as the weather would allow visual bombing. Spaatz immediately left Washington for Guam where his United States Army Strategic Air Forces headquarters had taken over the functions of the Washington headquarters of the Twentieth Air Force; he arrived there on July 29.

By August 1 it was just a matter of waiting for the 3rd, the earliest date set for the attack, and after that, for suitable bombing weather. There were now two bombs available; the scientists and technicians needed to handle them were on Tinian; the 509th had made 12 training strikes at targets in Japan; and the crew had been selected to deliver the first bomb.

Colonel Tibbets was going to lead the mission. He chose the plane and crew of Captain Robert Lewis, one of his instructors, to carry the bomb. With them would go one B-29 to measure the effect of the blast and one to carry camera equipment. In addition, three Superforts would precede Colonel Tibbets to check the weather, and there would be another Superfort waiting at Iwo Jima to take the bomb in case Tibbets' plane developed trouble.

On August 2 President Truman made his final decision

738

to use the bomb against Japan, and Lieutenant General Nathan Twining issued the field orders for the strike. The primary target was to be Hiroshima; the alternates were Kokura and Nagasaki. The bombing was to be visual, from 28,000 to 30,000 feet, the airspeed 200 miles per hour; the date was to be August 6.

The Superforts making the trip had their group insignia and names marked out. Tibbets later arranged to have Enola Gay, his mother's name, painted on the nose of the plane that was going to carry the bomb.

On August 4 the briefing of the crews began. At the first session they were shown pictures of the Alamogordo explosion and told that the bomb they were going to drop would have a force equal to 20,000 tons of TNT. The word "atomic" was not used to describe the bomb. Polaroid glasses were issued to all the men scheduled to go. They were given the details usual at a pre-mission briefing—take-off times, altitudes, routes, fuel loads. And they were given special instructions about avoiding clouds and keeping a critical distance from the target area after the bomb had been dropped.

The next day the Enola Gay was given a test run. Later she was taxied to a loading pit where the bomb waited. The five-ton "Little Boy" was raised by hydraulic jacks up into the forward bomb bay of the Superfort. The doors were closed and a sign posted to indicate that the plane was "cocked" and ready to go.

At midnight there was a weather briefing; the weather looked good. The crews were told of the arrangements that had been made for air-sea rescue and given final details on the procedures to be followed during the mission. Then came breakfast, and then the three weather planes took off. Take-off time for the Enola Gay was to be 2:45 a.m.

The crew started to assemble at the Enola Gay at two o'clock. Besides Colonel Tibbets there were Captain Robert A. Lewis, who was acting as copilot; Major Thomas W. Ferebee, the bombardier; Captain Theodore J. Van Kirk, the navigator; Lieutenant Jacob Beser, a radar countermeasures officer; Master Sergeant Wyatt E. Duzenbury, the flight engineer; Staff Sergeant Joe S. Stiborik, radar

739

operator; Sergeant George R. Caron, the tail gunner; Sergeant Robert A. Schumard, the waist gunner; and Pfc. Richard H. Nelson, radio operator. Also making the trip were Navy Captain William S. Parsons, who had worked at Los Alamos and was in charge of the bomb, and his assistant, Lieutenant Morris R. Jeppson.

After Army photographers had taken their pictures of the plane, the ground crew, and the crowd gathered to see them off, one by one the men climbed into the Superfort. Tibbets appeared at the pilot's window; he waved and started the four powerful engines one after another. Slowly the Enola Gay taxied to her runway. The camera plane, piloted by Captain George W. Marquardt, and Major Charles W. Sweeney's "Great Artiste," which had been transformed into a flying laboratory, were waiting for their take-off time. The Enola Gay left the ground at 2:45 to be followed at two-minute intervals by the other two planes. The "Little Boy" was on its way to Japan.

The bomb was still not armed. There had been a series of bad take-off crashes which had made everyone worry about having the Enola Gay take off with a live bomb on board. Captain Parsons had decided to put off the final assembly of the bomb until after they were safely airborne. To make sure that he would be able to do it smoothly when the time came, he had practiced putting the explosive charge in the end of the bomb over and over again. Now, as the Enola Gay leveled out over the Pacific, Parsons and Jeppson went to work in the bomb bay. The charge was inserted and the final connections made. The bomb would now explode after it had dropped to an altitude of 1,850 feet.

At Iwo Jima the Enola Gay began a slow climb to the altitude from which the bomb was to be dropped. The decision to strike the primary or the alternate targets rested with Colonel Tibbets and was to be made on the basis of information transmitted by the weather ships flying ahead of the Enola Gay.

At 8:15 the report on Hiroshima was received: "2/10 lower and middle lower, and 2/10 at 15,000 feet." Visual bombing conditions at the primary target! The decision was quickly made. Hiroshima!

740

The doomed city, Japan's eighth largest, was exactly what the Interim Committee had recommended as a target for the first atomic bomb—a military installation surrounded by houses and other buildings. It was an important army transport base and contained large ordnance, food, and clothing depots. It also had a shipbuilding yard, textile mills, oil-storage facilities, electrical works, and a large railroad yard. Because Hiroshima was on the list of targets reserved for the 509th, it had received so little damage that some of its residents had come to believe they were going to be spared the fate of Tokyo and Yokohama.

As the Enola Gay flew toward Hiroshima with her deadly cargo, the crew passed the time in various ways. Some of them tried to sleep, some read, some just sat and thought about the job that lay ahead. They were all a little awed by the bomb that rode in the forward bay. It was gray and long—close to ten feet—and about a yard in diameter. It was the biggest bomb they had ever seen.

Colonel Tibbets crawled back through the tunnel from the pilot's compartment to give the men in the rear a final briefing on the bomb. He asked the tail gunner, Sergeant George Caron, if he had figured it out yet.

Caron asked, "Is it some chemist's nightmare?"

Tibbets said it had nothing to do with chemistry. Then Caron recalled something he had read about a cyclotron and asked if it was a physicist's nightmare.

To this Colonel Tibbets replied, "I guess you could call it that."

As he started to return to the pilot's compartment Caron stopped him with another question: "Are we going to split atoms?"

The colonel just smiled and went back to his flying.

As the Enola Gay neared the Japanese coast, Captain Parsons went back to take one last look at the bomb. With Jeppson he had been keeping an electronic check on it from the forward compartment. Everything seemed to be all right. The bomb run was begun 25 miles out. Each man had his goggles ready to pull over his eyes when he heard the bombing signal. When they were 12 miles from target,

Ferebee, the bombardier, took over. Below he could see Hiroshima on the delta of the Ota River.

It was 8:15 in Hiroshima when the bomb was released. The continuous tone of the signal cut off, warning the crew and those in the accompanying Superforts that the bomb was away. The Enola Gay was at 31,600 feet, traveling at 328 miles per hour. It was clear and sunny. There were no enemy aircraft visible and the flak was far below them. The men sat behind their dark goggles and waited.

The bomb, set to go off above the ground to increase the effect of its blast, exploded in less than a minute. By that time Tibbets had put the Enola Gay into a steep, tight turn—the same turn he had practiced so often—and was leaving the target behind.

Far below, the 245,000 people who had not been evacuated from Hiroshima were up and beginning a new day. There had been an air-raid alert when the weather planes had passed over, but the all-clear had sounded. War workers were either en route or had already arrived at their destinations while others were busy building firebreaks and removing valuables to safety in the country. Probably few heard the Enola Gay as it passed over Hiroshima. The Japanese jammed in the vast Bushido Arsenal or hurrying through the heart of town to their jobs had no warning of the holocaust that was to envelop them.

Suddenly a light brighter than a thousand suns filled the sky. The world's first atomic bomb had exploded. At that moment, air became fire, walls crumbled to dust, and lives flickered out by the thousands.

The explosion started hundreds of fires almost simultaneously—fires whose intense heat sucked in air from all directions, creating a fire wind which helped to spread the numerous blazes. An area measuring 4.7 square miles in the heart of the city was completely destroyed. According to Japanese figures, 71,379 residents of Hiroshima were either dead or missing as a result of the bombing; almost that many more were injured. Many of the casualties were among the personnel of the Second Army and the Chucogu Regional Army units stationed in Hiroshima.

When the bomb exploded, the Enola Gay was racing away

742

from Hiroshima. In spite of the bright sunlight, the flash of the explosion lit up the inside of the Superfort. The crews of the two escort planes, observing the explosion through their protective goggles, reported that the flash after the explosion was deep purple, then reddish. It reached to almost 8,000 feet. The cloud, shaped like a mushroom, was up to 20,000 feet in one minute. Then the top part broke from the stem and eventually reached 40,000 feet.

Sergeant Caron, riding in the tail of the Enola Gay, was in the best position to view the effects of the blast. He saw a flash followed by a tremendous buildup of light which grew and then faded out.

"After what seemed like an eternity," Caron reported, "I saw shock waves coming up. I reported this to the Colonel and started taking pictures. He called back and told me to keep talking. I added that the shock waves resembled a series of circles like those caused from dropping pebbles in water. Seconds later they struck the airplane and one of the pilots asked if we had been hit by flak.

"Colonel Tibbets kept asking me what was going on. Then I saw the cloud and was never so busy in my life—trying to take pictures and keep the Colonel and the rest of the crew up to date on the blast.

"By the time the cloud rose slightly into the air we were far enough away and I could see the entire city. I commented that the whole area was covered with a thick, purplish mass that looked like fluid. It looked like it was a hundred or more feet thick and flooding out over the city from the center of the blast. Then flames started breaking up through the smoke and dust. The Colonel asked me to count them. I tried but lost track. In the meantime I was still taking pictures.

"Then Colonel Tibbets turned the Enola Gay so all crewmen could see and each gave his impression over the intercom and into the wire recorder. As we headed for home, the Colonel told me to keep my eye on the 'mushroom' and tell him when it disappeared from view. The crew for the most part was quiet on the return. I just sat there and watched that cloud. Finally, I called up that I was losing sight of it. We then were 363 miles from Hiroshima."

Captain Parsons later described what he was able to see: "A few fires were visible around the edges of the smoke, but we could see nothing of the city except the dock area where buildings were falling down. The boiling dust and debris continued for several minutes, as a white cloud plumed upward from the center to 40,000 feet and an angry dust cloud spread all around the city."

The crew felt a sense of relief that the bomb had been dropped successfully after their many months of training. But it was relief tinged with awe at the unearthly flash, the shock of the distant explosion, and the sight of a city disintegrating before their eyes.

The Superfort whose single bomb had destroyed Hiroshima sped back to Tinian, 1,600 miles away. So did The Great Artiste, whose instruments had measured the blast, and the B-29 camera plane. Messages had preceded them that the bomb had been dropped successfully.

The trip back was uneventful. Captain Lewis described their landing:

"I looked at 'Ole Bull' [Colonel Tibbets] and his eyes were bloodshot and he looked awful tired. He looked like the past ten months at Wendover and Washington and New Mexico and overseas had come up and hit him all at once. I said to him, 'Bull after such a beautiful job, you'd better make a beautiful landing.' And he did."

The Enola Gay touched down at 2:58 p.m., 12 hours and 13 minutes after she had taken off on her momentous journey into the Atomic Age. Close to 200 people were waiting as the Superfort taxied to her hardstand. Among them was General Spaatz, who pinned the Distinguished Service Cross on Tibbets' flying suit.

President Truman received news of the successful dropping of the bomb as he was returning from Potsdam on board the *Augusta*. His public announcement of the bombing was released in Washington 16 hours after it happened —still August 6 in the United States because of the time difference. The President again warned the Japanese people of what was in store for them.

The men in the Marianas received their first word of the powerful new bomb that had been dropped on Japan from the President's message. The 509th now became the center of attention, but the other B-29 units still had work to do. On the 7th, 131 Superforts struck at Tokokawa. The next day there was an incendiary attack on Yawata.

When no offer of surrender came from Japan, the decision was made to drop a second atomic bomb on the 9th. This time the primary target was to be Kokura in northern Kyushu, the site of a large army arsenal. Nagasaki was the secondary target. It was an industrial city covering a series of hills and valleys on the west coast of Kyushu.

"Fat Man," the plutonium bomb that had been tested at Alamogordo on July 16 and found to be more powerful than the one dropped on Hiroshima, was made ready and placed aboard the Superfort, "Bock's Car." Major Charles W. Sweeney, who had been in charge of one of the observation planes on the Hiroshima mission, was the pilot; his co-pilot was Lieutenant Frederick Olivi; the bombardier was Captain Kermit K. Beahan; and Captain James F. Van Pelt, Jr., was the navigator. Lieutenant Commander Frederick Ashworth was in charge of the bomb, which this time had to be armed before the plane took off.

Sweeney's regular B-29, The Great Artiste, which had been filled with instruments, accompanied Bock's Car as an observation plane and was flown by Captain Frederick Bock, who usually flew Bock's Car. This switch of planes between Sweeney and Bock led to confusion in stories about the dropping of the second atomic bomb. For years afterward there were accounts of the mission that had The Great Artiste carrying the bomb to Nagasaki.

Once more, in the early hours of an August morning, Superforts were prepared for take-off. Two observation planes went with Bock's Car; two weather planes were sent ahead to check bombing conditions at Kokura and at Nagasaki. A spare B-29 would be waiting at Iwo Jima in case Bock's Car couldn't make it all the way with the bomb.

The strike force got safely off at 3:49 a.m., much to the relief of the scientists, who feared a crash with the armed bomb would destroy half of Tinian. At 9 a.m. the report received from the Kokura weather plane indicated visual bombing conditions over the primary target. With orders

745

that called for a visual drop, Sweeney headed for Kokura.

But by the time Bock's Car arrived over the target, the weather had closed in and visual bombing was impossible. In his report Major Sweeney described what happened:

"The navigator made landfall perfectly. We passed over the primary target, but for some reason it was obscured by smoke. There was no flak. We took another run almost from the I.P. Again smoke hid the target. 'Look harder,' I said to the bombardier, but it was no use. Then I asked Commander Ashworth to come up for a little conference.

"We took a third run with no success. I had another conference with the Commander. We had now been fifty minutes over the target and wanted to drop our bomb in the ocean. Our gas was getting low. Six hundred gallons were trapped in one of the tanks.

"We decided to head for Nagasaki, the secondary target."

The report received from the Nagasaki weather plane at 9:19 had been "ceiling and visibility unlimited," but when Bock's Car reached there the target had a 8/10 cloud cover. Because of their fuel shortage Sweeney and Ashworth had decided to make one run and drop the bomb by radar if they had to. Commander Ashworth took the responsibility for the change in procedure.

The big ship was on instruments for 90 per cent of the bomb run. At the last moment Captain Beahan, the bombardier, called out, "I can see it, I can see the target!"

He took over and made a visual release of the bomb. It was 10:58 Nagasaki time. As the thundering Superfort turned in a tight arc and sped south, the city vanished in a sky-searing flash of light.

Nagasaki had had an air-raid alert at 7:45 a.m.; the all-clear had sounded at 8:30. When Bock's Car was sighted, the raid signal was given again but few people bothered to go to the shelters. If they had, the loss figures would have been less than the estimated 35,000 killed, 5,000 missing, and 60,000 injured.

The Nagasaki bomb's blast effect seemed greater than that at Hiroshima because of the difference in topography and the type of bomb used. The area totally destroyed was an oval 2.3 miles long and 1.9 miles wide; every building in it was destroyed, with severe damage extending in an irregular pattern beyond that. Over 68 per cent of Nagasaki's industrial area was destroyed.

The men in Bock's Car had donned their polaroid glasses before the bomb was dropped, but they were nearly blinded by the flash. Sergeant Raymond C. Gallagher, the assistant flight engineer, told of a tremendous white flash such as he had never seen before; this was followed by a black cloud which billowed up like a balloon.

The tail gunner, Staff Sergeant Albert T. Dehart, saw what looked like a big red ball coming up at him. On the ground was a big black cloud and out of it came a huge white cloud.

The shock of the explosion was felt by those in the strike plane. "The turbulence of the blast," said Major Sweeney, "was greater than that at Hiroshima. Even though we were prepared for what happened, it was unbelievable. Seven or eight miles from the city shock waves as visible as ripples on a pond overtook our plane, and concussion waves twice thumped against the plane, jolting it roughly.

"The underside of the great clouds over Nagasaki was amber-tinted, as though reflecting the conflagration at least six miles below. Beneath the top cloud mass, white in color, there gradually climbed a turbulent pillar of black smoke and dust which emitted a second fireball less vivid than the first. It rose as solid as a stump, its base dark purple, with a reddish hue in the center that paled to brown near the top."

The last look they got at Nagasaki showed a thick cone of dust covering half the city. On its rim near the harbor great fires were raging.

Aboard Bock's Car there was serious debate as to whether to bail out over an air-sea rescue craft in the Pacific or to try to reach Okinawa's Yontan airfield on their shrinking fuel supply. The decision was to make a run for Okinawa. As Bock's Car, practically dry of gasoline, descended to land at Okinawa, Sergeant Dehart, the tail gunner, saw smoke from Nagasaki 385 miles away.

The Emperor's Role

The question that continues to plague the world is whether dropping the bomb was an "immoral act." Could a more humane way have been found to settle the war without the atomic weapons. The obvious alternative—the invasion of Japan itself—is an equally chilling possibility. Admiral S. E. Morison describes what it could have been like:

"It was the Emperor who cut governmental red tape and made the great decision. This required courage. The Army chiefs and Admiral Toyoda were not greatly moved by the atomic explosions. They argued that the two bombs were probably all that the United States had; and if more were made we would not dare use them when invading Japan; that there was a fair chance of defeating the invasion by massed kamikaze attacks, and that in any event national honor demanded a last battle on Japanese soil. All the fighting hitherto had been little more than peripheral skirmishes; the way to victory was to "lure" the Americans ashore and "annihilate" them, as had been done by the original kamikaze "divine wind" to the hordes of Kublai Khan in A.D. 1281. Such had been the propaganda line given to the Japanese people to explain the series of defeats; they had no idea that Japan was really beaten.* Nothing less than an assertion of the Imperial will could have overcome these arguments and objections.

*Shigemitsu, *Japan and Her Destiny,* p. 334. An intelligent and patriotic French banker, M. Jacques Bardac, who was interned at Peiping through the entire war and cut off from all news and propaganda except Japanese, told me that it was so well done as to convince him up to the very last that Japan was winning. The older Japanese on Oahu, who could not understand English, believed even after the end of the war that Japan had won, and scores of them assembled one day on Aiea Heights to see the victorious Imperial Fleet enter Pearl Harbor. War Research Lab. Univ. of Hawaii, Report No. 8 of 1 Mar., 1946; Y. Kimura, "Rumor among the Japanese," *Social Process in Hawaii,* XI (1947), pp. 84-92.

"On the Allied side it has been argued that the maritime blockade, virtually complete by mid-August, would have strangled Japanese economy and that the B-29s and naval gunfire ships would have destroyed her principal cities and forced a surrender before long, without the aid of the atomic bombs, or of invasion. Fleet Admirals King and Leahy lent their distinguished advocacy to this view. Whether or not they were correct, not even time can tell. But of some facts one can be certain. The stepped-up B-29 bombings and naval bombardments, had they been continued after 15 August, would have cost the Japanese loss and suffering far, far greater than those inflicted by the two atomic bombs. And the probable effects of the projected invasions of Kyushu and Honshu in the fall and winter of 1945-1946, and of a desperate place-to-place defense of Japan, stagger the imagination. It is simply not true that Japan had no military capability left in mid-August. Although 2,550 kamikaze planes had been expended, there were 5,350 of them still left, together with as many more ready for orthodox use, and some 7,000 under repair or in storage; and 5,000 young men were training for the Kamikaze Corps. The plan was to disperse all aircraft on small grass strips in Kyushu, Shikoku and western Honshu, and in underground hangars and caves, and conserve them for kamikaze crashes on the Allied amphibious forces invading the home islands. Considering the number of planes, pilots and of potential targets, all within a short distance of principal airfields, it requires little imagination to depict the horrible losses that would have been inflicted on the invading forces, even before they got ashore. After accepting these losses there would have been protracted battles on Japanese soil, which would have cost each side very many more lives, and created a bitterness which even time could hardly have healed. Japan had plenty of ammunition left; the U.S. Army after the war found thousands of tons holed up in Hokkaido alone. And, as Russia would have been a full partner in this final campaign, there is a fair chance that Japan would have been divided like Germany and Korea, if not delivered completely to the mercy of the Communists.

"We must also point out that even after two atomic bombs had been dropped, the Potsdam Declaration clarified, the guards' insurrection defeated and the Emperor's will made known, it was touch and go whether the Japanese actually would surrender. Hirohito had to send members of the Imperial family to the principal Army commands to ensure compliance. His younger brother Prince Takamatsu was just in time to make the Atsugi airfield available for the first occupation

749

forces on 26 August, and to keep the kamikaze boys grounded. They were boasting that they would crash the *Missouri* when she entered Tokyo Bay. If these elements had had their way, the war would have been resumed with the Allies feeling that the Japanese were hopelessly treacherous, and with a savagery on both sides that is painful to contemplate.

"When these facts and events of the Japanese surrender are known and weighed, it will become evident that the atomic bomb was the keystone of a very fragile arch." *

*From *Victory in the Pacific*, pp. 351-354.